CUTTING ACROSS THE LANDS

Eveline Ferretti, Editor

CUTTING ACROSS THE LANDS

AN ANNOTATED BIBLIOGRAPHY ON NATURAL RESOURCE MANAGEMENT AND COMMUNITY DEVELOPMENT IN INDONESIA, THE PHILIPPINES, AND MALAYSIA

SOUTHEAST ASIA PROGRAM PUBLICATIONS
Southeast Asia Program
Cornell University
Ithaca, New York
1997

Editorial Board
Benedict Anderson
George Kahin
Stanley O'Connor
Keith Taylor
Oliver Wolters

Southeast Asia Program Series Number 16

Cornell Southeast Asia Program Publications
640 Stewart Avenue, Ithaca, NY 14850-3857

Printed in the United States of America

ISBN 0-87727-133-X

36829790

CONTENTS

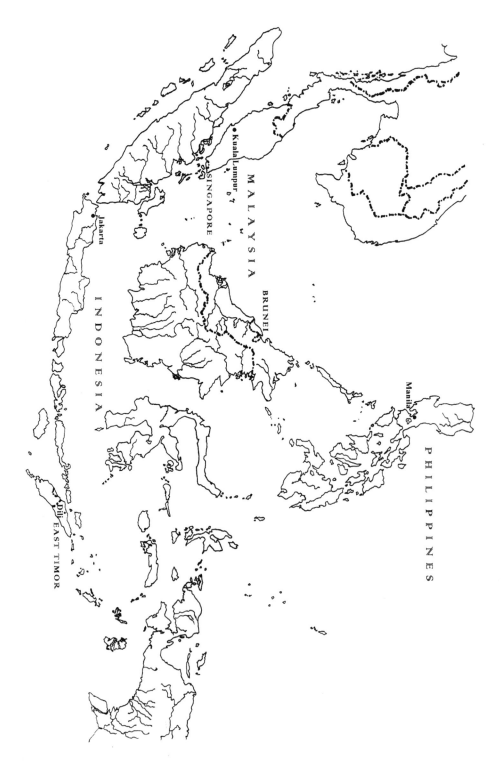

INSULAR SOUTHEAST ASIA

BIBLIOGRAPHY FOCUS AREA:
BORNEO and the SOUTHERN PHILIPPINES

Joe Baldwin, 1993

PREFACE

In a region that hosts some of the richest and most heavily exploited natural resources in the world, the tropical forests of Indonesia, Malaysia, and the Philippines have long been the focus of intense interest and concern. Over the years, this attention has generated a large body of literature, the very diversity of which reflects the varied and often contradictory perspectives, problems, and controversies associated with tropical forest land use and management in the region. As a bibliographic resource, the primary aim of *Cutting Across the Lands* is to identify the individual works that make up this literature and to highlight the different research and discussion foci that have characterized its development.

An explanatory note on the organizing principles which guided the development of this bibliography is likely to facilitate its use. The present volume incorporates and updates a bibliography first developed by an interdisciplinary group of researchers based at research institutes and universities in Southeast Asia and the United States. Aiming to contribute to informed policy development on tropical forest land management, the Southeast Asian Network on Upland and Logged-over Areas (SINULOG) was formed in 1991 to develop a comparative research program examining the dynamics of forest land transformation across different policy and socio-cultural environments. With this objective in mind, we selected Borneo and the Southern Philippines as our geographic focus of study.

The coherence of Borneo and the southern Philippines as a research focus was suggested by the shared biophysical characteristics and the similar patterns of forest resource exploitation evident on the islands of Cebu, Mindanao, Palawan, and Borneo—similarities which point to a commonality in the process of forest land transformation experienced in each area. Within this framework, the Borneo–Southern Philippines region could be conceptualized as a continuum of change, ranging from largely logged-out and heavily settled lands dominated by unirrigated farm fields and grasslands to more remote areas, which, while still sparsely populated and thickly forested, are now subject to accelerating pressures of resource exploitation and agricultural use. As envisioned by our research group, this framework would allow us to begin to identify and understand the changes affecting insular Southeast Asia's forest lands, drawing from the experience of those areas where forest land transformation was already advanced.

Despite the assumption of commonality, our research framework also sought to identify the ways in which different historical experiences and macropolicy environments influence the trajectory of environmental change in different localities. Thus, the research framework was conceived as accommodating two different yet mutually reinforcing functions: it would serve both as a research approach useful for gaining insight into common patterns of forest land transformation and as an illuminating perspective for identifying specific factors facilitating or constraining the processes by which different local agents manage forest resources.

As suggested by the concepts guiding the development of this bibliography, most of the work cited deals with research, analyses, and arguments directly and indirectly related to forest resource use and management in the Eastern Malaysian states of Sarawak and Sabah, the Indonesian Kalimantan provinces, and the Philippine islands of Palawan, Mindanao, and Cebu. The bibliography contains over 1,000 citations, culled from a wide range of disciplines and sources. Updates of the bibliography since the initial research framework was conceived have expanded the focus somewhat to include work that has focused on other regions of both insular and mainland Southeast Asia, yet which has substantive relevance to the issues at hand. Materials that shed light on processes of forest land use and transformation from the perspective of colonial and pre-colonial history are also included, although emphasis has been placed less on exhaustive coverage of historical and archaeological sources than on including key historical works that direct the reader to a wider range of work.

The complex character of the problems of forest land degradation in Southeast Asia presents a problem for organizing the bibliographic references in a way that allows readers to locate works relevant to their focus of interest quickly, yet which does not preclude fruitful interdisciplinary review of the works cited. To avoid unwieldy categorization of the literature, the bibliography's format has been kept simple, involving only seven sections. The first three are organized by country; materials cited are those which reflect research completed in Indonesia, Malaysia, and the Philippines, respectively. The fourth section covers work of different, Asia- and Southeast Asia-wide, or even global geographic scope, including various individual countries (India, Thailand, Vietnam, Laos, etc.). Citations for maps and other cartographic representations of forest land resources and demographic patterns of insular Southeast Asia (again with particular focus on the Southern Philippines–Borneo region) are grouped in Section Five. Section Six alerts readers to different journals that have particular relevance either to the study of forest land management in Southeast Asia in general, or to the study of different areas in Borneo and the southern Philippines in particular.

To assist readers in quickly finding works relevant to specific topics or fields of study, the seventh and final section of the bibliography offers a comprehensive subject index. Numbers following individual terms correspond to citations with the matching number in the bibliography proper. This index has been constructed on the basis of keywords included at the bottom of each reference, which indicate the specific geographic focus and summarize the main topics covered in each work. These terms will also alert readers to issues that, while possibly of only secondary focus in the material cited, are addressed in a manner that may be illuminating for readers with particular interest in them.

Most of the materials cited in this bibliography are accessible through conventional library channels, particularly those connected with institutes endowed with large Southeast Asian collections. However, because the original bibliography was compiled as a collaborative effort between researchers with access to the results of research and conference activities at different institutions, a portion of the references have more limited circulation. Readers interested in obtaining access to these materials are encouraged to inquire with the institution sponsoring, or otherwise associated with the work in question. For ephemeral materials having a particular geographic foci, it is also likely that the work cited will be accessible at the relevant institution participating in the initial SINULOG research effort (see contributors' list at back).

The task of developing an international collaborative research program devoted to systematic, comparative study of land transformation in insular Southeast Asia proved a daunting one to the SINULOG network, and the goals of our original initiative remain as yet unfulfilled. In the process of our efforts, however, a number of important lessons have been gleaned. Perhaps the most critical of these is an appreciation of the rapid changes and profound complexity of the land use pressures bearing on Southeast Asia's extensive forest lands. Ultimately, the ability to develop forest land management strategies that meet multifaceted environmental and economic needs requires the ability to critically synthesize insights from a wide range of fields and viewpoints, including those of the rural communities most directly affected by rapid changes in their forest land environments. It is the hope of those who have participated in the compilation of this bibliography that this work will make a substantive contribution towards this end.

Eveline Ferretti
Ithaca, New York

INDONESIA

1. **Abdoellah, O. S. 1993.** *Indonesian Transmigrants and Adaptation: An Ecological Anthropological Perspective.* Berkeley, Calif.: Center for South and Southeast Asian Studies, University of California.

   Indonesia/ South Kalimantan/ Land settlement and development/ Migration/ Household livelihood strategies/ Agriculture—Permanent/ Cultural ecology/ Indigenous and local communities—Forest land use and management practices.

2. **Adiningsih, J. S., A. Semali, S. Effendi, and S. Hadiwigeno. 1991.** "Resources and Problems Associated with the Development of Upland Areas in Indonesia." In Technologies for Sustainable Agriculture on Marginal Uplands in Southeast Asia. Proceedings of a seminar held at Ternate, Cavite, Philippines, 10–14 December 1990. Ed. G. Blair and R. Lefroy, pp. 45–54. Canberra: Australian Centre for International Agricultural Research (ACIAR).

   In a broad review of Indonesia's land resources, topography, soils and climate, and land utilization patterns, the authors discuss major constraints on agricultural development and sustainable land use in the uplands. Major findings from recent research on soil fertility management, soil conservation and erosion control, weed control (specifically *Imperata cylindrica*) and cropping systems are highlighted. The value of farming systems research for identifying socio-economic constraints on farmers against technology adoption is emphasized.

   Indonesia/ Agricultural development/ Land use—Patterns and planning/ Soil erosion and degradation/ Pest, weed, and crop disease management/ Farm management—Cropping systems/ Farming systems research/ State policy—Agricultural and rural development.

3. **Adjers, G., S. Hadengganan, J. Kuusipalo, K. Nuryanto, and L. Vesa. 1995.** "Enrichment Planting of Dipterocarps in Logged-over Secondary Forests: Effect of Width, Direction and Maintenance Method of Planting Line on Selected *Shorea* Species." *Forest Ecology and Management* 73 (1–3): 259–270.

   Indonesia/ South Kalimantan/ Forest regeneration/ Forest management—Commercial forestry and silviculture.

4. **Adnyana, M. O., and A. Rachim. 1994.** "Change in Food Consumption: Effects on Production and Use of Upland Crops in Indonesia." In *Changes in Food Consumption in Asia: Effects on Production and Use of Upland Crops.* Proceedings of a workshop held in Kandy, Sri Lanka, October 6–9, 1992. Ed. J. W. T. Bottema, G. A. C. De Silva, and D. R. Stoltz, pp. 33–44. Bogor: Regional Co-ordination Centre for Research and Development of Coarse

Grains, Pulses, Roots and Tuber Crops in the Humid Tropics of Asia and the Pacific (CGPRT Centre).

Following a description of land area, production, and yield of upland crops (maize, cassava, sweet potato, soybean, groundnut, and mungbean), the paper focuses on determinants of future food demand. These include demographic trends, per capita expenditure patterns, price elasticities of demand, and domestic use shares. Yield statistics cover the period from 1988 to 1992 and projected yields to the year 2000 are estimated.

Indonesia/ Agricultural development/ Agriculture—Smallholder cash crop farming/ Agricultural economics.

5.   **Ahmad, M. 1992.** "Rente ekonomi dalam eksploitasi hutan tropis." *Prisma* 21 (6): 3–17. [Economic Rent in the Exploitation of Tropical Forests.]

Ahmad assesses the Indonesian government's capacity to capture economic rents accruing from the timber industry based on statistics of the 1980s. When even the most favorable timber prices are used in the analysis, it appears that the Indonesian government was able to capture only 54% of potential rent in the timber sector by the late 1980s. Undervaluation of Indonesian timber reflected in this figure has in turn encouraged accelerated exploitation of the country's forest resources. Argues the author, appropriate adjustments in the government's mechanisms for capturing rent would lead to greater resource conservation [In Bahasa Indonesia].

Indonesia/ Timber industry—State policy and regulation/ Forest management—Economics/ State policy—Forest and natural resources.

6.   **Alrasjid, H. 1984.** "Virgin Forest and Sustained Yield of Logged-Over Forest at the River Baai Natural Forest Complex, East Kalimantan." Report to the Indonesian Center for Forest Research and Development [Bogor, West Java, Indonesia]: Pusat Penelitian dan Pengembangan Hutan Indonesia.

The Indonesian Selective Felling System (ISFS) is based on the assumption that sustained yield in natural forests can be achieved if the concession area contains adequate supplies of standard commercial trees (i.e., at densities of at least 25 per ha or more) with a diameter of at least 20 cm. The author assesses the relationship between the condition of logged-over forests and possibilities for sustained yield, comparing an unlogged natural forest, logged plots 5 years of age, and logged tracts 10 years of age in the River Baai area of East Kalimantan. While the natural forest boasted 28 mature commercial trees per ha (and thus could be considered eligible for ISFS), low average seedling and pole counts indicated that it would not regenerate these species on its own. Similarly, while the 5-yr-old logged-over forest had more than 25 commercial trees/ha, seedling and sapling densities were only 1000 and 882 per ha, respectively, indicating a failure at adequate natural regeneration. The 10 year old logging site showed more promise, with twenty-eight commercial trees per ha, a seedling count of over 1200/ha and a sapling density of 1103. Research results indicate a 10 year regeneration minimum for sustained yield, and the likelihood that even in this case, yields could not be sustained past the third rotation.

Indonesia/ East Kalimantan/ Timber industry—Logging/ Forest management—Commercial forestry and silviculture/ /Forest regeneration.

7.   **Ampt-Riksen, V. W. M. M., and J. W. van den Ven. 1992.** "A Crooked Balance: Agricultural Production and Nature Conservation: An Indonesian and a Dutch Area Compared." In *Law as a Resource in Agrarian Struggles.* Ed. F. v. B. Benda-Beckmann and M. van der Velde, pp. 191–218. Wageningen: Agricultural University.

The authors compare nature conservation legislation, its effects on nature and agriculture, and its embedded relationship to social life in contemporary Indonesia and the Netherlands. The study is based on the cases of the Kerinci National Park, Sumatra and the Winterswijk National Landscape Park, Netherlands. Four foci of the comparative study include the geophysical conditions influencing agricultural development, the history of land use and occupation around both park areas, legislation underlying the establishment and management of the two park areas, and general government policy concerning nature conservation and agricultural development.

Indonesia/ Sumatra/ Forest management—Parks and conservation areas/ State policy—Forest and natural resources/ Indigenous and local communities—Forest land use and management practices/ Indigenous and local communities—Land and resource tenure systems.

8.   **Anderson, B. R. O. 1987.** "The State and Minorities in Indonesia." In *Southeast Asian Tribal Groups and Ethnic Minorities: Prospects for the 80's and Beyond*, pp. 73–81. Cultural Survival Report, no. 22. Cambridge, Mass.: Cultural Survival.

The author traces the history of state policy on minority ethnic and religious groups in Indonesia from the colonial era through the present phase of the New Order regime. "Indonesianization" has been the primary aim of New Order policy on minority cultures, accompanied by militarization of the country's provinces as the state has sought to consolidate its political control over the archipelago.

Indonesia/ Indigenous and local communities—State policy/ Politics/ Political economy.

9.   **Angelsen, A. 1995.** "Shifting Cultivation and 'Deforestation': A Study from Indonesia." *World Development* 23 (10): 1713–1729.

Challenging conventional accounts of the process of deforestation in Indonesia, the author identifies basic factors in the expansion of shifting cultivation into the country's old-growth forest, drawing from a case study in Riau province, Sumatra. To assess pressures shaping forest land use in the study area a model assuming an open economy is deemed more appropriate than one assuming pure subsistence. Results of a household survey reveal current land use patterns as well as recent changes in the exogenous environment, related to government and plantation land claims, improved road access and higher local rubber prices, in-migration, and the displacement of customary land rights by the implementation of national land law. The combined impact of exogenous changes has been to increase local land rents and promote a race over property rights. Local farmers have responded by both intensifying use of existing farm land near villages and converting more distant standing forest to rubber groves. The study highlights the government's role in actively contributing towards the process of agricultural expansion.

Indonesia/ Sumatra/ Deforestation/ Agriculture—Shifting cultivation's environmental impacts/ Land use—Patterns and planning/ Indigenous and local communities—Forest land use and management practices/ State policy—Agricultural and rural development/ State policy—Land development/ Land settlement and development—Environmental impacts/ Land settlement and development—Impacts on local communities and economy/ Land tenure—Legislation and state policy.

Anon. 1990. "Indonesia: Second Forestry Institutions and Conservation Project." Photocopy. Staff Appraisal Report, no. 8603-IND. Washington, D.C.: World Bank.

This 79 page report outlines recent trends in Indonesia's forestry sector, discusses World Bank involvement, and highlights lessons learned. The focus is on the Second Forestry Institutions and Conservation Project, which will encompass concession management and inspection, reforestation (forest plantations), forestry research, conservation, policy advisory service, and the role of women. The option of engaging an external inspection agency to monitor timber concessions is also assessed.

Indonesia/ Forest management—Commercial forestry and silviculture/ Forest management—Forest resource conservation/ Timber plantations/ State policy—Forest and natural resources/ Project intervention—Forest management.

11.   **Anwar, A. 1992.** "Forestry and Forest Management Problems in Indonesia." Paper presented at the Study Meeting on New Trends in Environmental Management, 3–7 February 1992, in Tokyo, Japan. Photocopy.

An introductory section to this paper provides a broad overview of growth in the Indonesian forestry sector, the current extent of forest resources in the country, and the history of its forest management system, including the system's selective felling component. A second section focuses on problems of deforestation and environmental degradation. FAO estimates, considered to be among the most reliable for Indonesia, suggest that rates of deforestation during the early 1980s were between 600,000 ha to 1 million ha per year. Of this, roughly 80,000 per year have been attributed to logging, while the World Bank estimates that 200,000–300,000 ha are converted to government-sponsored tree crop plantations and transmigration settlements. Recent satellite imagery suggests that up to 500,000 ha of forestlands are converted to various types of agricultural use by shifting cultivators each year. This loss in forest cover signifies an approximate revenue loss of U.S.$1 billion per year.

Forest plantations comprise a promising venue for making forest land use more efficient in the country. The relatively successful history of teak plantations on Java is briefly discussed, as is the status of less extensive but still important productive and protective state forest plantations on the Outer Islands. In order to return degraded forest lands on Indonesia's Outer Islands to a more productive and environmentally stable state, the government of Indonesia initiated the Industrial Timber Estate program (Hutan Tanaman Industry or HTI) in 1984. Aimed at "accelerating the regeneration of secondary forest and degraded areas," the program grants private concession holders, state enterprises, and provincial forestry offices license to establish high yielding timber estates on public forest areas already transformed into shrublands, grasslands and degraded production forest with a stocking of less than 16 cubic meters per ha. Pulp plantations, linked to paper factories, are to figure prominently in this approach, and rattan plantations are also to be included. Since program inception, 68.7 thousand ha of plantations have been established, of which close to 2 thousand ha involve rattan. Roughly 80 percent of this acreage is located in Kalimantan. According to Program plans, by 1993, 1.5 million ha of forest plantations are to have been planted in the country, approximately 40 percent of which is to be in Kalimantan.

Though the plantation program is intended as a way to deal with forest land areas which have already been degraded, the author also notes the incentive the program may give to current interest groups to quickly clearcut and convert primary forest areas to plantation estates, given the returns from rapid timber extraction and the favorable conditions for good plantation performance created by clear-felling. In addition to more effective monitoring, greater technical expertise in forest and plantation development is needed to make the program work.

Indonesia/ Forest management—Commercial forestry and silviculture/ Forest management—Forest resource conservation/ Timber plantations/ Pulp and paper industry/ Rattan—Cultivation/ Deforestation/ State policy—Forest and natural resources/ Land settlement and development.

12.   **Anwarhan, H., S. Tairan, and R. Galib. 1984.** "Hasil penelitian pola tanam lahan kering di daerah transmigran Tajau Pecah, Kalimantan Selatan." In *Proceeding Pertemuan Teknis Penelitian Pola Usahatani Menunjang Transmigrasi.* Ed. H. Nataatmadja, pp. 234–243. Bogor, West Java, 27 February 1984. Bogor, Indonesia: Pusat Penelitian dan Pengembangan

Tanaman Pangan. [Research on Upland Cropping Patterns in the Transmigration Area of Tajau Pecah, South Kalimantan.]

Research on the upland cropping patterns in Tajau Pecah, South Kalimantan indicated the presence of Red-Yellow Podzolic soils with low N, P, K content and pH ranges between 5.3 and 6.5. The topsoil shows damage due to erosion. Average rainfall is 2533 mm/year. Wet months occur in the period between November and April. The research results show that cultivating maize I + upland rice / cassava–maize–kacang tunggak using low inputs is the most advisable cropping pattern. Using this pattern, total production (expressed in rice equivalents) reached 7.7 t with a net income of Rp. 246,140/year. [Summarized from vol. 1 (Farming System), Bibliografi, Pengembangan Sistem Informasi Pertanian Lahan Kering dan Konservasi Tanah, Bogor]. [In Bahasa Indonesia].

Indonesia/ South Kalimantan/ Agriculture—Permanent/ Farm management—Cropping systems/ Soils.

13.   **Appell, G. N. 1985.** "The Bulusu' of East Kalimantan: The Consequences of Resettlement." In *Modernization and the Emergence of Landless Peasantry: Essays on the Integration of Peripheries to Socioeconomic Centers.* Ed. G. N. Appell, pp. 186–242. Williamsburg, Va.: College of William and Mary.

Indonesia/ East Kalimantan/ Indigenous and local communities—State policy/ Resettlement.

14.   **—. 1986.** "Kayan Land Tenure and the Distribution of Devolvable Usufruct in Borneo." *Borneo Research Bulletin* 18 (2): 119–130.

Reviewing types of land tenure systems found among indigenous swidden farming communities of Borneo, Appell highlights in particular the characteristics of circulating and devolvable usufruct systems. While corporate (i.e., village-based) rights generally apply to all residual lands in most indigenous tenure systems, defining features of the village entity varies across Borneo's different tribal societies. The Kayan system of land tenure is characterized by devolvable usufruct. Evidence available to the author, however, does not yet clarify whether partitionable or divisible usufruct obtains. Appel suggests the application of several possible tests in further field work to distinguish between the two usufruct systems.

Indonesia/ Kalimantan/ Indigenous and local communities—Land and resource tenure systems.

15.   **Appell-Warren, L. P. 1985.** "Resettlement of the Bulusu' and Punan in Indonesian Borneo: Policy and History." *Borneo Research Bulletin* 17: 10–11.

Indonesia/ East Kalimantan/ Resettlement/ Indigenous and local communities—State policy.

16.   **Arndt, H. W. 1983.** "Transmigration: Achievement, Problems, Prospects." *Bulletin of Indonesian Economic Studies* 19 (3): 50–73.

Indonesia/ Land settlement and development/ Migration/ State policy—Land development.

17.   **Arndt, H. W., and R. M. Sundrum. 1977.** "Transmigration: Land Settlement or Regional Development?" *Bulletin of Indonesian Economic Studies* 13 (3): 72–90.

Indonesia/ Land settlement and development/ State policy—Land development/ Regional development.

18.   **Arnold, T. W. 1990.** "An Analysis of Trade Policies Relating to Indonesia's Forest Products." Indonesia/UTF/065/INS: Forestry Studies, Field Document no. V-4. Jakarta: Directorate General of Forest Utilization, Ministry of Forestry, Government of Indonesia; Food and Agricultural Organization of the United Nations.

Three main aspects of Indonesian trade policies have helped shape the development of the country's forest product export industry: 1) the opening up of the Indonesian economy to foreign investment in the late 1960s, setting off the timber boom in the Outer Islands; 2) an attempt to promote downstream processing of forest products through increasingly more restrictive taxes and bans on the export of raw materials; and 3) the impact of adjustment programs initiated by the government in response to the collapse of oil prices and the country's ensuing debt crisis in the early to mid-1980s. The author notes that Indonesia benefits favorably from the GSP preference granted on its exports of wood to developed countries, but has yet to capture a significant share of the GSP furniture market which promises further gains. However, recent restrictions on the export of raw materials appear likely to be only partially successful in promoting downstream processing industries. The greatest chance for success appears to lie in the country's plywood industry which has already managed to capture a large share of the world market. The author is less optimistic that similar trade policies will be as successful for other processed wood industries, where it does not appear likely that Indonesia will be able to achieve and maintain a solid market share over the long run. Overly restrictive trade policies may instead serve only to cause a long term loss in potential revenues while promoting inefficient domestic processing. Neither employment promotion nor resource conservation goals will be well served by this one policy thrust. The author suggests a number of possible policy alternatives, such as more effective tree pricing, selective product differentiation, marketing improvements, and skill upgrading at all levels of the forest industry labor force. Total report length is 53 pages.

Indonesia/ Timber industry—Trade and markets/ Timber industry—State policy and regulation/ State policy—Forest and natural resources/ Forest management—Economics.

19.   **Arsyad, S., I. Amien, T. Sheng, and W. Moldenhauer, eds. 1992.** *Conservation Policies for Sustainable Hillslope Farming*. Ankeny, Iowa: Soil and Water Conservation Society.

This monograph presents a collection of papers prepared for an international workshop on "Conservation Policies for Sustainable Hillslope Farming" held in Solo, Central Java in March 1991. Papers deal with a variety of issues related to soil conservation, including World Bank strategy in Asia (W. B. Margrath), recent approaches in soil conservation (D. W. Sanders), links between land tenure, land tenure legislation and soil conservation in Indonesia (S. M. P. Tjondronegoro; I. Soetiknjo; S. Soeromihardjo); experiences of soil conservation in Java (Yuwanti, Suyamni, and J. Levine) and the Philippines (R. Atienza); monitoring and evaluation (K. C. Lai); and forestry policy and soil conservation (N. P. Sharma). Papers are generally brief, providing broad overviews rather than research detail.

Asia/ Indonesia/ Soil erosion and degradation/ Project intervention—Soil conservation.

20.   **Aumeeruddy, Y. 1993.** "Agroforêts et aires de forêts protégées—représentations et pratiques agroforestières paysannes en périphérie du Parc National Kerinci Seblat, Sumatra, Indonésie." Ph.D. diss., Université Montpellier II, Montpellier, France.
[Agroforests and Protected Forest Areas: Peasant Agroforestry Systems and Practices on the Periphery of the Kerinci Seblat National Park.]

Indonesia/ Sumatra/ Agroforestry/ Indigenous and local communities—Forest land use and management practices/ Forest management—Parks and conservation areas.

21.   **Aumeeruddy, Y., and B. Sansonnens.** 1994. "Shifting from Simple to Complex Agroforestry Systems: An Example for Buffer Zone Management from Kerinci." *Agroforestry Systems* 28 (2): 113–141.

> A study of forest land use patterns was undertaken over an eighteen month period between 1990 and 1992 in Kerinci Valley, a densely populated valley surrounded by a natural park in Jambi province, Sumatra. While wet rice cultivation provides a major staple food crop, tree crop farming dominates the land use patterns of the region, accounting for 77% of the land resources used by the residents of the area, mostly on the hills surrounding flooded paddy area. Indigenous agroforestry systems associated with this land use include cash crops (coffee and cinnamon) grown in widely varying arrangements from monoculture fallow fields to multi-story gardens containing a rich variety of plant species. The study sought to examine the evolution of indigenous agroforestry practices in an area under increasing land pressure due to demographic growth as well as the requirements of park conservation. The authors summarize results of the study, describing local land use patterns, deforestation trends, and factors behind forest conversion to agriculture in the Kerinci Valley. A village case study highlights the shift being made in some parts of the valley from fallow-based agroforestry systems to more complex and intensively managed, multi-story gardens. Promotion of this trend is emphasized as an appropriate strategy to develop sustainable buffer zones around protected areas and to prevent the expansion of cash crop monoculture.

Indonesia/ Sumatra/ Indigenous and local communities—Forest land use and management practices/ Agricultural intensification/ Forest management—Parks and conservation areas/ Agroforestry.

22.   **Avé, J. B., V. T. King, and J. G. W. De Witt. 1983.** *West Kalimantan: A Bibliography.* Bibliographical Series, no. 13. Dordrecht, Netherlands: Koninklijk Instituut voor Taal-, Land- en Volkenkunde.

Indonesia/ West Kalimantan/ Bibliography.

23.   **Avé, J. B., and V. T. King. 1986.** *People of the Weeping Forest: Tradition and Change in Borneo.* Leiden, The Netherlands: National Museum of Ethnology.

Indonesia/ Malaysia/ Kalimantan/ Sabah/ Sarawak/ Indigenous and local communities/ Ethnography/ Indigenous and local communities—Commoditization.

24.   **Baas, P., K. Kalkman, and R. Geesink, eds. 1990.** *The Plant Diversity of Malesia.* Proceedings of the Flora Malesiana Symposium Commemorating Professor Dr. C. G. G. J. van Steenis, Leiden, August, 1989. Dordrecht: Kluwer Academic Publishers.

Malaysia/ Indonesia/ Forest flora/ Biodiversity.

25.   **Barber, C. V., and G. Churchill. 1987.** "Land Policy in Irian Jaya: Issues and Strategies." Project Report, no. INS/83/013. Jakarta: Government of Indonesia; United Nations Development Program; International Bank for Reconstruction and Development.

Indonesia/ Irian Jaya/ Land tenure—Legislation and state policy/ State policy—Land development/ Land use—Patterns and planning/ Indigenous and local communities—Land and resource tenure systems/ Indigenous and local communities—State policy.

26.   **Barber, C. V. 1989.** "The State, the Environment, and Development: The Genesis and Transformation of Social Forestry Policy in New Order Indonesia." Ph.D. diss., University of California, Berkeley, Calif.

Indonesia/ State policy—Forest and natural resources/ Social forestry/ Politics/ Political economy.

27.   **Barber, C. V., N. C. Johnson, and E. Hafild. 1994.** *Breaking the Logjam: Obstacles to Forest Policy Reform in Indonesia and the United States.* Washington, D.C.: World Resources Institute.

Noting some broad similarities between the rapid loss of primary forests in Indonesia during the past several decades and the fate of the once thickly covered forest areas of the U.S. during the 19th and early 20th centuries, the authors review the process of forest land degradation in both countries and propose options for policy reform. After a broad overview in the introductory chapter, the authors focus mainly on the timber industry's role in forest resource decline. In Chapter 2 patterns of forest land ownership are reviewed and their role in creating incentives to exploit forest resources at levels which seriously degrade local environments noted. In Indonesia, contradictions and inequities in the country's forest land legislation allow the state to lease sprawling concessions to timber industry giants while customary claims by local tribal groups are ignored. In the next chapter, the authors discuss economic dimensions of forest resource extraction, highlighting the ways in which Indonesian and U.S. economic development policies have either directly promoted forest clearing or impeded effective forest conservation. An underlying factor in this process, note the authors, has been consistent undervaluation of standing forest resources by policy-makers in both countries. Also notable in Indonesia has been the limited share of economic benefits from the forestry accruing to forest farming communities, even as local farmers are cut off from their traditional means of livelihood due to logging activities. Chapter 4 considers extant political economic conditions which shape current policy, highlighting who the particular beneficiaries have been and the mechanisms by which influence over the policy development process is exerted by dominant stakeholders in both countries. While thus stressing the deeply rooted, structural nature of exploitative forest land use in the U.S. and Indonesia, the authors conclude each section with recommendations for possible improvements in policy as well as for effective reform of the policy-making process itself. A final chapter provides a summary of conclusions and recommendations. The monograph provides an insightful synthesis of published and ephemeral literature dealing with the link between the timber industry, degradation of Indonesia's forests, and dislocation of local communities.

Indonesia/ Deforestation/ Timber industry—Logging/ Timber industry—Environmental impacts/ Timber industry—State policy and regulation/ State policy—Forest and natural resources/ Land tenure—Legislation and state policy.

28.   **Barbier, E. B. 1989.** "Cash Crops, Food Crops, and Sustainability: The Case of Indonesia." *World Development* 17 (6): 879–895.

Drawing from the case of Indonesia, Barbier argues that regardless of role in ensuring food self-sufficiency, economic policies formulated without specific consideration of environmental impact are likely to exacerbate resource degradation. Both Indonesia's pursuit of self-sufficiency during the early decades of the New Order regime and the government's more recent emphasis on export crop promotion have tended to increase environmentally destructive patterns of land and natural resources use. Barbier emphasizes the need for an alternative approach that integrates natural resource management concerns explicitly within the agricultural policy framework [Summarized from journal].

Indonesia/ State policy—Agricultural and rural development/ Deforestation/ Soil erosion and degradation/ State policy—Forest and natural resources/ Agriculture—Plantations/ Agriculture—Permanent.

29.   **Barlow, C. 1987.** "Developments in Plantation Agriculture and Smallholder Cash-crop Production." In *Indonesia: Resources, Ecology, and Environment.* Ed. J. Hardjono, pp. 85–103. Singapore: Oxford University Press.

Indonesia/ Sumatra/ Agricultural development/ Agriculture—Smallholder tree and perennial crop farming/ Agriculture—Smallholder cash crop farming/ Land settlement and development/ State policy—Agricultural and rural development.

30. **Barlow, C., and T. Tomich. 1991.** "Indonesian Agricultural Development: The Awkward Case of Smallholder Tree Crops." *Bulletin of Indonesian Economic Studies* 27 (3): 29–54.

Indonesia/ Agriculture—Smallholder tree and perennial crop farming/ Agriculture—Smallholder cash crop farming/ Agricultural development/ State policy—Agricultural and rural development.

31. **Basa, I., and H. Nataatmadja. 1984.** "Kemajuan penelitian usahatani di Semboja, Kaltim." In *Prosiding pertemuan teknis penelitian pola usaha tani menunjang Transmigrasi.* Ed. H. Nataatmadja, M. Bekti, M. Ismunadji, Soewardjo, E. S. Suryatna, and P. Sitorus, pp. 330–344. Cisarua, Bogor, West Java, 27 February 1984. Bogor, Indonesia: Badan Penelitian dan Pengembangan Pertanian. [Progress in Farming Systems Research in Semboja, East Kalimantan.]

Research in the Semboja transmigration area was aimed at finding an appropriate farming system and related technology in the Transmigration Area IV, East Kalimantan. The activities in Semboja were conducted as part of a wider research effort, with conservation measures as the main focus of soil-related work. Research showed that rice terracing at height intervals of 1.5 m is effective when followed by terrace-strengthening plants, such as *Leucaena* (3-month old seedlings planted on terrace risers) and grass planted along drainage canals. Cover crops like *Centrosema plumeri* and *Pueraria javanica* grew well and also contributed to effective soil conservation. Problems were encountered with soil fertility as well as heavy pest and disease infestation which affected all plant varieties used in the research trials. [Summarized from vol. 3 (Soil and Water Conservation), Bibliografi, Pengembangan Sistem Informasi Pertanian Lahan Kering dan Konservasi Tanah, Bogor]. [In Bahasa Indonesia].

Indonesia/ Kalimantan/ Agriculture—Permanent/ Project intervention—Soil conservation/ Farm management—Cropping systems.

32. **Basiago, A. D. 1995.** "Sustainable Development in Indonesia: A Case Study of an Indigenous Regime of Environmental Law and Policy." *International Journal of Sustainable Development and World Ecology* 2 (3): 199–211.

Basiago describes a number of examples of indigenous environmental management regimes in Indonesia and proposes their viability as models for sustainable resource use. These include the temple-based water management system of Bali, Javanese home-gardens, the *adat* and *sasi* systems of the Nusa Tenggara islands in eastern Indonesian and Maluku, land and forest resource tenure systems in West Kalimantan, swidden farming in East Kalimantan, and various forest-product collection regimes in the country.

Indonesia/ West Kalimantan/ Indigenous and local communities—Forest land use and management practices/ Indigenous and local communities—Forest products use and trade/ Indigenous and local communities—Land and resource tenure systems.

33. **Belsky, J. M. 1993.** "Household Food Security, Farm Trees, and Agroforestry: A Comparative Study in Indonesia and the Philippines." *Human Organization* 52 (2): 130–140.

Adoption of agroforestry is being hailed in the development literature as an increasingly widespread and important farm-level innovation to improve household food as well as cash security under conditions of growing land and labor constraints. Belsky argues for a regional and historical approach to examining factors in farm household decision-making on tree cultivation practices and patterns. Analysis of field research in the Philippines and Indonesia reveals the high value placed by households on rice consumption. It follows that in much of Southeast Asia, food security and upland farm decisions should be viewed within the broader context of the rice economy.

Indonesia/ Philippines/ Agroforestry/ Agricultural intensification/ Household livelihood strategies/ Indigenous and local communities—Forest land use and management practices/ Indigenous and local communities—Farming practices.

34.   ———. **1994.** "Soil Conservation and Poverty: Lessons from Upland Indonesia." *Society and Natural Resources* 7 (5): 429–443.

Since the colonial era, state soil conservation efforts in the Indonesian uplands have focused mainly on promoting bench terraces. Using current and historical data from the Kerinci district of Sumatra gathered during fieldwork in 1987–88, Belsky observes the resistance engaged by farmers against bench terrace construction and examines the reasons behind it. Reasons for the state's entrenched bias towards bench terracing rather than other, for farmers less costly soil conserving technologies are discussed. Belsky highlights in particular the role played by the Indonesian state's emphasis on "productivist and commodity-led agricultural development" as well as broader geopolitical institutions. These considerations cast doubt both on the likelihood for success of "economic remedies" (i.e., temporary state subsidization of soil conservation development) to problems of farming-induced soil erosion, and on the ability of the state to realize environmental and social changes that benefit the rural poor.

Indonesia/ Sumatra/ Soil erosion and degradation/ Project intervention—Soil conservation/ Watershed management/ Poverty/ Agriculture—Permanent/ Agriculture—Smallholder cash crop farming/ History—Colonial/ State policy—Agricultural and rural development/ State policy—Agricultural and rural development.

35.   **Bertault, J. G., and P. Sist. 1995.** "The Effects of Logging in Natural Forests." *Bois et Forêts des Tropiques* 245: 5–20.

The authors report the results of a study on damage to residual trees with different logging practices. The study comprised one part of the Silvicultural Techniques for the Regeneration of Logged Rainforest in East Kalimantan (STREK) project started in 1989. Particular focus was placed on assessing differences in conventional logging and reduced impact logging practices. The latter was shown to result in 18 percent less residual tree loss than the former, with significant implications for securing the sustainability of future tree harvests. Possible techniques for extrapolating sample plot-based data to much larger concession areas are discussed.

Indonesia/ East Kalimantan/ Timber industry—Logging/ Forest management—Commercial forestry and silviculture/ Forest management—Forest resource conservation/ Timber industry—Environmental impacts.

36.   **Blate, G. M. 1994.** "Post-dispersal Seed Predation by Terrestrial Vertebrates in Gunung Palung National Park, West Kalimantan, Indonesia." *TRI News* 1 (20–22).

Indonesia/ West Kalimantan/ Forest biology and ecology/ Forest fauna.

37.   **Blicher-Mathiesen, U. 1994.** "Borneo Illipe, a Fat Product from Different *Shorea* spp. (*Dipterocarpaceae*)." *Economic Botany* 48 (3): 231–242.

Fat extracted from the "illipe" nut—kernels of *Shorea* spp.—in the forests of Borneo and Sumatra have an important use in the fabrication of chocolate, particularly in face of rapid rise in cocoa butter prices in recent decades. During two field visits to East Sarawak (2–3 months each) in 1989 and 1991, Blicher-Mathiesen identified different, locally available *Shorea* species and collected fruit samples in order to compare fat quality. Distribution maps of naturally occurring tree populations for five different species are presented with the aim of assessing the potential to meet future demand sustainably.

Indonesia/ Malaysia/ Borneo/ Sumatra/ Forest flora/ Non-timber forest products.

38. **Bodmer, R. E., R. J. Mather, and D. J. Chivers. 1991.** "Rainforests in Central Borneo—Threatened by Modern Development." *Oryx* 25: 21–36.

The Fauna and Flora Preservation Society of the U.K. has recently embarked on the Red Alert Project with scientists from the Barito Ulu Project in northern Central Kalimantan, a collaborative research effort on forest regeneration being undertaken by U.K. and Indonesian scientists. The paper reports the results of preliminary wildlife and conservation surveys conducted in various watersheds of the Upper Barito River area. Local mammalian fauna, rainforest product collection and use by a number of small Dayak communities, and current problems of incursion into primary forests in the Upper Barito area are described. Though the surveys have shown the diversity of mammal species to be very high in the region, the density of these populations are quite low. With 2–4 km of logging roads being constructed in the Upper Barito region every week, the pressures on its rich but fragile ecosystems are great. The joint Red Alert Project effort will investigate potential solutions for the survival of Central Borneo rainforests, focusing on maintaining existing protected areas and encouraging the establishment of new ones.

Indonesia/ Central Kalimantan/ Forest flora/ Forest fauna/ Indigenous and local communities—Forest products use and trade/ Forest management—Parks and conservation areas/ Biodiversity.

39. **Bratawinata, A. A., and A. Sardjono. 1988.** "Inventarisasi sistem sistem agroforestry di Kalimantan Timur." In *Agroforestry untuk pengembangan daerah pedesaan di Kalimantan Timur.* Ed. A. Lahjie and B. Seibert, pp. 7–16. Samarinda, East Kalimantan, Indonesia: Department of Forestry, Mulawarman University; German Agency for Technical Cooperation (GTZ). [Inventory of Agroforestry Systems in East Kalimantan.]

Indonesia/ East Kalimantan/ Agroforestry/ Indigenous and local communities—Farming practices/ Indigenous and local communities—Forest land use and management practices.

40. **Bratawinata, A. A. 1991.** "Vegetation Analysis of the Tropical Forests on Mt. Embut and the Heath Forest on the Meratus Range, East Kalimantan with Special Reference to the Occurrence of *Agathis borneensis* in Relation to Edaphic Factors." In *Proceedings of the Fourth Round-Table Conference on Dipterocarps, 12–15 December 1989, Bogor, Indonesia.* Ed. I. Soerianegara, S. S. Tjitrosomo, R. C. Umaly, and I. Umboh, pp. 273–278. Bogor, Indonesia: SEAMEO BIOTROP.

Vegetative analysis was undertaken at two sites on Mt. Embut, Long Ampung and one site on the Meratus Mountain Range, Balikpapan to investigate the influence of edaphic factors on the occurrence of *Agathis borneensis*. On Mt. Embut, the study sites involved a hill tropical forest (480–800 m) with reddish brown to dark soil, rich in organic matter and of a sandy loam texture, and a montane tropical forest (800–1052 m), characterized by soil with lower litterfall and concentrations of nitrogen than lower lying forest. The hill site was found to contain 117 tree species at a density of 617 trees per ha. The importance value of *Agathis borneensis* at the tree, pole, and sapling stages equaled 31.17%, 22.19%, and 10%

respectively. At the montane site fewer trees of large girth predominated than at lower elevations. Number of tree species present was 105 with a density of 455 trees per ha. *Agathis borneensis* occurred commonly at all stages (tree, poles, and saplings), with importance values of 16.9, 31.54, and 10%, respectively. *Shorea platyclados*, a dipterocarp species, was found to be present, as also *Lithocarpus conocarpus, Eugenia sibulanensis* and *Quercus argentata* (in declining order of importance). At the Mt. Meratus, Balikpapan site (400 m), the soil is rich in organic matter, sandy-loam, dark and moist, despite the fact that it is derived from siliceous parent material. For this reason, the forest type is of a broad but not particularly marked heath (*kerangas*) type. Tree species diversity was found to be poor, despite a tree density of 465 per ha. Only 45 species were found at the tree stage, with a further 30 at the pole and 36 at the sapling stages. *Tristania obovata* and *Nepenthes* spp. occur commonly, while *Agathis borneensis* is of common occurrence in the tree stadium, with the Importance stadium at 1.2% only. Other extant species include *Artocarpus* spp., *Palaquium rostratum, Shorea parvifolia*, and *Cotylelobium* sp.

Indonesia/ Kalimantan/ Soils/ Vegetation analysis/ Forest flora/ Biodiversity.

41.   **Bremen, H. van, M. Iriansyah, and W. Andriesse. 1990.** "Detailed Soil Survey and Physical Land Evaluation in a Tropical Rain Forest, Indonesia: A Study of Soil and Site Characteristics in Twelve Permanent Plots in East Kalimantan." Tropenbos Technical Series, no. 6. Netherlands: Tropenbos Foundation.

The authors report on results of a study aimed at identifying soil and broad biophysical characteristics at 12 sites in East Kalimantan. Following an overview of climatological conditions, vegetation, land use, and other physical features, soil survey methods are described, and results of the analysis given. Twenty different land mapping units are identified based on geomorphological features, slope and drainage. The presence of only slight differences in chemico-physical characteristics between the units is noted. Results of the study are intended to assist in land evaluation and land use planning, particularly for purposes of forest protection and rehabilitation, and the authors emphasize "selective exploitation of natural forest" as the most suitable land use for the sites studied.

Indonesia/ East Kalimantan/ Soils/ Forest management—Forest resource conservation.

42.   **Broek, J. O. M. 1962.** "Place Names in the 16th and 17th Century Borneo." *Imago Mundi* 16.

Malaysia/ Indonesia/ Borneo/ History—Pre-colonial.

43.   **Brookfield, H., and Y. Byron. 1990.** "Deforestation and Timber Extraction in Borneo and the Malay Peninsula." *Global Environmental Change* 1 (1): 42–56.

The article begins with a review of general concerns regarding the timber industry, shifting cultivation, and land development for permanent settlement in Borneo and peninsular Malaysia. Due to the continuing lack of a standardized basis for imagery evaluation, remote sensing data remains unreliable as a means to gauge the range and rate of deforestation. The authors propose the use of timber export data as a proxy measurement for estimated forest cover loss in Borneo and Peninsular Malaysia. Timber export data from peninsular Malaysia and the different Malaysian and Indonesian political units of Borneo island (i.e., Sabah, Sarawak, West Kalimantan, Central Kalimantan, South Kalimantan, and East Kalimantan) are presented and analyzed, covering a 13 year period (1965 to 1987). In the mid-1980s, a decline in the export of sawlogs from Indonesia was compensated by a sharp increase in the export of plywood, indicating the continued rapid extraction of timber from ever more remote parts of Borneo island. The authors argue that the timber processing industry in Indonesia and more recently in Malaysia is expanding beyond sustainable limits. At present rates of extraction, the forests of Borneo are likely to be limited to the most inaccessible parts of the island. In short, a convergence between the present landscape of peninsular Malaysia and the future of Borneo is to be expected.

Malaysia/ Sabah/ Sarawak/ Indonesia/ Kalimantan/ Peninsular Malaysia/ Deforestation/ Timber industry—Logging/ Timber industry—Downstream processing/ Timber industry—Trade and markets.

44.   **Brookfield, H., F. J. Lian, L. Kwai-Sim, and L. Potter. 1990.** "Borneo and Malay Peninsula." In *The Earth as Transformed by Human Action.* Ed. B. L. Turner, W. C. Clark, J. F. Richards, W. B. Meyer, R. W. Kates, and J. T. Mathews, pp. 495–512. New York: Cambridge University Press.

This chapter presents a broad overview of the historical transformation of Borneo's resource frontier. Particular attention is given to the timber industry and its impact on forest ecology, while shifts from forest to agricultural land use, and changes in the local economies of indigenous communities are also reviewed. The main aim of the paper is "to characterize what happens to the land, its forests and its people when a resource-frontier ethos takes hold."

In their study of the Borneo island, the authors focus on the southeastern section of Kalimantan in Indonesia and Sarawak in Malaysia. To begin, past migration patterns, forest product trade networks, trends towards commodification, and traditional land use systems of this area are described, including non-irrigated wet-rice cultivation by Banjarese villagers in South Kalimantan, and forest product collection and swidden agriculture by indigenous tribal people (Kenyah Dayak in Kalimantan and Sarawak). The Dutch colonial administration began awarding scattered, mostly unsuccessful timber concessions to private investors in the early 1900s in East Kalimantan. However, larger scale commercial timber exploitation did not begin in the region until after independence in the 1970s. By 1975, roughly half of the world's total trade in tropical timber originated from Borneo island. The industry boomed as more species become marketable and new logging methods allow extraction from steeper slopes. Uniform logging and selective logging systems are employed in Malaysia and Indonesia respectively. Though both systems represent standard forestry practice, their ecological basis remains questionable. Damage to surrounding trees during extraction and road construction means that a far greater percentage of forests are disturbed than that which is actually extracted. Though the development of wood processing capacities has seemed to promise new opportunities for local employment, this has also served to exacerbate an ecologically destructive goldrush mentality in the region. In addition, though many male members of local communities are being attracted into timber-related industries at one time or another, current evidence suggests that downstream industries rely to a great degree on a flexibilized female and immigrant labor force, rather than offering real opportunities for steady employment.

A comparison of land use indicators of the mid-1980s with those of the 1920s suggest a marked expansion in wet rice cultivation in South Kalimantan as this province has become a net exporter of rice to the neighboring, 'resource frontier' Kalimantan provinces, despite serious ecological constraints. Also indicated are an expansion in the grassland and new pockets of poverty in the area. In the meantime, the timber-related boom in East Kalimantan has attracted increasing numbers of new settlers from South Kalimantan and beyond into that region, as unlicensed logging teams, cash-crop and quick-return oriented migrant farmers, and "carpet-bag" entrepreneurs seek to cash in on new opportunities. The combined effect of logging, profit-oriented shifting agriculture, and government-sponsored population resettlement schemes has been to undermine the ecological sustainability of the forest system. By the early 1980s, the "multiple damage" caused by logging concessionaires, expanded shifting cultivation and conversion had "created a fire hazard of unprecedented order" in Kalimantan, allowing huge tracts of the region to succumb to a disastrous forest fire in 1983–84.

All in all, while traditional human land use on Borneo and the Malay peninsula had "achieved compatibility between exploitation and conservation" in the past, today the region's forest resources are being quickly degraded by concessionaires, speculative entrepreneurs, and profit-driven migrant farmers. Increasingly cash-oriented indigenous shifting cultivators are also not immune to this tendency. "Viewed as a means of short-term gains," local forest resources will continue to be exploited unsustainably, "with costs externalized to others or to later generations." A more favorable state forest policy has been limited by excessive focus on priorities of population redistribution and economic growth, and hampered by a "dearth of real scientific knowledge" regarding forest regeneration. While the international environmental movement may have helped highlight current problems, "ultimately the most effective force for change" in countries like Indonesia and Malaysia will rest with "successful political pressure for conservation within these countries."

Indonesia/ Kalimantan/ Deforestation/ Timber industry—Development and structure/ Timber industry—Logging/ Timber industry—Environmental impacts/ Timber industry—Impacts on local communities and economy/ Migrant farmers and farming/ Land settlement and development/ Land use—Patterns and planning/ Indigenous and local communities—Economy/ Indigenous and local communities—Forest land use and management practices/ Indigenous and local communities—Commoditization/ State policy—Forest and natural resources.

45. **Brookfield, H., L. Potter, and Y. Byron. 1995.** In Place of the Forest: Environmental and Socio-economic Transformation in Borneo and the Eastern Malay Peninsula. Tokyo: United Nations University Press.

The authors present findings and analysis from a research project undertaken as part of the Clark University/United Nations University Project on Critical Environmental Situations and Regions. The monograph's focus is on Borneo as a resource frontier, while also incorporating an examination of the development of eastern peninsular Malaysia for purposes of comparison. The Borneo/Peninsular Malaysia study's aim has been to identify elements which indicate trends toward impoverished, endangered, or critical states of development. States of impoverishment, endangerment, and criticality are distinguished by the degree of environmental degradation. While impoverishment signifies a state in which environmental degradation has narrowed the range of possibilities for resource use, at the level of endangerment current trends bear negative implications for the continuation of extant resource use systems; at the state of criticality the preclusion of extant human use systems has become an immediate threat rather than simply an eventual possibility.

Part One of the monograph reviews the background of environmental and land management issues in Borneo and the peninsula as well a history of land transformation in the pre-modern, colonial, and post-World War II periods. Noting the extensive conversion of forest to agriculture and forest degradation due to timber extraction as key developments in the recent geographic history of both Borneo and Peninsular Malaysia, in Part Two the authors examine in greater detail trends whereby "endangerment" appears to be leading to "criticality." Seven specific foci provide the organizing framework for this theme: loss of biodiversity, deforestation and its relation to life-supporting functions of the environment, impacts of environmental change on forest people, deforestation and the global climate, problems of drought and fire with rapid forest land decline, the spread of weed-infested grasslands, and urban development. The monograph concludes with a review of main conclusions regarding the unsustainable nature of the current development trajectory in many parts of the region and the need to change attitudes and priorities of decision-making elites and government officials.

Indonesia/ Malaysia/ Sarawak/ Sabah/ Kalimantan/ Borneo/ Land use—Patterns and planning/ Deforestation/ Biodiversity/ Soil erosion and degradation/ Timber industry—Logging/ Timber industry—Environmental impacts/ Timber industry—Impacts on local communities and economy/ Forest management/ Land settlement and development/ Economic development/ Agriculture—Plantations/ Agriculture—Shifting cultivation's environmental impacts/ History—Colonial/ Indigenous and local communities—Forest products use and trade/ Indigenous and local communities—Commoditization/ Indigenous and local communities—Forest land use and management practices/ Indigenous and local communities—Land and resource tenure systems/ State policy—Forest and natural resources/ Indigenous and local communities—State policy/ State policy—Land development/ Land tenure—Legislation and state policy/ Drought/ Forest fires/ Grasslands.

46. **Bünning, E. 1947.** *In den Wäldern Nordsumatras: Reisebuch eines Biologen.*
     Bonn: Ferd. Dümmlers Verlag.
     [In the Forests of North Sumatra: A Biologist's Travel Log.]

     Indonesia/ Sumatra/ Forest flora/ Forest fauna/ History—Colonial.

47. **Bustomi, S., and K. Soemarna. 1986.** "Regeneration and Standing Stock Study
     on Logged-over Areas in Labanan Forest Complex, Forest District of Berau,
     East Kalimantan." *Buletin Penelitian Hutan, Pusat Penelitian dan
     Pengembangan Hutan* 479: 1–16.

     In a study of an area logged over in 1980–81, the authors find that natural regeneration
     of commercial tree species saplings and poles appeared sufficient. Distribution, however,
     was uneven, suggesting the need for enrichment planting.

     Indonesia/ East Kalimantan/ Forest regeneration/ Forest management—Commercial
     forestry and silviculture.

48. **Buurman, P., ed. 1980.** "Red Soils in Indonesia." SRI Bulletin, no. 5. Bogor,
     West Java, Indonesia: Soil Research Institute.

     Indonesia/ Soils.

49. **Byron, R. N., and M. A. Quintos. 1988.** "Log Export Restrictions and Forest
     Industries Development in South-east Asia (1975–1986): The Case of the
     Phillipines [sic]." In *Changing Tropical Forests: Historical Perspectives on
     Today's Challenges in Asia, Australasia, and Oceania.* Ed. J. Dargavel, K.
     Dixon, and N. Semple, pp. 427–446. Canberra, Australia: Centre for
     Resource and Environmental Studies.

     Regulating rates of timber extraction, limiting the export of unprocessed logs, and pro-
     moting the expansion of domestic downstream processing capacity have been common
     elements of national forestry policy in many timber-exporting countries of Southeast Asia.
     The authors critically assess the effects of these policies, with particular reference to
     Indonesia and the Philippines. While cautious about drawing premature conclusions, the
     authors suggest a number of key points: 1) These policies appear to have met with highly
     variable success across different countries. West Malaysia, on the one hand, has shown the
     strongest performance in terms of value-added, local employment and foreign exchange
     generated. By contrast, unsustainably high costs have characterized the development of
     downstream processing in Indonesia, and relatively few companies have responded to gov-
     ernment incentives in the Philippines; 2) Countries which have not implemented similar
     policies promoting the development of downstream processing industries have generally
     benefited from steps taken in Indonesia, West Malaysia, and the Philippines, given the re-
     sulting rise in international tropical timber prices; 3) Whatever the downstream industrial-
     ization policy, tropical forests of Southeast Asia appear to have been "consistently under-
     valued by the governments responsible for them," encouraging wasteful over-exploitation.
     Subsidies given to those engaged in downstream processing has tended only to exacerbate
     this problem, under-pricing existing forest stands even further.

     Philippines/ Indonesia/ Timber industry—Trade and markets/ Timber industry—
     Downstream processing/ Timber industry—Logging/ Timber industry—State policy and
     regulation.

50. **Campbell, J. L. 1992.** "Ecology of Bornean Orang-Utans (*Pongo pygmaeus*) in
     Drought- and Fire-affected Lowland Rainforest." Ph.D. diss., Pennsylvania
     State University, Pittsburgh, Pa.

Indonesia/ East Kalimantan/ Forest fauna/ Forest biology and ecology/ Drought/ Forest fires.

51.   **Cannon, C. H., D. R. Peart, M. Leighton, and K. Kartawinata. 1994.** "The Structure of Lowland Rainforest after Selective Logging in West Kalimantan, Indonesia." *Forest Ecology and Management* 67 (1–3): 49–68.

Indonesia/ West Kalimantan/ Forest regeneration/ Forest management—Commercial forestry and silviculture/ Vegetation analysis/ Timber industry—Environmental impacts.

52.   **Carter, J., M. Stockdale, F. Sanchez Roman, and A. Lawrence. 1995.** "Local People's Participation in Forest Resource Assessment: An Analysis of Recent Experience, with Case Studies from Indonesia and Mexico." *Commonwealth Forestry Review* 74 (4): 333–342.

The authors discuss the process of local people's participation in forest resource assessment based on case studies from Quintana Roo, Mexico, and the Kayan Mentarang Nature Reserve in East Kalimantan, Indonesia. Participatory assessment approaches are deemed necessary in order to integrate the varied objectives local communities and governments have in resource management. They are thus an important step towards instituting genuinely participatory resource management systems generally. Methods were developed by team members from the World Wide Fund for Nature involved in establishing participatory forest management efforts in both areas. Methods included preliminary site visits, participatory rural appraisal, preparation of river and watershed base maps, mapping workshops involving the entire community, drawing village resource maps by villagers, and discussing and drawing a management zonation model based on the village maps. Zone boundaries and management regulations are identified in a consensus-oriented decision-making process involving the entire village assembly. Improvements are made to the final zonation and regulation document through village feedback and tools such as GPS (Global Positioning Systems) and computerized data management. While forest resource assessment most frequently is a need perceived by outsiders rather than forest communities, the authors emphasize the importance of ensuring that collection and use of information on forest resources be conducted in a way that can be understood by local residents. Also important is the need to counter the tendency to place control over the analysis of forest assessment data exclusively in the hands of outside experts. The case of Quintana Roo offers a promising instance where outsiders filled the role of providing reasoned suggestions, while final decision-making has been left to the local people themselves.

Indonesia/ East Kalimantan/ Forest management—Parks and conservation areas/ Forest management—Forest resource conservation/ Indigenous and local communities—Forest land use and management practices/ Project intervention—Participatory methods/ Project intervention—Forest management.

53.   **Cense, A. A., and E. M. Uhlenbeck. 1958.** *Critical Survey of Studies on the Languages of Borneo.* Bibliographical Series, no. 2. The Hague: Koninklijk Inst. voor Taal-, Land- en Volkenkunde.

Indonesia/ Malaysia/ Borneo/ Indigenous and local communities/ Bibliography.

54.   **Centre for Agricultural Library and Research Communication. 1994.** *Indonesian Agricultural Bibliography.* Bogor, Indonesia: CALRC.

Covers information on agricultural and rural development in Indonesia added to the center's database in 1994.

Indonesia/ Bibliography/ Agricultural development/ Rural development.

55.   **Clauss, W., H. D. Evers, and S. Gerke. 1987.** "The Formation of a Peasant Society: Population Dynamics, Ethnic Relations and Trade among Javanese Transmigrants in East Kalimantan, Indonesia." Wirkungen der Transmigration, no. 2. Hamburg; Bielefeld, F.R.G: HWWA Institut für Wirtschaftsforschung; Forschungsschwerpunkt Entwicklungssoziologie, Fakultät für Soziologie, Universität Bielefeld.

The authors focus on the transmigration settlement of Rimbayu, East Kalimantan, which was established in stages from 1983 to 1986, receiving government-sponsored settlers from Java. Three aspects of the settlement site are investigated in particular: population dynamics, the development of a social structure, and the growth of trade and exchange networks. Transmigrant characteristics, motives for migrating, population structure of the settlement, and marriage and reproduction patterns are highlighted to examine how population dynamics are shaped. Developments in local social structure are described in terms of settlement administration, local organizations, and social dynamics, including socio-economic differentiation. Subsistence activities, exchange of both market and non-market type, local trading networks, the role of traders, and the influence of personal characteristics, culture and ethnicity, are examined to highlight the evolution of trade. The overall aim of the report is to achieve generalizable insights into the process by which peasant society evolve out of newly established settlement sites.

Indonesia/ East Kalimantan/ Land settlement and development/ Indigenous and local communities—Economy/ Indigenous and local communities—Social relations/ Indigenous and local communities—Commoditization/ Ethnicity and ethnic relations.

56.   **Cleary, M. C., and F. J. Lian. 1991.** "On the Geography of Borneo." *Progress in Human Geography* 15 (2): 163–175.

Malaysia/ Indonesia/ Borneo/ Geography.

57.   **Cleary, M. C., and P. Eaton. 1992.** *Borneo: Change and Development.* Singapore; Oxford, U.K.: Oxford University Press.

The authors provide a general overview of the geography, indigenous settlement, colonial history, demography, and recent socio-economic development history of Borneo island, including the East Malaysian states of Sabah and Sarawak, the Indonesian Kalimantan provinces, and Brunei. One chapter focuses briefly on the subsistence strategies associated with the swidden-based farming systems of the island's indigenous farmers, noting also the recent growth of a commercial agricultural sector. Separate chapters are devoted to current issues in natural resources management and conflicts between logging and customary land rights. The monograph provides a current, comprehensively researched introduction to a variety of aspects related to Borneo's socio-economic development, providing opportunity for some preliminary comparison between different countries and provinces.

Indonesia/ Kalimantan/ Malaysia/ Sabah/ Sarawak/ Geography/ History—Colonial/ Demography/ Agricultural development/ Economic development/ Indigenous and local communities—Farming practices/ Agriculture—Shifting cultivation/ Agriculture—Permanent/ Agriculture—Plantations/ Agriculture—Smallholder cash crop farming/ Agriculture—Smallholder tree and perennial crop farming/ Timber industry—Development and structure/ Timber industry—Impacts on local communities and economy/ Forest management—Commercial forestry and silviculture/ Forest management—Forest resource conservation.

58.   **Cohen, J. I., and C. Potter. 1990.** "Genetic Resource Conservation and Utilization in the Context of International Development." *Diversity* 6 (1): 18–21.

Reviews current efforts to integrate genetic resource conservation with agricultural development and general plant use practices. Cites project experiences in West Kalimantan and Sumatra, Indonesia, the Philippines, and Ecuador.

Indonesia/ West Kalimantan/ Philippines/ Biodiversity.

59. **Colfer, C. J. P. 1981.** "Women, Men, and Time in the Forests of East Kalimantan." *Borneo Research Bulletin* 13: 75–85.

A time allocation study of male and female members of an Uma' Jalan Kenyah community in East Kalimantan shows a division of labor more equal than any ever encountered by the author, where women are active decision-makers in local agroforestry practices. Kenyah livelihoods remain highly dependent on the Kalimantan forest. However, recent changes related to new economic development in the area are evident, as these forest communities clear larger swidden fields than before, use new technology (chainsaws and motorboats) and engage in male cash employment related to the timber industry. The author notes the negative implications these changes have for the forest ecology and for women's economic and social status within the Kenyah community.

Indonesia/ East Kalimantan/ Gender analysis/ Gender relations/ Indigenous and local communities—Commoditization/ Indigenous and local communities—Forest products use and trade/ Household livelihood strategies.

60. ————. **1983.** "Change and Indigenous Agroforestry in East Kalimantan." *Borneo Research Bulletin* 15: 3–20.

Comprising a chapter in a larger report completed by the Indonesia-U.S. Man and Biosphere Project in 1980, this paper summarizes the major findings of field research in a Kenyah swidden community of Long Segar, East Kalimantan of the late 1970s. The author discusses the important role that new technology is playing in indigenous community life, as male household members use chainsaws to clear forest swiddens more quickly than ever before. Also discussed is the role of new opportunities in off-farm employment as many Kenyah men find new sources of cash income through independent entrepreneurship in lumber processing. Profitability and flexibility are the main advantages that attract local villagers to these new forms of income generation. At the same time, however, traditional uses of the forest also continue. The influx of transmigrant settlers and the expanding activities of forest concessionaires portend future conflicts with indigenous populations for whom the forest remains a crucial, albeit increasingly commercialized means of livelihood.

Indonesia/ East Kalimantan/ Indigenous and local communities—Forest land use and management practices/ Indigenous and local communities—Commoditization/ Timber industry—Impacts on local communities and economy.

61. ————. **1983.** "Change and Indigenous Agroforestry in East Kalimantan, Cont'd." *Borneo Research Bulletin* 15: 70–80.

Continuation of essay contained in previous journal issue. See previous citation for abstract.

Indonesia/ East Kalimantan/ Indigenous and local communities—Forest land use and management practices/ Indigenous and local communities—Commoditization/ Timber industry—Impacts on local communities and economy.

62. ————. **1988.** "Kenyah Dayak Tree Cutting: In Context." In *Whose Trees?: Proprietary Dimensions of Forestry.* Ed. L. Fortmann and J. W. Bruce, pp. 172–175. Boulder, Colo.: Westview Press.

Excerpted from a final report completed in 1982 by the Indonesia-U.S. Man and the Biosphere Project, this paper attempts to place tree felling activities by local populations in East Kalimantan within the context of rapid socioeconomic changes being experienced by these communities. Tree-felling makes sense from the Kenyah perspective when multiple household needs are considered. The Kenyah cut trees both to produce food and necessary household goods, as well as to obtain cash income through casual labor for nearby, concession-holding timber companies. As the Kenyah continue traditional farming practices, opportunities offered by the timber companies have also become integral to their current lifestyles. The author suggests that current development practice in East Kalimantan must address both the agricultural and forestry-related functions that local land resources now have for indigenous communities.

Indonesia/ East Kalimantan/ Indigenous and local communities—Forest products use and trade/ Indigenous and local communities—Commoditization/ Timber industry—Impacts on local communities and economy.

63.   ———. **1991.** "Indigenous Rice and the Production and Subtleties of Culture Change: An Example from Borneo." *Agriculture and Human Values* 8 (Winter–Spring): 67–84.

This analysis is based on data collected during the author's field research among Uma' Jalan Kenyah Dayak villagers at Long Segar village in the late 1970s. Presently located 48 hours up the Telen River from Samarinda, Long Segar villagers migrated from much more isolated Long Ampung village on the Malaysia border in the early 1960s. The fact that Long Segar and Long Ampung residents share a common village origin enables the author to analyze the effects of the different geographical locations of the two communities on local patterns of rice production, land use and gender division of labor.

Markedly differing per household rice yields is the first significant difference highlighted between the two communities: average household rice yield was 850 kg per year in Long Ampung and 3,300 kg in Long Segar, despite the fact that modern fertilizer and pesticide inputs were not used in either community. Differences in the availability of extension services, soil quality, agricultural practices, and weather were either not evident or could not account for the rice yield differential. However, a marked difference in the size of rice fields cultivated, the type of forest cleared for rice farming, the availability of labor, and the type of technology used for clearing was evident. Long Segar residents not only appeared to clear significantly larger fields, but they cleared a much higher percentage of their fields from "old growth" than was evident among Long Ampung villagers. Two major factors in this different land use pattern were identified: 1) The greater availability of new technology (chainsaws and outboard motors) from places like Samarinda and nearby logging outposts for Long Segar villagers; and 2) The more consistent availability of male labor in Long Segar, since the village's closer proximity to off-farm wage opportunities enabled household men to return more frequently to help clear and harvest fields that were larger and located deeper in primary forest areas. The combined effect of both new technology and greater village accessibility has been to put more productive labor power at each household's disposal in Long Segar when compared with Long Ampung.

The author considers the effects that new land use and cropping patterns may have on the way labor is organized along gender lines among the Kenyah. Scattergrams and regression analysis comparing the proportion of female household members to household rice yields indicate that "women's contribution to production, relative to men's is less in Long Segar than in Long Ampung." Further analysis suggests that where female care of dependents did not appear to affect relative rice yields in Long Ampung, in Long Segar the reverse appeared to be true. In other words was, evidence indicates that agricultural production in Long Segar is now being organized in such a way that women's childcare and household role is becoming less compatible with active rice production. This change holds negative implications for women's overall social status in the village. Concludes the author, where the move to Long Segar may have made women's lives easier in terms of access to resources (i.e., greater rice yields), for the long term, "the seeds of growing sexual differentiation were obvious; and one could not escape the growing inequities between men's opportunities and resources, and women's."

Indonesia/ East Kalimantan/ Indigenous and local communities—Farming practices/ Indigenous and local communities—Forest land use and management practices/ Indigenous and local communities—Commoditization/ Gender relations.

64.   **———, with Richard G. Dudley. 1993.** *Shifting Cultivators of Indonesia: Marauders or Managers of the Forest?* Community Forestry Case Study Series, no. 6. Rome: Food and Agriculture Organization of the United Nations.

Drawing from statistical sources and field research spanning almost two decades, Colfer examines the shifting cultivation system of farming practiced by the Uma' Jalan Kenyah. Particular focus is given to tracing how this system has developed over time given changes associated with local socio-political history, the introduction of new technologies like chain saws and motorboats, marked environmental events such as drought and fire, and the expanding timber industry. Longitudinal data is examined from four villages representing remote, semi-remote, and accessible settlement conditions: Long Ampuh on the Kayan river in East Kalimantan's interior near the Sarawak border; Long Segar along the Telen River, a 2-day boat ride from Samarinda; Tanah Merah, located on an abandoned logging base camp two hours northeast of Samarinda; and Muara Wahau, a resettlement site located 6–8 hours by boat from Long Segar. Data on 28 years of migration, forest land use and clearing at each settlement site was gathered and analyzed to document the historical development of different patterns of forest land use and agroforestry management, and to identify some of the key factors shaping these patterns. Research findings related to issues of population growth, forest clearing, agroforestry productivity, and land tenure are also discussed and their implications for more appropriate policy development noted. Ten common misconceptions underlying current policy are rebutted based on the data gathered, and several alternative policy recommendations are made: institute better control of the timber industry, legitimize indigenous land claims, incorporate indigenous knowledge into agroforestry interventions, cease projects which promote in-migration to the Kalimantan provinces, and increase international funding for local forest management.

Indonesia/ East Kalimantan/ Agriculture—Shifting cultivation/ Indigenous and local communities—Forest land use and management practices/ Indigenous and local communities—Forest products use and trade/ Indigenous and local communities—Land and resource tenure systems/ Indigenous and local communities—Commoditization/ Migration/ Resettlement/ Population pressure/ Agroforestry/ Timber industry—Impacts on local communities and economy.

65.   **———. 1995.** "Beyond Slash and Burn: A Searching Look at Uma' Jalan Forest Knowledge." In *Adaptation and Development: Interdisciplinary Perspectives on Subsistence and Sustainability in Developing Countries*. Proceedings of the International Seminar on Indigenous Knowledge, 1994, Bandung, Indonesia. Ed. K. Admihardja, A. M. Kramadibrata, O. S. Abdoellah, and H. S. Martodirdjo, Bandung, Indonesia: Indonesian Resource Centre for Indigenous Knowledge, UPT, Padjadaran University.

Indonesia/ East Kalimantan/ Indigenous and local communities—Forest land use and management practices/ Indigenous and local communities—Land and resource tenure systems/ Indigenous and local communities—Religion and cosmology/ Indigenous and local communities—Social relations.

66.   **Collier, W. 1980.** "Fifty Years of Spontaneous and Government Sponsored Migrations in the Swampy Lands of Kalimantan: Past Results and Future Prospects." *Prisma* 18: 32–55.

Indonesia/ Kalimantan/ Land settlement and development/ Migration/ Land use—Patterns and planning.

67. **Cranbrook, G., Earl of. 1977.** *Mammals of Borneo: Field Keys and an Annotated Checklist.* Kuala Lumpur: Printed for MBRAS by Percetakan Mas Sdn. Bhd.

The author presents a descriptive checklist of mammals found in Malaysian and Indonesian Borneo.

Indonesia/ Kalimantan/ Malaysia/ Sabah/ Sarawak/ Forest fauna.

68. **Cribb, R. B. 1990.** "The Politics of Environmental Protection in Indonesia." Working Paper, No. 48. Clayton, Vic., Australia: Centre of Southeast Asian Studies, Monash University.

This working paper examines political and economic aspects of changing environmental policies in Indonesia from the colonial period to the present. While the New Order Indonesian government hosts a relatively high-profile Ministry of the Environment and other conservationist-oriented regulatory bodies within separate departments (Dept. of Forestry, etc.), the position of these agencies has been highly problematic. Considerable success was scored relatively early on with the establishment of a number of wildlife reserves throughout the country. However, efforts to enlarge the reserve area and problems of providing effective protection against commercial exploitation that is often illegal but unofficially sanctioned have pitted environmental concerns against those of powerful vested interests.

Although the Indonesian government has had to respond at least nominally to international environmentalist pressures being exerted on it through multilateral funding agencies like the World Bank, environmentalist branches within the government, lead by the current Minister of the Environment, Emil Salim, derive considerable legitimacy from technocratic arguments that connect conservation with sound economic development practice. Environmental protection is also being strengthened by Indonesia's growing middle class which has helped fuel the rise of a number of environmental NGOs. Links drawn between environmental issues and nationalist critiques of First World economic policies which make environmentally destructive development measures necessary has furthered the political legitimacy of many of these groups and the environmental technocrats working within the government.

Since the early 1980s, environmental politicking has moved from conservationist issues surrounding wildlife reserves to the regulation of a wider industrial segment in order to control urban and rural environmental pollution. The Basic Law on the Living Environment of 1982 and the Government Regulations on Environmental Impact Analyses of 1987 have been key developments in this regard. Industrial pollution in the Jakarta Bay and the planned development of nuclear power plants on Java also comprise important areas of contention where the real efficacy of the new laws will be tested.

While environmental concerns have gained some ascendancy within the Indonesian government, environmental regulation is also being recognized by state bureaucrats as a way to maintain control over a rising entrepreneurial class in face of growing pressures towards economic liberalization. In addition, environmentalist regulation appears to have become a means to implement greater government control and discipline over the Indonesian public itself, as cases of peasant resettlement and forced reforestation both on Java and the Outer Islands suggest. Environmentalism in Indonesia promises to be a heated issue in policy making and political maneuvering of the coming years. Its contradictory nature as a movement fueled both by "idealistic" concerns and bureaucratic self-interest will continue to be a central characteristic of its future development.

Indonesia/ State policy—Forest and natural resources/ State policy—Pollution control/ Social movements/ Politics.

69. **Curran, L. M. 1994.** "The Ecology and Evolution of Mast-Fruiting in Bornean *Dipterocarpacae*: A General Ectomycorrhizal Theory." Ph.D. diss., Princeton University, Princeton, N.J.

Indonesia/ West Kalimantan/ Forest flora/ Forest biology and ecology.

70.   **Curran, L. M., and M. Leighton. 1991.** "Why Mast? The Role of Generalized Insect and Vertebrate Seed Predators on the Reproductive Biology of Dipterocarpaceae in the Gunung Palung Nature Reserve, West Kalimantan." In *Proceedings of the Fourth Round-Table Conference on Dipterocarps, 12– 15 December 1989, Bogor, Indonesia*. Ed. I. Soerianegara, S. S. Tjitrosom, R. C. Umaly, and I. Umboh, pp. 541–542. Bogor, Indonesia: SEAMEO BIOTROP.
[Only an abstract of the authors' paper is provided in the monograph. For complete version, contact authors at Department of Biology, Princeton University (L. M. Curran) and the Peabody Museum, Harvard University (M. Leighton).]

Results of research on two major dipterocarp species fruiting episodes in Gunung Palung Nature Reserve in 1986 and 1987 respectively are described. These events "provided a 'natural experiment' to test Janzen's predator-satiation hypothesis." Research results lends support to the "hypothesis that long intermast intervals evolved in response to the predation by generalized migrant vertebrates. . . ." Drawing insights from the destruction of an entire crop (100,000 seeds/ha in the lowland forest) due to vertebrate consumption in 1986, the authors conclude that "in order to escape complete seed loss resulting from numerical and functional response of vertebrates, high proportions of dipterocarp species across large areas including all vegetation types must ripen fruit in tight synchrony" [Summarized from monograph abstract].

Indonesia/ West Kalimantan/ Forest biology and ecology.

71.   **Damiri, M., Johansyah, Erwyn, and Setiarno. 1993.** "Studi proses produksi lampit rotan irit (*Calamus trachycoleus*. BECC), pada CV. Cipta Karya, Kuala Kapuas, Kalimantan Tengah." Report prepared for the Faculty of Agriculture, Palangkaraya University, Palangkaraya, Central Kalimantan. Photocopy.
[A study of the rattan carpet production process at C.V. Cipta Karya, Kuala Kapuas, Central Kalimantan.]

C.V. Cipta Karya is a small rattan carpet factory of 51 employees in Kuala Kapuas, Central Kalimantan. Based on site observations and interviews undertaken over 1-1/2 months, the authors briefly describe 16 stages of carpet production at the factory, including the time required to finish carpets of various sizes.

Indonesia/ Central Kalimantan/ Rattan—Downstream processing.

72.   **Daroesman, R. 1979.** "An Economic Survey of East Kalimantan." *Bulletin of Indonesian Economic Studies* 15 (3): 43–106.

Daroesman analyzes the impact that revolutionary developments in the oil and timber industries have had on the East Kalimantan economy. With a flood of new foreign investment in timber extraction starting in the late 1960s, by the late 1970s East Kalimantan was producing nearly half of Indonesia's total timber exports. While the industry depended heavily on the import of foreign labor during the early years of the boom, by 1979 most of the work force in all firms were Indonesian nationals. A boom in oil and natural gas production began in the early 1970s as well, employing over 10,000 people by 1978. In 1979, the timber and oil industries together employed c. 12 percent of the provincial labor force. Spinoff effects of this rapid sectoral growth included rapid development of infrastructural facilities such as roads, ports, navigable riverways, airstrips, power stations, drinking water supply facilities, schools, and communications during the 1970s. The province also experienced considerable growth in manufacturing, construction, and other areas during this period as well. With rapid growth occurring in many non-farm sectors, the contribution of agriculture to regional income fell during the 1970s, and little development of irrigation facilities occurred, despite the boom-related population growth. This has necessitated the import of growing amounts of rice and other foods from other provinces. Though population growth occurred predominantly in three urban areas—Balikpapan, Samarinda, and Tarakan—migration into primary forests by cash-crop oriented Banjarese and Buginese settlers from South Kalimantan and South Sulawesi provinces occurred as well. Another development with major impact on East Kalimantan's economy has been the transmigration program which has relocated hundreds of thousands of government-sponsored settlers from Java and Bali as sedentary farmers in the province. Given the limited success these farmers have frequently faced in sustaining subsistence agriculture in the province, there has been a growing awareness of the need to more closely integrate transmigrant and local community development with the development of booming non-farm industries such as timber and oil. To address this issue, the Transmigration Area Development project was initiated in the mid-1970s with funding from GTZ (Gesellschaft für Technische Zusammenarbeit) which seeks to ensure substantive progress in regional development by matching measures aimed at sectoral growth with the needs of planned settler communities.

Indonesia/ East Kalimantan/ Timber industry—Development and structure/ Timber industry—Impacts on local communities and economy/ Regional development/ Land settlement and development.

73.   ———. **1981.** "Vegetative Elimination of Alang-alang." *Bulletin of Indonesian Economic Studies* 17 (1): 83–107.

[Daroesman reviews the problems involved in controlling and eliminating farm field and forest land infestation by *Imperata cylindrica* and reports on a recent approach involving the use of fast-growing legumes being tested in the context of the Indonesian Transmigration program. Findings of 1979 field tests conducted in Sumatra are discussed, including a comparison of costs and benefits with different specific techniques.]

Indonesia/ Sumatra/ Pest, weed, and crop disease management/ Grasslands/ Farm management—Economics/ Forest management—Economics.

74.   **Djamaludin. 1991.** "The Implementation of Indonesian Selective Cutting and Replanting (TPTI) Silviculture System for Timber Improvement in the Logged-Over Areas." In *Proceedings of the Fourth Round-Table Conference on Dipterocarps, 12–15 December 1989, Bogor, Indonesia.* Ed. I. Soerianegara, S. S. Tjitrosomo, R. C. Umaly, and I. Umboh, pp. 95–110. Bogor, Indonesia: SEAMEO BIOTROP.

Djamaludin describes the development of the Indonesian Selective Cutting and Replanting System (TPTI) since large-scale timber concessions were first assigned in the early 1970s. The system's function is to facilitate improved timber extraction over the long term. Constraints in ensuring that the TPTI system is consistently implemented are noted.

Indonesia/ Forest management—Commercial forestry and silviculture/ Timber industry—logging/ Timber industry—State policy and regulation.

75.   **Djuweng, S. 1992.** "The Conflicts between the Customary Land Rights and the Development Policy in West Kalimantan: The Case of Ngabang, Nobal, and Tumbang Titi." Paper prepared at the Institute of Dayakology Research and Development, Pontianak, 1992. Photocopy.

Djuweng describes conflicts over land use and ownership caused by tree crop (oil palm and rubber) plantation development at three sites in West Kalimantan. While formal agreements on customary land transfer were signed with local *adat* chiefs, these flew in face of the wishes of most community members, and were challenged as void and illegal. A critical position is taken on the actual benefits brought to local farmers by the plantation development initiatives, and the need to defend customary land rights is emphasized.

Indonesia/ West Kalimantan/ Land settlement and development—Impacts on local communities and economy/ Indigenous and local communities—Land and resource tenure systems.

76.   **Donner, W. 1987.** *Land Use and Environment in Indonesia.* Honolulu, Hawaii: University of Hawaii Press.

Indonesia/ Land use—Patterns and planning/ Land settlement and development/ Timber industry—Logging/ Agriculture—Shifting cultivation/ Agriculture—Shifting cultivation's environmental impacts/ Deforestation/ Forest management/ Land settlement and development—Environmental impacts/ Timber industry—Environmental impacts/ State policy—Forest and natural resources.

77.   **Dove, M. 1987.** "The Perception of Peasant Land Rights in Indonesian Development." In *Land, Trees and Tenure.* Ed. J. Raintree. Nairobi, Kenya; Madison, Wisc.: ICRAF; Land Tenure Center.

Indonesia/ Land tenure—Legislation and state policy/ Indigenous and local communities—Land and resource tenure systems/ Indigenous and local communities—State policy.

78.   ———. **1988.** *Sistem perladangan di Indonesia.* Yogyakarta, Indonesia: Gadjah Mada University Press.
[Swidden Systems in Indonesia.]

Indonesia/ Kalimantan/ Agriculture—Shifting cultivation/ Indigenous and local communities—Farming practices/ Indigenous and local communities—Forest land use and management practices / Cultural ecology.

79.   **Dove, M. R. n.d..** "Government Perceptions of Traditional Social Forestry in Indonesia: The History, Causes and Implications of State Policy on Swidden Agriculture." Photocopy Honolulu, Hawaii: East-West Center.

Shifting cultivation has long been an efficient "social forestry" system among indigenous forest dwellers of Indonesia. Yet modern government social forestry schemes take little if any account of these systems. This "oversight," argues the author, is due largely to the unsuitability of swidden agriculture for "control and extraction by central governments." The paper examines the history of government perceptions and policies towards swidden agriculture in Indonesia in this light.

Indonesia/ Indigenous and local communities—State policy/ Agriculture—Shifting cultivation/ State policy—Forest and natural resources/ Social forestry/ Political economy.

80.   ———. **1980.** "Development of Tribal Land Rights in Borneo: The Role of Ecological Factors." *Borneo Research Bulletin* 12 (1): 3–19.

Indonesia/ West Kalimantan/ Indigenous and local communities—Land and resource tenure systems/ Cultural ecology.

81.   ———. **1982.** "The Myth of the "Communal" Longhouse in Rural Development: The Kantu' of West Kalimantan." In *Too Rapid Rural Development: Perceptions and Perspectives from Southeast Asia.* Ed. C. MacAndrews and Chia Lin Sien, pp. 14–78. Athens, Ohio: Ohio University Press.

This paper presents a challenge to standard perceptions common among Indonesian government development planners about the "communal" nature of tribal and peasant life among the Kantu Dayaks of West Kalimantan. Dove discusses the nature of these perceptions and their impact on community development among the Kantu. To contrast with this outsider's view, Dove presents a description of the Kantu's own perceptions of life in the longhouse as well a functional analysis of its organization that seeks to "explain [the longhouse system] as a response to specific techno-environmental constraints."

Indonesia/ West Kalimantan/ Indigenous and local communities—Social relations/ Cultural ecology.

82.   ———. **1983.** "Swidden Systems and Their Potential Role in Agricultural Development: A Case-study from Kalimantan." *Prisma* 21: 81–100.

Approximately 3,800,000 households depend on swidden cultivation as their means of livelihood in Indonesia. This system of farming is still very poorly understood and needs to be given much greater research attention in order to include this segment of the population in current development advances. The author draws from extensive field research in West Kalimantan to describe the physical and social factors at play in local swidden systems, arguing that both play key roles. The author advocates that current development programs work with local populations to adapt swidden cultivation practices to a changing socio-economic milieu, rather than eliminating such practices altogether.

Indonesia/ West Kalimantan/ Agriculture—Shifting cultivation/ Indigenous and local communities—Farming practices/ Indigenous and local communities—Forest land use and management practices.

83.   ———. **1983.** "Theories of Swidden Agriculture, and the Political Economy of Ignorance." *Agroforestry Systems* 1: 85–99.

Current arguments regarding swidden agriculture in the humid tropics are based not on empirical data but on widely held myths. Three of the most common—1) the notion that swidden fields are communally owned; 2) the notion that swidden farming is "destructive" and "wasteful"; 3) the notion that swidden farming communities are purely subsistence-oriented with minimal involvement in a wider market economy—are examined and critically reviewed against the author's own findings from past field research in West and South Kalimantan, Indonesia. The author points out that swidden fields are commonly owned, cultivated and harvested by individual families, though principles of reciprocity may be used to share labor. Contrary to notions of swidden wastefulness, swidden farming is able to support a larger population than commercial logging. The succession of grasses including *Imperata cylindrica* within a swidden systems is affected by increasing population pressure and land shortage—often policy-related phenomena. Moreover, from the point of view of indigenous farming families, such succession is often welcomed for its role in soil rebuilding and providing cattle fodder. Finally, the planting and/or harvest of tradeable market products are a common component of swidden systems which have historically integrated many swidden agriculturalist communities into the world economy.

Noting the prevalence of common myths about swidden farming among development "experts," the author suggests that their use in invoking swidden reform programs points to underlying political motives: the desire to extend state control over commercially valuable forest areas.

Indonesia/ Kalimantan/ Agriculture—Shifting cultivation's environmental impacts/ Indigenous and local communities—Farming practices/ Indigenous and local communities—Forest land use and management practices/ Indigenous and local communities—Forest products use and trade/ Pest, weed, and crop disease management/ State policy—Forest and natural resources/ Political economy.

84.   ———. **1985.** "The Kantu' System of Land Tenure: The Evolution of Tribal Land Rights in Borneo." *Studies in Third World Societies* 33: 159–182.

Dove identifies specific ecological and historical factors shaping the land tenure system of the Kantu' Dayak of West Kalimantan. Household land rights among the Kantu are established by felling primary forest. These rights have unlimited duration as long as a household remains in the longhouse, although they are transferred to the parent's immediate offspring only. Third generation households no longer exercise any legitimate right to their to their grandparents land holdings, and are thus compelled to clear primary and other forest within the longhouse's territory to establish their own fields. Once a household moves, the rights to any land it has previously cleared are transferred back to the longhouse as a whole, returning this land to its original status as general longhouse territory.

The unlimited duration of Kantu land rights can be attributed in part to ecological factors. Annual rainfall in the Kantu' territory is relatively evenly dispersed. Those months during which the Kantu' must burn their fields are characterized by substantial rainfall, making burning more difficult here than elsewhere on Borneo. Greater value is thus placed on trees of secondary forests, which burn more readily than primary forest. Although more labor is needed to weed fields that have been cut from secondary growth than for those cut from primary forests, because it is beyond the Kantu's power to regulate rainfall, secondary forests remain relatively more desirable to the households of these communities, explaining in part why the right to return to such forests are held in perpetuity, rather than being returned to the larger community after being fallowed.

The author notes a difference between this pattern and land tenure patterns of earlier times among the Kantu'. Informant interviews revealed that there was a time within the last hundred years when "households did not hold exclusive rights to given sections of the forest" within the longhouse territory. There is no evidence to indicate that rainfall patterns then were any different than now, nor that the Kantu' had lived in another area of the Borneo island. Argues the author, one explanation for this different pattern of land tenure may be found in the greater incidence of warfare which prevailed at that time, making frequent moves necessary and lessening the appropriateness of long-term rights to land. Also, the demands of warfare conflicted with the greater labor requirements associated with weeding fields cut from secondary forests. Thus, cultivation of primary forests was preferable to secondary forests during this time. When tribal warfare ceased in the area, these conditions changed, giving primacy to the use of secondary forests and favoring the development of the Kantu's present land tenure system. In addition, cessation of warfare increased the population in the area, reducing the amount of primary forest open to any given longhouse community, and encouraging a tenure allocation system that excluded emigrating households from any further claim on their secondary forest plots, allowing these to reenter the community's resource pool.

The tendency towards increasing land scarcity continues today, portending further changes in indigenous tenure systems. In particular, it appears that same-generational households are formally dividing their inherited land rights between themselves, in order to share these with their new offspring, rather than relegate the latter to landlessness in face of growing resource scarcity. The complex history of land tenure among the Kantu' suggests the "fluidity" and "responsiveness" of local land tenure systems in face of an "ever-changing mix of relevant social, political and economic determinants."

Indonesia/ West Kalimantan/ Indigenous and local communities—Land and resource tenure systems/ Population pressure.

85.   ———. **1985.** "Plantation Development in West Kalimantan I: Extant Population/Lab Balances." *Borneo Research Bulletin* 17 (2): 95–105.

This paper examines problems faced by a People's Nucleus Estate (Perkebunan Inti Rakyat or PIR) being developed by a state-owned plantation corporation in Parindu district of West Kalimantan. Nucleus estates involve a large "nucleus" plantation owned by the state or a private firm, surrounded by small holdings, known as "plasma," which are owned by peasant households. Nucleus estates have been favored by the government as "a way of combining the efficiency of the old colonial model with the democracy and higher standard of living of independent and modernizing Indonesia." In recent years, the model has been seen as an alternative basis for transmigration settlement development, which had previously been organized around subsistence food cropping. Yet serious potential for conflict with local residents over land use exists.

In the case of Parindu district, the plantation corporation has based its plans on a faulty estimate of local land use patterns. More specifically, the amount of land being cultivated at any given time was estimated to be c. .51–.59 hectare per capita, meaning that only 2.4 percent of the district's total land area is being used by the indigenous population for farming. However, this figure does not take the amount of land lying fallow into account. Based on previous research among swidden agriculturalists of West Kalimantan, the author estimates when both actively cultivated and forest fallow lands are figured, the total amount of land involved in an indigenous swidden system is 6.63 hectare per capita. Applied to Parindu district, this means that up to 70 percent of the district land is already being used by the indigenous residents, representing up to 93 percent of the land that is actually arable. Despite this reality, the current plantation project plans to appropriate 315 square kilometers for PIR development, c. 30% of which will be managed by 4,500 new transmigrant households. Removing this land from the indigenous swidden systems will force a 20% reduction in the traditional fallow period, increasing the potential for resource degradation.

Given the negative implications of these changes for indigenous livelihood strategies, the author cautions that indigenous farmers will continue using plantation lands in defiance of expropriation efforts. Conflicts over land use could be avoided if adequate compensation was paid to farmers for swidden fallow as well as cultivated field, and if indigenous farmers themselves were encouraged to join in the project. For the long term, the author recommends that plantation development projects be sure to gather more accurate information about indigenous swidden farming systems in order better to accommodate their needs with new development initiatives.

Indonesia/ West Kalimantan/ Land settlement and development/ Land settlement and development—Impacts on local communities and economy/ Agriculture—Plantations/ Agriculture—Smallholder tree and perennial crop farming/ Agriculture—Smallholder cash crop farming/ Indigenous and local communities—Farming practices.

86. ———. **1985.** *Swidden Agriculture in Indonesia: The Subsistence Strategies of the Kalimantan Kantu'.* New Babylon Studies in the Social Sciences, no. 43. Berlin; New York: Mouton.

Indonesia/ West Kalimantan/ Agriculture—Shifting cultivation/ Indigenous and local communities—Farming practices/ Indigenous and local communities—Forest land use and management practices/ Indigenous and local communities—Forest products use and trade/ Indigenous and local communities—Land and resource tenure systems/ Indigenous and local communities—Religion and cosmology/ Indigenous and local communities—Social relations/ Cultural ecology/ Ethnography.

87. ———. **1986.** "The Ideology of Agricultural Development in Indonesia." In *Central Government and Local Development in Indonesia.* Ed. C. MacAndrews, pp. 221–247. Singapore: Oxford University Press.

The author highlights the role of ideology in government policy concerning swidden agriculture in Indonesia, suggesting that "latent goals" of the government official, donor agencies, and researchers addressing swidden agricultural systems are key factors in current land management problems in Indonesia. From this perspective, the "failure" of land management practices to preserve the landed resource base may be understood "in structural as opposed to simple instrumental terms."

Indonesia/ Agriculture—Shifting cultivation/ State policy—Agricultural and rural development/ State policy—Forest and natural resources/ Political economy.

88.   ———. **1986.** "Peasant vs. Government Perception and Use of the Environment: A Case Study of Banjarese Ecology and River Basin Development in South Kalimantan." *Journal of Southeast Asian Studies* 12 (1): 113–136.

Indonesia/ South Kalimantan/ Agriculture—Shifting cultivation's environmental impacts/ Indigenous and local communities—Farming practices/ Indigenous and local communities—Forest land use and management practices/ State policy—Forest and natural resources/ Political economy.

89.   ———. **1986.** "Plantation Development in West Kalimantan II: The Perceptions of the Indigenous Population." *Borneo Research Bulletin* 18 (1): 3–27.

Based on interviews with local residents and project staff, this chapter describes perceptions of local residents in Parindu districts, West Kalimantan regarding a plantation development project in their region. These perceptions include: concerns about inequitable distribution of the costs of the project given that local project participants will have had to sacrifice ancestral land claims to the project; concerns about vulnerability should local residents who have sold their land claims not be given the option to join the project; appreciation for the cash earning opportunities that wage labor for the plantation brings; reluctance to move to the plantation settlement and trade in their larger swidden holdings for a much smaller smallholder tree plots; concern about the loss of diversity in livelihood strategies in becoming a plantation-bound tree crop smallholder; a mistrust of official motivations and intentions behind the project; a sense that officials tend to discriminate against local residents in their hiring practices; a sense that project officials do not respect local residents. Given these strong local opinions regarding the plantation development, the author characterizes simple compensation of local community members for land lost as a mistaken policy. Instead, genuine efforts should be made to involve local community members in different ways—as smallholders within the formal project area, as smallholders on smaller schemes developed closer to traditional villages, as project managers, and finally as wage laborers for those who choose to remain in their traditional swidden systems yet still wish to benefit from new cash-earning opportunities. Presenting villagers with a diversity of adjustment strategies is seen to be key to cultivating a constructive relationship between indigenous residents, immigrant settlers and plantation developers.

Indonesia/ West Kalimantan/ Land settlement and development—Impacts on local communities and economy/ Agriculture—Plantations/ Agriculture—Smallholder tree and perennial crop farming/ Agriculture—Smallholder cash crop farming.

90.   ———. **1986.** "The Practical Reason of Weeds in Indonesia: Peasant Versus State Views of Imperata and Chromolaena." *Human Ecology* 14 (2): 163–190.

Indonesia/ Indigenous and local communities—Farming practices/ State policy—Forest and natural resources/ Cultural ecology/ Pest, weed, and crop disease management.

91.   ———. **1993.** "Smallholder Rubber and Swidden Agriculture in Borneo: A Sustainable Adaptation to the Ecology and Economy of the Tropical Forest." *Economic Botany* 47 (2): 136–147.

Dove examines the integration of Para rubber cultivation into Bornean systems of swidden farming. Based on fieldwork among the Kantu' Dayak of West Kalimantan, he highlights the way in which rubber cultivation occupies a niche in the local farm economy and agroecology that complements rather than competes with swidden-based rice farming. Given the dependence of Kantu' farmers on swidden fields for subsistence rice needs, the intensity of production on smallholder rubber groves is low, and may in some instances be inversely related to market prices. The complementary nature of rice and rubber cultivation enables Kantu' villagers to "participate in the market economy on their own terms," avoiding many of the risks of exclusive cash cropping. Given the obvious benefits to producers, this "composite" system of land and resource use deserves further attention from development researchers and planners.

Indonesia/ West Kalimantan/ Indigenous and local communities—Forest land use and management practices/ Agriculture—Shifting cultivation/ Agriculture—Smallholder tree and perennial crop farming/ Agriculture—Smallholder cash crop farming.

92.　　———. **1994.** "Transition from Native Forest Rubbers to *Hevea brasiliensis* (*Euphorbiaceae*) among Tribal Smallholders in Borneo." *Economic Botany* 48 (4): 382–396.

Indonesia/ West Kalimantan/ Agriculture—Smallholder tree and perennial crop farming/ Agriculture—Smallholder cash crop farming/ Indigenous and local communities— Commoditization/ Indigenous and local communities—Farming practices/ Indigenous and local communities—Forest land use and management practices.

93.　　———. **1995.** "The Impact of Cultivation on Peasant-State Relations in Forest Product Development: The Transition from Native Forest Latexes to the Introduced *Hevea* in Kalimantan." In *Society and Non-timber Forest Products in Tropical Asia*. Ed. J. Fox, pp. 55–72. East-West Center Occasional Papers: Environment Series, no. 19. Honolulu: East-West Center.

Dove examines the transition from the gathering of forest rubbers to the "agricultural" pursuit of Para rubber cultivation and tapping by indigenous swidden farmers in Kalimantan. Drawing from historical sources as well as fieldwork spanning over a decade between 1974 and 1984 among the Ibanic-speaking Kantu' of West Kalimantan, he reviews the technologies, land use patterns, and customary law arrangements associated with the exploitation of indigenous latex materials and those which developed with the introduction of *Hevea brasiliensis* to Borneo by Dutch and British colonial administrators in the late 19th century. Interested in maximizing its rent from rubber cultivation, the Dutch colonial government attempted to both promote and control rubber tapping on land under its domain. The shift to Para rubber thus may be said to represent a transition from tribal political-economic to peasant formation for Kalimantan swidden farmers. With this change, swiddeners became more deeply involved in the world market economy and more vulnerable to market changes and state intervention. At the same time, however, they also became more secure in their position vis à vis the colonial state by virtue of their ability to resist colonial production regimes and maintain a relative degree of control over their level of involvement in an emergent and at times quite lucrative agricultural sector. The stark differences in the history of rubber production in Borneo and Amazonia attest to the determinative role played by political-economic factors rather than merely biological and technical factors in the development of non-timber forest products in general.

Indonesia/ West Kalimantan/ Non-timber forest products/ Agriculture—Smallholder tree and perennial crop farming/ Agriculture—Smallholder cash crop farming/ History— Colonial/ Political economy.

94.　　———. **1995.** "Political vs. Techno-Economic Factors in the Development of Non-Timber Forest Products: Lessons from a Comparison of Natural and Cultivated Rubbers in Southeast Asia (and South America)." *Society and Natural Resources* 8 (3): 193–208.

Indonesia/ West Kalimantan/ Non-timber forest products/ Indigenous and local communities—Forest land use and management practices/ Agriculture—Smallholder tree and perennial crop farming/ Agriculture—Smallholder cash crop farming/ History—Colonial/ Political economy.

95.   **Dove, M. R., and S. Martopo, eds. 1987.** *Manusia dan alang-alang di Indonesia*. Yogyakarta, Indonesia: Gadjah Mada University Press. [Man and Imperata in Indonesia.]

Indonesia/ Kalimantan/ Agriculture—Shifting cultivation/ Indigenous and local communities—Forest land use and management practices/ Pest, weed, and crop disease management.

96.   **Drake, R. A. 1982.** "The Material Provisioning of Mualang Society in Hinterland Kalimantan Barat, Indonesia." Ph.D. diss., Michigan State University, East Lansing.

Indonesia/ West Kalimantan/ Indigenous and local communities—Economy/ Indigenous and local communities—Commoditization/ Ethnography.

97.   **Dransfield, J. 1986.** "Prospects for Rattan Cultivation." In *The Palm Tree of Life: Biology, Utilization and Conservation*. Proceedings of a symposium at the annual meeting of the Society for Economic Botany, New York Botanical Garden, Bronx, N.Y. Bronx, N.Y.: New York Botanical Garden.

As demand for rattan materials expand to supply a booming furniture and handicraft industry, the need to cultivate rattan is becoming more urgent. Swidden farmers in Kalimantan have traditionally cultivated small diameter rattan (*Calamus caesius and C. trachycoleus*) as a supplementary livelihood activity. Dransfield describes these practices as well as a government project to cultivate the same species on the Batu Putih Estate in eastern Sabah. While cultivating small diameter rattan appears to be feasible for humid areas, there is still little evidence that the same can be said for cane species of larger diameter.

Malaysia/ Sabah/ Indonesia/ Kalimantan/ Indigenous and local communities—Farming practices/ Indigenous and local communities—Forest products use and trade/ Rattan—Cultivation/ Non-timber forest products.

98.   **Eghenter, C. 1995.** "Knowledge, Action, and Planning: A Study of Long-Distance Migrations among the Kayan and Kenyah of East Kalimantan, Indonesia." Ph.D. diss., Rutgers University, New Brunswick, N.J.

Enghenter examines patterns of long-distance migration among Kayan and Kenyah Dayak communities in East Kalimantan with particular focus on the role that local ways of knowing and ways of planning shape migration behavior. This framework demonstrates the inseparability of considering cognitive performances, individual behavior, and environmental context. Cognitive activities may in turn be described as contingent upon stimuli in the physical and social environment, a body of shared experience and knowledge, and individual interpretation.

Indonesia/ East Kalimantan/ Migration/ Indigenous and local communities/ Indigenous and local communities—Social relations/ Cultural ecology.

99.   **Erbe, S., and K. Fasbender, eds. 1988.** *Selected Literature on Transmigration 1988*. Wirkungen der Transmigration, Supplementary volume to report no. 5. Hamburg; Bielefeld, Germany: HWWA Institut für Wirtschaftsforschung; Forschungsschwerpunkt Entwicklungssoziologie, Fakultät für Soziologie, Universität Bielefeld.

Supplements report no. 5 in the "Wirkungen der Transmigration" [Effects of Transmigration] series, providing copies of newspaper and journal articles on Indonesia's transmigration program that were published both in Indonesia and internationally in 1988.

Indonesia/ Land settlement and development.

100.   **Evensen, C. I., T. S. Dierolf, and R. S. Yost. 1994.** "Growth of Four Tree Species Managed as Hedgerows in Response to Liming on an Acid Soil in West Sumatra, Indonesia." *Agroforestry Systems* 27 (3): 207–222.

   While hedgerow intercropping with fast-growing, nitrogen-fixing tree species has been hailed as an important farming system strategy on relatively fertile tropical soils, little attention has been directed to the question of tree species adaptation to acid and infertile soils. A seven-year study was undertaken at Sitiung Vc, a transmigration settlement in West Sumatra to: 1) determine the tolerance of different tree species to Al; 2) identify factors related to soil fertility affecting tree growth; and 3) determine leaf and wood yields and longevity of different tree species in an intercropping arrangement. The tree species *Paraserianthes falcataria* and *Calliandra calothyrsus* grew well while *Gliricidia sepium* did not and was eventually replaced with *Flemingia macrophylla*. Lime treatment increased yields from *Calliandra* and *Flemingia* during the study's final years. Intensive pruning had an adverse effect on yields from *Paraserianthes* after four years, while *Calliandra* and *Flemingia* proved well adapted to the regime. [Summarized with modification from journal abstract].

   Indonesia/ Sumatra/ Agroforestry/ Farm management—Cropping systems.

101.   **Evers, H. D. 1988.** "The Emergence of Trade in a Peasant Society: Javanese Transmigrants in Kalimantan." Working Paper, no. 109. Bielefeld, Germany: Forschungsschwerpunkt Entwicklungssoziologie, Universität Bielefeld.

   Drawing from a 3-year field study, Evers details the characteristics of trading activities and networks which have developed at the Rimbayu transmigration settlement in Kutai District, East Kalimantan. Market outlets for farmers' goods include: the government-sponsored cooperative for rice, soybeans, corn, and other non-perishable foods; a trading post 8 km away where middlemen buy all types of produce; and peasant traders and shopkeepers dealing with the local food supply. Evers draws from case histories to identify the different types of traders (peasant traders and middlemen) with whom transmigrant farmers are likely to exchange goods for cash. Evers emphasizes the role of social, cultural as well as economic factors in the evolution of trading networks and the emergence of a peasant economy.

   Indonesia/ East Kalimantan/ Land settlement and development/ Indigenous and local communities—Commoditization.

102.   **Fasbender, K. 1987.** "Selected Articles on Transmigration 1987." Wirkungen der Transmigration, Supplementary volume to Report No. 4. Hamburg; Bielefeld, FRG: Institut für Wirtschaftsforschung; Forschungsschwerpunkt Entwicklungssoziologie, Fakultät für Soziologie, Universität Bielefeld.

   Supplements report no. 4 in the "Wirkungen der Transmigration" [Effects of Transmigration] series, providing copies of newspaper and periodical articles on the Indonesian Transmigration program published both in Indonesia and internationally in 1987.

   Indonesia/ East Kalimantan/ Land settlement and development.

103.   **Fasbender, K., and S. Erbe. 1988.** "Transmigration in East Kalimantan: The Indonesian Resettlement Programme and its Consequences for the Receiving Provinces." Wirkungen der Transmigration, no. 4. Hamburg; Bielefeld: HWWA Institut für Wirtschaftsforschung; Forschungsschwerpunkt Entwicklungssoziologie, Fakultät für Soziologie, Universität Bielefeld.

   Drawing from fieldwork in East Kalimantan, the authors describe the structure, achievements, and local consequences of Indonesian Transmigration sites, the motives of individual transmigrants, and the plans of those who come to established sites as spontaneous settlers. The East Kalimantan study is discussed in the broader context of the Transmigration program as a whole, with discussion of broad policy goals and Transmigration-related developments in other receiving provinces. As noted by the authors, there is growing evidence of significant impact of the program, both for regional economies and the national economy as a whole. [In German].

Indonesia/ East Kalimantan/ Land settlement and development—Impacts on local communities and economy.

104.   ———. **1990.** Towards a New Home: Indonesia's Managed Mass Migration. Transmigration between Poverty, Economics and Ecology. Hamburg, FRG: Verlag Weltarchiv.

Following a broad overview of the goals and different approaches of the Indonesian Transmigration program, Fasbender and Erbe assess the effects of government-sponsored land settlement specifically in East Kalimantan province. Number, size, and development of different Transmigration sites are noted, and their impact on local demography, economy, and ecology highlighted. Although the program appears to have catalyzed significant regional development in some provinces, the case of East Kalimantan demonstrates that better coordination of transmigration activities and greater attention to developing a cohesive regional development policy are needed.

Indonesia/ East Kalimantan/ Land settlement and development—Impacts on local communities and economy/ Land settlement and development—Environmental impacts.

105.   **Fitzgerald, D. P. 1972.** "Pioneer Settlement in Southern and East Kalimantan." *Borneo Research Bulletin* 4 (1): 9–12.

The author briefly reviews his research findings at numerous transmigration settlements in South and East Kalimantan provinces. Frontier farming is claiming a high percentage of actively farmed land in the region, as new fields produce cash crops that are sold regularly, while homestead garden plots provide subsistence needs. Adjustment on part of Javanese and Balinese settlers to the new farming environment as well as unfamiliar cultural milieu has been slow, and a significant share of transmigrants eventually leave their new homesteads due to the difficulties they face there. The most successful settlers appear to be those who arrive to the area on their own initiative. By contrast, government-sponsored transmigrants who are being encouraged to attempt Javanese-style rice production on their new farm plots appear to have met with much less success.

Indonesia/ East Kalimantan/ Land settlement and development/ Migrant farmers and farming.

106.   **Fried, S. 1995.** "Writing for Their Lives: Bentian Dayak Authors and Indonesian Development Discourse." Ph.D. diss., Cornell University, Ithaca, N.Y.

This dissertation focuses on the representations of indigenous forest land use and management systems being made by Bentian Dayak writers (city-dwelling members of a community organization for Bentian culture as well as rural rattan farmers). Fried describes and discusses documents written in the context of Bentian Dayak appeals and challenges to state forestry agencies concerning the viability of indigenous resource management systems and the validity of customary land rights. The first half of the dissertation sets the context for these writings, describing East Kalimantan's colonial history (i.e., early forest product trade, sultanate rule, Dutch administration, and missionary activities), the development of state-forest village relations under the New Order regime (particularly in relation to swidden farmers), and the rattan production regimes of the Middle Mahakam Bentian Dayak in East Kalimantan. Bentian Dayak writings are also placed in context of events surrounding the appropriation of Bentian swidden fields for the development of a privately-owned industrial forest plantation and a government-sponsored transmigration settlement site—a period during which struggles over the landgrabbing figured prominently in the local print news media. Concludes Fried, Bentian challenges to the state and agribusiness actions and self-representations as legitimate agents in forest resource management "reflect the attempts of a marginalized people to position themselves firmly as actors in the development discourse of Indonesia."

Indonesia/ East Kalimantan/ Ethnicity and ethnic relations/ Social movements/ Indigenous and local communities—Forest land use and management practices/ Indigenous and local communities—State policy/ Rattan—Cultivation/ Rattan—Collection and trade/ Pulp and paper industry/ State policy—Forest and natural resources/ Land settlement and development—Impacts on local communities and economy/ Timber industry—Impacts on local communities and economy/ Timber plantations/ Political economy.

107. **Fujisaka, S. 1994.** "Learning from Six Reasons Why Farmers Do Not Adopt Innovations Intended to Improve Sustainability of Upland Agriculture." *Agricultural Systems* 46 (4): 409–425.

Fujisaka examines seven upland project sites to identify the reasons for low rates of farmer adoption that often characterize upland agricultural development and conservation efforts. These include the IRRI/Philippine Department of Agriculture research site in Claveria, Misamis Oriental; a potential Integrated Social Forestry site at Calminoe, Philippines; the Upland Agriculture and Conservation Project on Java; the Forest Development and Watershed Management Project of the Lao government and FAO at Luang Prabang, Laos; the Philippine Bureau of Forest Development's (BFD) Allah Valley Watershed Development Project, Lake Sebu, South Cotabato, Philippines; the World Neighbor's Soil and Water Conservation Project in Cebu, Philippines; and the collaborative, IRRI-Government of Madagascar research project in the Madagascar Middle West and Central Highland. Six reasons farmers do not adopt the promoted technologies include: 1) the project targets a problem farmers themselves do not face; 2) the innovation promoted fails to work; 3) extension services are inadequate; 4) the innovation introduced is too expensive; social factors that impinge on attitudes towards and possibilities for adoption. Taking these considerations into account is likely to improve the extent and rate to which adaptation and adoption of erosion-controlling contour vegetative strips among Filipino farmers.

Philippines/ Mindanao/ Cebu/ Indonesia/ Project intervention—Soil conservation/ Project intervention—Social and community forestry.

108. **Fulcher, M. 1983.** "Resettlement and Replacement: Social Dynamics in East Kalimantan, Indonesia." Ph.D. diss., Northwestern University, Evanston, Ill.

Fulcher examines the dynamic of socio-economic change and interaction between settler and indigenous communities resulting from the Transmigration Program in East Kalimantan. Fieldwork was conducted in Melak district of East Kalimantan from June 1980 to September 1981. As agriculturalists, the transmigrated Javanese settlers as well as the indigenous Tunjung and Benuaq Dayak in the research area have competing interests over the question of access to land. This issue has served as a major source of tension between the settler and indigenous communities. Final resolution of resource-related tensions is made problematic by the lack of access to national institutions (i.e., courts) on the part of indigenous residents as well as the lack of official recognition of customary land law. Tensions are, however, diffused by the enclave nature of the transmigration settlement, informal institutions for consensus building within communities, as well as the balance struck between the settlers' relatively easier access to national courts and the indigenous population's association with local sources of magico-religious power (i.e., black magic). The author suggests a dynamic of avoidance deployed by both communities to prevent or manage conflict should it arise. This outcome is argued to be an outcome of the economic, social and political relationships characterizing the separate ethnic communities.

Indonesia/ Kalimantan/ Land settlement and development—Impacts on local communities and economy/ Land tenure—Legislation and state policy/ Indigenous and local communities—Land and resource tenure systems/ Ethnicity and ethnic relations.

109. **Gadas, S. R. 1995.** "A Hierarchical Approach to the Planning of Industrial Timber Plantations in Indonesia Using Timber Plantations in South Kalimantan as Test Case." Ph.D. diss., University of Washington, Seattle, Wash.

Indonesia/ South Kalimantan/ Forest management—Commercial forestry and silviculture/ Timber plantations.

110. **Gaither, Jr., J. C. 1994.** "Understorey of Avifauna of a Bornean Peat Swamp Forest: Is It Depauperate?" *Wilson Bulletin* 106 (2): 381–390.

Investigates bird populations and species composition in peat swamp and lowland dipterocarp forests of Gunung Palung Nature Reserve, West Kalimantan.

Indonesia/ West Kalimantan/ Forest fauna/ Biodiversity/ Forest biology and ecology.

111. **Galdikas, B. M. F. 1978.** "Orangutan Adaptation at Tanjung Puting Reserve, Central Borneo." Ph.D. diss., University of California, Los Angeles.

Indonesia/ Kalimantan/ Forest fauna/ Forest biology and ecology/ Forest management—Parks and conservation areas.

112. ———. **1982.** "Orangutan sebagai penyebar biji tanaman di Tanjung Puting, Kalimantan Tengah: Implikasinya terhadap pelestarian alam." *Ilmu dan Budaya* 2: 97–114.
[Orangutans as Disseminators of Plant Seeds in Tanjung Puting, Central Kalimantan: Implications for Environmental Conservation.]

Following a brief review of previous research on the influence of orangutans on forest ecology and structure, the author reports results of research conducted between January and June 1978 in Tanjung Puting nature reserve, Central Kalimantan, involving 644 hours of direct observation. Orangutans were observed to eat more than 50 different kinds of fruit (some only once or twice during the whole 6 month observation period), the leaves of 13 different plant species, and a variety of other plant food. Seeds were distributed over a wide area of the nature reserve (up to 10 km from the point of ingestion), by way of digestion as well as spitting, carrying the fruits some distance before consumption, and dropping tree-born fruits to the ground where they are picked up by other animals. Orangutans served the function of seed distribution for c. 70 percent of the plant species they consumed during the observation period. The author notes the importance of this dynamic for maintaining species diversity over a wide forest area in the nature reserve. [In Bahasa Indonesia].

Indonesia/ Central Kalimantan/ Forest fauna/ Forest biology and ecology/ Biodiversity.

113. ———. **1988.** "Orangutan diet, range and activities at Tanjung Pitung, central Borneo." *International Journal of Primatology* 9: 1–35.

Indonesia/ Kalimantan/ Forest fauna/ Forest biology and ecology/ Biodiversity.

114. **Garang, J. 1974.** Adat und Gesellschaft: Eine sozio-ethnologische Untersuchung zur Darstellung des Geistes- und Kulturlebens der Dajak in Kalimantan. Beiträge zur Südasienforschung, Südasien-Institut, Universität Heidelberg, Band 9. Wiesbaden, Germany: Franz Steiner Verlag.

[Adat and Society: A Socio-ethnological Study Towards the Representation of the Spiritual and Cultural Life of the Dayaks in Kalimantan.]

This monograph is a published version of the author's dissertation based on fieldwork among the Orang Ngaju of Tewah village, Gunung Mas sub-district, Central Kalimantan. Focus of the study included an ethnological investigation of the social organization and religious identity of the Ngaju people. [In German].

Indonesia/ Central Kalimantan/ Indigenous and local communities—Religion and cosmology/ Indigenous and local communities—Social relations/ Ethnography.

115. **Geertz, C. 1963.** *Agricultural Involution: The Process of Ecological Change in Indonesia.* Berkeley, Calif.: University of California Press.

Indonesia/ Agriculture—Shifting cultivation/ Agriculture—Permanent/ Agricultural intensification/ Indigenous and local communities—Farming practices.

116. **Geinitz, D. 1986.** Zielgruppenorienterte Förderung der kleinbäuerlichen Kautschukwirtschaft in Indonesien und Malaysia. Hamburg: Verlag Weltarchiv.
[Target Group-Oriented Promotion of Smallholder Rubber Production in Indonesia and Malaysia.]

Covering the 1960s through the early 1980s, Geinitz describes government programs aimed at increasing rubber production among smallholders in Malaysia and Indonesia. Achievements, strengths, and weaknesses of smallholder rubber programs in both countries are reviewed. The greater success at increasing rubber production and reducing poverty among smallholders in Malaysia as compared with Indonesia is noted, and possible factors contributing to this difference are suggested.

Indonesia/ Malaysia/ Agricultural development/ Agriculture—Smallholder tree and perennial crop farming/ Agriculture—Smallholder cash crop farming/ State policy—Agricultural and rural development/ Land settlement and development/ Poverty.

117. **German Forestry Group. 1990.** "Proceedings of Regional Seminar on Conservation for Development of Tropical Rain Forest in Kalimantan held in Samarinda, 18–19 October 1989." *GFG Report* 15 (Special Issue): 1–285.

24 papers are produced in this special issue of the *GFG Report* published by the German Forestry Group at Mulawarman University, Samarinda, East Kalimantan. Papers deal with various aspects of timber production from natural forests, plantation development, and forest resource conservation. [Most papers in Bahasa Indonesia].

Indonesia/ Kalimantan/ Timber industry—Logging/ Forest management—Commercial forestry and silviculture/ Forest management—Forest resource conservation/ Forest regeneration/ Timber plantations.

118. **Gillis, M. 1987.** "Multinational Enterprises and Environmental and Resource Management Issues in the Indonesian Tropical Forest Sector." In *MNCs, Environment, and the Third World.* Ed. C. Pearson, pp. 64–89. Durham, N.C.: Duke University Press.

The tropical timber industry has played a central role in the Indonesian economy since the early 1970s. Opened to foreign investment in the late 1960s, the timber industry rapidly boomed, mainly in Indonesia's Kalimantan provinces. By the mid-1970s timber was the nation's leading export, first eclipsed by the oil boom only by 1980. The author describes conflicts between foreign investors and the Indonesian government over changing state policies on export taxes, deepened downstream processing, domestic employment promotion and reforestation. Escalating government requirements led to a general withdrawal of American-based multi-national companies from Indonesia's timber sector in the early 1980s. By 1985, only Japanese, Malaysian, Philippine and other Southeast Asian timber corporations remained along with Indonesian investors. Ongoing shortcomings in the regulation of timber extraction and the dearth of technical information on tropical forest management have been major stumbling blocks. Argues the author, the withdrawal of large MNCs from Indonesia has left resource management in the hands of smaller firms with much less experience and no long term interest in the sustainable use of production forests.

Indonesia/ Timber industry—Development and structure/ Timber industry—Trade and markets/ Timber industry—State policy and regulation/ Forest management—Commercial forestry and silviculture/ Forest management—Forest resource conservation.

119.   ———. **1988.** "Indonesia: Public Policies, Resource Management, and the Tropical Forest." In *Public Policies and the Misuse of Forest Resources.* Ed. R. Repetto and M. Gillis, pp. 43–113. Cambridge, U.K.: Cambridge University Press.

Deforestation in Indonesia is proceeding rapidly. This paper assesses the role that the overall institutional environment and various government policies have played in this process. An introductory section reviews the composition of Indonesia's tropical rainforest stands and highlights factors other than government policy, including poverty, shifting cultivation, and fuelwood gathering, which appear to be accelerating the rate of degradation. In addition, the timber industry has figured very prominently in Indonesia's economic development since the late 1960s, and the author suggests that overemphasis on the productive rather than protective function of forest lands by government policymakers has been a key factor in the unsustainable rates of extraction and forest conversion characterizing the past several decades. Furthermore, a complex and ill-defined institutional framework has made for poor regulation of timber extraction as well as poor coordination of resource management. Inadequate levels of rent collected by the government on forest products has promoted wasteful resource use. Biased export tax structures, fiscal policies and government subsidies have skewed incentives, thus creating greater economic inefficiencies in forest use. Poorly planned resettlement programs have been another contributing factor in unsustainable land use. The authors conclude that, so far, both government policy and institutions have discouraged systematic resource conservation.

Indonesia/ Deforestation/ Timber industry—Logging/ Timber industry—State policy and regulation/ Timber industry—Environmental impacts/ Land settlement and development—Environmental impacts/ Forest management—Commercial forestry and silviculture/ Forest management—Forest resource conservation/ State policy—Forest and natural resources.

120.   **Godoy, R. A. 1990.** "The Economics of Traditional Rattan Cultivation." *Agroforestry Systems* 12: 163–172.

Indonesia/ Central Kalimantan/ Rattan—Cultivation/ Indigenous and local communities—Farming practices/ Farm management—Economics.

121.   **Godoy, R. A., and T. C. Feaw. 1991.** "Agricultural Diversification Among Smallholder Rattan Cultivators in Central Kalimantan, Indonesia." *Agroforestry Systems* 13: 27–40.

Godoy and Feaw examine the problem of over-dependence on a limited number of cash crops among farmers through a case study of smallholder rattan cultivators in Central Kalimantan. A poorly diversified portfolio of agricultural activities prevailed among the farmer studied. While farmers rely on rattan because of its current profitability, over-reliance results in excessive exposure to unfavorable market changes and environmental developments. This pattern is shaped by various economic and agronomic constraints that discourage farmers from diversifying out of rattan into other crops.

Indonesia/ Central Kalimantan/ Agriculture—Smallholder cash crop farming/ Agriculture—Smallholder tree and perennial crop farming/ Rattan—Cultivation/ Farm management—Economics.

122. **Goeltenbroth, F. 1992.** "Kerusakan hutan dan implikasi bagi kesinambugan daya dukung lingkungan." *Prisma* 21 (6): 31–51.
[Forest Destruction and Its Implications for Environmental Sustainability.]

The author provides a general overview of problems of deforestation in Indonesia resulting from timber industry, transmigration and population growth. Data is culled from various international as well as national (Indonesian) sources to briefly describe issues of biodiversity loss, erosion, and climate change. Also serious, notes the author, are problems of social and cultural dislocation resulting from rapid forest loss. [In Bahasa Indonesia].

Indonesia/ Deforestation/ Timber industry—Environmental impacts/ Land settlement and development—Environmental impacts/ Population pressure/ Soil erosion and degradation/ Biodiversity/ Timber industry—Impacts on local communities and economy.

123. **Government of Indonesia.** [1976]. "Peat and Podzolic Soils and their Potential for Agriculture in Indonesia: Proceedings ATA 106 Midterm Seminar, Tugu, October 13–14, 1976." *Bulletin Soil Research Institute* 19: 1–198.

Nine papers presented at the ATA 106 Midterm Seminar are reproduced in full in this Bulletin issue. Topics include appropriate approaches to promote agricultural development in Indonesia under tropical soil conditions as well as the impacts of shifting cultivation on areas of podzolic soil in the Kalimantan provinces. The bulletin is published by the Soil Research Institute of the Ministry of Agriculture.

Indonesia/ Kalimantan/ Soils/ Agriculture—Shifting cultivation's environmental impacts/ Forest management—Control of shifting cultivation/ Project intervention—Agricultural development.

124. ———. **1981.** "Proyek pemukiman transmigrasi non-pasang-surut, Teluk Dalam, Kecamatan Tenggarong, Kabupaten Kutai, Propinsi Kalimantan Timur." Photocopy. Jakarta: General Directorate of Transmigration.
[Transmigration Resettlement Project, Teluk Dalam, Tenggarong Sub-District, Kutai District, East Kalimantan.]

This typescript gives a brief description of various aspects of the Teluk Dalam transmigration settlement project in Kutai District, East Kalimantan. Includes data on the general setting, population, socio-economic and socio-cultural issues.

Indonesia/ East Kalimantan/ Land settlement and development.

125. ———. **1981.** "Proyek pemukiman transmigrasi non pasang-surut, Babulu Darat, Kecamatan Waru-Longsari, Kabupaten Pasir, Propinsi Kalimantan Timur." Photocopy. Jakarta: General Directorate of Transmigration.
[Transmigration Resettlement Project, Babulu Darat, Waru-Longsari Sub-District, Pasir District, East Kalimantan.]

This typescript provides a brief overview of the Babulu Darat transmigration resettlement project in Pasir district of East Kalimantan. The setting, population, socio-economic and socio-cultural issues as well as activities of the transmigration project are described.

Indonesia/ East Kalimantan/ Land settlement and development.

126.　——. **1985.** "A Review of Policies Affecting the Sustainable Development of Forestlands in Indonesia." 5 Volumes. Photocopy. Jakarta: Department of Forestry; State Ministry of Population, Environment and Development, Department of Interior; International Institute for Environment and Development.

This five volume report summarizes the findings of a comprehensive review of all government policies affecting the sustainable development of Indonesia's forest lands. A four member team completed the review and condensed its findings into the present form between 1983 and 1985. Vol. 1 (Discussion Document) outlines the main issues presented in the overall work, pointing to emerging problems in conflicting and inappropriate land and forestry utilization patterns. Vol. 2 reviews the issues identified in more specific detail. The team members conclude that four major issues should receive priority attention in forestry development by Indonesian policy makers: 1) developing more sustainable land use systems that direct a more appropriate pattern of forest-to-agriculture land conversion than has been the case under the government transmigration program and at the hands of spontaneous settlers; 2) devising ways that will better ensure the sustainability of protected as well as production forests; 3) developing policies and technology to increase the productivity of forest lands currently being used on an industrial basis; and 4) addressing the need for increasing socio-economic benefits from a preserved forest for both forest-dwelling and downstream rural communities through forest-based employment promotion. Volume 3 of the report (Background Paper) discusses the legislative and institutional framework under which Indonesian forest lands are controlled and put to productive use by the state, private investors and local communities.

The report is extensive and includes a number of appendices showing specific legislation, transmigration site assessment documents, an outline of least successful transmigration sites, as well as the forestry section of the 4th Five Year Development Plan (1984–1989). Data and information for the report were obtained largely from relevant policy documents, program studies (i.e., Transmigration program), and interviews with government officials rather than fieldwork documenting specific policy outcomes at the field level.

Indonesia/ Forest management—Commercial forestry and silviculture/ Forest management—Economics/ Forest management—Forest resource conservation/ Timber industry—Development and structure/ Timber industry—State policy and regulation/ Timber industry—Logging/ Timber industry—Environmental impacts/ Timber industry—Impacts on local communities and economy/ Timber plantations/ Land settlement and development/ Land settlement and development—Environmental impacts/ Land use—Patterns and planning/ Land tenure—Legislation and state policy/ State policy—Forest and natural resources/ State policy—Land development.

127.　——. **1990.** "Situation and Outlook of the Forestry Sector in Indonesia." 4 vols. Jakarta; Rome: Ministry of Forestry, Directorate General of Forest Utilization; Food and Agricultural Organization of the United Nations.

This four volume report is among the most comprehensive overviews of the forestry sector in Indonesia to date. Issues reviewed include forest-based processing industries; non-timber forest products; land use, the development of plantations and the conservation of natural forests; protection of the forest environment; legislation and policy concerning forest use. Proposals to improve performance in each of these areas are presented [Summarized from World Resources Institute, "1993 Directory of Country Environmental Studies: An Annotated Bibliography of Environmental and Natural Resource Profiles and Assessments" published by World Resources Institute, IIED, and IUCN, November 1992].

Indonesia/ Timber industry—Development and structure/ Timber industry—State policy and regulation/ Forest management—Commercial forestry and silviculture/ Forest management—Economics/ Timber plantations/ Forest management—Forest resource conservation/ Forest management—Parks and conservation areas/ Land use—Patterns and planning/ State policy—Forest and natural resources/ State policy—Land development/ Land tenure—Legislation and state policy/ Non-timber forest products.

128.　————. **1991.** "Biodiversity Action Plan for Indonesia." Jakarta; Washington, D.C.; Bogor, West Java, Indonesia: Ministry of Population and Environment; World Bank; Bogor Agricultural University, Faculty of Forestry.

An action plan for preserving biodiversity is presented in this 92 page report. Four components of the plan are described: development of parks and reserves and other protected areas for conservation; biodiversity conservation efforts on agricultural lands, in production forests and other areas not classified as formal protection zones; conservation of coast and sea resources; conservation efforts in the realm of policy and other "ex situ" areas. Program objectives and priorities are listed, as well as present and planned projects in conservation and sustainable development. [Summarized from World Resources Institute, "1993 Directory of Country Environmental Studies: An Annotated Bibliography of Environmental and Natural Resource Profiles and Assessments" published by WRI, IIED, and IUCN].

Indonesia/ Biodiversity/ Forest management—Parks and conservation areas/ Forest management—Forest resource conservation/ Conservation farming/ State policy—Forest and natural resources/ State policy—Pollution control.

129.　————. **1991.** "Indonesian Tropical Forestry Action Programme." 3 vols. Jakarta; Rome: Ministry of Forestry; Food and Agriculture Organization of the United Nations.

Current issues and government programs as well as planned programs and targets are presented in this three volume report. Special attention is given to the development of forest-based industries, development of a network of national parks and reserves, plantation development, and the role of government and private institutions in implementing the action plan. [Summarized from World Resources Institute, "1993 Directory of Country Environmental Studies: An Annotated Bibliography of Environmental and Natural Resource Profiles and Assessments" published by WRI, IUCN and IIED].

Indonesia/ Forest management—Commercial forestry and silviculture/ Timber industry—Development and structure/ Timber industry—Trade and markets/ Timber industry—State policy and regulation/ Timber industry—Downstream processing/ Forest management—Forest resource conservation/ Forest management—Parks and conservation areas/ State policy—Forest and natural resources.

130.　**Government of Indonesia. Agency for Agricultural Research and Development, and Asian Development Bank. 1991.** Marginal Farmer Community Development Project. Phase One Report.

The document represents a detailed report on the results of Phase I of Project No. 1400-INO undertaken by the Government of Indonesia's Agency for Agricultural Research and Development and the Asian Development Bank during Repelita V (National Five Year Development Plan No. 5). The overall aim of the project is to assist disadvantaged small farmers throughout the country. Carried out in association with Hunting Technical Services, Ltd. and P.T. Tricon Jaya, Phase I of the project aimed to develop a definition of marginal farmers, develop a methodology for identifying their location in Indonesia, apply the methodology to identify high concentrations of marginal farmers, and recommend policy guidelines for the integrated development of marginal farming communities. A community development approach is recommended for small farmer assistance in order "to improve adoption rates of new technologies and to ensure a more sustainable form of development."
　The report defines marginal farmers as "a community of small farmers who are exceeding the carrying capacity of their land because they are practicing traditional farming systems that fail to optimize the potential of that land, which forces them into a state of

poverty." The methodology developed for identifying high concentrations of marginal farmers draws from provincial poverty statistics as well as physical screening processes that identify both marginal land and areas of marginal land use on a provincial basis. Data was obtained through the RePPROT mapping program for the physical screening process. Summarizing RePPROT statistics, the report identifies 16 provinces to be prioritized in terms of marginal land use, 8 of which are characterized by shifting cultivation. These include Central, West and South Kalimantan, as well as Lampung, South Sumatra, Bengkulu, East Nusa Tenggara and East Timor provinces. Poverty statistics are then cited to identify concentrations of marginal farmers within these marginal land use areas. Based on this analysis, the report finds that major concentrations of marginal farmers are found in West and Central Kalimantan, Bengkulu, East Nusa Tengarra and East Timor as well as several other provinces marked by sedentary farming (i.e., all of Java, North Sumatra and South Sulawesi). This analysis is followed by a brief description of the processes and causes of marginality as well as existing policies affecting the problem in one way or another. A subsequent section is devoted to policy recommendations. Part II of the report describes the process used to select various sites for feasibility studies planned for Phase II of the project; Central and West Kalimantan provinces are among proposed project areas. The report includes a set of land use maps of the provinces surveyed.

Indonesia/ Central Kalimantan/ West Kalimantan/ South Kalimantan/ Poverty/ Agriculture—Shifting cultivation/ Land use—Patterns and planning/ Project intervention—Agricultural development.

131. **Gray, J. A., and S. Hadi. 1989.** "Forest Concessions in Indonesia: Institutional Aspects." Indonesia UTF/INS/065/INS: Forestry Studies, Field Document VI-I. Jakarta; Rome: Directorate General of Forest Utilization, Ministry of Forestry, Government of Indonesia/Food and Agriculture Organization of the United Nations.

Indonesia/ Timber industry—State policy and regulation/ Forest management—Commercial forestry and silviculture/ State policy—Forest and natural resources.

132. **Griffiths, M., and C. P. Van Schaik. 1993.** "The Impact of Human Traffic on the Abundance and Activity Periods of Sumatran Rain Forest Wildlife." *Conservation Biology* 7 (3): 623–626.

Griffiths and Van Schaik compare the large-mammal communities of two lowland areas in and around the Gunung Leuser National Park in northern Sumatra. One of the areas studied is hardly ever entered by people, while the other is subject to intensive use by researchers during daylight hours as well as by fishermen who work along the area's perimeter. Cameras were operated for seven to thirty months in each site respectively, and were set to be triggered only by passing larger animals. Study results indicate that some animals avoid heavily traveled areas and suggest that at least one animal species (the Malayan Sun Bear or *Helarctos malayanus*) tends to adopt nocturnal behavior when faced with frequent human disturbance. Some animals (primates, some squirrels, and hornbills) appear to have become habituated to human traffic, and there is some evidence in the literature that heavy human traffic reduces predation on habituated species, possibly resulting in significant ecological change. The findings present implications for ecotourism and field research that should be taken into consideration in project planning.

Indonesia/ Sumatra/ Forest fauna/ Forest biology and ecology/ Forest management—Parks and conservation areas.

133. **Guerreiro, A. J., and B. J. Sellato. 1984.** "Traditional Migration in Borneo: The Kenyah Context." *Borneo Research Bulletin* 16: 12–27.

Field research on migration patterns among the Kenyah of East Kalimantan reveal that Kenyah communities have tended to migrate for reasons other than the need for arable land.

Historically, competition and tension within Kenyah communities as well as warfare between different ethnic groups has been a major factor in the decision to form separate community groups and/or move to new settlement sites. More recently, the benefits offered by trading networks further downstream have been a major incentive to migrate. The Kenyah have proven themselves highly successful swidden farmers in the region, often crowding out other indigenous groups. The question remains as to whether they will be as successful in the transition to permanent agriculture.

Indonesia/ East Kalimantan/ Indigenous and local communities—Social relations/ Indigenous and local communities—Commoditization/ Migration/ Agricultural intensification.

134. **Hadi, S., S. Hadi, and R. Hidayat. 1985.** "Swidden Cultivation in East Kalimantan (Kenyah and Buginese)." In Swidden Cultivation in Asia: v. 3. Empirical Studies in Selected Swidden Communities: India, Indonesia, Malaysia, Philippines, Thailand. pp. 74–149. Social and Human Sciences in Asia and the Pacific; RUHSAP Series on Occasional Monographs and Papers, 12. Bangkok, Thailand: UNESCO Regional Office for Education in Asia and the Pacific.

The authors present the results of field study conducted in 1983 among swidden agriculturalists of East Kalimantan under the sponsorship of UNESCO's Man and Biosphere program. Data was collected through non-participant observation, unstructured and semi-structured interviews with community members, provincial leaders and government officials. The report is ethnographic, describing different aspects of village life and the agricultural cycle among two distinct ethnic groups: indigenous Kenyah (one tribe among what are collectively known as the Dayak of Kalimantan) and Buginese settlers who have migrated to Kalimantan from different parts of Sulawesi in search of land for cash cropping. The two ethnically distinct groups both practice shifting cultivation, although important differences in their respective cropping systems are noted. Government official perceptions of local swidden cultivators are also reported.

Indonesia/ East Kalimantan/ Indigenous and local communities—Farming practices/ Migrant farmers and farming/ Farm management—Cropping systems/ Agriculture—Shifting cultivation.

135. **Hadi, S., and Y. B. Ling. 1988.** "Swidden Cultivation among the Tunjung of East Kalimantan With Particular Emphasis on Socioeconomic Factors." *Sarawak Museum Journal* 39 (60): 111–148.

Hadi and Ling focus on the economics of shifting cultivation as practiced by residents of four villages in Kutai District, East Kalimantan. They describe village demographic structures, social organization and ethnic relations, agro-climatic conditions, methods for clearing and planting fields, cropping systems, and household income. While maize, rice and cassava comprise the main crops grown, cultivation of cash crops (coffee, cocoa, rubber, etc.) has increased since the late 1970s. Also highlighted are agricultural development projects in the area, involving provision of agricultural inputs (modern seed, fertilizer, and pesticides) and technical advice.

Indonesia/ East Kalimantan/ Indigenous and local communities—Economy/ Indigenous and local communities—Farming practices/ Agriculture—Smallholder cash crop farming/ Agriculture—Smallholder tree and perennial crop farming/ Project intervention—Agricultural development/ Farm management—Economics/ Farm management—Cropping systems.

136. **Haggarsson, J. E., U. Krynitz, and H. Strotz. 1994.** *Indonesian Forest Management with Emphasis on* Dipterocaraceae *and Their Ectomycorrhiza:*

A Minor Field Study. Working Paper—International Rural Development Centre, no. 248. Uppsala, Sweden: Swedish University of Agricultural Sciences, International Rural Development Center.

The authors present initial results on a study testing the polymerase chain reaction (PCR) method for identifying ectomycorrhiza species on *Dipterorcarpaceae* conducted in a forest concession owned by PT. Kiani Lestari in East Kalimantan. Issues of rain forest management in Kalimantan are reviewed in a lengthy appendix.

Indonesia/ East Kalimantan/ Forest management—Commercial forestry and silviculture.

137. **Hainsworth, G. B. 1985.** "Economic Growth, Basic Needs and Environment in Indonesia: The Search for Harmonious Development." *Southeast Asian Affairs* 1985: 152–173.

Indonesia/ State policy—Economic development/ State policy—Pollution control.

138. **Hall, P. 1991.** "Structure, Stand Dynamics, and Species Compositional Change in Three Mixed Dipterocarp Forests of Northwest Borneo." Ph.D. diss., Boston University, Brookline, Mass.

Indonesia/ East Kalimantan/ Forest flora/ Forest biology and ecology/ Vegetation analysis.

139. **Halos, S. C., F. F. Natividad, L. J. Escote-Carlson, G. L. Enriquez, and I. Umboh. 1994.** Proceedings of the Symposium on Biotechnological and Environmental Approaches to Forest Pest and Disease Management, Quezon City, Philippines, 28–30 April 1993. BIOTROP Special Publication, no. 53. Bogor, Indonesia: SEAMEO-BIOTROP.

Twenty papers discuss current problems in forest pest management in various parts of Asia and highlight recent strategies in biotechnological and environmentally-based pest control. Individual papers include, among others: "Inventory of Forest Damages at the Faperta UNCEN Experimental Gardens in Manokwari, Irian Jaya, Indonesia" by Matheus T. E. Kilmaskossu and Jan Piet Nerokouw; "Incidence of Dieback in Two *Acacia mangium* Plantation Sites in Sabah" by Mahmud Sudin; "Preliminary Observations on Insect Pests and Diseases Problems of *Gliricidia sepium* (Jacq.) Walp. germplasm collection in ViSCA and Its Implications for Genetic Improvement" by Ernesto C. Bumatay; "Biological and Environmental Pest and Disease Control Strategy in PICOP" by Emelio O. Anino; "Forest Pest and Diseases Research in the Philippines: An Overview" by Segundino V. Forondo and Marcelino U. Siladan; "Natural Enemies Associated with Some Insect Pests of Forest Plantations in Peninsular Malaysia" by Ahmad Said Sajap and Jaacob Abd. Wahab; "Preliminary Survey on Entomopathogenic Fungi in the Forest at Khao Yai National Park" by Pimpun Sommartya and Banpot Napometh; "Recent Insect Pest Outbreaks in Forest Plantations in Peninsular Malaysia" by Ab. Majid B. Ab. Rahman and Ahmad Said Sajap; and "Development of *Parmela* sp. in a *Pinus merkusii* stand affected by air pollutants at Puncak, West Java" by Dadang K. Permana, Soetrisno Hadi, and Simon T. Nuhamara.

Indonesia/ Malaysia/ Philippines/ Sabah/ Pest, weed, and crop disease management/ Forest management—Commercial forestry and silviculture/ Timber plantations.

140. **Hamzah, M. 1979.** *Pengaruh pengolahan tanah secara mekanis terhadap sifat phisik dan kimia tanah di Semboja dan Samarinda, Kalimantan Timur.* Banjarbaru, Indonesia: Departmen Pendudukan dan Kebudayan; Universitas Lambung Mangkurat, Fakultas Kehutanan.
[Effects of Mechanical Cultivation on Physical and Chemical Soil Properties in Sembaja and Samarinda, East Kalimantan.]

In Bahasa Indonesia.

Indonesia/ East Kalimantan/ Soils/ Soil erosion and degradation/ Land settlement and development—Environmental impacts.

141. **Hardjono, J. 1986.** "Transmigration: Looking to the Future." *Bulletin of Indonesian Economic Studies* 22 (2): 28–53.

Indonesia/ Land settlement and development/ Land settlement and development—Impacts on local communities and economy.

142. **———, ed. 1991.** *Indonesia: Resources, Human Ecology, and Environment.* Singapore; Oxford: Oxford University Press.

Ten papers on major environmental issues in Indonesia are presented, including: 1) The dimensions of Indonesia's environmental problems (J. Hardjono); 2) The utilization and management of land resources in Indonesia, 1970–1990 (S. M. P. Tjondonegoro); 3) Regional aspects of Indonesian agricultural growth (A. Booth); 4) Managing the ecology of rice production in Indonesia (J. Fox); 5) Developments in plantation agriculture and smallholder cash-crop production (C. Barlow); 6) Crisis and resilience in upland land use in Java (J. W. Nibbering); 7) Environment or employment: vegetable cultivation in West Java (J. Hardjono); 8) Environmental degradation, pollution, and the exploitation of Indonesia's fishery resources (R. C. Rice); 9) Environmental and social aspects of timber exploitation in Kalimantan, 1967–1989 (L. Potter, see this bibliography for abstract); 10) Human ecology in Indonesia: the search for sustainability in development (O. Soemarwoto).

Indonesia/ Deforestation/ Land use—Patterns and planning/ Agriculture—Permanent/ Agriculture—Plantations/ Agriculture—Smallholder cash crop farming/ Agriculture—Smallholder tree and perennial crop farming/ Soil erosion and degradation/ Timber industry—Development and structure/ Timber industry—Environmental impacts/ Timber industry—Impacts on local communities and economy/ Cultural ecology.

143. **Hardjono, J. M. 1977.** *Transmigration in Indonesia.* Kuala Lumpur, Malaysia: Oxford University Press.

Indonesia/ Land settlement and development/ Land settlement and development—Environmental impacts/ Land settlement and development—Impacts on local communities and economy.

144. **Harrer, H., ed. 1988.** "Borneo: Mensch und Kultur seit ihrer Steinzeit." Innsbruck: Pinguin-Verlag.

A series of brief papers and essays provide a broad overview of the geography, pre-history, material culture, cosmology, art history, archeology, flora and fauna, health status, and missionary history of Borneo island, covering local Dayak and Penan communities as well as the Brunei Sultanate. The papers draw from classic texts and historical materials in Borneo studies. [In German].

Malaysia/ Indonesia/ Borneo/ Geography/ Indigenous and local communities/ History—Colonial/ History—Pre-colonial/ Forest flora/ Forest fauna.

145. **Helbig, K. 1982.** Eine Durchquerung der Insel Borneo (Kalimantan): Nach den Tagebüchern aus dem Jahre 1937. 2 vols. Berlin, Germany: Dietrich Reimer Verlag.
[An Expedition Across Borneo Island (Kalimantan): Based on the Diaries of 1937.]

This monograph is comprised of the almost daily accounts kept by Helbig on a year-long tour taken with companion Erich Schreiter on foot through the Kalimantan provinces in 1937. The tour began in Pontianak, West Kalimantan, continued across the Müller mountain range in Central Kalimantan, through East Kalimantan to Samarinda, and then south, skirting the Meratus mountain range to Banjarmasin in South Kalimantan. The account is highly detailed, providing information on local geography, economy, geology, topography, flora, fauna, village settlements, diverse ethnic communities, farming practices, cultural practices, farming and resource use systems. Descriptions and discussions are carefully referenced, citing a rich body of literature developed in the course previous explorations and fieldwork by other foreign (mainly western) travelers, missionaries geographers, naturalists, colonial administrators, and natural scientists. As such, the monograph provides an excellent reference work to colonial-era observations on Borneo island. Includes a map detailing the 1937 Helbig-Schreiter tour and an extensive bibliography citing works from the early nineteenth through the early twentieth centuries. [In German].

Indonesia/ West Kalimantan/ Central Kalimantan/ East Kalimantan/ South Kalimantan/ History—Colonial/ Geography/ Topography/ Forest flora/ Forest fauna/ Indigenous and local communities.

146.   **Helbig, K. M. 1955.** "Die Insel Borneo in Forschung und Schrifttum." *Mitteilungen der Geographischen Gesellschaft in Hamburg* 52: n.g. [Research and Literature on Borneo Island.]

A bibliography on 19th and early 20th century research and literature on Borneo with particular emphasis on geography. [In German].

Indonesia/ Malaysia/ Borneo/ Bibliography/ Geography.

147.   **Hidayati, D. 1991.** "Effects of Development on the Expansion of Agricultural Land in East Kalimantan, Indonesia." *Borneo Review* 2: 28–50.

Hidayati provides a broad overview of changing population size, timber industry growth, government agricultural and resettlement programs, and area of cultivated land characterizing East Kalimantan's development since the early 1960s. Notes the author, the province's population size increased threefold between 1961 and 1987, largely due to in-migration of both spontaneous and government-sponsored transmigrants from other parts of Indonesia. Rural land use in the province is dominated by the timber industry, with 76 percent of its forests officially designated for forestry-related utilization. By 1984, 84 percent of the province's total forest area had been assigned to various private and state-owned agencies as timber concessions. Paralleling these developments, a rapid growth in the area of cultivated land occurred in the late 1970s and early 1980s, much of which is associated with shifting cultivation. According to agricultural census figures, between 1963 and 1983, the total area of land cultivated by small farmers in East Kalimantan grew from 105,000 ha to 196,000 ha, suggesting a 1.9 percent annual rate of increase. This has been accompanied by a large jump in the area of land designated for plantation development, which increased from 14,000 ha in 1963 to 333,922 ha in 1987, over two-thirds of which are owned by large-scale agribusiness entities rather than smallholders. The author concludes that the rapid expansion of land under cultivation in East Kalimantan may be attributed to the inter-action of different government policies, including its timber development, land settlement and plantation development policies. Lack of effective control of designated forest areas by the Forestry Department makes it difficult to prevent settlers who have had no success on government-sponsored settlement or plantation schemes from using logging roads to access new forest lands for conversion to agriculture.

Indonesia/ Kalimantan/ Land settlement and development/ Land use—Patterns and planning/ Timber industry—Impacts on local communities and economy/ Land settlement and development—Impacts on local communities and economy/ Agriculture—Plantations/ Migrant farmers and farming/ Migration/ Regional development.

148. **Hoffman, C. L. 1984.** "Punan Foragers in the Trading Networks of Southeast Asia." In *Past and Present in Hunter Gatherer Studies.* Ed. C. Schrire, pp. 123–149. Orlando.

Malaysia/ Indonesia/ Borneo/ Indigenous and local communities—Forest products use and trade/ History—Colonial.

149. ————. **1983.** "Punan." Ph.D. diss., University of Pennsylvania, Philadelphia, Pa.

Based on field research conducted August 1980 to November 1981, Hoffman contends that the hunter-gathering lifestyle of the Penan is actually a relatively recent "readaptation" from a livelihood system based on various forms of sedentary farming to one based on the collection of forest products. The Penan today are involved in a far-reaching network of forest product trade, that in turn includes Dayak, Malay, and Chinese consumers and traders. As such, they play a vital role in the economy of the region.

Indonesia/ West Kalimantan/ Ethnography/ Indigenous and local communities—Economy/ Indigenous and local communities—Forest products use and trade/ Ethnicity and ethnic relations.

150. **Holden, S., and H. Hvoslef. 1995.** "Transmigration Settlements in Seberida, Sumatra: Deterioration of Farming Systems in a Rain Forest Environment." *Agricultural Systems* 49 (3): 237–258.

To address the varied problems plaguing its ambitious Transmigration program, in recent years the Indonesian government has embarked on a "'second-stage' development" effort for some if the program's least successful sites. Holden and Hvoslef present results from research on one of these problem areas, the transmigration settlements in Seberida district, Riau province, Sumatra. Research was conducted with the aim of analyzing from both agroecological and socioeconomic perspective the cause and consequences of deteriorating farming systems found at the settlements. Research methods included preliminary rapid appraisal, a population census and migration study of all settlements, village-level structured interviews (all settlements), stratified random sample general household survey, and a survey of home gardens in three settlements, including studies of soils, erosion, biodiversity, productivity, and potential. Neither food nor tree crop-based farming system models introduced at the sites have been successful. Most of the settlers have failed to achieve self-sufficiency in food production. While upland rice farming methods introduced at the site have proved non-sustainable, overly small rubber plots and poor quality groves were found to undermine the viability of the tree-crop based systems as well. With up to 64 percent of the population falling below the poverty line, up to 30 percent of the original settlers have returned to Java. A large share of those remaining now seek off-farm sources of income, including nearby plantation work, forest product collection (particularly rattan), and swiddening in the adjacent rain forest area to make ends meet. The authors recommend that abandoned plots be ceded to remaining households and systematic tree replanting be undertaken to improve the viability of rubber production.

Indonesia/ Sumatra/ Land settlement and development/ Agriculture—Smallholder tree and perennial crop farming/ Agriculture—Smallholder cash crop farming/ Agriculture— Permanent/ Farm management—Economics.

151. **Horne, P. M., T. Ismail, and Chong Dai Thai. 1994.** "Agroforestry Plantation Systems: Sustainable Forage and Animal Production in Rubber and Oil Palm Plantations." In *Agroforestry and Animal Production for Human Welfare.* Proceedings of an international symposium held in association with the 7th AAAP Animal Science Congress, Bali, Indonesia, 11–16 July 1994. Ed. J. W.

Copland, A. Djajanegra, and M. Sabrani, pp. 89–98. ACIAR Proceedings, no. 55. Canberra: Australian Centre for International Agricultural Research.

Rising demand for meat means that demand for forage resources in Southeast Asia will double by year 2000. However, the land available for monoculture animal production is limited, indicating a growing need to integrate land uses between plantations and livestock production. The authors discuss the prospects for sustainable forage production in rubber and oil palm plantations in Indonesia, Malaysia and Thailand. Strategies for improving the forage resource on oil palm and rubber plantations are suggested, including introduction of improved forages and alternative plantation management regimes. The paper draws from an extensive review of the state of research literature.

Indonesia/ Malaysia/ Agricultural development/ Agroforestry/ Agriculture—Plantations/ Livestock management.

152.   **Hudson, A. B., and M. J. Hudson. 1967.** "Telang: A Maanjan Village of Central Kalimantan." In *Villages in Indonesia*. Ed. R. Koentjaraningrat. Ithaca, N.Y.: Cornell University Press.

Indonesia/ Central Kalimantan/ Ethnography/ Indigenous and local communities—Social relations.

153.   **Hugo, G. J. et al. 1987.** *The Demographic Dimension in Indonesian Development*. Singapore; New York: Oxford University Press.

Indonesia/ Demography/ Migration/ Land settlement and development/ Regional development.

154.   **Hunter, L. 1984.** "Tropical Forest Plantations and Natural Stand Management: A National Lesson from East Kalimantan." *Bulletin of Indonesian Economic Studies* 20 (1): 98–116.

The author aims to assess the probable effects of a log export ban and the resulting development of a domestic wood processing industry on East Kalimantan's tropical timber supply. A comparison is also made between the potential of two alternative land uses for meeting the projected industrial timber demand in Indonesia: maintaining and managing a natural forest versus establishing exotic tree plantations on the other. The paper concludes by discussing some of the wider implications of the two options.

Although the government of Indonesia appears determined to promote domestic forest-based processing industries, this policy may not necessarily lead to conservation of the resource, especially in the event of a recovery in the international processed forest product market. Analysis suggests that establishing fast-growing exotic tree plantations on smaller areas could complement sustained management of the natural forest. A profitability assessment of a program in East Kalimantan indicates that, even at lower timber prices, plantations could be as economically feasible as natural stand management. Finally, appropriate agreements between government and concessionaires could promote replanting, helping to remedy the problem of forest degradation and ensure continuing income streams.

Indonesia/ East Kalimantan/ Forest management—Commercial forestry and silviculture/ Forest management—Economics/ Timber plantations/ Timber industry—State policy and regulation.

155.   **IMBAS. 1988.** Indonesien: Irrweg Transmigrasi—Umsiedlung und Regionalplanung am Beispiel Ost Kalimantan. Frankfurt: IMBAS.
[Indonesia: The Mistaken Path of Transmigration—Resettlement and Regional Planning Based on the Example of East Kalimantan.]

Indonesia/ East Kalimantan/ Land settlement and development/ Land settlement and development—Impacts on local communities and economy/ Land settlement and development—Environmental impacts/ Regional development.

156. **Ingram, D. 1989.** "Analysis of the Revenue System for Forest Resources in Indonesia." Indonesia/UTF/065/INS: Forestry Studies, Field Document No. VI-2. Jakarta; Rome: Directorate General of Forest Utilization, Ministry of Forestry, Government of Indonesia/ Food and Agriculture Organization of the United Nations.

The author describes "the present forest revenue system in Indonesia and the historical changes in the level of forest revenues in relation to total potential rents." A discussion of the forest revenue system addresses a number of issues, including: volume-based charges; timber royalties; the reforestation guarantee deposit fund; sawtimber export taxes; and appropriate means for collecting forest revenue.

Indonesia/ Timber industry—State policy and regulation/ Forest management—Economics.

157. **Inoue, M., and A. M. Lahjie. 1990.** "Dynamics of Swidden Agriculture in East Kalimantan." *Agroforestry Systems* 12: 269–84.

This paper compares swidden agricultural systems in five Kenyah Dayak villages, two Benuaq Dayak villages, and two Javanese transmigrant villages. The authors observe the effects of increasing involvement in the cash economy on villager's utilization of forest land resources, noting increasing infiltration of cash in the village economy among villages closer to urban markets. Field studies of swidden cultivation patterns suggest that several of the Dayak communities studied who have moved closer to downstream urban centers tend to consume more cash and clear more primary forest than Dayak villagers still farming in the province's more remote interior. Though indigenous land use patterns thus appear to become more environmentally destructive with migration downstream, the incorporation of agroforestry components into local land use systems is also noted, giving some cause to believe that successful intervention is possible. This promise is substantiated by the farming practices of another cluster of Dayak villages with a longer history in the downstream area who have adopted a highly sustainable fallow cropping pattern involving the cultivation of rattan for profitable downstream trade. Least sustainable appear to be the practices of Buginese migrant farmers in the downstream region who clear primary forest for pepper cultivation, use little agroforestry, and often rely on the use of external inputs and laborers.

Indonesia/ East Kalimantan/ Agriculture—Shifting cultivation/ Agriculture—Shifting cultivation's environmental impacts/ Agroforestry/ Indigenous and local communities—Farming practices/ Indigenous and local communities—Forest land use and management practices/ Indigenous and local communities—Commoditization/ Migrant farmers and farming/ Agroforestry.

158. **Irawanti, S., M. Suharti, and I. M. Sulastiningshi. 1994.** "Kajian aspek demografi, sosial, dan ekonomi partisipasi tenaga kerja wanita di pabrik kayu lapis." *Jurnal Penelitian Hasil Hutan* 12 (4): 132–139.
[A Study of Demographic, Social and Economical Aspects of Women's Labor Force Participation in Plywood Mills.]

Indonesia/ Kalimantan/ Timber industry—Downstream processing/ Gender analysis.

159. **Irwin, G. 1955.** *Nineteenth Century Borneo: A Study in Diplomatic Rivalry.* 's-Gravenhage: Martinus Nijhoff.

Malaysia/ Indonesia/ Borneo/ History—Colonial/ Politics.

160.   **Ismail, G., M. Mohamed, and S. Omar, eds. 1992.** *Forest Biology and Conservation in Borneo.* Proceedings of the international conference, 30 July–3 August 1990, Kota Kinabalu, Sabah, Malaysia. Kota Kinabalu, Malaysia: Yayasan Sabah.

Organized by Yayasan Sabah, Universitii Kebangsaan Malaysia Sabah Campus, and the Sabah Ministry of Tourism and Environmental Development, the conference commemorated the 5th anniversary of the Danum Valley Rainforest Research and Training Programme and the 10th anniversary of UKB's Faculty of Science and Natural Resources. Conference papers focus largely on the biological aspects of Bornean rainforests though some attention was also given to forest management. Papers in the first section of the monograph focus on forest flora and botany, including: "Bamboos of Borneo and their Uses," Soejatmi Dransfield; "Rattans in Borneo: Botany and Utilisation," John Dransfield; "Species Diversity of Wild Fruit Trees in the Forests of Sabah as Illustrated by the Genera *Artocarpus, Durio* and *Mangifera*," William W., W. Wong and A. Lamb; "The Genus *Mangifera* in Borneo: Results of an IUCN-WWF/IBPGR Project," J.M. Bompard and A.J.G.H. Kostermans; "The Wild Relatives of Rice in Sabah," Masahuling B. Benong; "A Preliminary Survey of Orchids in Taman Bukit Tawau, Sabah," W. H. Lim and H. A. Saharan; "Problems and Prospects of *Rafflesia* Research in Borneo," Willem Meijer; "Distribution, Dispersal and Some Notes on *Rafflesia* around Kinabalu, Malaysia," Jamili Nais; "Phylogenetics of the Rafflesiaceae," R. S. Beaman, K. Mat-Salleh, W. Meijer and J. H. Beaman; "Specimen Databases and the Utilization for the Flora of Borneo," K. Mat-Salleh, J. H. Beaman and H. Beaman.

Papers in Part II of the proceedings discuss forest fauna, including descriptions of Borneo beetles, orangutans, proboscis monkey and other primates, as well as a paper on "Endemism in Bornean Mammals" by Colin P. Groves. Part III focuses on rainforest dynamics, ecology, and environmental degradation. Papers include, among others: "Hydrologic and Geomorphic Changes Following Rainforest Disturbance with Special Reference to Studies in Borneo," Ian Douglas; "Water Quality Scenario of Rivers in Sabah in Relation to Forest Operations," Murtedza Mohamed; "Conservation of Tropical Lowland Dipterocarp Forest to Plantations of *Acacia Mangium* Stands: Impact On Soil Physical Properties," Kamaruzaman Jusoff; "Species Diversity of Two Adjacent Minor Habitats in Mandor Nature Reserve of West Kalimantan," Herujono Hadisuproto and Syafruddin Said; "Use of Recently Logged Forest by Frugivorous Birds and Mammals," Mohammad Zakaria bin Hussin; "Wildlife Population Parameters As Indicators of the Sustainability of Timber Logging Operations," A. D. Johns and A. G. Marshall; "Hunting Patterns and their Significance in Sarawak," Julian Caldecott.

Part IV has a more varied focus, covering ecological, silvicultural, rural development, ethnobotanical, institutional, and policy-related aspects of forest resource management. Papers include, among others: "Ecological Approaches to Rural Development," G. N. Appell; "Dimensions of Rural Development: A Case of West Kalimantan, Indonesia," Syamsuni Arman; "Protected Areas in Borneo: The Institutional Framework," Peter Eaton; "Ecological Approaches to Commercial Dipterocarp Forestry," W. T. M. Smits, D. Leppe, I. Yasman and M. Noor; "Conservation in Safoda's Kinabatangan Rattan Plantation," P. S. Shim; "Kenyah Medicinal Plants: Beyond the Inventory," Danna J. Leaman, Razali Yusuf and J. Thor Arnason. A final section of the monograph presents abstracts of 35 additional papers given at the conference.

Malaysia/ Sabah/ Sarawak/ Indonesia/ Kalimantan/ Forest flora/ Forest fauna/ Forest biology and ecology/ Biodiversity/ Timber industry—Environmental impacts/ Timber plantations/ Hydrology/ Soil erosion and degradation/ Forest management—Commercial forestry and silviculture/ Forest management—Parks and conservation areas/ Forest management— Forest resource conservation/ Project intervention—Rural development/ Indigenous and local communities—Forest products use and trade/ Rattan—Resource management and conservation/ Rattan—Cultivation/ Non- timber forest products.

161.   **Jay, S. 1989.** "The Basir and Tukang Sangiang: Two Kinds of Shaman Among the Ngaju Dayak." *Indonesia Circle* 49 (June): 31–44.

The paper briefly describes the cosmology of the Orang Ngaju, a Dayak tribal group concentrated along the Kahayan and Rungan rivers of Central Kalimantan. This is followed by a detailed description of the role of shamanism, more specifically, of two types of shamanistic figures—*basirs* and *tukang sangiang*—in Ngaju community life. The close association between *tukang sangiang* and charismatic female figures in the Ngaju community is noted. In a closing discussion, the role of both figures is placed within the context of the wider struggle by Dayak communities for official acceptance of their cultural and religious identity. After persistent advocacy by Dayak leaders, Dayak *Kaharingan* was recognized by the Indonesian government as a Hindu sect in 1980—a classification based on the erroneous notion that *Kaharingan* is an ancient form of Hinduism. One outcome of this development was the establishment of an official Great Council for the *Kaharingan* Religion charged with codifying and standardizing customary beliefs and rituals. The author suggests that the persistence of the *tukang sangiang* role in Dayak religious tradition has represented a means to resist the male-dominated bias and government control represented by the *Kaharingan* Council.

Indonesia/ Central Kalimantan/ Indigenous and local communities—Religion and cosmology/ Gender relations/ Social movements/ Ethnicity and ethnic relations.

162. **Jessup, T. 1981.** "Why Do Apo Kayan Shifting Cultivators Move?" *Borneo Research Bulletin* 13 (1): 16–32.

Drawing from field observations among the East Kalimantan Dayak, Jessup investigates various factors that motivate Dayak shifting cultivators to migrate to different regions of the island's interior. Migration has had a long history among the region's shifting cultivators; often different tribes have moved into secondary forest once cleared by previous cultivators using indigenous systems of land rights transfer. The author distinguishes between "different kinds of moving" by indigenous groups and suggests a variety of reasons for specific migration patterns, many related to involvement in trade. Migration may be seen as a rational response to changing conditions, including increasing opportunities for downriver trade and new opportunities for cash employment alongside farming. However, in most cases farming remains a central means of livelihood for the Dayak, making spontaneous resettlement to cities and increasingly urbanized villages unlikely. Government resettlement policy and plans should recognize these considerations and work to "attract" rather than force Dayak cultivators into sedentary settlements.

Indonesia/ East Kalimantan/ Migration/ Indigenous and local communities—Economy/ Indigenous and local communities—Commoditization.

163. **Jessup, T. E., and N. L. Peluso. 1986.** "Minor Forest Products as Common Property Resources in East Kalimantan, Indonesia." In *Proceedings of the Conference on Common Property Resource Management, 21–26 April 1985, Office of International Affairs, National Research Council, Washington, D.C.* pp. 505– 532. Washington, D.C.: National Academy Press.

Indonesia/ East Kalimantan/ Non-timber forest products/ Indigenous and local communities—Land and resource tenure systems/ Indigenous and local communities—Forest products use and trade/ Forest management—Forest resource conservation.

164. **Kartawinata, K. 1978.** "Biological Changes after Logging in a Lowland Dipterocarp Forest." In *Proceedings of the Symposium on the Long-term Effects of Logging in Southeast Asia*. Ed. R. S. Suparto, pp. 25–34. Bogor, West Java, Indonesia: BIOTROP.

Indonesia/ Kalimantan/ Timber industry—Environmental impacts/ Forest regeneration/ Forest biology and ecology.

165. ————. **1980.** "East Kalimantan: A Comment." *Bulletin of Indonesian Economic Studies* 16 (3):120–121.

> Responding critically to earlier assessments of the contribution which East Kalimantan's forests could make to the country's timber industry, the author cites evidence showing the damage which the current selective felling system is having on the province's forest ecosystem. While felling selected trees already has a potentially negative impact on the surrounding forest, the process of extracting these large trunks from the felling site seriously exacerbates the damage. A review of current felling and extraction practices is called for.

> Indonesia/ East Kalimantan/ Timber industry—Logging/ Timber industry—Environmental impacts.

166. ————. **1984.** "The Impact of Development on Interactions between People and Forests in East Kalimantan: Comparison of Two Areas of Kenyah Dayak Settlement." *The Environmentalist* 4 (7): 87–95.

> Indonesia/ East Kalimantan/ Indigenous and local communities—Commoditization/ Indigenous and local communities—Forest products use and trade/ Indigenous and local communities—Forest land use and management practices/ Indigenous and local communities—Farming practices/ Agriculture—Shifting cultivation's environmental impacts/ Cultural ecology.

167. **Kartawinata, K., T. C. Jessup, and A. P. Vayda. 1989.** "Exploitation in Southeast Asia." In *Tropical Rainforest Ecosystems.* Ed. H. Leith and M. J. A. Werger. Ecosystems of the World, no. 14A. Amsterdam: Elsevier Science Publishers B.V.

> Indonesia/ East Kalimantan/ Timber industry—Logging/ Timber industry—Environmental impacts/ Agriculture—Shifting cultivation's environmental impacts/ Deforestation.

168. **Kartawinata, K., S. Riswan, and H. Soedjito. 1980.** "The Floristic Change after Disturbance in Lowland Dipterocarp Forest in East Kalimantan." In *Tropical Ecology and Development.* Proceedings of the Vth International Symposium of Tropical Ecology, 16–21 April 1979, Kuala Lumpur, Malaysia. Ed. J. L. Furtado, pp. 47–54. Kuala Lumpur: International Society for Tropical Ecology.

> Indonesia/ East Kalimantan/ Vegetation analysis/ Timber industry—Environmental impacts/ Forest regeneration/ Forest biology and ecology.

169. **Kartawinata, K., and O. Satjapradja. 1983.** "Prospects for Agro-Forestry and the Rehabilitation of Degraded Forest Land in Indonesia." *Mountain Research and Development* 3 (4): 414–417.

> Agro-forestry has long been practiced by farmers in Indonesia, although scientific recognition of agroforestry technology as a means of agricultural development with resource conservation is only a recent phenomenon. Currently, a growing amount of research is being directed at identifying promising agroforestry strategies. Kartawinata and Satjaprada emphasize the resources offered by existing agroforestry practices, which differ in their form and purpose in different parts of the country and have involved use of a great variety of tree species, including fruit trees. One particular fruit tree known locally as *tengkawang* (*Shorea spp.*) is highlighted for its great potential as an income-earning crop in agroforestry-based systems. Many other species of fast-growing trees easily found in Indonesia's secondary and primary forests also show good prospects for rehabilitating degraded lands, *Imperata*-infested grasslands, and logged-over forests.

Indonesia/ Agroforestry/ Indigenous and local communities—Farming practices/ Indigenous and local communities—Forest land use and management practices/ Non-timber forest products.

170. **Kartawinata, K., A. P. Vayda, and R. S. Wirakusumah. 1978.** "East Kalimantan and the Man and Biosphere Program." *Borneo Research Bulletin* 10: 28–40.

Indonesia/ East Kalimantan/ Forest management—Forest resource conservation/ Project intervention—Forest management.

171. **Kartawinata, K., and A. P. Vayda. 1984.** "Forest Conversion in East Kalimantan, Indonesia: The Activities and Impact of Timber Companies, Shifting Cultivators, Migrant Pepper-farmers, and Others." In *Ecology in Practice, part I: Ecosystem Management.* Ed. F. di Castri, F. W. G. Baker, and M. Hadley, pp. 98–126. Dublin; Paris: Tycooly International Publishing/ UNESCO.

Kartawinata and Vayda report on the results of integrated social and biological research at several tropical forest locations East Kalimantan, Indonesia. The research found considerable variation in forest land and resource use patterns among different types of farmers and forest users studied—shifting cultivators, migrant pepper farmers, and unlicensed wood cutters. Economic considerations were found to play a dominant role in choices regarding resource use among all subjects. In all cases except for that of impoverished Javanese transmigrants, environmentally-damaging patterns of forest land use were pursued not out of need but because they were perceived as profitable alternatives to other activities. Greatest environmental damage was shown be caused by the mechanical timber harvesting practices of large timber companies, which resulted in "genetic erosion, reduction in species diversity, and very slow recovery of the forest." Least damaging was the impact of non-commoditized swidden farming communities living in more remote forest areas. These as well as the more environmentally benign innovations being practiced by downstream-dwelling farmers may provide insights into resource-conserving forest use technologies acceptable to local communities [Summarized from monograph abstract].

Indonesia/ East Kalimantan/ Indigenous and local communities—Farming practices/ Indigenous and local communities—Forest land use and management practices/ Agriculture—Shifting cultivation's environmental impacts/ Migrant farmers and farming/ Land settlement and development—Environmental impacts/ Timber industry—Environmental impacts.

172. **Karyono, O. K., H. Dwiprabowo, and B. M. Purnama. 1994.** "Kajian ekonomi pengusahaan minyak tengkawang di Kalimantan Barat: kasus Batu Layang." *Jurnal Penelitian Hasil Hutan* 12 (3): 104–108.
[Economic Analysis of the *Tengkawang* (Illipe) Oil Industry: Case of Batu Layang, West Kalimantan.]

Indonesia/ West Kalimantan/ Non-timber forest products/ Indigenous and local communities—Forest products use and trade/ Agricultural economics.

173. **Kebschull, D., K. Fasbender, H. D. Evers, and W. Clauss. 1987.** "The Economic and Social Effects of Transmigration in Indonesia: The Subject of Research." Wirkungen der Transmigration, no. 1. Bielefeld; Hamburg, FRG: Fakultät für Soziologie, Universität Bielefeld; Abteilung Entwickslungsländer, Institut für Wirtschaftsforschung.

In the first of a series of reports on the effects of the Indonesian Transmigration program, the authors describe the aims, scope, field sites, and methodology of the study. In the first of the report's two sections, these issues are discussed in relation to the study's economic component. Economic concerns related to the Indonesian government's land settlement initiatives are discussed, including the effects of organized settlement efforts on agricultural production, the organization of labor, and rural development. The report's second section focuses on social issues in the transmigration process—the other major component of the study series. Past research in this area is briefly reviewed, the social environment of the study area described, and the study focus is placed in the context of current theories and concepts of transmigration and land settlement. Sociological and anthropological studies of societies in Java, Bali, Madura, and East Kalimantan are also reviewed as background. Case studies of individual Transmigration sites which provide the basis for analysis are described.

Indonesia/ East Kalimantan/ Land settlement and development/ Land settlement and development—Impacts on local communities and economy.

174. **Kennedy, R. 1962.** *Bibliography of Indonesian Peoples and Cultures*. Ed. T. W. Maretzki and H. T. Fisher, New Haven, Conn.: Human Relations Area Files.

Indonesia/ Indigenous and local communities/ Bibliography.

175. **Kessler, P. J. A., and K. Sidayasa. 1994.** *Trees of the Balikpapan-Samarinda Area, East Kalimantan, Indonesia: A Manual to 280 Selected Species*. Tropenbos Series, no. 7. Wageningen, Netherlands: Tropenbos Foundation.

Intended as a guide to the primary lowland forest of East Kalimantan, the monograph describes the flora at six sites in the undulating plains and rugged hills between Balikpapan and Samarinda. The compilation was conducted as part of the International MOF Tropenbos-Kalimantan Project, a collaborative effort between the Indonesian Ministry of Forestry, the Tropenbos Foundation, and Rijksherbarium/Hortus Botanicus, Leiden.

Indonesia/ East Kalimantan/ Forest flora.

176. **King, V. T. 1975.** "Further Problems in Bornean Land Tenure Systems: Comments on an Argument." *Borneo Research Bulletin* 7: 12–15.

Indonesia/ Kalimantan/ Indigenous and local communities—Land and resource tenure systems.

177. **———. 1993.** *Peoples of Borneo*. Cambridge, Mass.: Blackwell Publishers.

The author describes the diverse cultural communities of Borneo island drawing from archaeological, anthropological and historical sources as well has his own fieldwork in the region. Individual chapters address: General perspectives on Borneo island, the Dayak and other cultural communities, Borneo's prehistory, influences of India, China and Islam, the island's history under European colonialism, major economic systems (hunting-gathering, swidden farming, coastal economies), socio-political organizations (with a focus on egalitarian societies of the Iban and Bidayuh, stratified societies of the Kayan and Kenyah, longhouses, and state formation under the sultanate of Brunei), worldview and religion, material culture, and modernization and development. The book presents a great deal of detail and enables comparison across national and regional boundaries. An extensive 20 page reference list is provided.

Indonesia/ Kalimantan/ Malaysia/ Sarawak/ Sabah/ Ethnography/ Indigenous and local communities—Economy/ Indigenous and local communities—Social relations/ Indigenous and local communities—Religion and cosmology/ Indigenous and local communities—Commoditization/ Indigenous and local communities—Farming practices/ Agriculture—Shifting cultivation/ History—Colonial/ History—Pre-colonial/ State policy—Agricultural and rural development/ Indigenous and local communities—State policy.

178. ———, ed. **1994.** *Tourism in Borneo: Issues and Perspectives.* Williamsburg, Va.: Borneo Research Council.

Indonesia/ Malaysia/ Borneo/ Regional development/ Economic development.

179. **Kochler, K. G. 1972.** "Wood Processing in East Kalimantan." *Bulletin of Indonesian Economic Studies* 8 (3): 93–129.

This article explores the prospects for wood processing industries development in East Kalimantan. Indonesian government policies are geared to promoting rapid industrialization in order to create more employment opportunities. At the same time, Indonesian planners note that the need for large-scale investment to help promote this development must be balanced with the need to minimize the social costs of foreign involvement. Planners hope to steer a course that takes both needs into consideration.

Indonesia/ East Kalimantan/ Timber industry—Downstream processing/ Timber industry—State policy and regulation.

180. **Korpelainen, H., G. Ådjers, J. Kuusipalo, K. Nuryanto, and A. Otsamo. 1995.** "Profitability of Rehabilitation of Overlogged Dipterocarp Forest: A Case Study from South Kalimantan, Indonesia." *Forest Ecology and Management* 79 (3): 207–215.

Indonesia/ South Kalimantan/ Reforestation/ Forest management—Economics.

181. **Kramadibrata, P., and J. Dransfield. 1992.** "*Calamus inops (Palmae: Calamoideae)* and its Relatives." *Kew Bulletin* 47: 581–593.

The authors provide a detailed description of the rattan palm, *Calamus inops* Becc. and the related taxa *C. pedicellatus* Becc. and *C. orthostachyus* Furt., along with their relationship to other species of *Calamus*. They find that local names given to rattan plants are frequently unreliable, suggesting the need for some scientific supervision of rattan-related research. [Summarized from journal abstract].

Indonesia/ Sulawesi/ Forest flora/ Rattan—Growth and distribution.

182. **Kuusipalo, J., G. Adjers, Y. Jafarsidik, A. Otsamo, K. Tuomela, and R. Vuokko. 1995.** "Restoration of Natural Vegetation in Degraded *Imperata cylindrica* Grassland: Understorey Development in Forest Plantations." *Journal of Vegetation Science* 6 (2): 205–210.

The authors examine the strategy of restoring natural forest cover on degraded grassland areas through cultivation of a "sacrifice fallow crop" of fast-growing tree species. The regeneration process on plots of different tree species is assessed in a grassland area of Riam Kiwa, South Kalimantan. Tree plots with *Acacia mangium* were found to promote the highest number of indigenous trees in their understorey, while other species were associated with more diverse grass and herb vegetation. The high proportion of evergreen woody vegetation on the plots examined was found to decrease fire risk and grass competition, thus facilitating succession to natural forest.

Indonesia/ South Kalimantan/ Forest regeneration/ Reforestation/ Grasslands.

183. **Kuusipalo, J., Y. Jafarsidik, G. Ådjers, and K. Tuomela. 1996.** "Population Dynamics of Tree Seedlings in a Mixed Dipterocarp Rainforest Before and After Logging and Crown Liberation." *Forest Ecology and Management* 81 (1–3): 85–94.

Liberation cutting of pioneer/secondary forest trees comprises a standard silvicultural practice aimed at facilitating commercially viable forest regeneration in logged-over forest stands. The authors assess the actual benefits of this practice by examining the structure and development of seedling stock of three stands of mixed dipterocarp forests (12 year old logged-over forest treated with crown liberation, untreated logged-over forest, and unlogged, untreated forest) over a two year period in Kintap subdistrict, South Kalimantan. Study results indicated that, contrary to purported aim, crown liberation conducted uniformly over a logged-over site favors light-demanding pioneer species rather than dipterocarp. A more successful and cost-effective method for facilitating growth of commercially valuable species would involve creating artificial gaps in the pioneer tree canopy specifically over patches of abundant dipterocarp seedlings.

Indonesia/ South Kalimantan/ Forest regeneration/ Forest management—Commercial forestry and silviculture/ Vegetation analysis/ Timber industry—Environmental impacts.

184.   **Lahjie, A. 1991.** *Dilemma kehutanan dan pembangunan pedesaan di Kalimantan Timur.* Samarinda, Indonesia: Fakultas Kehutanan Universitas Mulawarman.
[The Dilemma Between Forestry and Rural Development in East Kalimantan.]

In Bahasa Indonesia.

Indonesia/ East Kalimantan/ Rural development/ Forest management—Commercial forestry and silviculture/ Forest management—Forest resource conservation/ Land use—Patterns and planning/ State policy—Forest and natural resources.

185.   **Lahjie, A. M., and B. Seibert, ed. 1988.** Agroforestry untuk pengembangan daerah pedesaan di Kalimantan Timur: prosiding seminar kehutanan, 19–21 September 1988, Samarinda, East Kalimantan. Samarinda, East Kalimantan: Department of Forestry, Mulawarman University; GTZ.
[Agroforestry for the Development of Rural Areas in East Kalimantan: Proceedings of a Forestry Seminar.]

Contains two dozen papers presented at a regional seminar on agroforestry in rural development held at Mulawarman University in 1988. Individual papers discuss a variety of aspects of agroforestry development in East Kalimantan, including an inventory of existing agroforestry systems practiced by local indigenous and settler communities, integration of agroforestry in Transmigration sites, integration of agroforestry with timber plantation development, palm and rattan cultivation and management by local farmers, integrating the perennial crops (coffee, chocolate, pepper, charcoal) into agroforestry systems, agroforestry-oriented land use systems (particularly honey production) traditionally used by indigenous residents of East Kalimantan, and their potential for *in-situ* preservation of genetic resources. [In Bahasa Indonesia with English abstracts].

Indonesia/ East Kalimantan/ Agroforestry/ Rural development/ Land settlement and development/ Rattan—Cultivation/ Agriculture—Smallholder cash crop farming/ Agriculture—Smallholder tree and perennial crop farming/ Agriculture—Shifting cultivation/ Indigenous and local communities—Forest land use and management practices/ Indigenous and local communities—Forest products use and trade/ Non-timber forest products/ Biodiversity.

186.   ———. **1990.** "Honey Gathering by People in the Interior of East Kalimantan." *Bee World* 71 (4): 153–157.

Describes the honey harvesting methods of indigenous farmers in East Kalimantan, highlighting favored tree species for nest building by *Apis dorsata*, harvest timing, tree-climbing and honey-retrieval techniques, as well as associated rituals and beliefs.

Indonesia/ East Kalimantan/ Non-timber forest products/ Indigenous and local communities—Forest products use and trade.

187. **Laman, T. G. 1995.** "*Ficus stupenda* Germination and Seedling Establishment in a Bornean Rain Forest Canopy." *Ecology* 76 (8): 2617–2626.

Indonesia/ West Kalimantan/ Forest biology and ecology/ Forest flora.

188. ———. **1994.** "The Ecology of Strangler Figs (*Hemiepiphytic ficus* spp.) in the Rain Forest Canopy of Borneo." Ph.D. diss., Harvard University, Cambridge, Mass.

Indonesia/ West Kalimantan/ Forest flora/ Forest biology and ecology/ Vegetation analysis.

189. **Lambert, D. 1975.** "Bibliography on Hunter Gatherers in Borneo." *Borneo Research Bulletin* 7: 25–27.

Indonesia/ Malaysia/ Indigenous and local communities/ Bibliography.

190. **Lambert, K., S. Suryanto, L. Baert, and J. Vanderdeelen. 1990.** "The Agricultural Value of the Peat Soils in Kalimantan." *Mededelingen van de Faculteit Landbouwwetenschappen, Rijksuniversiteit Gent* 55 (1): 1–9.

The authors review the major peat types found in four specific settings in the Kalimantan provinces: topogenous peats in river valley and coastal areas, and ombrogenous peats in basin and upland areas. The fragile forest ecosystems and podzolic soils characteristic of peatland settings pose serious constraints to agriculture. Also highlighted are the soil management implications of traditional agricultural methods.

Indonesia/ East Kalimantan/ Soils/ Indigenous and local communities—Farming practices/ Agricultural development.

191. **Lawrence, D. C., M. Leighton, and D. R. Peart. 1995.** "Availability and Extraction of Forest Products in Managed and Primary Forest around a Dayak Village in West Kalimantan, Indonesia." *Conservation Biology* 9 (1): 76–88.

Patterns of secondary forest management and forest product collection by residents of Kembera, a Dayak village on the outskirts of Gunung Palung National Park, West Kalimantan, were observed from April 1991 through April 1992. The research methodology involved measuring the density of marketable and locally useful tree species in discrete plots of managed secondary forest, conducting interviews, and obtaining tree density and product data from primary forest locations for purposes of comparison. The four main products harvested by villagers included *tengkawang* seeds (*Shorea stenoptera*), durian fruits of various *Durio* species, rubber (*Hevea brasiliensis*), and timber, particularly Bornean ironwood (*Eusideroxylon zwageri*). While the total abundance of these products was greater in surrounding primary forest areas, the density of harvestable tree species was much higher in the managed fallow areas, and villagers showed a marked preference for harvesting from the latter areas. The authors suggest this pattern to reveal a greater efficiency of forest product collection in managed fallows, which in turn is likely to be motivating villagers to develop tree groves of useful species on fallowed land. The pattern raises questions about the appropriateness of extractive reserves or buffer zones as a means to encourage sustainable production of forest products since these may lack sufficient efficiency to interest local villagers.

Indonesia/ West Kalimantan/ Indigenous and local communities—Forest land use and management practices/ Indigenous and local communities—Forest products use and trade/ Non-timber forest products/ Forest management—Parks and conservation areas.

192. **Leighton, M. 1984.** "The El-Ni–o Southern Oscillation Event in Southeast Asia: Effects of Drought and Fire on Tropical Forests in Eastern Borneo." Report prepared for Project US-293. Photocopy. Geneva, Switzerland: IUCN/WWF.

Indonesia/ East Kalimantan/ Forest fires/ Drought/ Forest regeneration.

193. **Lindblad, J. T. 1985.** "Economic Change in Southeast Kalimantan 1880–1940." *Bulletin of Indonesian Economic Studies* 21 (3): 69–103.

This article analyzes the economic development of Southeast Kalimantan from 1880–1940 within the context of the international debate on economic dualism. From about 1900, Southeast Kalimantan experienced spectacular economic expansion, due to rapidly increasing oil, rubber, coal and timber and non-timber forest products (mostly rattan and damar) exports. This economic development was characterized by the formation of highly insular, Western-market oriented enclaves such as the oil industry. At the same time, rapid influxes of cash into the area as well as consolidation of Dutch control over local government administration and external trade meant that growth in economic activity pursued by indigenous smallholders and swidden farmers (e.g. rubber tapping and forest product collection) paralleled growth occurring in foreign-dominated enclaves. Argues the author, this combination of parallelism and insularity did not provide the ideal basis for the region's future economic growth. Parallelism is here defined as a special case of dualism in which both the indigenous and Western sectors of the economy are dynamic but are distinguished by different degrees of technological development.

Indonesia/ East Kalimantan/ History—Colonial/ Regional development/ Timber industry—Development and structure/ Indigenous and local communities—Economy/ Indigenous and local communities—Forest products use and trade/ Agriculture—Smallholder tree and perennial crop farming/ Agriculture—Smallholder cash crop farming/ Rattan—Collection and trade.

194. ———. **1988.** *Between Dayak and Dutch: The Economic History of Southeast Kalimantan, 1880–1942.* Dordrecht, Holland: Foris Publications.

Indonesia/ East Kalimantan/ History—Colonial/ Regional development/ Timber industry—Development and structure/ Timber industry—Logging/ Indigenous and local communities—Economy/ Agriculture—Smallholder tree and perennial crop farming/ Agriculture—Smallholder cash crop farming/ Indigenous and local communities—Forest products use and trade/ Rattan—Collection and trade.

195. **Lorenz, C., and A. Errington. 1991.** "Achieving Sustainability in Cropping Systems: The Labour Requirements of a Mulch Rotation System in Kalimantan, Indonesia." *Tropical Agriculture* 68 (3): 249–254.

On-farm trials of a mulch rotation system (MRS) in a transmigrant settlement in Kutai district, East Kalimantan confirm its greater sustainability over alternative cropping systems. The MRS system was shown to require less inorganic fertilizer than existing practices, while at the same time proving adaptable to the labor availability and schedules faced by farmers at the settlement. The research underscores to address issues of labor requirements and constraints in field trials for new cropping systems.

Indonesia/ East Kalimantan/ Conservation farming/ Farming systems research/ Farm management—Cropping systems/ Land settlement and development.

196. **Lynch, O. J. 1984.** "The Ancestral Land Rights of Tribal Indonesians: A Comparison with the Philippines." Photocopy. New Haven, Conn.: School of Forestry, Yale University.

Indigenous people's land rights are receiving increasing attention in current discussions of sustainable development. In this 36 page essay the author investigates the status of tribal land rights in modern Indonesia, drawing comparisons to similar issues in the Philippines. Current land law in Indonesia is based largely on laws of the colonial era and often fail to benefit indigenous communities. Although theoretically recognized in the Indonesia's Basic Agrarian Law, in practice, tribal land rights in East Kalimantan are consistently ignored. The author notes the similarity between this and the plight of tribal peoples in the Philippines.

Indonesia/ Kalimantan/ Land tenure—Legislation and state policy/ Indigenous and local communities—Land and resource tenure systems.

197.   **MacAndrews, C. 1986.** *Land Policy in Modern Indonesia.* Boston, Mass.: Oelgeschlager, Gunn Hain.

Indonesia/ State policy—Land development/ Land tenure—Legislation and state policy/ State policy—Agricultural and rural development/ Economic development/ Land settlement and development.

198.   **Mackie, C. 1984.** "The Lessons behind East Kalimantan's Forest Fires." *Borneo Research Bulletin* 16: 63–74.

Indonesia/ East Kalimantan/ Forest fires/ Agriculture—Shifting cultivation's environmental impacts/ Timber industry—Environmental impacts/ Forest management—Forest resource conservation.

199.   **———. 1987.** "Disturbance and Succession Resulting from Shifting Cultivation in an Upland Rainforest in Indonesian Borneo." Ph.D. diss., Rutgers University, New Brunswick, N.J.

Mackie investigates the disturbance in forest dynamics imposed by shifting cultivation activities, as measured by spatial pattern, frequency, predictability and severity. Swidden farming patterns of the Kenyah Dayak in East Kalimantan comprised the focus of study. Rice fields and successional vegetation established in the swidden process formed clusters of forest gaps up to up to 30 ha in size. Decisions regarding site, size and fallow age of fields cut varied from household to household, reflecting differences in household structure, age composition, and other circumstances. Fallowed fields were found to regenerate rapidly into secondary forest cover, and were often managed by households to yield useful tree products. Forest species diversity declined steeply in sites that had been cultivated for many years consecutively, with exotic weed species becoming dominant. The effects of shifting cultivation were compared with other gap-forming disturbances, including landslides. The latter were found to result in much more severe, though far less extensive disturbance than swidden farming. As agricultural activities tended to be clustered around specific sites, primary forest was found to still dominate large tracts of land around the study area. Clear-cut assessments regarding disturbance impacts were thus difficult to make on the basis of single variables (gap frequency or gap size), suggesting the need to incorporate greater complexity and dynamism for more reliable disturbance analysis.

Indonesia/ East Kalimantan/ Agriculture—Shifting cultivation's environmental impacts/ Indigenous and local communities—Farming practices/ Indigenous and local communities—Forest land use and management practices/ Forest regeneration.

200.   **MacKinnon, J. R., and K. MacKinnon. 1986.** *Review of the Protected Areas System in the Indo-Malayan Realm.* Cambridge, UK; Gland, Switzerland: IUCN.

Indonesia/ Malaysia/ Forest management—Parks and conservation areas/ Biodiversity.

201.   **Mackinnon, J. R., and K. Phillipps. 1993.** *A Field Guide to the Birds of Borneo, Sumatra, Java, and Bali.* Oxford: Oxford University Press.

> The guide covers 820 birds with color illustrations and family and species descriptions. Introductory sections provide a broad overview of the biogeography of the region, with a list of Indonesian national parks. Appendices list endemic and endangered species in main reserves and by island, land birds found on offshore island groups, Bornean montane birds by mountain group, bird call sonosketches, regional ornithological clubs and other sources for relevant information.

> Malaysia/ Indonesia/ Borneo/ Forest fauna.

202.   **MacKinnon K., A. Irving, and M. A. Bachruddin. 1994.** "A Last Chance for Kutai National Park—Local Industry Support for Conservation." *Oryx* 28 (3): 191–198.

> Discusses the surprisingly supportive role played by a coal mine along the northern boundary of Kutai National Park in the process of enhancing park protection and management.

> Indonesia/ East Kalimantan/ Forest management—Parks and conservation areas/ Mining.

203.   **Magenda, B. 1991.** *East Kalimantan: The Decline of a Commercial Aristocracy.* Cornell Modern Indonesia Project Monograph Series, no. 70. Ithaca, N.Y.: Southeast Asia Program, Cornell University.

> Indonesia/ East Kalimantan/ Politics/ History—Colonial/ Regional development/ Timber industry—Development and structure.

204.   **Manning, C. 1971.** "The Timber Boom, With Special Reference to East Kalimantan." *Bulletin of Indonesion Economic Studies* 2 (3): 30–60.

> Manning describes the history, development and effects of the timber boom in East Kalimantan during the early years of the New Order government. Since the late 1960s, the province has played a major role in Indonesia's timber sector. Already by 1970, East Kalimantan accounted for 25 percent of total production and 50 percent of total log exports from Indonesia due to the high value of its indigenous timber species (*meranti, kruing,* and *agathus*) on the world market. Japanese buyers based in Samarinda played a major role in the early years of the timber boom as patrons of small loggers and collectors of other forest products (rattan, damar, etc.) under the *banjir kap* or unmechanized extraction system. Through the early 1970s, most timber was exported in log form, with Japan absorbing 80 percent of Indonesia's log exports. The boom brought many economic benefits to the country and region, but also some serious costs including: rapid degradation of forest resource in interest of short term profits, threatening the long-term viability of the industry; damage to the local ecology by unplanned and uncontrolled exploitation; and penetration of economic activities into the province's remote interior, with negative impact on the previously isolated communities living there. In the interest of minimizing social costs while maximizing benefits, the government consolidated formal control over all national forest areas by the early 1970s. While one state-owned timber company has itself been involved in timber production in the region, most of the forest area has been assigned to private concessionaires, often involving joint partnerships between foreign and domestic firms. All private concessionaires are responsible for managing the resource according to government guidelines.
> The author identifies a number of issues that require government attention: 1) Rapid exploitation of the resource occurred during early years of the boom, prompting the government to institute a selective and sustained yield cutting policy. In reality, however, the policy is not uniformly applied by all concessionaires; 2) The timber industry has considerable revenue-generating potential which the government attempts to tap through a system of royalties, export taxes, and license fees; 3) The employment potential in the industry is

quite large. As many as 20,000 people are estimated to find work within the industry in East Kalimantan alone, although the skilled laborers are typically recruited from the Philippines and Malaysia; 4) While government regulations require that community and social service development accompany timber extraction, existing rules are not explicit, and few services are actually provided; in addition, the interests of local communities are often negatively impacted by concessionaire activity in their areas; 5) While most domestic concessionaires depend on partnerships with foreign investors, transfer of technology to domestic partner firms is not guaranteed by the present policy. In only 3 of 12 joint venture partnerships are Indonesian partners actively involved in production management decision-making.

Already by these early years of the industry's development, the Indonesian government looked to the booming timber sector as a basis for future industrialization. The abundance of timber resources, continuing strong external demand for wood products, the labor-intensive nature of the industry to match Indonesia's abundant labor supply, and the government's growing ability to develop supporting power facilities are cited by the author as promising factors for downstream development of the country's processing capacity. However, in addition to the problems cited above, the author notes a number of additional concerns, including: 1) Over-dependence on a small number of foreign buyers for Indonesia's wood products; 2) The problem of controlling and enforcing government logging guidelines among a very large number of small private concessionaires; and 3) The involvement of many concession-owners who have no real business expertise or sincere business orientation (i.e., military and para-military organizations); 4) Conflicts between concession- holders and the East Kalimantan government and between concession-holders themselves due to concession-border disputes.

Indonesia/ East Kalimantan/ Timber industry—Development and structure/ Timber industry—Logging/ Timber industry—Impacts on local communities and economy/ Timber industry—State policy and regulation/ Timber industry—Downstream processing/ Forest management—Commercial forestry and silviculture.

205. **Marsono, D. 1980.** "The Effect of Indonesia Selective Cutting (TPI) on the Structure and Regeneration of Lowland Tropical Dipterocarp Forests in East Kalimantan, Indonesia." Ph.D. diss., University of the Philippines, Los Ba–os, Philippines.

Indonesia/ East Kalimantan/ Timber industry—Environmental impacts/ Forest regeneration/ Forest management—Commercial forestry and silviculture.

206. **Mas'ud, F. A., and Ag. Pudjiharta. 1977.** *Peranan reboisasi dan penghijauan terhadap tata air di Daera Aliran Sungai Riam Kanan - Kalimantan Selatan.* Bogor, Indonesia: Lembaga Penelitian Hutan.
[The Role of Afforestation and Regreening in the Hydrology of the Riam Kana River Basin, South Kalimantan.]

Research was aimed at discovering the effect of the reforestation and regreening on the hydrological system of the Riam Kanan watershed. 48.98% of the watershed is covered by dense forest, 36.73% by alang-alang (imperata grass), and 14.71% by other plant species. Data was collected by PLN (National Electricity Corporation) along the Barito river from January to June 1975 and from January to June 1976. The research shows that reforestation and regreening with one-year old seedlings had no effect on the hydrological system of the study area. [Adapted from vol. 2 (Forestry/Agroforestry), Bibliografi, Pengembangan Sistem Informasi Pertanian Lahan Kering dan Konservasi Tanah, Bogor].

Indonesia/ South Kalimantan/ Hydrology/ Reforestation/ Watershed management.

207. **Massing, A. 1981.** "The Journey to Paradise: Funerary Rites of the Benuaq Dayak of East Kalimantan." *Borneo Research Bulletin* 13: 85–104.

Detailed information on the funerary rites of the Benuaq Dayak are provided, including the economic costs of the ceremony.

Indonesia/ East Kalimantan/ Indigenous and local communities—Religion and cosmology/ Indigenous and local communities—Economy.

208.   **Matius, P., and Y. Okimori. 1991.** "Floristic Composition and Dynamics of Lowland Dipterocarps Forest Largely Burned in Bukit Soeharto Protection Forest East Kalimantan." In *Proceedings of the Fourth Round-Table Conference on Dipterocarps, Bogor, Indonesia, 12–15 December 1989.* Ed. I. Soerianegara, S. S. Tjitrosomo, R. C. Umaly, and I. Umboh, pp. 257–271. Bogor, Indonesia: SEAMEO BIOTROP.

A vegetation survey and analysis of 3 plots in Bukit Soeharto Protection Forest, East Kalimantan aimed to assess the damage inflicted on local lowland dipterocarp forests by past fire, to clarify the succession process, and to evaluate the forest's potential for rehabilitation. The three plots studied (1 ha, .72 ha, and .36 ha in size, respectively) corresponded with three states of disturbance: (a) lightly disturbed, (b) moderately disturbed, and (c) heavily disturbed. The survey methodology involved species identification and size measurement of mature trees, saplings, and seedlings. Analysis of tree community dynamics was based on the Importance Value (IV), and level of damage was verified in all tall trees.
Results were as follows: (1) Floristic composition: Plot (a) was found to contain 310 trees (98.7% of which were primary vegetation), 130 species and 32 families, with the *Dipterocarp* species dominant. Plot (b) was found to have 320 trees (53.8% primary vegetation), 86 species, with *Macaranga gigantea* as the dominant species. Plot (c) had 210 trees (82% primary vegetation), 37 species, and 17 families, with *Macaranga gigantea* also dominant.
(2) Presence of rotting trees: Plot (a) contained 22% rotting trees, plot (b) 48%, and plot (c) 42%.
(3) Natural regeneration: In plot (a), all young trees were dominated by the primary species. Plot (c) had no dipterocarp species at any regeneration stage. In plot (b), trees of primary species equaled trees of pioneer species at the young tree and sapling stages. At the seedlings stage, however, the trees of primary species outnumbered the pioneers.
(4) Growth increment: The growth increment (total basal area) of forest stand increased in the moderate and heavily disturbed forest, but decreased in the forest only lightly disturbed by fire. As pioneer species invaded the former two forest stands, high growth rates resulted. In the lightly disturbed forest, a number of fallen tall trees had been affected by forest fire, and their loss outweighed the growth increment of remaining advanced trees. [Summarized from monograph abstract].

Indonesia/ Kalimantan/ Forest regeneration/ Forest fires/ Vegetation analysis.

209.   **Maydell, H. J. von. 1988.** "Penelitian terapan dalam agroforestry." In *Agroforestry untuk pengembangan daerah pedesaan di Kalimantan Timur.* Ed. A. Lahjie and B. Seibert, pp. 3–7. Samarinda, East Kalimantan, Indonesia: Department of Forestry, Mulawarman University; German Agency for Technical Cooperation (GTZ).
[Interdisciplinary Research in Agroforestry.]

Indonesia/ East Kalimantan/ Agroforestry.

210.   **Mayer, J. 1988.** Letter to Peter Bird Martin, Institute of Current World Affairs. Unpublished correspondence.

Describes field visits to rattan-cultivating villages and logging sites in Pesesir, East Kalimantan.

Indonesia/ East Kalimantan/ Indigenous and local communities—Farming practices/ Indigenous and local communities—Forest land use and management practices/ Land settlement and development—Impacts on local communities and economy/ Rattan—Cultivation/ Timber industry—Impacts on local communities and economy.

211. ———. **1990.** "Penanaman rotan, ekonomi keluarga dan pemanfaatan lahan: suatu kasus dari Pasir, Kalimantan Timur." In *Agroforestry untuk pengembangan daerah pedesaan di Kalimantan Timur*. Ed. A. M. Lahjie and B. Seibert, pp. 141–158. Samarinda, East Kalimantan, Indonesia: Department of Forestry, Mulawarman University; German Agency for Technical Cooperation (GTZ).
[Rattan Cultivation, Household Economics and Land Use: A Case Study from Pasir, East Kalimantan.]

Indonesia/ East Kalimantan/ Indigenous and local communities—Economy/ Indigenous and local communities—Forest land use and management practices/ Household livelihood strategies/ Rattan—Cultivation/ Agroforestry/ Agriculture—Shifting cultivation.

212. **Medway, Lord. 1965.** *Mammals of Borneo*. Singapore: Royal Asiatic Society.

The author presents a broad descriptive guide to the mammals of Borneo island.

Indonesia/ Kalimantan/ Malaysia/ Sabah/ Sarawak/ Forest fauna.

213. **Meyer, C. 1993.** "Environmental and Natural Resource Accounting: Where to Begin?" WRI Issues in Development, Washington, D.C.: Center for International Development and Environment, World Resources Institute.

Meyer presents an overview of the concept of environmental and natural resources accounting and its development. The report describes recent precedents in order to provide some initial guidelines for those interested in pursuing the further development of green accounting methods by national governments. The report describes the U.N.'s progress in this area, provides case studies of natural resource accounting undertaken by WRI and its collaborators in Indonesia and Costa Rica, and reviews the application of the emerging U.N. green accounting system to national accounting in Mexico and Papua New Guinea. A less in-depth survey of other countries' experiences is provided as well, followed by a concluding section highlighting probable future directions in environmental accounting.

Indonesia/ Forest management—Economics.

214. **Michon, G. 1985.** "De l'homme de la forêt au paysan de l'arbre: Agroforesteries Indonesiennes." Ph.D. diss., Université de Montpellier, Montepellier, France.
[From Forest Dweller to Tree Farmer: Indonesian Agroforestry.]

Indonesia/ Agroforestry/ Indigenous and local communities—Forest land use and management practices.

215. **Mile, M. Y. 1980.** Hasil dan evaluasi kegiatan proyek resettlement penduduk Miau Baru, propinsi dati i Kalimantan Timur. Bogor, West Java, Indonesia: Lembaga Penelitian Hutan.
[Result and Evaluation of Population Resettlement Project Activity at Miau Baru, East Kalimantan.]

In Bahasa Indonesia.

Indonesia/ East Kalimantan/ Resettlement.

216. **Moekiyat, W., H. Hitam, and R. S. Wirakusumah. 1970.** "Menaksir masa bera perladangan perpindah-pindah di Kaltim." Paper presented at a National Seminar on Development and Environment, 5–6 June 1970, in Jakarta. Photocopy.
[Estimation of Fallow Periods in Shifting Cultivation, East Kalimantan.]

This paper describes an approach taken by the authors to estimate most sustainable fallow periods using biomass analysis. A fallow period of 10 years was estimated to be most suitable for the site surveyed. Better estimates of adequate fallow periods may help to assess the productivity of different land areas.

Indonesia/ East Kalimantan/ Agriculture—Shifting cultivation.

217. **Mogea, J. P. 1991.** "Indonesia: Palm Utilization and Conservation." In *Palms for Human Needs in Asia: Palm Utilization and Conservation in India, Indonesia, Malaysia and the Philippines.* Ed. D. Johnson, pp. 37–75. Rotterdam: A. A. Balkema.

This report summarizes results of one part of a study of palm utilization in Asia undertaken as part of a wider research effort on wild palm conservation funded by the World-Wide Fund for Nature (WWF). The project's overall aim was to identify the most economically important as well as most threatened wild palm species in Asia, develop appropriate action plans for their conservation, and raise public and policy-maker awareness of current conservation needs. The Indonesian section of the report summarizes the origin, native habitat, derived products and services, yield, and conservation status of 39 palm taxa found throughout the archipelago. Local names for each taxa are provided. Noting that considerable research on the silviculture and conservation techniques for rattan is already underway in Indonesia, the author recommends further focus on three additional palm taxa, namely salak palms, sugar palms and lontar palms. An extensive list of palm species is provided and their distribution noted. Similar reports describing local palm utilization and conservation problems were prepared for other areas of Asia. Reports for Sabah, Sarawak (East Malaysia), and the Philippines have been abstracted separately.

Indonesia/ Rattan—Growth and distribution/ Rattan—Collection and trade/ Rattan—Cultivation/ Rattan—Resource management and conservation/ Forest management—Forest resource conservation/ Non-timber forest products.

218. **Momberg, F. 1993.** *Indigenous Knowledge Systems—Potentials for Social Forestry Development: Resource Management of Land-Dayaks in West Kalimantan.* Berliner Beiträge zu Umwelt und Entwicklung, no. 3. Berlin: Technische Universität Berlin.

In a study of indigenous knowledge systems of Dayak farmers in Sanggau District, West Kalimantan, Momberg argues that these systems should be legitimized by forestry planners and policymakers, and that indigenous people should be empowered to control and manage local forests based on their own institutions and tenure arrangements. The monograph presents data gathered through a survey of several villages in Sanggau District. Study villages were selected to reflect different environmental settings and the potential to participate in a social forestry development project currently being planned by the Indonesian Directorate for Reforestation and Land Rehabilitation (under the Ministry of Forestry) in cooperation with the Deutsche Gesellschaft für Technische Zusammenarbeit (GTZ). In the first of the monograph's three sections, Momberg draws from a wide body of literature to provide a broad overview of issues in deforestation in Indonesia's outer islands, human ecological approaches to forest management, indigenous knowledge systems, and community empowerment. Section 2 describes the study area, planned social forestry project activities, study methodology, as well as results of the agroecological analysis of indigenous agroforestry system and the socio-economic survey of local Dayak resource management systems. Section 3 lists major study findings, including the high degree of skill with which local farmers manage forest resources through a variety of strategies, and a number of technical points salient to developing suitable social forestry approaches.

Indonesia/ West Kalimantan/ Indigenous and local communities—Forest land use and management practices/ Indigenous and local communities—Land and resource tenure systems/ Cultural ecology/ Project intervention—Social and community forestry.

219.   **Mori, S., and Marjenah. 1994.** "Effect of Charcoaled Rice Husks on the Growth of Dipterocarpaceae Seedlings in East Kalimantan, with Special Reference to Ectomycorrhiza Formation." *Journal of the Japanese Forestry Society* 76 (5): 462–464.

Indonesia/ East Kalimantan/ Forest management—Commercial forestry and silviculture/ Reforestation.

220.   **Mubyarto, and A. S. Dewanta. 1991.** *Karet: Kajian Sosial-Ekonomi.* Yogyakarta: Penerbit Aditya Media.
[Rubber: A Socio-Economic Study.]

Indonesia/ Agricultural development/ Agriculture—Smallholder tree and perennial crop farming/ Agriculture—Smallholder cash crop farming/ Agriculture—Plantations/ State policy—Agricultural and rural development/ Land settlement and development.

221.   **Mubyarto, L. Soetrisno, Putu Sudito, S. A. Awing, Sulistiyo, A. S. Dewanta, Ninik Sri Rejeki, and E. Pratiwi. 1991.** *Kajian sosial ekonomi desa-desa perbatasan di Kalimantan Timur.* Yogyakarta, Central Java, Indonesia: P3PK, Gadjah Mada University; Aditya Media.
[Socio-Economic Analysis of Rural Villages in East Kalimantan.]

Providing a general introduction to East Kalimantan as well as a brief description of the region's economy and the development of its oil- and tropical timber-based sectors, the authors highlight the impact this development has had on the economic life of the province's indigenous communities. While physical isolation may be partly to blame for some of the poverty among indigenous communities in the area, top-down development policy has been unable to offer any real solutions. In fact, the traditional government perception that shifting cultivators cause forest destruction has meant that government programs appear less geared to supporting indigenous communities than to controlling their traditional farming activities. In addition, the Dayak communities face new problems which threaten to undermine their way of life and their long-term well-being. While indigenous inhabitants have not benefited economically from the timber and forest-based industry that has entrenched itself in the province, rapid development of logging activities has already seriously impacted the local environment and traditional farming systems, causing a decline in harvests from shifting cultivation as well as the income derived from the collection of forest products. While the area is still rich in a number of non-timber forest resources, their commercial exploitation requires access to capital, technology and managerial expertise, all of which is available only to outsiders; at best, indigenous forest dwellers gain access to these resources through a dependent relationship with outside brokers. The lack of transportation facilities hampers the availability of basic consumer goods from towns and cities, driving up their price, even as indigenous communities have become increasingly dependent on such products. This in turn has prompted many community members to migrate, seeking paid employment outside the area, mainly in Sarawak.

These problems highlight the need for the regional government to take a more active role in defending the Dayak side in the conflict between their economic interests and those of the modern sector. Development policy must involve the indigenous people of the area in a participatory and integrated way. [In Bahasa Indonesia].

Indonesia/ East Kalimantan/ Indigenous and local communities—Economy/ Indigenous and local communities—Forest products use and trade/ Indigenous and local communities— Farming practices/ Timber industry—Logging/ Timber industry—Impacts on local communities and economy/ Indigenous and local communities—Commoditization/ Indigenous and local communities—State policy/ Forest management—Control of shifting cultivation/ Agriculture—Shifting cultivation.

222.   **Mubyarto, Sulistiyo, and San Afri Awang, eds. 1992.** *Perekonomian rakyat Kalimantan: prosiding Seminar Nasional Pengembangan Perekonomian Rakyat Kalimantan, 4–8 August 1991, Pontianak, West Kalimantan.* Yogyakarta, Indonesia: Aditya Media.
[Local Kalimantan Economy: Proceedings of the National Seminar on Local Community Development in Kalimantan.]

22 papers presented at a national seminar are provided. Subjects discussed include: general strategies for local community development in Kalimantan, Dayak social organization and material culture, shifting cultivation as a food production and land use system, effects of plantation crop development on local communities, effects of transmigration, current status and future possibilities for social forestry in the region, and the role of women and NGOs in the local development process. While many papers discuss these issues in general terms, several are based on results of local fieldwork. Publication of the proceedings was sponsored by Yayasan Agro Ekonomika based in Yogyakarta. [In Bahasa Indonesia].

Indonesia/ Kalimantan/ Indigenous and local communities—Economy/ Indigenous and local communities—Social relations/ Indigenous and local communities—Farming practices/ Indigenous and local communities—Forest land use and management practices/ Indigenous and local communities—Economy/ Land settlement and development—Impacts on local communities and economy/ Social forestry/ Gender analysis/ Non-governmental organizations/ Project intervention—Fallow improvement.

223.   **Needham, R. 1972.** "Penan." In *Ethnic Groups of Insular Southeast Asia.* Ed. F. M. Lebar, pp. 176–180. New Haven.

Malaysia/ Indonesia/ Sarawak/ Kalimantan/ Ethnography/ Indigenous and local communities.

224.   **Ngo, T. H. G. M. 1989.** "Antara pemilik dan pemanfaat: Kisah penguasaan lahan Orang Kayan di Kalimantan Barat." *Prisma* 4: 73– 86.
[Between Ownership and Usufruct: A Report on Land Management among the Orang Kayan in West Kalimantan.]

National land policy in Indonesia has assumed an overly uniform and legalistic approach to issues of customary land tenure. Ngo argues that this approach fails to come to terms with the diversity and variability characteristic of traditional land tenure patterns among Indonesia's many tribal communities. As an example, he describes conflicts which have emerged over forest lands along the Sungai Mendalam and Sungai Sambus, both tributaries of Kapuas river in West Kalimantan. Forests along the river contain a high density of Illipe nut trees (*Shorea spp.*), long managed and harvested by the Orang Kayan, a local Dayak community, for purposes of trade and home use. Increasingly, however, these groves are being harvested by Melayu newcomers recently settled along Sungai Sambus, who have also become interested in cashing in on the lucrative trade in Illipe nuts. Although access to and harvest of the groves has long been regulated by indigenous Dayak tenure regimes, the Orang Kayan are finding themselves increasingly unable to prevent incursions by outsiders.

Appeals to local authorities have been ineffective, given the lack of official certificates of ownership and the lack of active agricultural cultivation in the disputed groves.

A broad overview is provided on the history of the Orang Kayan's presence along the Sungai Mendalam, describes the local community structure, the traditional resource tenure regimes, as well as the general problem of conflicts of land between the Orang Kayan and recent Melayu newcomers to the area. Contrary to conclusions drawn by previous researchers in the area (i.e., Jérôme Rousseau), Ngo argues that local Orang Kayan do recognize individual ownership and devolvable usufruct rights over specific resources, which often involve specific trees in a given community-controlled area. This system differs from other indigenous tenure regimes in Kalimantan. The author concludes with an appeal for greater rigor in documenting existing land tenure regimes in Kalimantan in order to correct the simplistic and misleading notions currently underlying government mediations of the emerging land tenure disputes in the region. [In Bahasa Indonesia].

Indonesia/ West Kalimantan/ Indigenous and local communities—Land and resource tenure systems/ Indigenous and local communities—Forest land use and management practices/ Land settlement and development—Impacts on local communities and economy/ Land tenure—Legislation and state policy/ Ethnicity and ethnic relations.

225.   ———. **1992.** "Hak ulayat masyarakat setempat: pelajaran dari Orang Kayan dan Limbai." *Prisma* 21 (6): 53–65.
[Local Customary Land Tenure: Lessons from the Orang Kayan and Limbai.]

The article summarizes research findings from fieldwork conducted among the Orang Kayan and Orang Limbai, two Dayak communities along the West Kalimantan and Central Kalimantan borders. Fieldwork was conducted in July 1986–February 1987 and January – February 1990 respectively. Ngo provides a brief overview of tribal history, social structure, livelihood strategies as well as land use systems. Particular attention is given to describing the indigenous land tenure systems characteristic of each group. Significant differences between Orang Kayan and Orang Limbai are noted especially in terms of the recognition of individual ownership, devolvable use rights, and maintenance of enriched versus non-enriched fallows. In both cases, however, the extant indigenous land tenure and land use system is given little formal recognition by national authorities, who base their reading of local ownership on the national land law. This situation is facilitating the gradual expropriation of customary lands, which are increasingly falling under the formal control of immigrant farmers and state development projects. Attempts to promote agroforestry in the region will need to adequately address this problem in order to achieve success among local indigenous communities. [In Bahasa Indonesia].

Indonesia/ West Kalimantan/ Central Kalimantan/ Indigenous and local communities— Land and resource tenure systems/ Indigenous and local communities—Forest land use and management practices/ Land settlement and development—Impacts on local communities and economy/ Land tenure—Legislation and state policy.

226.   **Ohta, S., and S. Effendi. 1992.** "Ultisols of "Lowland Dipterocarp Forest" in East Kalimantan, Indonesia. I. Morphology and Physical Properties." *Soil Science and Plant Nutrition* 38 (2): 197–207.

Reporting on investigation into the morphological and physical properties of 35 typic Paleudults and Typic Hapludults, the major soils of lowland *Dipterocarp* forests in East Kalimantan, Ohta and Syarif describe appearance, color, and texture at different strata. Differences in clay migration and silt translocation are noted between soils of different texture, and the relationship between physical properties and soil texture and depth highlighted. [Summarized from journal abstract].

Indonesia/ Kalimantan/ Soils.

227.   ———. **1992.** "Ultisols of "Lowland *Dipterocarp* Forest" in East Kalimantan, Indonesia. II. Status of Carbon, Nitrogen, and Phosphorus." *Soil Science and Plant Nutrition* 38 (2): 207–216.

In Part 2 of a investigation of 35 typic Paleudults and Hapludults dominant in lowland *Dipterocarp* forests of East Kalimantan, Indonesia, Ohta and Syarif focus on results of chemical analysis, noting in particular the status of C, N, and P (including available forms of the latter elements). Sharply declining C, N, and P contents were noted in the top 15–20 cm of soil, and were directly correlated with the clay content in each horizon group. Higher C, N, and P contents in the finer soils may be linked to the stabilizing influence of clay particles on organic matter as well as the higher mobility of organic matter in the finer soils. Available N content was directly correlated with the total N content, and N availability was the highest when the C:N ratio ranged between 10 and 15. Nitrification was not as pronounced as ammonification. Available P correlated closely with the total C content. No marked difference in available P appeared between texture types; however, availability did decrease with increasing exchangeable Al, dithionite citrate soluble Fe, and clay. Finer soils were found to store larger amounts of C and total and available N and P, which "were distributed more largely in the subsoils (30–150 cm) than it has been believed." [Summarized from journal abstract].

Indonesia/ Kalimantan/ Soils.

228.   **Otsamo, A., G. Adjers, T. S. Hadi, J. Kuusipalo, K. Tuomela, and R. Vuokko. 1995.** "Effect of Site Preparation and Initial Fertilization on the Establishment and Growth of Four Plantation Tree Species Used in Reforestation of *Imperata cylindrica* Dominated Grasslands." *Forest Ecology and Management* 73 (1–3): 271–277.

Examines the effects of various site preparation techniques, including strip plowing, complete plowing, herbicide treatments, and application of NPK fertilizers on performance of various tree species. Tree species used include *Acacia mangium*, *Gmelina arborea*, *Paraserianthes falcataria*, and *Swietenia macrophylla*.

Indonesia/ South Kalimantan/ Reforestation/ Pest, weed, and crop disease management/ Forest management—Commercial forestry and silviculture/ Grasslands.

229.   **Otten, M. 1986.** *Transmigrasi: Myths and Realities: Indonesian Resettlement Policy, 1965–1985.* IWGIA Document, no. 57. Copenhagen: International Work Group for Indigenous Affairs.

Indonesia/ Land settlement and development—Impacts on local communities and economy/ Land settlement and development—Environmental impacts/ Indigenous and local communities—State policy/ State policy—Land development/ Ethnicity and ethnic relations.

230.   **Padoch, C. 1983.** "Agricultural Practices of the Kerayan Lun Dayeh." *Borneo Research Bulletin* 15 (1): 33–38.

While the Kerayan Lun Dayeh of East Kalimantan are conventionally known as shifting cultivators, they have also long been involved in the cultivation of irrigated rice. Padoch argues that the shift to irrigated rice cultivation makes sense given the relative labor requirements of shifting cultivation and "intensive pond-field farming." In this remote part of Borneo island, the latter can be shown to yield not only more crop per hectare but also more crop per person-day of work than swiddening. Factors behind this phenomenon include: 1) a less marked dry season in the region; 2) isolation from market trade which made procurement of useful technology for swidden farming (iron and steel implements) more difficult than for other Dayak groups in Kalimantan; 3) a local topography conducive to flooding; 4) the relatively limited threat of outsider invasion. Under these conditions, the labor required for constructing dikes, seeding, weeding and harvesting rice is less than that required by shifting cultivation for similar yields, thus making intensive wet rice cultivation a rational choice.

Indonesia/ East Kalimantan/ Indigenous and local communities—Farming practices/ Agricultural intensification.

231.   ————. **1985.** "Labor Efficiency and Intensity of Land Use in Rice Production: An Example from Kalimantan." *Human Ecology* 13 (3): 271–289.

Drawing from earlier fieldwork among the Kerayan Lun Dayeh of East Kalimantan, Padoch challenges the generalizability of the 'Boserup hypothesis.' Boserup has argued a close correlation between population density and the transition to land-intensive systems, suggesting that in sparsely populated environments, land extensive methods will predominate. Flying in face of this prediction, in a remote and lightly populated region of East Kalimantan, the Kerayan Lun Dayeh have long been practicing labor-intensive wet rice cultivation. Padoch reviews the factors that make this a rational farming system choice. The analysis highlights the role of environmental (both social and natural) circumstances other than simply population density in promoting different agricultural forms.

Indonesia/ East Kalimantan/ Indigenous and local communities—Farming practices/ Indigenous and local communities—Forest land use and management practices/ Agricultural intensification.

232.   ————. **1987.** "A Study of a Bornean System of Intensive Agriculture as a Model for Development." In *People and the Tropical Forest: A Research Report from the United States Man and the Biosphere Program*. Ed. A. Lugo et al., pp. 10–11. Washington, D.C: U.S. Dept. of State.

Indonesia/ East Kalimantan/ Indigenous and local communities—Farming practices/ Agricultural intensification.

233.   ————. **1995.** "Creating the Forest: Dayak Resource Management in Kalimantan." In *Society and Non-Timber Forest Products in Tropical Asia*. Ed. J. Fox, pp. 3–12. East-West Center Occasional Papers, Environment series, no. 19. Honolulu: East-West Center.

Noting the relative dearth of studies on Dayak forest management systems, Padoch describes the forest land use and maintenance patterns of the Tara'n Dayaks, a previously undescribed tribal group residing north of the Kapuas river in Balai subdistrict, Sanggau, West Kalimantan. The description draws from fieldwork in the territory of Tae, a village of five hamlets covering 16 km2 and supporting about 88 people/km2. A trend toward decreasing dependence on swidden-based rice farming, increasing dependence on irrigated and rain-fed permanent paddy farming, as well as increasing conversion of hillside areas to managed forest vegetation is noted for Tae village. Three principal types of managed forest vegetation kept by the Tara'n Dayaks are identified: 1) *tembawang* or former house sites where forest-gardens have been promoted on formerly cleared areas as a source of fruit, rubber, construction timbers, rattan and medicinal fibers; 2) *tanah adat* or land that has never yet been cleared, yet which is known to fall under the domain of customary law and which has been managed in ways similar to *tembawang* land; and 3) *tanah usaha* or enterprise plots planted to highly marketable tree species such as rubber. Though carefully managed and central to the livelihood systems of Tae villagers, managed forest areas among Dayaks generally have remained largely invisible to timber concession holders and government agencies. Padoch emphasizes the need to recognize and legitimate these indigenous forest use and management systems.

Indonesia/ West Kalimantan/ Indigenous and local communities—Forest land use and management practices.

234.   **Padoch, C., and N. L. Peluso, eds. 1996.** *Borneo in Transition: People, Forests, Conservation, and Development.* Kuala Lumpur: Oxford University Press.

Indonesia/ Malaysia/ Kalimantan/ Sarawak/ Sabah/ Borneo/ Regional development/ Agricultural development/ Forest biology and ecology/ Deforestation/ Forest management—Forest resource conservation/ Forest management—Parks and conservation areas/ Indigenous and local communities—Economy/ Indigenous and local communities—Commoditization/ Indigenous and local communities—Forest land use and management practices/ Indigenous and local communities—Land and resource tenure systems/ Land settlement and development/ Land settlement and development—Impacts on local communities and economy/ Land tenure—Legislation and state policy/ Timber industry—Logging/ Timber industry—Impacts on local communities and economy/ State policy—Forest and natural resources.

235.   **Padoch, C., and A. Vayda. 1983.** "Patterns of Resource Use and Human Settlement in Tropical Forests." In *Tropical Rainforest Ecosystems, Part A.* Ed. F. Golley, pp. 301–313. Amsterdam: Elsiever.

Indonesia/ Kalimantan/ Indigenous and local communities—Forest land use and management practices/ Indigenous and local communities—Forest products use and trade.

236.   **Pangetsu, M. 1989.** "East Kalimantan: Beyond the Timber and Oil Boom." In *Unity and Diversity: Regional Economic Development in Indonesian Since 1970.* Ed. H. Hill, pp. 152–175. Singapore: Oxford University Press.

Indonesia/ East Kalimantan/ Regional development/ Timber industry—Development and structure.

237.   **Pantir, T. 1990.** "Hak milik menurut hukum adat ditinjau dari UUPA No. 5/1960." Paper presented to the Seminar on Dayak Tribal Custom, 9–11 November 1990, in Kutai Regency, East Kalimantan.
[Land Ownership Rights According to Customary Law Considered from the Perspective of National Agrarian Law No. 5/1960.]

Titus Pantir cites specific legislation in the Indonesian land code to argue that customary land rights are clearly guaranteed by Indonesian law. As such, the main question remains not whether tribal communities are entitled to their land (they clearly are), but how to best execute the existing law in order to delegate genuine control over customary lands to the country's tribal communities. To this end the author recommends the formation of village cooperatives and the promotion of indigenous community development. Also examined more closely are questions of traditional rights of direct ownership. Most often, local officials have recognized these rights only when proof of continuous cultivation is presented. However, this approach involves an overly exclusive definition of customary ownership, conflicting with the more inclusive concept of customary land rights. More specifically, the latter concept refers to any land under long-term tribal control as standing forest, not merely as cultivated area.

In recent years, certificates of ownership, land classification schemes, and land reform laws have been used by outside speculators to expropriate traditional forest farmers. Indonesian land laws specify the maximum number of hectares a traditional farmer may maintain given extant population density, in excess of which the government maintains the right to purchase by eminent domain for purposes of distribution to landless farmers. The effect has been to progressively expropriate indigenous farmers in the Kalimantan farmers in face of government-sponsored resettlement and land development schemes. The author also critically assesses the role of timber concessions in the expropriation process, calling for a review of the concession system to identify where concession claims conflict with traditional claims of customary land and to allow local communities usufruct rights within valid concession areas. Though much maligned, traditional shifting cultivation among East

Kalimantan farmers remains the only system of agricultural production that involves routinely allowing cultivated lands to return to the biological diversity characteristic of the original forest stands from which they were originally cut. Research by Potter and Brookfield is cited to note that accelerated soil erosion appears to be more characteristic of lands disturbed by logging than those which have been under traditional swidden agriculture for decades. The author concludes with a number of recommendations relating to achieving full recognition of customary land rights as required by Indonesian law. Written by a member of the Dayak Foundation. [In Bahasa Indonesia].

Indonesia/ Kalimantan/ Indigenous and local communities—Land and resource tenure systems/ Indigenous and local communities—Forest land use and management practices/ Land tenure—Legislation and state policy.

238. **Partohardjono, S. 1994.** "Upland Agriculture in Indonesia: Recent Trends and Issues." In *Upland Agriculture in Asia*. Proceedings of a workshop held in Bogor, Indonesia April 6–8, 1993. Ed. J. W. T. Bottema, and D. R. Stoltz, pp. 17–36. Bogor: Regional Co-ordination Centre for Research and Development of Coarse Grains, Pulses, Roots and Tuber Crops in the Humid Tropics of Asia and the Pacific (CGPRT Centre).

Partohardjono presents a broad review of recent trends in land resources, production and productivity of major commodities, key biophysical issues, and field experience in upland agricultural development in Indonesia. The extent and distribution of various land types (irrigated lowland, rainfed lowland, dryland, upland and tidal swamp) as also growth trends in irrigated lands are described. Data are presented on corn, soybean and cassava yields as Indonesia's major upland crops. Also discussed are the results of intervention efforts, covering release of improved varieties of soybean, peanut and mungbean, results of field experiments in crop and cropping system improvements, as well as progress achieved in increasing per hectare yields of different upland crops (corn, peanuts, cassava, soybean, wetland and dryland rice) on a national level.

Indonesia/ Agricultural development/ Land use—Patterns and planning/ Agriculture—Smallholder cash crop farming/ State policy—Agricultural and rural development/ Project intervention—Agricultural development/ Farm management—Cropping systems.

239. **Partomihardjo, T. 1987.** "The Ulin Wood Which Is Threatened to Extinction." *Duta Rimba* 13 (87): 87–88.

Partomihardjo describes the biology, uses, regeneration dynamics, and silviculture of *ulin*, also known as Bornean iron wood (*Eusideroxylon zwageri*). Due to its strength and durability, ulin is a popular and over-exploited wood species in the Kalimantan provinces and southern Sumatra. Effects of over-exploitation are exacerbated by its slow rate of natural regeneration. Controls on ulin felling and trading as well as promotion of ulin silviculture are needed to preserve this resource.

Indonesia/ Kalimantan/ Forest flora/ Non-timber forest products/ Forest management—Forest resource conservation/ Forest management—Commercial forestry and silviculture.

240. **Patay, M., and G. Aditjondro. 1987.** "Dampak ekologis dan sosial penebangan hutan rawa dan hutan bakau oleh pemegang HPH di Sawa-Er Asmat dan Babo." Photocopy. Jayapura, Irian Jaya, Indonesia: Yayasan Pengembangan Masyarakat Desa Irian Jaya.
[Ecological and Social Effects of Logging of Swamp and Mangrove Forests by Concession-Holders in Sawa-Er Asmat and Babo, Manokwari District, Irian Jaya.]

In Bahasa Indonesia.

Indonesia/ Irian Jaya/ Timber industry—Environmental impacts/ Timber industry—Impacts on local communities and economy.

241.   **Payne, J., and C. M. Francis. 1985.** *A Field Guide to the Mammals of Borneo.* Kota Kinabalu; Kuala Lumpur, Malaysia: World Wildlife Fund Malaysia.

Malaysia/ Sabah/ Sarawak/ Indonesia/ Borneo/ Kalimantan/ Forest fauna.

242.   **Peluso, N. L. Forthcoming.** "Changing Forms of Access to Rattan Collection and Trade in East Kalimantan." In *Interactions Between People and Forests in East Kalimantan.* Ed. T. Jessup, Kuswata Kartawinata, and A. P. Vayda. Jakarta: UNESCO.

Indonesia/ East Kalimantan/ Indigenous and local communities—Forest products use and trade/ Rattan—Collection and trade/ Indigenous and local communities—Land and resource tenure systems.

243.   ———. **1983.** "Networking in the Commons: A Tragedy for Rattan?" *Indonesia* 35 (April): 95–108.

Indonesia/ East Kalimantan/ Rattan—Collection and trade/ Rattan—Resource management and conservation/ Indigenous and local communities—Forest products use and trade.

244.   ———. **1983.** "Traders and Merchants: The Forest Products Trade of East Kalimantan in Historical Perspective." Master's thesis, Cornell University, Ithaca, N.Y.

Indonesia/ East Kalimantan/ Non-timber forest products/ Indigenous and local communities—Forest products use and trade/ History—Colonial.

245.   ———. **1989.** "The Role of Non-timber Forest Products in Shifting Cultivation Communities and Households: Current Knowledge and Prospects for Development." Indonesia; UTF/INS/O65/ INS Forestry Studies, Field Document No. II-2. Jakarta: Directorate General of Forest Utilization, Ministry of Forestry, Government of Indonesia; Food and Agriculture Organization of the United Nations.

The commercial and subsistence-related roles of non-timber forest products (NTFP) within shifting cultivator communities of Indonesia's Outer Islands are described. Commercialization has brought many changes to the economies of indigenous Outer Island communities, but little statistical data exists on the social and economic impacts of this change on the subsistence use of NTFP. The author draws from a number of project documents, ethnographic research, and sector studies to describe what may be learned about NTFP use from these secondary sources so far. The study was commissioned in the context of developing the potential of these products to generate more income for shifting cultivators. The author observes that more specific information is needed about the potential impact of such efforts on indigenous forest product use. The role of other factors (such as land tenure, labor scarcity, etc.) on patterns of resource exploitation needs deeper understanding as well.

Indonesia/ Non-timber forest products/ Indigenous and local communities—Forest products use and trade/ Indigenous and local communities—Commoditization.

246.   ———. **1991.** "Forest Dependence and Vulnerability: The Role of Differential Access to Forests and Trees." Photocopy. Rome: Community Forestry Unit, Food and Agriculture Organization of the United Nations.

This 100 pp. report presents detailed case studies of two forest villages in West Kalimantan, focusing specifically on access to and dependence on forests and trees. Each case study describes: the evolution of current patterns of access; forest- and agroforestry-related land use; local forest and land use terms; access to forest and tree products; labor (general; division of labor; seasonality); resource conflicts. An Appendix also details research methods for comparative case studies on access.

Indonesia/ West Kalimantan/ Indigenous and local communities—Forest products use and trade/ Indigenous and local communities—Forest land use and management practices/ Indigenous and local communities—Land and resource tenure systems/ Indigenous and local communities—Commoditization/ Gender analysis.

247.   ———. **1991.** "Merchants, Manipulation, and Minor Forest Products on the Mahakam: Bugis Political-economic Strategies in Pre-colonial Kutai." In *Authority and Leadership in the Bugis World.* Ed. K. Van Dijk and G. Acciaioli. Leiden, Netherlands: Koninklijk Instituut voor Taal-, Land en Volkenkunde.

Indonesia/ East Kalimantan/ History—Pre-colonial/ Non-timber forest products/ Indigenous and local communities—Forest products use and trade.

248.   ———. **1992.** "The Ironwood Problem: (Mis-)management and Development of an Extractive Rainforest Product." *Conservation Biology* 6: 210–219.

Peluso examines the role that government forestry policies have played in the decline of local ironwood supplies in the dipterocarp forests of West Kalimantan. Because customary institutions for forest resource management are not recognized as viable by the government, local people's claims to ironwood are given little protection. Timber companies are granted the rights to control forest resources in their given concessions, yet "have little incentive or capacity to manage the activities of numerous villages within these territories." Peluso suggests the suitability of joint management arrangements involving government, timber companies, and empowered traditional institutions to ensure the protection both of forest resources and local people's legitimate claims to them.

Indonesia/ West Kalimantan/ Forest management—Forest resource conservation/ Indigenous and local communities—Forest products use and trade/ Indigenous and local communities—Forest land use and management practices/ State policy—Forest and natural resources/ Non-timber forest products.

249.   ———. **1992.** "The Political Ecology of Extraction and Extractive Reserves in East Kalimantan." *Development and Change* 23 (4): 49–74.

The extractive reserve model has gained ascendance in the current discourse over sustainable rainforest development. The author aims to examine the potential viability of this model in Indonesia through a discussion of the political ecology of rattan extraction in the country's province of East Kalimantan. While the collection of rattan for commercial trade has had a long history in the Southeast Asian region, larger scale extraction first developed in Indonesia during the late 1960s with the onset of the New Order regime's aggressive pursuit of resource-based industrialization. During this time, the state asserted effective control over the Indonesia's forest lands, overriding the traditional tenure arrangements operative among the indigenous forest-dependent communities of the country. With the conjuncture of national and international developments relating to the state's forest management policies and the international rattan market, the profitability of rattan trading soared in the early 1970s, attracting increasing numbers of downstream traders into the business. The effect of these developments has been to deplete rattan stocks in many areas of East Kalimantan once richly endowed with the resource. Resource depletion, drought, fire, and increasing government regulation of rattan collection and export in the 1980s have threatened to undermine the rattan-based livelihoods of many indigenous communities in Kalimantan. Also noted is the increasing semi-proletarianization of upstream rattan producers who now collect and bundle rattan directly for downstream, foreign-owned rattan carpet factories.

In this context, the establishment of extractive reserves to secure the rattan resource base for long-term community welfare appears one possible option. A review of the existing legislation concerning rattan collection suggests that a legal framework for a reserve system is in fact in place in Indonesia. However, organizing and empowerment of local communities would also be necessary to ensure that small-scale production is not undermined by large scale rattan plantations also being planned. Enabling effective territorial and tenurial claims over rattan producing areas by small-scale producers would thus be a key component of any extractive reserve system in Indonesia.

Indonesia/ Kalimantan/ Indigenous and local communities—Forest products use and trade/ Forest management—Forest resource conservation/ Rattan—Collection and trade/ Rattan—Resource management and conservation/ State policy—Forest and natural resources.

250.   ——. **1992.** "The Rattan Trade in East Kalimantan, Indonesia: Can Extraction Be Reserved?" In *Non-timber Products from Tropical Forests: Evolution of a Conservation and Development Strategy.* Ed. D. Nepstad and S. Schwartzman, pp. 117–127. New York: New York Botanical Garden.

This paper discusses the pressures on the trade in the non-timber forest products of East Kalimantan and considers both the potential for and the constraints on creating extractive reserves in this political-economic context. It is argued "that the notion of extractive reserves is an attractive one, particularly given the rapidity with which East Kalimantan's forests are being destroyed. However, the difficulties of defining access rights, the political climate in Indonesia, and the realities of enforcing exclusion call for the creation of village extractive reserves rather than a labor-based organization of forest product extractors across a whole region."

Indonesia/ East Kalimantan/ Rattan—Collection and trade/ Rattan—Resource management and conservation/ Indigenous and local communities—Forest products use and trade/ Forest management—Forest resource conservation.

251.   ——. **1992.** *Rich Forests, Poor People: Resource Control and Resistance in Java.* Ithaca, N.Y.: Cornell University Press.

Sixty-seven percent of Indonesia's population are concentrated on Java, 23.2% of which is officially designated as forest land owned by the state. Java's state forests are today managed by a large parastatal enterprise (*Perum Perhutani*) largely for purposes of commercial teak and pine production. With 1/3 of the rural population classified as "forest villages," and hundreds of thousands landless farmers on the island, use of and access to the rich resources harbored in Java's state forests pose a continuous flashpoint for conflict between state and local villager interests. Drawing from careful archival research and fieldwork at numerous forest village sites, Peluso analyzes the means by which the Indonesian state maintains its control over forest land resources in Java, as well as the processes by which this control is resisted daily, and sometimes openly challenged by rural villagers. Following an introductory chapter that sets the contextual and theoretical framework, Peluso traces the pre-colonial and colonial legacies of the current state forestry regime on Java, noting the imposition of principles of "scientific forestry" by Dutch colonial administrators, which secured control over forest lands for the state, and today underlies the Indonesian state's exclusion of traditional uses of forest land and timber. The following section explores the changing nature of the Indonesian state, the evolving political economy of forestry in the Indonesia, and the processes by which these developments have shaped the specifics of forest management practice in the country. A third focus involves case studies of villager resistance to state forest control in both teak and non-teak production areas, highlighting the ecological, socio-historical and cultural circumstances of these challenges, as well as the process by which customary forest access continues to be criminalized. In a concluding chapter, Peluso considers possible approaches to forest management that integrate both commercial production and local villager interests (i.e., social forestry), noting the specific constraints and conditions that need to be addressed to make such alternatives truly viable.

Indonesia/ Java/ State policy—Forest and natural resources/ Forest management—Commercial forestry and silviculture/ Timber plantations/ Indigenous and local communities—Economy/ Indigenous and local communities—Forest products use and trade/ Indigenous and local communities—Forest land use and management practices/ Indigenous and local communities—State policy/ History—Colonial/ Political economy/ Social forestry.

252.   ———. **1995.** "Extraction Interactions: Logging Tropical Timbers in West Kalimantan, Indonesia." In *Society and Non-timber Forest Products in Tropical Asia.* Ed. J. Fox, pp. 73–96. East-West Center Occasional Papers: Environment Series, no. 19. Honolulu: East-West Center.

Interactions between competing systems of forest resource use, such as large-scale timber extraction and community-based regimes for forest product collection, are still poorly understood by tropical forestry specialists. Peluso attempts to redress this lacunae through a study of the production, trade and management of highly termite-resistant Bornean ironwood by West Kalimantan forest villagers, with a particular focus on the impacts of the timber industry on this system. The paper begins with a broad overview of issues in customary law, forest product collection and trade by forest villages in Kalimantan, national land law, and the forest concession system in Indonesia. The specific features of Bornean ironwood (*Eusideroxylon zwageri*, locally known as *belian*) and its collection and management under both customary tenure and the official minor forest product concession arrangements are then discussed. A case study of one West Kalimantan village is presented, showing the growing commercialization of ironwood trade with the expanding timber industry and the changes in tenure and trading arrangements this development has brought. The potentially positive benefits of developing entrepreneurship around ironwood trade have been largely negated by the problem of overexploitation, as government initiatives to "modernize" customary tenure arrangements have proceeded halfheartedly, without adequate planning and support. Peluso emphasizes the need for a "more explicit approach to joint management" of forest lands between villagers and government agencies, requiring in turn "a more solid legal backing for traditional management institutions."

Indonesia/ West Kalimantan/ Non-timber forest products/ Indigenous and local communities—Forest products use and trade/ Indigenous and local communities—Land and resource tenure systems/ Timber industry—Impacts on local communities and economy/ State policy—Forest and natural resources/ Land tenure—Legislation and state policy/ Forest management—Forest resource conservation.

253.   **Pelzer, K. 1945.** *Pioneer Settlement in the Asiatic Tropics.* Special Publication, no. 29. New York: American Geographical Society.

Population distribution in the Asian tropics is considered, with particular focus on the Philippines and Indonesia. The author argues that population is poorly distributed in the region, with islands like Java and Luzon suffering increasingly serious over-population and declining person:land ratios, while other islands remain sparsely settled by "primitive" swidden farmers. Government assistance is needed to encourage the migration of households from over-populated areas to areas where arable land is still plentiful. Case studies of government-sponsored resettlement schemes in Mindanao, the Philippines, and Lampung province on Sumatra, Indonesia are presented.

Asia/ Philippines/ Mindanao/ Indonesia/ Sumatra/ Migration/ Land settlement and development/ State policy—Land development/ History—Colonial.

254.   **Persoons, G. 1989.** "Modified Hunting and Gathering: Symbiotic Relations with Malay Farmers." In *Women, Migrants and Tribals*. Ed. G. K. Lieten, O. Niewenhuys, and L. Schenk-Sandbergen, pp. 31–46. New Delhi: Manohar.

The Kubu are a nomadic people of Southern Sumatra (Jambi and Palembang provinces). Today they number c. 20,000, and continue to follow a largely hunter-gatherer lifestyle, although development in the region has brought changes. Due to rapid forest encroachment, contact between the Kubu and sedentary ethnic Malay farmers in S. Sumatra has become commonplace, and the Kubu can no longer subsist on forest products alone. Yet, notes the author, despite their shrinking resource base, the Kubu have not been assimilated in the increasingly predominant peasant culture. Rather, a "grafting" process has taken place, whereby forest product collection and trade, barter, and begging have replaced hunting and gathering as the Kubu's main means of livelihood. The author notes that replacement of S. Sumatra's presently varied land use patterns with monoculture estates or other exclusionary uses will reduce livelihood options for the Kubu only further, leaving complete assimilation or exclusive focus on roadside and in-town begging as the only remaining alternatives.

Indonesia/ Sumatra/ Indigenous and local communities—Economy/ Indigenous and local communities—Forest products use and trade/ Indigenous and local communities—Commoditization/ Land settlement and development—Impacts on local communities and economy.

255.   **Potter, L. 1985.** "Management, Enterprise and Politics in the Development of the Tropical Rain Forest Lands: Degradation, Innovation and Social Welfare in the Riam Kiwa Valley, Kalimantan, Indonesia." *Tyranny of the Household: Investigative Essays on Women's Work*. Ed. D. Jain, and N. Banerjee. New Delhi: Shakti Books.

Indonesia/ South Kalimantan/ Regional development/ Land use—Patterns and planning/ Political economy/ Agricultural intensification/ State policy—Agricultural and rural development/ State policy—Land development.

256.   ———. **1988.** "Indigenes and Colonisers: Dutch Forest Policy in South and East Borneo (Kalimantan) 1900 to 1950." In *Changing Tropical Forests: Historical Perspectives on Today's Challenges in Asia/Austral Asia and Oceania*. Ed. J. Dargavel, K. Dixon, and N. Semple, pp. 127–53. Canberra: Centre for Resource and Environmental Studies, Australian National University.

Indonesia/ East Kalimantan/ History—Colonial/ State policy—Forest and natural resources/ State policy—Land development/ Timber industry—Development and structure.

257.   ———. **1990.** "Forest Classification, Policy and Land-use Planning in Kalimantan." *Borneo Review* 1 (1): 91–128.

Potter reviews state of current research on the condition of Kalimantan's forests and critically examines the Indonesian government's forest classification system. To be sustainable, land use planning must appropriately balance contrasting needs and interests concerning watershed and ecosystem protection, timber production to supply a growing downstream processing sector, and agricultural expansion. The effectiveness of present policies to meet these needs is evaluated, and suggestions made for changes in the direction of greater resource sustainability.

Indonesia/ East Kalimantan/ Land use—Patterns and planning/ State policy—Forest and natural resources/ State policy—Land development/ Timber industry—Development and structure.

258.   ————. **1991.** "Environmental and Social Aspects of Timber Exploitation in Kalimantan, 1967–1989." In *Indonesia: Resources, Ecology and Environment.* Ed. J. Hardjono, pp. 177–211. Singapore; Oxford: Oxford University Press.

This paper sketches a short, analytical history of timber exploitation in East Kalimantan since the ascendance of the New Order state in Indonesia. A liberalized foreign investment policy of the time opened Outer Island forests to both foreign and domestic private concessionaires on a large scale, bringing on a massive logging spree that enabled Indonesia to capture 41% of the world tropical log market by 1979. Logging activities, associated agricultural conversion projects, and an influx of spontaneous settlers with newly opened logging roads have contributed to a drastic reduction of existing forest cover in much of the country's forested provinces. Given the changes this has wrought on local environments, the author stresses the urgent need for a "reassessment of land-use allocation in the designated forest areas" to ensure more sustainable land use practices in the future.

The paper is divided into 3 main sections. The first two review existing studies and forestry data to describe main issues which emerged among forestry planners and observers during early (1967–1979) and later phases (1980–1989) of timber extraction in the province. These include: 1) The application of the Basic Forestry Law to the logging industry, logging practices by concessionaires, and the failure of timber companies to heed existing forestry regulations; 2) The damage to the local ecology done by mechanized logging techniques and the selective logging system; 3) The impact of the industry on local populations in terms of land tenure conflicts and degradation of their livelihood systems; 4) The benefits as well as negative impacts of downstream processing development; 5) Problems encountered in the conversion of large forest tracts to agricultural uses both within the Transmigration Programme and by spontaneous settlers from other islands.

The final section of the paper is devoted to discussing major needs that must be addressed for a sustainable land use plan in East Kalimantan, given the conditions imposed by the province's logging history. In particular, the author cites an urgent need for forest category reclassification, in order to better match agricultural conversion policies with actual physical and social conditions. How much land is actually available and needed for specific timber production and forest conversion targets comprises another question needing further clarification. The author highlights the results of the RePPProt land use and suitability study completed for East Kalimantan in 1987, the IIED/GOI review of Indonesia's production forest needs and policies, current plans for timber estate expansion, and current debates on rates of forest destruction by both indigenous and immigrant residents.

The paper concludes that given present pressures and attitudes of those "currently entrusted with the 'management' of the forests," the outlook is bleak for more sustainable land use practices in East Kalimantan. Some relief from pressures to exploit the forest beyond sustainable levels may be available if Western nations agree to classify the genetic resources of tropical forests as invaluable commodities which they must help pay to protect. For places like East Kalimantan, these kinds of revenues may provide an alternative source of earnings and help develop alternative sources of industrial employment.

Indonesia/ East Kalimantan/ Deforestation/ Timber industry—Development and structure/ Timber industry—Logging/ Timber industry—Impacts on local communities and economy/ Timber industry—Environmental impacts/ Timber industry—State policy and regulation/ Land settlement and development—Environmental impacts/ Land settlement and development—Impacts on local communities and economy/ State policy—Forest and natural resources/ State policy—Land development/ Forest management—Forest resource conservation/ Land use—Patterns and planning.

259.   **Priyono, R., W. Smits, S. Priasukmana, and J. Mayer. 1988.** "Palm and Rattan Species in Agroforestry Systems in East Kalimantan." In *Agroforestry untuk pengembangan daerah pedesaan di Kalimantan Timur: Prosiding seminar kehutanan, 19–21 September 1988, Samarinda, East Kalimantan.* Ed. A. M. Lahjie and B. Seibert, Samarinda, Indonesia: Department of Forestry, Universitas Mulawarman; GTZ.

[Agroforestry for Rural Development in East Kalimantan: Proceedings of a Forestry Seminar.]

Papers presented in this proceedings section focus on various agroforestry and integrated farming approaches using different crops. Individual papers include: Development of hybrid coconut in integrated farming systems in the transmigration area Rimba Ayu, Kota Bangun, Kutai District, East Kalimantan (R. Priyono); The utilization of sugar palm (*Arenga pinnata*) in agroforestry (W. Smits); The utilization of sugar palm and the possibility for its development on the riverbank areas in the middle Mahakam Area, Kutai District, East Kalimantan (R. Priyono); Rattan gardens as an agroforestry system for development in East Kalimantan (S. Priasukmana); and Rattan cultivation, family economy and land use: a case study from Pasir District, East Kalimantan (J. Mayer, J.). [In Bahasa Indonesia].

Indonesia/ East Kalimantan/ Agroforestry/ Project intervention—Agroforestry/ Indigenous and local communities—Forest products use and trade/ Indigenous and local communities—Farming practices/ Indigenous and local communities—Forest land use and management practices/ Farm management—Cropping systems.

260.   **Provinse, J. H. 1937.** "Cooperative Ricefield Cultivation among the Siang Dyaks of Central Borneo." *American Anthropologist* 39 (1): 77–102.

Based on three months of fieldwork, Provinse describes the swidden paddy cultivation system of the Siang Dayak located northward of Poeroek Tjahoe on the Upper Barito river in Central Borneo. Particular emphasis is placed on identifying the cooperative forms of labor organization and labor allocation patterns involved in the community's subsistence rice production. It is argued that among the Siang Dayak cooperative swidden farming efforts are less motivated by "external social and religious forces" than by the "motive power" of these efforts as shaped by utilitarian, household economic objectives. An appendix records the activity of six men and one woman in one village over two fortnightly periods during field preparation season.

Indonesia/ Kalimantan/ Indigenous and local communities—Farming practices/ Indigenous and local communities—Economy.

261.   **Putz, F. E., and A. Susilo. 1994.** "Figs and Fire." *Biotropica* 26 (4): 468–469.

Putz and Susilo observe and discuss the persistence of hemiephytic figs in areas affected by fire, based on data gathered from Borneo and Venezuela.

Indonesia/ Malaysia/ Borneo/ Forest flora/ Forest biology and ecology/ Forest fires.

262.   **Rabinowitz, A. 1995.** "Helping a Species Go Extinct: The Sumatran Rhino in Borneo." *Conservation Biology* 9 (3): 482–488.

Current efforts to reverse the steep decline of rhinoceros populations in Asia have tended to emphasize ex-situ conservation methods, mainly through captive breeding programs. Rabinowitz characterizes this approach as a costly failure, as evidenced by the poor results of the Sumatran Rhino Trust which succeeded in capturing only 35 rhinos from forest areas of Sumatra, Borneo, and Peninsular Malaysia between 1987 and 1993, 12 of which have died in captivity, and none of which have produced offspring. The situation of rhinos in Sabah, the East Malaysian state containing the most important populations of Sumatran rhino outside Sumatra and Peninsular Malaysia, is presented as a case study of the rhinos' declining numbers, shrinking habitat, and ineffective conservation efforts. The new conservation strategy being promoted by the Global Environmental Facility, focusing on wild population protection, sanctuary management, captive propagation, and gene-bank technologies, also appears flawed by an over-reliance on high-tech, ex-situ measures. Rabinowitz emphasizes the need to focus efforts much less on captive breeding and much more on "intensive, on-the-ground protection and management activities."

Malaysia/ Indonesia/ Sabah/ Forest fauna/ Wildlife management.

263. **Rahardjo, D. 1972.** "Kedudukan dan peranan sektor kehutanan dalam pembangunan daerah Kalimantan Timur." *Prisma* 1 (2): 27–33.
[The Position and Role of the Forestry Sector in the Regional Development of East Kalimantan.]

Timber production in East Kalimantan plays an important role both in the regional and national economies. This suggests close cooperation between the provincial and the national governments is needed. Forestry sector planning should be integrated with that of other sectors to ensure support for both forestry and forestry-derived or related industries. [In Bahasa Indonesia].

Indonesia/ East Kalimantan/ Timber industry—Development and structure/ Regional development/ State policy—Forest and natural resources/ Timber industry—State policy and regulation.

264. **Raintree, J. B., and H. A. Francisco, eds. 1994.** *Marketing of Multipurpose Tree Products in Asia.* Proceedings of an international workshop held in Baguio City, Philippines, 6–9 December 1993. Bangkok: Winrock International.

Eight sections cover different themes related to multipurpose tree product marketing in different Southeast Asian countries, at different scales of operation, and in connection with different products. Section themes include: 1) Marketing of multipurpose tree products; 2) Woodfuel and timber markets; 3) Marketing of multipurpose food trees; 4) Industrial markets; 5) Impacts of markets on rural development: farm forestry, agroforestry and non-timber forest products; 6) Market information systems; 7) Innovative approaches (including case studies of green marketing, plantation development and marketing in West Sumatra, and MPT product marketing by the Ikalahan in the Cordilleras of Northern Luzon); and 8) Working group reports. Products discussed include fuelwood in Cebu and Asia, timber in Sri Lanka, *Parka speciosa* fruits in Peninsular Malaysia, jackfruit in the Central Visayas, *Artocarpus* species in Nepal, industrial wood in Pakistan, India, Thailand, and the Philippines, and *kapok* in West Sumatra.

Asia/ Indonesia/ Sumatra/ Kalimantan/ Philippines/ Cebu/ Palawan/ Agroforestry/ Non-timber forest products/ Indigenous and local communities—Forest products use and trade/ Fuelwood/ Agricultural economics.

265. **Ramli, R. 1992.** "Intervensi langsung negara dalam industri kayu lapis." *Prisma* 21 (6): 19–28.
[Direct State Intervention in the Plywood Industry.]

Ramli focuses on the Indonesian government's ban on the export of raw timber put into effect by the Indonesian government during the mid-1980s. The relative costs and benefits of royalties on raw timber versus an outright ban are assessed as two policy alternatives for promoting greater downstream processing. While the government's choice to implement an export ban made strategic sense as a means to rapidly develop a domestic plywood industry, capture a large share of the international plywood market, and force the closure of many competing plywood factories in other Asian countries (South Korea, Singapore, Japan), it has also had some serious negative effects. More specifically these include greater inefficiency in the use of raw timber by domestic producers than might have been the case had downstream processing been more gradually promoted through timber royalties as well as the growing concentration of ownership within the timber industry. The lack of effective mechanisms to divert economic rent from the timber industry to the public sector has allowed the rent generated from Indonesia's export ban to benefit a small group of large entrepreneurs who now exert quasi-oligopolistic control over the industry. The author suggests the potential value of a timber tax to rectify this imbalance, internalize the negative externalities of timber extraction on the natural and socio-cultural environment, and compensate local communities who bear the brunt of the industry's environmental impacts. [In Bahasa Indonesia].

Indonesia/ Timber industry—Development and structure/ Timber industry—State policy and regulation/ Timber industry—Downstream processing.

266.   **Retnowati, E., and O. Satjapradja. 1988.** "Erosion, Runoff, and Rainfall Characteristics of the Tropical Rain Forest in East Kalimantan." *Buletin Penelitian Hutan* 511 (9–16).

The authors report on data collected in 1985/86 in a lowland tropical rain forest near Samarinda, East Kalimantan. The study sought to describe the relationship between rainfall, runoff, rainfall characteristics, as well as the quality of vegetative cover. [In Bahasa Indonesia].

Indonesia/ Kalimantan/ Soil erosion and degradation.

267.   **Richardson, S. D. 1990.** "Forestry Institutions and Policy." Indonesia UTF/INS/065/INS: Forestry Studies, Field Document No. VI-5. Jakarta: Directorate General of Forest Utilization, Ministry of Forestry, Government of Indonesia/Food and Agriculture Organization of the United Nations.

This report examines forestry sector administration at the national level. Individual chapters address: forestry institutions and policy; administration and policy development; specific policy issues, including sustainable development and the environment; natural resource depletion; forest management; plantation forestry; forest-based industries; and support services. Policy recommendations and informal proposals are included.

Indonesia/ State policy—Forest and natural resources/ Timber industry—Downstream processing/ Forest management—Forest resource conservation.

268.   **Riswan, S. 1982.** "Ecological Studies in Primary, Secondary, and Experimentally Cleared Mixed Dipterocarp Forest and Kerangas Forest in East Kalimantan, Indonesia." Ph.D. diss., University of Aberdeen, Aberdeen, U.K.

Indonesia/ East Kalimantan/ Forest biology and ecology/ Forest regeneration/ Timber industry—Impacts on local communities and economy.

269.   ———. **1989.** "Trend of Soil Nutrient Movements in Two Different Soil Types after Clear-Cut With or Without Burning in Kalimantan, Indonesia." In *Nutrient Management for Food Crop Production in Tropical Farming Systems.* Ed. J. van der Heide, pp. 261–270. Malang, East Java; Haren, Netherlands: University of Brawijaya; Institute for Soil Fertility.

A 1.5 year study on soil nutrient movement in burned and unburned clear-cut forest areas of East Kalimantan where Red- Yellow Podzolic soil (Ultisol) and a Podzol (Spodosol) dominate showed significant variation in soil property dynamics. Dynamics differed between burned and unburned areas in mixed Dipterocarp forest, while no differences were evident in forest areas of the *kerangas* (heath forest) type. Soil conditions had recovered in the mixed Dipterocarp forest after only 1.5 years, while in the heath forest, significant soil degradation had occurred. Research results suggest the advisability of maintaining a natural forest state on extremely poor soils (Podzols).

Indonesia/ East Kalimantan/ Forest regeneration/ Soil erosion and degradation/ Forest management—Forest resource conservation/ Forest fires.

270.   ———. **1991.** "Kerangas Forest at Gunung Pasir, Samboja, East Kalimantan: Status of Nutrient in the Leaves." In *Proceedings of the Fourth Round-Table Conference on Dipterocarps, 12–15 December 1989, Bogor, Indonesia.* Ed. I. Soerianegara, S. S. Tjitrosomo, R. C. Umaly, and I. Umboh, pp. 279–294. Bogor, Indonesia: SEAMEO BIOTROP.

A *kerangas* (heath) forest in Samboja, East Kalimantan was examined for the status of tree leaf nutrients, including nitrogen, phosphorus, potassium, calcium, magnesium and sodium. Average leaf nutrient contents are not poor, and for P, K, and Ca appear to be higher than in mixed dipterocarp forest. While the dominant tree species has an average leaf nutrient status, some rare and nondominant tree species have higher levels. No direct impact on controlling the status of nutrients in the forest ecosystem results, however; rather the individual tree species vary in their efficiency in taking up nutrients from the environment and thus conserving them in the forest ecosystem. [Summarized from monograph abstract].

Indonesia/ East Kalimantan/ Forest biology and ecology/ Forest flora/ Vegetation analysis.

271.   **Riswan, S., and K. Kartawinata. 1988.** "A Lowland Dipterocarp Forest 35 Years After Pepper Plantation in East Kalimantan, Indonesia." *Some Ecological Aspects of Tropical Forest of East Kalimantan: A Collection of Research Reports.* Ed. S. Soemodihardjo. pp. 1–40. Man and Biosphere Indonesia Contribution, no. 48. Jakarta: Indonesian Institute of Sciences; Indonesian National MAB Committee.

The paper reports the results of one study undertaken as part of the Man and Biosphere research program in East Kalimantan in the late 1970s and early 1980s. The structure, floristic composition and vegetation dynamics of a lowland dipterocarp forest plot 35 years after abandonment as a pepper plantation are described. The authors estimate that returning the disturbed forest plot to a state similar to primary forest stands would require c. 150–500 years.

Indonesia/ East Kalimantan/ Forest regeneration/ Migrant farmers and farming.

272.   ———. **1988.** "Regeneration After Disturbance in a Kerangas (Heath) Forest In East Kalimantan, Indonesia." *Some Ecological Aspects of Tropical Forest of East Kalimantan: A Collection of Research Reports.* Ed. S. Soemodihardjo. pp. 61–80. Man and Biosphere Indonesia Contribution, no. 48. Jakarta: Indonesian Institute of Sciences; Indonesian National MAB Committee.

As part of a larger report on the results of individual studies undertaken in the Man and Biosphere research program in East Kalimantan in the late 1970s and early 1980s, this essay focuses on regeneration of heath forests in East Kalimantan after disturbance by clearcutting and clearcutting followed by burning respectively. The authors find that most regeneration in both cases appears to take place via resprouting rather than reseeding, indicating that the quality of the soil itself rather than the burning process has greater influence on "the direction and rate of secondary succession."

Indonesia/ East Kalimantan/ Forest regeneration/ Forest fires.

273.   ———. **1991.** "Regeneration after Disturbance in a Lowland Mixed Dipterocarp Forest in East Kalimantan, Indonesia." In *Rain Forest Regeneration and Management.* Ed. A. G—mez-Pampa, T. C. Whitmore, and M. Hadley, pp. 295–302. Man and the Biosphere Series, no. 6. Paris: UNESCO; Parthenon Publishing Group.

A study on regeneration after clear-cutting and burning in primary lowland forest in Lempake, East Kalimantan, Indonesia involved comparison of two (0.5 ha each) contiguous clear-cut plots, one of which was burnt. Observations spanned a 78 week period. Seedlings were found to play a more important role than sprouts in the early stage of succession, and the unburned plot showed better performance in the number of species, percentage of cover and frequency of seedlings and resprouts, as well as the number of primary forest species. The dominant species in the unburnt and burnt plots differed, even though the plots were adjacent. The presence of an undisturbed seed bank in the unburned soil area may be a key factor in regeneration.

Indonesia/ East Kalimantan/ Forest regeneration.

274.   **Rodman, B. 1978.** "Diets, Density and Distribution of Borneon Primates." In *Ecology of Arboreal Florivores.* Ed. G. Montgomery, pp. 465–478. Washington, D.C.: Smithsonian Institute Press.

The author reports on observations made between May 1970 and July 1971 and July 1978 through August 1978 in a 3 km2 area of Kutai National Park, East Kalimantan. The study focused on five species of primates sympatric to orang utans, documenting their diet and distribution. Two habitat zones could be distinguished—riverine and deep forest—based on the different proportions of leaves and mature fruit present. The author observed that the primates studied inhabited the two habitat zones at different densities, reflecting the differing density of food material available.

Indonesia/ Kalimantan/ Forest fauna/ Forest biology and ecology.

275.   **Ross, M. S. 1980.** "The Role of Land Clearing in Indonesia's Transmigration Programme." *Bulletin of Indonesian Economic Studies* 16 (1): 75–85.

The author discusses specific problems related to land clearing for transmigration settlement development, proposing a number of possible remedies. In particular the author stresses that land clearing teams should follow proper soil conserving practices. The use of heavy equipment should be highly discouraged; soils should not be exposed directly to rain, wind and sunlight; tree roots should be left in the ground to preserve the soil structure. Further studies of proper land clearing techniques are discussed including, investigations into biomass resources, methods for recovering cleared biomass without damaging the soils, and involving transmigrant participation in land clearing.

Indonesia/ East Kalimantan/ Land settlement and development—Environmental impacts/ Soil erosion and degradation.

276.   ———. **1984.** *Forestry in Land Use Policy for Indonesia.* Trinity Term, U.K.: Green College.

Although a total of 143 million hectares of land are designated as forest land officially under the jurisdiction of the Ministry of Forestry, estimates of the early 1980s indicate that only approximately 122 million hectares of closed forest still exist in Indonesia. Roughly 99% of these forest lands are located on the country's "Outer Islands." Ross identifies two conflicting pressures on this resource: the demand of the country's developing forestry sector for raw materials and the need for agricultural land to sustain Indonesia's growing and still largely agriculturally based population. 21 million hectares of new agricultural lands will be needed by the year 2000 according to one estimate of 1981. At the same time, the author estimates that between 7.2 million to 71 million ha of natural forests would be needed to supply the country's forestry industries over the next 50 years, depending on demand and the level of productivity achieved within the industry. By contrast, only 0.55 million to 5.2 million ha of forest plantations would be needed to supply the same volume of timber, although problems of "controlling" encroachment by "local populations" operating under principles of local customary land rights would require special attention.

The author stresses that intensification of current forestry activities to increase per area unit productivity would be a key means to resolve current conflicts between forestry-related and agricultural land use needs. A re-classification of forest lands to more accurately reflect agricultural suitability is suggested in detail. The manuscript contains province-specific empirical data on land use, broad background information on relevant institutions and legislation, and projections of future land and timber needs. The thesis upon which this work is based was written in the context of providing supportive policy suggestions for Indonesia's Transmigration program.

Indonesia/ Land use—Patterns and planning/ Forest management—Commercial forestry and silviculture/ State policy—Forest and natural resources/ State policy—Land development/ Timber plantations/ Deforestation.

277.   **Rousseau, J. 1987.** "Kayan Land Tenure." *Borneo Research Bulletin* 19: 47–56.

Rousseau continues a debate with anthropologist Appell on the question of devolvable usufructuary rights among the Kayan Dayak of Malaysia. Drawing from fieldwork conducted in different parts of Kayan territory, he points out the variability of usufructuary rights assignment among the Kayan: while the middle Baluy Kayan do not generally recognize a kin group's right to fallow land it once cultivated, other Kayan groups along the Mahakam, Baram, and Kayan rivers do. Argues Rousseau, the field data suggests that land tenure systems are strongly influenced by the availability of land, and thus are likely to change as land becomes more or less scarce. Among the Baluy Kayan it appears that labor investment rather than simply tree felling represents a key condition for assuming usufructuary rights.

Malaysia/ Indonesia/ Borneo/ Indigenous and local communities—Land and resource tenure systems.

278.   ———. **1988.** "Central Borneo: A Bibliography." *The Sarawak Museum Journal* n.s., 38 (59): 1–274.

Indonesia/ Malaysia/ Sarawak/ Bibliography.

279.   ———. **1990.** *Central Borneo: Ethnic Identity and Social Life in a Stratified Society.* Oxford: Clarendon Press.

In a detailed ethnography, Rousseau characterizes central Borneo as distinct social unit marked by great ethnic diversity yet with a common history and social system cutting across ethnic boundaries. The Kayan form the most homogeneous ethnic category, their social organization appears to be a model for others, and their language the lingua franca of the region. Also present, however, are Kenyah, Kajang, Kelabit, Penan, Bukat, and many more indigenous tribal groups. Rousseau draws from written sources as well as fieldwork of the early 1970s and 1984 to describe the ethnic distribution in historical context, outlining early migrations and pre-colonial history as well as developments in more recent periods. The social organization of Central Borneo agriculturalists, including settlement patterns, village economy, and political structures, are characterized by a stratified system of social hierarchy involving high aristocrats, low aristocrats, commoners, and, in the past, slaves. The migrations, settlement, and economy, of Central Borneo nomads are also described, along with their egalitarian political organization in which nomadic leaders have little formal authority and rely largely on persuasive skills to influence group decisions and conduct.

Another focus of the ethnography is a study of the relations and interactions between swiddeners and nomads, between different swidden groups, and between Central Borneo peoples and coastal communities. Swiddener-nomad relations pivot around trade in forest products, while sometimes also involving alliances forged in face of invasion from other groups or downriver forces. Nomads are largely subordinated to settled swiddeners, and the heads of the latter command a position as "overlord" over the former. Nomads are typically seen as "serving" more powerful swiddeners, yet they are also able to escape oppressive relationships by switching allegiance to other groups. A major source of power enjoyed by swiddeners in their economic relationship with nomadic groups is the former's larger population size, access to outside resources, and propensity towards asserting hierarchical relations of power. Among agriculturalists, "the relatively rigid local power structure articulates with a more flexible regional system" such as informal councils in which different members exert varying degrees of clout. In sum, in describing Central Borneo as an integrated social unit, Rousseau presents ethnicity as one component within this unit; that is, as "people's conceptualization of their social and cultural life" but not necessarily "the inescapable frame of social relations." The analysis places into question the salience of ethnic units as unit of analysis in social research on Borneo.

Indonesia/ Malaysia/ Borneo/ Ethnography/ Indigenous and local communities—Social relations/ Indigenous and local communities—Economy/ Indigenous and local communities—Forest products use and trade/ Indigenous and local communities—Land and resource tenure systems/ Ethnicity and ethnic relations.

280.   **Ruslim, Y. 1994.** *Der Beitrag eines planmässigen Erschliessungs- und Nutzungkonzeptes zur pfleglichen Holzernte im tropischen Regenwald, untersucht am Beispiel eines Dipterocarpaceenwaldes in Ostkalimantan.* Göttinger Beiträge zur Land- und Forstwirtschaft in den Tropen und Subtropen, no. 95. Göttingen, Germany: Institut für Pflanzenbau und Tierhygiene in den Tropen und Subtropen.
[The Contribution of a Planned Access and Utilization Scheme to Orderly Timber Harvest in Tropical Rainforests Based on the Example of a Dipterocarp Forest in East Kalimantan.]

Based on a case study of a concession owned by the International Timber Corporation Indonesia (ITCI) in East Kalimantan, Ruslim compares different strategies for developing access to timber sites and suggests the superior effectiveness of "planned intimate" access systems for reducing forest damage from logging.

Indonesia/ East Kalimantan/ Timber industry—Logging/ Timber industry—State policy and regulation/ Forest management—Commercial forestry and silviculture/ Forest management—Forest resource conservation.

281.   **Ruzicka, I. 1979.** "Rent Appropriation in Indonesian Logging: East Kalimantan, 1972/73–1976/77." *Bulletin of Indonesian Economic Studies* 15 (2): 45–74.

This paper discusses two related issues in the Indonesian forestry sector: 1) Profits made from logging operations; and 2) The current taxation arrangements aimed at channeling resource rents to the central and provincial governments. Ruzicka assesses the efficiency of the current tax arrangements in capturing appropriate amounts of timber profits for public coffers during the years 1972/73 through 1976/77. The analysis shows that the government captured only a modest share of total timber rents during this period. In the boom year of 1973/74, when world timber prices peaked, the government appropriated less than one-quarter of total timber rents generated by medium-sized producers; only about one-third of total timber rents was appropriated during the next peak in world prices, 1976/77.

Indonesia/ East Kalimantan/ Timber industry—Logging/ Timber industry—State policy and regulation.

282.   **Sabrani, A., and Y. Saepudin. 1994.** "Agroforestry, Resettlement and Shifting Cultivation." In *Agroforestry and Animal Production for Human Welfare.* Proceedings of an international symposium held in association with the 7th AAAP Animal Science Congress, Bali, Indonesia, 11–16 July 1994. Ed. J. W. Copland, A. Djajanegra, and M. Sabrani, pp. 50–54. ACIAR Proceedings, no. 55. Canberra: Australian Centre for International Agricultural Research.

Following a brief description of the extent of shifting cultivation in Indonesia and problems associated with it, the authors note that resettlement is one of the main government strategies for dealing with the issue. Resettlement efforts are now being improved with a new focus on incorporating an agroforestry component into resettlement sites. Major models in this new orientation are described, including allowing farmers to temporarily intercrop food in young forest plantation (i.e. teak) areas, the *Amarasi* model developed on Timor island involving the use of the tree legume *lamtoro* (*Leucaena leucocephala*) interplanted between rows of maize and legumes, plantation agroforestry (intercropping food with tree crops like rubber, oil palm, coffee, cocoa), industrial agroforestry involving fast growing trees around natural forests to produce timber and pulp products, and livestock-tree crop combination in upland areas, involving planting of grass and tree legumes to produce fodder for intensified animal husbandry.

Indonesia/ Project intervention—Agroforestry/ Resettlement/ Forest management—Control of shifting cultivation.

283.   **Saccheri, I., and D. Walker. 1991.** "Subsistence and Environment of a Highland Kenyah Community." *Sarawak Museum Journal* 42 (63 (n.s.)): 193–250.

The article draws from a six week period of field research in Long Payau, Kenyah community in Apo Kayan region between Kayan and Mahakam rivers in East Kalimantan. One of the main aims of the study was to examine questions addressed by Chin (1985) in an earlier paper on a lowland rainforest Kenyah community, regarding the Kenyah's ability to maintain traditional forms of resource use and management in a changing socioeconomic environment. The authors sought to determine whether Chin's claim concerning the adaptiveness of traditional Kenyah systems also hold specifically a highland setting.

A brief review of the area's history and demography reveals that the area has undergone significant depopulation in recent decades as many households and whole communities have moved to more developed areas of East Kalimantan. The current demographic structure, physical environment, traditional land tenure arrangements, food and diet, swidden farming system, and ecological limitations to crop production are described. Also noted is the community's use of different plants and animals, and non-food items derived from the forest as well as its purchase of goods imported from downriver. While specific sources of food are subject to failure, the diversity of the Kenyah diet allows villagers to consistently meet their food and other material needs. In contrast to lowland Kenyah communities, no goods or foodstuffs are produced solely for sale by the upland Kenyah, though surplus food such as pork, vegetables, rice and honey are sold. In addition to woven rattan products, various forest products, usually related to medicinal uses, are traded for cash. Long Payau residents participate in a more significant way in the cash economy as a source of male labor for logging camps and cash crop plantations in Sarawak and other parts of the Kalimantan provinces. Still all adults present in the community are skilled in a wide variety of tasks, and as such each household can subsist effectively with little need to purchase goods or services from other sources. In conclusion, the author's note that the community appears cohesive, with most of the present community committed to an ongoing presence in the area. There is even indication that some of those who have migrated out of the area to procure an education are in the process of returning as village teachers and other resource persons. As with the case of lowland Kenyah communities in Chin's research, there is little to suggest that the Long Payau community will not be able to maintain stable institutions over the long run.

Indonesia/ Kalimantan/ Indigenous and local communities—Economy/ Indigenous and local communities—Commoditization/ Household livelihood strategies/ Indigenous and local communities—Forest products use and trade/ Indigenous and local communities—Forest land use and management practices.

284.   **Saharjo, B. H. 1994.** "Deforestation with Reference to Indonesia." *Wallaceana* 73: 7–12.

Saharjo examines the problem of deforestation in Indonesia, using data on the 1950 to 1982 period. Discussion includes issues of defining deforestation, causes and impacts of forest loss, and methods for forest land rehabilitation.

Indonesia/ Deforestation.

285.   **Salafsky, N. 1993.** "The Forest Garden Project: An Ecological and Economic Study of a Locally Developed Land-use System in West Kalimantan, Indonesia." Ph.D. diss., School of the Environment, Duke University, North Carolina.

Salafsky presents the results of an ecological and economic study of forest garden systems and associated land uses being maintained by indigenous and immigrant farming communities around the Gunung Palung Park, West Kalimantan.

Indonesia/ West Kalimantan/ Agroforestry/ Indigenous and local communities—Forest land use and management practices/ Indigenous and local communities—Forest products use and trade/ Forest management—Forest resource conservation/ Forest management—Parks and conservation areas.

286.   ———. **1993.** "Mammalian Use of a Buffer Zone Agroforestry System Bordering Gunung Palung National Park, West Kalimantan, Indonesia." *Conservation Biology* 7 (4): 928–933.

Salafsky draws from interviews with local villagers around the Gunung Palung National Park, West Kalimantan to estimate mammalian use of forest garden and farm habitats, document local villagers' perceptions of crop damage caused by mammals, and examine villagers' knowledge about local mammals and their behavior. The study was undertaken as part of the author's doctoral dissertation fieldwork in Benawai Agung township, Ketapang Regency, West Kalimantan. Households in the village numbered about 560, and included residents of mainly Malay, Chinese, Balinese, and Javanese origin. As with neighboring indigenous Dayak villages, forest gardens comprise an important component of the local land use system. Observations gathered in the context of the larger dissertation research project suggested the "socio-buffering" function of the forest gardens, that is, their role in providing goods and services to local villagers. Results of the mammalian use study component in turn suggest that in conjunction with this function, forest gardens and associated habitats are used by many mammals, and thus are likely to serve the multiple-aims of a buffer zone area around a limited-access core nature reserve. Study results also suggested the presence of net costs for local villagers associated with mammal entry into forest gardens, highlighting the need to take these into consideration in designing viable buffer zone strategies.

Indonesia/ West Kalimantan/ Indigenous and local communities—Forest land use and management practices/ Wildlife management/ Forest biology and ecology/ Forest fauna/ Forest management—Parks and conservation areas.

287.   ———. **1994.** "Drought in the Rain Forest: Effects of the 1991 El Ni–o-southern Oscillation Event on a Rural Economy in West Kalimantan, Indonesia." *Climatic Change* 27 (4): 373–396.

Indonesia/ West Kalimantan/ Drought.

288.   ———.**1994.** "Forest Gardens in the Gunung Palung Region of West Kalimantan, Indonesia: Defining a Locally-Developed, Market-Oriented Agroforestry System." *Agroforestry Systems* 28 (3): 237–268.

Based on a multidisciplinary study of forest land use systems involving farms, home gardens, forest gardens, and forest extraction areas around an established nature reserve, Salafsky concludes that forest gardens may be understood as a type of home garden that has been developed by local communities in response to new economic markets. An overview of Benawai Agung, Sukadana district, West Kalimantan is provided along with details on the different types of forest gardens found in the area, including the mixed fruit and plantation crops cultivated (durian, coffee, rubber, *Arenga pinnata*) and others. In addition to management techniques, socioeconomic aspects of forest gardening are also discussed, including issues of tenure, markets, and prices. Salafsky highlights the need for future work in understanding the role of forest gardens in tropical forest management in general.

Indonesia/ West Kalimantan/ Land use—Patterns and planning/ Indigenous and local communities—Forest land use and management practices/ Indigenous and local communities—Forest products use and trade/ Agroforestry/ Agriculture—Smallholder tree and perennial crop farming/ Agriculture—Smallholder cash crop farming/ Agriculture—Smallholder cash crop farming.

289.　———. **1995.** "Ecological Factors Affecting Durian Production in the Forest Gardens of West Kalimantan, Indonesia." *Agroforestry Systems* 32 (1): 63–79.

Beliefs of forest garden owners concerning ecological and economic factors in durian fruit production are examined using a geographic information system-based analysis. Interviews and mapping were conducted during three 2–5 month long field sessions in the township of Benawai Agung, Sukadana District, West Kalimantan from 1990 to 1992. Factors examined included tree characteristics, micro-site factors, species association, and position of garden. Salafsky finds that farmer perceptions about ecological factors in durian production are generally accurate. The analysis leads to specific recommendations for improving durian yields at other sites, while also highlighting the specific strengths of GIS analysis for the study of slow-growing, complex agroforestry systems.

Indonesia/ West Kalimantan/ Indigenous and local communities—Forest land use and management practices/ Agriculture—Smallholder tree and perennial crop farming/ Agriculture—Smallholder cash crop farming.

290.　**Salafsky, N., B. I. Dugelby, and J. W. Terborgh. 1993.** "Can Extractive Reserves Save the Rain Forest? An Ecological and Socioeconomic Comparison of Nontimber Forest Product Extraction Systems in Petén, Guatemala, and West Kalimantan, Indonesia." *Conservation Biology* 7 (1): 39–52.

The authors examine and compare ecological, socioeconomic, and political factors determining the viability of forest production extraction systems in the Maya Biosphere Reserve, Petén, Guatemala and near the Gunung Palung National Park, West Kalimantan, Indonesia. The analysis is based on observations made during research visits in 1990 and earlier fieldwork. Primary forest products gathered by residents of Uaxactun and Carmelita villages in Petén are traded to export markets and include chicle (latex from *Manilkara zapota* trees, *xate* (fronds from *Chamaedorea spp.* palms), and allspice (fruits from *Pimenta dioica* trees). In West Kalimantan, extraction systems are less formally organized than in Petén, but nevertheless involve regular part-time collection of a variety of non-timber forest products, including rattan (*Calamus*), *gaharu* (a resin gleaned from infected heartwood or *Aquilaria* spp.), *illipe* nuts (*Shorea* spp.), ironwood (*Eusideroxylon zwageri*), *medang* (bark from the mid-canopy tree *Litsea* spp.), and various wild fruits. Ecological factors affecting the viability of these systems include density of the exploited species, temporal availability of products, product and ecosystem sustainability. Socioeconomic and political factors include resource tenure and conservation incentives, physical and social infrastructure, product demand, pressures for alternative land uses, and political power. Comparative analysis suggests that conditions in Petén are conducive to the viability of extractive reserve systems, while in West Kalimantan, relevant factors are less promising. In the latter case, alternative land use systems which are already present in the area, involving diverse, extensive, and well-managed forest gardens, are likely to have a larger role to play in preserving rainforest areas.

Indonesia/ West Kalimantan/ Indigenous and local communities—Forest products use and trade/ Indigenous and local communities—Forest land use and management practices/ Non-timber forest products/ Forest management—Parks and conservation areas.

291.   **Saman, E., A. L. P. Hutapea, and Wailayatiningsih. 1993.** *Politik hukum pengusahaan hutan di Indonesia.* Jakarta: Wahana Linkungan Hidup Indonesia (WALHI).
[The Politics of Law on the Forestry Industry in Indonesia.]

Describes state policy, relevant laws and presidential decrees governing timber concessions, forest product collection permits, and timber plantations, and other aspects of the forestry industry in Indonesia. Critically assesses the implementation of forestry laws and policy, highlighting conflicts generated with sustainable forest use practices of local farmers, failure of forest product collection permits to benefit local communities, and the displacement of local farmers caused by plantation development. Recommendations are given for improving existing laws to resolve serious problems.

Indonesia/ Forest management—Commercial forestry and silviculture/ State policy—Forest and natural resources/ Timber industry—State policy and regulation/ Land tenure—Legislation and state policy.

292.   **Sansonnens, B. 1994.** "Structure et dynamique agroforestières en Asie tropicale humide. Analyse comparée de deux études de cas, à Sumatra (Indonésie) et au Sri Lanka." Ph.D. diss., Université de Lausanne, Lucerne, Switzerland.
[Agroforestry Structure and Dynamics in the Humid Tropics of Asia: Comparative Analysis of Two Case Studies in Sumatra (Indonesia) and Sri Lanka.]

Indonesia/ Sumatra/ Agroforestry/ Indigenous and local communities—Forest land use and management practices.

293.   **Sardjono, M. A. 1988.** "Lembo: sistem pemanfaatan lahan tradisional di Kalimantan Timur." In *Agroforestry untuk pengembangan daerah pedesaan di Kalimantan Timur: prosiding seminar kehutanan.* Ed. A. M. Lahjie and B. Seibert, pp. 253–267. Samarinda, East Kalimantan, 19–21 September 1988. Samarinda, Indonesia: Department of Forestry, Universitas Mulawarman; GTZ.
[Lembo: Traditional Land Use System in East Kalimantan.]

"*Lembo*" is a term widely used among the Tunjung, Benuaq, and other indigenous groups of East Kalimantan to describe groves of fruit trees managed by local communities in nearby fallow fields. Sardjono describes the evolution and structure of this indigenous form of agroforestry and details its role in the local economy and diet. Data is drawn from fieldwork in Tunjung and Benuaq Dayak villages in Kutai district, as well as among Javanese transmigrants who appear to have adopted this resource management pattern from their indigenous neighbors.

Indonesia/ East Kalimantan/ Indigenous and local communities—Forest products use and trade/ Indigenous and local communities—Forest land use and management practices/ Agroforestry.

294. ———. **1990.** "Die Lembo-Kultur in Ost-Kalimantan: Ein Modell für die Entwicklung der Feuchttropen." Ph.D. diss., Universität Hamburg, Fachbereich Biologie, Hamburg, Germany.
[Lembo-culture in East Kalimantan: A Model for Development in Moist Tropical Environments.]

Indonesia/ East Kalimantan/ Indigenous and local communities—Forest land use and management practices/ Indigenous and local communities—Forest products use and trade/ Indigenous and local communities—Land and resource tenure systems/ Agroforestry/ Forest biology and ecology/ Non-timber forest products/ Forest management—Forest resource conservation/ Project intervention—Fallow improvement.

295. **Sastrawinata, H. A., B. Soehirlan, and O. Satjapradja. 1981.** "Pengembangan pola usaha tani kehutanan (agroforestry) di Kesatuan Pemangkuan Hutan Balikpapan - Kalimantan Timur." Laporan Lembaga Penelitian Hutan, no. 370. Bogor, West Java, Indonesia: Lembaga Penelitian Hutan.
[The Development of Agroforestry in Balikpapan Forest Service, East Kalimantan.]

The authors describe the swidden farming patterns of local communities in the protected forest areas around Balikpapan and Batakan. Effects of swidden activities on the forest environment are noted. Possibilities of strengthening the agroforestry components of local forest land use patterns in order to improve forest conservation are considered.

Indonesia/ East Kalimantan/ Agriculture—Shifting cultivation/ Indigenous and local communities—Farming practices/ Indigenous and local communities—Forest land use and management practices/ Agroforestry/ Project intervention—Fallow improvement.

296. **Schindele, W., Thoma W., and K. Panzer. 1989.** "Investigation of the Steps Needed to Rehabilitate the Areas of East Kalimantan Seriously Affected by Fire." In *The Forest Fire 1982–1983 in East Kalimantan Part I: The Fire, the Effects, the Damage, and Technical Solutions*. GTZ-ITTO Forestry Research Report, no. 5. Samarinda, East Kalimantan, Indonesia: GTZ-ITTO.

Indonesia/ East Kalimantan/ Forest fires/ Forest regeneration.

297. **Schneider, W. M., and M. J. Schneider. 1988.** "Food and Factions: The Local Politics of Selako Agricultural Development." *Human Organization* 47 (1): 58–64.

The authors describe a government-sponsored agricultural development project involving irrigated rice cultivation in West Kalimantan. The analysis focuses on the implications of factionalism within the project's target communities, two Selako Dayak communities along the Indonesian-Malaysian border, for project development. The authors argue a major factor behind the project's success was the fact that socio-political realities characterizing the target communities, including a long history of factionalism and the centralized nature of power relationships in the local village structure were integrated into the project design.

Indonesia/ West Kalimantan/ Indigenous and local communities—Social relations/ Project intervention—Agricultural development.

298. **Schulze, P. C., M. Leighton, and D. R. Peart. 1994.** "Enrichment Planting in Selectively Logged Rain Forest: A Combined Ecological and Economic Analysis." *Ecological Applications* 4 (3): 581–592.

Financial appraisal taking into consideration both economic and ecological variables is applied to the strategy of enrichment planting of native fruit-producing genera in logged forest areas of Kalimantan. Consideration of eight ecological parameters (survival, growth rate, etc.) and eleven economic parameters (costs, market prices, etc.) allow for the selection of genera and species that both complement the process of forest regeneration as well as promise substantial returns economically based on net present value projections. The latter are observed to depend on fruit price, fruit production, age of first reproduction, survival rates, and harvesting and marketing costs.

Indonesia/ Kalimantan/ Forest management—Economics/ Forest regeneration/ Agroforestry/ Project intervention—Fallow improvement.

299.   **Searle, G. 1987.** Major World Bank Projects: Their Impact on People, Society and the Environment. Cornwall, U.K.: Wadebridge Ecological Centre.

Drawing from internal World Bank documents, Searle discusses the environmental and socioeconomic impacts of the Indonesian Transmigration program in Sumatra, Kalimantan, and Irian Jaya, funded by a combination of national revenues, World Bank, and foreign government assistance. Other case studies in the report include the Narmada River Basin Projects in northern India, and the Northwest Region Integrated Development Program in Polonoreste, Brazil.

Indonesia/ Land settlement and development—Environmental impacts/ Land settlement and development—Impacts on local communities and economy.

300.   **Seavoy, R. E. 1975.** "The Origin of Tropical Grasslands in Kalimantan, Indonesia." *Journal of Tropical Geography* 40: 48–52.

The uncontrolled burning of *lalang* (*Imperata*) grasslands to aid hunting has rapidly reduced the area of secondary forest suitable for shifting cultivation. Under conditions of controlled grazing the grasses *Axonopus compressus* and *Chrysopogon aciculatus* tend to replace the Imperata. When an area of secondary forest has declined to the point of drastically reduced agricultural yields and periodic hunger, the villages will move into the interior, where forest is still available.

Indonesia/ Kalimantan/ Agriculture—Shifting cultivation's environmental impacts/ Indigenous and local communities—Forest land use and management practices/ Pest, weed, and crop disease management/ Grasslands.

301.   ———. **1980.** "Population Pressure and Land Use Change: From Tree Crops to Sawah in Northwestern Kalimantan, Indonesia." *Singapore Journal of Tropical Geography* 1 (2): 61–67.

Indonesia/ Kalimantan/ Agricultural intensification/ Land use—Patterns and planning/ Population pressure/ Indigenous and local communities—Farming practices.

302.   **Seibert, B. 1989.** "Agroforestry for the Conservation of Genetic Resources." *GFG [German Forestry Group] Report* 13: 55–71.

Seibert briefly describes the agroforestry systems of traditional swidden farmers in Borneo. The biological diversity of these systems suggest the possibility of a community-oriented approach to genetic conservation that does not conflict with existing land use systems. Scientific names and local uses for different plant species found in traditional Borneo agroforestry systems are given.

Indonesia/ Kalimantan/ Indigenous and local communities—Farming practices/ Indigenous and local communities—Forest land use and management practices/ Indigenous and local communities—Forest products use and trade/ Agroforestry/ Biodiversity.

303. ———. **1990.** "Butter aus dem Regenwald—Die Tengkawangs auf Borneo."
        Forstarchiv 61 (6): 115–119.
        [Butter from the Rainforest—The Tengkawangs on Borneo.]

        Indonesia/ Kalimantan/ Indigenous and local communities—Forest products use and trade/
        Indigenous and local communities—Forest land use and management practices/ Non-timber
        forest products.

304. **Sellato, B. 1993.** "Myth, History and Modern Cultural Identity Among Hunter-
        Gatherers: A Borneo Case Study." *Journal of Southeast Asian Studies* 24 (1):
        18–43.

        The Bukat people of West Kalimantan are an indigenous hunter-gatherer community of
        West Kalimantan (Kapuas Hulu regency), who have been gradually adopting a sedentary,
        farming lifestyle. The author examines one Bukat legend and its interpretation by a Bukat
        notable to illuminate "an in-the-process manipulation of the historical tradition by a hunt-
        ing-gathering society, in a multi-staged sequence involving ancient and modern factors of a
        different nature—political, cultural, and religious—and displaying internal contradictions
        that are to be related to the ongoing alteration of the mode of subsistence, from forest hunt-
        ing-gathering to swidden agriculture."

        Indonesia/ West Kalimantan/ Indigenous and local communities—Religion and cosmology/
        Indigenous and local communities—Forest products use and trade/ Indigenous and local
        communities—Farming practices/ Indigenous and local communities—Commoditization.

305. ———. **1994.** *Nomads of the Borneo Rainforest: The Economics, Politics and
        Ideology of Settling Down.* Trans. S. Morgan. Honolulu: University of
        Hawaii Press.

        Reflecting twelve years of field research, this monograph focuses on processes of trans-
        formation undergone by the Punan of Borneo—the collective name given to the island's
        nomadic hunter-gather societies—over the past two centuries. Following a brief but com-
        prehensive overview highlighting different groups among the Punan and Dayak peoples of
        the Borneo interior, Sellato recounts the history of migration, settlement, inter- and intra-
        group relations of two specific Punan groups—the Bukat of West and East Kalimantan and
        the Kereho of Central Kalimantan. This section of the monograph draws mainly from oral
        histories told by Bukat and Kereho informants themselves, demonstrating generally the re-
        liability of oral traditions for historical research, and more specifically the strong sense of
        cultural identity that continues to be emphasized by Punan groups based on the idea of
        common ancestral homelands. In the monograph's second part, Sellato draws from a wide
        variety of multidisciplinary sources to analyze the subsistence economy of traditional
        nomadism among the Punan, based on sago exploitation and hunting of wild game.
        Processes of change are described in a separate chapter which highlights a reorientation
        from subsistence forest product collecting to collecting for the market. Sellato argues that
        the ultimate impetus for this change can be traced to growing coastal markets for various
        forest products over the past 200 years, which have prompted settled and semi-settled farm-
        ing communities to cultivate stable and exclusive trading relations with the Punan, often
        based on unequal relations of power between the politically subordinated Punan and their
        downstream trading partners. These relations have in turn entrenched the use of metal tools
        and other labor-saving technology among the Punan, who now barter for desired manufac-
        tured goods with marketable forest products. This reorientation has in turn involved greater
        reliance on rice cultivation among the Punan, corresponding to less far-ranging patterns of
        movement and greater interaction with settled rice growers. At the same time, the degree of
        change varies considerably among different groups, and the Punan as a whole do not appear
        to be becoming exclusive rice farmers. Rather, they demonstrate a distinct preference for
        "mixed subsistence economy, based on a combination of cultivated crops and wild sago."
        Sellato's analysis presents a challenge to assuming an inherent opposition between rice
        farmers and nomads, demonstrating instead "that there exists a continuum of [stable and

functional] economic situations, based on various combinations of rice farming, horticulture, hunting, and gathering." In sum, the history of Punan transformations shows a complex interplay between forces of economic change and the ongoing salience of Punan values and cultural identity.

Indonesia/ West Kalimantan/ East Kalimantan/ Central Kalimantan/ Ethnography/ Indigenous and local communities—Social relations/ Indigenous and local communities—Economy/ Indigenous and local communities—Forest products use and trade/ Indigenous and local communities—Forest land use and management practices/ Indigenous and local communities—Land and resource tenure systems/ Migration/ History—Pre-colonial/ History—Colonial/ Ethnicity and ethnic relations.

306.   **Shapiro, J. S. 1995.** "Morphometric Variation in the Orang Utan (*Pongo pygameus*), with a Comparison to Inter- and Intraspecific Variability in the African Apes." Ph.D. diss., Columbia University, New York, N.Y.

Indonesia/ Sumatra/ Kalimantan/ Forest fauna/ Forest biology and ecology.

307.   **Sidiyasa, K., U. Sutisna, Marfuah-Sutiyono, T. Kalima-Sutrasno, and T. C. Whitmore, comp. 1990.** *Tree Flora of Indonesia: Check List for Kalimantan.* Ed. T. C. Whitmore, I. G. M. Tantra, and U. Sutisna, Bogor, Indonesia: Forest Research and Development Centre, Ministry of Forestry, Agency for Forestry Research and Development.

Three volumes (Part I, Part II.1 and Part II.2) list tree families and genera found in Kalimantan; vernacular names of the region's tree species. A final volume lists and illustrates the *dipterocarpae* and other major tree species found in the Kalimantan provinces.

Indonesia/ Kalimantan/ Forest flora.

308.   **Siebert, S. F. 1995.** "Prospects for Sustained-yield Harvesting of Rattan (*Calamus* spp.) in Two Indonesian National Parks." *Society and Natural Resources* 8 (3): 209–218.

Reporting on a study conducted in Kerinci-Seblat National Park (KSNP), Sumatra, and Dumoga-Bone National Park, Sulawesi between 1987 and 1992, Siebert describes the population densities and growth rates of naturally occurring *Calamus exilis* and *Calamus zollingeri* species. Efforts to cultivate these particular species have thus far met with little success, making natural stands the only viable source of this material for now. Following criteria proposed by Salafsky, ecological factors, socio-economic factors, and political factors are evaluated to assess the possibilities for sustained-yield management of natural rattan stands. Ecological aspects appear promising, and effectively managed rattan harvesting may reduce incentives to convert forest to farmland. However, social and political factors such as poorly determined resource access regimes and tenure arrangements, lack of effective village-based management organizations and harvesting guidelines, and the weak position of rattan collectors in relation to external commercial interests, pose some important constraints. These insights suggest the need for further research on appropriate harvesting regimes, development of new tenure arrangements, regulatory reform to allow sustainable extraction of forest products from protected areas, and the development of effective local organizations for the locally-based regulation of cane harvesting.

Indonesia/ Sumatra/ Sulawesi/ Rattan—Growth and distribution/ Rattan—Resource management and conservation/ Forest management—Parks and conservation areas/ Non-timber forest products.

309.   ———. **1995.** "Rattan Management for Forest Conservation in Indonesian National Parks and Preserve Buffer Zones." In *Society and Non-timber Forest Products in Tropical Asia.* Ed. J. Fox, pp. 97–107. East-West Center Occasional Papers: Environment Series, no. 19. Honolulu: East-West Center.

Siebert reports on research conducted on *Calamus exilis* (rattan) in Kerinci-Seblat National Park in Sumatra, Indonesia. Demographic characteristics of the species were examined in primary forest at 1,200–1,400 meters altitude by sampling rattan plant and cane abundance and environmental factors in forty plots 0.05 ha in size. While cultivation trials of the *C. exilis* species failed, at observed plant densities and harvesting methods, rattan collection appears promising as a sustainable use of standing forest areas, with little or no effect on other forest flora and fauna. Collection and processing of rattan into handicraft items provide an important and much appreciated source of income for more than seventy households around the Kerinci park. Study results support the claim that "the cultivation and management of rattan and other non-timber forest products represent possible means of meeting conservation and development objectives."

Indonesia/ Sumatra/ Non-timber forest products/ Rattan—Growth and distribution/ Rattan—Collection and trade/ Rattan—Resource management and conservation/ Forest management—Parks and conservation areas.

310.   ———. **1986.** "Notes on Rattan Collection and Trade in the Masamba District, Sulawesi Selatan." *Borneo Research Bulletin* 18: 59–64.

Indonesia/ Rattan—Collection and trade/ Rattan—Resource management and conservation/ Indigenous and local communities—Forest products use and trade/ Non-timber forest products.

311.   ———. **1990.** "Hillside Farming, Soil Erosion, and Forest Conversion in Two Southeast Asian National Parks." *Mountain Research and Development* 10 (1): 64–72.

Comparing the Bayhang watershed near Leyte Mountains National Park, Philippines and the Sungai Ning watershed near Kerinci-Seblat National Park, Indonesia, Siebert examines the relationship between soil erosion on hillside farms and forest conversion to farmland in adjacent national parks. Evidence of accelerated erosion in both watersheds based on a random sample of hillside farms is noted. In Bayhang, mean soil losses were about 422 t/ha during the first six months of cultivation, while in Sungai Ning loss equaled 3.8 t/ha during the cropping year on continuously cultivated farms. Research also demonstrated declining soil productivity as a result of soil erosion. As farmers' fields become degraded, new forest is cleared for agricultural use in the Leyte National Park. In Kerinci, farmers substituted cassava for crops with higher fertility requirements and also turned to the adjacent national park for access to fresh farmland. Possibilities for the introduction of soil-conserving technologies and alternative livelihood opportunities are discussed.

Philippines/ Indonesia/ Soil erosion and degradation/ Agriculture—Shifting cultivation's environmental impacts/ Migrant farmers and farming/ Indigenous and local communities—Forest land use and management practices/ Agricultural intensification/ Forest management—Parks and conservation areas.

312.   ———. **1990.** "Soil Erosion and Conservation Farming in Kerinci, Sumatra." Ph.D. diss., Cornell University, Ithaca, N.Y.

Indonesia/ Agriculture—Shifting cultivation's environmental impacts/ Soil erosion and degradation/ Soils/ Conservation farming/ Forest management—Forest resource conservation/ Forest management—Parks and conservation areas.

313.   ———. **1991.** "Rattan: The Key to Natural Forest Management in Southeast
        Asia." Paper presented at the International Forestry Working Group Technical
        Session at the SAF National Convention, 4–7 August 1991, in San Francisco,
        Calif. Photocopy.

> Attempts to implement natural forest management systems in tropical Southeast Asia
> confront serious ecological, economic and social constraints. Managed rattan harvesting is
> examined as a potential means of ameliorating these constraints. The abundance, site pref-
> erences and management potential of economically-important rattan species were examined
> in Kerinci-Seblat National Park (KSNP), Indonesia. Primary forests in KSNP contained
> approximately $15 worth of *Calamus exilis* per hectare. If harvested on a sustainable basis,
> *C. exilis* could produce approximately $5 worth of unprocessed cane per hectare per year.
> Rattan harvesting may be compatible with a variety of natural forest management systems.
> However, the value of rattan is significantly lower than alternative land uses, particularly
> the cultivation of perennial cash crops and thus cannot ensure natural forest management.
> Nevertheless, managed rattan harvesting warrants greater research and development consid-
> eration throughout Southeast Asia. [Quoted from paper].

> Indonesia/ Sumatra/ Rattan—Collection and trade/ Forest management—Forest resource
> conservation/ Non-timber forest products.

314.   **Siebert, S., and T. W. Scott. 1990.** "Influence of Topsoil Removal and Fertilizer
        Application on Peanut Yields from an Indonesian Ultisol." *Agriculture,
        Ecosystems, and Environment* 32: 213–221.

> Indonesia/ Soils/ Soil erosion and degradation.

315.   **Silitonga, T. 1994.** "Tropical Forest Conservation in Indonesia: Problems and
        Solutions." In *Agroforestry and Animal Production for Human Welfare*.
        Proceedings of an international symposium held in association with the 7th
        AAAP Animal Science Congress, Bali, Indonesia, 11–16 July 1994. Ed. J. W.
        Copland, A. Djajanegra, and M. Sabrani, pp. 39–41. ACIAR Proceedings,
        no. 55. Canberra: Australian Centre for International Agricultural Research.

> Describes national policy on forest, particularly in regards to broad aims and principles
> in forest conservation.

> Indonesia/ State policy—Forest and natural resources/ Forest management—Forest resource
> conservation.

316.   **Simpson, R. B. 1995.** "Nepenthes and Conservation." *Curtis's Botanical
        Magazine* 12 (2): 111–118.

> Indonesia/ Malaysia/ Borneo/ Non-timber forest products/ Forest flora/ Biodiversity.

317.   **Sirait, M., S. Prasodjo, N. Podger, A. Flavelle, and J. Fox. 1994.** "Mapping
        Customary Land in East Kalimantan, Indonesia: A Tool for Forest
        Management." *Ambio* 23 (7): 411–417.

> The authors discuss the benefits and constraints of participatory mapping strategies that
> involve social scientists, map makers, and local residents in identifying customary land use
> systems. The discussion draws from the experience of the Kayan Mentarang Project in East
> Kalimantan. Methodology components include oral histories, collaborative sketch maps,
> Global Positioning System (GPS), and Geographic Information System (GIS) technologies.

> Indonesia/ East Kalimantan/ Indigenous and local communities—Forest land use and man-
> agement practices/ Indigenous and local communities—Land and resource tenure systems/

Project intervention—Participatory methods/ Forest management—Parks and conservation areas.

318. **Siswanto, B. E., and K. Soemarna. 1990.** "Metode inventarisasi rotan die kelompok hutan Sungai Tapen/Biangan, KPH Barito selatan, Kalimantan tengah." *Buletin Penelitian Hutan* 527: 9–20.
    [Inventory of Rattan in the Sungai Tapen/Biangan Forest District of South Barito, Central Kalimantan.]

    Indonesia/ Central Kalimantan/ Rattan—Growth and distribution/ Non-timber forest products.

319. **Slamet-Velsink, I. E. 1986.** Emerging Hierarchies, Processes of Stratification and Early State Formation in the Indonesian Archipelago: Prehistory and the Ethnographic Present. Leiden.

    Indonesia/ Kalimantan/ History—Pre-colonial/ Indigenous and local communities—Social relations.

320. **Smythies, B. E. 1981.** *The Birds of Borneo.* Kota Kinabalu; Kuala Lumpur, Malaysia: Sabah Society; Malayan Nature Society.

    Malaysia/ Indonesia/ Borneo/ Forest fauna.

321. **Soedirman, S. 1991.** "Study on the Changes of Forest Condition in Bukit Soeharto Dipterocarp Forest Area, East Kalimantan, using Aerial Photographs." In *Proceedings of the Fourth Round-Table Conference on Dipterocarps, 12–15 December 1989, Bogor, Indonesia.* Ed. I. Soerianegara, S. S. Tjitrosomo, R. C. Umaly, and I. Umboh, pp. 221–246. Bogor, Indonesia: SEAMEO BIOTROP.

    Soedirman estimates changes in the forest condition of the *Taman Hutan Raya Bukit Soeharto* (Bukit Soeharto Protected Area) resulting from the activities of communities surrounding the forest. Data is based on aerial photographs.

    Indonesia/ East Kalimantan/ Deforestation/ Indigenous and local communities—Forest land use and management practices/ Forest management—Control of shifting cultivation.

322. **Soedjito, H. 1985.** Succession and Nutrient Dynamics Following Shifting Cultivation in Long Sungai Barang, East Kalimantan, Indonesia. New Brunswick, New Jersey: Master's thesis, Rutgers University.

    Indonesia/ East Kalimantan/ Forest regeneration/ Agriculture—Shifting cultivation's environmental impacts/ Forest biology and ecology.

323. ———. **1988.** "Spatial Patterns, Biomass, and Nutrient Concentrations of Root Systems in Primary and Secondary Forest Trees of a Tropical Rainforest in Kalimantan, Indonesia." In *Some Ecological Aspects of Tropical Forest of East Kalimantan: A Collection of Research Reports.* Ed. S. Soemodihardjo, pp. 41–60. Man and Biosphere Indonesia Contribution, no. 48. Jakarta: Indonesian Institute of Sciences; Indonesian National MAB Committee.

    Reporting results of a study undertaken as part of the Man and Biosphere research program in East Kalimantan in the early 1980s, Soedjito describes major differences found between root systems of primary and secondary forest trees. Roots of secondary forest trees are found to penetrate deeper into the soil, have longer lateral roots, contain higher levels of nutrients, and have greater biomass than trees of primary forests. The findings demonstrate the importance of these trees in nutrient conservation.

Indonesia/ East Kalimantan/ Forest biology and ecology/ Forest regeneration.

324.   ————. 1990. "Root System of Successional and Old Growth Forest Species and its Roles on Nutrient Dynamics Within a Tropical Rain Forest in Indonesia." Ph.D. diss., Rutgers University, New Brunswick, New Jersey.

Indonesia/ East Kalimantan/ Forest biology and ecology/ Forest regeneration.

325.   **Soedjito, H., and C. J. P. Colfer. 1988.** "On Resettlement from the Bottom Up." *Some Ecological Aspects of Tropical Forest of East Kalimantan: A Collection of Research Reports.* Ed. S. Soemodihardjo, pp. 87–105. Man and Biosphere Indonesia Contribution, no. 48. Jakarta: Indonesian Institute of Sciences; Indonesian National MAB Committee.

As part of a monograph presenting results of a study series in the East Kalimantan Man and Biosphere research program, this paper comprises a critical appraisal of Indonesian government resettlement programs aimed at indigenous communities. Drawing from field-work at a resettlement site, Soedjito and Colfer observe that government policy on the development of new resettlement sites was issued from a centralized office that appeared only superficially aware of the quality of indigenous community life. This centralized system of planning and policy-making has tended to result in the building of resettlement villages and new farming systems which indigenous communities are reluctant to accept. In particular, government plans to transform the dry rice farmers of Long Segar to livestock-raising wet rice cultivators appeared doomed to failure from the start, given extant soil conditions and labor availability. The authors urge more careful study of local ecological conditions and villager needs in connection with resettlement promotion, suggesting several specific improvements in agricultural systems and employment opportunities being offered to resettled villagers.

Indonesia/ East Kalimantan/ Resettlement/ Project intervention—Agricultural development/ Indigenous and local communities—State policy.

326.   **Soekotjo. 1981.** "Diameter Growth of Residual Stands in Logged Over Areas in East Kalimantan Tropical Rainforest, Indonesia." Ph.D. diss., Michigan State University, East Lansing, Mich.

Indonesia/ East Kalimantan/ Forest regeneration.

327.   **Soemodihardjo, S., ed. 1988.** *Some Ecological Aspects of Tropical Forest of East Kalimantan: A Collection of Research Reports.* MAB Indonesia, Contribution no. 48. Jakarta: Indonesian Institute of Sciences; Indonesian National MAB Committee.

This monograph contains four research papers summarizing the results of research conducted in conjunction with the Man and Biosphere research program in East Kalimantan during late 1970s and early 1980s. The general theme of the MAB program focused on the "environmental effects of different kind of land use" taking place in East Kalimantan. Papers included are by Soedarsono Riswan and Kuswata Kartawinata; Herwasono Soedjito; Soedarsono Riswan and Kuswata Kartawinata; Carol J.P. Colfer and Herwasono Soedjito. All have been abstracted separately in this bibliography.

Indonesia/ East Kalimantan/ Agriculture—Shifting cultivation's environmental impacts/ Land settlement and development—Environmental impacts/ Timber industry—

Environmental impacts/ Forest biology and ecology/ Deforestation/ Soil erosion and degradation/ Forest management—Forest resource conservation.

328. **Stadtmüller, T. 1989.** "Soil Erosion in East Kalimantan, Indonesia." *GFG Report* 13: 11–28.

The main issues relevant to the problem of soil erosion in East Kalimantan, Indonesia are discussed.

Indonesia/ East Kalimantan/ Soil erosion and degradation/ Deforestation.

329. **———. 1990.** "Soil Erosion in East Kalimantan, Indonesia." In *Research Needs and Applications to Reduce Erosion and Sedimentation in Tropical Steeplands.* Ed. R. R. Ziemar, C. L. O'Loughlin, and L. S. Hamilton, pp. 221–230. Oxfordshire, U.K.: International Association of Hydrological Sciences.

Increased soil erosion and land degradation in East Kalimantan has been attributed to progressive loss of the province's virgin forest cover. Stadtmüller discusses some of the major land uses which have been associated with this degradation process, including logging, shifting cultivation, vegetable farming on erosion-prone hillsides, mono-crop plantations, and mining. A discussion of the effects of the large forest fire that occurred in Borneo in 1982/83 is also included.

Indonesia/ Kalimantan/ Soil erosion and degradation/ Deforestation/ Forest fires/ Mining/ Timber industry—Environmental impacts/ Land settlement and development—Environmental impacts/ Agriculture—Shifting cultivation's environmental impacts.

330. **Stockdale, M. C., and B. Ambrose. In press.** "Mapping and NFTP Inventory: New Participatory Methods for Forest Dwelling Communities in East Kalimantan." In *Recent Approaches to Participatory Forest Resource Assessment.* Ed. J. Carter. London: Overseas Development Institute.

Indonesia/ East Kalimantan/ Non-timber forest products/ Project intervention—Participatory methods/ Forest management—Forest resource conservation.

331. **Sukardjo, S. 1990.** "The Secondary Forest of Tanah Grogot, East Kalimantan, Indonesia." In *The Plant Diversity of Malesia.* Proceedings of the Flora Malesiana Symposium Commemorating Professor Dr. C.G.G.J. van Steenis, August 1989, Leiden, Netherlands. Ed. P. Baas, K. Kalkman, and Gersnick, pp. 213–224. Dordrecht, Netherlands; Boston, Mass.: Kluwer Academic Publishers.

Sukardjo describes the structure and floristic composition of a 0.25 ha plot of young secondary forest at Tanah Grogot, East Kalimantan. Twenty-six species of trees were found, as well as 47 sapling and 56 ground vegetation species. While the tree species diversity is low compared with findings in other lowland secondary forests in the area, at 592 trees, 4,736 saplings, and 130,400 ground vegetation pieces per hectare, the density of individuals is high. *Vitex pinnata-Genusia furfuracea* dominates the community. [Summarized from monograph abstract].

Indonesia/ East Kalimantan/ Vegetation analysis/ Forest flora/ Forest regeneration/ Biodiversity.

332. **Sukmana, S., A. Abdurachman, and A. Syarifuddin Karama. 1994.** "Strategies to Develop Sustainable Livestock on Marginal Land." In *Agroforestry and*

Animal Production for Human Welfare. Proceedings of an international symposium held in association with the 7th AAAP Animal Science Congress, Bali, Indonesia, 11–16 July 1994. Ed. J. W. Copland, A. Djajanegra, and M. Sabrani, pp. 55–61. ACIAR Proceedings, no. 55. Canberra: Australian Centre for International Agricultural Research.

The authors describe the animal husbandry improvement component of the Upland Agriculture and Conservation Project (UACP) implemented in Jratunseluna (central Java) and Brantas (east Java) from 1984 through 1993, involving the introduction of high-yielding grasses and legumes. The general project activities and farming systems characteristics are highlighted, the potential for livestock development assessed for the area, and appropriate approaches and organizational structures to facilitate this aim are proposed. Also noted are study results showing improvement in the animal carrying capacity from 1 animal unit per ha to 4–6 with the introduction of grasses and legumes appropriate for use as fodder.

Indonesia/ Project intervention—Soil conservation/ Livestock management.

333.   **Sutisna, U., H. C. Soeyatman, and S. Sutomo. 1988.** "Tree Species Composition Analysis of Rain Forests at Pemantas and Batu Ampar, East Kalimantan." *Buletin Penelitian Hutan* 500: 35–51.

The authors report the results of an enumeration of tree species at sapling, pole and tree stages in virgin and logged-over forest areas (2 and 5 years old) in the Pemantas and Batu Ampar areas of East Kalimantan. In both areas, the tree species count was highest in the virgin forests, exceeding those of logged-over areas by 9.2 to 15.3%. Differences in tree species composition for the Pemantas and Batu Ampar areas were also indicated, with *Shorea johorensis* dominating in the virgin forest of the former, and *Shorea laevis* in the latter. [In Bahasa Indonesia with English tables and captions].

Indonesia/ East Kalimantan/ Forest flora/ Forest regeneration/ Vegetation analysis.

334.   **Sutiyono, D. Durahim, and A. Muzani. 1988.** "Traditional Cultivation of *Calamus caesius* (Sega Rattan) in Loksado, South Kalimantan." *Buletin Penelitian Hutan* 511: 41–51.

The authors describe the siting, propagation, management and harvesting of rattan plants by traditional producers in South Kalimantan. Cultivated in a variety of locations, including abandoned swiddens, hilly areas, and river banks, rattan plants yield remunerative harvests after c. 10–15 years, and may be harvested repeatedly after this at 2–3 year intervals. Farmers use household as well as hired labor. [In Bahasa Indonesia].

Indonesia/ South Kalimantan/ Rattan—Cultivation/ Indigenous and local communities—Farming practices.

335.   **Sutlive, V. H., ed. 1993.** *Change and Development in Borneo.* Selected papers from the First Extraordinary Conference of the Borneo Research Council, August 4–9, 1990. Williamsburg, Va.: Borneo Research Council.

Indonesia/ Malaysia/ Borneo/ Indigenous and local communities—Economy/ Indigenous and local communities—Commoditization/ Indigenous and local communities—Land and resource tenure systems/ Indigenous and local communities—Social relations/ Ethnicity and ethnic relations.

336.   **Tagawan, H., and N. Wirawan, eds. 1988.** A Research on the Process of Earlier Recovery of Tropical Rain Forest after a Large Scale Fire in Kalimantan Timur, Indonesia: Report of the Grant-in-Aid for Scientific Research

(Overseas Scientific Survey) in 1986 and 1987. Occasional Paper, no. 14. Kagoshima, Japan: Kagoshima University, Research Center for the South Pacific.

Several papers summarize the results of field research in Kutai National Park, East Kalimantan to measure the effects of the large forest fire of 1982/83 which affected over 3.1 million ha of rainforest in Borneo. Specific paper foci include: results of soil erosion measurements; preliminary data on vegetational disturbances; changes in terrestrial invertebrate community structure; and changes in the mammal population of burnt park areas.

Indonesia/ East Kalimantan/ Forest fires/ Forest regeneration/ Soil erosion and degradation.

337. **Tarrant, J. et al., eds. 1987.** "Natural Resources and Environmental Management in Indonesia: An Overview." Report prepared for U.S.A.I.D. Jakarta: U.S. Agency for International Development.

Indonesia/ Forest management—Forest resource conservation/ State policy—Forest and natural resources/ State policy—Pollution control/ Deforestation.

338. **Thiollay, J. 1995.** "The Role of Traditional Agroforests in the Conservation of Rain Forest Bird Diversity in Sumatra." *Conservation Biology* 9 (2): 335–353.

In May–June 1991 and July 1992 (breeding season) Thiollay observed the bird community composition and structure in three different types of managed agroforests and nearby primary forests along the western slopes of Bukit Barisan Selatan National Park, southwestern Lampung province, Sumatra. While the agroforests demonstrated a rich diversity of trees and plants, bird species richness, diversity, and equitability were found to be 12% to 62% less in these areas than in primary forest. Coefficients of similarity between the natural and managed forest communities were found to be low (0.43–0.55). Of the 216 total species identified in the samples, 56% significantly decreased or disappeared from the agroforest areas, while only 22% either appeared or increased. Large frugivores and insectivores and terrestrial forest specialists were the most severely affected. Small frugivores, foliage insectivores, and nectarivores, on the other hand, appeared to thrive in the agroforest environment. Factors affecting biodiversity in agroforests are discussed. The research findings demonstrate that agroforests do not equal the biodiversity of primary forest areas. Nevertheless, they represent "a valuable compromise between conservation of tropical forest biodiversity and sustainable use of natural resources" while also functioning as buffer zones between protected forest and densely populated areas.

Indonesia/ Sumatra/ Forest fauna/ Agroforestry/ Indigenous and local communities—Forest land use and management practices/ Biodiversity/ Forest management—Parks and conservation areas.

339. **Tinal, U. K., and J. L. Palenewen. 1978.** "Mechanical Logging Damage after Selective Cutting in the Lowland Dipterocarp Forest at Beloro, East Kalimantan." In *Proceedings of the Symposium on the Long-Term Effects of Logging in Southeast Asia.* Ed. S. Rahardjo et al., Bogor, West Java, Indonesia: BIOTROP.

Indonesia/ Timber industry—Logging/ Timber industry—Environmental impacts.

340. **Tomich, T. P., and M. v. Noordwijk. 1995.** "What Drives Deforestation in Sumatra? Paper presented at the Regional Symposium on Montane Mainland Southeast Asia in Transition, Chiang Mai, Thailand, 13–16 November 1995. Photocopy."

The authors present various hypotheses on the main factors behind deforestation as well as on possible solutions. Local household, community, and regional migration level hypotheses are outlined, current research supporting or challenging individual hypotheses are briefly cited, and areas of further research need highlighted. The paper was prepared in the context of a current focus on shifting cultivation by the Bogor, Indonesia branch of the International Centre for Research on Agroforestry as well as the current "Alternatives to Slash-and-Burn" research and development initiative being conducted in Indonesia under the rubric of the Global Environment Facility.

Indonesia/ Sumatra/ Deforestation/ Forest management—Economics/ Agriculture—Shifting cultivation's environmental impacts.

341. **Tsing, A. L. 1993.** *In the Realm of the Diamond Queen: Marginality in an Out-of-the-Way Place.* Princeton, N.J.: Princeton University Press.

Tsing presents an ethnography of the Meratus Dayak of South Kalimantan drawing from dissertation fieldwork completed in September 1979 through August 1981 and a return visit in 1986. She explores "the making of a marginal culture" as a process that involves both state projects of incorporation and marginalization as well as local community reinterpretations of and challenges to externally imposed dichotomies and power hierarchies. One of the central aims of the ethnography is thus to "situate local commentaries [reflecting social identity] . . . within wider negotiations of meaning and power at the same time as recognizing local stakes and specificities." Also central to the narrative is the perspective of gender, as the author attempts to "show the connections between intercommunity divisions, including gender differences, and Meratus regional and national marginality." The ethnography is divided into three main sections and contains rich ethnographic detail of Meratus Dayak household and community life.

Indonesia/ South Kalimantan/ Indigenous and local communities/ Ethnography/ Indigenous and local communities—Religion and cosmology/ Indigenous and local communities—Forest land use and management practices/ Indigenous and local communities—Social relations/ Indigenous and local communities—State policy/ Ethnicity and ethnic relations/ Gender relations/ Social movements.

342. **Tuomela, K., J. Kuusipalo, L. Vesa, K. Nuryanto, and A. P. S. Sagala. 1996.** "Growth of Dipterocarp Seedlings in Artificial Gaps: An Experiment in a Logged-Over Rainforest in South Kalimantan, Indonesia." *Forest Ecology and Management* 81 (1–3): 95–100.

The authors assess the feasibility of using gap simulation to facilitate the regeneration of dipterocarp forest after logging. While creating gap openings was found to have a positive impact on dipterocarp development, gaps of less than 500m2 appeared to be optimal. The species *Shorea parviflora* was found to grow faster than *S. fallax* in gaps. The data indicate that gap simulation provides a more cost-effective means to facilitate commercially viable forest regeneration while also helping to maintain the natural mosaic structure of rain forests.

Indonesia/ South Kalimantan/ Forest regeneration/ Forest management—Commercial forestry and silviculture.

343. **Ukur, F. 1975.** "Mengenal Suku Dayak di Kabupaten Bulongan Kalimantan Timur." *Peninjau* 1: 20–34.
[Introducing the Dayak Tribes of Bulongan Province, East Kalimantan.]

The author provides a concise description of Dayak communities in northern East Kalimantan, an area sharing a mountainous border with the state of Sabah, Malaysia. The names and approximate location of different tribal groups, geographical characteristics of the areas listed, characteristics of the material culture, cosmology, rituals and customs are noted. A helpful cultural and geographical overview of the region. [In Bahasa Indonesia].

Indonesia/ Kalimantan/ Ethnography/ Indigenous and local communities/ Geography.

344. **Vargas, D. M. 1984.** "Interface of Customary and National Law in East Kalimantan, Indonesia." Ph.D. diss., Yale University, New Haven, Conn.

Indonesia/ East Kalimantan/ Land tenure—Legislation and state policy/ Indigenous and local communities—Land and resource tenure systems.

345. **Vayda, A. P. 1981.** "Research in East Kalimantan on Interactions between People and Forest: A Preliminary Report." *Borneo Research Bulletin* 13 (1): 3–15.

The author briefly describes current research activities being undertaken under the Man and Biosphere program at three main locations in East Kalimantan: 1) Apo Kayan in the forest interior; 2) Talen River lowland area; 3) in the vicinity of the provincial capital, Samarinda.
The research aims to show: 1) the range of people's forest-related knowledge; 2) their repertoire of forest-related activities; 3) the variety of situations in which decisions to engage in these activities or to change them are made; and 4) the environmental and socioeconomic effects that these activities have.

Indonesia/ East Kalimantan/ Indigenous and local communities—Forest products use and trade/ Indigenous and local communities—Forest land use and management practices/ Migrant farmers and farming/ Timber industry—Environmental impacts/ Cultural ecology.

346. ———. **1987.** "Self-Managed Land Colonization in Indonesia." *Community Management: Asian Experience and Perspectives*. Ed. D. C. Korten, pp. 113–124. West Hartford, Conn.: Kumarian Press.

Indonesia/ Migrant farmers and farming/ Land settlement and development.

347. ———. **1987.** "Shifting Cultivation and Patch Dynamics in an Upland Forest in East Kalimantan, Indonesia." In *People and the Tropical Forest: A Research Report from the United States Man and the Biosphere Program*. Ed. A. E. Lugo et al., pp. 16–17. Washington, D.C.: U.S. Dept. of State.

Indonesia/ East Kalimantan/ Agriculture—Shifting cultivation's environmental impacts/ Indigenous and local communities—Forest land use and management practices/ Forest regeneration/ Forest biology and ecology.

348. **Vayda, A. P., and T. C. Jessup. 1985.** "Tropical Forest Migrations: Case Studies of Movements by Kenyah and Bugis People in Indonesia." *Wallaceana* 45: 3–5.

This article summarizes the main points of a paper presented in the Symposium on Historical Ecology at the 8th Annual Meeting of the American Anthropological Association, December 1985, Washington, D.C. Various reasons underlie patterns of migration among the Bugis of Southeast Sulawesi, among them the variable price of pepper, failure to obtain adequate farmland on Sulawesi, ready opportunities for acquiring farmland on other islands, and the destruction of pepper plantations on East Kalimantan in the great forest fire of 1983–84. Responding to these factors, the Buginese farmers seek new farmland in forest areas to begin the cultivation of pepper and other cash crops, steadily expanding the area extent of their impact on the forest.

Somewhat different patterns of resource use may be observed among the indigenous Kenyah. To begin, migration appears to have increased among upriver Kenyah, as these seek more accessible trading routes downriver. As the Kenyah move downstream, the extent of forest clearing for swidden fields drops among those who remain behind. At the same time, however, as the Kenyah acquire new technology and become more deeply involved in cash exchange, small scale timber felling is undertaken more frequently. Both ethnic groups are thus involved in changing patterns of forest use, often with negative implications for forest conservation.

Indonesia/ East Kalimantan/ Agriculture—Shifting cultivation/ Migrant farmers and farming/ Indigenous and local communities—Forest land use and management practices/ Indigenous and local communities—Farming practices/ Migration/ Deforestation.

349. **Vayda, A. P., C. J. P. Colfer, and M. Brotokusumo. 1980.** "Interactions Between People and Forests in East Kalimantan." *Impact of Science on Society* 30 (3): 179–190.

This article describes the early stages of research conducted in East Kalimantan as part of the UNESCO Man and Biosphere Program. Three sites were chosen for study to examine significant differences in shifting cultivation and forest use among different communities. These were the Apo Kayan on an inland plateau, still far removed from commercial activity such as logging; the Telen River lowland area, where inland Dayaks have migrated in search of easier trading routes, and where commercial timber activity has been accelerating; and an area just outside the booming provincial city of Samarinda. The authors describe the use of a situational approach to their research, whereby a particular behavior (such as tree cutting) is studied for significant underlying influences and external impacts. In particular, the authors emphasize the responsiveness of local actors as they rationally adjust farming and income-earning practices to make the most of changing local conditions. Some preliminary findings are described in order to illustrate the usefulness of a situational approach for making sense of how people interact with their forest environment, and for formulating appropriate development plans.

Indonesia/ East Kalimantan/ Indigenous and local communities—Forest land use and management practices/ Indigenous and local communities—Commoditization/ Migrant farmers and farming/ Timber industry—Environmental impacts/ Agriculture—Shifting cultivation's environmental impacts.

350. **Vayda, A. P., and A. Sahur. 1985.** "Forest Clearing and Pepper Farming by Bugis Migrants in East Kalimantan: Antecedents and Impact." *Indonesia* 39: 93–110.

Indonesia/ Migrant farmers and farming/ Agriculture—Shifting cultivation's environmental impacts/ Deforestation.

351. **Verlaat, E. 1995.** "'We Don't Want a Road, It Will Bring Development': Management of Natural Vegetation by Indigenous People." *BOS Nieuwsletter* 14 (2 (31)): 46–57.

The forest and vegetation management techniques of the Karen people of Thailand, the Tukano and Kayapo of Brazil, and the Punan of Kalimantan provide examples of effective management strategies that build on rather than ignore or negate indigenous knowledge and points of view. Without this orientation, forestry development projects quickly become forces that undermine indigenous cultures rather than assist local communities.

Indonesia/ Kalimantan/ Indigenous and local communities—Forest land use and management practices.

352. **Vondal, P. J. 1987.** "Intensification Through Diversified Resource Use: The Human Ecology of a Successful Agricultural Industry in Indonesian Borneo." *Human Ecology* 15 (1): 27–51.

    Indonesia/ East Kalimantan/ Agricultural intensification/ Indigenous and local communities—Commoditization/ Indigenous and local communities—Forest land use and management practices/ Agricultural development.

353. **Wahana Informasi Masyarakat (WIM). 1994.** PIR: anugerah atau bencana; Studi kasus sengketa agraria antara negara dan rakyat pada proyek PIR. Medan, Indonesia: WIM.
    [Nucleus-Estate Smallholder Programs: Blessing or Disaster: Case Studies of Agrarian Conflicts between People and the State Concerning NES Projects.]

    This study reviews the development of *perusahaan inti-rakyat* (PIR), or nucleus-estate smallholder development projects in Indonesia within the context of a global trend towards contract farming between small-scale producers and large international agribusiness enterprises. The nucleus-estate smallholder model has been developed and pursued by the Indonesian government since the 1970s, and presently comprises a major thrust in its agricultural development, smallholder promotion, and land development efforts on Sumatra, Kalimantan, and other islands beyond Java and Bali. A major problem associated with this approach concerns the frequent conflicts between state development agencies and local farmers over land appropriated for PIR projects. Following a review of the general history as well as policy and legal underpinnings of the land issue in PIR programs, three case studies of conflicts of land taken for nucleus estate development are provided, all in North Sumatra province. A closing analytical section identifies common patterns and specific factors promoting conflict with local residents in the process of PIR development.

    Indonesia/ Sumatra/ Land settlement and development/ Agriculture—Plantations/ Agriculture—Smallholder tree and perennial crop farming/ Agriculture—Smallholder cash crop farming/ State policy—Agricultural and rural development/ State policy—Land development/ Land tenure—Legislation and state policy.

354. Wahana Lingkungan Hidup Indonesia (WALHI), and Yayasan Lembaga Bantuan Hukum Indonesia (YLBHI). 1992. *Mistaking Plantations for the [sic] Indonesia's Tropical Forest.* Jakarta: WALHI.

    In recent years, development of a dynamic pulp and paper industry based on a secure supply of raw material from tree plantations has been promoted by the Indonesian government as a promising strategy for sustainable forest land management. By offering incentives to logging concessionaires to develop commercial plantations and downstream pulp and paper processing industries, the government's stated hope is to reduce logging in the country's virgin forest areas. Serious questions remain, however, about this strategy's environmental and social impacts. This short monograph reviews these concerns, providing a brief history of deforestation and the timber industry in Indonesia, an overview of the targeted international pulp and paper market, a summary of problems related to timber plantation development, including accelerated loss of natural forests, monoculturalization, pollution, and social impacts. A case study of PT. Inti Indorayon Utama, a privately owned company involved in establishing an extensive eucalyptus plantation in the Lake Toba watershed of Northern Sumatra province, is presented. The struggle of residents at Sugapa village against the expropriation of their land by the company, which resulted in well-publicized court proceedings against resisting women, is described. The study highlights that while timber plantations do in theory offer some important benefits in the way of sustainable land use, adequate consideration must be given to mitigating adverse environmental effects and ensuring that real benefits accrue to local communities as well.

    Indonesia/ Sumatra/ Timber plantations/ Timber industry—Impacts on local communities and economy/ Deforestation/ Social movements/ Pulp and paper industry.

355. **Wahana Lingkungan Hidup Indonesia (WALHI) Research Team. 1993.** *HPH dan ekonomi regional kasus Kalimantan Timur*. Jakarta: WALHI.
[Timber Concessions and the Regional Economy: The Case of East Kalimantan.]

There have long been many concerns about the system by which timber concession rights (*Hak Pengusahaan Hutan* or HPH) have been granted and used in Indonesia since the system's inception in 1967. Addressing these concerns, a team of researchers at WALHI (a leading environmental advocacy organization in Indonesia) and the World Resources Institute (WRI) embarked on a case study of the concession system's impact on the environment and regional economy of East Kalimantan. The study involves both macro- and micro-level analyses, drawing from regional development indicators, labor force and industrial statistics, fiscal records, as well as two months of field research in Jelmu Sibak, a village located on the Lawa river in Kutai district and surrounded by three different concession areas. Study results confirm the presence of troubling problems in the way timber concessions are being managed in East Kalimantan with some serious implications for the future state of the timber industry in the region. Moreover, even as timber extraction appears likely only to decline in its ability to contribute to regional economic and job growth, the timber concessions studied were found to provide little in the way of new and sustainable sources of income for Jelmu Sibak villagers, and in some cases appear to be threatening the existing income generating opportunities villagers now gain from their surrounding forest resources. [In Bahasa Indonesia].

Indonesia/ East Kalimantan/ Timber industry—Impacts on local communities and economy.

356. **Warren, J. F. 1987.** *At the Edge of Southeast Asian History*. Quezon City: New Day Publishers.

The monograph presents a collection of essays written between the late 1970s and the mid-1980s. Several essays focus on the role of trade and slave trading in the development of the Sulu Zone under the Sulu sultanate during the 19th century. Incorporating the Sulu archipelago between the Southern Philippines, Northern Borneo and Northern Sulawesi island, the Sulu sultanate commanded great control over inter-island trade throughout insular Southeast Asia during the first half of the 19th century. Warren links vigorous slave raiding by sultan forces throughout the Southeast Asian islands to booming Western demand for jungle products such as gutta-perche (raw rubber) and rattan as well as the infusion of Western-made arms and munitions to the area. Booming trade with the West through Singapore and other entrepot cities made command over adequate labor supplies to procure tradeable goods vital to the economic and political dominance of the Sulu sultanate, encouraging in turn the procurement of labor through slave-raiding. Access to a constant supply of weapons made this procurement possible.

These forces had an impact on local populations and ethnic relations far beyond the area directly controlled by the Sultanate. Also important was the role of Western traders who were able to manipulate connections with coastal sultans in eastern Borneo to establish lucrative trading links with shifting cultivator communities located far upstream in the Borneo interior. Both the Sulu sultanate and these early Western trade monopolies were eventually usurped from their dominant commercial position in the area by the arrival of Arab traders using steamboats. The control exerted by Sulu sultanates in the region was also severely diminished by the end of the 19th century after vigorous military attacks by both Spanish and English naval fleets. A concerted resettlement campaign was started by colonial authorities, aimed at transforming the seafaring coastal communities of the region into sedentary agriculturalists. With these essays, the author seeks to highlight the impact of global forces linked to industrialization in the West on communities conventionally perceived to be on the periphery of modern history.

Indonesia/ Malaysia/ Philippines/ History—Colonial/ Non-timber forest products/ Ethnicity and ethnic relations/ Resettlement.

357. **Weidelt, H. J. 1993.** "Dorfwälder im tropischen Asien—Zwischen Nutzung und Kult." *Forstarchiv* 64 (6): 300–307.
[Village Forests in Tropical Asia—Utilization and Cultural Role.]

Describes structure and composition of forest gardens maintained by Dayak villagers of East Kalimantan and the village forests and sacred tree groves kept by the Dai in Yunnan, southwestern China. In addition to their cultural and economic value, the ecological and biodiversity functions of both garden forms are noted.

Indonesia/ East Kalimantan/ Indigenous and local communities—Forest land use and management practices/ Indigenous and local communities—Forest products use and trade/ Biodiversity.

358. **Weinstock, J. A. 1979.** "Land Tenure Practices of the Swidden Cultivators of Borneo." M.Sc. thesis, Cornell University, Ithaca, N.Y.

Indonesia/ Kalimantan/ Indigenous and local communities—Land and resource tenure systems/ Indigenous and local communities—Forest land use and management practices/ Indigenous and local communities—Farming practices.

359. ———. **1981.** "Weighing Environmental Factors as Determinates of Dayak Land Tenure." *Borneo Research Bulletin* 13: 107–113.

Weinstock attempts to help clarify the relationship between soil conditions, precipitation, and other ecological factors on the one hand and Dayak land tenure patterns on the other. The article is framed as a critical response to points raised in an earlier analysis by Dove.

Indonesia/ East Kalimantan/ Indigenous and local communities—Land and resource tenure systems.

360. ———. **1983.** "Keharingan and the Luangan Dayaks: Religion and Identity in Central-East Borneo." Ph.D. diss., Cornell University, Ithaca, N.Y.

This study focuses on the Luangan Dayaks, who inhabit the region between the middle Barito River in Central Kalimantan and the middle Mahakam River in East Kalimantan. The study presents the basic tenets of *keharingan*, the indigenous religion of southern Borneo. Social organization and the political structure are viewed as they exist within the Luangan perceptual sphere of *keharingan*. Economic activities, primarily those of agriculture, are described and explained as they operate also within the framework of *keharingan*. [Summarized from author's abstract].

Indonesia/ East Kalimantan/ Central Kalimantan/ Indigenous and local communities—Religion and cosmology/ Indigenous and local communities—Economy/ Indigenous and local communities—Farming practices/ Indigenous and local communities—Social relations.

361. ———. **1983.** "Rattan: Ecological Balance in a Borneo Rainforest Swidden." *Economic Botany* 37: 58–68.

Indonesia/ Kalimantan/ Rattan—Cultivation/ Indigenous and local communities—Forest products use and trade/ Indigenous and local communities—Forest land use and management practices/ Agriculture—Smallholder cash crop farming/ Agriculture—Smallholder tree and perennial crop farming.

362. ———. **1994.** "Smallholder Silvopastoralism in Indonesia." In *Agroforestry and Animal Production for Human Welfare.* Proceedings of an international sym-

posium held in association with the 7th AAAP Animal Science Congress, Bali, Indonesia, 11–16 July 1994. Ed. J. W. Copland, A. Djajanegra, and M. Sabrani, pp. 119–122. ACIAR Proceedings, no. 55. Canberra: Australian Centre for International Agricultural Research.

Weinstock summarizes the general history of silvopastoralism in Indonesia, with particular attention to government efforts to promote leucaena planting since the early 1980s, and the problems encountered in the process. Two case studies are included: 1) Smallholder livestock management patterns in West Java, which have been largely subsistence oriented, using goats and sheep (small ruminants) and have increasingly involved the cultivation of variety of grasses along roads, fields and village lanes, as well as cultivation of variety of leguminous tree species; 2) West Timor, where land is more abundant and people tend to have larger ruminants like cattle, manage the latter for purposes of cash sales of meat, and have greater reliance on leucaena (*lamtorogung*), first promoted by missionaries in the 1930s. In the case of West Timor, the monoculture-nature of leucaena production resulted in serious losses due to psyllid infestation in mid-1980s. The case studies shows important differences in the local development of silvopastoral systems due to differing biophysical characteristics, as well as socio-cultural and economic factors.

Indonesia/ Java/ East Nusa Tenggara/ Indigenous and local communities—Forest land use and management practices/ Agroforestry/ Livestock management.

363. **Weinstock, J. A., and Satyawan Sunito. 1989.** "Review of Shifting Cultivation in Indonesia." Indonesia UTF/INS/065/INS: Forestry Studies, Field Document II–1. Jakarta; Rome: Directorate General of Forest Utilization, Ministry of Forestry, Government of Indonesia/Food and Agriculture Organization of the United Nations.

The authors present a detailed overview of shifting cultivation in Indonesia. Individual chapters address: definition and typology of shifting cultivation; analysis of situation and trends (including a critical analysis of existing statistical and qualitative data); government programs (Ministries of Forestry; Agriculture; Transmigration; Social Affairs; Home Affairs); government laws and legislation; traditional law (adat); experience from other countries (including comparisons with Philippines and East Malaysia); and survey proposal.

Indonesia/ Agriculture—Shifting cultivation/ Indigenous and local communities—Farming practices/ Migrant farmers and farming/ Indigenous and local communities—Land and resource tenure systems/ Indigenous and local communities—Land and resource tenure systems/ Forest management—Control of Shifting cultivation/ Land tenure—Legislation and state policy/ Resettlement/ Indigenous and local communities—State policy.

364. **Weinstock, J. A., and N. T. Vergara. 1987.** "Land or Plants: Agricultural Tenure in Agroforestry Systems." *Economic Botany* 41: 312–322.

The distinction made by the Luangans of Borneo between tenure rights in land and tenure rights in forest products is described. The authors stress that complex indigenous tenure systems have important implications for agroforestry and forest resource management.

Indonesia/ Indigenous and local communities—Land and resource tenure systems/ Indigenous and local communities—Forest products use and trade/ Forest management—Forest resource conservation.

365. **Whitten, A. J. 1987.** "Indonesia's Transmigration Program and its Role in the Loss of Tropical Rain Forest." *Conservation Biology* 1: 239–246.

Indonesia/ Land settlement and development—Environmental impacts/ Deforestation.

366. **Whittier, H. L. 1973.** "Social Organization and Symbol of Social Differentiation: An Ethnographic Study of the Kenyah Dayak of East Kalimantan (Borneo)." Ph.D. diss., Michigan State University, East Lansing, Mich.

Indonesia/ East Kalimantan/ Ethnography/ Indigenous and local communities—Social relations/ Indigenous and local communities—Religion and cosmology.

367. ———. **1974.** "The Distribution of the Punan in East Kalimantan." *Borneo Research Bulletin* 6: 42–48.

This paper provides a short description of Punan settlement locations in East Kalimantan, focusing on a number of sub- districts in Bulungan and Berau districts.

Indonesia/ East Kalimantan/ Indigenous and local communities.

368. **Widjaja, E. A., and T. C. Jessup. 1986.** "Short Description of Indigenous Rice from East Kalimantan, Indonesia." *Plant Genetic Resources Newsletter* 67: 102–111.

The authors draw from fieldwork in East Kalimantan to describe 22 ordinary (*padei latak*) and 13 glutinous (*padei ubek*) rice varieties grown by the Kenyah Dayak. Names are given in the Lepo' Tukung dialect of the Kenyah Dayak language.

Indonesia/ East Kalimantan/ Indigenous and local communities—Farming practices.

369. **Wilson, C. C., and L. Wilson. 1975.** "The Influence of Selective Logging on Primates and Some Other Animals in East Kalimantan." *Folia Primatologica* 23: 243–274.

The authors conducted a brief survey in East Kalimantan as well as state-of-current-research literature review to assess the impact of selective logging operations on primate populations, birds and squirrels. Research results suggest that primate species density is not particularly impacted by moderate forest disturbance due to selective logging, although the breeding population of some species may be more seriously affected than others. Rain forest birds and squirrels appear to be most at risk. Also noted is the potentially more serious implications of human encroachment following logging for local wildlife populations. Further research is recommended to address knowledge gaps, and more preservation areas are needed to ensure protection of core habitat areas. [Summarized from journal abstract].

Indonesia/ Kalimantan/ Forest fauna/ Timber industry—Environmental impacts.

370. **Wilson, W. L., and A. D. Johns. 1982.** "Diversity and Abundance of Selected Animal Species in Undisturbed Forest, Selectively Logged Forest and Plantations in East Kalimantan, Indonesia." *Biological Conservation* 24: 205–218.

Indonesia/ Kalimantan/ Forest fauna/ Timber industry—Environmental impacts/ Biodiversity.

371. **Wind, J. 1991.** *Buffer Zones.* Vol. 1. A Concept for Park Protection and Community Participation. Bogor, Indonesia: Government of Indonesia. Ministry of Forestry and Director General of Nature Conservation and Forest Protection.

Indonesia/ Forest management—Parks and conservation areas/ Project intervention—Participatory methods.

372. **Wirawan, N. 1987.** "Good Forest within the Burned Forest Area in East Kalimantan." In *Proceedings of the Third Round Table Conference on Dipterocarps.* Ed. A. J. G. H. Kostermans, pp. 367–387. Jakarta: UNESCO.

   Indonesia/ East Kalimantan/ Forest fires/ Forest regeneration.

373. **World Bank. 1988.** Indonesia—Adjustment, Growth, and Sustainable Development. Washington D.C.: World Bank.

   Indonesia/ Economic development/ State policy—Agricultural and rural development/ State policy—Pollution control/ State policy—Forest and natural resources/ State policy—Land development.

374. ———. **1988.** Indonesia: The Transmigration Program in Perspective. Washington, D.C.: World Bank.

   Provides a comprehensive review of the major components, achievements, and problems of the Indonesian transmigration program, arguably the country's most ambitious upland development effort since the late 1970s. Among the assessment's major findings are the low returns and settler incomes achieved at a large share of transmigration sites. Frequent critiques of the program also concern the adverse environmental impacts of poorly managed land clearing, the introduction of farming systems poorly suited to upland environments, and social tensions created by program development vis á vis local communities. As the report also argues, however, despite program shortcomings, economic prospects have improved for most settlers relative to the poverty trap they faced on Java, and available indicators suggest positive program impacts on local employment and regional development. Given its pressing economic and population-related development, the Indonesian government will have to continue a focus on sustainable land development in its forested Outer Islands. The report closes with a number of recommendations for helping to ensure better success in the focus for the future, including scaling back the scope of the program to more manageable target numbers, engaging a focus on strengthening existing sites rather than developing new ones, shifting focus to tree crop rather than upland food crop-based farming systems as a more sustainable land use type for the receiving areas, greater attention to supporting spontaneous settlers, and greater consideration of institutional, environmental, and social impact issues.

   Indonesia/ Land settlement and development/ Land settlement and development—Environmental impacts/ Land settlement and development—Impacts on local communities and economy/ Agricultural development/ Agriculture—Smallholder tree and perennial crop farming/ Agriculture—Smallholder cash crop farming/ State policy—Land development.

375. ———. **1990.** Indonesia: Sustainable Development of Forests, Land and Water. Washington, D.C.: World Bank.

   Indonesia/ Economic development/ State policy—Forest and natural resources/ State policy—Pollution control/ State policy—Land development/ Timber industry—State policy and regulation/ Forest management—Commercial forestry and silviculture/ Forest management—Forest resource conservation/ Forest management—Economics.

376. **Yamakura, I., A. Hagihara, S. Sukardjo, and H. Ogawa. 1987.** "Tree Form in a Mixed Dipterocarp Forest in Indonesian Borneo." *Ecological Research* 2 (3): 215–227.

   Pipe model theory is applied to data on the production structure of 47 species in a tropical rain forest stand in Sebulu, E. Kalimantan. The analysis explains crown shapes and a mathematical model for stem form.

Indonesia/ East Kalimantan/ Forest biology and ecology.

377. **Yeager, C. P. 1992.** "Changes in Proboscis Monkey (*Nasalis larvatus*) Group Size and Density at Tanjung Puting National Park, Kalimantan Tengah, Indonesia." *Tropical Biodiversity* 1 (1): 49–55.

> Declining group size and density of a population of proboscis monkeys (*Nasalis larvatus*) at Tanjung Puting National Park, Kalimantan Tengah Indonesia appears to be linked to increasing habitat disturbance, particularly growing boat traffic. Data were collected in 1984/1985, 1989 and 1991, and the authors emphasize the need for longer-term study for more accurate assessments. [Summarized from journal].

Indonesia/ Kalimantan/ Forest fauna/ Forest management—Parks and conservation areas/ Wildlife management.

378. **Yunus, M., and R. S. Wirakusumah. 1978.** "Sedikit pandangan sosiologis proses resetelmen penduduk Kalimantan Timur." Paper presented at the National Workshop on Population Resettlement, 5–6 May 1978, in Cibogo, West Java. Photocopy.
[Some Sociological Considerations on the Resettlement Process, East Kalimantan.]

> This paper describes the East Kalimantan Resettlement Project as it enters its sixth year of implementation. Thus far, the project has resettled 3,942 households in ten locations. The article highlights different adjustment processes which are expected to occur as transmigrants settle in to their new communities.

Indonesia/ East Kalimantan/ Land settlement and development.

379. **Zerner, C. 1990.** "Community Rights, Customary Law, and the Law of Timber Concessions in Indonesia's Forests: Legal Options and Alternatives in Designing the Commons." UTF/INS/065/Forestry Studies Report. Jakarta; Rome: Directorate General of Forest Utilisation, Ministry of Forestry; Food and Agriculture Organisation of the United Nations.

> This report provides a critical discussion of the relationship between community rights and national law in managing Indonesia's forest resources. Subject headings include: 1) problems and issues in forest concession management; 2) an outline of the legal and regulatory framework for forest production in Indonesia; 3) the role and status of community rights (*hak ulayat*) and customary law (*hukum adat*) rights in Indonesia's legal and regulatory framework for forest concessions; 4) designing the commons; 5) recommendations on the law of forest concessions and on the law of community rights and customary law. The report is followed by three appendices, one of which discusses resource management practices of the Kenyah and Kayan peoples of the interior of East Kalimantan.

Indonesia/ East Kalimantan/ Timber industry—State policy and regulation/ Land tenure—Legislation and state policy/ Indigenous and local communities—Land and resource tenure systems/ Indigenous and local communities—Forest land use and management practices.

380. **Zoefri, H. 1978.** "Some Observations on the Effects of Mechanical Logging on Regeneration, Soil and Hydrological Conditions in East Kalimantan." In *Proceedings of the Symposium on the Long-term Effects of Logging in Southeast Asia*. Ed. S. Rahardjo. Bogor, West Java, Indonesia: BIOTROP.

Indonesia/ Kalimantan/ Timber industry—Environmental impacts/ Forest regeneration/ Soil erosion and degradation/ Hydrology.

MALAYSIA

381. **Abdul Rahim, N. 1990.** "Effects of Selective Logging Methods on Hydrological Parameters in Peninsular Malaysia." Ph.D. diss., University College of North Wales, Bangor, Wales, U.K.

Malaysia/ Peninsular Malaysia/ Timber industry—Logging/ Timber industry—Environmental impacts/ Hydrology.

382. **Abdullah, A. R. 1991.** "Centre-Periphery Relations: Its Implications on Smallholder Farmers in Sarawak." *Sarawak Gazette* 118 (1516): 20–24.

The author makes an appeal for greater local input into policy-making. Thus far, agricultural and regional development policy in Sarawak, as exemplified by the Sarawak Land Development Board, has been strongly biased towards promoting large-scale land development, plantation-based agriculture and highly specialized farming. This approach has ignored the adaptability and diversity of traditional, albeit semi-commercialized, Iban farming which has proven quite successful at dealing with variable market conditions. Rigidity in much of the state's agricultural development programs has yielded unsuccessful results so far. The author suggests that the greater flexibility shown by the Sawarak Land Consolidation and Rehabilitation Authority may offer a more promising means to promote increased farmer productivity over the long run.

Malaysia/ Sarawak/ State policy—Agricultural and rural development/ State policy—Land development/ Indigenous and local communities—Farming practices/ Indigenous and local communities—Commoditization/ Agriculture—Shifting cultivation/ Agriculture—Smallholder cash crop farming/ Land settlement and development.

383. **Ahmad, F. B. 1993.** "Medicinal Plants Used by Kadayan Community in Sarawak." *Sarawak Museum Journal* 44 (65 (n.s.)).

Five herbalists from the Kadayan community in Lawas/Limbang, Sarawak were interviewed to identify commonly used medicinal plants. Traditional uses for 53 plant species were documented and phytochemical studies performed to analyze component elements and antibacterial properties.

Malaysia/ Sarawak/ Indigenous and local communities—Forest products use and trade/ Non-timber forest products.

384. **Aiken, R. S., and C. H. Leigh. 1992.** *Vanishing Rain Forests: The Ecological Transition in Malaysia.* Oxford: Clarendon Press.

The monograph is divided into several major sections. The first provides a general description of the distribution and ecology of tropical rain forests, different patterns of resource use (both traditional and modern), the impact of human activities in terms of forest conversion, and emerging conservation and sustainable development issues relating to sustainable tropical forestry, sustainable forest farming, and park and protected area management. In a subsequent chapter, Aiken and Leigh describe in closer detail the vegetative formations, flora and fauna, and the soil and hydrology systems of Malaysian rainforests in particular. A history of forest resource utilization in Malaysia is presented, including colonial and post-colonial forestry, changing patterns of shifting cultivation, plantation and other land development schemes. The impact of these activities on forest hydrology, soil erosion, biological resource loss, and indigenous communities is described. The authors follow with a discussion of resource conservation in Malaysia in historical perspective, describing colonial and post-colonial conservation strategies, specific conflicts over land use and recent efforts in integrated forest management and protected park systems. The monograph represents an excellent overview and summary of published research on tropical forest resource management in Malaysia, from a technical as well as policy-oriented socio-economic perspective.

Malaysia/ Forest flora/ Forest fauna/ Forest biology and ecology/ Timber industry—Logging/ Timber industry—Environmental impacts/ Agriculture—Plantations/ Agriculture—Shifting cultivation's environmental impacts/ Land settlement and development—Environmental impacts/ Hydrology/ Soil erosion and degradation/ Biodiversity/ Forest management—Commercial forestry and silviculture/ Forest management—Forest resource conservation/ Watershed management/ Forest management—Parks and conservation areas/ State policy—Forest and natural resources/ History—Colonial.

385. **Aiken, R. S. et al. 1982.** *Development and Environment in Peninsular Malaysia.* Singapore: McGraw-Hill International Book Co.

Malaysia/ Peninsular Malaysia/ Regional development/ Land use—Patterns and planning/ Geography/ Agricultural development/ Agriculture—Plantations/ Land settlement and development/ Migration/ Timber industry—Development and structure/ Timber industry—State policy and regulation/ Forest management—Commercial forestry and silviculture/ Forest management—Forest resource conservation/ Pest, weed, and crop disease management/ State policy—Agricultural and rural development/ State policy—Forest and natural resources/ State policy—Pollution control.

386. **Aminuddin, B. Y., W. T. Chow, and T. T. Ng. 1991.** "Resources and Problems Associated with Sustainable Development of Upland Areas in Malaysia." In *Technologies for Sustainable Agriculture on Marginal Uplands in Southeast Asia.* Proceedings of a seminar held at Ternate, Cavite, Philippines, 10–14 December 1990. Ed. G. Blair and R. Lefroy, pp. 55–61. Canberra: Australian Centre for International Agricultural Research (ACIAR).

Data are presented on demographic pressure, government policy goals, and land suitable and unsuitable for farming in Peninsula Malaysia, Sarawak, and Sabah. Accelerated soil loss under different uses, poor soils, land tenure disputes, labor shortages, poverty, and poorly developed infrastructure are identified as major constraints to technology adoption. Possible strategies and supporting research findings to address these constraints are noted.

Malaysia/ Agricultural development/ Rural development/ Population pressure/ Land use—Patterns and planning/ Agriculture—Smallholder tree and perennial crop farming/ Soil erosion and degradation/ Agriculture—Smallholder cash crop farming/ State policy—Agricultural and rural development.

387. **Andau, P. M., and J. Payne. 1982.** "The Plight of the Sumatran Rhinoceros in Sabah." *Malaysian Forester* 45 (4): 548-557.

The Silabukan and Lumerau Forest Reserves in eastern Sabah feature a limited number of the near extinct rhinoceros species *Dicerorhinus sumatrensis*. The 15–30 rhinoceros remaining in the area, however, are under serious pressure due to the combined impacts of timber extraction, conversion of forest lands to agricultural use, and hunting. Noting the problems associated with relocating the breeding population to a more remote site, the authors propose a possible in situ conservation strategy involving the protection of a core area of virgin forest as undisturbed rhinocerous habitat and the management of the surrounding commercial forests according to sound forestry principles.

Malaysia/ Sabah/ Forest management—Parks and conservation areas/ Forest fauna/ Wildlife management.

388. **Andriesse, J. P., and T. Koopmans. 1984.** "A Monitoring Study on Nutrient Cycles in Soils Used for Shifting Cultivation Under Various Climatic Conditions in Tropical Asia: I. The Influence of Simulated Burning on Farm and Availability of Plant Nutrients." *Agriculture, Ecosystems, Environment* 12: 1–16.

Andriesse and Koopmans report the results of lab-based simulation of burning aimed at identifying physical, chemical and microbiological processes involved in shifting cultivation. Using soil samples from a forest site in Sarawak, Malaysia, the simulation demonstrated the role played by burning in decreasing cation exchange capacity and increasing pH, electric conductivity, base saturation, available phosphorus and other nutrients released from organic matter. Where temperatures reached over 150 degrees, a significant decrease in exchangeable aluminum occurred, while calcium and magnesium appeared to exist as salts between 150 and 250 degrees. Temperatures did not generally reach more than 150 degrees below a range of 2 inches, well above the rooting range for annual crops. Study results thus suggest that "microbiological changes from heating are probably of greater importance than the chemical ones."

Malaysia/ Sarawak/ Soils/ Agriculture—Shifting cultivation's environmental impacts.

389. **Andriesse, J. P., and R. M. Schelhaas. 1987.** "A Monitoring Study of Nutrient Cycles in Soils Used for Shifting Cultivation under Various Climatic Conditions in Tropical Asia: II. Nutrient Stores in Biomass and Soil—Results of Baseline Studies." *Agriculture, Ecosystems, and Environment* 19: 285–310.

The authors report the results of soil analyses on samples taken from sites in Sri Lanka and Sarawak, Malaysia undertaken to provide baseline information for a series of soil monitoring studies. Qualitative difference in macronutrients (Ca, MG. K, N, P and S) of different nutrient reservoirs are noted in vegetation, litter, roots and soils up to .75m below the surface. These differences appear to be related to differing climatic conditions and parent materials, and indicate different nutrient recycling processes occurring in the sites studied. In both cases, however, it appears that maintaining tree vegetation and avoiding the destruction of valuable tree trunks during the cropping period play a key role in preventing the loss of nutrients through leaching. The accumulated analytical base will be the reference for subsequent monitoring studies.

Malaysia/ Sarawak/ Agriculture—Shifting cultivation's environmental impacts/ Soils.

390. **———. 1987.** "A Monitoring Study on Nutrient Cycles in Soils Used for Shifting Cultivation Under Various Climatic Conditions in Tropical Asia: III. The Effects of Land Clearing through Burning on Fertility Level." *Agriculture, Ecosystems and Environment* 19: 311–332.

The authors studied the impact of burning felled vegetation on soil nutrient levels (C, N, P, K, Ca, Mg, S) and physical properties (CEC, pH, and EC) at sites in Sri Lanka, Thailand, and Sarawak, Malaysia. Important differences were found between complete burns conducted in Sri Lanka and Thailand and incomplete burns conducted in Sarawak. In the former, burning was associated with a 20–25 percent decline in organic carbon, 5–10 percent decline in CEC, and less than a 10 percent decline in organic phosphorus. No significant change was observed in soil nitrogen levels, though N levels in biomass dropped steeply, probably due to volatilization. Incomplete burning in Sarawak resulted in a 20 percent increase in carbon and nitrogen, a 10 percent increase in CEC, and a 4 percent increase in organic phosphorus. Incomplete burning was also associated with nitrogen conservation through the addition of organic matter to the soil. In all cases, fertility increases were noted up to 75 cm below the surface, though most markedly so up to 5 cm. Piling of vegetation was shown to have a negative effect on maintaining organic matter and N due to higher soil temperatures with burning, and also appeared to increase alkalinity, thus constraining crop production. Nutrient leaching was noted in the Sri Lankan soil within 4 months of burning.

Malaysia/ Sarawak/ Agriculture—Shifting cultivation's environmental impacts/ Soils.

391. **Anon. n.d.** "Copper Development Agreement (in respect to the Mamut Copper Project) between the Government of Malaysia and the Overseas Mineral Resources Development Sabah Berhad." Photocopy.

Malaysia/ Sabah/ State policy—Forest and natural resources/ Mining.

392. ———. **1979.** "Forest Resource Base, Policy and Legislation of Sabah." *Malaysian Forester* 42 (4): 286–310.

Malaysia/ Sabah/ State policy—Forest and natural resources/ Timber industry—State policy and regulation/ Land tenure.

393. ———. **1991.** "The Cocoa Boom and Its Subsequent Dilemma with Particular Reference to Sabah." *Planter* 67: 397–401.

In the late 1970s and early 1980s an outbreak of the cocoa shoot virus in major cocoa-producing countries set off a boom in land development for cocoa production in Sabah, Malaysia. Rapid land development occurred, however, without adequate attention to ensuring suitable shading conditions and planting materials needed for successful cocoa production. The authors discuss the impact of these constraints on cocoa harvests, highlighting the diseases afflicting Sabah's cocoa fields as a result of poor inputs. Suggestions for technological measures to deal with the problem are given.

Malaysia/ Sabah/ Agriculture—Plantations/ Pest, weed, and crop disease management.

394. **Appell, G. N. 1963.** "Myths and Legends about the Rungus of the Kudat District." *Journal of the Sabah Society* 1 (4): 9–15.

Four myths are considered regarding the socio-cultural traits and economic status of the Rungus in Kudat. Common misconceptions include: 1) the notion that the natives of Kudat, including the Rungus, can be ethnologically termed as 'Dusuns'; 2) that the Rungus longhouses must be broken to facilitate their economic improvement; 3) that wet rice cultivation is alien among the Rungus and therefore must be introduced; and 4) that the Rungus are half starved throughout the year and therefore have to forage for food in the jungle.

The author contends that the Rungus are a group of people with distinct culture and traditions, and, in any case, the term 'Dusun' is really an exonym. Furthermore, notes the author, breaking up the longhouse will likely retard rather than facilitate economic development among this group of people for the simple reason that a disintegrating society is much less able to cope with changing circumstances that an ongoing one. Wet "padi" cultivation is not alien to the Rungus people, although many are prevented from entering this activity for lack of suitable land and irrigation/drainage facilities and unpredictable climatic patterns in the area. Finally, the Rungus custom to forage for food in the jungle does not so much suggest an inadequate food supply than a means to obtain a highly varied and nutritious diet.

Access to and ownership of agricultural land among the Rungus people are also discussed. In the traditional Rungus system, the individual does not hold residual ownership rights in land. These rights are lodged with the village as a corporate unit. The right to use land for agricultural purposes by the individual family unit is concomitant to residence rights in the village. It is also argued that shifting cultivation as practiced by the Rungus is remarkably efficient given present technology.

Malaysia/ Sabah/ Indigenous and local communities—Social relations/ Indigenous and local communities—Land and resource tenure systems/ Indigenous and local communities—Forest products use and trade/ Agriculture—Shifting cultivation.

395.   ———. **1965.** "The Nature of Social Groupings Among the Rungus of Sabah, Malaysia." Ph.D. diss., Australian National University, Canberra, A.C.T., Australia.

Malaysia/ Sabah/ Indigenous and local communities—Social relations.

396.   ———. **1966.** "Residence and Ties of Kinship in a Cognitive Society: The Rungus of Sabah, Malaysia." *Southwestern Journal of Anthropology* 22 (2): 280–301.

Malaysia/ Sabah/ Indigenous and local communities—Social relations.

397.   ———. **1971.** "System of Land Tenure in Borneo: A Problem in Ecological Determinism." *Borneo Research Bulletin* 3: 17–20.

Malaysia/ Sabah/ Indigenous and local communities—Land and resource tenure systems.

398.   ———. **1972.** "Rungus Dusun." In *Insular Southeast Asia: Ethnographic Studies. Section 3. Borneo and Moluccas.* Comp. F. M. LeBar, vol. 1. New Haven, Conn.: Human Relations Area Files.

Malaysia/ Sabah/ Indigenous and local communities/ Ethnography.

399.   ———. **1974.** "The Analysis of Property Systems: The Creation and Devolution of Property Interests among the Rungus of Borneo." A paper presented at the Conference of the Association of Social Anthropologists in Social Anthropology and Law, March, 1974, at the University of Keele. Photocopy.

Malaysia/ Sabah/ Indigenous and local communities—Land and resource tenure systems.

400.   ———. **1986.** "Social Anthropological Research among the Rungus Dusun: A Talk for the Sabah Society." *Journal of the Sabah Society* 8 (2): 194–209.

Divided into two main parts, this article discusses 1) the main features of Rungus culture and 2) the process of social change in the community. Part I provides an insight into the Rungus domestic family, the long house, the Rungus village agriculture and land tenure system, and their traditional religion. Part two presents some evidence of the adverse impact of modernization on the Rungus people, which includes the bulldozing of sacred graves and historical places, a steady decline in the number of people with skills in arts and crafts, and the loss of oral literature, the emergence of nucleated settlement patterns replacing longhouses; land shortages; religious and moral decadence; alcoholism; loss of reverence for elders and of life. In short, the Rungus appear to be facing a breakdown of the cultural structures that bind people and allow them to identify with each other. The author blames much of this decay on the country's education system and emphasizes the need to perceive modernization as involving basic changes in conceptual frameworks rather than simply access to new material goods.

Malaysia/ Indigenous and local communities—Social relations/ Indigenous and local communities—Commoditization.

401. ———. **1987.** "Social Determinants of Rungus and Bulusu' Settlement Patterns." *Borneo Research Bulletin* 19: 161–169.

> The Rungus, a Dusunic speaking group of East Malaysia has fared somewhat better at the hands of the Malaysian government than have the Bulusu' people of East Kalimantan at those of the Indonesian state. In the former case, relatively good social service facilities (medical, schools) have been provided, although the government has caused problems by ignoring customary land ownership and expropriating swidden fields. In East Kalimantan, enforced resettlement under an authoritarian regime has displaced the Bulusu' from lands being claimed by the timber industry and imposed a situation of economic decline. The Rungus have had greater opportunity than the Bulusu' to express views on economic and political developments, and have been thus in a better position both to challenge unfair government policies and to demand better services.

Malaysia/ Sabah/ Indigenous and local communities—State policy/ Resettlement.

402. **Avé, J. B., and V. T. King. 1986.** *People of the Weeping Forest: Tradition and Change in Borneo.* Leiden, The Netherlands: National Museum of Ethnology.

Indonesia/ Malaysia/ Kalimantan/ Sabah/ Sarawak/ Indigenous and local communities/ Ethnography/ Indigenous and local communities—Commoditization.

403. **Baas, P., K. Kalkman, and R. Geesink, eds. 1990.** *The Plant Diversity of Malesia.* Proceedings of the Flora Malesiana Symposium Commemorating Professor Dr. C. G. G. J. van Steenis, Leiden, August, 1989. Dordrecht: Kluwer Academic Publishers.

Malaysia/ Indonesia/ Forest flora/ Biodiversity.

404. **Bahrin, T. S., and Lee Boon Thong. 1988.** *FELDA: 3 Decades of Evolution.* Kuala Lumpur: Federal Land Development Authority.

Malaysia/ Agricultural development/ Agriculture—Plantations/ Agriculture—Smallholder tree and perennial crop farming/ Agriculture—Smallholder cash crop farming/ Land settlement and development/ State policy—Agricultural and rural development/ State policy— Land development.

405. **Bailes, C. 1985.** "Kinabalu—Mountain of Contrasts." *Kew Magazine* 2: 273– 284.

Malaysia/ Sabah/ Forest flora/ Forest fauna/ Forest biology and ecology/ Forest management—Parks and conservation areas.

406. **Baillie, I. C. 1976.** "Further Studies on Drought in Sarawak, East Malaysia." *Journal of Tropical Geography* 43: 20–29.

Malaysia/ Sarawak/ Forest biology and ecology/ Drought.

407.   **Baillie, I. C., and M. I. Ahmed. 1984.** "The Variability of Red Yellow Podzolic Soils Under Mixed Dipterocarp Forest in Sarawak, Malaysia." *Malaysian Journal of Tropical Geography* 9: 1-13.

Malaysia/ Sarawak/ Soils.

408.   **Baring-Gould, S., and C. A. Bampfylde. 1909.** *A History of Sarawak under Its Two White Rajahs, 1839–1909.* London: Henry Sotheran.

Malaysia/ Sarawak/ History—Colonial.

409.   **Barlow, C. 1978.** *The Natural Rubber Industry: Its Development, Technology, and Economy in Malaysia.* Kuala Lumpur: Oxford University Press.

Malaysia/ Agricultural development/ Agriculture—Smallholder tree and perennial crop farming/ Agriculture—Smallholder cash crop farming/ Agriculture—Plantations/ Land settlement and development/ State policy—Land development/ State policy—Agricultural and rural development.

410.   **Barlow, H. S. 1994.** "Malaysia and Carbon Offsets." *Planter* 70 (819): 278–281.

Reports on two carbon offset arrangements involving a) the Innoprise Corporation Sdn Bhd (ICSB) (a subsidiary of the Sabah Foundation) and the Forests Absorbing Carbon-dioxide Emissions (FACE) Foundation, Netherlands (set up by the Dutch Electricity Generating Board), and b) ICSB and the New England Electric Services (NEES) company of Massachusetts, U.S.A. In both cases, the power utilities involved are attempting to offset carbon dioxide emissions produced in the course of their operations by assisting in forest conservation and rehabilitation in Sabah. Project activities include assisting ICSB in reforestation and developing a reduced-impact logging regime.

Malaysia/ Sabah/ Project intervention—Forest management/ Forest management—Forest resource conservation/ Reforestation.

411.   **Beaman, J. H., and R. S. Beaman. 1990.** "Diversity and Distribution Patterns in the Flora of Mount Kinabalu." In *The Plant Diversity of Malesia.* Proceedings of the Flora Malesiana Symposium Commemorating Professor Dr. C.G.G.J. van Steenis, August 1989, Leiden, Netherlands. Ed. P. Baas, K. Kalkman, and R. Gersnick, pp. 147–160. Dordrecht, Netherlands; Boston, Mass.: Kluwer Academic Publishers.

Mount Kinabalu in northern Borneo is among the most biologically diverse areas of the world. The authors describe the range of flora found in the mountain's forested hillsides, noting the often restricted distribution of many of its native plant species. In addition to climatic variability, key factors shaping this diversity include "numerous geologically recent habitats on a diversity of substrates (particularly ultramafic outcrops), regularly recurring El Niño droughts that may drive catastrophic selection, precipitous topography resulting in strong reproductive isolation over short distances, and small population size for many species which may be susceptible to genetic drift." While a manifestation of the mountain's biological richness, the restricted spatial distribution of many plant species make the mountain's flora susceptible to the destructive effects of various environmental threats, including uncontrolled agricultural encroachment on forest lands, mining activities, and government development programs. [Summarized from paper abstract].

Malaysia/ Sabah/ Forest flora/ Forest biology and ecology/ Forest management—Parks and conservation areas.

412. **Beaman, R. S., J. H. Beaman, C. W. Marsh, and P. V. Woods. 1985.** "Drought and Forest Fires in Sabah in 1983." *Journal of the Sabah Society* 8: 10–30.

Malaysia/ Sabah/ Forest biology and ecology/ Drought/ Forest fires.

413. **Beaman, R. S., J. H. Beaman, C. Marsh, and P. V. Woods. 1986.** "Drought and Forest Fire in Sabah in 1983." *Sains Malaysiana* 15 (3): 295–314.

Extreme drought experienced in Sabah and much of the rest of Borneo island during the early 1980s was linked to the El Niño/ Southern Oscillation phenomenon of 1982–1983. With rainfall only 15 percent of normal at the drought's height (1983), expansive, human-caused fires swept through the region, destroying over one million ha of forest lands, 85 percent of which consisted of logged-over forest. The authors describe the fire's huge economic and ecological costs, as well as those caused by the drought itself in form of farm losses, tree mortality, water shortages, increased human disease, and poor atmospheric quality. Better plans for handling drought-and fire-related emergencies are needed, as well as greater attention to developing and maintaining protected areas.

Malaysia/ Sabah/ Drought/ Forest fires.

414. **Beccari, O. n.d.** "Proposals for Studies on Environmental Impact of Logging in Sabah." Photocopy. Kota Kinabalu, Malaysia: UKM, Sabah Campus.

Malaysia/ Sabah/ Timber industry—Logging/ Timber industry—Environmental impacts.

415. **———. n.d.** *Reforestation at Sabah Softwoods, Sdn.* Kota Kinabalu, Sabah: Sabah Foundation.

Malaysia/ Sabah/ Reforestation.

416. **———. 1988.** "Sabah's Future Hinges on Reforestation." *Timber Trade Review* 19 (31): 12–30.

Malaysia/ Sabah/ Forest management—Commercial forestry and silviculture/ Reforestation.

417. **Best, J. R. 1988.** "Change Over Time in a Farming System Based on Shifting Cultivation of Hill Rice in Sarawak, Malaysia." *Agricultural Administration and Extension* 29: 69–83.

In 1973/74 a socio-economic study of three villages in Sarawak, Malaysia predicted that farmers would increasingly turn from subsistence swidden farming to sedentary cash crop production as population density increased in the region. Best reports the results of a re-survey in the early 1980s, which contradicts this prediction. Rather than increasing cash crop production, farm households appear to have expanded the area of swidden fields under food crops (mainly rice), while in at least one village income from off-farm employment (largely migrant remittances) had taken the place of income from cash crops. Contrary to common observations on the declining viability of swidden farming communities with population growth, living standards appeared not to have declined. Fallow periods do show signs of approaching a critical minimum, however, and Best urges government attention to the promotion of appropriate land-saving agricultural technologies. [Summarized from journal abstract].

Malaysia/ Sarawak/ Agriculture—Shifting cultivation/ Population pressure/ Agricultural intensification/ Agriculture—Smallholder cash crop farming/ Indigenous and local communities—Farming practices.

418.   **Bevis, W. W. 1995.** *Borneo Log: The Struggle for Sarawak's Forests.* Seattle: University of Washington Press.

> Bevis presents a narrative account of a year-long investigation into logging, the timber trade, and their impacts on the environment and indigenous peoples of Sarawak. The narrative draws from observations, and interviews conducted during visits to logging sites and the Sarawak interior, from local media coverage of current events, as well from background research on the colonial and natural history of the region. One section of the monograph focuses in particular on the Japanese timber trade, and its role in Sarawak's forest loss, drawing from observations made during investigative visits to corporate headquarters as well as environmental activist non-governmental organizations in Japan. The destructive nature of the timber industry and the urgency of local as well as international struggles against its wanton advance are emphasized.

> Malaysia/ Sarawak/ Timber industry—Logging/ Timber industry—Development and structure/ Timber industry—Trade and markets/ Timber industry—Impacts on local communities and economy/ Timber industry—Environmental impacts/ Social movements/ Nongovernmental organizations/ Politics/ Political economy.

419.   **Bhargava, S. K., and D. Chai. 1988.** "Development of Forest Sector Planning: An Appraisal of Forest Management in Sabah." Photocopy. Sandakan, Sabah, Malaysia: Sabah Forest Department.

> This consultancy report, jointly commissioned by FAO/UNDP and the Sabah State Forest Department, provides alternative policy suggestions on the use of forest land, reforestation and development of forest industries in Sabah, consistent with the 'sustainable yield' production objectives of the government. The authors find that in spite of the good intentions expressed in Sabah's declared forest policy, the forest resource is clearly not being managed in conformity with the basic principle of sustained yield. Politicians and bureaucrats do not appear to recognize or be sufficiently concerned about the seriousness of the situation and its inevitable consequences in relation to the State's economy. Based on its findings, the report proposes a number of recommendations, including: 1) a reduction in the log export quota by 1 million meters annually for 3 years to 3 million meters by 1990; 2) clearer specification of sound logging practices and implementation of effective controls on logging activities to reduce damage and avoid timber wastage in the forest; and 3) preparation of an action plan for bringing commercial forest resources under sustained yield management as rapidly as possible.

> Malaysia/ State policy—Forest and natural resources/ Timber industry—State policy and regulation/ Forest management—Commercial forestry and silviculture.

420.   **Billington, D. R. 1979.** "Soil Erosion and Logging: A Review Paper." Photocopy. Sandakan, Sabah, Malaysia: Sabah Forest Department.

> Malaysia/ Timber industry—Logging/ Timber industry—Environmental impacts/ Soil erosion and degradation.

421.   **Blicher-Mathiesen, U. 1994.** "Borneo Illipe, a Fat Product from Different *Shorea* spp. (*Dipterocarpaceae*)." *Economic Botany* 48 (3): 231–242.

> Fat extracted from the "illipe" nut—kernels of *Shorea* spp.—in the forests of Borneo and Sumatra have an important use in the fabrication of chocolate, particularly in face of rapid rise in cocoa butter prices in recent decades. During two field visits to East Sarawak (2–3 months each) in 1989 and 1991, Blicher-Mathiesen identified different, locally available *Shorea* species and collected fruit samples in order to compare fat quality. Distribution maps of naturally occurring tree populations for five different species are presented with the aim of assessing the potential to meet future demand sustainably.

Indonesia/ Malaysia/ Borneo/ Sumatra/ Forest flora/ Non-timber forest products.

422. **Bossel, H., and H. Krieger. 1994.** "Simulation of Multi-species Tropical Forest Dynamics Using a Vertically and Horizontally Structured Model." *Forest Ecology and Management* 69 (1–3): 123–144.

Malaysia/ Sabah/ Forest biology and ecology/ Forest regeneration/ Vegetation analysis.

423. **Broek, J. O. M. 1962.** "Place Names in the 16th and 17th Century Borneo." *Imago Mundi* 16.

Malaysia/ Indonesia/ Borneo/ History—Pre-colonial.

424. **Brookfield, H. 1994.** "The End of the 'Resource Frontier.'" In *Transformation with Industrialization in Peninsular Malaysia*. Ed. Harold Brookfield, with the assistance of Loene Doube, and Barbara Banks, pp. 82–94. Kuala Lumpur: Oxford University Press.

Malaysia/ Peninsular Malaysia/ Deforestation/ Timber industry—Development and structure/ Regional development.

425. **Brookfield, H., and Y. Byron. 1990.** "Deforestation and Timber Extraction in Borneo and the Malay Peninsula." *Global Environmental Change* 1 (1): 42–56.

The article begins with a review of general concerns regarding the timber industry, shifting cultivation, and land development for permanent settlement in Borneo and peninsular Malaysia. Due to the continuing lack of a standardized basis for imagery evaluation, remote sensing data remains unreliable as a means to gauge the range and rate of deforestation. The authors propose the use of timber export data as a proxy measurement for estimated forest cover loss in Borneo and Peninsular Malaysia. Timber export data from peninsular Malaysia and the different Malaysian and Indonesian political units of Borneo island (i.e., Sabah, Sarawak, West Kalimantan, Central Kalimantan, South Kalimantan, and East Kalimantan) are presented and analyzed, covering a 13 year period (1965 to 1987). In the mid-1980s, a decline in the export of sawlogs from Indonesia was compensated by a sharp increase in the export of plywood, indicating the continued rapid extraction of timber from ever more remote parts of Borneo island. The authors argue that the timber processing industry in Indonesia and more recently in Malaysia is expanding beyond sustainable limits. At present rates of extraction, the forests of Borneo are likely to be limited to the most in-accessible parts of the island. In short, a convergence between the present landscape of peninsular Malaysia and the future of Borneo is to be expected.

Malaysia/ Sabah/ Sarawak/ Indonesia/ Kalimantan/ Peninsular Malaysia/ Deforestation/ Timber industry—Logging/ Timber industry—Downstream processing/ Timber industry—Trade and markets.

426. **Brookfield, H., L. Potter, and Y. Byron. 1995.** *In Place of the Forest: Environmental and Socio-economic Transformation in Borneo and the Eastern Malay Peninsula*. Tokyo: United Nations University Press.

The authors present findings and analysis from a research project undertaken as part of the Clark University/United Nations University Project on Critical Environmental Situations and Regions. The monograph's focus is on Borneo as a resource frontier, while also incorporating an examination of the development of eastern peninsular Malaysia for purposes of comparison. The Borneo/Peninsular Malaysia study's aim has been to identify elements which indicate trends toward impoverished, endangered, or critical states of development. States of impoverishment, endangerment, and criticality are distinguished by the degree of environmental degradation. While impoverishment signifies a state in which environmental degradation has narrowed the range of possibilities for resource use, at the level of endangerment current trends bear negative implications for the continuation of extant resource use systems; at the state of criticality the preclusion of extant human use systems has become an immediate threat rather than simply an eventual possibility.

Part One of the monograph reviews the background of environmental and land management issues in Borneo and the peninsula as well as a history of land transformation in the pre-modern, colonial, and post-World War II periods. Noting the extensive conversion of forest to agriculture and forest degradation due to timber extraction as key developments in the recent geographic history of the both Borneo and Peninsular Malaysia, in Part Two the authors examine in greater detail trends whereby "endangerment" appears to be leading to "criticality." Seven specific foci provide the organizing framework for this theme: loss of biodiversity, deforestation and its relation to life-supporting functions of the environment, impacts of environmental change on forest people, deforestation and the global climate, problems of drought and fire with rapid forest land decline, the spread of weed-infested grasslands, and urban development. The monograph concludes with a review of main conclusions regarding the unsustainable nature of the current development trajectory in many parts of the region and the need to change attitudes and priorities of decision-making elites and government officials.

Indonesia/ Malaysia/ Sarawak/ Sabah/ Kalimantan/ Borneo/ Land use—Patterns and planning/ Deforestation/ Biodiversity/ Soil erosion and degradation/ Timber industry—Logging/ Timber industry—Environmental impacts/ Timber industry—Impacts on local communities and economy/ Forest management/ Land settlement and development/ Economic development/ Agriculture—Plantations/ Agriculture—Shifting cultivation's environmental impacts/ History—Colonial/ Indigenous and local communities—Forest products use and trade/ Indigenous and local communities—Commoditization/ Indigenous and local communities—Forest land use and management practices/ Indigenous and local communities—Land and resource tenure systems/ State policy—Forest and natural resources/ Indigenous and local communities—State policy/ State policy—Land development/ Land tenure—Legislation and state policy/ Drought/ Forest fires/ Grasslands.

427. **Brooks, S. M., K. S. Richards, and R. Nussbaum. 1994.** "Simulator Experiments of the Varied Consequences of Rain Forest Logging for Runoff and Erosion." *Geografiska Annaler. Series A, Physical Geography* 76 (3): 143–152.

Malaysia/ Sabah/ Soil erosion and degradation/ Hydrology/ Timber industry—Environmental impacts.

428. **Brooks, S. M., and T. Spencer. 1995.** "Vegetation Modification of Rainfall Characteristics: Implications for Rainfall Erosivity Following Logging in Sabah, Malaysia." *Journal of Tropical Forest Science* 7 (3): 435–446.

Malaysia/ Sabah/ Soil erosion and degradation/ Timber industry—Environmental impacts/ Forest regeneration.

429. **Brosius, J. P. 1986.** "River, Forest, and Mountain: The Penan Gang Landscape." *Sarawak Museum Journal* n.s., 36 (57): 172–184.

Malaysia/ Indigenous and local communities—Forest products use and trade/ Indigenous and local communities—Forest land use and management practices.

430. ———. **1992.** "The Axiological Presence of Death: Penan Gang Death-Names." Ph.D. diss., University of Michigan, Ann Arbor, Mich.

Malaysia/ Sarawak/ Indigenous and local communities—Religion and cosmology/ Indigenous and local communities—Social relations.

431.   ————. **1992.** "Perspectives on Penan Development in Sarawak." *Sarawak Gazette* 119 (1579): 5–21.

The paper was first presented at the Workshop on Penan Development sponsored by the Angkatan Zaman Mansang (AZAM), 20-21 January 1991, in Marudi, Sarawak. The author provides a brief ethnographic description of the Penan, a hunter-gathering people indigenous to Borneo, noting the distinctions which exist between Eastern and Western Penan. This section is followed by a discussion of the Penan's point of view on development, including the paternalistic relationship the Penan identify between themselves and the state government. Also noted is the Penan's overriding concern about logging as a central threat to their long-term survival. Brosius recommends that special attention be given to a number of issues that will shape processes of socio-economic change among the Penan. These include the wide degree of variation in the extent to which different Penan groups are involved in agriculture (i.e., sago cultivation) and the cash economy (i.e., through trade of forest products); the greater suitability of establishing service centers within the Penan's traditional settlement area rather than outright resettlement as a means to bring the benefits of development closer to the Penan people; the need to conserve the Penan's forest resource base in order to ensure their successful integration into the cash economy; and, finally, the need to ensure the Penan's participation as active agents in rather than passive recipients of development policy making.

Malaysia/ Sarawak/ Indigenous and local communities—Forest products use and trade/ Indigenous and local communities—Farming practices/ Indigenous and local communities—Commoditization/ Timber industry—Impacts on local communities and economy/ Indigenous and local communities—State policy.

432.   ————. **1995.** "Bornean Forest Trade in Historical and Regional Perspective: The Case of Penan Hunter-Gatherers of Sarawak." In *Society and Non-Timber Forest Products in Tropical Asia.* Ed. J. Fox, pp. 13–26. East-West Center Occasional Papers, Environment series, no. 19. Honolulu: East-West Center.

Focusing on the collection and trade of forest products by Penan hunter-gatherers in Sarawak, Brosius highlights the changes in these activities across time and space. A historical view of Penan trading practices is provided by a review of the rich oral historical tradition of the Penan, which contain detailed descriptions of forest product trade. While camphor, ironwood shingles, and rhinoceros horn, damar (resin produced from *Agathis borneensis*, and *jelutong* (a hard latex derived from trees of the genus *Dyera*) figured prominently among goods traded by the Penan in the past, more currently Penan have been increasingly engaged in producing and trading fine woven rattan mats and baskets. Trade in *kayu gaharu* or aromatic wood from the genus *Aquilaria* still occurs, though less than in previous decades. Patterns of trading relations appear to be changing as well, with Penan now frequently trading directly with downriver traders than their traditional longhouse-based Dayak partners. Changes in trade over time may be linked to changing market values for different products, resource depletion, and the acquisition of new skills. Considerable variation also obtains between Penan in different parts of Borneo island today, and may be linked to resource variability, differing local population densities of foragers, and different local traditions in skill development.

Malaysia/ Sarawak/ Indigenous and local communities—Forest products use and trade/ History—Colonial.

433. **Brown, N. 1993.** "The Implications of Climate and Gap Microclimate for Seedling Growth Conditions in a Bornean Lowland Rain Forest." *Journal of Tropical Ecology* 9 (2): 153–168.

A study of microclimates of closed canopy forest and ten differently-sized canopy gaps in a lowland dipterocarp forest of Sabah reveals the complex nature of the relationship between microclimate and gap size. Gaps of different size were found to vary considerably in microclimate across time and space. Similarly-sized gaps may have different microclimates and favor the growth of different tree species. Study results highlight the role of randomness in the location and timing of gap creation and its importance for processes of forest regeneration.

Malaysia/ Sabah/ Forest biology and ecology/ Forest regeneration/ Vegetation analysis.

434. **Brown, N., and M. Press. 1992.** "Logging Rainforests the Natural Way?" *New Scientist* March 14: 25–29.

Preliminary results are given for a long-term study undertaken by a team of researchers from Britain and Southeast Asia on the impact of natural disturbances to the rainforest canopy on rainforest ecology. The Danum Valley, Sabah study examined the dynamics of vegetative regeneration on the forest floor once small gaps in the forest canopy are created by falling trees. Broadly stated, study results show that seedlings of different tree species are favored by both different sizes in the canopy gap created and different frequencies with which the forest canopy is disturbed. These results carry some important implications for sustainable logging practices. To preserve the biological diversity of a rainforest, seedlings of different tree species must have relatively equal chances of survival. To ensure this, logging and other human activity in the forest must be conducted in such a way that recreates the high variability in patterns of natural forest disturbance. As conducted today, however, modern logging practice typically tends to create only one kind of invasive canopy disturbance, thus creating conditions that favor the regeneration only of a few pioneer species. Logging activities must be modified to become geared more towards "varying not only the size of the gaps they make, but also how often they disturb different parts of the forest." It appears that "the success of the healing" from logging activity depends both on reducing the "size of the gaps" made in forest canopies, as well as on varying "the frequency with which the [logging] wounds are inflicted."

Malaysia/ Sabah/ Forest biology and ecology/ Forest regeneration/ Forest management— Commercial forestry and silviculture/ Biodiversity.

435. **Bruenig, E. F. 1991.** "Pattern and Structure Along Gradients in Natural Forests in Borneo and in Amazonia: Their Significance for the Interpretation of Stand Dynamics and Functioning." In *Rain Forest Regeneration and Management.* Ed. A. Gómez-Pompa, T. C. Whitmore, and M. Hadley, pp. 235–244. Paris: UNESCO; Parthenon Publishing Group.

Soil types, soil structure, climatic conditions, forest physiognomic features, and tree species distribution patterns are compared for two areas of tropical rain forests in San Carlos de Rio Negro in Venezuela and Sabal Forest Reserve in Sarawak, Malaysia. Significant differences in soil types and tree species distribution patterns are noted, suggesting important variation in forest dynamics and regeneration. The implications for research and management are discussed. Further comparative work in Sabal (Sarawak), Danum (Sabah), Bawang Ling/Hainan (China), and San Carlos de Rio Negro (Venezuela) is planned to examine links between pattern and dynamics, and the suitability of the former for indicating regeneration mechanisms and phasic developments [Summarized from chapter abstract].

Malaysia/ Sarawak/ Soils/ Vegetation analysis/ Forest biology and ecology/ Forest regeneration/ Biodiversity.

436.   ———. **1996.** *Conservation and the Management of Tropical Rainforests: An Integrated Approach to Sustainability.* Wallingford, Oxfordshire, U.K.: CAB International.

Bruenig synthesizes a wide body of literature on rain forest ecology and discusses issues in holistic, integrated resource conservation and management. Particular attention is paid to the interaction between natural and socio-cultural systems. Examples are drawn from Sarawak, where Bruenig has conducted much fieldwork, as well as Amazonia. Details are provided on the history of forestry in Sarawak as well as promising recent developments in community-oriented, "naturalistic" rainforest management approaches pioneered in the area.

Malaysia/ Sarawak/ Forest management—Forest resource conservation/ Forest management—Commercial forestry and silviculture/ Timber industry—Logging/ Timber industry—Environmental impacts/ Project intervention—Social and community forestry.

437.   **Bruenig, E. F., and Huang Y.-W. 1989.** "Patterns of Tree Species Diversity and Canopy Structure and Dynamics in Human Tropical Evergreen Forests on Borneo and in China." In *Tropical Forests: Botanical Dynamics, Speciation and Diversity.* Ed. L. B. Holm-Nielsen, I. C. Nielsen, and H. Balslev, pp. 76–88. London: Academic Press.

Malaysia/ Sarawak/ Forest biology and ecology/ Vegetation analysis/ Biodiversity.

438.   **Bruijnzeel, L. A., M. J. Waterloo, J. Proctor, A. T. Kuiters, and B. Kotterink. 1993.** "Hydrological Observations in Montane Rain Forests on Gunung Silam, Sabah, Malaysia, with Special Reference to the 'Massenerhebung' Effect." *Journal of Ecology* 81 (1): 145–167.

Malaysia/ Sabah/ Forest biology and ecology/ Hydrology/ Soils.

439.   **Burgers, P. P. M. 1993.** "Rainforest and Rural Economy." *Sarawak Museum Journal* 44 (65 (n.s.)).

In Malaysia generally and in Sarawak state particularly, national and state-level development policies aim at sometimes contradictory goals of effective forest land management, state revenue maximization, promotion of growth in the agricultural sector, and protection of native peoples. In implementing national agricultural policy, the Sarawak government has as one of its main goals "to replace 'traditional' systems of hill rice production by more efficient, productive and market-oriented production methods," although this approach neglects the ecological functionality of fallow-based farming on tropical soils. Results of a survey-based study of Bidayuh communities in Teng Bukap Subdistrict of Kuching Division are described to illuminate key aspects of the local rural economy and appropriate approaches to agricultural development. Shifting cultivation of hill rice is the main agricultural practice of the region; cash crops, primarily pepper and cocoa, are also cultivated, with rubber cultivation of declining importance in the local economy. A wide range of forest products are collected, including ferns, palm products, fungi, fruits, bamboo, game, fish, honey, insects, and materials suitable for housing construction. While most of these are used primarily for home consumption, some (i.e., rattan and hardwoods) have been a source of cash income for a long time, and others, such as butterflies and birds provide opportunity for new income streams. Changing patterns of forest product sales, production structure, collection, and management are described, and the impacts of government administrative policies, land development, and invasive logging on local access to forest products are noted. Noting a conflict between growing dependence on cash income and local farmers'

declining access to commercially valuable forest products, Burgers recommends development of appropriate agroforestry systems to increase supplies on a sustainable basis.

Malaysia/ Sarawak/ Indigenous and local communities—Economy/ Indigenous and local
communities—Forest products use and trade/ Indigenous and local communities—
Commoditization/ State policy—Agricultural and rural development.

440.   **Burghouts, T. B. A., E. J. F. Campbell, and P. J. Kolderman. 1994.** "Effects of
Tree Species Heterogeneity on Leaf Fall in Primary and Logged Dipterocarp
Forest in the Ulu Segama Forest Reserve, Sabah, Malaysia." *Journal of
Tropical Ecology* 10 (1).

Malaysia/ Sabah/ Forest regeneration/ Forest biology and ecology/ Timber industry—
Environmental impacts/ Vegetation analysis.

441.   **Burrough, J. B., and A. Jamin. 1972.** "Traditional Methods of Susun Rice
Cultivation." *Journal of the Sabah Society* 5 (4): n.g.

The authors describe different hillpadi and wetpadi cultivation systems in Sabah and the
cultural traditions associated with them. Particular attention is placed on the role of
'bambarayon' or the rice spirit as the medium through which the people can seek interces-
sion from the gods to secure an abundant harvest. The authors also compare the amount of
physical labor required and unit area yield for hillpadi and wetpadi cultivation respectively.

Malaysia/ Agriculture—Shifting cultivation/ Indigenous and local communities—Farming
practices/ Indigenous and local communities—Religion and cosmology.

442.   **Caldecott, J. O. 1988.** *Hunting and Wildlife Management in Sarawak*. Gland,
Switzerland: International Union for the Conservation of Nature (IUCN).

Malaysia/ Sarawak/ Forest fauna/ Indigenous and local communities/ Wildlife management.

443.   **Campbell, E. J. F., and D. M. Newbery. 1993.** "Ecological Relationships between Lianas and Trees in Lowland Rain forest in Sabah, East Malaysia."
Journal of Tropical Ecology 9 (4): 469-490.

Malaysia/ Sabah/ Forest biology and ecology/ Forest flora.

444.   **Cense, A. A., and E. M. Uhlenbeck. 1958.** *Critical Survey of Studies on the
Languages of Borneo*. Bibliographical Series, no. 2. The Hague: Koninklijk
Inst. voor Taal-, Land-en Volkenkunde.

Indonesia/ Malaysia/ Borneo/ Indigenous and local communities/ Bibliography.

445.   **Chai, D. 1979.** "Reforestation of Logged Areas." Paper presented at the Seminar
on Fertility and Management of Deforested Land, 1979, in Kota Kinabalu.
Photocopy.

Malaysia/ Sabah/ Reforestation.

446.   **Chai, D., and M. P. Urdabe. 1977.** "The Effectiveness of Current Silviculture
Practice in Sabah." *Malaysian Forester* 40: 27–35.

Malaysia/ Sabah/ Forest management—Commercial forestry and silviculture.

447. **Chandler, G. 1991.** "Confronting Change: Interaction between the Timber Industry and Villagers in the Interior of Sabah." In *Images of Malaysia.* Ed. M. I. Said and J. Saravanamuttu, pp. 37–57. Kuala Lumpur, Malaysia: Persatuan Sains Sosial Malaysia.

The author examines the employment opportunities, market opportunities for agricultural produce, infrastructural development (roads, etc.) as well as environmental changes brought to rural villagers in two districts of Sabah's interior during the mid-1980s. Fieldwork for the paper was conducted in 1985–86, and involved interviews with Forestry Department officials, staff from other government departments, timber company workers and administrative staff, as well as local villagers. The author notes that although timber companies offer many job opportunities, few members of the indigenous communities were attracted to long-term employment in the industry, given the labor demands of swidden farming and regular obligations to participate in time-consuming ritual celebrations, weddings, etc. Concludes the author, the cultural values held by local villagers are different from those necessary for full-time off-farm labor. Contracted buyers supply local canteens and timber camp workers with fresh produce and meats largely imported from outside the area, thus restricting demand for locally grown goods. Moreover, indigenous farmers in the area rarely produce enough surplus crops to provide regular supplies of food to the timber camp. The greatest impact of logging activities on local villagers results from the environmental consequences of road construction (i.e., water pollution from serious soil erosion and oil spills), the loss of wildlife and wild forest plants due to disturbances caused by logging, and degradation of the primary forest area's potential as swidden land. These impacts create considerable antagonism between local villagers and the timber companies. Road construction does bring the benefit of easier access to larger population and market centers, but this was usually true only for the most well-located villages. The author's findings raise questions regarding the equitability in the current distribution of costs and benefits of economic development derived from the timber industry.

Malaysia/ Sabah/ Timber industry—Logging/ Timber industry—Impacts on local communities and economy.

448. **Chandler, G. N. 1989.** *Access to Education in the Interior of Sabah.* Clayton, Vic., Australia: Centre of Southeast Asian Studies, Monash University.

Malaysia/ Sabah/ Indigenous and local communities—State policy/ Rural development.

449. ———. **1989.** *Agricultural Development in Sabah.* Clayton, Vic., Australia: Development Studies Centre Publications.

Malaysia/ Sabah/ State policy—Agricultural and rural development/ Agricultural development/ Rural development/ Regional development.

450. ———. **1989.** "Isolation and Access to the Interior of Sabah." Ph.D. diss., Monash University, Melbourne, Australia.

Murut and Dusun shifting cultivators of Keningau and Nabawan/ Pensiangan districts in the interior of Sabah need road access to gain any real benefits from development initiatives such as new health care services, education and commercial opportunities. The government is encouraging shifting cultivators to move to more accessible areas where they can be provided with government facilities at a relatively low cost. The need for a more participatory development planning process in the area is emphasized. Agriculture development projects in the form of resettlement, settlement and in-situ development projects aimed at replacing shifting cultivation with cash crop production remain generally top-down in nature and do not take sufficient account of the needs of the Murut and Dusun people they serve. Argues the author, "until there is more consultation in all stages in the development of these projects, and a greater willingness to accept the priorities of the shifting cultivators, the expectations of the government will continue not to be met."

Malaysia/ Indigenous and local communities—State policy/ Resettlement/ Rural development/ State policy—Agricultural and rural development/ Project intervention—Agricultural development/ Forest management—Control of shifting cultivation.

451.   **Chatfield, G. A. 1969.** "The People of Sabah: Planning and Preparation of an Ethnographic Map." *Journal of Sabah Society* n.s., 5 (1).

Describing the geographical and demographic make-up of Sabah, this article identifies the main ethnic groups in Sabah, distinguishing between indigenous (native) and immigrant residents of the province. Over several decades, the Muruts, who depend on the forest for much of their subsistence needs, have been steadily pushed into the hinterlands of the province's hilly interior, while the Kadazans clear lowland forests for wet padi cultivation.

Malaysia/ Indigenous and local communities/ Ethnography/ Indigenous and local communities—Forest land use and management practices/ Ethnicity and ethnic relations.

452.   **Cheng, T. u. 1969.** *Archaeology in Sarawak*. Cambridge, U.K.: W. Heffer Sons.

Malaysia/ Sarawak/ History—Pre-colonial.

453.   **Chey, V. K. 1989.** *A Survey of Termites in Sabah Forests*. Sandakan, Sabah: Sabah Forest Department.

Malaysia/ Sabah/ Forest fauna/ Forest management—Commercial forestry and silviculture/ Pest, weed, and crop disease management.

454.   **Chin, S. C. 1982.** "The Significance of Rubber as Cash Crop in Kenyah Swidden Village in Sarawak." *Federation Museum Journal* 27: 23–37.

Malaysia/ Sarawak/ Indigenous and local communities—Farming practices/ Agriculture—Shifting cultivation/ Agriculture—Smallholder cash crop farming/ Agriculture—Smallholder tree and perennial crop farming/ Indigenous and local communities—Commoditization.

455.   ———. **1984.** "Agriculture and Subsistence in a Lowland Rainforest Kenya Community." Ph.D. diss., Yale University, New Haven, Conn.

Malaysia/ Sarawak/ Indigenous and local communities—Forest land use and management practices/ Indigenous and local communities—Farming practices/ Household livelihood strategies/ Agriculture—Shifting cultivation.

456.   ———. **1985.** "Agriculture and Resource Utilization in a Lowland Rainforest Kenyah Community." *Sarawak Museum Journal* 35 (56): 1–322.

Resource use strategies of a Sarawak Kenyah community are described in detail. The author notes the stability and compatibility of Kenyah livelihood patterns with the complex rainforest ecosystem. Pressures toward change are being exerted by population growth and a growing integration with the cash economy, bringing new opportunities, needs, and expectations. Though the potential for disequilibrium exists, the author is optimistic about the ability of the Kenyah to effectively manage these pressures while also retaining many aspects of their traditional material culture as well as value system.

Malaysia/ Sarawak/ Indigenous and local communities—Forest products use and trade/ Indigenous and local communities—Farming practices/ Indigenous and local communities—Forest land use and management practices/ Indigenous and local communities—Commoditization/ Agriculture—Shifting cultivation/ Population pressure/ Agricultural intensification.

457.   ———. **1989.** "Managing Malaysia's Forests for Sustained Production." *Wallaceana* 55–56: 1–11.

The author assesses the extent and quality of Malaysian forests and timber resources, noting their contribution to government revenues and rural community livelihoods. Different management systems used at different times and in different areas of Malaysia this century are described, including: 1) a regeneration system practiced in the 1920s and 1930s which incorporated the use of seed cuttings; (2) the Malayan Uniform System (MUS), relying on natural regeneration and a 70-year felling cycle; and (3) the Selective Management System (SMS) in use in peninsular Malaysia for the past two decades, limiting felling to a minimum diameter for different tree species as well as a maximum number of trees to be extracted per hectare. The failure for real cutting practices to match ideal guidelines, and resulting forest damage and soil erosion are noted. Argues Chin, felling rates must be reduced in order to sustain primary forests as a timber source past the next 8 years. Recommendations concerning alternative silvicultural systems and plantation development measures are noted.

Malaysia/ Sabah/ Timber industry—Logging/ Forest management—Commercial forestry and silviculture/ State policy—Forest and natural resources/ Timber industry—State policy and regulation.

458.   ———. **1992.** "Shifting Cultivation and Logging in Sarawak." In *Logging Against the Natives of Sarawak*. Ed. Institute of Social Analysis (INSAN), pp. 57–62. Kuala Lumpur, Malaysia: INSAN.

The author addresses several concerns raised about the impact of shifting cultivation on Sarawak's forest lands. In contrast to conventional stereotype of the destructiveness of shifting cultivation, the low level of tillage associated with this farming system among Sarawak's indigenous communities helps prevent erosion on newly cleared fields. Studies completed by the author suggest that each of the state's c. 36,000 swidden farming households clears only 5 acres of land for agriculture each year for a total of 180,000 across the entire state. Only c. 5 percent of this (9,000 acres) is cut from primary forests, far less than the 150,000 acres of primary forest cover loss often attributed to swidden farmers by government officials. Standing forest continues to be a critical component of the life-support system for many of the state's indigenous forest-farming communities, who derive as much as 47–64 percent of their diet as well as much of their cash income from collected forest products. As such, these communities have a great stake in preserving the forest but are seriously threatened by invasive logging which had already affected 670,000 acres in Sarawak by 1987. Given these statistics, the author stresses that shifting cultivation poses no threat to Sarawak's forests, while better control over the state's timber industry is urgently needed.

Malaysia/ Sarawak/ Agriculture—Shifting cultivation's environmental impacts/ Indigenous and local communities—Forest land use and management practices/ Indigenous and local communities—Forest products use and trade/ Timber industry—Logging/ Timber industry—Impacts on local communities and economy.

459.   **Cho, G. 1990.** The Malaysian Economy: Spatial Perspectives. London: Routledge.

Malaysia/ Geography/ Economic development/ Regional development/ State policy—Economic development/ State policy—Agricultural and rural development.

460. **Christensen, H., and O. Mertz. 1993.** "The Risk Avoidance Strategy of Traditional Shifting Cultivation in Borneo." *The Sarawak Museum Journal* 44 (65 (n.s.)).

   Christensen and Mertz document the swidden-based farming practices of two Bukit and Taboyan communities in Sarawak. They find that the households studied manage four different farming environments simultaneously: home gardens, farm gardens, swiddens, and fallow areas. Particularly noted is the rich diversity of cultigens cultivated by Bukit and Taboyan farmers. Ninety-two different cultigens are identified, many of which are found in several varieties, and some of which are harvested from old swidden fields several years after being left to fallow. The risk-management function of this crop diversity is emphasized, along with its contribution to ecological and economic sustainability of indigenous farming systems. Two tables list the names—both scientific and native—as well as location of the cultigens identified.

   Malaysia/ Sarawak/ Indigenous and local communities—Farming practices/ Indigenous and local communities—Forest land use and management practices/ Indigenous and local communities—Forest products use and trade.

461. **Chung, A. Y. C. 1995.** *Common Lowland Rainforest Ants of Sabah.* Borneo Nature Series, no. 1. Sandakan, Malaysia: Sabah Forest Department.

   Malaysia/ Sabah/ Forest fauna/ Forest biology and ecology.

462. **Chung, C. S. 1990.** "The System Must Change: The Promotion of Sustainable Forest Management in Sarawak." *Wallaceana* 61: 1–8.

   Chung critically reviews a report by the International Tropical Timber Council ("The Promotion of Sustainable Forest Management: A Case Study in Sarawak, Malaysia") prepared for the ITTO conference in Bali, Indonesia 1990. Based on ITTO's own conclusion, present timber harvesting practices in Sarawak are unsustainable. However, the author observes, the ITTO report goes on to recommend harvest levels that will only continue to undermine the state's forest resource base. More genuinely conservative management strategies are urgently needed.

   Malaysia/ Sarawak/ Timber industry—Logging/ Deforestation/ Forest management—Commercial forestry and silviculture/ Forest management—Forest resource conservation.

463. **Cleary, M. C., and F. J. Lian. 1991.** "On the Geography of Borneo." *Progress in Human Geography* 15 (2): 163–175.

   Malaysia/ Indonesia/ Borneo/ Geography.

464. **Cleary, M. C., and P. Eaton. 1992.** *Borneo: Change and Development.* Singapore; Oxford, U.K.: Oxford University Press.

   The authors provide a general overview of the geography, indigenous settlement, colonial history, demography, and recent socio-economic development history of Borneo island, including the East Malaysian states of Sabah and Sarawak, the Indonesian Kalimantan provinces, and Brunei. One chapter focuses briefly on the subsistence strategies associated with the swidden-based farming systems of the island's indigenous farmers, noting also the recent growth of a commercial agricultural sector. Separate chapters are devoted to current issues in natural resources management and conflicts between logging and customary land rights. The monograph provides a current, comprehensively researched introduction to a variety of aspects related to Borneo's socio-economic development, providing opportunity for some preliminary comparison between different countries and provinces.

Indonesia/ Kalimantan/ Malaysia/ Sabah/ Sarawak/ Geography/ History—Colonial/ Demography/ Agricultural development/ Economic development/ Indigenous and local communities—Farming practices/ Agriculture—Shifting cultivation/ Agriculture—Permanent/ Agriculture—Plantations/ Agriculture—Smallholder cash crop farming/ Agriculture—Smallholder tree and perennial crop farming/ Timber industry—Development and structure/ Timber industry—Impacts on local communities and economy/ Forest management—Commercial forestry and silviculture/ Forest management—Forest resource conservation.

465. **Cobb, D. D. 1988.** "Iban Shifting Cultivation: A Bioregional Perspective." Ph.D. diss., Arizona State University, Tempe, Ariz.

This dissertation takes a somewhat unconventional form as an advocacy statement on behalf of the indigenous system of shifting cultivation practiced by the Iban of Sarawak. It examines their traditional system of farming from a bioregionalist perspective and presents information which indicates that well-managed shifting cultivation is an appropriate agricultural technology for much of Sarawak's interior. An analysis of development trends in Malaysia, from the micro to the macro levels, synthesizes information concerning the possible benefits as well as the social and environmental costs of such development to Iban shifting cultivators. The author's research involved 1) soil sampling to establish the appropriateness of swidden agriculture for the local environment; 2) a detailed study of a longhouse community in Sarawak to examine the way resident needs are met through indigenous livelihood strategies; and 3) bioregional analysis to assess shifting cultivation as a component of a local cultural ecology. [Summarized from author's abstract].

Malaysia/ Sarawak/ Indigenous and local communities—Farming practices/Indigenous and local communities—Economy/ Indigenous and local communities—Forest land use and management practices/ Indigenous and local communities—Forest products use and trade/ Indigenous and local communities—Social relations/ Agriculture—Shifting cultivation/ Soils/ Cultural ecology.

466. **Cockburn, P. F. 1976.** *Trees of Sabah*. Sabah Forest Record, no. 10. Kuching, Sarawak, Borneo: Borneo Literature for Forest Dept. Sabah.

Malaysia/ Sabah/ Forest flora.

467. **Colchester, M. 1992.** *Pirates, Squatters and Poachers: The Political Ecology of Dispossession of the Native Peoples of Sarawak*. London; Selangor, Malaysia: Survival International; Institute for Social Analysis (INSAN).

The author describes the loss of effective control over Sarawak's land and forest resources by the state's indigenous communities. Challenging conventional notions of the wastefulness of indigenous land use practices, the author traces the roots of the land crisis presently faced by local communities to colonial land administration policy and British military repression of native resistance. Post-colonial development policies have further weakened indigenous land claims and caused serious degradation of the natural environment. The position of most indigenous farmers as "squatters" on state-controlled land is thus presented as an outcome of systematic state policy that has undermined local livelihood systems. Nevertheless, the recent expansion of grassroots activism towards reclaiming land ownership provides some cause for hope. Future improvements in local communities' position vis-a-vis modernization will be possible only through further strengthening of grassroots networking.

Malaysia/ Sarawak/ Timber industry—Impacts on local communities and economy/ Land tenure—Legislation and state policy/ State policy—Land development/ History—Colonial/ Social movements/ Political economy.

468.   **Collenette, P. 1963.** "A Physiographic Classification for North Borneo." *Journal of the Sabah Society* 1 (4): 9–15.

   The author proposes the physiographical classification of Sabah into four regions, namely 1) the Western Lowlands; 2) the Western Cordillera; 3) the Central Uplands; and 4) the Eastern Lowlands. Each region is divided into several sub-regions, and the main features of each subregion are briefly described.

   Malaysia/ Sabah/ Geography.

469.   **Conway, G. R., and E. B. Tay. n.d.** "Crop Pests in Sabah, Malaysia and Their Control." Photocopy. Kota Kinabalu, Sabah, Malaysia: Department of Agriculture.

   Malaysia/ Sabah/ Pest, weed, and crop disease management.

470.   **Corner, E. J. H. 1988.** *Wayside Trees of Malaya.* Kuala Lumpur, Malaysia: Malayan Nature Society.

   The author describes trees found in secondary forest, farm field, way-side and other non-forest areas across the Malaysian peninsula and archipelago. A 2-volume work.

   Malaysia/ Forest flora.

471.   **Cotter, Conrad Patrick, with S. Saito. 1965.** *Bibliography of English Language Sources on Human Ecology, Eastern Malaysia and Brunei.* Honolulu, Hawaii: Asian Studies Department, University of Hawaii.

   Malaysia/ Sabah/ Sarawak/ Bibliography/ Cultural ecology.

472.   **Courtenay, P. P. 1977.** "The Role of the Plantation in Economic Development." Paper presented at the Conference on South East Asian Studies, 22–26 November 1977, at the University of Malaya, Kota Kinabalu. Photocopy.

   Malaysia/ Agriculture—Plantations/ State policy—Agricultural and rural development.

473.   **Cramb, R. A. 1985.** "The Importance of Secondary Crops in Iban Hill Rice Farming." *Sarawak Museum Journal* 34 (55): 37–46.

   Malaysia/ Sarawak/ Indigenous and local communities—Farming practices/ Agriculture—Shifting cultivation/ Agriculture—Smallholder cash crop farming/ Agriculture—Smallholder tree and perennial crop farming/ Farm management—Economics.

474.   ———. **1987.** "The Evolution of Iban Land Tenure: A Study in Institutional Economics." Ph.D. diss., Monash University, Melbourne, Australia.

   Malaysia/ Indigenous and local communities—Land and resource tenure systems/ Farm management—Economics.

475.   ———. **1988.** "The Commercialization of Iban Agriculture." In *Development in Sarawak: Historical and Contemporary Perspectives.* Ed. R. A. Cramb and R. H. W. Reece, pp. 105-134. Monash Paper on Southeast Asia, no. 17. Clayton, Vic., Australia: Monash University, Centre of Southeast Asian Studies.

Malaysia/ Sarawak/ Indigenous and local communities—Commoditization/ Agriculture—
Shifting cultivation/ Agricultural intensification.

476. ———. **1988.** "The Role of Smallholder Agriculture in the Development of
Sarawak: 1963–88." In *Socio-Economic Development in Sarawak: Policies
and Strategies for the 1990s*. Ed. A. M. M. Salleh, H. Solhee, and M. Y.
Kasim, pp. 83–110. Kuching, Sarawak, Malaysia: Angkatan Zaman Mansang
(AZAM).

Smallholders predominate in Sarawak's agricultural sector, producing all of the state's
rice, coconut, sago, and pepper as well as most of its rubber and cocoa. Cramb reviews the
characteristics and patterns of change in smallholder production, describing developments
in hill rice cultivation, wet rice cultivation, and cash crop production respectively. Though
agriculture's share of the state's economic output has declined over recent decades due to
expansion in the timber and other sectors, in absolute terms, the real value of agricultural
output has increased, largely due to cash-crop oriented intensification, "self-financed" by
local smallholders. The author challenges the contention that hill rice cultivation by swidden farmers is extending ever deeper into the state's primary forests, noting that primary
forests account for only a small proportion of the area cleared for cultivation each year (10–
20 percent), and that average rice field sizes among the state's swidden farmers have actually declined in recent decades. The author notes a recent shift in government policy toward
large scale, centrally managed development of cash crop production, although most of these
programs have fallen well short of production targets thus far. Given these difficulties in
organized, large scale land development, the author suggests that the government build on
the agricultural intensification being spontaneously pursued by the state's smallholders, and
develop a decentralized, village-based strategy for improving productivity and farmer
incomes.

Malaysia/ Sarawak/ Indigenous and local communities—Farming practices/ Indigenous and
local communities—Commoditization/ Agriculture—Shifting cultivation/ Agriculture—
Permanent/ Agricultural intensification/ State policy—Agricultural and rural development.

477. ———. **1989.** "Shifting Cultivation and Resource Degradation in Sarawak:
Perceptions and Policies." *Borneo Research Bulletin* 21 (1): 22–49.

The ideological basis for dominant views on shifting cultivation in East Malaysia is
suggested. The paper traces the development of negative government attitudes towards Iban
farming practices from the period of the Brooke dynasty, when these were misunderstood as
"inefficient" forms of food production, through the interwar colonial period, when shifting
cultivation was summarily characterized by British administrators as irrational and destructive of a valuable forest resource, to the contemporary period where old notions have been
carried over by Malay and Chinese government administrators. The author notes that little
real evidence exists to support these negative views of indigenous agriculture in Sarawak.
Citing emerging documentation that shifting cultivation can, under certain circumstances,
comprise a sustainable and ecologically appropriate form of resource use, the author suggests that negative views on shifting cultivators on the part of non-indigenous populations is
a matter of cultural and political bias. Behind past and current government efforts to seden-
tarize shifting cultivators and rationalize their "destructive" farming systems may lie the
need to "concentrate rural dwellers in accessible locations and link them to government
administration and services to facilitate political control." Such control becomes even more
important given the needs of government's own "development program based on extensive
plantation agriculture and rapid timber exploitation."

Malaysia/ Sarawak/ Agriculture—Shifting cultivation's environmental impacts/
Deforestation/ Forest management—Control of shifting cultivation.

478. ———. **1989.** "The Use and Productivity of Labour in Shifting Cultivation: An
East Malaysian Case Study." *Agricultural Systems* 29: 97–115.

Labor use and labor productivity associated with shifting cultivation in the Saribas District, Sarawak in East Malaysia are examined. Cramb argues that real opportunities exceed opportunity costs in swidden farming, ensuring its persistence despite increasing commercialization. [Summarized from journal abstract].

Malaysia/ Sarawak/ Agriculture—Shifting cultivation/ Indigenous and local communities—Farming practices/ Indigenous and local communities—Commoditization/ Farm management—Economics.

479.   ———. **1990.** "Reply to John Palmer." *Borneo Research Bulletin* 22 (1): 44–45.

The author replies to challenge by J. Palmer in the same journal issue on the effects of Iban shifting cultivation in Sarawak. Village level surveys reveal that the area of primary forest cleared by Iban shifting cultivators is relatively limited, equaling roughly 5,000 hectares per year and representing only a 0.2 percent increase in total land area under forest-fallow systems. The author notes that logging companies 'go through this much primary forest in a week.'' Shifting cultivators actively manage their fallow plots, using a variety of agroforestry schemes. Notions of an expanding "green desert" in the rainforest are based on inaccurate readings of the ethno-ecological context of Iban communities which is still only poorly understood by foreign scientists and policy makers.

Sarawak/ Malaysia/ Agriculture—Shifting cultivation's environmental impacts/ Deforestation.

480.   ———. **1991.** "The Changing Agricultural Economy of the Saribas." In *Images of Malaysia.* Ed. M. I. Said, and J. Saravanamuttu, pp. 8–37. Kuala Lumpur, Malaysia: Persatuan Sains Sosial Malaysia.

Major changes in the Iban economy of Sarawak due to population growth, spread of commercial agriculture, and increase in government services, make it likely that studies of Iban agriculture by Freeman are no longer representative of the wide majority. The author examines recent changes in the Iban agricultural economy based on a case study of two longhouse communities in the Nanga Spak area of Saribas district in Sarawak where field-work was conducted in 1979–1980. Population and settlement patterns, land use history, village economies, hill rice, pepper and rubber production patterns are described for each community. The author finds that Iban agricultural production strategies are flexible and responsive to new opportunities and constraints, as evidenced by the emergence of a patterns of diversified, semi-commercial agriculture supplemented by income from off-farm work. Differences between the two villages are noted, including different population pressures, differing degrees of accessibility to markets, and differing degrees of specialization. The accumulation of a greater degree of productive capital in one village in the form of area planted to rubber and greater access to remunerative off-farm work appeared to give members of this community a greater range of options than those of the other village during times of sudden economic downturn or environmental stress. These differences correspond to somewhat contrasting views among members of the two villages concerning the desirability of various government-sponsored development programs. The author recommends a decentralized approach towards rural development among the Iban address the specific local demands and assists communities in expanding their livelihood options through diversified farming.

Malaysia/ Sarawak/ Indigenous and local communities—Farming practices/ Indigenous and local communities—Commoditization/ Agricultural intensification/ State policy—Agricultural and rural development.

481.   ———. **1992.** "The Evolution of Property Rights to Land in Sarawak: An Institutionalist Perspective." Photocopy. Ithaca, N.Y.: Southeast Asia Program, Cornell University.

Malaysia/ Sarawak/ Indigenous and local communities—Land and resource tenure systems/ Agriculture—Shifting cultivation.

482. ———. **1992.** "The Impact of the Japanese Occupation (1941-45) on Agricultural Development in Sarawak." Draft manuscript. Photocopy.

Following a brief overview of the administrative, political and economic structures introduced by the occupying Japanese forces in Sarawak in the early 1940s, the author describes the food production programs pursued by the Brooke and the Japanese regimes respectively. Despite concerted efforts to promote padi cultivation in Sarawak on the part of the Brooke regime, padi cultivation first boomed in the region during a sustained downturn in the price for more remunerative agricultural commodities during the depression years 1930–33. Agricultural programs pursued by the Japanese were successful in achieving rice self-sufficiency in the state, but only by imposing monopolistic purchasing rights and forced deliveries. While the Japanese policies generated funds to support war activities, they did so at the cost of forcing an unsustainable expansion of marginal land under padi cultivation and undermining the local export economy based on rubber, pepper, sago and coconut production.

Malaysia/ Sarawak/ State policy—Agricultural and rural development/ State policy—Land development/ History—Colonial.

483. **Cramb, R. A., and I. R. Wills. 1990.** "The Role of Traditional Institutions in Rural Development: Community-Based Land Tenure and Government Land Policy in Sarawak, Malaysia." *World Development* 18 (3): 347–360.

Cramb and Wills challenge the view that traditional institutions, particularly those related to tenure, are incompatible with economic development. The community-based land tenure system of the Iban in Sarawak is examined and its adaptability to changing circumstance is noted. The authors argue for incorporating traditional institutions as "building blocks of a modern, development-oriented institutional structure" [Summarized from journal abstract].

Malaysia/ Sarawak/ Indigenous and local communities—Land and resource tenure systems/ Indigenous and local communities—State policy.

484. **Cranbrook, G., Earl of. 1977.** *Mammals of Borneo: Field Keys and an Annotated Checklist.* Kuala Lumpur: Printed for MBRAS by Percetakan Mas Sdn. Bhd.

The author presents a descriptive checklist of mammals found in Malaysian and Indonesian Borneo.

Indonesia/ Kalimantan/ Malaysia/ Sabah/ Sarawak/ Forest fauna.

485. **Dahlan, H. M. 1983.** "Group Ethos and Leadership Attributes: The Characterological Change of the Illanun Community?" In *Sabah: Traces of Change.* Ed. H. M. Dahlan, pp. 110–131. Kajian Etnografi Sabah Jilid, no. 3. Selangor, Malaysia: Universiti Kebangsaan Malaysia-Yayasan Sabah.

Malaysia/ Sabah/ Indigenous and local communities—Social relations.

486. **Deegan, J. L. 1973.** "Change Among the Lun Bawang, a Borneo People." Ph.D. diss., University of Washington, Seattle, Wash.

Malaysia/ Sarawak/ Indigenous and local communities/ Indigenous and local communities—Commoditization/ Ethnography.

487.   ————. **1974.** "Community Fragmentation Among the Lun Bawang." *Sarawak Museum Journal* 22 (43): 229–247.

Malaysia/ Sarawak/ Indigenous and local communities—Social relations/ Indigenous and local communities—Commoditization.

488.   **Dixon, G. 1974.** "Dayak Land Tenure." *Borneo Research Bulletin* 6: 5–15.

Malaysia/ Sarawak/ Indigenous and local communities—Land and resource tenure systems.

489.   **Douglas, I., T. Greer, K. Bidin, and W. Sinun. 1993.** "Impact of Roads and Compacted Ground on Post-logging Sediment Yield in a Small Drainage Basin, Sabah, Malaysia." *CSIRO Water Resources Series* 12: 213–218.

Malaysia/ Sabah/ Soil erosion and degradation/ Hydrology/ Timber industry—Environmental impacts.

490.   **Douglas, I., T. Greer, W. M. Wong, T. Spencer, and W. Sinun. 1990.** "The Impact of Commercial Logging on a Small Rainforest Catchment in Ulu Segama, Sabah, Malaysia." In *Research Needs and Applications to Reduce Erosion and Sedimentation in Tropical Steeplands.* Ed. R. R. Ziemar, C. L. O'Loughlin, and L. S. Hamilton, pp. 165–173. IAHS Publication, no. 192. Wallingford, Oxfordshire, U.K.: International Association of Hydrological Scientists.

A study was conducted in the Sungei Steyshen Baru catchment, Sabah, to determine the effects of different stages of logging activity on total suspended sediment yield. Substantial increases in sediment yield were noted in association with the initial logging phase, i.e., road construction. Further increases were noted in association with subsequent stages involving extraction along and extensification of the logged area beyond the road respectively. The study revealed total increases in sedimentation as well as heightened soil loss during observed storms. Specific measurement results are provided.

Malaysia/ Sabah/ Soil erosion and degradation/ Timber industry—Environmental impacts/ Hydrology.

491.   **Dransfield, J. 1984.** *The Rattans of Sabah.* Sabah Forestry Record, no. 13. Sandakan, Sabah, Malaysia: Sabah Forest Department.

Malaysia/ Sabah/ Rattan—Growth and distribution/ Forest flora/ Non-timber forest products.

492.   ————. **1986.** "Prospects for Rattan Cultivation." In *The Palm Tree of Life: Biology, Utilization and Conservation.* Proceedings of a symposium at the annual meeting of the Society for Economic Botany, New York Botanical Garden, Bronx, N.Y. Bronx, N.Y.: New York Botanical Garden.

As demand for rattan materials expand to supply a booming furniture and handicraft industry, the need to cultivate rattan is becoming more urgent. Swidden farmers in Kalimantan have traditionally cultivated small diameter rattan (*Calamus caesius and C. trachycoleus*) as a supplementary livelihood activity. Dransfield describes these practices as well as a government project to cultivate the same species on the Batu Putih Estate in eastern Sabah. While cultivating small diameter rattan appears to be feasible for humid areas, there is still little evidence that the same can be said for cane species of larger diameter.

Malaysia/ Sabah/ Indonesia/ Kalimantan/ Indigenous and local communities—Farming practices/ Indigenous and local communities—Forest products use and trade/ Rattan—Cultivation/ Non-timber forest products.

493. ———. **1990.** "Notes on Rattans *(Palmae: Calamoideae)* Occurring in Sarawak, Borneo." *Kew Bulletin* 45: 73–99.

Malaysia/ Sarawak/ Forest flora/ Rattan—Growth and distribution/ Non-timber forest products.

494. ———. **1991.** "Notes on *Pinanga (Palmae)* in Sarawak." *Kew Bulletin* 46: 691–698.

Dransfield provides a brief account of three palms recently identified in Borneo, including *Pinanga cucullata, P. rupestris* and *P. pachypylla.* The palm *P. malaiana* var. *barramensis* is suggested to be synonymous with *P. mirabilis.*

Malaysia/ Sarawak/ Forest flora/ Rattan—Growth and distribution/ Non-timber forest products.

495. ———. **1992.** *The Rattans of Sarawak.* Richmond, Surrey, U.K. Kuching, Sarawak, Malaysia: Kew Royal Botanic Gardens; Sarawak Forest Department.

Drawing from fieldwork conducted with Sarawak Forest Herbarium, the author has compiled a guidebook (233 pp.) for identifying the rattans of Sarawak. Separate chapters deal with 8 different genera of palms: *Korthalsia, Daemonorops, Calamus, Pogontium, Ceratolobus, Retispatha, Plectocomiopsis, Plectocomia.* Detailed illustrations accompany the descriptions given for each species within the genera. The guidebook ends with a short bibliography of selected further readings as well as a checklist of Sarawak rattans.

Malaysia/ Sarawak/ Forest flora/ Rattan—Growth and distribution/ Non-timber forest products.

496. **Dransfield, S. 1992.** *The Bamboos of Sabah.* Sabah Forest Records, no. 14. Kuala Lumpur: Forestry Department.

Following a brief discussion of the general morphology of bamboo plants, Dransfield describes ten genera and their individual species. Genera covered include: *Bambusa, Dendrocalamus, Dinochloa, Gigantochloa, Racemobambos, Schizostachyum, Sphaerobambos, Thyrostachys, Yushania,* and *"Bambusa"* sp. (related to *B. wrayi* Stapf). Illustrations, checklist of bamboos in Sabah, index to scientific names, and index to vernacular names are included.

Malaysia/ Sabah/ Forest flora/ Non-timber forest products.

497. **Duff, A. B., R. A. Hall, and C. W. Marsh. 1984.** "A Survey of Wildlife in and around a Commercial Tree Plantation in Sabah." *Malaysian Forester* 47 (3–4): 197–213.

Malaysia/ Sabah/ Forest fauna/ Forest management—Commercial forestry and silviculture/ Wildlife management.

498. **Dunn, F. L. 1975.** *Rain-forest Collectors and Traders: A Study of Resource Utilization in Modern and Ancient Malaya.* Monographs of the Malaysian Branch of the Royal Asiatic Society, no. 5. Kuala Lumpur: Royal Asiatic Society.

Malaysia/ Indigenous and local communities—Forest products use and trade/ Non-timber forest products/ History—Pre-colonial/ History—Colonial.

499.   **Esteve, J. 1988.** "La productivité forestière dans l'État de Sabah (Malaysia)." *Bois et Forêts des Tropiques* 218: 78–87.

Esteve documents the history of commercial forestry in Sabah, Malaysia since the late 19th century colonial period. The transition from manual logging ("kuda-kuda") using water buffalo for timber extraction to mechanized logging in the 1960s is described. Particular attention is also given to developments of the last decade, when Sabah became a major timber-exporting region of the world. Implications for the forestry industry's future are noted. [In French].

Malaysia/ Sabah/ Timber industry—Development and structure/ Timber industry—Logging/ History—Colonial.

500.   **Foo, N. K. A. 1986.** "Land Classification and Land Tenure in Sarawak in Relation to Land Development." *Sarawak Gazette* 112 (1496): 17–21.

Malaysia/ Sarawak/ Land use—Patterns and planning/ Land tenure—Legislation and state policy/ State policy—Land development.

501.   **Food and Agricultural Organization (FAO). 1987.** "Report of the Mission to Malaysia on Tropical Forestry Action Plan (24–29 November 1986)." Photocopy. Rome: Food and Agricultural Organization.

A 55 page mission report on the progress being made towards a Tropical Forest Action Plan (TFAP) by the Malaysia Government in cooperation with FAO.

Malaysia/ State policy—Forest and natural resources/ Forest management.

502.   **Fox, J. E. D. n.d.** "Natural Vegetation of Sabah and Natural Regeneration of the Dipterocarp Forest." Photocopy. Bangor, Wales: University of Bangor.

Malaysia/ Sabah/ Forest flora/ Forest biology and ecology/ Forest regeneration/ Forest management—Commercial forestry and silviculture.

503.   **———. n.d.** "Production in Regenerating Forest." Photocopy. Sandakan, Sabah, Malaysia: Sabah Forest Research Department.

Malaysia/ Timber industry—Logging/ Forest management—Commercial forestry and silviculture/ Forest regeneration.

504.   **———. 1968.** Logging Damage and the Influence of Climber Cutting Prior to Logging in the Lowland Dipterocarp Forest in Sabah. Kuala Lumpur, Malaysia: Public Printers.

The author examines the level of damage from logging activities due to climbers, with particular reference to the damage suffered by pole-sized commercial species. A comparative analysis of the damage with and without poisoning the climbers prior to felling the trees is presented.

Malaysia/ Timber industry—Logging/ Forest management—Commercial forestry and silviculture/ Timber industry—Environmental impacts.

505.   ————. **1970.** *Preferred Check-list of Sabah Trees.* Sabah Forest Record, no. 7. Kuching, Sarawak, Malaysia: Borneo Literature Bureau for Forest Dept. Sabah.

Malaysia/ Sabah/ Forest flora/ Forest management—Commercial forestry and silviculture.

506.   ————. **1978.** "The Natural Vegetation of Sabah, Malaysia: 1. The Physical Environment and Classification." *Tropical Ecology* 19: 218–239.

Fox gives a broad overview of the climate, geology, soils, and vegetation of Sabah, the East Malaysian state lying in northern Borneo. The terrain is mountainous and the region is characterized by relatively little seasonal change and steady temperatures, particularly in heavily forested areas. Lithosols predominate at higher elevations in the west (comprising 41 percent of the region), while red/yellow latosols and podsolics are found in the lower-lying main river valleys of the east (36 percent). Fox summarizes various classifications worked out for the state's vegetation and integrates ecological and soil reconnaissance data to suggest a more general scheme. Sabah's forests are dominated by Dipterocarpaceae, 160 species of which may be found in the state. Based on various ecological considerations, seven types of dipterocarp forest may be identified.

Malaysia/ Sabah/ Forest flora/ Soils/ Forest management—Commercial forestry and silviculture.

507.   ————. **1983.** "The Natural Vegetation of Sabah, Malaysia: 2. The Parashorea Forests of the Lowlands." *Tropical Ecology* 23: 94-112.

Malaysia/ Sabah/ Forest flora/ Forest management—Commercial forestry and silviculture.

508.   **Fox, J. E. D., and T. H. Hing. 1971.** "Soils and Forest on an Ultrabasic Hill Northeast of Sabah." *Journal of Tropical Geography* 32: 38–48.

Malaysia/ Sabah/ Forest flora/ Soils.

509.   **Fox, J. E. D. 1969.** "Soil Damage Factor in Present Day Logging in Sabah." *Journal of the Sabah Society* n.s., 5 (1): n.g.

The author examines the changes in the physical landscape and the ecosystem of the forest arising from logging activities. Soil damage has become serious in recent years due to extensive use of heavy machinery in the logging industry. Adversely affected are the rate of growth and range of species which can grow back in the forest. The impact of this soil damage on the land's potential to yield cash crops is discussed. Various management alternatives are suggested to minimize soil and ecosystem damage to the forest.

Malaysia/ Sabah/ Timber industry—Logging/ Timber industry—Environmental impacts/ Soil erosion and degradation/ Forest management—Commercial forestry and silviculture.

510.   **Freeman, D. 1992.** *The Iban of Borneo.* London School of Economics Monographs on Social Anthropology, no. 41. Kuala Lumpur: S. Abdul Majeed.
[Reprint of the new edition of Freeman's Report on the Iban of Sarawak published in 1955 by the Government of Sarawak.]

This monograph represents a modified excerpt from Freeman's report, *Iban Agriculture*, published in 1955 on contract with the Colonial Social Science Research Council. Fieldwork took place among the Ulu Ai Iban in the Baleh region of Kapit District, Third Division, Sarawak, and was aimed at presenting a comprehensive account of Iban methods of dry rice cultivation on a swidden farming basis. Noting that Iban land use and management methods can only be properly understood in the context of the social groups that make up Iban society, Freeman begins the report with two chapters on Iban social organization, distinguishing between the basic household unit or *bilek-family* (the economically self-sufficient kin unit defined by shared living space), the larger longhouse-community to which the *bilek-family* belongs, and the tribe, defined as "a diffuse [though endogamous] territorial grouping dispersed along the banks of a major river and its diverging tributaries." Chapter Three reviews Iban land tenure patterns, noting among other details, the Iban's historical propensity to migrate and claim new territory, the equal rights of access to land held by individual Iban bilek-families within the long-house territory, and the claim to ownership of land secured by bilek families through forest clearing. A detailed account of Iban agriculture and economy follows in Chapters Four and Five, providing a description of farming methods, labor input, harvest yields, average household ability to meet food requirements, and income from rubber production. The sixth and final chapter discusses Iban land use patterns, noting the Iban "predilection" for virgin forest that is cultivated two years in succession or three times within first 5–7 years after clearing. It is this "prodigious" use of land, argues Freeman, that earns the Iban the title of "mangeurs de bois." Given the accelerated soil erosion associated with the practice of cultivating virgin forest for 2 or more years consecutively, Iban methods shifting cultivation are "wasteful and dangerous," and "frequently produce deleterious results." Emphasizes the author, measures are needed to "stabilize" Iban farming practices in order to ensure the viability of future agricultural and forestry development.

Malaysia/ Sarawak/ Ethnography/ Indigenous and local communities—Farming practices/ Indigenous and local communities—Economy/ Indigenous and local communities—Religion and cosmology/ Indigenous and local communities—Social relations/ Indigenous and local communities—Forest land use and management practices/ Indigenous and local communities—Land and resource tenure systems.

511.   **Freeman, J. D. 1955.** *Iban Agriculture: A Report on the Shifting Cultivation of Hill Rice by the Iban of Sarawak.* London: Her Majesty's Printing Office.

Malaysia/ Sarawak/ Indigenous and local communities—Farming practices/ Indigenous and local communities—Forest land use and management practices/ Migration/ Agriculture—Shifting cultivation.

512.   **Gait, B. A. 1988.** "Effects of Logging on Rural Communities: A Proposed Community Forestry Program for the Two Village in Ulu Kinabatangan, Sabah, Malaysia." RECOFTC Paper, no. 9. Bangkok: Regional Community Forestry Training Center, Faculty of Forestry, Kasetsart University.

This publication reports the results of a two-month study of two Kinabatangan river communities—Kuala Karamuak and Inarad—conducted in 1987 to examine the role of forests for traditional economies and the impact of logging activities on rural communities. The study was undertaken in connection in an attempt to forge a better relationship between local villagers and the Yayasan Sabah concession located in the area. The sites were chosen for study because of the different degree of exposure to logging activity experienced by each community. Most of the land around Karamuak had been logged during the 1970s, while at Inarad, located further upstream on the Kinabatangan, logging had taken place for a brief while, from 1984 to 1987, with no further activity since then.

The paper notes the contradictory implications of timber industry development in the area. On the one hand, poor logging techniques seriously disturb local wildlife and plant populations, as well as hydrological systems, leaving communities with impoverished natural environments and a declining quality of water sources. On the other hand, logging activity in Kuala Karamuak has introduced the possibility of new ways of earning cash income, including, illegal timber felling, government employment and easier access to markets to trade forest products. While these new income opportunities appear to be welcomed by many villagers, failing any improvements in local infrastructure and skill training, they introduce a boom-and-bust pattern of economic development, as layoffs occur when the timber industry slumps, road access is undermined by poor maintenance, and local stocks of commercially valuable commodities, such as rattan, are rapidly depleted. Facing declining opportunities for cash income in a village that has now become much more cash-dependent, growing numbers of young villagers migrate downstream to search for work elsewhere.

Given that Inarad and Kuala Karamuak lie at very different points along this continuum of environmental and socio-economic change, the paper recommends different approaches to supporting sustainable community development in each location. The relatively self-sufficient village economy at Inarad may be supported simply by ensuring that better medical, educational, and agricultural extension services are provided. At Kuala Karamuak, however, "more comprehensive assistance" is required, including road development, issuing of formal land titles, and sustained agricultural extension to promote intensive, irrigated rice cultivation, and small-holder rattan or rubber plantation development. In particular, the author also suggests that "exposing potential farmers to the farming system practiced in another agricultural oriented district" may be a promising means to promote remunerative and sustainable farming practices locally.

Malaysia/ Sabah/ Timber industry—Impacts on local communities and economy/ Indigenous and local communities—Forest products use and trade/ Indigenous and local communities—Commoditization/ Timber industry—Logging/ Agriculture—Shifting cultivation/ Non-timber forest products/ Migration/ Indigenous and local communities—State policy.

513. **Geddes, W. R. 1954.** *The Land Dayaks of Sarawak.* Colonial Research Study, no. 14. London: H.M.S.O.

Malaysia/ Sarawak/ Ethnography/ Indigenous and local communities—Social relations/ Indigenous and local communities—Economy/ Indigenous and local communities—Farming practices/ Indigenous and local communities—Land and resource tenure systems/ Indigenous and local communities—Religion and cosmology.

514. ———. **1957.** *Nine Dayak Nights.* Melbourne, Australia: Oxford University Press.

Malaysia/ Sarawak/ Ethnography/ Indigenous and local communities—Social relations/ Indigenous and local communities—Religion and cosmology.

515. **Geinitz, D. 1986.** Zielgruppenorienterte Förderung der kleinbäuerlichen Kautschukwirtschaft in Indonesien und Malaysia. Hamburg: Verlag Weltarchiv.
[Target Group-Oriented Promotion of Smallholder Rubber Production in Indonesia and Malaysia.]

Covering the 1960s through the early 1980s, Geinitz describes government programs aimed at increasing rubber production among smallholders in Malaysia and Indonesia. Achievements, strengths, and weaknesses of smallholder rubber programs in both countries are reviewed. The greater success at increasing rubber production and reducing poverty among smallholders in Malaysia as compared with Indonesia is noted, and possible factors contributing to this difference are suggested.

Indonesia/ Malaysia/ Agricultural development/ Agriculture—Smallholder tree and perennial crop farming/ Agriculture—Smallholder cash crop farming/ State policy—Agricultural and rural development/ Land settlement and development/ Poverty.

516. **Ghani, A. N. A., N. M. N. A. Majid, C. P. M. Chellapan, and M. N. Shamsuddin. 1994.** "Plantation-based Agroforestry Systems for Livestock Production on Tin Tailings in Peninsular Malaysia." In *Agroforestry and*

Animal Production for Human Welfare. Proceedings of an international symposium held in association with the 7th AAAP Animal Science Congress, Bali, Indonesia, 11–16 July 1994. Ed. J. W. Copland, A. Djajanegra, and M. Sabrani, pp. 67–81. ACIAR Proceedings, no. 55. Canberra: Australian Centre for International Agricultural Research.

Wastelands composed of tin tailings represent .86% of total land area in Malaysia, and are concentrated in Perak and Selangor states. Agroforestry systems may be a feasible way to make productive use of these areas, integrating timber, agricultural crops, and animals. The authors report on the results of a study of agrosilvopastoral and silvopastoral systems in two tin tailings in Selangor, evaluating economic viability of each system based on tangible outputs produced during project cycle. The net present value (NPV) is found to be positive in both cases, and the internal rates of return were found to be greater than the marginal economic opportunity cost of capital in mid-1980s, demonstrating the economic viability of both systems. The silvopastoral system involving timber and pasture appeared slightly more profitable than the agrosilvopastoral system (which included crop production trees) due to better resource utilization.

Malaysia/ Peninsular Malaysia/ Agroforestry/ Farm management—Economics/ Livestock management.

517.   **Gillis, M. 1988.** "Malaysia: Public Policies and the Tropical Forest." In *Public Policies and the Misuse of Forest Resources*. Ed. R. Repetto and M. Gillis, pp. 115–164. New York: World Resources Institute.

Supplying roughly 40% of the world trade in tropical timber, between 1976 and 1985 Malaysia experienced an annual rate of deforestation in Malaysia of 250,000 ha, equaling roughly 1% of the country's total forest area. Though relatively low by world standards, this rate appears to have increased markedly during the 1980s, especially in the East Malaysia states of Sabah and Sarawak. As in Indonesia, major factors behind loss of forest cover in Malaysia are "poverty, institutions, and public policies" although, notes Gillis, "the relative roles of these factors have been quite different" in these two countries. Significant differences also exist between Peninsular Malaysia, Sabah and Sarawak, due in large part to different forest resource endowments, different demographic and socio-economic profiles, and the large degree of autonomy each state possesses over the management of the forestry sector. Divided into three sections, this paper examines general forest endowments and forestry policy in Malaysia as a whole, as well as the specific background, current conditions and policies which apply in Sabah and Sarawak in particular.

In an analysis of forest use and policy in Sabah, the author observes the central role shifting cultivation is commonly cited to play in the state's deforestation problem. By 1980 almost 3, 650,000 ha of Sabah's forests is estimated to have been "affected" by shifting cultivation; by contrast, only 1,280,000 ha of land had been logged over for timber extraction by 1985. Suggests the author, opening up of interior forest lands by logging roads, poverty (in 1982, 51.2% of the Sabah population fell below the poverty line, as compared with 37.7% nationally), and local tenure and land use laws, by which any native to Sabah may gain formal title to land by clearing it for cultivation, appear to be among the main incentives behind this extensive use of forest lands by Sabah swiddeners. As regards to the local timber industry, the Sabah government has consistently captured a much higher share of the rent from commercial timber extraction (ranging between 70.4% and 93.1% between 1979 and 1983) than Indonesia and the neighboring state of Sarawak, largely through more aggressive collection of taxes and timber royalties. Despite this apparent disincentive to rapid resource extraction, local timber resources have still been quickly depleted in the state, with the extent of unlogged forest dropping from 55% in 1973 to less than 25% by 1983.

A discussion of forest use, forest sector development, forestry and non-forestry policies in Sarawak and Peninsular Malaysia follows. Accurate estimates of forest cover loss is scant for Sarawak. Still, as in Sabah, shifting cultivation is cited to be the prime cause of deforestation in the state; existing evidence suggests that as much as 1/3 of the state's total forest area (9,434,000 ha) is under shifting cultivation. Though the state's forest fee system does a poor job of rent capture overall, a lower effective royalty rate has been at least in part responsible for discouraging high-grading within the industry, resulting in a much lower rate of damage to logged-over stands than elsewhere (i.e., Indonesia or even Sabah).

In Peninsular Malaysia, deforestation has proceeded rapidly since the turn of the century, due in part to extensive logging between 1955 and 1980, but more significantly in recent years to conversion of remaining forest lands to agriculture (largely tree crops). Though this development has preserved the productive value of previous forest lands in the region, it also implies a worrisome loss of the forest's protective role and "the irreversible loss of the value of the forest's non-wood products." The paper concludes with a brief note on the effect of Malaysia's exchange rate policy on forest land use, observing that a consistently undervalued Malaysian dollar during the 1970s and early 1980s allowed timber producers an artificially high return on log exports, thus promoting overly extensive and wasteful timber extraction across the country.

Malaysia/ Sabah/ Sarawak/ Deforestation/ Timber industry—Development and structure/ Timber industry—Environmental impacts/ Timber industry—State policy and regulation/ Agriculture—Shifting cultivation/ Land settlement and development—Environmental impacts/ Forest management—Commercial forestry and silviculture/ Forest management—Control of shifting cultivation/ State policy—Forest and natural resources/ Land tenure—Legislation and state policy.

518. **Golingi, F., and Chua Min Hiung. 1969.** "Socio-Cultural Issues Encountered in the Implementation of In-situ Rural Development Programmes." *Socio-Cultural Dimensions of Development.* Ed. Mohammad Yaakub Hj. Johari. Kota Kinabalu, Sabah: Institute for Development Studies.

The authors identify key socio-cultural factors that inhibit the successful implementation of on-site income generating projects in Sabah attempted by the Rural Development Corporation, a major rural development agency of the State. Among the factors cited are the limited and highly seasonal attraction of rural labor to wage employment in the agricultural sector; low labor productivity arising from what appears at the surface to be lethargy; disruption of project implementation due to competing rights to land coming from the rural people based on their unofficially recognized customary rights to the property; interference by local leaders in the management of the project; poor labor mobility arising from parochialism/xenophobia; slow adoption of technology due to illiteracy; and retrenchment difficulty where rural people take the loss of job as equivalent to loss of face and retaliate by willfully destroying the property of the project. The authors conclude that social viability of all proposed in-situ rural development projects in Sabah should be assessed in addition to their technical and economic viability.

Malaysia/ Sabah/ Project intervention—Rural development.

519. **Golingi, F., and M. D. Ismail. 1988.** "Opportunities for Smallholders to Participate in Modern Agriculture Sector." *Towards Modernizing Smallholder Agriculture in Sabah.* Ed. T. C. Chuan, and W. Yee. Kota Kinabalu, Sabah: Institute for Development Studies.

Different ways in which smallholder farmers and shifting cultivators in Sabah might transform their production activities from subsistence to commercial production are proposed and examined. The authors suggest that important income generating opportunities are present in a number of areas, namely: 1) in the production of import-substituting crops such as coffee, poultry, eggs, meat, tropical and temperate table fruits, padi and other grains/tubers for animal feed; 2) in the cultivation of export crops such as cocoa and oil palm; and 3) in small-scale agro-based processing. Such opportunities can be effectively realized by helping smallholders to participate in government sponsored settlement schemes or by organizing them at the local level to undertake cooperative production methods. However, the article also notes a number of constraints that would have to be removed to effect smooth transition -lack of knowledge and capital on the part of the smallholder; land-holdings of uneconomic size; inadequate household labor; and inadequate physical and market infrastructures.

Malaysia/ Sabah/ Project intervention—Agricultural development/ Agriculture—Smallholder cash crop farming/ Agriculture—Smallholder tree and perennial crop farming/ Land settlement and development.

520. **Golokin, S. L., and P. K. Cassels. 1989.** "An Appraisal of Sabah Softwoods Sdn. Bhd. 12 Years after Establishment." *Planter* 65 (760): 301–310.

Golokin and Cassels describe the progress scored by Sabah Softwoods Sdn. Bhd. (SSSB), a joint venture between the Sabah Foundation and North Borneo Timbers Bhd. involving over 60,000 ha of land. Founded in 1973 SSSB first aimed to plant most of its land to short-rotation Pinus caribaea, and process the product into pulpwood. Slow growth rates and high costs associated with this species, however, soon prompted the project management to switch its emphasis to broadleaved species, including *Albizia falcataria*, *Gmelina arborea* and *Acacia mangium*, and the production of sawlogs. By 1987, almost 27,000 ha had been planted. Though a limited number of hectares were planted to cocoa, oil palm, rubber, and coffee the more intensive management requirements of these agricultural crops have discouraged expansion of this project component. The authors cover various aspects of SSSB's development, including various research initiatives and problems of pests, diseases, fires, and economic viability.

Malaysia/ Sabah/ Timber plantations/ Forest management—Commercial forestry and silviculture.

521. **Gonzales, M. et al. 1988.** "Shifting Cultivation of the Murut in Sabah, Malaysia: A Socio-Economic and Physical Study in 7 Selected Villages in Mukim Nabawan." Photocopy. Utrecht, Netherlands: Department of Geography of Developing Countries, University of Utrecht.

This paper presents an in-depth case study of seven Murut villages in Sabah province, focusing on socio-economic characteristics of shifting cultivators in the villages and the impact of government-initiated projects to encourage a transition from shifting to sedentary farming. The availability of natural resources and alternative employment opportunities is also examined to assess the potential for local economic development.

The authors conclude that while people have benefited from the various public facilities and amenities that have accompanied the government-initiated projects (with a number of villagers enjoying higher cash income than ever before), there is little sign that the Murut are ready to give up shifting cultivation. The main reason for this is that most government projects so far have failed to provide local residents with an alternative source of food, the most basic household need of all, to replace hillpadi rice cultivated on hilly swiddens. Subsistence farming continues to be a high priority in the utilization of household labor, often at the expense of the people's participation in the various government-initiated development projects in the area.

Malaysia/ Sabah/ Project intervention—Agricultural development/ Indigenous and local communities—Economy/ Indigenous and local communities—Farming practices.

522. **Grip, H., A. Malmer, and F. K. Wong. 1994.** "Converting Tropical Rainforest to Forest Plantation in Sabah, Malaysia. I. Dynamics and Net Losses of Nutrients in Control Catchment Streams." *Hydrological Processes* 8 (3): 179–194.

Malaysia/ Sabah/ Timber plantations/ Timber industry—Environmental impacts/ Hydrology/ Soil erosion and degradation.

523. **Guerreiro, A. 1988.** "Cash Crops and Subsistence Strategies: Towards a Comparison of Kayan and Lahanan Economies." *Sarawak Museum Journal* 39 (60): 15–37.

> The Kayan and Lahanan social systems are characterized as rigidly stratified with little social mobility between the aristocratic and lower class members of a longhouse community. Due to the closed nature of these communities, little change has been apparent in the indigenous agricultural systems. Recently, government programs have been directed at promoting more productive agricultural practices to which the Kayan and Lahanan have responded favorably. Yet, forest product gathering, fishing, and small-scale horticulture remain the main means of subsistence. The author recognizes the social and symbolic nature of agricultural systems, and predicts changes in the society and culture of the Kayan and Lahanan as these organized development efforts proceed.

> Malaysia/ Sarawak/ Indigenous and local communities—Economy/ Indigenous and local communities—Farming practices/ Indigenous and local communities—Social relations/ Indigenous and local communities—State policy/ Agriculture—Shifting cultivation/ State policy—Agricultural and rural development.

524. ————. **1992.** "Some Aspects of Change among the Baluy Kayan." *Sarawak Journal* 43 (64 (n.s.)): 47–105.

> The author draws from fieldwork undertaken during 1986–1987 in 3 Kayan communities in Long Murum, Belaga District, Sarawak, one of which was the site Jérôme Rousseau's fieldwork in the early 1970s. Statistical data drawn from district-level socio-economic and agricultural surveys is with data drawn from a household-level survey completed during fieldwork. The author first presents a broad ethnographic overview of the Belaga District Kayan, including a detailed examination of local land tenure patterns. This is followed by more specific description of the communities studied, with special focus on broad changes in the local economy as well as local village political processes.
>
> Notes the author, in one community surveyed, the formal population increased by 30 percent between 1971 and 1987; however, at the time of survey, 43 percent of the local population was away from the village for schooling, university-level study, or employment purposes. 3.6 percent of the population appeared to be routinely involved in temporary migration related to employment, although this figure is higher in other communities. Also noted was a trend towards smaller swiddens and decreased amount of time devoted to food crop cultivation, when the present data is compared with that of Rousseau. The author suggests that such developments may be explained by an increasing proportion of labor devoted to cash crop cultivation. Despite significant economic and ideological changes over the past 20 years, many features of the socio-political fabric remain the same, including the cultural value placed on village hierarchy and hereditary ranking. As a result, many local political processes remain largely under control by village chiefs. These contradictory changes may signify pressure for educated village members of commoner lineage to migrate to larger towns downstream where there is less potential for conflict with traditional village elites.

> Malaysia/ Sarawak/ Indigenous and local communities—Social relations/ Indigenous and local communities—Farming practices/ Indigenous and local communities—Commoditization/ Migration/ Agriculture—Shifting cultivation/ Agriculture—Smallholder cash crop farming.

525. **Guntavid, P. J. 1983.** "Tinjauan awal tumbuhan ubatan tradisional Negeri Sabah." Bachelor of Science thesis, [Sabah].
[Preliminary Survey of Traditional Herbal Medicines in Sabah.]

> Malaysia/ Sabah/ Non-timber forest products/ Indigenous and local communities—Forest products use and trade.

526. **Halos, S. C., F. F. Natividad, L. J. Escote-Carlson, G. L. Enriquez, and I. Umboh. 1994.** Proceedings of the Symposium on Biotechnological and Environmental Approaches to Forest Pest and Disease Management, Quezon City, Philippines, 28–30 April 1993. BIOTROP Special Publication, no. 53. Bogor, Indonesia: SEAMEO-BIOTROP.

Twenty papers discuss current problems in forest pest management in various parts of Asia and highlight recent strategies in biotechnological and environmentally-based pest control. Individual papers include, among others: "Inventory of Forest Damages at the Faperta UNCEN Experimental Gardens in Manokwari, Irian Jaya, Indonesia" by Matheus T. E. Kilmaskossu and Jan Piet Nerokouw; "Incidence of Dieback in Two *Acacia mangium* Plantation Sites in Sabah" by Mahmud Sudin; "Preliminary Observations on Insect Pests and Diseases Problems of *Gliricidia sepium* (Jacq.) Walp. germplasm collection in ViSCA and Its Implications for Genetic Improvement" by Ernesto C. Bumatay; "Biological and Environmental Pest and Disease Control Strategy in PICOP" by Emelio O. Anino; "Forest Pest and Diseases Research in the Philippines: An Overview" by Segundino V. Forondo and Marcelino U. Siladan; "Natural Enemies Associated with Some Insect Pests of Forest Plantations in Peninsular Malaysia" by Ahmad Said Sajap and Jaacob Abd. Wahab; "Preliminary Survey on Entomopathogenic Fungi in the Forest at Khao Yai National Park" by Pimpun Sommartya and Banpot Napometh; "Recent Insect Pest Outbreaks in Forest Plantations in Peninsular Malaysia" by Ab. Majid B. Ab. Rahman and Ahmad Said Sajap; and "Development of *Parmela* sp. in a *Pinus merkusii* stand affected by air pollutants at Puncak, West Java" by Dadang K. Permana, Soetrisno Hadi, and Simon T. Nuhamara.

Indonesia/ Malaysia/ Philippines/ Sabah/ Pest, weed, and crop disease management/ Forest management—Commercial forestry and silviculture/ Timber plantations.

527. **Hamer, W. I., and L. L. Kitingan. 1982.** *Agricultural Development in Tambunan, Sabah, Malaysia.* Environmental Report, no. 11. Melbourne, Australia: Graduate School of Environmental Science, Monash University.

Despite government initiatives to provide modern rice strains, fertilizers and other inputs to farmers of Sabah, there has been little if any increase in production. The authors examine this problem through land capability evaluation and socio-economic fieldwork in Tambunan, an inland-lying agricultural area of Sabah state. They find that most of the land suitable for irrigated rice farming has already been developed and farmers have generally failed to use the modern farming inputs made available to them, due in part to underdeveloped extension services and the lack of fit with traditional farming methods. Possible program approach modifications are recommended, including greater emphasis on encouraging diversified farming, better training, and greater involvement of local agency staff in the design and development process.

Malaysia/ Sabah/ State policy—Agricultural and rural development/ Project intervention—Agricultural development.

528. **Harrer, H., ed. 1988.** "Borneo: Mensch und Kultur seit ihrer Steinzeit." Innsbruck: Pinguin-Verlag.

A series of brief papers and essays provide a broad overview of the geography, pre-history, material culture, cosmology, art history, archeology, flora and fauna, health status, and missionary history of Borneo island, covering local Dayak and Penan communities as well as the Brunei Sultanate. The papers draw from classic texts and historical materials in Borneo studies. [In German].

Malaysia/ Indonesia/ Borneo/ Geography/ Indigenous and local communities/ History—Colonial/ History—Pre-colonial/ Forest flora/ Forest fauna.

529.   **Harrisson, T. 1970.** "The Prehistory of Borneo." *Asian Perspectives* 13: 17–45.

   Harrisson provides a broad overview of archeological sites and findings primarily in Sarawak and Sabah. He summarizes the key insights these archaeological materials provide on Borneo's pre-historic human settlements, flora and fauna as well as pre-colonial trade, migration, and inter-island contact. The article closes with an outline highlighting what this information reveals about the development of indigenous material culture and the long history of contact between local communities in Borneo and the peoples and cultures beyond.

   Malaysia/ Sarawak/ Sabah/ History—Pre-colonial/ Indigenous and local communities/ Migration.

530.   **Harrisson, T., and B. Harrisson. 1969.** *The Prehistory of Sabah*. Sabah Society Journal Monograph, vol. 4. Kota Kinabalu: Sabah Society.

   Following an outline of major aspects of Sabah's pre-colonial history (defined as the state's historical development prior to documentation by written record), the authors identify major archaeological sites and artifactual findings (stone tools, earthenware, metal tools, stonewares, and beads). The concluding chapter describes Sabah's "oldest" document, written in the coastal Idahan language using Arabi Jawi script, telling the Idahan story of origin from a mythical ancestor on the Kinabatangan River.

   Malaysia/ Sabah/ History—Pre-colonial.

531.   **Hatch, T. 1980.** "Shifting Cultivation in Sarawak: Past, Present, and Future." In *Tropical Ecology and Development*. Proceedings of the Fifth International Symposium of Tropical Ecology, 16–21 April 1979, Kuala Lumpur. Ed. J. I. Furtado, pp. 483–496. Kuala Lumpur: International Society of Tropical Ecology.

   Although shifting cultivation evolved as food production system well suited to the tropical forest environment, increasing population pressure is making the swidden-based livelihoods of the Iban and Dayak farmers of Sarawak increasingly less viable. The bush/fallow period has been declining in recent decades throughout the state, resulting in falling rice yields, increased soil erosion, and decreasing soil fertility. Swidden farming has the added negative effect of damaging large areas of valuable timber resources. With about 20% of Sarawak's land area under shifting cultivation, and some evidence that this area is being steadily extended, these economic and ecological problems are of widespread impact. Research and development activities will have to aim at devising ways of improving the shifting cultivation system within the context of the hilly, often remote areas in which swidden activities usually take place. Recent attention has been directed to dry terracing and agro-forestry as among the most appropriate means for developing more viable, intensified systems of rice production.

   Malaysia/ Sarawak/ Agriculture—Shifting cultivation's environmental impacts/ Indigenous and local communities—Farming practices/ Indigenous and local communities—Forest land use and management practices/ Agricultural intensification/ Project intervention—Soil conservation/ Project intervention—Fallow improvement.

532.   ———. **1982.** "Shifting Cultivation in Sarawak—A Review." Technical Paper, no. 8. Kuching, Sarawak, Malaysia: Soils Division, Research Branch, Department of Agriculture, Sarawak.

   Malaysia/ Sarawak/ Agriculture—Shifting cultivation/ Agriculture—Shifting cultivation's environmental impacts/ Indigenous and local communities—Farming practices/ Indigenous and local communities—Forest land use and management practices/ Indigenous and local communities—Land and resource tenure systems/ Agricultural intensification/ Poverty/

Project intervention—Fallow improvement/ State policy—Agricultural and rural development/ State policy—Forest and natural resources.

533.   **Helbig, K. M. 1955.** "Die Insel Borneo in Forschung und Schrifttum." *Mitteilungen der Geographischen Gesellschaft in Hamburg* 52: n.g. [Research and Literature on Borneo Island.]

A bibliography on 19th and early 20th century research and literature on Borneo with particular emphasis on geography. [In German].

Indonesia/ Malaysia/ Borneo/ Bibliography/ Geography.

534.   **Hewgill, A. C., and R. A. Cramb. 1992.** "Rural Development in Sabah: A Preliminary Bibliography." Agricultural Economics Discussion Paper, no. 2/92. Brisbane, Queensland, Australia: Department of Agriculture, University of Queensland.

Malaysia/ Sabah/ Bibliography/ Rural development.

535.   **Heydon, M. J., and P. Bulloh. 1996.** "The Impact of Selective Logging on Sympatric Civet Species in Borneo." *Oryx* 30 (1): 31-36.

Heydon and Bulloh summarize results of a study on sympatric civet species in primary and selectively logged forests of the Ulu Segama Forest Reserve, Sabah, from January 1992 to December 1993. The density of the civet population was found to be considerably lower in the logged forest (6.4 per km2) than in the primary forest (31.5 per km2). This difference is likely to be linked primarily to the impact of timber industry activities, as little hunting is known to occur in the area.

Malaysia/ Sabah/ Forest fauna/ Timber industry—Environmental impacts.

536.   **Hoffman, C. L. 1984.** "Punan Foragers in the Trading Networks of Southeast Asia." In *Past and Present in Hunter Gatherer Studies.* Ed. C. Schrire, pp. 123–149. Orlando.

Malaysia/ Indonesia/ Borneo/ Indigenous and local communities—Forest products use and trade/ History—Colonial.

537.   **Hon Tat Tang. 1987.** "Problems and Strategies for Regenerating Dipterocarp Forests in Malaysia." In *Natural Management of Tropical Moist Forests: Silvicultural and Management Prospects of Sustained Utilization.* Ed. F. Mergen and J. R. Vincent, pp. 23–46. New Haven, Conn.: Yale University School of Forestry and Environmental Studies.

Timber production in Malaysia is expected to decline by the late 1990s due to loss of forest resources. Given this trend, plantations are likely to play a central role in the timber industry in the future, replacing natural forests as the main source of raw materials. However, it is projected that at least 8 million ha of natural primary forest will remain in the country and will continue to play a significant, albeit more limited role in timber production. There remains a dearth of scientific evidence on the dynamics of change and regeneration in the natural forest; also poorly understood is to what degree current management prescriptions are truly useful and sustainable over the long run in a silvicultural and economic sense. The author concludes that given present limitations in the availability of reliable data, it appears that an integration of modified versions of the Malayan Uniform System and the Selective Management System comprises the best option for sustainable forest management. Appropriate research programs and information dissemination systems must be instituted to provide a sounder basis upon which this approach may be developed.

Malaysia/ Forest management—Commercial forestry and silviculture/ Forest regeneration.

538. **Hong, E. 1987.** *Natives of Sarawak: Survival in Borneo's Vanishing Forest.* Penang, Malaysia: Institut Masyarakat.

   The author examines in detail the impact of current logging activities on indigenous forest dwellers of Sarawak, focusing largely on the Dayak swidden cultivators of the region. Local swidden farming practices are described. Once a highly sustainable form of land use in the Borneo forests, swidden farming is being undermined by the onset of large-scale, commercial timber extraction. A review of Malaysian land and forestry law, government land development policy, forest policy and dam development is included. Struggles of indigenous forest dwellers to resist encroachment by state agencies and timber companies are highlighted.

   Malaysia/ Sarawak/ Timber industry—Logging/ Timber industry—Impacts on local communities and economy/ Timber industry—Environmental impacts/ Indigenous and local communities—Farming practices/ Indigenous and local communities—Forest land use and management practices/ Indigenous and local communities—Forest products use and trade/ State policy—Forest and natural resources/ State policy—Land development/ Land tenure—Legislation and state policy/ Social movements.

539. **Horne, P. M., T. Ismail, and Chong Dai Thai. 1994.** "Agroforestry Plantation Systems: Sustainable Forage and Animal Production in Rubber and Oil Palm Plantations." In *Agroforestry and Animal Production for Human Welfare.* Proceedings of an international symposium held in association with the 7th AAAP Animal Science Congress, Bali, Indonesia, 11–16 July 1994. Ed. J. W. Copland, A. Djajanegra, and M. Sabrani, pp. 89–98. ACIAR Proceedings, no. 55. Canberra: Australian Centre for International Agricultural Research.

   Rising demand for meat means that demand for forage resources in Southeast Asia will double by year 2000. However, the land available for monoculture animal production is limited, indicating a growing need to integrate land uses between plantations and livestock production. The authors discuss the prospects for sustainable forage production in rubber and oil palm plantations in Indonesia, Malaysia and Thailand. Strategies for improving the forage resource on oil palm and rubber plantations are suggested, including introduction of improved forages and alternative plantation management regimes. The paper draws from an extensive review of the state of research literature.

   Indonesia/ Malaysia/ Agricultural development/ Agroforestry/ Agriculture—Plantations/ Livestock management.

540. **Huang, Y. W., and E. F. Bruenig. 1989.** "Species Richness, Diversity, Structure and Pattern Changes along Ecological Gradients: 1. Preliminary Borneo-Hainan Comparison." *Borneo Research Bulletin* 21 (1): 3–21.

   Malaysia/ Sarawak/ Forest flora/ Forest biology and ecology/ Biodiversity.

541. **Ibrahim Hj. Moh. Kassim. 1984.** "Mamut Copper Mine Pollution, 1977–1982: The Effectiveness of Anti-Pollution Control Measures." Master's thesis, University of San Francisco, San Francisco, Calif.

   Malaysia/ Sabah/ State policy—Pollution control/ Mining.

542.   **Institute of Social Analysis (INSAN). 1992.** *Logging against the Natives of Sarawak*. Kuala Lumpur, Malaysia: INSAN.

The monograph consists of a collection of essays on logging and its impact on local communities and their natural environment in Sarawak. Papers include: "The Continuing Pillage of Sarawak's Forest" (Jomo K. S.); "Logging in Sarawak: The Belaga Experience" (Sarawak Study Group); "Logging Accidents in Sarawak" (Jeyakumar Devaraj); "Shifting Cultivation and Logging in Sarawak" (S. C. Chin); "Sarawak Pribumi Land Rights, Development and 'Primitive' Lifestyles: Lessons for Other Malaysians" (Khoo Khay Jin). See separate entries for abstracts of papers by Jomo K. S. and S. C. Chin.

Malaysia/ Sarawak/ Timber industry—Logging/ Timber industry—Environmental impacts/ Timber industry—Impacts on local communities and economy/ State policy—Forest and natural resources/ Agriculture—Shifting cultivation/ Land tenure/ Social movements/ Political economy.

543.   **Irwin, G. 1955.** Nineteenth Century Borneo: A Study in Diplomatic Rivalry. 's-Gravenhage: Martinus Nijhoff.

Malaysia/ Indonesia/ Borneo/ History—Colonial/ Politics.

544.   **Ismail, G., M. Mohamed, and S. Omar, eds. 1992.** *Forest Biology and Conservation in Borneo*. Proceedings of the international conference, 30 July-3 August 1990, Kota Kinabalu, Sabah, Malaysia. Kota Kinabalu, Malaysia: Yayasan Sabah.

Organized by Yayasan Sabah, Universitii Kebangsaan Malaysia Sabah Campus, and the Sabah Ministry of Tourism and Environmental Development, the conference commemorated the 5th anniversary of the Danum Valley Rainforest Research and Training Programme and the 10th anniversary of UKB's Faculty of Science and Natural Resources. Conference papers focus largely on the biological aspects of Bornean rainforests though some attention was also given to forest management. Papers in the first section of the monograph focus on forest flora and botany, including: "Bamboos of Borneo and their Uses," Soejatmi Dransfield; "Rattans in Borneo: Botany and Utilisation," John Dransfield; "Species Diversity of Wild Fruit Trees in the Forests of Sabah as Illustrated by the Genera *Artocarpus*, *Durio* and *Mangifera*," William W., W. Wong and A. Lamb; "The Genus *Mangifera* in Borneo: Results of an IUCN-WWF/IBPGR Project," J.M. Bompard and A.J.G.H. Kostermans; "The Wild Relatives of Rice in Sabah," Masahuling B. Benong; "A Preliminary Survey of Orchids in Taman Bukit Tawau, Sabah," W. H. Lim and H. A. Saharan; "Problems and Prospects of *Rafflesia* Research in Borneo," Willem Meijer; "Distribution, Dispersal and Some Notes on *Rafflesia* around Kinabalu, Malaysia," Jamili Nais; "Phylogenetics of the Rafflesiaceae," R. S. Beaman, K. Mat-Salleh, W. Meijer and J. H. Beaman; "Specimen Databases and the Utilization for the Flora of Borneo," K. Mat-Salleh, J. H. Beaman and H. Beaman.

Papers in Part II of the proceedings discuss forest fauna, including descriptions of Borneo beetles, orangutans, proboscis monkey and other primates, as well as a paper on "Endemism in Bornean Mammals" by Colin P. Groves. Part III focuses on rainforest dynamics, ecology, and environmental degradation. Papers include, among others: "Hydrologic and Geomorphic Changes Following Rainforest Disturbance with Special Reference to Studies in Borneo," Ian Douglas; "Water Quality Scenario of Rivers in Sabah in Relation to Forest Operations," Murtedza Mohamed; "Conservation of Tropical Lowland Dipterocarp Forest to Plantations of *Acacia Mangium* Stands: Impact On Soil Physical Properties," Kamaruzaman Jusoff; "Species Diversity of Two Adjacent Minor Habitats in Mandor Nature Reserve of West Kalimantan," Herujono Hadisuproto and Syafruddin Said; "Use of Recently Logged Forest by Frugivorous Birds and Mammals," Mohammad Zakaria bin Hussin; "Wildlife Population Parameters As Indicators of the Sustainability of Timber Logging Operations," A. D. Johns and A. G. Marshall; "Hunting Patterns and their Significance in Sarawak," Julian Caldecott.

Part IV has a more varied focus, covering ecological, silvicultural, rural development, ethnobotanical, institutional, and policy-related aspects of forest resource management. Papers include, among others: "Ecological Approaches to Rural Development," G. N. Appell; "Dimensions of Rural Development: A Case of West Kalimantan, Indonesia," Syamsuni Arman; "Protected Areas in Borneo: The Institutional Framework," Peter Eaton; "Ecological Approaches to Commercial Dipterocarp Forestry," W. T. M. Smits, D. Leppe, I. Yasman and M. Noor; "Conservation in Safoda's Kinabatangan Rattan Plantation," P. S. Shim; "Kenyah Medicinal Plants: Beyond the Inventory," Danna J. Leaman, Razali Yusuf and J. Thor Arnason. A final section of the monograph presents abstracts of 35 additional papers given at the conference.

Malaysia/ Sabah/ Sarawak/ Indonesia/ Kalimantan/ Forest flora/ Forest fauna/ Forest biology and ecology/ Biodiversity/ Timber industry—Environmental impacts/ Timber plantations/ Hydrology/ Soil erosion and degradation/ Forest management—Commercial forestry and silviculture/ Forest management—Parks and conservation areas/ Forest management—Forest resource conservation/ Project intervention—Rural development/ Indigenous and local communities—Forest products use and trade/ Rattan—Resource management and conservation/ Rattan—Cultivation/ Non-timber forest products.

545. **Itoh, A., T. Yamakura, K. Ogino, and Lea Hua Seng. 1995.** "Survivorship and Growth of Seedlings of Four Dipterocarp Species in a Tropical Rainforest of Sarawak, East Malaysia." *Ecological Research* 10 (3): 327–338.

Malaysia/ Sarawak/ Forest biology and ecology/ Forest regeneration.

546. **Jakhro, A. A. 1982.** "Evaluation of the Fertility of Grass Land—Twenty Four Paddocks at Tambang Menggaris." *Bulletin of the Society of Agricultural Scientists Sabah* 6 (1): n.g.

Malaysia/ Sabah/ Soils.

547. **Janowski, M. H. 1988.** "The Motivating Forces Behind Recent Changes in the Wet Rice Agricultural System in the Kelabit Highlands." *Sarawak Gazette* 114 (1504): 9–21.

Malaysia/ Sarawak/ Indigenous and local communities—Farming practices/ Agriculture—Permanent/ Agricultural intensification.

548. **Jenkins, G. P. 1989.** Trade, Exchange Rate, and Agricultural Pricing Policies in Malaysia. Washington, D.C.: World Bank.

Malaysia/ State policy—Agricultural and rural development/ Agricultural development.

549. **Joekes, S., with N. Heyzer, R. Oniang'o, and V. Salles. 1994.** "Gender, Environment, and Population." In *Development and Environment: Sustaining People and Nature.* Ed. D. Ghai, pp. 137–166. Oxford: Blackwell.

Critical of "Women in Development" (WID) and "ecofeminist" approaches that posit an assumed, immutable relationship between women and environmental protection, the authors propose a framework of inquiry that problematizes notions of gender and nature and sees both concepts as constructs emerging from the social relations underlying the organization of society. They also place under critical review the direct causal relationship link assumed to exist directly between population growth and environmental degradation. Implied instead is the possibility of the reverse relationship: processes of environmental degradation may themselves have a negative impact on women's status and thus pose an indirect but growing constraint on fertility decline. Gender aspects of social adaptations to environmental change are explored within this framework, based on field data gathered among Kelabit, Murut and

Iban groups in Limbang District, Sarawak, among rural villages of Embu District, Kenya, and among residents of a low-income, peri-urban community in Xochimilco, Mexico. In each case, the paper identifies the gender-specific health and nutritional impacts of environmental change, explores the role played by changing environments on women's interest in fertility and childrearing, and addresses the question of how women's status is affected by environmental change. Evidence from the case studies suggest women's direct exposure to the negative effects of environmental decline, and at least in the case of Sarawak, a pattern of gender-differentiated access to non-resource based livelihood access emerging with rapid economic development. Trends in East Malaysia appear to be towards greater social stratification of gender, as women lack access to the emergent labor market even as traditional forms of forest-resource based livelihoods and cultural activities are being devalued. Findings indicate the need to supplement progress being made in women's education with the provision of other resources (improved agricultural techniques, family planning services, etc.) directly to women.

Malaysia/ Sarawak/ Timber industry—Impacts on local communities and economy/ Indigenous and local communities—Commoditization/ Gender relations/ Gender analysis.

550.   **Johansson, E., and M. Kluge. 1995.** *Natural Rehabilitation of Tractor Disturbed Soils in Tropical Rain Forest in Sabah, Malaysia.* International Rural Development Centre Working Paper, no. 285. Uppsala, Sweden: International Rural Development Centre, Swedish University of Agricultural Sciences.

Malaysia/ Sabah/ Soil erosion and degradation/ Timber industry—Environmental impacts/ Forest regeneration.

551.   **Johari, M. Y. Hj. 1991.** *Issues and Strategies in Rural Development.* Kota Kinabalu, Sabah: Institute for Development Studies.

Papers delivered at a 1989 seminar on issues and strategies in rural development in Kota Kinabalu, Sabah are presented. The seminar was organized to examine the strengths and weaknesses of past rural development strategies and programs and to formulate a more effective, efficient, and consistent rural development plan for the 1990s. Four of the collected papers outline the rural development experiences of the Sabah Foundation and Rural Development Authority respectively, describing how each is responding to the call for more effective intervention strategies for improving the economic welfare of the rural people. While specific approaches vary from one agency to another, one shared characteristic is the persistent belief that rural people are prevented from responding satisfactorily to government initiatives due to a myriad of socio-cultural factors characteristic of local communities (including a high sense of economic dependency syndrome). These factors must be taken into better account in planning for rural development projects in Sabah.

Malaysia/ Sabah/ Project intervention—Rural development.

552.   **Johns, A. G. 1996.** "Bird Population Persistence in Sabah Logging Concessions." *Biological Conservation* 75 (1): 3–10.

In a comparison of three unlogged and six selectively logged forests in southeast Sabah, bird species richness was found to be greatest in the logged areas, probably due to the forest edge effect. At the same time, six particular species appeared consistently vulnerable to the impacts of logging. Noting that these species persisted in scattered, small blocks of unlogged forest and showed little likelihood of eventually colonizing regenerating logged areas, Johns stresses the importance of ensuring that small refuge areas are maintained within logging concessions.

Malaysia/ Sabah/ Forest fauna/ Timber industry—Environmental impactsm/ Biodiversity.

553.   **Jomo K. S. 1992.** "Child Welfare in Sarawak." *Borneo Review* 3: 234–258.

Malaysia/ Sarawak/ Health and nutrition/ Indigenous and local communities—Commoditization/ Poverty.

554.   **———. 1992.** "The Continuing Pillage of Sarawak's Forests." In *Logging Against the Natives of Sarawak.* Ed. Institute for Social Analysis (INSAN), pp. i–ix. Kuala Lumpur, Malaysia: INSAN.

In an introduction to the INSAN monograph, Jomo K. S. provides a brief overview of the timber industry's expansion in East Malaysia. The political economy of invasive timber extraction in Sarawak may be traced back to the state's incorporation into the Malaysia federation, as the British government helped facilitate the transfer of its lucrative colonial possessions into "safe hands" through the granting of privileges, including control over concession disbursement, to the East Malaysian state governments. Political disputes between political contenders in the Sarawak government involving access to logging rights since the early 1980s are described. While politicians and well-connected businessmen profit greatly from the industry, industry workers are poorly compensated and local communities bear the brunt of its environmental costs.

Malaysia/ Sarawak/ Timber industry—Development and structure/ Timber industry—State policy and regulation/ Timber industry—Impacts on local communities and economy/ History—Colonial/ Political economy.

555.   **Jonish, J. 1992.** *Sustainable Development and Employment: Forestry in Malaysia.* World Employment Programme Working Paper, WEP 2-22/WP. 234. Geneva, Switzerland: International Labour Office.

Malaysia/ Timber industry—Development and structure/ Forest management—Economics/ State policy—Forest and natural resources/ Timber industry—State policy and regulation.

556.   **Kahin, A. 1992.** "Crisis on the Periphery: The Rift Between Kuala Lumpur and Sabah." *Pacific Viewpoint* 65 (1): 30–49.

This paper presents an analysis of the current relations between Malaysia's prime minister Dr. Mahathir Mohamad and the state government of Sabah headed by Datuk Joseph Pairin Kitingan, who represents the multiracial Sabah Unity Party (PBS). Kahin suggests that the current state of "near open warfare" between Kuala Lumpur and Kota Kinabalu is a "revival, albeit in intensified form, of dissatisfactions long expressed by Sabah's population at the erosion of the rights they hoped to receive within the Malaysian federation." The federal government has successfully prevailed in at least two previous eruptions of open tensions over the question of Sabah's autonomy. The present crisis, however, has continued for a strikingly long time, with the PBS in control of the state government for the past seven years, voicing a sustained call for greater state's rights.

Datuk Pairin Kitingan has been noted for his skillful diffusion of potentially volatile situations which would have given the central power the needed legitimacy for more direct intervention in the state's government. Another source of strength for the PBS has been the party's multiethnic appeal which has been able to forge important political solidarity between the state's Christian Kadzan and Chinese communities with even some Muslim support. Weaknesses, however, include persistent charges of corruption relating to profits gained from land speculation and the timber industry, fissures within the party leading to splinter groups, and the political strength gleaned by the federal government as a result of its success in putting down earlier challenges from the Sabah government. Although the political future of the PBS party in Sabah is thus in question, the federal government is still faced with the problem of managing open resentment of central government rule among the general population in Sabah. Under these circumstances, blatant heavy-handedness by the federal government is only likely to bolster the PBS power base. In order to diffuse rather than heighten any potential secessionary momentum in Sabah, the federal government would be wiser to address specific grievances of the Sabah population, such as uncontrolled immigration, the small number of local officials in the state bureaucracy, and the desire for a locally-based university.

Malaysia/ Sabah/ Politics/ Ethnicity and ethnic relations/ Social movements.

557.   **Kalsi, M. S., and L. Felix. 1979.** "Soils in Sabah—With Some Collected Crop Yield Data." *Bulletin of the Society of Agricultural Scientists Sabah* 11 (11): n.g.

Malaysia/ Sabah/ Soils.

558.   **Kamil, N. F. 1994.** "Diversification and Commercialization of Upland Agriculture: The Malaysian Experience." In *Upland Agriculture in Asia.* Proceedings of a workshop held in Bogor, Indonesia April 6–8, 1993. Ed. J. W. T. Bottema and D. R. Stoltz, pp. 43–52. Bogor: Regional Co-ordination Centre for Research and Development of Coarse Grains, Pulses, Roots and Tuber Crops in the Humid Tropics of Asia and the Pacific (CGPRT Centre).

Kamil reviews past performance of highland agriculture in Malaysia with a focus on prospects for diversification and commercialization. The paper focuses on the development of the Cameron Highlands in Peninsular as the major location for highland agriculture. Tea, vegetables, flowers, and fruits are most important highland crops with income earning potential. The market trends for these crops is assessed and strategies for future development suggested.

Malaysia/ Peninsular Malaysia/ Agricultural development/ Agriculture—Smallholder cash crop farming/ Agriculture—Smallholder tree and perennial crop farming/ Agricultural economics.

559.   **Kasim bin Ali, A. 1994.** "Change in Food Consumption: The Situation in Malaysia." In *Changes in Food Consumption in Asia: Effects on Production and Use of Upland Crops.* Proceedings of a workshop held in Kandy, Sri Lanka October 6–9, 1992. Ed. J. W. T. Bottema, G. A. C. De Silva, and D. R. Stoltz, pp. 21–32. Bogor: Regional Co-ordination Centre for Research and Development of Coarse Grains, Pulses, Roots and Tuber Crops in the Humid Tropics of Asia and the Pacific (CGPRT Centre).

The author describes supply potential as well as market situation and outlook for maize, soybean, groundnut, cassava. Also reviewed is the situation in the processing sector for these different crops.

Malaysia/ Agricultural development/ Agriculture—Smallholder cash crop farming/ Agricultural economics.

560.   **Kasolan, J. 1988.** "A Preliminary Study of More Economic Land Use of Yayasan Concession Area in Sabah, Malaysia." Master's thesis. Cranfield Institute of Technology, Silsoe College, Silsoe, U.K.

Malaysia/ Sabah/ Land use—Patterns and planning/ Timber industry—Logging/ Forest management—Commercial forestry and silviculture/ Forest management—Economics.

561.   **Kato, M., T. Inoue, and T. Nagamitsu. 1995.** "Pollination Biology of *Gnetum* (*Gnetaceae*) in a Lowland Mixed Dipterocarp Forest in Sarawak." *American Journal of Botany* 82 (7): 862–868.

Malaysia/ Sarawak/ Forest biology and ecology/ Forest flora.

562.   **Kavanagh, M., A. A. Rahim, and C. J. Hails. 1989.** *Rainforest Conservation in Sarawak: An International Policy for WWF.* Kuala Lumpur, Malaysia; Gland, Switzerland: WWF Malaysia; WWF International.

The report is divided into 9 major sections covering 1) Overall national and international contexts in which controversies over forestry development in Sarawak have taken place; 2) Sarawak's forest status; 3) Natural habitats and their protection; 4) Forest sector policy and planning; 5) Production forest management and exploitation; 6) Indigenous people and land-use; 7) Overview of necessary measures to secure forest conservation in Sarawak; 8) Discussion of current and recommended WWF policy in Sarawak; 9) A list of recommended actions for WWF to undertake in order to implement the report's recommended policies. A 4-page bibliography provides a number of published and non-published references relevant to forestry and resource conservation in Sarawak.

Malaysia/ Sarawak/ Deforestation/ Forest management—Commercial forestry and silviculture/ Forest management—Parks and conservation areas/ State policy—Forest and natural resources/ Indigenous and local communities—Forest land use and management practices.

563.   **Kedit, P. M. 1994.** "Use of Plants for Architecture and Decorative Purposes of the Iban in Sarawak." *Sarawak Gazette* 121 (1528): 25–31.

Noting the role of the rainforest environment as a source of useful plants and plant materials, Kedit examines the way in which the design and structure of Iban longhouses as well as various art forms (decorations, tatoos, carvings, and weavings) are informed by both the plants available to Iban villagers as well as by the diversity, nutrient cycling dynamics, and structure of the rainforest.

Malaysia/ Sarawak/ Indigenous and local communities—Forest products use and trade.

564.   **Kee, K. P. 1990.** "Forest Biology and Conservation in Borneo: A Bibliography." Paper presented at the Conference on Forest Biology and Conservation in Borneo, 30 July-3 August 1990, in Kota Kinabalu, Sabah. Photocopy.

Malaysia/ Sabah/ Bibliography/ Forest management—Forest resource conservation/ Biodiversity.

565.   **King, V. T. 1990.** "Land Settlement Programmes in Sarawak: A Mistaken Strategy." In *Margins and Minorities: The Peripheral Areas and Peoples of Malaysia.* Ed. V. T. King and M. J. G. Parnwell, pp. 163–183. Hull, U.K.: Hull University Press.

Malaysia/ Sarawak/ Land settlement and development/ Resettlement/ Indigenous and local communities—State policy.

566.   ———. **1990.** "Why is Sarawak Peripheral?" In *Margins and Minorities: The Peripheral Areas and Peoples of Malaysia.* Ed. V. T. King and M. J. G. Parnwell, pp. 110–129. Hull, U.K.: Hull University Press.

Malaysia/ Sarawak/ Regional development/ State policy—Economic development.

567.   ———. **1993.** *Peoples of Borneo.* Cambridge, Mass.: Blackwell Publishers.

The author describes the diverse cultural communities of Borneo island drawing from archaeological, anthropological and historical sources as well has his own fieldwork in the region. Individual chapters address: General perspectives on Borneo island, the Dayak and other cultural communities, Borneo's prehistory, influences of India, China and Islam, the island's history under European colonialism, major economic systems (hunting-gathering, swidden farming, coastal economies), socio-political organizations (with a focus on egalitarian societies of the Iban and Bidayuh, stratified societies of the Kayan and Kenyah, longhouses, and state formation under the sultanate of Brunei), worldview and religion, material culture, and modernization and development. The book presents a great deal of detail and enables comparison across national and regional boundaries. An extensive 20 page reference list is provided.

Indonesia/ Kalimantan/ Malaysia/ Sarawak/ Sabah/ Ethnography/ Indigenous and local communities—Economy/ Indigenous and local communities—Social relations/ Indigenous and local communities—Religion and cosmology/ Indigenous and local communities— Commoditization/ Indigenous and local communities—Farming practices/ Agriculture— Shifting cultivation/ History—Colonial/ History—Pre-colonial/ State policy—Agricultural and rural development/ Indigenous and local communities—State policy.

568.   ———, ed. **1994.** *Tourism in Borneo: Issues and Perspectives.* Williamsburg, Va.: Borneo Research Council.

Indonesia/ Malaysia/ Borneo/ Regional development/ Economic development.

569.   **Kitingan, J. G., and M. J. Ongkili, eds. 1989.** *Sabah 25 Years Later.* Kota Kinabalu, Sabah: Institute for Development Studies.

Malaysia/ Sabah/ Regional development/ Demography/ Indigenous and local communities/ Rural development/ Agricultural development.

570.   **Kleine, M., and J. Heuveldop. 1993.** "A Management Planning Concept for Sustained Yield of Tropical Forests in Sabah, Malaysia." *Forest Ecology and Management* 61 (3/4): 277–297.

Commercial dipterocarp forests account for about 40 percent of the total land area of Sabah. Procedures have recently been developed for the sustainable management of timber production in these forests based on sustained yield approaches successfully applied in other parts of the world. Under the new regime, planning will proceed at both the enterprise and compartment levels. The system is being adopted with the aim of a successful transition to more sustainable forestry practices than has characterized the more purely exploitation-oriented approaches of past decades.

Malaysia/ Sabah/ Forest management—Commercial forestry and silviculture/ Timber industry—State policy and regulation/ Forest management—Forest resource conservation.

571.   **Koeniger, N., G. Koeniger, S. Tingek, A. Kalitu, and M. Mardan. 1994.** "Drones of *Apis dorsata* (Fabricius 1793) Congregate under the Canopy of Tall Emergent Trees in Borneo." *Apidologie* 25 (2): 249–264.

Malaysia/ Sabah/ Forest biology and ecology/ Forest fauna.

572.   **Kumar, R. 1982.** "A Quantitative Analysis of the Elasticities of Export and Home Demand of Key Malaysian Wood Products." *Kajian Ekonomi Malaysia* 19 (1): 35–45.

Using data from 1960 through 1976, Kumar finds low elasticity of demand for sawlogs as compared with various processed wood products, including sawed timber, plywood, and particleboard. Prospects for industry appear fairly good as long as a focus on downstream processing continues, and timber extraction is appropriately managed to ensure that supply meets demand.

Malaysia/ Timber industry—Trade and markets.

573.   ———. **1986.** *The Forest Resources of Malaysia: Their Economics and Development.* Singapore: Oxford University Press.

Kumar presents a comprehensive review of the development of the Malaysian forestry sector from the colonial period to the present. Providing 15 percent of national export earnings in 1980, and over one-half of the provincial revenue in Sabah, forestry is of central importance to Malaysia's economic development, and particularly so to that of the East Malaysian states. Noting the scarcity of adequate research on Malaysia's forestry sector, the author addresses some major issues in this area both substantively and critically.

Two issues emerge from the analysis in particular. First, the government policy to promote rural development to benefit *bumiputera* (indigenous Malay and East Malaysian residents) has resulted in rapid conversion of forest lands to agricultural use, and these policies have been uncoordinated and ad hoc in nature. Second, government policy on forest land development has been to open land rapidly and maximize short-term economic gain; as a result logging has outstripped agricultural conversion and afforestation capacity, leaving large tracts of logged over land exposed to erosion. This has seriously limited the possibility of natural regeneration and promises to cause a progressive shortage of raw lumber for the developing forest-based industries in the future.

Specific historical factors have been a major factor behind the present lack of a clearly defined forest management system in the country. Among the most important of these was an early separation in the British colonial government between the central Forest Department charged with forest protection and the District Forest Offices charged with administration and revenue collection. A similar separation between administrator and professional forester obtains today. The separation between conservation-minded foresters and revenue-minded administrators has meant that classification of forest areas into productive and protective areas is has been largely ignored, as forest protection has succumbed to growing pressures for commercial forest utilization. The result is growing expanses of stripped land that remain idle and bare. In short, ecological issues have been made peripheral to the economic growth strategy in Malaysia, with some seriously negative implications for forest conservation.

The history of timber extraction and forest land use more specifically in East Malaysia is also described. Most lowland forest in Sabah has already been destroyed. Much of forest cover now set aside as permanent production forest is on hills, where the opportunity cost in terms of agricultural conversion is low, but where regeneration will most certainly need to be artificially introduced at a high cost.

Econometric forecasts for the timber market suggest the urgency of improved forest management practices in order to ensure product quality and quantity in the future. Modifications to the existing system which seem most promising include: 1) Phased privatization of specific facets of forestry sector, especially its capital intensive complexes, which should be attached to long concession leases managed according to guidelines; 2) Increasing the competitiveness of the present concession-bidding system by removing barriers to entry and extending leases to several harvesting cycles; and 3) Thorough review and reform of forest administration, as begun by the new National Forest Policy, to better meet conservation and regeneration needs. A far less politically feasible option would be that of making forestry a federally managed rather than state managed sector, a step which could serve only to coordinate the supply of timber, and not guarantee protection of the resource's renewability.

Malaysia/ Timber industry—Development and structure/ Timber industry—Logging/ Timber industry—State policy and regulation/ Forest management—Commercial forestry and silviculture/ Forest management—Economics/ Forest management—Forest resource conservation/ State policy—Forest and natural resources/ History—Colonial.

574.   **Lamb, A. 1976.** "A Preliminary Report on the Progress of Cocoa Smallholding Development in Sabah." *Journal of the Incorporated Society of Planters* [56]: n.g.

Malaysia/ Sabah/ Agriculture—Permanent/ Agriculture—Smallholder cash crop farming/ Agriculture—Smallholder tree and perennial crop farming/ Agricultural development.

575.   **Lambert, D. 1975.** "Bibliography on Hunter Gatherers in Borneo." *Borneo Research Bulletin* 7: 25–27.

Indonesia/ Malaysia/ Indigenous and local communities/ Bibliography.

576.   **Lee, C. H. 1982.** "Development of Timber Plantations in Sabah." *Journal of Incorporated Society of Planters* 62 (1): n.g.

Lee discusses the growth potential of various 'softwood' tree species based on soil quality as found in the concession areas of Sabah Softwood Sdn.Bhd., a major forest plantation company in Sabah located in Tawau. Potential end-uses and commercial value of these species are suggested. The species with the most promise for the company are estimated to be: a) *Albizia Falcataria*; b) *Eucalyptus Deglupta*; c) *Gmelinz Arbonsa*; and d) *Acacia Mangium*. The establishment of fast growing wood species is possible in Sabah as demonstrated by Sabah Softwood Sdn. Bhd. Much could be gained with the use of improved planting material, proper silvicultural practices, and the implementation of soil surveys and mapping to match tree species to soil type.

Malaysia/ Timber plantations/ Forest management—Commercial forestry and silviculture.

577.   **Lee, L. 1989.** "An Evaluation of a Dairy Farm in Kundasang, Sabah." Dr. Vet. Med. thesis. Universiti Pertanian Malaysia, Serdang Selangor, Malaysia.

Malaysia/ Sabah/ Agriculture—Permanent/ Livestock management.

578.   **Lee, T. 1966.** "The Dayaks of Sarawak." *Journal of Tropical Geography* 23: 28–39.

Malaysia/ Sarawak/ Indigenous and local communities—Economy/ Indigenous and local communities—Forest land use and management practices.

579.   **Lee, Y. C. 1968.** "Land Use in Sarawak." *Sarawak Museum Journal* 16 (3233): 282–308.

Malaysia/ Sarawak/ Land use—Patterns and planning.

580.   **Lee, Y. F. 1994.** "Some Models for Estimating Rattan Growth and Yields." *Journal of Tropical Forest Science* 6 (3): 346–355.

Lee describes ten models for estimating length, volume, and weight of rattan stems and stands, noting results of tests conducted using data from a *Calamus caesius* plot in Kabili-Sepilok Forest Reserve, Sabah.

Malaysia/ Sabah/ Rattan—Growth and distribution/ Rattan—Cultivation.

581.   **Lee, Y. F., and A. Gibot. 1986.** *Indigenous Edible Plants of Sabah.* Sandakan, Sabah: Sabah Forest Department.

Malaysia/ Sabah/ Non-timber forest products/ Indigenous and local communities—Forest products use and trade.

582. **Lee Yong Leng. 1968.** "Population Changes in Sabah, 1951–1960." *Journal of Tropical Geography* 26: 55–68.

Malaysia/ Sabah/ Demography/ Migration.

583. **Leigh, M. Forthcoming.** *The Political Economy of Timber in Sarawak.* Ithaca, N.Y.: Cornell University Press.

Malaysia/ Sarawak/ Timber industry—Development and structure/ Timber industry—Logging/ Timber industry—State policy and regulation/ Political economy/ Social movements/ Ethnicity and ethnic relations.

584. ———. **1966.** "Checklist of Holdings on Borneo in the Cornell University Libraries." Data Paper, no. 62. Ithaca, N.Y.: Southeast Asia Program, Department of Asian Studies, Cornell University.

Malaysia/ Sabah/ Sarawak/ Bibliography.

585. ———. **1974.** *The Rising Moon: Political Change in Sarawak.* Sydney, Australia: Australian National University Press.

Malaysia/ Sarawak/ Politics/ Ethnicity and ethnic relations.

586. ———. **1982.** "Is There Development in Sarawak?: Political Goals and Practice." In *Issues in Malaysian Development.* Ed. J. C. Jackson and M. Rudner, pp. 339–374. Singapore: Heinemann Educational Books (Asia).

Malaysia/ Sarawak/ Regional development/ State policy—Economic development/ Politics.

587. ———. **1990.** "The Socio-Political Dimension: Development in Sarawak." In *Socio-Economic Development in Sarawak: Policies and Strategies for the 1990s.* Proceedings of a seminar, 10–12 October 1988, Kuching, Sarawak. Ed. A. M. M. Salleh et al., pp. 219–225. Kuching, Sarawak: Angkatan Zaman Mansang.

Malaysia/ Sarawak/ Regional development/ State policy—Economic development/ Politics/ Political economy.

588. ———. **1991.** "Money Politics and Dayak Nationalism: The 1987 Sarawak State Election." In *Images of Malaysia.* Ed. M. I. Said and J. Saravanamuttu, pp. 180–202. Kuala Lumpur, Malaysia: Persatuan Sains Sosial Malaysia.

Leigh examines the significance of the 1987 state elections as a turning point in the political alliances between and among the Dayak, Chinese and Muslim communities in Sarawak state. Sarawak politics in the years leading to the 1987 election are discussed and election results analyzed to highlight the ethnic composition of the total votes cast for different parties. Despite growing calls for more equitable distribution of the benefits of Malaysia's New Economic Policy, unlike the situation in Sabah, Dayak nationalists in Sarawak appeared unable to galvanize the Dayak vote while at the same time alienating the state's Chinese constituency. Political cleavages within the state's Muslim leadership provided opportunity for new Dayak-Muslim alliance building yet to some degree also weakened the position of this alliance within the election. Against these tensions, the Federal Government continued to provide key support to the incumbent Muslim-led Coalition

Government which emerged victorious in the election. Nevertheless, Leigh notes the significance of the emerging division within the Muslim leadership of the state which was accompanied by much publicity concerning charges of corruption against incumbent government officials. Coupled with emerging concerns about the neglect of Dayak interests and the increasingly evident degradation of the state's natural resources, such criticism "foreshadows a rather more fundamental questioning of political leaders in future campaigns."

Malaysia/ Sarawak/ Politics/ Social movements/ Ethnicity and ethnic relations.

589.   **Lian, F. J. 1988.** "The Economics and Ecology of the Production of the Tropical Rainforest Resources by Tribal Groups of Sarawak." In *Changing Tropical Forests: Historical Perspectives on Today's Challenges in Asia, Australasia and Oceania.* Ed. J. Dargavel, K. Dixon, and N. Semple, pp. 113–127. Canberra, Australia: Centre for Resource and Environmental Studies.

The paper has four main foci: 1) A history of the status of forest products in the economy of Southeast Asian countries and the involvement of indigenous peoples; 2) The importance of trading of jungle products in the economy of tribal people; 3) The system used by the Kenyah tribe of Borneo to sustain the production of forest resources; and 4) Kenyah perspectives on the influence of political factors on their care for the forest. Earlier generations of Kenyah communities harvested forest products and cultivated land for food production in a sustainable manner, with limited negative impact on the forest ecology in Sarawak. Today, however, Kenyah timber fellers and farmers tend to clear wider areas, and harvest immature trees and other forest products, aggravating the negative effects of logging on the environment. With the loss of control over forest resources to external agents, such as the Sarawak government, the Kenyah presently have little incentive to preserve the forest resource base. "Indigenizing the forest industry" and recognizing traditional tenure claims to put indigenous people back in control over their local resources may be important policy options for ensuring more sustainable forest management.

Malaysia/ Sarawak/ Indigenous and local communities—Economy/ Indigenous and local communities—Forest products use and trade/ Indigenous and local communities—Forest land use and management practices/ Indigenous and local communities—Farming practices/ Non-timber forest products/ State policy—Forest and natural resources/ Land tenure—Legislation and state policy.

590.   ———. **1987.** "Farmer's Perceptions and Economic Change: The Case of Kenyah Swidden Farmers in Sarawak, East Malaysia." Ph.D. diss., Australian National University, Canberra, Australia.

Malaysia/ Sarawak/ Indigenous and local communities—Economy/ Indigenous and local communities—Farming practices/ Indigenous and local communities—Forest land use and management practices/ Indigenous and local communities—Commoditization/ Agriculture—Shifting cultivation.

591.   ———. **1988.** "The Timber Industry and Economic Development in Sarawak: Some Contemporary Trends and Proposals for 1990 and Beyond." In *Socio-Economic Development in Sarawak: Policies and Strategies for the 1990s.* Ed. A. M. M. Salleh, H. Solhee, and M. Y. Kasim, pp. 118–137. Kuching, Sarawak, Malaysia: Angkatan Zaman Mansang (AZAM).

Lian evaluates the performance of the timber industry as one of Sarawak state's leading economic sectors. Though rich in a diversity of plant species, the actual commercial potential of Sarawak's forests is relatively low, given the low density of merchantable species in the region. Even so, Sarawak is presently the main exporter of tropical timber, having overtaken Indonesia since the mid-1980s. Yet the share of returns captured from downstream processing is low, and economic benefits derived from the industry is unevenly distributed, benefiting only a small portion of the state's population. It is likely that present rates of timber extraction are unsustainable, undermining the sector's long-term potential to continue contributing to the state's economy. A series of measures to improve the industry's performance are described, including legislative reform, reform of timber licensing procedures, better regulation of logging operations, and intensification of silvicultural activities to rehabilitate and conserve existing production forests. A number of factors make the development of timber plantations in the state a less than optimal but potentially also necessary option. Specific measures to increase local returns from downstream processing as well as to distribute the benefits derived from the industry more equitably are also recommended.

Malaysia/ Sarawak/ Timber industry—Development and structure/ Timber industry— Logging/ Timber industry—State policy and regulation/ Timber industry—Impacts on local communities and economy/ Timber plantations/ Forest management—Commercial forestry and silviculture.

592. **Liew, T. C., ed. 1984.** *Proceedings of the Seminar on Forest Plantation Development in Malaysia.* Sandakan, Sabah: Sabah Forest Department.

Malaysia/ Timber plantations.

593. **————. 1987.** "Forest Plantations in Sabah, Malaysia." *Klinkii* 3 (3): 2–10.

Describes plantation-related programs of the Sabah Forest Development Authority, Sabah Softwoods Sdn Bhd, and Sabah Forest Industries Sdn Bhd.

Malaysia/ Sabah/ Timber plantations.

594. **Loi, K. S., L. J. Uyo, R. G. Eilers, and R. H. Louie. 1985.** "Terrain Classification in Sarawak." *Malaysian Journal of Tropical Geography* 11: 12–31.

Malaysia/ Sarawak/ Geography/ Soils.

595. **Low, H. 1848.** *Sarawak: Its Inhabitants and Productions.* London: Richard Bentley.

Malaysia/ Sarawak/ History—Colonial/ Ethnography/ Indigenous and local communities— Economy/ Indigenous and local communities—Social relations/ Indigenous and local communities—Religion and cosmology.

596. **MacKinnon, J. R., and K. MacKinnon. 1986.** *Review of the Protected Areas System in the Indo-Malayan Realm.* Cambridge, UK; Gland, Switzerland: IUCN.

Indonesia/ Malaysia/ Forest management—Parks and conservation areas/ Biodiversity.

597. **Mackinnon, J. R., and K. Phillipps. 1993.** *A Field Guide to the Birds of Borneo, Sumatra, Java, and Bali.* Oxford: Oxford University Press.

The guide covers 820 birds with color illustrations and family and species descriptions. Introductory sections provide a broad overview of the biogeography of the region, with a list of Indonesian national parks. Appendices list endemic and endangered species in main reserves and by island, land birds found on offshore island groups, Bornean montane birds by mountain group, bird call sonosketches, regional ornithological clubs and other sources for relevant information.

Malaysia/ Indonesia/ Borneo/ Forest fauna.

598. **Majid, Z. 1985.** "Swidden Cultivation in Sarawak (Iban)." In Swidden Cultivation in Asia: v. 3: Empirical Studies in Selected Swidden Communities: India, Indonesia, Malaysia, Philippines, Thailand. UNESCO Regional Office for Education in Asia and the Pacific, pp. 150–212. Social and Human Sciences in Asia and the Pacific; RUSHAP Series on Occasional Monographs and Papers, no. 12. Bangkok, Thailand: UNESCO Regional Office for Education in Asia and the Pacific.

The author presents results from a UNESCO-sponsored Man and the Biosphere (MAB) field study of swidden cultivators in Sarawak, Malaysia. In 1982 a cluster of five indigenous (Iban) swidden communities were studied for the impact of development on these villages, mutual perceptions between the communities and local government officials/extension agents, interaction between the communities and the natural environment. The study reports empirical findings (income, land use, crop production, labor inputs, farming system management), briefly describes development plans for the area, and discusses participant/extension agent perceptions. The rational economic basis for swidden agricultural practices is emphasized.

Malaysia/ Sarawak/ Agriculture—Shifting cultivation/ Indigenous and local communities—Farming practices/ Household livelihood strategies/ Land use—Patterns and planning/ Project intervention—Rural development/ Cultural ecology.

599. **Malingreau, J. P., G. Stephens, and L. Fellows. 1985.** "Remote Sensing of Forest Fires: Kalimantan and North Borneo in 1982–83." *Ambio* 14 (6): 314–321.

Malaysia/ Sabah/ Forest fires.

600. **Malmer, A. 1990.** "Stream Suspended Sediment Load After Clear-Felling and Different Forestry Treatments in Tropical Rainforest, Sabah, Malaysia." *Research Needs and Applications to Reduce Erosion and Sedimentation in Tropical Steeplands.* Ed. R. R. Ziemer, C. L. O'Loughlin, and L. S. Hamilton, pp. 62–71. IAHS Publication, no. 192. Wallingford, Oxfordshire, U.K.: International Association of Hydrological Sciences Publication.

The authors report on a paired catchment experiment in Mendolong, Sabah investigating the effects of different timber harvesting practices on local water and soil flow regimes. The highest rate of sediment soil loss (3.9 t/ha) was recorded in association with tractor-based timber extraction. Implications for timber harvest management are discussed.

Malaysia/ Sabah/ Timber industry—Logging/ Timber industry—Environmental impacts/ Soil erosion and degradation/ Hydrology.

601. ———. **1992.** "Water Yield Changes after Clear-Felling Tropical Rainforest and Establishment of Forest Plantation in Sabah, Malaysia." *Journal of Hydrology* 134: 77–94.

The paper reports on a paired catchment experiment begun in 1985 in Mendolong, Sabah. The study's aim has been to assess changes in hydrological regime, measured by water flow, hydrochemical, soil and biomass changes, resulting from various timber harvesting strategies and cultivation of fast-growing tree species in plantation stands. Specific results are reported and implications discussed.

Malaysia/ Sabah/ Timber industry—Logging/ Timber plantations/ Timber industry—Environmental impacts/ Hydrology.

602. ———. **1993.** Dynamics of Hydrology and Nutrient Losses as Response to Establishment of Forest Plantation: A Case Study on Tropical Forest Land in Sabah, Malaysia. Ph.D. diss., Swedish University of Agricultural Sciences, Umeå, Sweden.

Malaysia/ Sabah/ Timber plantations/ Hydrology/ Soil erosion and degradation.

603. ———. **1996.** "Hydrological Effects and Nutrient Losses of Forest Plantation Establishment on Tropical Rainforest Land in Sabah, Malaysia." *Journal of Hydrology* 174 (1/2): 129–148.

Malaysia/ Sabah/ Soil erosion and degradation/ Hydrology/ Timber industry—Environmental impacts/ Timber plantations.

604. **Malmer, A., and H. Grip. 1990.** "Soil Disturbance and Loss of Infiltrability Caused by Mechanized and Manual Extraction of Tropical Rainforest in Sabah, Malaysia." *Forest Ecology and Management* 38 (1): 1–2.

Malmer and Grip investigate indicators of soil infiltrability (soil density, infiltration rate, and sorptivity) on two watersheds in Sabah with a history of both selective and clear felling since 1981. Soil density was significantly higher and steady-state infiltrability and sorptivity significantly lower in areas felled using tractors for log removal, when compared with unlogged forest and areas felled using chainsaws and wooden rail skidding (i.e., the 'kuda-kuda' method). These differentials were found to persist even on 6-year old tractor tracks. The research results provide empirical data on the adverse impacts of tractor use in tree felling, particularly for soils with high clay content, and suggest the need to make greater use of alternative methods, including cable yard logging or manual extraction systems.

Malaysia/ Sabah/ Timber industry—Logging/ Timber industry—Environmental impacts/ Soil erosion and degradation/ Hydrology.

605. ———. **1994.** "Converting Tropical Rainforest to Forest Plantation in Sabah, Malaysia. II. Effects on Nutrient Dynamics and Net Losses in Streamwater." *Hydrological Processes* 8 (3): 195–209.

Malaysia/ Sabah/ Timber plantations/ Timber industry—Environmental impacts/ Soil erosion and degradation/ Hydrology.

606. **Maluda, J. W. 1992.** "The People in the Uplands of Sabah and the Twin Issues of Environmental Degradation and Sustainable Agriculture." Report prepared for the Working Meeting on the MacArthur Planning Grant on Strategies for Sustaining Agriculture, Natural Resources, and Communities in the Uplands of the Insular Economies of Southeast Asia, 2–11 January 1992, in Cebu City, Cebu. Photocopy.

Malaysia/ Sabah/ Indigenous and local communities—Farming practices/ Migrant farmers and farming/ Agriculture—Shifting cultivation's environmental impacts/ Agriculture—Permanent/ Agriculture—Smallholder cash crop farming/ Indigenous and local communities—Commoditization/ Poverty/ Project intervention—Agricultural development/ State policy—Agricultural and rural development/ Forest management—Forest resource conservation.

607. ———. **1992.** "The Socio-Cultural, Economic and Political Characteristics of Hillpadi Farmers in Sabah, Malaysia." Photocopy. Kota Kinabalu, Sabah, Malaysia: Institute for Development Studies.

The author provides an interpretative analysis of the data collected from field interviews of some 1,370 shifting cultivators located in various parts of Sabah in 1989. Data collected and analyzed related to the age distribution of heads of households; marital status, ethnicity and religious affiliations; family size and formal education attainment of children; access to health, education and potable water supply; house and land ownership status; main economic activities; availability of government assistance; access to market; incidence of migration; and main sources of information about government policies. Information gained was used by the Institute of Development Studies to formulate a separate development policy for shifting cultivators in Sabah.

Malaysia/ Sabah/ Agriculture—Shifting cultivation/ Indigenous and local communities—Economy/ Indigenous and local communities—Farming practices/ Ethnicity and ethnic relations/ Indigenous and local communities—State policy.

608. **Marsh, C., and B. Gait. 1988.** "Effects of Logging on Rural Communities: A Comparative Study." *Journal of the Sabah Society* n.s., 7: 394–434.

The authors summarize the results of a comparative study on the physical, biological, and socio-economic condition between two villages along the Kinabatangan river in the east coast of Sabah. In Inarad, a remote village relatively untouched by logging, a stable condition exists based on a subsistence economy involving food production and petty cash income from riverborne trade in rattan and other forest products. In Karamuak, on the other hand, after an economic boom brought by widespread logging, the subsistence economy became dislocated, and sources of cash income have become scarce due to the destruction of non-timber forest product resources. Results of these developments have included a high rate of emigration and heightened dependency on the government in the village.

Malaysia/ Sabah/ Timber industry—Impacts on local communities and economy/ Indigenous and local communities—Economy/ Indigenous and local communities—Commoditization/ Indigenous and local communities—Forest products use and trade/ Migration.

609. **Martin, R. A. 1988.** *Deforestation and Community Forestry in Sabah, Malaysia.* RECOFTC Paper, no. 15. Bangkok: Regional Community Forestry Training Center, Faculty of Forestry, Kasetsart University.

A 35 page report describing current community forestry efforts in Sabah, Malaysia.

Malaysia/ Sabah/ Deforestation/ Reforestation/ Project intervention—Social and community forestry.

610. **Martyn, H. S. 1966.** "Silviculture Technique in Sabah." *Malaysian Forester* 29 (4): n.g.

Malaysia/ Sabah/ Forest management—Commercial forestry and silviculture.

611. **Mason, R. 1995.** "Parti Bansa Dayak Sarawak and the Sarawak State Elections of 1987 and 1991." *Kajian Malaysia* 13 (1): 26–58.
Malaysia/ Sarawak/ Politics/ Ethnicity and ethnic relations/ Social movements.

612. **Mead, D. J. 1989.** "Malaysia's 'New' Plantations." *New Zealand Forestry* 33 (4): 12–14.

Mead describes recent efforts in Malaysia to ensure timber supply through the development of timber plantations using fast-growing species (mainly *Acacia mangium*, *Paraserianthes falcataria*, and *Gmelina aborea*). Describing characteristics of these species, Mead also summarizes progress made thus far: In Peninsular Malaysia, a total of 29,000 ha have been planted under the 'Compensatory Forest Plantation Programme," which aims to develop a total of 188,000 ha of timber plantations by the mid-1990s. In Sabah, a total of c. 70,000 ha have been planted through three separate schemes since the mid-1980s: Sabah Softwoods Sdn. Bhd., the Sabah Forest Development Authority, and Sabah Forest Industries Sdn. Bhd., though some setbacks have been experienced due to forest fires.

Malaysia/ Sabah/ Timber plantations.

613. **Medway, Lord. 1965.** *Mammals of Borneo.* Singapore: Royal Asiatic Society.

The author presents a broad descriptive guide to the mammals of Borneo island.

Indonesia/ Kalimantan/ Malaysia/ Sabah/ Sarawak/ Forest fauna.

614. **Meijer, W. 1963.** "Forest Types in Sabah and Their Economic Aspects." A paper presented at the UNESCO Humid Tropics Symposium, July 1963, in Kuching, Sarawak. Photocopy.

Malaysia/ Sabah/ Forest flora/ Forest management—Commercial forestry and silviculture.

615. **Mitchell, A. H. 1994.** "Ecology of Hose's Langur, *Presbytis hosei*, in Mixed Logged and Unlogged Dipterocarp Forest of Northeast Borneo." Ph.D. diss., Yale University, New Haven, Conn.

Malaysia/ Sabah/ Forest fauna/ Forest biology and ecology/ Timber industry—Environmental impacts.

616. **Moll, H. A. J. 1987.** "Oil Palm in Malaysia." In *The Economics of Oil Palm.* pp. 135–166. Wageningen, Netherlands: Centre for Agricultural Publishing and Documentation.

Moll discusses key factors that have contributed to Malaysia's success in developing its palm oil industry since 1960, including abundance of land resources, environmental suitability, ease in switching from rubber to oil palm cultivation, technological advances in both primary production and processing, and palm oil's relative profitability as compared to rubber. The development of the sector has been based on both the development of large, privately owned estates as well as smallholder production organized through government land development schemes. Production has been concentrated mainly in Peninsular Malaysia, accounting for 88% of output, though development has also proceeded fairly rapidly in Sabah and Sarawak in recent years, which today account for 10% and 2% of output respectively. As a whole, Malaysia produces 56% of the world's palm oil, and is responsible for 85% of global exports. The importance of research to support successful technological innovation as well as of institutional factors promoting farmer adoption is noted. Extant conditions are likely to promote further growth.

Malaysia/ Sabah/ Agriculture—Plantations/ Agriculture—Smallholder tree and perennial crop farming/ Agriculture—Smallholder cash crop farming/ Land settlement and development.

617. **Molukun, J. 1962.** "Monogit—A Native Custom." *Journal of the Sabah Society* 1 (2): 17–19.

The Kadazan/Dusun people in Penampang, Sabah perform a number of "monogit" or sacrifice rituals to invoke and appease the "god of agriculture" in order to ensure that the year's harvest is abundant. The author describes one of these sacrifice rituals in closer detail. Performed on a biennial basis, immediately after planting, this ritual is usually conducted by three *bobohizans* (priestesses) who specialize in this sort of traditional worship.

Malaysia/ Sabah/ Indigenous and local communities—Farming practices/ Indigenous and local communities—Religion and cosmology.

618. **Montgomery, P. J. 1984.** "Feasibility of Growing Certain Crops in Sabah." *Journal of Incorporated Society of Planters* September: n.g.

The author assesses the economic and technical feasibility of growing rubber, oil palm, and cocoa under coconut on a large plantation basis in Sabah. Based on experiences of major Malaysian plantation companies who also have properties in Sabah, the pre-tax profit per mature hectare for each crop in 1980 were: Rubber—M$500; Oil Palm—M$1,200; and Cocoa/Copra—M$2,500. Analysis findings suggest that the larger the plantation, the more profitable the enterprise would be on a per mature hectare basis. Given this situation, significant incentives towards plantation consolidation exist.

Malaysia/ Sabah/ Agriculture—Plantations/ Agricultural economics.

619. **Morningstar, O. R., and N. M. Knight. 1990.** "Implementing Agroforestry in Sarawak: A Final Report on the Sabal Pilot Agroforestry Project." Forest Research Report, no. RR 1. Kuching, Malaysia: Reforestation Unit, Forest Department.

A 76 page report describing implementation process and outcome of a pilot agroforestry project in Sabal, Sarawak.

Malaysia/ Sarawak/ Agroforestry/ Project intervention—Agroforestry/ Project intervention—Fallow improvement.

620. **Morrison, A. 1993.** *Fair Land Sarawak: Some Recollections of an Expatriate Official.* Ithaca, N.Y.: Southeast Asia Program, Cornell University.

The author presents a narrative account of his experiences as a Government Information Officer with the British administration in Sarawak in the late 1940s and 1950s. During this period the author was closely involved with preparing the transition to Malaysian independence from colonial rule. The monograph provides both an insightful view of British colonial government in East Malaysia of this period from the perspective of an individual closely affiliated with its administration.

Malaysia/ Sarawak/ History—Colonial/ Politics.

621. **Murtedza, M., and T. T. Chuan. 1991.** "Effects of Deforestation with Special Reference to East Malaysia." *Borneo Review* 2: 122–144.

The opening sections of the paper sketch out the status of East Malaysia's forest resources and their economic significance to the region. This is followed by a summary of news reports and recent research documenting suspended solid loads in rivers associated with logging activities. The data reveals significant increases in sediment loads due to logging and the authors suggest the need for appropriate management responses.

Malaysia/ Sabah/ Sarawak/ Deforestation/ Timber industry—Environmental impacts/ Soil erosion and degradation.

622. **Murtezda, A. 1990.** "Estimation of Sediment Yields of Major Watersheds in Sabah." In *Proceedings of the IHP/UPM/UNESCO Workshop on Watershed Development and Management for Asia and the Pacific*. Kuala Lumpur, Malaysia: University Pertanian Malaysia.

Universiti Pertanian Malaysia, Kuala Lumpur, Malaysia.

Malaysia/ Sabah/ Soil erosion and degradation/ Hydrology/ Timber industry—Environmental impacts.

623. **Mustapha, Z. Hj. 1990.** "Agricultural Transformation and Rural Development in East Malaysia: Aspects of Structural Change and Poverty Among Rural Communities in Sabah." In *Margins and Minorities: The Peripheral Areas and Peoples of Malaysia*. Ed. V. T. King and M. J. G. Parnwell, pp. 227–257. Hull, U.K.: Hull University Press.

Mustapha analyzes changes in the economy of Sabah from the perspective of the traditional agricultural sector and that of the regional economy as a whole. Analysis of structural shifts in the economies of subsistence farming communities is followed by a look at broader changes in the structure of the Sabah economy and the policies associated with them. While significant improvements have been scored in overall agricultural productivity, problems of underdevelopment, poverty and income imbalances still prevail in many areas of the state.

Malaysia/ Sabah/ Regional development/ Poverty/ Indigenous and local communities—Economy/ Indigenous and local communities—Commoditization/ State policy—Agricultural and rural development.

624. **Nasi, R. 1993.** "Analysis of the Spatial Structure of a Rattan Population in a Mixed Dipterocarp Forest of Sabah (Malaysia)." *Acta Oecologica* 14 (1): 73–85.

Malaysia/ Sabah/ Rattan—Growth and distribution.

625. **Needham, R. 1972.** "Penan." In *Ethnic Groups of Insular Southeast Asia*. Ed. F. M. Lebar, pp. 176–180. New Haven.

Malaysia/ Indonesia/ Sarawak/ Kalimantan/ Ethnography/ Indigenous and local communities.

626. **Neun, P. et al. 1991.** "Appropriate Land Use Systems for Shifting Cultivators: Technical and Institutional Proposals for the Rural Community Development Programme Based on Participatory Approach in Kota Marudu district, Sabah." Report prepared for the Centre for Advanced Training in Agricultural Development, Technical University of Berlin. Photocopy. Berlin, Germany: Centre for Advanced Training in Agricultural Development, Technical University of Berlin.

A proposal for an economically and socially viable, as well as environmentally sound pilot project in rural development is presented for the hill areas of Koromoka and Tg. Babu Darat, where residents are mainly shifting cultivators, and land has been seriously degraded due to intensive logging and hillpadi farming activities. The project model was developed after a three month field study by a group of post graduate students from the Technical University of Berlin. Specific components of the model include 1) selection of land use for individual sites within the project based on the site's topography, soil depth, the state of degradation and the distance of the land from the homestead, and 2) recognition of the need to create an institution that would facilitate the active participation of the people in planning and implementation of projects.

Four preliminary suggestions are given for land use selection: 1) In areas with a slope of up to 30 degrees, with a soil depth of more than 30 cm., and soil suitable for agriculture but not requiring intensive conservation measures, crop choices are coconut and rubber to be planted under the sloping agriculture land technology (SALT). 2) In areas with slope of 10 to 60 degrees, soil depth of less than 30 cm, and soil suitable for agriculture but not requiring intensive conservation measures, an appropriate crop choice would be rubber alone to be planted under SALT system or on terraces. 3) In areas with slope of up to 60 degrees and soil not suitable for agriculture due to degradation, an appropriate land use would be tree farming. 4) On hilltops and in areas with slope of more than 60 degrees with soil not suitable for agriculture but important as watershed areas, an appropriate land use would be to maintain protection forest.

Malaysia/ Sabah/ Project intervention—Rural development/ Project intervention—Soil conservation/ Project intervention—Fallow improvement/ Land use—Patterns and planning/ Conservation farming.

627.   **Nicolaisen, I. 1983.** "Change Without Development: The Transformation of Punan Bah Economy." *Sarawak Museum Journal* n.s., 32 (53): 191–230.

Malaysia/ Sarawak/ Indigenous and local communities—Commoditization/ Indigenous and local communities—Forest products use and trade/ Timber industry—Impacts on local communities and economy/ Land settlement and development—Impacts on local communities and economy.

628.   **Nolten, M. et al. 1986.** "The Socio-Economic Status of Shifting Cultivators in 7 Selected Villages in Mukim Nabawan, Sabah." Photocopy. Utrecht, Netherlands: Department of Geography of Developing Countries, State University of Utrecht.

The authors describe the swidden-based farming systems in 7 villages of Nabawan district, Sabah, drawing from data gathered in a 1985–86 socio-economic survey. Fallow periods average about 6 years among the farmers studied, with rice, cassava, maize the most important food crops. Coffee and cacao are also grown to obtain cash income. While vegetables and fish-ponds appear promising options for the development of appropriate agricultural projects in the area, conditions of low fertility and poor soil drainage pose serious obstacles to a complete switch from shifting cultivation to permanent agriculture.

Malaysia/ Sabah/ Agriculture—Shifting cultivation/ Agriculture—Smallholder cash crop farming/ Agriculture—Smallholder tree and perennial crop farming/ Indigenous and local communities—Farming practices/ Farming systems research/ Farm management—Economics/ Project intervention—Fallow improvement.

629.   **Nomura, J. 1984.** "Prospects for the Marketing and Utilization of Fast Growing Plantation Timber from Japanese Viewpoint." In *Proceedings of the Seminar on Forest Plantation Development in Malaysia.* Ed. L. T. Chim. Sandakan. Sabah: Sandakan Forest Department.

Malaysia/ Sabah/ Timber plantations/ Timber industry—Trade and markets.

630.   **Nussbaum, R., J. Anderson, and T. Spencer. 1995.** "Factors Limiting the Growth of Indigenous Tree Seedlings Planted on Degraded Rainforest Soils in Sabah, Malaysia." *Forest Ecology and Management* 74 (1–3).

Malaysia/ Sabah/ Soil erosion and degradation/ Timber industry—Environmental impacts/ Forest regeneration.

631.   **Nykvist, N. 1994.** "An Environmental Impact Study on Establishment of Forest Plantations in Sabah, Malaysia." *IRD Currents* 8: 25–27.

>   Nykvist summarizes results of a two-year study on the effects of logging and forest plantation development (using *A. mangium*) in six watersheds in Sabah, Malaysia undertaken in the mid-1980s. Soil erosion is gauged on land subject to different treatments (manual logging and extraction, manual logging with tractor-based extraction followed by burning, and no logging). Soil erosion was 4.9 tons per ha in the plots subjected to tractor use and burning as compared with 2.2 tons per ha on the manually treated areas. While costs of clearing and plantation establishment proved higher in the manually treated plots, these areas were also characterized by richer growth of *A. mangium*.

>   Malaysia/ Sabah/ Timber plantations/ Soil erosion and degradation/ Timber industry—Environmental impacts.

632.   **Nykvist, N., H. Grip, Sim, Boom Liang, A. Malmer, and F. K. Wong. 1994.** "Nutrient Losses in Forest Plantations in Sabah." *Ambio* 23 (3): 210–215.

>   The authors report on research aimed at assessing inorganic nutrient losses from the soil on areas subjected to different methods of clear felling (tractor logging with subsequent burning and manual logging with no burning). Unburned, manually logged areas showed far less soil disturbance than those where tractors had been used; nutrient losses in the former were 50% less than those in the latter. Also significant was the thicker weed infestation that occurred in burned areas, signifying higher costs associated with plantation development. The authors propose various methods for limiting nutrient losses during clear felling of tropical forests. [Summarized from journal abstract].

>   Malaysia/ Sabah/ Timber industry—Environmental impacts/ Timber plantations/ Soil erosion and degradation.

633.   **Oelze, K. A., and M. Heinrich. 1994.** "Documentation, Effectivity, and Importance in Forestry of Medicinal Plants from Sabah, Malaysia." *Angewandte Botanik* 68 (5/6): 177–186.

>   Oelze and Heinrich report on a 1990 ethnobotanical study documenting medicinal plant use by residents of Rompon village near Mt. Kinabalu, Sabah. Villagers were found to use 106 plants for 120 uses. Effectivity for each use was assessed on a ranked scale by integrating ethnobotanical, phytochemical, and pharmacological data. About 65 percent of the medicinal plant species identified were found to be possibly or probably effective.

>   Malaysia/ Sabah/ Indigenous and local communities—Forest products use and trade/ Nontimber forest products.

634.   **Olander, L. 1995.** "The Role of Nutrient Dynamics in Maintaining Tree Species Diversity at Lambir Hills National Park, Sarawak, Malaysia." *TRI News* 14 (1): pp. 23–26.

>   Malaysia/ Sarawak/ Forest biology and ecology/ Biodiversity.

635.   **Padoch, C. 1980.** "The Environmental and Demographic Effects of Alternative Cash-Producing Activities Among Shifting Cultivators in Sarawak." In *Tropical Ecology and Development, 16–21 April 1979, Kuala Lumpur.* Proceedings of the Fifth International Symposium of Tropical Ecology. Ed. J. I. Furtado, pp. 475–481. Kuala Lumpur: International Society of Tropical Ecology.

Alternative methods of earning cash income are shown to have significantly different implications for population growth and forest land degradation. Off-farm wage labor away from home involves long absences of large numbers of men from the village and appears to be associated with reduced population growth and less population pressure on the land than in areas where wage labor plays little or no role in the village economy. Villages were a large portion of cash income is derived from the collection and sale of forest products appear to grow more rapidly. Cash cropping tends to aggravate this pressure, particularly in the case of some export crops, by leading to soil deterioration. Results of the research suggest issues related to economic development that should be given greater attention in considering appropriate natural resources and development policy options.

Malaysia/ Sarawak/ Household livelihood strategies/ Indigenous and local communities— Economy/ Indigenous and local communities—Commoditization/ Indigenous and local communities—Farming practices/ Indigenous and local communities—Forest products use and trade/ Indigenous and local communities—Forest land use and management practices/ Population pressure/ Agriculture—Shifting cultivation's environmental impacts/ Agriculture—Smallholder cash crop farming.

636.   ———. 1982. "Land Use in New and Old Areas of Iban Settlement." *Borneo Research Bulletin* 14: 1–16.

Malaysia/ Sarawak/ Indigenous and local communities—Forest land use and management practices/ Agriculture—Shifting cultivation/ Migration.

637.   ———. 1982. *Migration and its Alternatives among the Iban of Sarawak.* Verhandelingen van het Koninklijk Institut voor Taal-, Land-en Volkenkunde, no. 98. The Hague, Netherlands: M. Nijhoff.

Malaysia/ Sarawak/ Indigenous and local communities—Farming practices/ Indigenous and local communities—Forest land use and management practices/ Indigenous and local communities—Social relations/ Indigenous and local communities—Land and resource tenure systems/ Agriculture—Shifting cultivation/ Population pressure/ Migration.

638.   ———. 1984. "The Iban of Engkari: A History of Migration and Settlement." *Sarawak Museum Journal* 33: 1–13.

Malaysia/ Sarawak/ Indigenous and local communities—Farming practices/ Agriculture— Shifting cultivation/ Migration/ Population pressure.

639.   **Padoch, C., and N. L. Peluso, eds. 1996.** *Borneo in Transition: People, Forests, Conservation, and Development.* Kuala Lumpur: Oxford University Press.

Indonesia/ Malaysia/ Kalimantan/ Sarawak/ Sabah/ Borneo/ Regional development/ Agricultural development/ Forest biology and ecology/ Deforestation/ Forest management—Forest resource conservation/ Forest management—Parks and conservation areas/ Indigenous and local communities—Economy/ Indigenous and local communities— Commoditization/ Indigenous and local communities—Forest land use and management practices/ Indigenous and local communities—Land and resource tenure systems/ Land settlement and development/ Land settlement and development—Impacts on local communities and economy/ Land tenure—Legislation and state policy/ Timber industry— Logging/ Timber industry—Impacts on local communities and economy/ State policy— Forest and natural resources.

640.   **Palmer, J. R. 1990.** "Forestry and Land Use in Sarawak." *Borneo Research Bulletin* 22: 42–43.

The author challenges R. Cramb for "partial use of evidence" in an earlier paper on the effects of shifting cultivation in the Sarawak rainforest. Contrary to Cramb's argument, the author maintains that substantial loss of primary rainforest may be attributed directly to "deliberately excessive clearing" by indigenous forest dwellers interested in later compensation when government land development plans are implemented. Aerial photographs and ecological studies by the Malaysian Forest Research Institute are cited to substantiate this claim.

Malaysia/ Sarawak/ Deforestation/ Forest management—Control of shifting cultivation.

641. **Payne, J., and C. M. Francis. 1985.** *A Field Guide to the Mammals of Borneo.* Kota Kinabalu; Kuala Lumpur, Malaysia: World Wildlife Fund Malaysia.

Malaysia/ Sabah/ Sarawak/ Indonesia/ Borneo/ Kalimantan/ Forest fauna.

642. **Petch, B. 1986.** "Alternatives to Shifting Cultivation: The Sabal Agroforestry Project." Forest Research Report, no. SS 15. Kuching, Sarawak: Forest Department.

A 34 page report describing the aims, structure and progress of a pilot agroforestry project in Sabal, Sarawak.

Malaysia/ Sarawak/ Project intervention—Agroforestry/ Project intervention—Fallow improvement.

643. **Phelan, P. R. 1988.** "Native Law in Sabah: Its Administrators—Headman and Native Chief." *Journal of the Sabah Society* 8 (4): 475–501.

The author provides a historical account of the evolution of the local chieftain system, an institution which at one time was a dominant part of the daily life of rural people in Sabah. The historical as well as contemporary role played by native chiefs in maintaining law and order, dispensation of native justice, land allocation and cooperative economic activities is outlined. In the past, when land was still largely communally owned, the authority to allocate land to subsistence agriculture resided with the native chiefs. This conferred much reverence and social status to those occupying this position. Today, however, most of the land in rural areas is under residual ownership which in turn has reduced the status of native chiefs within local communities.

Malaysia/ Sabah/ Indigenous and local communities—Social relations/ Indigenous and local communities—Land and resource tenure systems.

644. **Phillips, C. 1987.** "Preliminary Observations on the Effects of Logging on a Hill Forest in Sabah." In *Impact of Man's Activities on Tropical Upland Forest Ecosystems.* Ed. Y. Hadi, K. Awang, N. Muhamad Majid, and S. Mohamed, pp. 187–215. Serdang, Selangor, Malaysia: Universiti Pertanian Malaysia.

This paper presents the findings of research conducted on Research Plot 467 near Keniangau regarding damage to soil and vegetation arising from selective logging activities. Research findings indicate that some 12.42% of the area was bared by tractor tracks. Removal of commercial wood average 54m/ha but about 43% of dipterocarp trees more than 10 cm dbh were damaged in the process. Logging activities also increased fire hazard in the area by leaving 66 m/ha of the 120m/ha of wood felled on the forest floor. The paper suggests that residual stocking would need 70 years or more to yield 15 trees per ha in the next harvest, and that shorter harvest cycles are possible if treatments are carried out and/or if more species becomes marketable.

Malaysia/ Sabah/ Timber industry—Environmental impacts/ Soil erosion and degradation.

645.   **Pinard, M. A., and F. E. Putz. 1994.** "Vine Infestation of Large Remnant Trees in Logged Forest in Sabah, Malaysia: Biomechanical Facilitation in Vine Succession." *Journal of Tropical Forest Science* 6 (3): 302–309.

       Malaysia/ Sabah/ Forest regeneration/ Forest biology and ecology/ Vegetation analysis.

646.   **Pinard, M. A., F. E. Putz, J. Tay, and T. E. Sullivan. 1995.** "Creating Timber Harvest Guidelines for a Reduced-Impact Logging Project in Malaysia." *Journal of Forestry* 93 (10): 41–45.

       The authors describe a carbon-offset arrangement between a U.S. power company and a forest concessionaire in Sabah. Guidelines are being developed to reduce logging damage to both soils and standing trees with the aim of decreasing greenhouse gas emissions resulting from excessive tree loss.

       Malaysia/ Sabah/ Forest management—Commercial forestry and silviculture/ Forest management—Forest resource conservation.

647.   **Ping, K. K. et al. 1990.** *Forest Biology and Conservation in Borneo: A Bibliography.* Kota Kinabalu: Yayasan Sabah.

       Malaysia/ Sabah/ Forest biology and ecology/ Forest management—Parks and conservation areas/ Biodiversity/ Bibliography.

648.   **Plas, M. C. van der, and L. A. Bruijnzeel. 1993.** "Impact of Mechanized Selective Logging of Rainforest on Topsoil Infiltrability in the Upper Segama Area, Sabah, Malaysia." In *Hydrology of Warm Humid Regions.* Proceedings of an international symposium held at Yokohama, Japan, 13–15 July 1993. Ed. J. S. Gladwell, pp. 203–211. Wallingford, Oxfordshire, U.K.: IAHS Press.

       Malaysia/ Sabah/ Soil erosion and degradation/ Hydrology/ Timber industry—Environmental impacts.

649.   **Primack, R. B. 1991.** "Logging, Conservation, and Native Rights in Sarawak Forests from Different Viewpoints." *Borneo Research Bulletin* 23: 3–13.

       The author reviews the ITTO report on selective logging in Sarawak prepared in early 1990. This is followed by a brief account of the Sarawak government's response, which, suggests the authors, appeared to reflect a cautious acceptance of the report's major conclusions.

       Malaysia/ Sarawak/ Timber industry—Logging/ Forest management—Forest resource conservation/ Indigenous and local communities—Land and resource tenure systems/ Land tenure—Legislation and state policy.

650.   **Primack, R. B., and F. Tieh. 1994.** "Long-term Timber Harvesting in Bornean Forests: The Yong Khow Case." *Journal of Tropical Forest Science* 7 (2): 262–279.

       The Yong Khow Sons timber concession comprises the oldest concession operating in the hill forests of Sarawak. Primack and Tieh highlight the relative success achieved by the concession in sustainable forest extraction, noting the good condition of the forests in the concession despite the 3–4 felling cycles which have occurred since 1938. Factors behind this successful performance are discussed, as well as recent problems concerning agricultural conversion within the timber concession area.

Malaysia/ Sarawak/ Timber industry—Logging/ Forest management—Commercial forestry and silviculture/ Forest management—Control of shifting cultivation.

651. **Pringle, R. 1970.** *Rajahs and Rebels: The Ibans of Sarawak under Brooke Rule, 1841–1941.* London: Macmillan.

Malaysia/ Sarawak/ History—Colonial/ Indigenous and local communities—Social relations/ Ethnicity and ethnic relations/ Social movements.

652. **Proctor, J. et al. 1988.** "Ecological Studies on Gunung Silam, A Small Ultrabasic Mountain in Sabah, Malaysia. I. Environment, Forest Structure and Floristics." *Journal of Ecology* 76: 320–340.

Reporting on ecological fieldwork conducted in 1983–84, the authors describe the local climate, geology, soils, and vegetation of Gunung Silam in Sabah. Changes in species composition with rising elevation are highlighted.

Malaysia/ Sabah/ Forest biology and ecology/ Soils/ Forest flora.

653. ———. **1989.** "Ecological Studies on Gunung Silam, A Small Ultrabasic Mountain in Sabah, Malaysia. II. Some Forest Processes." *Journal of Ecology* 77: 317–331.

Following an earlier paper on basic geologic, climatic, vegetative, and distinctive soils-related characteristics of Gunung Silam given in a previous paper, the authors now describe key forest processes, involving herbivory, mortality, diameter increment, litterfall, and foliar nutrients.

Malaysia/ Sabah/ Forest biology and ecology.

654. **Putz, F. E., and A. Susilo. 1994.** "Figs and Fire." *Biotropica* 26 (4): 468–469.

Putz and Susilo observe and discuss the persistence of hemiephytic figs in areas affected by fire, based on data gathered from Borneo and Venezuela.

Indonesia/ Malaysia/ Borneo/ Forest flora/ Forest biology and ecology/ Forest fires.

655. **Rabinowitz, A. 1995.** "Helping a Species Go Extinct: The Sumatran Rhino in Borneo." *Conservation Biology* 9 (3): 482–488.

Current efforts to reverse the steep decline of rhinoceros populations in Asia have tended to emphasize ex-situ conservation methods, mainly through captive breeding programs. Rabinowitz characterizes this approach as a costly failure, as evidenced by the poor results of the Sumatran Rhino Trust which succeeded in capturing only 35 rhinos from forest areas of Sumatra, Borneo, and Peninsular Malaysia between 1987 and 1993, 12 of which have died in captivity, and none of which have produced offspring. The situation of rhinos in Sabah, the East Malaysian state containing the most important populations of Sumatran rhino outside Sumatra and Peninsular Malaysia, is presented as a case study of the rhinos' declining numbers, shrinking habitat, and ineffective conservation efforts. The new conservation strategy being promoted by the Global Environmental Facility, focusing on wild population protection, sanctuary management, captive propagation, and gene-bank technologies, also appears flawed by an over-reliance on high-tech, ex-situ measures. Rabinowitz emphasizes the need to focus efforts much less on captive breeding and much more on "intensive, on-the-ground protection and management activities."

Malaysia/ Indonesia/ Sabah/ Forest fauna/ Wildlife management.

656.   **Rahim, S., and M. Anuar. 1987.** *Promoting the Concept of Agroforestry to Small Farmers in Sabah: A Preliminary Experience.* FRC Publication, no. 38. Sandakan, Malaysia: Forest Research Agency, Sabah Forest Department.

Rahim and Anuar describe two recent agroforestry projects of the Sabah Forest Department: a demonstration plot set up at Sungai Darling in the Segaliud Forest Reserve in 1983, and the agroforestry component of a resettlement project started in central Sabah in 1984. The demonstration 64.5 ha plot in Sungai Darling involves a number of different models, including: 1) cultivation of *Coffea liberica* and *Coffea robusta* under *Gliricidia sepium* and durian trees in an advanced fallow plot; 2) simultaneous cultivation of numerous multipurpose species (*Durio, Shorea macrophylla, Dyera costulata, Macadamia,* and *Cinnamomum*); 3) the intercropping of various forest trees with various fruit trees (rambutans, mawa mangosteens, mawa coconut, and others); and 4) use of various other perennial trees, such as bamboo, pinang, avocado and banana, in different constellations as borders or plantations.

The central Sabah resettlement project aimed at discouraging shifting cultivation by establishing viable farming system alternatives, including 1) intercropping of cocoa and coffee with fast-growing tree species (*Gmelina aborea, Acacia mangium, Paraserianthes falcataria, Leucaena leucocephala,* and *Parkia*); (2) integrated plantations using multipurpose and fruit trees; and 3) rattan and bamboo plantations.

Malaysia/ Sabah/ Project intervention—Agroforestry/ Resettlement/ Forest management—Control of shifting cultivation.

657.   **Raich, J. W. 1987.** "Canopy Openings, Seed Germination, and Tree Regeneration in Malaysian Coastal Hill Dipterocarp Forest." Ph.D. diss., Duke University, Durham, N.C.

Raich assesses the effects of treefall gaps on microclimates, the influence of gap size on tree seed germination, the influence of light on seedling growth, and factors influencing seedling distribution in forest gaps based on a study of coastal hill dipterocarp forest in Pantai Acheh Forest Reserve, Penang, Malaysia.

Malaysia/ Peninsular Malaysia/ Forest biology and ecology/ Forest regeneration/ Vegetation analysis.

658.   **Rambo, T. A. 1982.** "Orang Asli Adaptive Strategies: Implications for Malaysian Natural Resource Development Planning." In *Too Rapid Rural Development: Perceptions and Perspectives from Southeast Asia.* Ed. C. MacAndrews and Chia Lim Sien, pp. 250–299. Athens, Ohio: Ohio University Press.

Conversion of tropical forest lands on peninsular Malaysia to agricultural use has proceeded at a rapid pace since independence. Private agents and state development authorities have both played central roles in this process. Indigenous forest-dwelling communities on the peninsula have been severely affected, often to their detriment. This paper describes the nature of Orang Asli (Semang and Senoi) social systems as adapted to life in the rain forest. Given the ability of the Semang and Senoi to maintain their communities without damaging the forests around them, the author advises government policies that preserves the adaptability and sustainability of the indigenous way of life and livelihood.

Malaysia/ Peninsular Malaysia/ Indigenous and local communities—Social relations/ Indigenous and local communities—Forest products use and trade/ Indigenous and local communities—Forest land use and management practices/ Land settlement and development—Impacts on local communities and economy.

659. **Regis, P. 1989.** "Demography." In *Sabah 25 Years Later*. Ed. J. P. Kitingan and M. J. Ongkili, pp. 405–450. Kota Kinabalu, Sabah: Institute for Development Studies.

Malaysia/ Sabah/ Demography.

660. **Renterghem, O. van. 1988.** "From Independence to Incorporation: Shifting Cultivation in Transition." Report prepared for the University of Utrecht. Utrecht, Netherlands: University of Utrecht.

Reporting on the effects of modernization on Rungus swidden farming communities of Sabah, Renterghem suggests that recent developments have tended to polarize two groups in village community life: young households who take opportunities offered by modernization to increase their cash income and accumulated wealth; and older households, who are less involved in cash transactions. Such change notwithstanding, the role of swidden farming continues to be central in the village economy, particularly to meet basic food needs. Renterghem's analysis is based on fieldwork in the Kudat and Pitas Districts of northern Sabah.

Malaysia/ Sabah/ Indigenous and local communities—Commoditization/ Household livelihood strategies/ Agriculture—Shifting cultivation.

661. **Rhys, W. T. 1962.** "Tambunan Dusun Social Structure." *Sociologus* n.s., 12: 51–63.

Malaysia/ Sabah/ Indigenous and local communities—Social relations/ Ethnography.

662. **Roth, H. L. February 1896.** *The Natives of Sarawak and British North Borneo.* London: Truslove and Hanson.

Malaysia/ Sabah/ Sarawak/ History—Colonial/ Ethnography/ Indigenous and local communities.

663. **Rousseau, J. 1987.** "Kayan Land Tenure." *Borneo Research Bulletin* 19: 47–56.

Rousseau continues a debate with anthropologist Appell on the question of devolvable usufructuary rights among the Kayan Dayak of Malaysia. Drawing from fieldwork conducted in different parts of Kayan territory, he points out the variability of usufructuary rights assignment among the Kayan: while the middle Baluy Kayan do not generally recognize a kin group's right to fallowed land it once cultivated land, other Kayan groups along the Mahakam, Baram, and Kayan rivers do. Argues Rousseau, the field data suggests that land tenure systems are strongly influenced by the availability of land, and thus are likely to change as land becomes more or less scarce. Among the Baluy Kayan it appears that labor investment rather than simply tree felling represents a key condition for assuming usufructuary rights.

Malaysia/ Indonesia/ Borneo/ Indigenous and local communities—Land and resource tenure systems.

664. ———. **1988.** "Central Borneo: A Bibliography." *The Sarawak Museum Journal* n.s., 38 (59): 1–274.

Indonesia/ Malaysia/ Sarawak/ Bibliography.

665. ———. **1990.** *Central Borneo: Ethnic Identity and Social Life in a Stratified Society.* Oxford: Clarendon Press.

In a detailed ethnography, Rousseau characterizes central Borneo as distinct social unit marked by great ethnic diversity yet with a common history and social system cutting across ethnic boundaries. The Kayan form the most homogeneous ethnic category, their social organization appears to be a model for others, and their language the lingua franca of the region. Also present, however, are Kenyah, Kajang, Kelabit, Penan, Bukat, and many more indigenous tribal groups. Rousseau draws from written sources as well as fieldwork of the early 1970s and 1984 to describe the ethnic distribution in historical context, outlining early migrations and pre-colonial history as well as developments in more recent periods. The social organization of Central Borneo agriculturalists, including settlement patterns, village economy, and political structures, are characterized by a stratified system of social hierarchy involving high aristocrats, low aristocrats, commoners, and, in the past, slaves. The migrations, settlement, and economy, of Central Borneo nomads are also described, along with their egalitarian political organization in which nomadic leaders have little formal authority and rely largely on persuasive skills to influence group decisions and conduct.

Another focus of the ethnography is a study of the relations and interactions between swiddeners and nomads, between different swidden groups, and between Central Borneo peoples and coastal communities. Swiddener-nomad relations pivot around trade in forest products, while sometimes also involving alliances forged in face of invasion from other groups or downriver forces. Nomads are largely subordinated to settled swiddeners, and the heads of the latter command a position as "overlord" over the former. Nomads are typically seen as "serving" more powerful swiddeners, yet they are also able to escape oppressive relationships by switching allegiance to other groups. A major source of power enjoyed by swiddeners in their economic relationship with nomadic groups is the former's larger population size,, access to outside resources, and propensity towards asserting hierarchical relations of power. Among agriculturalists, "the relatively rigid local power structure articulates with a more flexible regional system" such as informal councils in which different members exert varying degrees of clout. In sum, in describing Central Borneo as an integrated social unit, Rousseau presents ethnicity as one component within this unit; that is, as "people's conceptualization of their social and cultural life" but not necessarily "the inescapable frame of social relations." The analysis places into question the salience of ethnic units as unit of analysis in social research on Borneo.

Indonesia/ Malaysia/ Borneo/ Ethnography/ Indigenous and local communities—Social relations/ Indigenous and local communities—Economy/ Indigenous and local communities—Forest products use and trade/ Indigenous and local communities—Land and resource tenure systems/ Ethnicity and ethnic relations.

666. **Sahabat Alam Malaysia. 1989.** *The Battle for Sarawak's Forests.* Penang, Malaysia: World Rainforest Movement; Sahabat Alam Malaysia.

Malaysia/ Sarawak/ Timber industry—Impacts on local communities and economy/ Timber industry—Logging/ Politics/ Social movements.

667. ———. **1990.** *Solving Sarawak's Forest and Native Problem.* Penang, Malaysia: Sahabat Alam Malaysia.

This short book (43 pp.) provides a brief background account of logging in Sarawak, a description of customary tenure regimes, a summary of legal cases dealing with traditional land rights, and a chronology of the Penang blockade of Sarawak logging roads. A number of measures to resolve the confrontation between loggers and indigenous people in Sarawak are recommended, including: official and legally effective recognition of customary land rights; an immediate moratorium on all logging on customary lands; establishment of a national park system; active measures to restore the ecological health of the state's forest lands; development programs geared towards the specific needs of local Penang communities; and the establishment of a communally managed forest reserve system. A final section includes a copy of the first revised text of the Draft of Universal Declaration on the Rights of Indigenous Peoples developed by the United Nations.

Malaysia/ Sarawak/ Timber industry—Impacts on local communities and economy/ Timber industry—Logging/ Indigenous and local communities—Land and resource tenure systems/ Social movements.

668. **Sakandar, H. A. 1981.** *Resource Allocation on Vegetable Farms at Kundasang, Bundu Tuhan, Sabah, Malaysia Timur.* Bogor, Indonesia: Institut Pertanian Bogor.

Malaysia/ Sabah/ Agriculture—Permanent/ Agriculture—Smallholder cash crop farming/ Farm management—Economics.

669. **Sandin, B. 1969.** *The Sea Dayaks of Borneo before White Rajah Rule.* London: Macmillan.

Malaysia/ Sarawak/ History—Pre-colonial/ Migration/ Indigenous and local communities.

670. ———. **1994.** "Sources of Iban Traditional History." *Sarawak Museum Journal* 46 (67 (n.s.)): 1–300.

Issued as special monograph in the *Sarawak Museum Journal* volume series, this work comprises an ethnohistory of the Iban of Borneo complementing Sandin's earlier publication, *The Sea Dayaks of Borneo before White Rajah Rule* (1967) focusing on the protohistoric migration of the Iban to Sarawak. The present work draws from oral traditions among the Iban. Parts One and Two and focus on Iban mythology of ancestral origins and very early migrations. Parts Three and Four recount historical events between 1841 and 1900 (the first half-century of Brooke rule) and those associated with the beginning of Iban economic development in the early twentieth century through the period of Japanese occupation. Various aspects of Iban history in addition to migration, such as inter-regional conflicts, warfare, and struggles over leadership, are highlighted. A lengthy introduction by Clifford Sather reviews the state of written documentation on Iban history, providing a comprehensive overview of Iban migration, early history, trade and settlement patterns, and genealogies.

Malaysia/ Sarawak/ Indigenous and local communities—Social relations/ Indigenous and local communities—Economy/ Migration/ History—Pre-colonial/ History—Colonial.

671. **Sani, H. B. 1989.** "Agroforestry in Sarawak, Malaysia: Recent Development." In *Symposium on Agroforestry Systems and Technologies.* Biotrop Special Publications, no. 39. Bogor, Indonesia: SEAMEO.

Malaysia/ Sarawak/ Project intervention—Agroforestry/ Project intervention—Fallow improvement.

672. **Sani, S., ed. 1987.** *Environmental Conservation in Sabah: Issues and Strategies.* Proceedings of a seminar, 20–21 January 1987, Kundasang, Sabah. Kota Kinabalu, Sabah: Institute for Development Studies.

Malaysia/ Sabah/ Deforestation/ State policy—Forest and natural resources/ Forest management—Forest resource conservation.

673. **Sarawak Study Group. [1990].** *Logging in Sarawak: The Belaga Experience.* Petaling Jaya, Malaysia: Institute for Social Analysis.

Logging has become a central component of the Sarawak regional economy. This book explores the development of this industry in one district of Sarawak's interior (Belaga) and the effects the industry is having on the region's indigenous swidden agriculturalist and hunter gatherer communities. While these communities enjoy few of the benefits derived from the timber industry, they are bearing a disproportionate share of its external costs. The publication emphasizes the need to protect indigenous rights and ensure that their interests are also met. Specific means to achieve this goal are proposed.

Malaysia/ Sarawak/ Timber industry—Logging/ Timber industry—Impacts on local communities and economy/ Social movements.

674.   **Sather, C. 1990.** "Trees and Tree Tenure in Paku Iban Society: The Management of Secondary Forest Resources in a Long Established Iban Community." *Borneo Review* 1 (1): 16–40.

Sather examines Iban farming in the Paku River region in Sarawak (Second Division), noting that the Iban have continuously occupied the area for more than fourteen generations. With the longhouse as the main unit organizing forest management, the Iban set aside communal forest to be used as communal cemeteries, fruit tree reserves, river corridors and sacred forest groves. Temporary bans on tree clearing are observed around working ricefields. Heritable rights over individual trees and useful plants are acknowledged and traced through oral history. This tenurial system thus "transcends the primary units of everyday social experience, contributes to the maintenance of intra-regional relations, and historicizes the landscape that surrounds each local community." The research results highlight the sustainability of Iban forest management regimes and support recent challenges made against the conventional view of Iban farmers as "eaters of the forest."

Malaysia/ Sarawak/ Indigenous and local communities—Land and resource tenure systems/ Indigenous and local communities—Forest land use and management practices.

675.   **Seethalakshmi, K. K. 1987.** "Prospects of Cane Plantations—Malaysian Experience." *Evergreen Trichur* 18: 24–25.

Seethalakshmi describes briefly the Kinabatangan rattan project, of the Sabah Forest Development Authority (SAFODA). Initiated in 1978 to address the problem of declining rattan resources, the project involves establishing rattan plantations on logged-over forest areas. Susceptibility of *Calamus caesius* to the effects of flooding limits its usefulness in all but hilly areas. With naturally spreading stolons as well as suckers, *C. trachycoleus* has proved itself of more widespread applicability. Planting technique used by SAFODA for seedlings of *C. trachycoleus* are described.

Malaysia/ Sabah/ Rattan—Cultivation/ Rattan—Cultivation/ Non-timber forest products.

676.   **Sesser, S. 1991.** "Logging the Rainforest." *New Yorker* 67 (May 27): 42–67.

The impact of rainforest logging on East Malaysia's environment and people is described, drawing from conversations with Dayak (Kayan) villagers, Penan forest dwellers, and community activists. The author describes how local communities experience extensive damage to the ecosystem upon which they depend for their livelihood. As logging continues at a rapid rate in East Malaysia, resistance to timber company intrusions is also mounting, and a number of villagers and forest dwellers have been arrested and made to stand trial in provincial courts. The author stresses the links between rapid deforestation, political favoritism, corruption among local officials, and the accelerating demand for tropical wood-based plywood in Japan where environmental organizations have yet to secure a wider audience in their call for greater conservation.

Malaysia/ Sarawak/ Timber industry—Logging/ Timber industry—Trade and markets/ Timber industry—Impacts on local communities and economy/ Timber industry—Environmental impacts/ Social movements/ Politics.

677. **Sibat, P. 1982.** "The Effect of Land Management Practices on Soil Erodibility in Sarawak, Malaysia." Master's thesis, Cramfield Inst. of Technology, National College of Agricultural Engineering, Silsoe, United Kingdom.

Malaysia/ Sarawak/ Soil erosion and degradation/ /Land use—Patterns and planning/ Forest management—Forest resource conservation.

678. **Sim, H. C. 1990.** "Agrarian Change and Gender Relations: Rural Iban Women and the Batang Ai Resettlement Scheme, Sarawak." Ph.D. diss., University of Malaya, Kuala Lumpur.

In the early 1980s, Iban villagers of the upper Batang Ai river area were resettlement by the government in order to make way for a large hydroelectric dam in the area. As Sim highlights resettlement and incorporation into an agricultural program administered by the Sarawak Land Consolidation and Rehabilitation Authority (SALCRA) catapulted the subsistence farmers into a highly monetized economy. Drawing from field research at the resettlement site in the late 1980s, the author shows how this sudden shift in the villagers' economic relations was accompanied by an erosion of women's status. More specifically, the once complementary gender division of labor characteristic of the Batang Ai Iban was replaced by a rigid division between men's work in cash crop production and women's work in food crop production, bringing about a cultural devaluation of women's contribution to the household and village economy, an association of women with low-value work, and a displacement of women to the bottom of the village wage structure. Also apparent was growing stratification between women, as those whose families were able to prosper through resettlement became able to hire the labor of less well-off women. The author notes the role of social ideology in shaping women's changing position in Batang Ai Iban society. Despite women's high legal status in traditional Iban culture, greater cultural value is typically associated with male gender identity. Argues the author, this cultural asymmetry has articulated with recent socio-economic changes in Batang Ai, allowing for the internalization and firm entrenchment of lower female socio-economic status within everyday village life.

Malaysia/ Sarawak/ Resettlement/ Indigenous and local communities—Commoditization/ Gender analysis/ Gender relations.

679. **Simpson, R. B. 1995.** "Nepenthes and Conservation." *Curtis's Botanical Magazine* 12 (2): 111–118.

Indonesia/ Malaysia/ Borneo/ Non-timber forest products/ Forest flora/ Biodiversity.

680. **Sinidol, F., and M. Benggon. 1961.** "The Creation of a Folk Story from Penampang." *Journal of the Sabah Society* 1 (1): 42–48.

This paper describes the mythical belief among the Kadazan/ Dusan people in Sabah about the creation of the universe and how the gods brought the first padi seeds to the community. The authors link this mythical belief to many traditional rituals and practices associated with padi cultivation in Sabah, particularly religious sacrifices to appease the gods to ensure the continued abundance of harvest. The famous 'Kaamatan' festival, celebrated annually on a grand scale in Sabah, finds its origin in this mythical belief.

Malaysia/ Sabah/ Indigenous and local communities—Farming practices/ Indigenous and local communities—Religion and cosmology.

681. **Smith, J. M. B. 1977.** "An Ecological Comparison of Two Tropical High Mountains." *Journal of Tropical Geography* 44: 71–80.

Compares the forest ecology of Mount Kinabalu, Sabah with that of Mount Wilhelm, Papua New Guinea to develop an appropriate classification scheme.

Malaysia/ Sabah/ Forest biology and ecology.

682.   **Smythies, B. E. 1981.** *The Birds of Borneo*. Kota Kinabalu; Kuala Lumpur, Malaysia: Sabah Society; Malayan Nature Society.

Malaysia/ Indonesia/ Borneo/ Forest fauna.

683.   **Soepadmo, E., and K. M. Wong, eds. 1995.** *Tree Flora of Sabah and Sarawak.* . Vol. 1. Sandakan, Malaysia: Sabah Forestry Department.

First of eight volumes being produced by the Tree Flora of Sabah and Sarawak Project, a 10-year project undertaken by the Forest Research Institute Malaysia and the Sabah and Sarawak Malaysian governments, focusing on 109 tree families and 3,000 species. Introductory chapters to the volume proper contain a review of the project's background, a brief history of botanical research on Borneo, and a description of local biogeography and ecology. Thirty-one tree families are then covered in separate chapters.

Malaysia/ Sabah/ Sarawak/ Forest flora.

684.   **Songan, P. 1992.** "Perceived Motivations and Deterrents Associated with Participation of Peasants in Rural Development Programs in Sarawak, Malaysia." Ph.D. diss., Cornell University, Ithaca, N.Y.

Malaysia/ Sarawak/ Project intervention—Rural development.

685.   **Spindler, G. 1965.** *The Dusun, a North Borneo Society*. Stanford, Calif.: Stanford University Press.

The author investigates Dusun customary behavior, conceptions of natural and supernatural world, and how these relate to sickness and death. The social and economic relationships among this group of people are also examined.

Malaysia/ Sabah/ Ethnography/ Indigenous and local communities—Social relations/ Indigenous and local communities—Religion and cosmology/ Indigenous and local communities—Economy/ Indigenous and local communities—Farming practices.

686.   **Strickland, S. S. 1986.** "Long Term Development of Kejamin Subsistence: An Ecological Study." *Sarawak Museum Journal* n.s., 36 (57): 117–172.

Geographers and anthropologists have contended that rice cultivation is relatively new in much of Southeast Asia, having replaced older sago-yam-taro cropping systems among the region's indigenous shifting cultivator communities. The author examines possible ecological factors behind this transition. It is suggested that reasons of local ecology and demography are insufficient to explain why the transition may have occurred. Instead, the author contends that indigenous subsistence cultivators in Sarawak may have adopted rice as their main food crop for reasons of prestige, influenced by contact with other groups who associated a sense of superiority with rice consumption.

Malaysia/ Sarawak/ Indigenous and local communities—Farming practices/ History—Colonial.

687.   **Strickland, S. S., and S. J. Ulijaszek. 1994.** "Iban Energy, Nutrition, and Shifting Agriculture." *Ecology of Food and Nutrition* 33 (1–2): 75–92.

In a cross-sectional anthropometric study conducted at harvest time in an Iban village, the authors find indicators of lower nutritional status among adults of households engaging in long-fallow shifting cultivation than those engaging in short-fallow farming regimes. The study results contradict the usual assumptions about declining household health with shortened fallow periods and calls into question conventional ideas about population pressure and carrying capacity.

Malaysia/ Sarawak/ Agriculture—Shifting cultivation/ Indigenous and local communities—Farming practices/ Agricultural intensification/ Health and nutrition.

688. **Sutlive, V. H. 1985.** "Urban Migration into Sibu, Sarawak I." *Borneo Research Bulletin* 17: 85–94.

Malaysia/ Sarawak/ Indigenous and local communities/ Migration.

689. ———. **1986.** "Urban Migration into Sibu, Sarawak II." *Borneo Research Bulletin* 18: 27–45.

Malaysia/ Sarawak/ Indigenous and local communities/ Migration.

690. ———, **ed. 1993.** *Change and Development in Borneo.* Selected papers from the First Extraordinary Conference of the Borneo Research Council, August 4–9, 1990. Williamsburg, Va.: Borneo Research Council.

Indonesia/ Malaysia/ Borneo/ Indigenous and local communities—Economy/ Indigenous and local communities—Commoditization/ Indigenous and local communities—Land and resource tenure systems/ Indigenous and local communities—Social relations/ Ethnicity and ethnic relations.

691. **Sutton, K. 1988.** "Land Settlement in Sabah: From the Sabah Land Development Board to the Federal Land Development Authority." *Malaysian Journal of Tropical Geography* 18: 48–58.

In recent years, the Sabah Land Development Board has increasingly abdicated much of its responsibility for land settlement in Sabah to the Federal Land Development Authority. The SLDB now maintains a focus on policy development related to agribusiness expansion based on large-scale plantations. Providing a brief overview of these changes, Sutton critically assesses FELDA plans in Sabah in light of the only limited success scored by the SLDB in smallholder-based land development. These plans, notes the author, have been modeled largely after FELDA's approach in Peninsular Malaysia. While highly successful in the latter case, the FELDA approach will face some very different circumstances in Sabah. Should these differences not be taken into adequate account, it is likely that FELDA will face many of the same failures experienced by the SLDB.

Malaysia/ Sabah/ Land settlement and development/ Agriculture—Plantations/ Agriculture—Smallholder cash crop farming/ Agriculture—Smallholder tree and perennial crop farming/ State policy—Agricultural and rural development/ State policy—Land development.

692. ———. **1989.** "Malaysia's FELDA Land Settlement Model in Time and Space." *Geoforum* 20 (3): 339–354.

Sutton describes the successful history of Malaysia's Federal Land Development Authority (FELDA) in land settlement and smallholder plantation expansion. Particular focus is placed on recent developments, including plans for devolving management authority to settlers, and a switch from individual land titles to a system of shared ownership. Problems involving settler grievances and failure to realize settler self-reliance and self-management on older schemes are noted. Success of the FELDA model in East Malaysia as well as other developing countries is likely to depend on the Authority's ability and willingness to make appropriate modifications to suit local circumstance.

Malaysia/ Land settlement and development/ Agriculture—Plantations/ Agriculture—Smallholder tree and perennial crop farming/ Agriculture—Smallholder cash crop farming/ State policy—Agricultural and rural development/ State policy—Land development.

693.   **Symington, C. F. 1974.** *Foresters' Manual of Dipterocarps.* Malayan Forest Records, No. 16, Kuala Lumpur, Malaysia: Penerbit University Malaya.

This work was first published in 1943 by the Raffles Museum, Singapore.

Southeast Asia/ Malaysia/ Forest flora/ Forest management—Commercial forestry and silviculture.

694.   **Tamin, N. M., ed. 1993.** *Ecological Economics in Relation to Forest Conservation and Management.* Proceedings of the International Conference on Ecological Economics, Pulau Langkawi, 20–22 July 1992. Kuala Lumpur: Syarikat Datar Raya Sdn Bhd.

Contains ten papers dealing with various issues in ecological economics and forest conservation, including biodiversity conservation, economics of conservation, rainforest management in Papua New Guinea, timber resource management in Sri Lanka, forest pathogens in Thailand, forest regeneration in Sabah, natural resource accounting for forest values, ecology and economic role of Toona in Malaysia, and information access and dissemination.

Asia/ Malaysia/ Sabah/ Forest management—Forest resource conservation/ Forest management—Economics/ Forest regeneration/ Biodiversity.

695.   **Tan, K. C., and N. Jones. 1982.** "Fast Growing Hardwood Plantations on Logged-over Forest Sites in Sabah." *Malaysian Forester* 45: 558–575.

Malaysia/ Sabah/ Timber plantations.

696.   **Tarling, N. 1969.** *British Policy in the Malay Peninsula and Archipelago, 1824–1871.* Kuala Lumpur: Oxford University Press.

Malaysia/ Peninsular Malaysia/ History—Colonial/ Politics.

697.   **Taylor, D. M., D. Hortin, M. J. G. Parnwell, and T. K. Marsden. 1994.** "The Degradation of Rainforests in Sarawak, East Malaysia, and Its Implications for Future Management Policies." *Geoforum* 25 (3).

Malaysia/ Sarawak/ Deforestation/ Timber industry—Environmental impacts/ Agriculture—Shifting cultivation's environmental impacts/ Forest management—Forest resource conservation/ State policy—Forest and natural resources.

698.   **Thai-Tsung, N., T. Yui-Long, and H. Kueh, eds. 1991.** *Towards Greater Advancement of the Sago Industry in the '90s.* Proceedings of the Fourth International Sago Symposium, 6–9 August 1990, Kuching, Sarawak, Malaysia. Kuching, Sarawak, Malaysia: Ministry of Agriculture and Community Development and Department of Agriculture.

As reflected in the Symposium's title, the focus of the papers included in the proceedings is on the technical aspects of increasing sago yields, in line with government efforts in the Southeast Asia region to increase plantation-based sago cultivation. Several of the papers presented also focus on describing the environmental conditions associated with sago production, the ecology of sago in Sarawak, the variety and diversity and genetic importance of sago palms generally, and traditional sago palm management by indigenous communities in Papua New Guinea.

Southeast Asia/ Malaysia/ Sarawak/ Non-timber forest products/ Forest flora/ Agriculture—Plantations/ Agricultural development/ Forest biology and ecology/ Indigenous and local communities—Forest products use and trade/ Indigenous and local communities—Forest land use and management practices/ State policy—Agricultural and rural development.

699. **Tham, C. K., and L. T. Chim. 1978.** "Prospect of Forest Plantation in the Tropics with Particular Reference to Sabah." Photocopy. Sandakan, Malaysia: Sandakan Forestry Department.

Malaysia/ Sabah/ Timber plantations.

700. **Thang, H. C. 1987.** "Can the Existing Wood Resources in Malaysia Meet Future Domestic Requirements?" *Malaysian Forester* 50: 217–234.

Thang estimates both Malaysia's roundwood supply needs and production capacity for the 1986–2000 period, using data on extant availability, production plans, and management systems likely to be required by the government. Malaysia as a whole will produce a little over 29 million cubic meters of roundwood per year between 1986 and 2000, more than covering projected needs in the country's wood processing sector, in which capacity is likely to be about 22 cubic meters per year. Spatial differences do obtain however, with Peninsular Malaysia and Sabah expected to fall short of meeting their own supply needs in the wood processing sector; production from Sarawak is likely to make up the shortfall.

Overall domestic wood requirements are also likely to be fully met by production within the country: in Peninsular Malaysia, rubberwood harvesting will play a significant role in meeting local domestic needs, while in both Sabah and Sarawak, rubberwood harvesting is negligible, and hardwood will continue to dominate the local markets.

Malaysia/ Timber industry—Trade and markets/ Timber industry—Downstream processing.

701. **Thong, L. B., and T. S. Bahrin. 1993.** "The Bario Exodus: A Conception of Sarawak Urbanisation." *Borneo Review* 4 (2): 114–128.

The authors discuss the spatial dimension of urbanization in Sarawak, focusing on the growing migration among Kelabits and other indigenous groups from Sarawak's highland interior to lowland urban centers. Outside influences and the introduction of education have raised expectations of interior dwelling residents, prompting migration downriver in search of jobs and higher schooling. Migration patterns in the Kelabit Highlands show a "destination bias in favor of urban areas in the Baram valley" to which the highland interior is linked via major river ways. This pattern results from the lack of interconnected surface infrastructure between river basins, producing "independent urban subsystems" that contribute to the diffusion of innovation and development into interior areas. A potential down-side of this pattern, however, is the possibility of economic inertia and weak integration with the wider regional economy associated with lack of linkages between different subsystems. The pending completion of the Pan-Borneo Highway from Semantan to Lawas can be expected to counter this tendency and contribute "to the development of a more integrated holistic urban space."

Malaysia/ Sarawak/ Migration/ Regional development.

702.   **Thu, E. R. 1981.** "Religious Belief and Practices of the Rungus People." *Journal of the Sabah Society* n.s., 7 (2): 113–122.

> The author describes the manner in which the Rungus people conduct their worship of various celestial and terrestrial deities, both good and evil, describing also the variety of festivals (harvest festival, 'magahau' festival, 'bumoran' festival, 'moginum' festival) which form an integral part of this worship. Most of these events are in one way or another associated with padi cultivation, indicating the dominance of this activity in the life of the Rungus people.

> Malaysia/ Sabah/ Indigenous and local communities—Religion and cosmology/ Indigenous and local communities—Farming practices.

703.   **Ti, T. C., and W. M. Tangau. 1991.** *Cultivated and Potential Forest Plantation Tree Species with Special Reference to Sabah.* Kota Kinabalu, Sabah, Malaysia: Institute for Development Studies.

> Aiming to provide the necessary technical information to private investors interested in the possibility of future investment in commercial tree planting, the authors describe the biological features and growth attributes of a range of fast-growing tropical wood species which are either already cultivated or thought to have cultivation potential in Sabah. In addition, the commercial viability of forest plantation development in Sabah is estimated. Under normal circumstances, an Internal Rate of Return of 5.9 percent is estimated to be likely. This rate of return is unattractive to investors and it would be necessary for the government to provide additional fiscal incentives if it wants to see more private investment in commercial tree planting.

> Malaysia/ Sabah/ Timber plantations/ Forest management—Commercial forestry and silviculture/ Forest management—Economics.

704.   **Ti, T. C., and W. Yee, eds. 1989.** *Revitalization of Industrial Crops in Sabah.* Kota Kinabalu, Sabah: Institute for Development Studies.

> Papers presented at a 1986 IDS seminar focused on formulating individual strategies for revitalizing the development of oil palm, cocoa, coconut, rubber and coffee crops in Sabah. An overview of the financial and marketing problems faced by these crops is also provided.

> Malaysia/ Sabah/ Agriculture—Plantations/ Land settlement and development/ Agricultural development/ Agricultural economics.

705.   **Tiing, L. B. 1979.** "The Effects of Shifting Cultivation on Sustained Yield Management in Sarawak's National Forests." *Malaysian Forester* 42 (4): 418–422.

> Malaysia/ Sarawak/ Agriculture—Shifting cultivation's environmental impacts/ Forest management—Commercial forestry and silviculture/ Forest management—Control of shifting cultivation/ Deforestation.

706.   **Timbuong, R. B. 1986.** "Kajian sosio-ekonomi keatas penanam padi bukit di daerah Kota Marudu, Sabah." Bachelor of Science thesis, [Kota Kinabalu, Sabah].
[Socio-economic study of hillpadi rice cultivators in Kota Maruda District, Sabah.]

> In Bahasa Melayu.

> Malaysia/ Sabah/ Indigenous and local communities—Economy/ Indigenous and local communities—Farming practices/ Agriculture—Shifting cultivation.

707. **Treseder, K. K., D. W. Davidson, and J. R. Ehleringer. 1995.** "Absorption of Ant-provided Carbon Dioxide and Nitrogen by a Tropical Epiphyte." *Nature* 375 (6527): 137–139.

Malaysia/ Sarawak/ Forest biology and ecology/ Forest flora.

708. **Udarbe, M. P. 1985.** "Economic Considerations in Forest Plantation Development: A Case Study of the Activities of the Sabah Forestry Development Authority (SAFODA)." *International Tree Crops Journal* 3 (2–3): 85–99.

Establishing forest plantations has become a major focus of the Sabah Forestry Development Authority as a means both of meeting local production needs and of catalyzing rural development among impoverished farmers. Udarbe describes two major projects undertaken by SAFODA under this broad aim: the Bengkoka afforestation and resettlement project and a major reforestation effort. Project aims in Bengkoka include resettling 2000 families and involving these in the development of 3600 ha of timber plantations. The wasteland reforestation effort focuses on planting 10 to 1000 ha sized tracts of abandoned scrub- and grassland to fast-growing tree species (*A. mangium*, *Pinus caribaea*, and *P. oucarpa*) as well as 835 ha of old and abandoned rubber groves with rattan. Aspects of project financing and economics are discussed in detail.

Malaysia/ Sabah/ Timber plantations/ Resettlement/ Reforestation/ Project intervention—Rural development/ Rattan—Cultivation/ Forest management—Economics.

709. **———. 1987.** "The Future Role of *Acacia Mangium* in the Pulp and Paper Industry in Sabah." *APPITA* 40 (6): n.g.

Malaysia/ Sabah/ Timber plantations/ Forest management—Economics.

710. **———. 1989.** "Social Forestry in Sabah: A Learning Experience." In *Social Forestry in Asia: Factors That Influence Program Implementation*. Ed. N. T. Vergara and R. A. Fernandez, pp. 209–223. Los Baños, Laguna, The Philippines: Southeast Asian Ministers of Education Organization, Regional Center for Graduate Study and Research in Agriculture.

Udarbe describes recent social forestry experiences by the Sabah Forestry Development Authority. These have had have three main foci: establishing large-scale forest plantations involving resettled smallholders; afforesting scattered wastelands through the employment of local villagers; and tree farming on private smallholder lots. Institutional and socioeconomic problems encountered in these three approaches are described and responses by the Sabah Forestry Development Authority noted.

Malaysia/ Sabah/ Project intervention—Social and community forestry/ Reforestation/ Resettlement/ Timber plantations.

711. **Udarbe, M. P., K. Uebelhör, C. D. Klemp, M. Kleine, B. von der Heyde, R. Glauner, and W. Benneckendorf. 1994.** "Standards for Sustainable Management of Natural Forests in Sabah." In *Forestry and Forest Products Research*. Proceedings of a conference, 1–2 November 1993. Ed. S. Appanah, K. C. Khoo, H. T. Chan, and L. T. Hong, pp. 28–50. Kuala Lumpur: Forest Research Institute Malaysia.

Identifies the full range of standards for various activities needed to meet requirements of sustainable natural forest management in Sabah, based on the requirements of environmental impact assessments and expected international product-label certification schemes.

Standards for forest zoning, yield regulation, timber harvesting, and organizational development are discussed in greater detail.

Malaysia/ Sabah/ Forest management—Commercial forestry and silviculture/ Forest management—Forest resource conservation/ Timber industry—Logging.

712. **Van Der Plas, M. 1990.** "Hydrological Characteristics of the Forest Floor in Undisturbed and Logged-Over Rain Forest, Danum Valley, Sabah, Malaysia." Ph.D. diss., Free University, Amsterdam, Netherlands.

Malaysia/ Sabah/ Hydrology/ Soil erosion and degradation/ Timber industry—Environmental impacts.

713. **Van Leur, M. et al. 1987.** "Shifting Cultivation of the Rungus in Sabah, Malaysia—A Way of Life." Report prepared for the Department of Agriculture, Sabah. Kota Kinabalu, Malaysia: Department of Agriculture.

This case study of a number of Rungus villages in Kudat division, Sabah highlights the socio-economic traits of this particular ethnic group, their access to education and health facilities, and current patterns of urban migration. Particular attention is given to problems of subsistence, the introduction of commercial farming and non-sustainable farming practices in the division where poor soil conditions prevail.

Malaysia/ Sabah/ Indigenous and local communities—Economy/ Indigenous and local communities—Commoditization/ Indigenous and local communities—Farming practices/ Soil erosion and degradation.

714. **Voon, P. K. 1983.** "Patterns of Population Movements in the Districts of Sabah, Malaysia, with Reference to the 1960s." *Journal of the Sabah Society* 7 (3): 213–243.

Voon highlights several features of population movement into and within Sabah in the period 1960–1970. Three out of every ten persons in the State changed their place of residence during the period. A notable number of people involved in these demographic shifts are immigrants from neighboring countries who came to Sabah as economic or political refugees. Among native inhabitants, relocation is either within a home district or to adjacent districts, the latter accounting for most movement by local residents. It is argued that the volume and direction of population movement during the 1960–1970 period was determined by the interplay of several factors, namely the socio-cultural background of the migrants, their ethno-linguistic identity, the physical geography of the state, and the availability of economic opportunities in the receiving area.

Among those immigrating from neighboring countries, these factors have promoted their concentration on the east coast of Sabah, where it is more likely that relatives who were earlier immigrants are already settled, and where employment opportunities are relatively abundant. Among local inhabitants of the province, choice of migration destiny was primarily determined by socio-cultural and ethno-linguistic considerations. As a result, the majority of migrating local residents relocated within their home district, or moved to an adjacent district regardless of the extent of economic opportunities available there. These factors have given rise to a growing maldistribution between growing populations of local inhabitants and areas of growing economic opportunity within the state of Sabah. As a result, the province's east coast, is characterized by a marked shortage of local labor.

Malaysia/ Sabah/ Demography/ Migration.

715. **Voon, P. K., and S. H. Khoo. 1980.** "Upland Development and Settlement in Malaysia." *Malaysian Journal of Tropical Geography* 1: 43–56.

Malaysia/ Migration/ Land settlement and development/ State policy—Agricultural and rural development/ State policy—Land development.

716.   **Voon Phin Keong. 1981.** "The Rural Development Programme in Sabah, Malaysia, With Reference to the 1970s." *Malaysian Journal of Tropical Geography* 3: 53–67.

Malaysia/ Sabah/ Project intervention—Rural development.

717.   **Voris, H. K., and R. F. Inger. 1995.** "Frog Abundance Along Streams in Bornean Forests." *Conservation Biology* 9 (3): 679–683.

The authors report results of a study on 22 species of stream frogs inhabiting rain-forest streams in two locations in Sarawak and Sabah states, respectively. Sampling was completed in 1962, 1970, and 1984, allowing the analysis to take on a time series perspective otherwise not well represented in the current literature on declining amphibian populations. Fifteen common species of frogs representing four families were found to account for 89% and 90% of the sampled frogs in the Sabah and Sarawak sites respectively. The data do not indicate an systematic decline in the overall frog numbers at the observed sites, with individual species variously showing increases, decreases, or a steady state.

Malaysia/ Sabah/ Sarawak/ Forest fauna/ Biodiversity/ Forest biology and ecology.

718.   **Wallace, A. R. 1869.** *The Malay Archipelago.* London: Macmillan.

Malaysia/ Sarawak/ Forest flora/ Forest fauna/ History—Colonial.

719.   **Walton, J. R. 1990.** "The Economic Structure of Sabah." *Margins and Minorities: The Peripheral Areas and Peoples of Malaysia.* Ed. V. T. King and M. J. G. Parnwell, pp. 208–226. Hull, U.K.: Hull University Press.

Drawing from statistics of the 1960s through mid-and late-1980s, this paper gives a broad overview of the economic structure of Sabah. In particular, the authors note the state's heavy dependence on a narrow range of primary products (timber, petroleum and agriculture), low labor productivity, and poverty among indigenous, subsistence-oriented inhabitants. Diversification of the state's economic base, education, and infrastructural development have been given high priority in the state development planning process. Despite improved irrigation and promotion of double-cropping, rice production in the state fell by 26 percent between 1970 and 1986, and Sabah continues to import rice to cover local consumption needs. Palm oil and cocoa production have been heavily promoted in the State, converting previous forest lands into plantation areas. By 1987, the amount of land under oil palm and cocoa cultivation (228,00 ha and 184, 000 ha respectively) well exceeded the area devoted either to rubber (80,000 ha) or to rice production (ca. 41,400 ha). While over half of the palm oil acreage is managed by smallholders, cocoa remains an estate crop, and by the mid-1980s Sabah accounted for 61 percent of the Malaysia's cocoa production overall. Land settlement schemes have involved relatively minor programs to support existing farmers on their own holdings as well as much larger efforts to re-settle landless and shifting cultivators as well as "small-holders with plots of uneconomic size." Much of the rapid increase in oil palm expansion is attributed to such land development schemes.

In 1985, 61 percent of Sabah's total land are was still classified as forest (c. 44,870 sq km). Timber exports provide the bulk of the state's revenue, exceeding oil in the late 1980s. It is estimated that 80 percent of the state's timber is exported in unprocessed sawlog form (as of 1987), despite the steady rise in the number of operational timber mills. Japan purchases c. 2/ 3 of Sabah's timber exports, suggesting a worrisome vulnerability to fluctuations in the Japanese timber market. The Sabah Foundation and the Sabah Forestry Development Authority remain largely in control of local timber development and plans for diversifying the industry with the development of downstream processing facilities have been drafted. With a mandate to promote educational opportunities for Sabah's indigenous peoples, the Sabah Foundation funds its activities through its own timber, wood processing and plantation activities. Agencies active among indigenous settlements include the Rural Development Corporation (Korporasi Pembangunan Desa) and its subsidiary, the Sabah Marketing Authority (SAMA).

The paper gives further details on the status of other economic sectors in the state, including mining, fisheries, manufacturing, trade, infrastructure and public utilities. Though the state's industrial base is still small and dominated by food- and wood-processing, a number of state industrial development agencies are present to promote the sector. Crude oil and timber, accounting for roughly 70 percent of the area's exports, provide the state with a large balance of trade surplus, averaging M$1,755 per year. By 1985, Sabah boasted 6,500 km of roads, of which 32 percent were paved and the rest remain graveled.

In conclusion, the authors note a number of problems facing the state, including the need for greater conservation in the forestry sector, low levels of skill within the local population, high local prices due to the area's dependence on mainland Malaysia for manufactured goods, and ongoing poverty among the indigenous residents, exacerbated by the arrival of foreign migrants. The local state government has recently initiated a new planning approach with the completion of the Sabah Action Blueprint (SAB) aimed at coordinated development policies and activities in all sectors. The overall aim of the blueprint is "to provide the necessary framework to bring about a transition from a commodity-based economy to a diversified and valued added economy."

Malaysia/ Sabah/ Regional development/ Agricultural development/ Agriculture—Permanent/ Agriculture—Plantations/ Land settlement and development/ Timber industry—Development and structure/ Poverty/ State policy—Agricultural and rural development/ State policy—Land development/ State policy—Economic development.

720.   ———. **1990.** "The Economic Structure of Sarawak." *Margins and Minorities: The Peripheral Areas and Peoples of Malaysia.* Ed. V. T. King and M. J. G. Parnwell, pp. 114–135. Hull, U.K.: Hull University Press.

Malaysia/ Sarawak/ Regional development/ Agriculture—Permanent/ Agriculture—Plantations/ Agriculture—Shifting cultivation/ Timber industry—Development and structure/ Land settlement and development/ Poverty/ Agricultural development/ State policy—Agricultural and rural development/ State policy—Economic development.

721.   **Warren, J. F. 1987.** *At the Edge of Southeast Asian History.* Quezon City: New Day Publishers.

The monograph presents a collection of essays written between the late 1970s and the mid-1980s. Several essays focus on the role of trade and slave trading in the development of the Sulu Zone under the Sulu sultanate during the 19th century. Incorporating the Sulu archipelago between the Southern Philippines, Northern Borneo and Northern Sulawesi island, the Sulu sultanate commanded great control over inter-island trade throughout insular Southeast Asia during the first half of the 19th century. Warren links vigorous slave raiding by sultan forces throughout the Southeast Asian islands to booming Western demand for jungle products such as gutta-perche (raw rubber) and rattan as well as the infusion of Western-made arms and munitions to the area. Booming trade with the West through Singapore and other entrepot cities made command over adequate labor supplies to procure tradeable goods vital to the economic and political dominance of the Sulu sultanate, encouraging in turn the procurement of labor through slave-raiding. Access to a constant supply of weapons made this procurement possible.

These forces had an impact on local populations and ethnic relations far beyond the area directly controlled by the Sultanate. Also important was the role of Western traders who were able to manipulate connections with coastal sultans in eastern Borneo to establish lucrative trading links with shifting cultivator communities located far upstream in the Borneo interior. Both the Sulu sultanate and these early Western trade monopolies were eventually usurped from their dominant commercial position in the area by the arrival of Arab traders using steamboats. The control exerted by Sulu sultanates in the region was also severely diminished by the end of the 19th century after vigorous military attacks by both Spanish and English naval fleets. A concerted resettlement campaign was started by colonial authorities, aimed at transforming the seafaring coastal communities of the region into sedentary agriculturalists. With these essays, the author seeks to highlight the impact of global forces linked to industrialization in the West on communities conventionally perceived to be on the periphery of modern history.

Indonesia/ Malaysia/ Philippines/ History—Colonial/ Non-timber forest products/ Ethnicity and ethnic relations/ Resettlement.

722. **Watson, D. J. 1989.** "The Evolution of Appropriate Resource-management Systems." In *Common Property Resources: Ecology and Community-Based Sustainable Development.* Ed. F. Berkes, pp. 55–69. London: Belhaven Press.

Increased demand for agricultural land resulting in decreased fallow periods poses serious problems for current shifting cultivation systems in Sarawak, Malaysia. The author describes the situation as one of a "passive system for [resource] management" that is facing rapid socio-economic change. 20% of Sarawak's population—40,000 households involving 250,000 people—currently earns its livelihood through shifting cultivation. 23% of the province's total land area is claimed by swidden cultivation. Much of this is hilly land is not well suited for agricultural use and yields a per-hectare economic return that is much lower than that offered by production forests in the same area. The author challenges current "fascination" with overly romanticized communal property regimes, citing the low productivity of most collective farms. More appropriate resource policy, argues the author, would include active promotion of intensified land use, new knowledge to replace old ideas, and more productive land management practices among indigenous forest dwellers.

Malaysia/ Sarawak/ Indigenous and local communities—Forest land use and management practices/ Indigenous and local communities—Land and resource tenure systems/ Agriculture—Shifting cultivation.

723. **Wells, G. 1963.** "Sabah's Mountain Road to Prosperity." *Borneo Bulletin* 10 (19): n.g.

Malaysia/ Sabah/ State policy—Agricultural and rural development/ Regional development.

724. **Whinfrey-Koepping, E. 1988.** "The Family in a Changing Agricultural Economy: A Longitudinal Study of an East Sabah Village." Working Paper, no. 47. Clayton, Australia: Centre of Southeast Asian Studies, Monash University.

This paper draws from data collected through anthropological fieldwork in one ethnic Kadzan village in Lower Labuk Valley, East Sabah, between 1966 and 1986. Whinfrey-Koepping traces changes in the local economy and how these have affected gender relations within the household. More specifically, she notes the growing inability of local families to maintain household self-sufficiency in rice production. As nearby forest lands are claimed by timber companies and thus become off-limits to local farmers, villagers have been forced to continue farming on degraded soils despite decreasing yields. Involvement in commodity exchange to make up for the rice shortfall has deepened. In addition, with the advent of the timber industry, more men began finding employment outside the village while women remained central to household rice production and thus achieve a greater degree of control over the household economy. Household tension and the incidence of domestic violence grew, however, with the return of many men to the village during a recession in the timber industry and other external changes. A sudden influx of government programs to develop the village as a "model kampong" increased the incidence of wage labor, eroded the importance of farming, and with it women's household status. With a collapse of the government's ecologically inappropriate development schemes, household farming re-assumed its former importance. The opening of a road to the coast allowed a number of families to scatter beyond the village yet maintain easy access to it. This provided villagers with access to new land, and eased pressure on nearby land resources, thus improving productivity. The author suggests that with these changes a more "acceptable, though altered, pattern" of gender relations returned to the community, establishing "a more equable economic balance between spouses in accordance with Kadzan expectations."

Malaysia/ Sabah/ Indigenous and local communities—Commoditization/ Indigenous and local communities—Farming practices/ Indigenous and local communities—Forest land use and management practices/ Timber industry—Impacts on local communities and economy/ Gender analysis/ Gender relations/ Project intervention—Rural development.

725.   **Williams, T. R. 1965.** *The Dusun, a North Borneo Society.* New York: Rhinehart and Winston.

Malaysia/ Sabah/ Indigenous and local communities/ Ethnography.

726.   **Woods, P. 1987.** "Drought and Fire in Tropical Forests in Sabah—An Analysis of Rainfall Patterns and Some Ecological Effects." In *Proceedings of the Third Round Table Conference on Dipterocarps.* Ed. A. J. G. H. Kostermans, pp. 367–387. Jakarta: UNESCO.

Malaysia/ Sabah/ Forest fires/ Drought/ Forest biology and ecology.

727.   **———. 1989.** "Effects of Logging, Drought, and Fire on Structure and Composition of Tropical Forests in Sabah, Malaysia." *Biotropica* 21 (4): 290–298.

Woods estimates the impact of severe environmental disturbance caused by decades of logging, the extended El Niño drought of 1983, and the widespread fires facilitated by these factors in Sabah's tropical forest during 1983–84. Comparison of fire and drought damage in plots of logged and primary forest areas showed significant differences in mortality rates of mature trees, which ranged between 38–94% in the logged areas, and 19–71% in unlogged sites. Sapling mortality, however, was more than 80% in both cases. Coupled with more complete loss of canopy cover, high rates of sapling mortality severely stunted forest regeneration in both older and newer logged sites, increasing likelihood of widespread conversion of these areas to unproductive grasslands. Canopy species suffered much less damage in primary forests, reducing the density of invading grasses. In the latter case, while species composition may have been permanently altered through sapling loss, greater chances of recovering the forest structure obtained.

Malaysia/ Sabah/ Forest fires/ Drought/ Timber industry—Environmental impacts/ Forest regeneration/ Biodiversity/ Vegetation analysis.

728.   **World Conservation Monitoring Center. 1988.** "Sabah and Sarawak: Conservation of Biological Diversity." Cambridge, U.K.; Gland, Switzerland: World Conservation Monitoring Centre; International Union for Conservation of Nature and Natural Resources, Tropical Forest Program.

Problems in rapid deforestation, forest conversion, and uncontrolled commercial and recreational exploitation of forest resources in Sabah and Sarawak are highlighted in this 21 page report. The paper suggests specific actions to address these issues and lists all protected areas in the region. [Summarized from World Resources Institute, "1993 Directory of Country Environmental Studies: An Annotated Bibliography of Environmental and Natural Resource Profiles and Assessments" published by WRI, IIED, and IUCN].

Malaysia/ Sarawak/ Sabah/ Forest management—Parks and conservation areas/ Biodiversity.

729. **Yaakub, N. F., A. M. Ayob, and T. Noweg. 1993.** "Dayak Bidayuh of the Bau-Lundu Region: Demographic Profile and the Perception of Educational Amenities." *Sarawak Museum Journal* 44 (65 (n.s.)).

  In a subsection of a larger feasibility study, the authors describe the demographic and educational characteristics of Bidayuh communities in Bau-Lundu who are potential participants in several land development schemes proposed for the area under authority of the Sarawak Land Consolidation and Rehabilitation Authority (SALCRA). Particular attention is given to local perceptions concerning educational facilities and the degree of priority assigned to children's schooling among community members.

  Malaysia/ Sarawak/ Indigenous and local communities/ Resettlement.

730. **Yahya, N. 1993.** *Local History Collection: An Annotated Bibliography.* Kota Kinabalu, Malaysia: Sabah State Library.

  Malaysia/ Sabah/ Bibliography/ History—Colonial/ History—Pre-colonial.

731. **Yap, S. W., C. V. Chak, L. Majuakim, M. Anuar, and F. E. Putz. 1995.** "Climbing Bamboo (*Dinochloa* spp.) in Deramakot Forest Reserve, Sabah: Biomechanical Characteristics, Modes of Ascent, and Abundance in a Logged-over Forest." *Journal of Tropical Forest Science* 8 (2): 196–202.

  Describes the characteristics and climbing patterns of various bamboo species in a forest site selectively logged in 1975. Highlights dynamics by which climbing bamboo are able to dominate logged-over forest areas.

  Malaysia/ Sabah/ Forest regeneration.

732. **Yong, P. 1994.** "Challenges and Opportunities in Sarawak's Tourism Industry." *Sarawak Gazette* 121 (1530): 16–22.

  Malaysia/ Sarawak/ Regional development.

733. **Yusuf, H. et al., eds. 1986.** Proceedings of Workshop on "Impact of Man's Activities on Tropical Upland Forest Ecosystems, " 3–6 February 1986, Serdang, Selangor. Serdang, Selangor, Malaysia: Faculty of Forestry, Universiti Pertanian Malaysia.

  A collection of papers delivered at workshop on the impact of human activity on forest ecosystems. Paper topics include: tropical silviculture; management of forest resources; development of plantation forestry; timber extraction; development of plantation crops and livestock rearing; watershed conservation measures; and shifting cultivation. The papers generally observe the disturbance of forest ecosystems caused by human use of forest lands. Without appropriate action, forest land destruction may ultimately cancel out any short-term material benefits derived from current human action. Ways of minimizing the adverse impact of development are proposed.

  Malaysia/ Sabah/ Timber industry—Environmental impacts/ Forest management—Commercial forestry and silviculture/ Timber plantations/ Agriculture—Shifting cultivation's environmental impacts/ Agriculture—Plantations/ Agriculture—Permanent/ Watershed management/ Forest biology and ecology.

PHILIPPINES

734. **Abad, R. C. 1981.** "Internal Migration in the Philippines: A Review of Research Findings." *Philippine Studies* 29: 129–143.

   Philippines/ Demography/ Migration.

735. **Abregana, B. C. 1983.** "Human Disturbances in a Tropical Rainforest: Nature, Views and Approaches." In *Research on the Impact of Development on Human Activity Systems in Southeast Asia*. Dumaguete City, Philippines: Siliman University.

   Philippines/ Agriculture—Shifting cultivation's environmental impacts/ Migrant farmers and farming/ Deforestation/ Timber industry—Environmental impacts/ Timber industry—Impacts on local communities and economy.

736. **————. 1983.** "Land Use in a Tropical Rain Forest: The Balinsasayao Swidden Farmers." Photocopy. Manila: Research Center, De La Salle University.

   The author describes the Balinsasayao project of Silliman University still underway at the time of writing. The project is multidimensional, involving "studies in soil analysis, forestry, agriculture, vertebrate fauna, and social components that dealt with the kaingeros' perception of life conditions, view of the forest, decision-making, . . . rites and rituals, health, and nutrition." Some initial findings of a sample survey are provided focusing on cropping patterns in particular. Results indicate that population as well as kaingin activities have expanded rapidly in the area. Many farmers are eager to clear new plots in the belief that this will eventually lead the government to award them clear property rights. Original ("pioneer") settlers feel that their standard of living is declining, while more recent settlers perceive less change to be taking place. Major problems cited were economic in nature; difficulties in utilizing social services (schools, health centers) were also mentioned frequently. In general, local residents are becoming more aware of the need for forest conservation and developing alternatives to shifting cultivation. Noting that agroforestry appears to be among the most promising of current forest conservation alternatives in the area, the author describes various components of Silliman University's agroforestry program.

   Philippines/ Agriculture—Shifting cultivation/ Land use—Patterns and planning/ Migrant farmers and farming/ Indigenous and local communities—Forest land use and management practices/ Population pressure/ Project intervention—Agroforestry.

737. **Acosta, J. R. N. O. 1994.** "Loss, Emergence, and Retribalization: The Politics of Lumad Ethnicity in Northern Mindanao." Ph.D. diss., University of Hawaii, Honolulu.

Philippines/ Mindanao/ Indigenous and local communities—Social relations/ Ethnicity and ethnic relations/ Politics.

738. **Agrarian Reform Institute. 1986.** *An Analysis of Rural Organizations in the Philippines: Typologies, Problems and Issues, and Policy Alternatives.* College, Laguna, Philippines: Agrarian Reform Institute, College of Development Economics and Management, University of the Philippines at Los Ba–os.

Philippines/ Social movements/ Project intervention—Agricultural development/ Project intervention—Rural development.

739. **Aguilar, F. V. 1982.** *Social Forestry for Upland Development: Lessons From Four Case Studies.* Quezon City, Philippines: Institute of Philippine Culture, Ateneo de Manila University.

Philippines/ Project intervention—Social and community forestry.

740. **———. 1983.** "Blueprints and Realities: The Experience of Upland Development Projects." Paper presented at the Conference on Upland Development: Policies and Issues, 22–25 August 1983, at the Center for Policy and Development Studies, University of the Philippines at Los Ba–os. Photocopy.

As of 1981, there were 252 ongoing social forestry related projects in the Philippines, all government-affiliated, a trend signifying "the 'greatest reversal' in forestry circles" in the Philippines in recent decades. This development could prove either "a triumph for those who are concerned that meaningful social development should accompany the processes of economic growth" or merely a "remedial action adopted out of expediency." Aguilar first provides a general description of typical upland development projects and their underlying theory, including general goals, arrangements for access to land, recruitment of project personnel, and policies on community organization associated with social forestry. Empirical observation of existing projects, however, reveals a number of areas where reality does not match expected performance. To begin, most projects still cover only a limited area. The Ilocos Region seems to exhibit an "overconcentration" of these projects, while Region VIII (Eastern Visayas) has the least. Actual intervention strategies often differ considerably from social forestry "blueprints," and project performance still frequently falls far short of expected standards. At least six factors appear to underlie these problems: problems of tenure insecurity, the primacy of basic needs, constraints in technology transfer, difficulties in maintaining project development and tensions surrounding the role of the community in this process, shortages in project staffing, and various bureaucratic constraints.

Philippines/ Project intervention—Social and community forestry/ Social forestry.

741. **———. 1983.** "The Task Ahead: Developing the Uplands through Social Forestry." *Philippine Studies* 31: 409–429.

Philippines/ Social forestry/ Agricultural development/ State policy—Forest and natural resources.

742. **Alukino, J. M. et al. n.d.** "The Effects of the Logging Ban: Region VIII." Report prepared for the Training and Development Issues Project. Photocopy. Makati, Metro Manila: National Economic Development Authority.

The government's moratorium on logging is assessed with regard to its effects in the Eastern Visayas region of the country. For logging firms, operations did slow down considerably, displacing workers and reducing the volume of forest products. As unemployment rates have risen steeply among logging workers incomes have declined, dietary intake has been reduced, and many loggers are now planning to migrate elsewhere.

Timber-related industries (e.g., furniture) were not substantially affected by the ban because there has been an increase in raw materials supplied by small permit-holders and other suppliers since the logging ban. There does not appear to have been an increase in kaingin-making during the period studied, indicating that displaced logging workers did not generally take up this means of livelihood. At the same time, evidence does suggest a steep rise in illegal logging.

Philippines/ Timber industry—Logging/ Timber industry—Trade and markets/ Timber industry—Downstream processing/ Timber industry—State policy and regulation.

743. **Anderson, J. N. 1982.** "Rapid Rural 'Development' Performance and Consequences in the Philippines." In *Too Rapid Rural Development: Perceptions and Perspectives from Southeast Asia*. Ed. C. MacAndrews and Chia Lin Sien, pp. 122–171. Athens, Ohio: Ohio University Press.

The author provides a broad summary of past studies of current development needs and trends in rural Philippines. Changes that are affecting the natural environment, rural standards of living and people's options for future improvement are discussed. In conclusion, the author cites the need for an integrating analysis of what is already known about rural development in the Philippines in order better to understand links between different factors.

Philippines/ Rural development.

744. **Anon. 1985.** "The Naaland Style of Upland Farming in Naga, Cebu, Philippines: A Case of an Indigenous Agroforestry Scheme." In *Report on the Third ICRAF/USAID Agroforestry Course*. Ed. E. Zulberti, pp. 71–108. Universiti Pertanian Malaysia, Sedang, Selangor, Malaysia, 1–19 October 1984. Sedang, Selangor, Malaysia: International Center for Research on Agro-Forestry; U.S. Agency for International Development.

Philippines/ Agroforestry/ Indigenous and local communities—Farming practices.

745. **Aquino, D. M., G. Pollet, and E. Wakker. 1991.** "Rattan Utilization in a Sierra Madre Community: The San Mariano Case." Paper presented at the First Cagayan Valley Programme on Environment and Development Conference, 26–29 August 1991, in Cabagan, Isabele, Philippines. Photocopy.

This analysis deals with the rattan industry in San Mariano, Isabela, noting that studies of forest destruction should also give some emphasis to non-timber products. Three sections review patterns of rattan collection and use, issues of resource exhaustion, and possible options for improved forest management.

Philippines/ Non-timber forest products/ Rattan—Collection and trade/ Rattan—Resource management and conservation.

746. **Aquino, R. M. 1983.** "Lessons from Experiences in Social Forestry: Findings from Nine Selected Case Studies." Working Papers in Social Forestry Series, Manila: Integrated Research Center, De La Salle University.

Aquino presents a synthesis of main lessons learned from case studies of nine successful social forestry initiatives in the Philippines. A review of socio-economic conditions in the communities involved reveals low income levels, chronic indebtedness, limited services, highly unfavorable terms of trade for upland farm products, and widespread fear of eviction. Greater security of tenure is a major goal.

The objectives and accomplishments of the nine social forestry projects under study are described. Key lessons are highlighted: (1) Upland communities are poor and distinct; (2) Individual people as well as communities have different needs; (3) Indigenous organizations and land management technologies already exist in the uplands; (4) Communities want security of tenure; and (5) Various precedents for necessary steps towards successful project initiation, development, monitoring, budgeting, sustainability, and capability building do exist as outlined in the paper. Concludes the author, "there is a need to help upland communities, but we should let the uplanders write the terms of reference."

Philippines/ Project intervention—Social and community forestry.

747. **Aquino, R. M. et al. 1987.** "Mounting a National Social Forestry Program: Lessons Learned from the Philippine Experience." EAPI Working Paper, no. 87–9. Honolulu, Hawaii: East West Center.

Philippines/ Social forestry/ State policy—Forest and natural resources/ Project intervention—Social and community forestry.

748. **Area Research and Training Center. University of San Carlos. 1985.** "Process Documentation Reports to the Central Visayas Regional Project (CVRPO-I)." Cebu City, Philippines: ARTC, University of San Carlos.

A 10-volume report series on upland agriculture, social forestry and nearshore fisheries projects. Each volume includes: executive summary; collated field supervisors reports; site reports.

Philippines/ Cebu/ Project intervention—Agricultural development/ Project intervention— Soil conservation/ Project intervention—Social and community forestry.

749. **Atienza, C. S., and R. S. Marte. 1994.** "Changes in Food Consumption in the Philippines: Effects on Production and Use of Upland Crops." In *Changes in Food Consumption in Asia: Effects on Production and Use of Upland Crops.* Proceedings of a Workshop Held in Kandy, Sri Lanka October 6–9, 1992. Ed. J. W. T. Bottema, G. A. C. De Silva, and D. R. Stoltz, pp. 3–21. Bogor: Regional Co-ordination Centre for Research and Development of Coarse Grains, Pulses, Roots and Tuber Crops in the Humid Tropics of Asia and the Pacific (CGPRT Centre).

The authors presents and discuss food balance sheets showing utilization amounts for various uses (feed, seed, industry, food, etc.) and total supply. The data covers maize, sweet potato, cassava, white potato, gabi, other roots, mungbeans, groundnuts, soybeans, and dried beans.

Philippines/ Agricultural development/ Agricultural economics.

750. **Baconguis, S. R., and A. M. Dano. 1984.** "Some Geomorphological Characteristics and Infiltration Capacities of the Different Land-uses at the Buhisan Watershed." *Sylvatrop* 9 (1): 1–2.

Results of a study comparing geomorphological characteristics as well as infiltration capacities across different land uses in the Buhisan Watershed near Cebu City are presented. Land utilization types included a variety of plantations of differing duration, ungrazed grassland and pasture. The highest level of infiltration was found on a plantation of *G. aborea*, while the lowest was on grassland heavily used for cattle pasture.

Philippines/ Cebu/ Land use—Patterns and planning/ Soil erosion and degradation/ Soils/ Hydrology/ Land settlement and development—Environmental impacts/ Grasslands.

751.   **Bagadion, B. 1990.** "Trees, Monies, Rebels and Cronies: The Case of the Chellophil Resources Corporation." Ph.D. diss., Cornell University, Ithaca, N.Y.

The Cellophil Resources Corporation was founded in 1973 to develop a large-scale logging and pulp manufacturing enterprise. Transfer of concession rights to large tracts of forest lands in Northern Luzon conflicted directly with tribal land tenure claimed by the Tinggian, an upland farming people indigenous to the area. Although the company was never able to produce pulp on a commercial scale, its logging operations had a severe impact on the local ecology and subsistence production systems of the Tinggian, as documented by the author. While CRC's failure as a commercial enterprise has conventionally been attributed to popular unrest and armed insurgency in the area, Bagadion's research shows that "managerial, technical, and financial problems brought about by 'crony capitalism' were the major factors behind [its] collapse. . . ." [Summarized from author's abstract].

Philippines/ Timber industry—Logging/ Timber industry—Environmental impacts/ Timber industry—Impacts on local communities and economy/ State policy—Forest and natural resources/ Politics/ Political economy.

752.   **Barker, T. C. 1984.** "Shifting Cultivation among the Ikalahans." Working Paper, Series 1. College, Laguna, Philippines: Program on Environmental Science and Management, University of the Philippines at Los Ba–os College.

This paper presents the results of three years of research in the early 1980s among the Ikalahans of Imugan, Nueva Vizcaya, summarizing the Ikalahan shifting cultivation (*inuman*) practices. The Ikalahan have wide recognition in the Philippines as the one of the earliest forest-dwelling communities to be involved in community-based forestry and land stewardship on a pilot project basis. The project has been managed by the Kalahan Educational Foundation, an Ikalahan organization formed to oversee the management of tribal lands in cooperation with the Bureau of Forest Development as well as a number of other community development initiatives.

While traditional Ikalahan shifting cultivation practices were well adapted to local conditions in the past, new pressures are coming to bear on this system, including a growing population and more intensive use of forestlands. These changes threaten the sustainability of local food production systems, as soil and nutrient loss is accelerated, forest land regeneration is increasingly constrained, and problems of weeds, plant pathologies, and insects become more intractable. As the Ikalahan themselves have recognized these problems, general community support of agroforestry and other soil-conserving programs has grown. To support the Ikalahans' search for new soil conservation approaches, more research is needed on the question: "If fallows are shortened as shifting cultivation is intensified [sic], how do we maintain soil fertility?" Additional areas of concern include: control over diseases, weeds, insects, and conservation of the necessary physical properties of the soil.

Philippines/ Agriculture—Shifting cultivation/ Indigenous and local communities—Farming practices/ Indigenous and local communities—Forest land use and management practices/ Agricultural intensification/ Soil erosion and degradation/ Project intervention—Soil conservation/ Project intervention—Agroforestry/ Pest, weed, and crop disease management.

753.   **Barrios, H. T. 1984.** "Impact Assessment of a Forest Occupancy Management Project." *Journal of Philippine Development* 11 (1): 26–42.

Presidential Decree No. 705 provides for a "Forest Occupancy Management Program," the chief aspects of which are summarized by the author. The present study is intended to assess the extent to which this program has succeeded, as shown by a case study of the Angat Watershed Reservation Area (Dona Remedios Trindad, Balacan). Different stages of project execution are described, as are some characteristics of the persons (household heads) living in the area.

Project results were mixed. Income did increase between 1980 and 1981, at least partially because the cultivation of fruit trees was encouraged. Deforestation in and in-migration to the area have slowed. Reforestation, however, has been delayed "because the people must first meet their basic needs." Many households have not given up shifting cultivation due mainly to economic reasons. Farmers have also experienced difficulties in getting their crops to market, and farm-to-market roads ranked highest on a survey question which asked respondents to specify their priority concerns.

Philippines/ Forest management—Control of shifting cultivation/ Project intervention—Soil conservation/ Reforestation/ Watershed management.

754. **Bautista, Ma. L., ed. 1982.** *Perspectives in Social Forestry Papers*. Manila: De La Salle University; University of the Philippines.

This collection of papers contains presentations given at a workshop organized by De La Salle University to "orient (De La Salle) faculty members on social forestry, to learn from the experts, and to establish closer links with agencies doing related work especially those in the Bureau of Forest Development Upland Development Working Group." The following papers are presented: 1) Domingo, V. Jacalva, "Possible Technologies for Upland Development;" 2) Delfin, J. Ganapin, Jr., "Social Forestry: The Forester's Point of View"; 3) Harold Olofson, "Social Forestry from One Anthropologist's Point of View"; 4) Jaime B. Veneracion, "Social Forestry: A Social Scientist's View"; 5) Neptale Q. Zabala, "Development Plans for Makiling Forest"; 6) Percy E. Sajise, "Strategies for Transdisciplinary Research on Natural Resource Development: The Case of the UPLB Upland Hydroecology Program"; and 7) Roberto P. Ropera, "An Overview of Systems Analysis and Its Application to Forestry."

Philippines/ Social forestry/ Watershed management/ Project intervention—Soil conservation/ Project intervention—Social and community forestry.

755. **Belsky, J. M. 1984.** "Stratification among Migrant Hillside Farmers and Some Implications for Agroforestry Programs: A Case Study in Leyte, Philippines." Master's thesis, Cornell University, Ithaca, N.Y.

Philippines/ Migrant farmers and farming/ Indigenous and local communities—Social relations/ Project intervention—Agroforestry.

756. ———. **1993.** "Household Food Security, Farm Trees, and Agroforestry: A Comparative Study in Indonesia and the Philippines." *Human Organization* 52 (2): 130–140.

Adoption of agroforestry is being hailed in the development literature as an increasingly widespread and important farm-level innovation to improve household food as well as cash security under conditions of growing land and labor constraints. Belsky argues for a regional and historical approach to examining factors in farm household decision-making on tree cultivation practices and patterns. Analysis of field research in the Philippines and Indonesia reveals the high value placed by households on rice consumption. It follows that in much of Southeast Asia, food security and upland farm decisions should be viewed within the broader context of the rice economy.

Indonesia/ Philippines/ Agroforestry/ Agricultural intensification/ Household livelihood strategies/ Indigenous and local communities—Forest land use and management practices/ Indigenous and local communities—Farming practices.

757.   **Belsky, J. M., and S. F. Siebert. 1983.** "Household Responses to Drought in Two Subsistence Leyte Villages." *Philippine Quarterly of Culture and Society* 11: 237–256.

   The paper describes two upland villages which are alike in several ways save that one (Karila) is situated in an area with "wide access to abundant forest resources" while the other (San Pablo) is not. As a result of this difference, the two communities underwent very different experiences during the severe drought of 1982–83. Karila's well forested watershed sustained stream flows at levels sufficient to meet all drinking, washing, and most importantly, irrigation needs. The forests also provided both food and nonfood products. Is San Pablo, the opposite situation prevailed. Its residents experienced increased poverty, malnutrition, and indebtedness. Short-term out-migration from this community also increased significantly. The findings suggests the importance of forest resources to rural communities as insurance against drought, poor weather, pest infestation and other natural disasters.

   Philippines/ Indigenous and local communities—Forest land use and management practices/ Household livelihood strategies/ Non timber forest products/ Drought/ Poverty/ Watershed management.

758.   **Bennagen, P. L. 1985.** "Swidden Cultivation among the Dumagat." In Swidden Cultivation in Asia, v. 3: Empirical Studies in Selected Swidden Communities: India, Indonesia, Malaysia, Philippines, Thailand. pp. 213–268. Social and Human Sciences in Asia and the Pacific; RUSHAP Series on Occasional Monographs and Papers, no. 12. Bangkok, Thailand: UNESCO Regional Office for Education in Asia and the Pacific.

   The author presents the results of a two-year field study sponsored by UNESCO's Man and the Biosphere (MAB) program. From 1973 to 1975 a cluster of indigenous Dumagat and immigrant swidden communities in a mountainous region northeast of Metro Manila was studied for interrelationships between environmental factors, culture and government policy on environmental and social change. The report draws from both survey and ethnographic research, describing the swidden cycle, labor allocation, income, and land use patterns. The impact of development projects, the external market, and government intervention is also described. The need for structural improvement in the external socioeconomic environment to ensure equity for swidden cultivator communities is noted.

   Philippines/ Agriculture—Shifting cultivation/ Indigenous and local communities—Farming practices/ Indigenous and local communities—Forest land use and management practices/ Migrant farmers and farming/ Household livelihood strategies/ Cultural ecology/ Indigenous and local communities—State policy.

759.   **Bensel, T. G., and E. M. Remedio. 1993.** *Patterns of Commercial Woodfuel Supply, Distribution and Use in the City and Province of Cebu, Philippines.* [Bangkok]: Regional Wood Energy Development Programme in Asia, Food and Agricultural Organization.

   Bensel and Remedio provide a detail report on the results of a two-year (1991–93) study on the commercial woodfuel system in the city and province of Cebu, Philippines. The study focused on patterns of woodfuel demand, production, and distribution. As highlighted in the report, woodfuel represents a significant share of energy consumption on Cebu, even in urban areas. Consumers include households, small restaurants and foodstalls, as well as larger-scale bakeries and industrial enterprises, which are supplied through well-established, competitive woodfuel trading networks. Supply appears assured by a sustainable production pattern involving the cultivation of trees that are fast-growing, well-suited to regular coppicing, and grown on private land. The study findings highlight potential ways to improve the woodfuel situation through further research and policy development, as well as the need to rethink common assumptions about links between woodfuel use and forest land degradation.

Philippines/ Cebu/ Non-timber forest products/ Fuelwood.

760. **Boado, E. L. 1988.** "Incentive Policies and Forest Use in the Philippines." In *Public Policies and the Misuse of Forest Resources*. Ed. R. Repetto and M. Gillis, pp. 165–203. Cambridge, U.K.: Cambridge University Press.

There is little disagreement that deforestation in the Philippines has been proceeding at a very rapid rate since the second World War (roughly 172,000 ha per year between the late 1950s through 1973), though estimates differ as to exactly how much of the country's total area still remains covered by primary or secondary forest. Landsat images of the early 1980s indicate that total forest area in the Philippines had declined to 7.8–8.3 million ha by 1983 (of the archipelago's roughly 33 million ha land area in total), down from 8.5–9 million ha in 1976, while the extent of remaining virgin forest may be as low as .2–.7 million ha. While this alarming loss of forest cover has been due in part to deliberate conversion following reclassification, "destructive logging and shifting cultivation" are cited as the "major persistent causes." A broad description of the timber industry's history, the country's growth in timber exports, the illegal timber trade, and the results of the selective logging system mandated by government forest policy is provided. A number of key issues in forest policy are considered. The government's revenue collection systems is cited as a major factor behind rapid forest cover loss due to logging. With formal authority over 98 percent of the country's forests, the Philippine government awards timber rights to the private sector through its licensing system. Failing to capture more than a small share of potential rent from timber extraction between 1950 and 1970, this system provided the conditions for a destructive boom in logging activities during this period. Short-term concession leases, weak enforcement of license terms, and political patronage are cited as additional factors.

Promotion of the forest products industry has been another important force behind forest loss in the country, as processing requirements, tax credits and exemptions, and other incentives encouraged inefficient use of valuable timber resources by downstream processors. Third, the author cites the role of forest land conversion to agricultural use. Although politically expedient, the government's policy to open up virgin forest lands to settlement by landless farmers, rather than reduce concentration of ownership in the more fertile lowlands, caused vast tracts of forest to be converted to agriculture in the 1950s and 1960s, at a rate of 200,000 ha per year. Additional pressure on the country's forests resulted from land speculation and the opening of virgin forest areas by logging roads, allowing the uncontrolled entry of increasing numbers of incipient shifting cultivators since the 1970s. Soil erosion, watershed degradation, and conversion of large expanses of forest to unproductive, cogon-infested grassland have been among the most serious outcomes of this pressure.

The author concludes with a brief note on some of the major lessons learned from the Philippine experience. Particular attention needs to be paid to reinforcing the government's forestry staff to effect better supervision of forest use, devising more appropriate licensing and taxation systems, reducing protection of inefficient wood processing industries, and effecting a more equitable land ownership pattern through redistribution of arable land in lowland areas rather than encroachment into fragile upland forests. Plantation development, social forestry, systematic conservation enforcement, and other measures have an important role to play in fulfilling a critical need to make use of Philippines' remaining forest lands more efficient and sustainable over the long term.

Philippines/ Deforestation/ Timber industry—Development and structure/ Timber industry—Trade and markets/ Timber industry—Logging/ Timber industry—State policy and regulation/ Land settlement and development—Environmental impacts/ Agriculture—Shifting cultivation's environmental impacts/ Forest management—Forest resource conservation/ State policy—Forest and natural resources.

761.   **Borlagdan, S. B. 1987.** "Working with People in the Uplands: The Bulolakaw Social Forestry Experience." Photocopy. Quezon City, Philippines: Institute of Philippine Culture, Ateneo de Manila.

This document serves as the final report for the first 25 months of process documentation research completed by the Institute of Philippine Culture in the Bulolakaw Upland Development Program (UPD) pilot program. The purpose of the research was to assist the BFD personnel to develop their capacity and skill in participatory upland resource management within the context of its Integrated Social Forestry (ISF) program. The report summarizes the key activities, issues, and problems that occurred in the Bulolakaw pilot project and highlights the lessons that can be learned from them. The following concerns are discussed: organizing the upland farmers, providing farm security, promoting upland development technologies to improve local livelihood conditions, and responding to basic needs [Modified executive summary].

Philippines/ Project intervention—Social and community forestry/ Project intervention—Participatory methods.

762.   ———. **1989.** "Process Documentation Research on Participatory Social Forestry." In *A Decade of Process Documentation Research: Reflections and Synthesis.* Ed. C. C. Veneracion. Quezon City, Philippines: Institute of Philippine Culture, Ateneo de Manila University.

The implementation and results of process documentation during a participatory social forestry project in Alcoy, Cebu are summarized. An early problem identified by the process documentation report (PDR) was that farmers felt that they were not participating fully in the stewardship land surveys. A second issue involved conflicting land claims between farmer occupants and absentee-claimants (i.e., absentee landlords). A third dealt with an initial tendency to exclude women from the project-sponsored community organization. Still a fourth problem revolved around competition between different subgroups for access to agroforestry inputs. Some suggestions for ways in which PDR might be improved and implemented for upland development are given.

Philippines/ Project intervention—Social and community forestry/ Project intervention—Participatory methods.

763.   **Borlagdan, S. B. 1990.** "Social Forestry in Upland Cebu." In *Keepers of the Forest: Land Management Alternatives in Southeast Asia.* Ed. M. Poffenberger, pp. 266–276. West Hartford, Conn.: Kumarian Press.

This paper describes the Ford Foundation-assisted Upland Development Project in Bulolakaw, Alcoy, Cebu.

Philippines/ Cebu/ Project intervention—Social and community forestry.

764.   **Borlagdan, S. B. et al. 1990.** "The Cebu Integrated Social Forestry Project." Network Paper, no. 10c. London, U.K.: Overseas Development Institute, Social Forestry Network.

Philippines/ Cebu/ Project intervention—Social and community forestry.

765.   **Bouis, H. E., and L. J. Haddad. 1990.** "Effects of Agricultural Commercialization on Land Tenure, Household Resource Allocation, and Nutrition in the Philippines." IFPRI Research Report, no. 79. Washington, D.C.: International Food Policy Research Institute.

Periodic surveys of 500 households involved in maize and sugar production in Bukidnon, Mindanao completed during 1984 and 1985 collected data on holding size, incomes, spending, consumption, and nutrition. A variety of household types were covered, including landless, smallholder, and tenant farmers. Study results indicate that as cash cropping of sugar cane for export increased since the establishment of a sugar mill in 1977, land consolidation also increased, while subsistence maize farming, access to land for tenant farmers, and women's participation in own farm production all declined. Incomes have improved somewhat for those smallholders growing sugar cane. However, very little nutritional improvement appears to have resulted, owing largely to high levels of morbidity among preschoolers of sugarcane growing households. The results point to some serious health and sanitation problems blocking the nutritional gains that might have been expected from higher incomes.

Philippines/ Mindanao/ Agricultural development/ Agriculture—Permanent/ Agriculture—Smallholder cash crop farming/ Poverty/ Household livelihood strategies/ Indigenous and local communities—Commoditization/ Health and nutrition.

766.   ———. **1994.** "The Nutrition Effects of Sugarcane Cropping in a Southern Philippine Province." In *Agricultural Commercialization, Economic Development, and Nutrition.* Ed. Braun, J. von, and E. Kennedy, pp. 204–217. Baltimore, Md.: Johns Hopkins University Press.

Philippines/ Mindanao/ Agricultural development/ Agriculture—Smallholder cash crop farming/ Health and nutrition.

767.   **Broad, R., and J. Cavanagh. 1993.** *Plundering Paradise: The Struggle for the Environment in the Philippines.* Berkeley, Calif.: University of California Press.

Drawing from interviews and field visits made to different parts of the Philippines over a one year period (August 1988 August 1989), as well as from experiences gained during repeated research visits since 1977, the authors provide a narrative account of current conflicts over natural resource exploitation and industrial pollution in the country. While resource exploitation has been rampant in the Philippines, the vast majority of the country's population has obtained little if any of the benefits derived from this development, and in many cases, bear the direct costs of resulting environmental degradation. Field visits and direct interviews with local residents on Mindanao, Palawan, Northern Luzon and Bataan are cited to show how soil erosion due to loss of forest cover, disrupted stream flows, flooding, and dwindling fisheries impact directly and most adversely upon the already meager livelihoods of growing numbers of Filipino farming and fishing households. The authors focus on several cases of community-based action taken against logging companies, the Philippine government, industrial polluters, and commercial fisheries, highlighting the main features of a growing though loosely knit "sustainable development" movement in the Philippines. In the wake of communism's decline during the last several years, growing activism by citizen and indigenous people's groups in the Philippines suggest the emergence of a new debate within development economics between adherents of "the free-market school" and "the growing ranks promoting an alternative vision of sustainable and equitable development."

Philippines/ Social movements/ Timber industry—Logging/ Timber industry—Environmental impacts/ Timber industry—Impacts on local communities and economy/ Deforestation/ State policy—Economic development/ Politics/ Non-governmental organizations.

768.   **Brosius, J. P. 1990.** *After Duwagan: Deforestation, Succession, and Adaptation in Upland Luzon, Philippines.* Michigan Studies of South and Southeast Asia,

no. 2. Ann Arbor, Mich.: Center for South and Southeast Asian Studies, University of Michigan.

Brosius applies succession theory to the analysis of the changing landscape and "ecosystemic relations" among the Ayta of upland Zambales, Philippines. In contrast to other approaches in human ecology which seek to de-emphasize the role of "historical vicissitude," the author stresses the goal of achieving a better understanding of local histori- cal factors in the process of landscape change. The study aims, in short, to "account for historical uniqueness of an ecosystem while at the same time avoiding a particularistic per- spective." Drawing from the results of field research From January to August 1980, the author analyzes the parameters of three types of disturbance: 1) swiddening; 2) logging; and 3) burning (mainly of grasslands) to define a sequence of change in local ecosystems that is both initiated and experienced by human actors.

The analysis highlights the diversity of swidden farming systems and their differing implications for resulting forest land transformations. Parameters of disturbance—i.e., fre- quency, intensity, and scale—may be used to characterize these differences. Also important, however, are extant contextual factors, such as rainfall seasonality, local physiography, and local floral portfolio, which combine with parameters of disturbance to shape local biotic environments. Concludes the author, centuries of swidden farming by the Ayta practiced in the presence of specific contextual factors (i.e., extreme seasonality) have resulted in a land- scape largely devoid of its original forest cover, and now covered with early secondary vegetation. Though destructive of the original forest cover, by maintaining this early secondary forest land environment, the Ayta have been able to maintain an economically productive habitat capable of sustaining their livelihood over the long-term. The analysis provides an approach for clarifying the specific factors—summarized here as parameters of disturbance and contextual factors—in the still poorly understood process of forest land transformation.

Philippines/ Deforestation/ Agriculture—Shifting cultivation's environmental impacts/ Indigenous and local communities—Forest land use and management practices/ Cultural ecology/ Grasslands.

769.   **Brown, E. C. 1991.** "Tribal Peoples and Land Settlement: The Effects of Philippine Capitalist Development on the Palawan." Ph.D. diss., State University of New York, Binghamton, N.Y.

Based on a village census and interviews, Brown explores the settlement history, social relations, economic development, and environmental problems of southern Palawan island, with particular focus on the areas indigenous residents, the Palawan. Steady in-migration since World War II has involved the progressive settlement of the region's coastal plains and the displacement of the Palawan to upland areas. Though still comprising a numeric majority in the area, the Palawan occupy a subordinated and less visible status than non- Palawan households who have arrived on the island over the last fifty years, who now dominate local administrative structures, export agriculture, and the economy in general. Agricultural intensification and increased intercropping has accompanied the decline in available land resources. To compensate for declining rice yields, Palawan villagers increasingly engage in off-farm employment; at the same time, they face discrimination and unequal access to technology and information. While "deculturation" and "aculturation" are proceeding among the Palawan, they maintain an ethnic distinctiveness due to their resistance against domination by outsiders.

Philippines/ Palawan/ Land settlement and development/ Land settlement and develop- ment—Impacts on local communities and economy/ Migration/ Indigenous and local com- munities—Economy/ Indigenous and local communities—Commoditization/ Indigenous and local communities—Farming practices/ Indigenous and local communities—Social relations/ Ethnicity and ethnic relations.

770.   **Burton, E. 1983.** "The Impact of Modern Medical Intervention on the Agusan Manobo Medical System." Ph.D. diss., University of Pittsburgh, Pittsburgh, Penn.

While focused on the process and implications of modern medical interventions, this dissertation includes a description and analysis of the current food production system of the Agusan Manobo on Mindanao island. In particular, the author observes that the harvests from Manobo upland swiddens are bountiful and rich in nutrients, even when compared to their lowland counterparts. Lowland farms, notes the authors, appear less diverse in nutritional resources and more likely to be subject to attack by a variety of pests, including rats and locusts.

Philippines/ Indigenous and local communities—Farming practices/ Health and nutrition.

771.   **Byron, R. N., and M. A. Quintos. 1988.** "Log Export Restrictions and Forest Industries Development in South-east Asia (1975–1986): The Case of the Phillipines [*sic*]." In *Changing Tropical Forests: Historical Perspectives on Today's Challenges in Asia, Australasia, and Oceania.* Ed. J. Dargavel, K. Dixon and N. Semple, pp. 427–446. Canberra, Australia: Centre for Resource and Environmental Studies.

Regulating rates of timber extraction, limiting the export of unprocessed logs, and promoting the expansion of domestic downstream processing capacity have been common elements of national forestry policy in many timber-exporting countries of Southeast Asia. The authors critically assess the effects of these policies, with particular reference to Indonesia and the Philippines. While cautious about drawing premature conclusions, the authors suggest a number of key points: 1) These policies appear to have met with highly variable success across different countries. West Malaysia, on the one hand, has shown the strongest performance in terms of value-added, local employment and foreign exchange generated. By contrast, unsustainably high costs have characterized the development of downstream processing in Indonesia, and relatively few companies have responded to government incentives in the Philippines; 2) Countries which have not implemented similar policies promoting the development of downstream processing industries have generally benefited from steps taken in Indonesia, West Malaysia, and the Philippines, given the resulting rise in international tropical timber prices; 3) Whatever the downstream industrialization policy, tropical forests of Southeast Asia appear to have been "consistently undervalued by the governments responsible for them," encouraging wasteful over-exploitation. Subsidies given to those engaged in downstream processing has tended only to exacerbate this problem, under-pricing existing forest stands even further.

Philippines/ Indonesia/ Timber industry—Trade and markets/ Timber industry—Downstream processing/ Timber industry—Logging/ Timber industry—State policy and regulation.

772.   **Cabrido, C. A. 1984.** "Fuelwood Management by Rural Households." *Canopy International* 10 (4): 3–5.

Fuelwood is the basic energy source for most rural households in the Third World. This paper reviews findings on the topic with a view towards identifying current "research gaps" in the field. Fuelwood consumption in the Philippines is relatively high, while, unfortunately, sustainable forest yield has been low. As a result, fuelwood scarcity is bound to become increasingly critical in the years to come. Among likely side effects of this development will be increasing labor requirements for finding fuelwood (usually affecting women and children the most) as well as accelerated forest-ecosystems disturbance. Some suggestions are made to address this situation, ranging from the use of specific plant varieties for speedier forest regeneration to ideas about fuel-efficient cook stoves. There is a need for the Philippines government to come up with a systematic program for fuelwood management. Better statistics on the problem are also needed, though are not easy to collect in practice.

Philippines/ Non-timber forest products/ Fuelwood.

773. ————. **1985.** "An Assessment of National Soil Erosion Control Management Problems in the Philippines." In *Soil Erosion Management*. Proceedings of a workshop held at PCARRD, Los Ba–os, Philippines, 3–5 December 1984. Ed. E. T. Craswell, J. V. Remenyi, and L. G. Nallana, pp. 13–20. Canberra: Australian Center for International Agricultural Research.

Philippines/ Soil erosion and degradation.

774. ————. **1989.** "Population, Natural Resources and Environment: Present Crisis and Alternative Paths to Sustainable Development." *PSSC Social Science Information* 17 (2): 11–13.

This article gives a broad overview of the country's present environmental crisis. A minimum set of nine policy measures "which should be undertaken simultaneously in order to attain the goal of sustainable development" is presented. The role of women and of population variables is also stressed and a brief agenda of critical research topics is given.

Philippines/ Deforestation/ Soil erosion and degradation/ Population pressure.

775. **Cadelina, R. V. 1982.** "Batak Interhousehold Food Sharing: A Systematic Analysis of Food Management of Marginal Agriculturalists in the Philippines." Ph.D. diss., University of Hawaii, Honolulu, Hawaii.

Philippines/ Palawan/ Indigenous and local communities—Economy/ Household livelihood strategies.

776. ————. **1983.** "Domestic Development Cycle Stage and Expansion of Swidden Fields: A Theoretical Perspective." Paper presented at the Symposium on Research and Impact of Development on Human Activity Systems in Southeast Asia, 8–11 August 1983, in Bandung, West Java, Indonesia. Photocopy.

An initial distinction is made between "lowlanders-turned-uplanders" and indigenous upland groups. Immigrant lowlanders in upland environments are generally associated with a more extensive and destructive use of forest lands than indigenous uplanders. Data from the Lake Balinsasayo uplands study is used to look at reasons behind farmers' decisions to expand their swidden. The influence of household stage in the domestic life cycle is noted. When children are first being born, caloric needs increase. The swidden may not yet be enlarged, however, since the mother must spend more time in child care; labor input into swidden field is still constant or even declining at this time. During the "middle stage" of the family cycle, caloric needs are higher still (thus a need to expand) while labor inputs expand as children reach adolescence (thus the ability to expand). Data collected from twelve kaingero households generally support the thesis. Implications for the country's Social Forestry Programs are suggested.

Philippines/ Agriculture—Shifting cultivation/ Migrant farmers and farming/ Indigenous and local communities—Forest land use and management practices/ Household livelihood strategies.

777.   ————. **1983.** "Social Forestry Program: Prospects and Implications on the Community and Household Level." Paper presented at the First ASEAN Forestry Congress, 10–15 October 1983, in Manila, Philippines. Photocopy.

This paper attempts a constructive critique of the present social forestry program in the Philippines. The author begins by emphasizing that upland households are not homogenous. As discussed in an earlier paper, the land needs of individual households differ during successive phases of the family life cycle. "Middle stage" households have a higher calorie need (typically this becomes a calorie deficit) and are found to be cultivating more plots. Project interventions should therefore focus on "these critical households," keeping in mind their higher food needs than households in other life cycle stages. In addition, program planners and project workers must be sure to place "obvious" needs in specific local context. For example, most uplanders do want increased agricultural production, but if the new inputs are too expensive they won't use them. "Community participation" is often invoked to ensure that social forestry projects address and handle issues from a community-level perspective. Yet, heterogeneity in community-level factors must also be taken into greater account. More specifically, indigenous upland groups tend to be more organized as communities than "lowlanders-turned-uplanders," and the latter are more likely to need greater help in community organizing. To be a constructive concept, community participation must be more rigorously defined and operationalized. Finally, a third mistake frequently made in social forestry is to view the community as a single, isolated entity. To address local resource management problems in more realistic terms, one must also take into account the socio-economic and ecological relationships that exist between communities.

Philippines/ Indigenous and local communities—Farming practices/ Indigenous and local communities—Forest land use and management practices/ Household livelihood strategies/ Project intervention—Social and community forestry/ Project intervention—Participatory methods.

778.   ————. **1986.** "Philippine Poverty Studies: Concepts, Problems and an Alternative Approach." In *Faces of Philippine Poverty: Four Cases from the Visayas*. Ed. R. G. Abad, C. V. Rowe, and V. Lopez-Gonzaga, pp. 187–224. Metro Manila: Philippine Social Science Council.

Cadelina examines problems of poverty among four main groups, including plantation workers as well as upland shifting cultivators. When poverty is viewed as a condition, upland swiddeners appear to fare better than other groups due to a variety of subsistence strategies that supplement cash incomes and their access to the means of production (i.e., land, even if through squatting, livestock, and simple farm tools). When poverty is viewed as process, however, the salience of a distinct world view held by uplanders becomes apparent, as the latter appear more amenable than sugarcane workers to economic risk-taking and less willing to subject themselves to loss of personal freedom. In addition, the importance of historical antecedents and structural factors that vary among the four groups becomes evident. For migrant farmers in the uplands, these include the lack of service provisions and tenure security characteristic of frontier areas, unfavorable terms of trade, ecological constraints, demographic pressures, and forest loss. Emphasizes Cadelina, the processual model views poor people as rational decision makers and allows researcher to propose poverty programs which can work within the prevailing system rather than unrealistically requiring "ownership" of the means of production. Implications of this model for the current situation of Philippine poverty groups are explored.

Philippines/ Migrant farmers and farming/ Poverty.

779.   ————. **1986.** "Poverty in the Upland: Lowland Migrant Swiddeners in the Balinsasayao Forest, Negros Oriental." In *Faces of Philippine Poverty: Four Cases from the Visayas*. Ed. R. G. Abad, R. V. Cadelina, and V. Lopez-Gonzaga, pp. 165–188. Metro Manila: Philippine Social Science Council.

This is a study of "lowlander-turned uplanders," as set in an upland area located about 25 kilometers northwest of Dumaguete City, Negros Oriental. Data were collected by means of both a sample survey and participant observation. The demographic and socioeconomic characteristics of the respondents are described along with health/nutritional variables and their views about their situation and problems. While most respondents are poor, this particular group does not fare quite so badly as some of the others analyzed in the present volume. The main reason for this is that "compared to other upland groups, this population has a more diversified and wider niche base" (e.g., access to Lake Balinsasayao). However, "their levels of aspirations . . . seem to be relatively low . . . (whether as due to satisfaction or resignation)." In addition, the author argues that lowland farming techniques employed by the immigrant farmers in their new upland environment has contributed to a decline in farm production, declining soil fertility, and receding forests. Inappropriate farming practices are, in short, also a major factor in keeping the immigrant farmers economically depressed.

Philippines/ Migrant farmers and farming/ Agriculture—Shifting cultivation/ Poverty/ Household livelihood strategies/ Health and nutrition.

780. **Canlas, E. S., and Elmer V. Sayre. 1986.** "The Tobacco Farmers of an Upland Philippine Province: Will Their Dreams Go Up in Smoke?" Research report prepared for the International Development Research Centre. Photocopy. Cagayan de Oro, Mindanao: Research Institute for Mindanao Culture.

This study documents tobacco cultivation and its implications among traditional corn farmers in a land reform-linked project area in upland Bukidnon, Mindanao. The project studied involved an agroforestry dimension insofar as the planting of ipil-ipil was encouraged along with other trees to provide fuel for tobacco-curing operations. In general, more farmers lost more money on the venture than they were able to gain. Loan repayments were very irregular, as were amortization payments under the land reform program. There is less risk associated with corn than tobacco, though profitability is also less. Farmers were not particularly eager to go into tree-farming. Some thought that the Bureau of Forest Development (BFD) would evict them once the trees were grown. Others were not interested in a crop which could not promise a quick economic return. As of the study date, there was also no "ready market" for the trees. Most respondents understood that a clear trend towards deforestation had taken place during the past few decades. Many also realized that this may result in decreased rainfall, additional soil erosion and the like.

Philippines/ Agriculture—Smallholder cash crop farming/ Project intervention—Agroforestry.

781. **Capistrano, A. D., and Sam Fujisaka. 1984.** "Tenure, Technology and Productivity of Agroforestry Schemes." Working Paper, no. 84-06. Manila: Philippine Institute for Development Studies.

The authors review the literature on agroforestry-based technologies being promoted in social forestry efforts, with a particular focus on issues of productivity and land tenure policies. The authors' analysis raises a number of questions regarding the productivity actually being achieved by current agroforestry schemes, the forces constraining agroforestry yields, the appropriateness of the recommended agroforestry technology, the influence of land holdings size and tenure security on farmer decisions to adopt agroforestry technology, as well as marketing considerations. These questions point to a number of problems in current efforts to promote agroforestry, suggesting that Bureau of Forestry Development upland programs and policies are still far from effective.

Philippines/ Agroforestry/ Land tenure/ Project intervention—Agroforestry.

782. **Carner, G. 1981.** "Survival, Interdependence and Competition among the Philippine Rural Poor." *Philippine Sociological Review* 29 (4): 45–57.

Despite lack of clarity on the concept of poverty, it is possible to identify who the poor are and what specific factors underlie their impoverished state. In the Philippines, three broad groups may be distinguished as most disadvantaged: landless agricultural workers, upland farmers and sustenance fishermen. Their survival strategies reveal significant differences and disparities in socioeconomic outcomes. Despite the resourcefulness the poor show in managing limited productive assets, their livelihood strategies are seriously undermined by a vicious cycle of population pressure, environmental decline, and the growth cycle itself. In order to begin breaking these structures of poverty down, appropriate policies and targeting of specific needs among different groups are urgently needed. [Modified author's abstract].

Philippines/ Poverty/ Household livelihood strategies/ Population pressure/ Deforestation/ Soil erosion and degradation.

783. **Castillo, R. A. del, and F. V. Cagampang. 1977.** "The Case of Mt. Makiling Kaingero." Paper presented at KALAHI Symposium, 11 February 1977, sponsored by Forest Research Institute and Binbining Filipinas Charities, Inc., College, Laguna, Philippines. Photocopy.

Following a brief sketch of the environmental side-effects of deforestation on Mt. Makiling, the authors summarize the findings of the first survey of illegal occupants living in Mt. Makiling conducted in 1972 along with data from researcher Duldulao's survey in 1975. Using this data, patterns of in-migration, land tenure, and socio-economic characteristics are described. In the second section, the authors describe the activities of various government offices (including the University of the Philippines, Los Ba–os) in the Mt. Makiling region, highlighting resettlement projects for Makiling squatters in particular. Though difficulties have been many, note the authors, the Resettlement Committee remains "committed" to its goal of clearing the Makiling Forest of all squatters, as mandated by "the order of the President and the goals of a compassionate society."

Philippines/ Forest management—Control of shifting cultivation/ Migrant farmers and farming/ Resettlement.

784. **Castro, C. P. 1989.** "Facilitating and Constraining Factors in the Implementation of Social Forestry in the Philippines." In *Social Forestry in Asia: Factors That Influence Program Implementation*. Ed. N. T. Vergara and R. A. Fernandez, pp. 287–299. College, Laguna, Philippines: Southeast Asian Regional Center for Graduate Study and Research in Agriculture.

Castro presents an "insider's" view of social forestry in the Philippines as an official with the Bureau of Forest Development. As of December 1986, only 170,542 households in the Philippines had joined the program, and of this number only 61,124 had received the promised certificates of stewardship. This disappointing performance may in part be linked to the BFD's neglect of past lessons, of indigenous social forestry practices, and of potentially supportive non-BFD government agencies. Direct obstacles to the program include: the negative image of foresters among the rural population; resistance by traditional foresters; and an overly narrow focus on particular areas and agroforestry technologies.

Philippines/ Social forestry/ Project intervention—Social and community forestry.

785. **Central Visayas Resource Management Project. 1982.** "Project Preparation Report." 3 vols. Cebu City, Cebu: Central Visayas Resource Management Project, Cebu, Philippines.

This 3-volume report presents feasibility studies dealing with watershed management, social forestry, infrastructure, nearshore marine fish habitat management, institution building, research training, technical assistance, and rural organization of credit and marketing.

Philippines/ Cebu/ Project intervention—Rural development/ Project intervention—Social and community forestry/ Watershed management.

786.   **Cohen, J. I., and C. Potter. 1990.** "Genetic Resource Conservation and Utilization in the Context of International Development." *Diversity* 6 (1): 18–21.

Reviews current efforts to integrate genetic resource conservation with agricultural development and general plant use practices. Cites project experiences in West Kalimantan and Sumatra, Indonesia, the Philippines, and Ecuador.

Indonesia/ West Kalimantan/ Philippines/ Biodiversity.

787.   **Conelly, W. T. 1982.** "Economic Adaptation in an Upland Environment in Palawan: A Preliminary Survey of Field Research." *Philippine Sociological Review* 30 (1–4): 51–62.

This paper asks in what ways and how effectively do settlers in an upland community like Napsaan, Palawan, utilize resources in exploiting the environment. Time allocation patterns across a range of different economic activities are highlighted, and the productivity and returns to labor of the three most important activities (shifting cultivation, tree farming, and forest product gathering) are assessed. Based on research findings, Conelly concludes that the most successful adaptations to rapidly changing upland environments are those which include a diverse set of livelihood strategies. Over-reliance upon non-food producing activities or those which are remunerated strictly in cash are generally counter-productive. [Modified author's abstract].

Philippines/ Palawan/ Migrant farmers and farming/ Agriculture—Shifting cultivation/ Indigenous and local communities—Forest land use and management practices/ Indigenous and local communities—Forest products use and trade/ Indigenous and local communities—Economy/ Non-timber forest products.

788.   ———. **1983.** "Upland Development in the Tropics: Alternative Economic Strategies in a Philippine Frontier Community." Ph.D. diss., University of California at Santa Barbara, Santa Barbara, Calif.

Throughout the Southeast Asian tropics, upland farmers have begun to alter their traditional swidden farming and foraging practices in order to cope with the pressures of growing population density, land scarcity, and the increasing importance of the market economy. This dissertation attempts a policy-oriented analysis of adaptive strategies of contemporary upland farmers in a frontier settlement on the island of Palawan, Philippines. The focus is on alternative economic strategies employed by settlers in exploiting the area's diverse environment. Subsistence choices within the community studied are highly varied; major options include short fallow shifting cultivation, forest collecting, ocean fishing, small-scale irrigated rice cultivation, and tree crop farming. Based on documented returns to labor for each option, the author attempts to explain the economic and social factors that lead individuals to make the subsistence decisions that they do. The author places these decision-making processes within the context of economic change and the transition from long fallow shifting cultivation to intensive irrigated rice farming, critically examining many assumptions about the adaptiveness of traditional swidden agriculture and assessing alternative explanations for the transition process. Finally, policy implications of the research findings are considered for a broader upland development context. [Summarized from author's abstract].

Philippines/ Agriculture—Shifting cultivation/ Agricultural intensification/ Migrant farmers and farming/ Indigenous and local communities—Economy/ Indigenous and local communities—Farming practices/ Indigenous and local communities—Forest products use and trade/ Indigenous and local communities—Forest land use and management practices/ Household livelihood strategies/ Non-timber forest products/ Agriculture—Smallholder tree and perennial crop farming/ Agriculture—Smallholder cash crop farming.

789.   ———. **1985.** "Copal and Rattan Collecting in the Philippines." *Economic Botany* 39 (1): 39–46.

Minor forest products such as rattan and Manila copal have long been an important source of cash income for indigenous forest collectors in Southeast Asia. Focusing on the Tagbanua of Palawan Island in the Philippines, the history and economic significance of forest collecting in the region are described. The paper also documents the growing scarcity of forest products in Palawan and discusses several policy options intended to help preserve rattan and copal resources.

Philippines/ Palawan/ Indigenous and local communities—Forest products use and trade/ Non-timber forest products/ Rattan—Collection and trade/ Rattan—Resource management and conservation.

790.   **Conklin, H. C. 1957.** "Hanunoo Agriculture: A Report on an Integral System of Shifting Agriculture in the Philippines." Forestry Development Papers, no. 12. Rome: Food and Agriculture Organization of the United Nations.

In a ground-breaking analysis of the swidden cropping system of the Hanunoo tribe in the uplands of Mindoro island, Conklin describes the complex patterns of land use by the Hanunoo. More specifically, the author observes that a variety of techniques for slashing and controlled burning are employed by the Hanunoo to clear new swiddens, depending on extant field conditions. Once actively cropped swiddens decline in productivity, they are succeeded by different stages of managed fallow, rather than simply abandoned. Dispelling earlier theories of the wanton and destructive nature of indigenous swidden farming, the author concludes that Hanunoo agricultural practices represent an ecologically sound and finely tuned system of land use in the Southeast Asian tropics that is able to yield higher volumes of rice on a sustained basis per acre than that produced by lowland farmers.

Philippines/ Agriculture—Shifting cultivation/ Indigenous and local communities—Farming practices/ Indigenous and local communities—Forest land use and management practices/ Cultural ecology.

791.   **Contreras, A. P. 1989.** "The Discourse of Development: Some Implications for Local Power/Knowledge in the Philippine Uplands." *Philippine Sociological Review* 37 (1–2): 12–25.

Although development may "appear compassionate and empowering, " in reality it usually operates to the advantage of those already in power. Neither "radical leftism" nor "liberal revisionism" can overcome "the hegemony of a unified and totalizing form of development." The solution rather, must begin at the grassroots. Plural movements which possess "an equivalent agenda" can bring about change. The Philippine uplands is taken as a case study. State policy toward upland "squatters" was initially punitive and subsequently more compassionate, as evidenced in the transition towards an integrated social forestry agenda in the Bureau of Forest Development. However, neither approach has worked, and in response "more and more, local people are beginning to organize themselves in order to assert their rights." Yet the threat of co-optation should not be ignored, and attention should be devoted to strengthening linkages among local groups.

Philippines/ Social movements/ State policy—Forest and natural resources/ Political economy.

792. **Cornista, L. 1985.** "Land Tenure System in the Philippine Uplands: Its Implications to Agroforestry." In *Land, Trees, and Tenure*. Proceedings of an International Workshop on Tenure Issues in Agroforestry, 27–31 May 1985, Nairobi, Kenya. Ed. J. B. Raintree, pp. 277–281. College, Laguna, Philippines: Agrarian Reform Institute, College of Development Economics and Management, University of the Philippines at Los Ba–os.

Philippines/ Indigenous and local communities—Land and resource tenure systems/ Land tenure—Legislation and state policy/ Agroforestry/ Project intervention—Agroforestry.

793. ———. **1985.** "Land Tenure and Resource Use among Upland Farmers." Agrarian Reform Institute Paper Series, no. 2. College, Laguna, Philippines: Agrarian Reform Institute, College of Development Economics and Management, University of the Philippines at Los Ba–os.

Philippines/ Indigenous and local communities—Land and resource tenure systems/ Indigenous and local communities—Forest land use and management practices.

794. **Cornista, L. B., and E. F. Escueta. 1991.** "Communal Forest Leases as a Tenurial Option in the Philippines Uplands." IAST Occasional Papers Series, No. 36. College, Laguna, Philippines: Institute of Agrarian Studies, College of Economics and Management, University of the Philippines.

Philippines/ Social forestry/ Land tenure.

795. Corpuz, E. 1984. "A Comparative Economic Study of Traditional Kaingin, Modified Cropping Patterns and Tree Farming in Mt. Makiling." Master's thesis, University of the Philippines, Los Ba–os, College, Laguna, Philippines.

The author argues that the economic viability and sustainable productivity of traditional kaingin are lower than modified cropping patterns which have been adopted by some farmers in the uplands to meet current conditions.

Philippines/ Agriculture—Shifting cultivation/ Agricultural intensification/ Agriculture—Smallholder tree and perennial crop farming/ Agriculture—Smallholder cash crop farming/ Farm management—Economics.

796. **Costello, M. A. n.d.** "Trends in Farm Size and Structure, Northern Mindanao, 1970–1980." Final report on the Population and Development Planning and Research Project submitted to the National Economic Development Authority. Cagayan de Oro, Mindanao: RIMCU, Xavier University.

This paper presents an analysis of major changes in Northern Mindanao's agricultural sector using data from the 1970 and 1980 census. Major topics covered include rural and urban population growth, employment in agriculture, tenure status, changes in farm size and in the total area under cultivation, corporate farming enterprises, equity issues in land ownership, and cropping patterns.

Philippines/ Population pressure/ Agricultural development/ Agricultural intensification/ Land tenure.

797. ———. **1984.** "Social Change in Mindanao: A Review of the Research of a Decade." *Kinadman* 6 (1): 1–41.

Philippines/ Mindanao/ Economic development/ Ethnicity and ethnic relations/ Social movements/ Politics.

798.   ————. **1988.** "Levels of Living and Their Geographic Context: Northern Mindanao, 1960–1980." Final report on the Population and Development Planning and Research project submitted to the National Economic Development Authority, Region X. Cagayan de Oro, Mindanao: RIMCU, Xavier University.

Philippines/ Mindanao/ Demography/ Migration/ Poverty.

799.   ————. **1992.** "The Demography of Mindanao." In *Mindanao: Land of Unfulfilled Promise*. Ed. M. Turner, R. J. May, and L. R. Turner, pp. 31–60. Quezon City, Philippines: New Day Publishers.

Costello explores major demographic developments on Mindanao island during the 20th century. Island-wide and subregional time series data are provided on population growth rates, population density, urbanization and fertility rates. Statistics are also provided for specific characteristics of Mindanao's population, including age structure, educational status, and occupational categories. While Mindanao's population growth rates were generally much higher than the rest of the Philippines in the first half of the 20th century, over the last two decades, this difference has narrowed significantly. By the 1975–80 intercensal period, the population growth rate for Mindanao was only 2.6 percent, compared with 2.5 percent for all of the Philippines. Population density increased from 6.58 persons/km2 in 1903 to 138.04 persons/km2 in 1990. Recent agricultural research suggests that this dramatic increase in population density has been accompanied by a substantial drop in the average farm size, from 12 ha in 1963 to only 4 ha in 1980.

Against this general background, important variation among the island's subregions and subpopulations also obtain, and rates of change have shifted between different areas. The data suggests an accelerated rate of urbanization in Mindanao, exceeding that of the rest of the country, while growth rates in the uplands remain high though declining. In sum, Mindanao's demographic profile has become increasingly complex during this century, making generalizations on an island-wide basis difficult, and requiring greater attention to the direction and implications of subregional trends.

Philippines/ Mindanao/ Demography/ Migration.

800.   ————. **1993.** *People, Places and Time: The Population Factor in Sustainable Agriculture*. Paper presented at the Seminar/ Workshop on Reporting Sustainable Agriculture, 30 March 1993, at SEARSOLIN, Cagayan de Oro City.

Philippines/ Demography/ Agricultural intensification.

801.   ————. **1993.** "Rural Population Growth and Environmental Problems: Focus on Region X." Paper presented at the Seminar on Population and the Environment: Sustainable Development from a Regional Perspective, 14 August 1993, in Cagayan de Oro City. Photocopy.

Costello reviews current theories of the interrelationship between demographic pressure and environment degradation, contrasting the Malthusian and Cornucopian views of population growth. Demographic statistics on Mindanao are examined to assess the applicability of each theory. These indicators suggest that while population growth has been high in the past, Northern Mindanao is experiencing a net outflow of persons through migration. Urbanization has accelerated, due at least in part to the reclassification of formerly rural barangays to officially urban ones. Due to the offsetting factor of high fertility, however, the island's rural population has continued to grow, though at a slower pace than seen in previous decades. Agricultural statistics show an increase in the number of farmers in Northern Mindanao coupled with a steady decline in the average farm size over the past decade.

Other indicators suggest that demographic growth has been accompanied by accelerated forest cover loss and a marked decline in soil productivity (measured by annual crop yields).

While the region-wide statistics for Northern Mindanao suggest some cause for concern, the author also notes the need to recognize variability within the region. In particular, it is hypothesized that given the strong attraction exerted by the region's urban centers on current migrants, upland areas which have already been settled over a prolonged period of time may be experiencing significant net out-migration. Upland in-migration is thus now limited largely to the region's remaining more sparsely settled mountainous areas. Concluding remarks reflect on the need to qualify concerns about an inevitable population crisis and to replace alarmist theories with greater efforts towards a well-developed family planning and family health program.

Philippines/ Mindanao/ Population pressure/ Agricultural intensification/ Migration/ Deforestation/ Soil erosion and degradation.

802.   **Costello, M. A., and P. L. Ferrer. 1992.** "Net Migration in the Philippines: 1980–1990." Project Report to the ILO-Japan-DOLE Multilateral Project on Strategic Approaches Toward Employment Promotion, no. 1. Cagayan de Oro, Philippines: Research Institute for Mindanao Culture, Xavier University.

Philippines/ Demography/ Migration.

803.   **Costello, M. B. ,. E. 1992.** "Report to the MacArthur Planning Grant Workshop." Report prepared for the Working Meeting of the MacArthur Planning Grant on Strategies for Sustaining Agriculture, Natural Resources, and Communities in the Uplands of the Insular Economies of Southeast Asia, 2–11 January 1992, in Cebu City, Cebu. Photocopy.

A report outlining current issues in upland communities, upland development, demography, and forest land use in Mindanao. Includes an extensive, largely annotated bibliography.

Philippines/ Mindanao/ Agriculture—Shifting cultivation/ Agricultural development/ Rural development/ Land use—Patterns and planning/ Demography/ Forest management—Forest resource conservation.

804.   **Cramb, R. A., and G. C. Saguiguit Jr. 1994.** *Socioeconomic Evaluation of Soil Conservation Technologies for Upland Farming Systems in the Philippines: Project Overview*. SEARCA-UQ Uplands Research Project, Working Paper no. 1. Los Ba–os, Philippines: SEARCA-UQ Uplands Research Project.

Cramb and Saguiguit describe the objectives and methodology of a collaborative project on upland soil conservation technologies undertaken by the SEAMEO Regional Center for Graduate Study and Research in Agriculture (SEARCA) and the University of Queensland. The project focuses on the study of on eight upland sites throughout the Philippines where a major project-based attempt to introduce soil conservation technologies among farmers has been made. Rapid rural appraisal techniques are planned to obtain farmer feedback on technology adoption and adaptation. This feedback is intended to be of immediate value to researchers and development workers, while also serving as basis upon which to develop a more general socioeconomic model of technology adoption in upland environments. Description of the project's methodological framework is followed by a review of progress made in the development and dissemination of soil conservation technology in the Philippines. The paper ends with more detailed project outline, including specific objectives, hypotheses, and planned methodological strategies.

Philippines/ Project intervention—Soil conservation.

805. **Cruz, Ma. C. 1984.** "Population Pressure, Migration and Markets: Implications for Upland Development." Working Paper, no. 84-05. Makati, Metro Manila: Philippine Institute for Development Studies.

> Cruz presents demographic data on the Philippines to argue the importance of markets and gradual change in shaping the link between population and agricultural intensification. Lending support to Boserup's hypothesis, there has been an apparent trend towards shorter fallow periods in the uplands, as population has steadily increased due largely to in-migration. The data also indicates that recent and relatively short-distant (within region) migration is becoming the predominant upland pattern. Currently one third of all upland residents are migrants (with the greatest proportion residing in Mindanao, regions 10, 11, and 12). In the case of the Philippines, the government has played a major role in migration to the uplands through its settlement programs and land titling system. Also important has been the role of external commercial markets, as transitions to a market economy occur first in those areas which are located closer to trading centers and cities. In general, then, both government decisions and market forces will affect population distribution in the uplands. These factors should be taken into account in designing social forestry programs.

> Philippines/ Population pressure/ Agricultural intensification/ Migration / Land settlement and development/ Agricultural economics.

806. **Cruz, Ma. C. J., I. Zosa-Feranil, and C. L. Goce. 1988.** "Population Pressure and Migration: Implications for Upland Development in the Philippines." *Journal of Philippine Development* 15 (1): 15–46.

> A procedure for identifying upland municipalities is first described, and population growth patterns for those communities are computed. Note the authors, increasingly critical levels of population pressure appear to be building up in the uplands, as population density levels have reached the carrying capacity limit of 200 persons/km2 in some provinces. Somewhat surprisingly, three of the eight highest density upland provinces are from Mindanao: Misamis Oriental, Misamis Occidental and Lanao del Sur. Migration streams from upland areas are heaviest from the Central and Western Visayas, while those areas receiving most newcomers are in Mindanao. Information on migration circumstances, socioeconomic characteristics of migrants, and descriptions of the migrant adjustment process are presented in a case study of three villages in Mount Makiling, Laguna province. Statistical analysis suggests that land availability is a more significant factor encouraging upland in-migration than factors like economic hardship in the originating area. Other significant variables are population density, age at time of movement, and education. The paper ends with policy recommendations and suggestions for future research.

> Philippines/ Population pressure/ Migration.

807. **Cruz, M. C. J. 1986.** "Population Pressure and Migration in Philippine Upland Communities." In *Man, Agriculture and the Tropical Forests: Change and Development in the Philippine Uplands*. Ed. S. Fujisaka, P. Sajise, and R. del Castillo. Bangkok: Winrock International Institute for Agricultural Development.

> Philippines/ Demography/ Population pressure/ Migration.

808. **Cruz, M. C. J., C. A. Meyer, R. Repetto, and R. Woodward. 1992.** *Population Growth, Poverty, and Environmental Stress: Frontier Migration in the Philippines and Costa Rica.* Washington, D.C.: World Resources Institute.

> The authors present two detailed case studies examining the links between degradation of fragile upland (i.e., "frontier") environments, population pressure, and economic as well as land tenure policies in the Philippines and Costa Rica respectively. With a population

density of more than 200 people per sq. km. and a population growth rate of 2.5% p.a. between 1950 and 1985, the Philippines is in critical need of arable land to sustain adequate food production. Widespread poverty is particularly critical in the Philippines where as much as 57% of the population lives below the poverty line. Facing rapidly shrinking prospects in lowland areas, growing numbers of impoverished farmers as well as urban dwellers have little recourse but to seek better fortune elsewhere, mostly in upland areas. In the early 1980s, the Philippine debt crisis and accompanying structural adjustment program seriously aggravated the incidence of poverty in both rural and urban areas and intensified the flow of migrants into the country's beleaguered uplands; net migration into upland areas increased from 9.4% of the upland population between 1975 and 1980 to 14.5% in the early 1980s, for the first time exceeding migration flows from rural to urban areas. As of 1985, an estimated 32% of the country's people lived in areas officially categorized as upland, and it is projected that at current rates, the number of people in upland areas will increase by at least one million each year over the next ten years. The area of cultivated forest lands increased from 582,000 ha in 1960 to over 3.9 million ha in 1987. While total cultivated area expanded by 2.7 million ha between 1980 and 1987, 60% of this increase derived from expansion of agriculture into formerly forested areas with a slope of between 18 and 30%.

Another major factor contributing to the flow of impoverished migrants seeking agricultural livelihood in highly fragile environments has been the highly inequitable distribution of land ownership and land use rights in the country's lowlands, creating a growing class of landless farmers. In addition, while land with a slope over 18% is officially classified as public domain under the authority of the federal government, lack of both forestry field staff and any clear system for property titling in upland areas has in effect invited growing numbers of otherwise landless farmers to cultivate new land as squatters, while providing little incentive for investment in long-term soil conservation strategies. Countless migrants have been attracted to still forested frontier environments by infrastructural development accompanying government resettlement programs especially in Mindanao during the 1950s through 1970s. Logging roads and timber clearing by timber concessionaires have facilitated the uncontrolled settlement of forest lands in other areas.

Migration in search of arable land has had a distinctly regional pattern in the Philippines as well, with most movement during the 1960 through 1970 period occurring a) intra-Luzon; b) intra-Mindanao (mostly into areas near logging concessions) and c) Visayas to Luzon and Mindanao. The spin-off amenities offered by organized government resettlement attracted large numbers of spontaneous migrants to Mindanao in particular, where more than 950,000 ha of forest lands were converted to cropping between 1960 and 1970. While urbanward migration dominated the 1970s, as noted above, the early 1980s saw a sharp increase in the migration flow to upland areas. In contrast to migration of the 1960s, however, recent flows of migrants have targeted areas already quite densely populated, have involved growing numbers of urban as well as rural migrants, and have contributed to the rapid growth of upland urban population. Finally, where earlier migrants had primarily been farmers with some capital for initial investment into new homesteads, a far greater proportion of the present migration flow into the Philippine uplands have been much poorer, financing access to arable land in already settled upland areas by exchanging labor for usufruct rights.

In view of the findings of the case studies provided, the authors note that successfully mitigating the stress on an already highly strained upland resource base will require that the "interconnectedness" of "rapid population growth, environmental degradation, poverty, and tenurial policies" be recognized. Effective policies and measures must be developed on all fronts simultaneously. In the Philippines, particular attention should be given to establishing clear property rights in land, especially for indigenous upland cultivators, pursuing effective as well as equitable economic growth to provide alternative employment for growing numbers of people, and making important improvements in the accessibility of health and family planning services.

Philippines/ Population pressure/ Migration/ State policy—Forest and natural resources/ State policy—Economic development/ Migrant farmers and farming/ Land settlement and development/ Land tenure—Legislation and state policy.

809. **Cruz, W., ed. 1984.** Economic Policies for Forest Resources Management: Summary of the Papers and Proceedings of the Seminar-Workshop on Economic Policies for Forest Resources Management. Calamba, Laguna: Philippine Institute for Development Studies.

> This brief summary is divided into three parts. The first section presents a research framework for forest resources management providing an economist's perspective on the changing role of the forest sector in the national economy. Part II presents brief summaries of the workshop papers and of the comments made by the discussants. The eight papers include: "Forest Land Management in the Context of National Land Use," by A. V. Revilla; 2) "Policy Issues on Commercial Forest Management, " by C. A. Cruz M. Segura de los Angeles; 3)"Trade and Fiscal Policies for Forest-based Commercial Sector," by C. David; 4) "Economic Policies and Pressures on Forest Resources," by G. C. Nelson; 5) "Population Pressure, Migration and Markets: Implications for Upland Development," by M. C. Cruz; 6) Tenure, Technology, and Productivity in the Uplands," by S. Fujisaka and A. D. Capistrano; 7) "Assessment of Environmental Effects of Watershed Management," by W. P. David; and 8) "Management of Costs of Watershed Reforestation," by J. Galvez. The final portion of the report presents a research agenda derived from the workshop presentations and discussions.

> Philippines/ Forest management—Economics/ Timber industry—State policy and regulation/ State policy—Forest and natural resources/ Land use—Patterns and planning/ Population pressure/ Land tenure—Legislation and state policy/ Reforestation/ Watershed management.

810. **Cruz, W., H. A. Francisco, and Z. T. Conway. 1988.** "The On-Site and Downstream Costs of Soil Erosion in the Magat and Pantabangan Watersheds." *Journal of Philippine Development* 5 (1): 85–111.

> The authors propose and apply a methodology for assessing the impact of soil erosion on the Magat and Pantabangan watersheds. A substantial decrease in forest cover is documented for both, resulting in an annual loss of soil nutrients costing more than P3,000 per hectare. Downstream costs of soil erosion are also discussed. More specifically, the authors assess the losses that will be incurred due to declining capacity for irrigation and power generation resulting from accelerated sedimentation of the Pantabangan and Magat reservoirs.

> Philippines/ Soil erosion and degradation/ Watershed management/ Forest management—Economics.

811. **Cruz, W., and M. Segura delos Angeles. 1988.** "Forest and Upland Resources Management: A Policy Framework." *Journal of Philippine Development* 15 (1): 1–14.

> Philippines/ Forest management—Economics/ Watershed management/ State policy—Forest and natural resources.

812. Dalmacio, M. V., and Rolando L. Metin. 1986. "The Community-Based Forest Research and Development Project." *Canopy International* 12 (6): 1–4, 10–11.

> The background and rationale of the Community-Based Forest Research and Development Project are discussed. A basic goal of the project is to ensure that forest research is made more relevant to upland inhabitants, (for example, by engaging uplanders in data collection, by translating the results of academic research into layperson's language). In addition, project methodology stresses a "participatory approach" to development planning. The project has four major features: 1) Forestry research may be used as an entry point to

the community; 2) The project emphasizes community capability building; 3) Economic livelihood is stressed; 4) A mutual partnership between the people and their government is envisioned. Some examples of Philippine upland communities where the project has been introduced are given along with sixteen "lessons learned." In sum, where forest researchers have had little to do with upland communities in the past, this project attempts to bridge this gap, bringing researchers into upland communities to forge a closer working relationship for the future.

Philippines/ Project intervention—Social and community forestry/ Project intervention—Participatory methods.

813.   **Dames and Moore, Intl., Louis Berger, Intl., and Institute of Development Anthropology. 1989.** "Sustainable Natural Resources Assessment—Philippines." Report prepared for the U.S. Agency for International Development. Manila: U.S. Agency for International Development.

Philippines/ Forest management—Forest resource conservation/ Forest management—Commercial forestry and silviculture/ Deforestation/ State policy—Forest and natural resources.

814.   **Dano, A. M. 1990.** "Effect of Burning and Reforestation on Grassland Watersheds in the Philippines." In *Research Needs and Applications to Reduce Erosion and Sedimentation in Tropical Steeplands.* Ed. R. R. Ziemer, C. L. O. O'Loughlin, and L. S. Hamilton, pp. 53–61. IAHS Publication, no. 192. Wallingford, Oxfordshire, U.K.: International Association of Hydrological Sciences.

Philippines/ Watershed management/ Reforestation/ Hydrology/ Soil erosion and degradation/ Grasslands.

815.   **David, W. P. 1988.** "Soil and Water Conservation Planning: Policy Issues and Recommendations." *Journal of Philippine Development* 15 (1): 47–84.

The problem of soil erosion in the Philippines is reviewed along with various approaches to conservation planning. Studies show that erosion rates from hilly areas increase markedly when the natural forest cover is disturbed. However, natural grass cover also offers good soil protection; therefore, tree plantations which make extensive use of weeding may cause more harm than good. Steepness of slope, soil properties and rainfall patterns also affect erodibility. Estimates of the impact of soil conservation practices upon erodibility are presented and incorporated with the other factors into a more general model. The sedimentation problem is then reviewed briefly, followed by a discussion of land use and conservation planning issues. Some of the problematic issues now affecting policy are 1) the presence of unrealistic policies and regulation, 2) rural poverty, 3) ineffective land use planning and allocation, 4) lack of popular support and 5) various implementation problems. A new system for classifying lands in the country is proposed, along with a new land use planning and allocation scheme.

Philippines/ Soil erosion and degradation/ Land use—Patterns and planning.

816.   **de los Angeles, M. S., and E. Rodriguez. 1992.** "Measuring Benefits from Natural Resource Conservation: The Case of the Central Visayas Regional Projects—I." Working Paper Series, No. 92-03. Manila: Philippine Institute for Development Studies.

In a brief report, the authors present the results of a monitoring study on Phase I of the Central Visayas Regional Projects. Conducted in 1989, the study aimed to measure benefits from the project for individual participants, measure the adoption of practices recognized to have a positive impact on the resource base, and provide a basis for further impact evaluation. The methodology used, hypotheses posed, and empirical results derived from the study are described. The authors found that the CVRP-I appeared generally successful in motivating resource management among project participants, with significant spread effects to non-formal participants also noted. Cooperators were found to implement conservation strategies more often than non-cooperators. However, problems in achieving successful results for nearshore fishery sites were encountered. Statistical differences in income were noted between cooperators and non-cooperators for the upland agriculture site, but not for the social forestry sites. More time is needed to assess the long-term effects of the project on quality of life.

Philippines/ Cebu/ Project intervention—Soil conservation/ Project intervention—Social and community forestry.

817. **dela Torres, Ma. I. G. 1993.** *Tales from the Darker Side of IFPs: A Briefing Paper on the Integrated Forestry Management Agreement.* LRC-KSK Issue Paper, no. 93-10. Quezon City: Legal Rights and Natural Resources Center-Kasama sa Kalikasan (LRC-KSK/ Friends of the Earth-Philippines.

Dela Torre provides a brief overview of recent developments in Philippines forest management and commercial forestry policy, examining in particular the history of the Industrial Forest Plantation effort, one of several tree farming programs undertaken by the government to manage the country's residual forest areas. About 22,500 ha of tree plantations are to be established per year from 1987 to 2000 under the IFP program, involving 25-year Industrial Forest Management Agreements between the Department of Environment and Natural Resources and any "qualified person or corporation, partnership, association, or community organization." Problems in implementing the program are discussed, and the markedly commercial rather than forest protective bias of the program is noted.

Philippines/ State policy—Forest and natural resources/ Forest management—Commercial forestry and silviculture/ Forest management—Forest resource conservation/ Timber plantations/ Reforestation.

818. **Derecho, E. O., and M. J. Caberos. 1981.** "A Study on the Attitude of Selected Kaingeros in Bataan and Zambles Towards the BFD's Forest Occupancy (Kaingin) Management Program." Photocopy. Quezon City, Philippines: Watershed Management Division, Bureau of Forest Development, Government of the Philippines.

In this paper, the authors report results of a study covering a sample of fifty kaingeros from two study sites (Bataan and Zambales). Study findings suggest the following characteristics as typical of local household heads: 41–50 years of age, male 3 or 4 dependents, elementary education, farmers (with an additional occupation), married, Tagalog, with a 3–4 hectare farm, in residence for 31 or more years, and with an income of less than P2,000 per year.
Attitudes toward Forest Occupancy Management Program appeared almost universally favorable among respondents. Most seem to see the program as working to help them obtain title to their land. The specific subcomponents of the program (except for communal tree farming and relocation in a government resettlement area) were also given strong support by the respondents. Highest priority for government assistance was given to road construction, follow-up for improved tenure status, and loans for livestock production.

Philippines/ Forest management—Control of shifting cultivation/ Project intervention—Social and community forestry/ Resettlement/ Project intervention—Forest management.

819. **Diokno, G. 1981.** "Home is the Kaingero on the Hill." *Habitat* 1 (3): 116–118.

Diokno sketches a sympathetic portrait of the kaingero—a man who "only asks for opportunity not merely to exist but to live." A visit to a Community Tree Farm project site shows that kaingeros are suspicious of strangers—a sentiment that is unfortunately all too often confirmed by personal experience. The author notes the importance of certain age-old rituals and beliefs to the villagers concerning their forest environment. Regarding the forest as an important source of livelihood, local villagers appear basically sympathetic to forest preservation efforts.

Philippines/ Migrant farmers and farming/ Project intervention—Social and community forestry/ Forest management—Control of shifting cultivation.

820.   **Dizon, E. L. 1986.** "The Reforestation Project in Nabuklod Reservation." *Philippine Studies* 34 (4): 409–435.

Factors influencing the effectiveness of the Family Approach Reforestation Project, as was carried out in the Baluga Reservation (Floridablanca, Pamapanga), are examined. Interviews were conducted with two key informants, twenty-three project participants and fifteen non-participants. On-site observations were also made along with an analysis of project documents and interviews with Bureau of Forestry Development (BFD) personnel.

Overall, the evaluation exercise showed the project had made few gains. Most of the participants dropped out of the project before a year had finished. Numerous factors appeared to contribute to this poor performance. To begin with, the seminomadic subsistence pattern adopted by the Baluga was not conducive to ongoing project participation. In addition, the program did not respond closely to the felt needs of the people. Wages were low and payments came late. The Balugas (a poorly educated tribal group) generally did not understand well how to handle money. Overall, it was more of a temporary "relief" project than one which helped them to gain the capacity of solving their own problems. Indeed, pre-existing mechanisms for doing this (e.g., subsistence shifting cultivation) were somewhat weakened by the introduction of a market/cash economy.

Lines of communication between the BFD personnel and the Baluga were generally not strong. The project was not conceptualized in consultation with the people. Miscommunication and mistrust was common. There were also problems within the BFD. Responsibilities concerning project implementation were not clear. Leadership (if defined as the ability to redesign specific program components in order better to meet local needs) was weak. "Thus, while the Project generated some temporary benefits . . . it also quite ironically, led the people to greater dependency and exploitation."

Philippines/ Project intervention—Forest management/ Reforestation.

821.   **Drijver, C., and P. Sajise. 1991.** "Community-Based Resource Management and Environmental Action Research." Paper presented at First Cagayan Valley Programme on Environment and Development, 26–29 August 1991, Cabagan, Isabela, Philippines. Photocopy.

This paper examines the role of environmental science in the design of policies and action. Seven cases of environmental action projects (four from the Philippines, three from Africa) are reviewed. Argue the authors, the most fundamental lesson learned from these case studies concerns "the pivotal role of local communities in environmental action." In general, government agencies and NGOs do not have the capacity to protect or sustainably manage resources, especially those located in remote areas. Hence the role of local communities remains critical. The authors then explain five basic principles of Community Based Forest Resource Management, noting also the role of environmental action research (EAR) in promoting these principles. Although EAR boasts no pre-defined methodological blueprint, it is possible to identify some common steps typically followed with this approach.

Philippines/ Project intervention—Forest management/ Project intervention—Social and community forestry.

822. **Duldulao, A. C. 1978.** "Kaingin, Erosion, and Kaingin Management." *Forestry Digest* 5 (2): 52–63.

Philippines/ Migrant farmers and farming/ Agriculture—Shifting cultivation's environmental impacts/ Forest management—Control of shifting cultivation.

823. ———. **1978.** "Resettlement Within the Concept of Human Settlement and Kaingin Management." Paper presented at the Third Kaingin Management Seminar-Workshop, December 1978, Cebu City. Photocopy.

Arguing that kaingin-making is "the worst enemy of forest conservation" the author suggests four possible strategies for its eradication. The first approach is "the punitive measure." This is not effective because kaingineros would rather go to jail than watch their children go hungry. A second strategy is the family tree planting subsidy. This, however, is a "mere palliative."

In more recent years, considerable attention has been given to programs designed to resettle kaingineros. Program success along these lines, however, would require a very complex and expensive agenda of activities which may well be beyond Bureau of Forestry Development (BFD) capacity. A fourth and final option is that of kaingin management (or "forest occupancy management"), that takes an integrated socio-economic approach. Research findings suggest that the latter option holds the most promise for success, although, again, the requirements for program success are many. The author discusses specific problems and constraints. The need for increased manpower at the BFD is noted in particular. Despite these caveats, the authors conclude that the "potentials of kaingin management" are considerable.

Philippines/ Forest management—Control of shifting cultivation/ Resettlement/ Project intervention—Social and community forestry.

824. ———. **1981.** *An Integrated Project for Kaingin Control in the Philippines: A New Approach to Forest Conservation.* Manila, Philippines: Bureau of Forestry Development.

The integrated project for kaingin control lasted for five years (1977–1981). Some 484 project cooperators were interviewed for this report and some of the major findings presented. These deal with migration, land tenure, respondent/household profile, employment and income, agricultural and agro-forestry practices, major problems faced by the farmer-respondents, participation in cooperatives, attitudes toward and participation in the project and environmental values/attitudes. Suggestions are given by participants as to what could be done to improve the project and facilitate reforestation.

Philippines/ Forest management—Control of shifting cultivation/ Reforestation.

825. ———. **1981.** "The Kaininero as Focus of Development." *Philippine Sociological Review* 29 (1–4): 153–158.

Different types of kaingineros are described and strategies to engage shifting cultivators in national development efforts discussed. Agroforestry is proposed as the most suitable means for simultaneously improving farmer welfare as well as promoting active partnership in natural resources protection and development.

Philippines/ Migrant farmers and farming/ Forest management—Control of shifting cultivation/ Agroforestry.

826. **Eder, J. F. 1987.** *On the Road to Tribal Extinction: Depopulation, Deculturation, and Adaptive Well-being among the Batak of the Philippines.* Berkeley: University of California Press.

Eder examines the process by which a once-thriving hunter-gatherer Batak community on Palawan is being threatened by the impact of modernization and contact with the outside world. The study draws from fieldwork spanning fifteen years during which Eder visited or at various times lived among the Batak. It also includes results of two censa taken eight years apart, recording time allocation patterns, health indicators, cultural beliefs and institutions, and settlement patterns of local communities. Particular attention is paid to the role of human motivation behind current behavior and the sense of ethnic identity fostering it.

Eder's analysis focuses on the finding that the Batak of Palawan are not reproducing at a rate sufficient to ensure the long-term replacement of their populace. The immediate cause of this development is identified as dysfunctional social and economic behavior. The ultimate cause shaping this immediate factor, however, is the process of articulation with the outside world. It is argued that the latter is resulting in a level of social stress high enough to destabilize indigenous institutions and beliefs, leading to attitudes and behavior which do not serve the interest of the Batak's long term survival.

The monograph begins with an overview of the Batak community prior to intensive contact with foreign settlers. This is followed by a description of current social and economic life, an investigation into demographic and physiological indicators of Batak community decline, and a discussion of various indicators of the declining viability of local social institutions. Eder argues a causal link between erosion of ethnic identity and "desultory nature of Batak material life." That is, while the Batak do appear to have means at their disposal to ensure a more successful outcome of current socio-economic change, they do not avail of them. An important factor in this self-destructive inertia has been a problematic change in the Batak identity of themselves as a distinct ethnic group. This identity is increasingly being redefined "in terms of those practices and values related to collection and sale of forest resources and wage labor on lowland farms" and is thus serving to entrench a highly dependent position on the local socio-economy.

Philippines/ Palawan/ Indigenous and local communities—Commoditization/ Indigenous and local communities—Forest products use and trade/ Indigenous and local communities—Social relations/ Health and nutrition/ Poverty/ Ethnicity and ethnic relations.

827.   ———. 1991. "Agricultural Intensification and Labor Productivity in a Philippine Vegetable Gardening Community: A Longitudinal Study." *Human Organization* 50 (3): 245–255.

Philippines/ Agricultural intensification/ Agriculture—Smallholder cash crop farming/ Farm management—Economics.

828.   **Edgerton, R. K.** "Frontier Society on the Bukidnon Plateau." In *Philippine Social History: Global Trade and Local Transformations.* A. W. McCoy and E. C. de Jesus, pp. 361–389. Quezon City, Philippines: Ateneo de Manila University Press.

Philippines/ Mindanao/ History—Colonial/ Land settlement and development.

829.   **Edralin, D. M., and A. D. Lupdag. 1988.** "Promoting Upland Development: The Cebu Soil and Water Conservation Projects Five Years After." Final Report submitted to World Neighbors. Manila: Research Center, De La Salle University. Photocopy.

Philippines/ Cebu/ Project intervention—Soil conservation/ Watershed management.

830.   **Ellevera-Lamberte, E. 1983.** "Macro-level Indicators of Upland Poverty: The Case of the Delivery and Access to Services in Upland Areas." *Philippine Sociological Review* 31 (1–2): 19–52.

Drawing from government data, the authors identify predominantly upland provinces and in the Philippines and evaluate the level and quality of service delivery to these areas. Major disadvantages faced by upland provinces in access to services are highlighted, and a need for a change in government bias against upland areas is noted.

Philippines/ Poverty/ Rural development.

831.   ———. **1984.** "Indicators of Upland Poverty." In *Upland and Uplanders: Proceedings of the First National Conference on Research in the Uplands*. Ed. C. P. Castro. Quezon City, Philippines: BFD-Upland Development Program.

One important contribution of this paper is its attempt to present a coherent classification system for upland and lowland environments on a province by province basis in the Philippines. The authors identify at least five criteria upon which a distinction between upland and lowland may be made: 1) average slope of the province as indicated by existing soil maps; 2) proportion of total provincial land under forest cover; 3) proportion of total households in province who are kaingin households; 4) proportion of total province currently being irrigated; 5) level of productivity.

Philippines/ Poverty/ Agriculture—Shifting cultivation/ Rural development.

832.   **Factoran, F. S., Jr. 1990.** "Population Resources and the Future of the Philippines." *Populi* 17 (4): 20–29.

The history of Philippine forestry is presented as a case study of the complex interaction between economics, demographics, and ecology. Included in the analysis is a description of the Integrated Social Forestry program of the Bureau of Forest Development. Highlighting past and projected rates of deforestation, Factoran identifies population growth, in-migration to the uplands and an undervitalized population program as among the most immediate factors in the country's forestry-related problems. Over the long term, there is also the need to consider political economic issues underlying the highly uneven distribution of access to natural resources. At the planning level, appropriate measures would be facilitated if the loss of natural resources are factored into the national accounts.

Philippines/ Deforestation/ State policy—Forest and natural resources/ Population pressure/ Political economy.

833.   **Flieger, W. SVD, and J. Avila. 1991.** "What is Happening in CUP Country?: A First Assessment of Socioeconomic Changes Among Upland Farmers to the Cebu Upland Project between 1987 and 1990." Photocopy. Cebu City, Cebu, Philippines: GTZ.

Philippines/ Cebu/ Project intervention—Rural development/ Poverty.

834.   **Forest Management Bureau. 1988.** "Natural Forestry Resources of the Philippines." Photocopy. Manila, Philippines: Philippine-German Forest Resource Inventory Project.

Philippines/ Forest management—Economics.

835.   **Foronda, S. U., M. T. Rondolo, and M. U. Siladan. 1991.** "Status of Dipterocarp Research in the Philippines." In *Proceedings of the Fourth Round-Table Conference on Dipterocarps, 12-15 December 1989, Bogor, Indonesia*. Ed. I. Soerianegara, S. S. Tjitrosomo, R. C. Umaly, and Umboh Irene, pp. 49–64. Bogor, Indonesia: SEAMEO BIOTROP.

The authors briefly describe current as well as planned research programs in the production and utilization aspects of dipterocarp forests. A ten page bibliography is provided.

Philippines/ Forest management—Commercial forestry and silviculture.

836.   **Frake, C. 1955.** "Social Organization and Shifting Cultivation among the Sindangan Subanon." Ph.D. diss., Yale University, New Haven, Conn.

Frake examines the relationship between shifting cultivation and problems of population density, settlement patterns, organization of labor, and land tenure. Of primary concern among the Sindangan Subanon is the need to maintain spatial mobility of a family swiddening unit in order to engage swidden-based farming technology most productively. As a result, swidden farming as a food production systems does little to stimulate the growth of complex socio-political structures that are otherwise often associated with agrarian communities.

Philippines/ Agriculture—Shifting cultivation/ Indigenous and local communities—Farming practices/ Indigenous and local communities—Social relations/ Ethnography.

837.   ———. **1962.** "Cultural Ecology and Ethnography." *American Anthropologist* 64 (1): 53–59.

Examining the cultural ecology of Subanon settlements, the author examines the spatial pattern in which Subanon swidden fields and houses are located. The Subanon tend to open swidden fields as close as possible to existing fields in order to maximize their ability to protect crops against wild animals. At the same time, the Subanon avoid locating family houses close to other neighbors. The author notes that these locational arrangements tend to create more or less unbroken expanses of swidden fields in the tropical forest, making natural reforestation more difficult and promoting the spread of grasslands.

Philippines/ Indigenous and local communities—Forest land use and management practices/ Agriculture—Shifting cultivation's environmental impacts/ Cultural ecology.

838.   **Frossard, D. 1994.** "A Peasant Ecological Critique of 'Green Revolution' in the Philippines." Unpublished draft paper. University of California, Irvine. Photocopy.

Frossard describes findings from a recent dissertation case study of MASIPAG, a Philippine farmers' association promoting organic farming among the country's peasant farmers. Key concerns about fertilizer and pesticide use associated with green revolution technology among farmers in Nueva Ecija of Central Luzon are discussed. Notes the author, advocacy for sustainable agriculture and "peasant science" under the MASIPAG framework appear to be less a manifestation of "traditional" peasant values than an insightful example of Philippine farmers' use of environmentalist rhetoric to promote their political and ecological aims.

Philippines/ Social movements/ Conservation farming.

839.   **Fujisaka, S. 1986.** "Philippine Social Forestry: The Participatory Approach Conceptual Model." In *Participatory Approaches to Development: Experiences in the Philippines.* Ed. T. S. Osteria, and J. Okamura, pp. 77–101. Manila: Research Center, De la Salle University.

The social forestry model which seems to be currently in use in the Philippines is described. "Social forestry is . . . forestry encompassing people, community development, the curbing of forest degradation, serious and complex realities, and certain activities and culture-bearing, symbol-sharing groups." There has been a major (and correct) emphasis upon participatory approaches. As corollaries, community organization, "felt needs" and participation in decision-making have been stressed. Recent case studies also show a number of important (and perhaps incorrect) implicit assumptions underlying current social forestry efforts. These include assuming a strictly local approach to problem solving, as well as the belief that upland communities are presently unorganized and their inhabitants "traditional."

An expanded conceptual model should include both the explicit and implicit assumptions of social forestry, since "implicit assumptions may be the source of some project difficulties and provide the basis for suggestions for project planners and implementors." Criteria for project success need to be established. Similarly, factors which contribute to project failure and/or success must be recognized and comparatively examined. Specific suggestions along are given are presented along these lines. Findings from the author's own research (in an ISF project set in Calminor, Laguna) are used to examine more closely the proposed conceptual model.

Philippines/ Social forestry/ Project intervention—Social and community forestry/ Project intervention—Participatory methods.

840.   ———. **1986.** "Pioneer Shifting Cultivators, Upland Ecosystem, and 'Social Forestry' Policy in the Philippines." *Philippine Sociological Review* 34 (1): 26–36.

Fujisaka describes research focused on the adaptations of pioneer shifting cultivators to local agroecosystem change in four upland communities. The research findings highlights important lessons for social forestry policy in the Philippines. These lessons draw attention to the importance of policy flexibility, demographic change, technology development and adaptation to local conditions for increasing social forestry program success.

Philippines/ Agriculture—Shifting cultivation/ Agricultural intensification/ Population pressure/ Migrant farmers and farming/ Social forestry/ Indigenous and local communities—Forest land use and management practices.

841.   ———. **1986.** "Pioneer Shifting Cultivation, Farmer Knowledge, and an Upland Ecosystem: Co-evolution and Systems Sustainability in Calminoe, Philippines." *Philippine Quarterly of Culture and Society* 14: 137–164.

Philippines/ Agriculture—Shifting cultivation/ Agricultural intensification/ Migrant farmers and farming/ Indigenous and local communities—Forest land use and management practices.

842.   ———. **1989.** "A Method for Farmer-participatory Research and Technology Transfer: Upland Soil Conservation in the Philippines." *Experimental Agriculture* 25: 423–433.

Fujisaka describes the use of a participatory method focused on incorporating farmers' perceptions in determining research priorities. The method is intended to integrate the concerns and contributions of both farmers and scientists with farmer-to-farmer technology transfer. Emphasis on participatory methods is needed in view of the persistent lack of farmer participation in most on-farm adaptive research.

Philippines/ Project intervention—Soil conservation/ Project intervention—Participatory methods.

843.   ———. **1989.** "The Need to Build Upon Farmer Practice and Knowledge: Reminders from Selected Upland Conservation Projects and Policies." *Agroforestry Systems* 9: 141–153.

Four agroforestry projects are examined to assess why farmer adoption has not been more widespread. Included in the assessment are: the Upland Agriculture and Conservation Project, central-east Java, Indonesia; 2) Allah Valley Watershed Development Project, Lake Sebu, South Cotabato, Philippines; 3) World Neighbor's Project on Cebu, Philippines; 4) Forest Development and Watershed Management Project, Luang Prabang, northern Lao. All projects involved agroforestry and conservation farming components. Also evaluated are two policy approaches towards the problem of farm ecosystem degradation: 1) prohibiting the burning of pasture land, and 2) promotion of social forestry in the Philippines after earlier, largely unsuccessful attempts at preventing forest land settlement and (later) granting of land leases in return for improved management. The need to ensure a genuinely participatory approach and to avoid a bias towards pre-determined technologies is emphasized as a key lesson learned.

Philippines/ Mindanao/ Cebu/ Project intervention—Soil conservation/ Project intervention—Agroforestry/ Project intervention—Social and community forestry/ Project intervention—Participatory methods.

844. ————. **1994.** "Learning from Six Reasons Why Farmers Do Not Adopt Innovations Intended to Improve Sustainability of Upland Agriculture." *Agricultural Systems* 46 (4): 409–425.

Fujisaka examines seven upland project sites to identify the reasons for low rates of farmer adoption that often characterize upland agricultural development and conservation efforts. These include the IRRI/Philippine Department of Agriculture research site in Claveria, Misamis Oriental; a potential Integrated Social Forestry site at Calminoe, Philippines; the Upland Agriculture and Conservation Project on Java; the Forest Development and Watershed Management Project of the Lao government and FAO at Luang Prabang, Laos; the Philippine Bureau of Forest Development's (BFD) Allah Valley Watershed Development Project, Lake Sebu, South Cotabato, Philippines; the World Neighbor's Soil and Water Conservation Project in Cebu, Philippines; and the collaborative, IRRI-Government of Madagascar research project in the Madagascar Middle West and Central Highland. Six reasons farmers do not adopt the promoted technologies include: 1) the project targets a problem farmers themselves do not face; 2) the innovation promoted fails to work; 3) extension services are inadequate; 4) the innovation introduced is too expensive; social factors that impinge on attitudes towards and possibilities for adoption. Taking these considerations into account is likely to improve the extent and rate to which adaptation and adoption of erosion-controlling contour vegetative strips among Filipino farmers.

Philippines/ Mindanao/ Cebu/ Indonesia/ Project intervention—Soil conservation/ Project intervention—Social and community forestry.

845. **Fujisaka, S., P. E. Sajise, and R. A. del Castillo, eds. 1986.** *Man, Agriculture and the Tropical Forest: Change and Development in the Philippine Uplands.* Bangkok: Winrock International Institute for Agricultural Development.

This monograph contains an interdisciplinary collection of papers dealing with different aspects of upland development in the Philippines. Individual papers discuss change and development, population and migration, indigenous communities, economics of upland development, land use, agroforestry and social forestry strategies, land tenure and government natural resource policy. Contributing authors include Filomena Aguilar, Sam Fujisaka, Percy Sajise, Filomeno Torres, John Raintree, Ma. Concepcion J. Cruz, Owen Lynch. A final chapter by Fujisaka and Sajise attempts a synthesis of the different issues and perspectives presented, highlights interrelationships and discusses areas where more research appears most necessary.

Philippines/ Forest management/ Population pressure/ Migration/ Agricultural economics/ Agriculture—Shifting cultivation/ Agriculture—Shifting cultivation's environmental impacts/ Indigenous and local communities/ Migrant farmers and farming/ Land use—Patterns and planning/ Land tenure/ Social forestry/ Conservation farming/ Agroforestry/ State policy—Forest and natural resources.

846. **Fujisaka, S., and E. Wollenberg. 1991.** "From Forest to Agroforest and Logger to Agroforester: A Case Study." *Agroforestry Systems* 14: 113–129.

Fujisaka and Wollenberg examine the process by which migrant farmers in frontier forest environments adapt to an ecosystem being rapidly transformed by human action (logging, small-scale resource extraction, agricultural expansion). Though standing forests disappeared, a rapid rate of natural succession also occurred due to high rainfall and vigorous forest feed stock. Facing serious pest and soil problems, farmers shifted from annual cereal cropping to root and mixed perennials. Supported in part by income derived from small-scale logging and charcoal fabrication, this spontaneous transition to more sustainable farming arrangements took place despite unfavorable social conditions.

Philippines/ Agriculture—Shifting cultivation/ Migrant farmers and farming/ Indigenous and local communities—Farming practices/ Indigenous and local communities—Forest land use and management practices/ Agriculture—Smallholder tree and perennial crop farming/ Fuelwood/ Agroforestry.

847. **Ganapin, D. J., Jr. n.d.** "Livelihood and Appropriate Technology in the Uplands." Participatory Approaches to Development, Series II. Manila: Integrated Research Center, De la Salle University.

Even though uplanders are poor, poverty is not inherent in the uplands. The forest is a rich resource which has so far only benefited the elite. For livelihood strategies to be successful, they must work to bring about social justice. Swidden farming provides most kaingineros with a good living, and, thus, they are not eager to take other jobs, especially since most alternative employment is scarce and/or very poorly remunerated. Development approaches should therefore concentrate on on-site livelihood strategies. In addition, these must match the kainginero's perceived needs and constraints.

Ganapin describes specific constraints of upland cropping systems. Because the possibility of achieving and sustaining a high income is uncertain, even with technical assistance and agricultural inputs, the kainginero typically supplements swidden farming with income derived from off-farm work. In light of this, marketing co-ops and agroforestry have frequently been suggested as good development strategies. Nevertheless, these will not always be accepted by the uplanders because of certain constraints. Other income generating strategies (livestock raising, tree farming, "carabao" logging, fuelwood production, fishing, hired labor cottage industries, etc.) are discussed. The author concludes the paper by presenting ten suggestions for development planners concerned with improving conditions in the Philippine uplands.

Philippines/ Poverty/ Project intervention—Rural development/ Agriculture—Shifting cultivation/ Indigenous and local communities—Farming practices/ Farm management—Cropping systems.

848. ———. **1987.** "Forest Resources and Timber Trade." *Solidarity* 115 (November–December): 53–64.

The author draws from various data sources and research reports to estimate loss of forest cover in the Philippines between the early 1930s and early 1970s and to highlight the impact of this process on the country's biological diversity, soil resources as well as tribal community welfare. While shifting cultivation, agribusiness and logging are arguably the immediate causes of deforestation in the Philippines, these are themselves only symptoms of a socio-economic system conducive to forest destruction. To successfully arrest current trends, the author emphasizes the need for "historical analysis, a holistic approach, long-term solutions and continuous vigilance" in addition to "united action by citizens at the local and international levels."

Philippines/ Deforestation/ Political economy/ Timber industry—Environmental impacts/ Agriculture—Shifting cultivation's environmental impacts/ Agriculture—Plantations.

849. **Gapas, J. R. 1990.** "The Environmental Situation of Northern Mindanao." *Mindanet* 2 (4): 64.

Writing as the Regional Director for the Northern Mindanao Department of Energy and Natural Resources, Gapas gives a general overview of current environmental problems in Northern Mindanao: deforestation, soil erosion, small-scale mining, the growing number of potential sources of pollution such as industrial establishments and automobiles.

Philippines/ Mindanao/ Deforestation/ Soil erosion and degradation/ Mining.

850. **Garilao, E., and D. Noval-Morales. 1982.** "Non-government Organizations in the Uplands: Issues and Projects." Report prepared for Participatory Uplands Management Programs. Photocopy. Manila: De la Salle University.

The paper begins with a profile of the Philippine upland farmer. Income education levels and access to social services are all low, and upland households frequently suffer from a seasonal "hunger gap." The remoteness of upland farmers makes it difficult for NGOs to work with them. Nevertheless, Philippine Business for Social Progress (PBSP) has assisted thirty-four uplands projects and now has access to a network of upland NGOs. Most such projects deal with agriculture or education; few have an agroforestry component.

Having identified a number of specific issues as central to upland development planning (including problems of land tenure, productivity, ecology and community organization), PBSP continues to grapple with finding realistic means to grapple with these questions. PBSP's present strategy is to work mainly with credit cooperatives. In addition, the organization is also focusing on helping NGOs to do a better job with regard to technology transfer and community organizing.

Philippines/ Poverty/ Non-governmental organizations/ Project intervention—Rural development.

851. **Garrity, D. P., and P. C. Augustin. 1995.** "Historical Land Use Evolution in a Tropical Acid Upland Agroecosystem." *Agriculture, Ecosystems, and Environment* 53 (1): 83–95.

Garrity and Augustin report results of a study on land use changes among upland farmers in Claveria, Mindanao over a 40 year period. The site is characterized by slight to steeply sloping topography and volcanic Oxisols. Aerial photographs taken in 1949 and 1967 as well as a ground survey of 1988 provide macro-level data on changing land use patterns. Other secondary sources provide information on the regional development history. While the area of cultivated land increased from 9 to 20 percent between 1949 and 1967, sharply accelerated inmigration in more recent decades led to increasingly rapid forest land conversion. By 1988, 41 percent of the local area was under cultivation, and only 1 percent of forest lands remained. A mixture of field crop and perennial cash crop production has expanded on steeply sloping lands in the area. The study provides a broad overview of the pressures coming to bear over time on local upland and forest land areas, and may provide important background to assess research needs in conservation farming in sloping environments.

Philippines/ Mindanao/ Land settlement and development/ Indigenous and local communities—Forest land use and management practices/ Deforestation.

852. **Garrity, D. P., D. K. Kummer, and E. S. Guiang. 1993.** "The Philippines." In *Sustainable Agriculture and the Environment in the Humid Tropics*. Comp.

N. R. C. Committee on Sustainable Agriculture and the Environment in the Humid Tropics, pp. 549-624. Washington, D.C.: National Academy Press.

As contributors to a study on agricultural sustainability and the humid tropics commissioned by the National Research Council, the authors review major issues in uplands ecosystem management in the Philippines. Trends in land use, population growth, agriculture, upland migration, intensification of rice production, and upland farming systems are discussed in the paper's first section. A discussion of problems of deforestation in the Philippines follows, describing extent and causes. A third major section focuses on various approaches to achieving land use sustainability in the uplands, including, among others, various conservation farming techniques on sloping lands, new tenure arrangements, fallow improvement, reforestation, and sustainable forestry. The authors close with a discussion of future policy, research, and institutional imperatives needed to achieve genuine sustainability.

Philippines/ Deforestation/ Land use—Patterns and planning/ Population pressure/ Conservation farming/ Reforestation/ Forest management—Forest resource conservation/ Forest management—Commercial forestry and silviculture/ Timber industry—Logging/ Land tenure—Legislation and state policy.

853. **Garrity, D. P., and A. R. Mercado. 1994.** "Nitrogen Fixation Capacity in the Component Species of Contour Hedgerows: How Important?" *Agroforestry Systems* 27 (3): 241–258.

A four-year experimental study undertaken on the International Rice Research Institute's on-farm upland research site in Claveria, northern Mindanao from 1988 to 1991 aimed at determining the actual significance of nitrogen fixation for crop productivity. Annual crop yields were compared when intercropped with *Gliricidia sepium* (a nitrogen-fixing tree legume), *Senna spectabilis* (a nitrogen-fixing tree), and *Pennisetum purpureum* (a forage grass). Also measured were hedgerow biomass and nutrient yields from leaf and green stem prunings. Grass hedgerows were found to reduce maize yields by 86 percent by the second year. Hedgerow tree species showed no significant effect on grain yields (rice and maize), although less competitive effects were indicated with the nitrogen-fixing tree and annual crops grown in adjacent rows. Study results suggest the absence of any significant advantages in crop productivity associated with the use of nitrogen-fixing hedgerow systems, and the importance of factors other than nitrogen fixation for optimal species choice.

Philippines/ Mindanao/ Agriculture—Permanent/ Farm management—Cropping systems.

854. **Garrity, D., and A. Mercado. 1994.** "Reforestation through Agroforestry: Market Driven Small-Holder Timber Production on the Frontier." In *Marketing of Multipurpose Tree Products in Asia*. Proceedings of an International Workshop Held in Baguio City, Philippines, 6–9 December 1993. Ed. J. B. Raintree and H. A. Francisco, pp. 265–268. Bangkok: Winrock International.

In recent years, pioneer farmers in north-central Mindanao have begun to farm timber trees on infertile grassland soils in the uplands, making this a dominant enterprise within their farming systems and using their own capital resources to do it. Garrity and Mercado examine this trend through a two-pronged focus on the timber marketing system centered in Cagayan de Oro city and on the tree farming activities of a sample set of farmers in Claveria, Misamis Oriental (about 25 km from Cagayan de Oro city). A steady increase in prices for medium-sized logs is noted as a major factor encouraging local tree farming. The area planted to trees by interviewed farmers ranged from 0.5 to 3.0 ha, or 17 to 100 percent of the farm, with trees planted as intercrops to maize, rice, and cassava. Most timber harvesting is done on bulk contract basis, with the sawmill or timber trader responsible for actual felling. The data challenges conventional assumptions about farmer reluctance to plant trees, and "may suggest a powerful model for reforesting the uplands."

Philippines/ Mindanao/ Agroforestry/ Reforestation/ Agriculture—Smallholder tree and perennial crop farming/ Agriculture—Smallholder cash crop farming/ Indigenous and local communities—Forest land use and management practices.

855.   **Garvan, J. M. 1929.** *The Eastern Manóbo of Agusan.* Washington, D.C.: Bureau of Ethnology.

This monograph represents one of the most comprehensive ethnographic works ever done of any of Mindanao's indigenous groups. The Manóbo are the largest cultural group in Mindanao, divided today into 10 distinct subgroups found in the northern, eastern and southern regions of the island. Garvan describes cultural patterns among the Eastern Manóbo of Agusan province in detail, including subsistence farming practices, which at the time of writing included a combination of swidden cultivation, hunting, fishing, and gathering of wild forest products. Swidden fields are cultivated for an average of two years, after which they are left to fallow for at least seven. Included in the ethnography is a description of the complex religious beliefs that guide local decisions about specific agricultural practices, such as tree felling and swidden field location.

Philippines/ Mindanao/ Ethnography/ Indigenous and local communities—Farming practices/ Indigenous and local communities—Forest land use and management practices/ Indigenous and local communities—Forest products use and trade/ Indigenous and local communities—Land and resource tenure systems/Indigenous and local communities—Religion and cosmology/ Indigenous and local communities—Social relations/ Agriculture—Shifting cultivation.

856.   ————. **1931.** *The Manóbos of Mindanao.* Memoirs of the National Academy of Sciences, vol. 23, 1st memoir. Washington, D. C.: Government Printing Office.

Garvan presents a detailed ethnography of the Manóbos of Eastern Mindanao island. Part 1 describes the geographical distribution of the Manóbos and other major ethnic groups in Mindanao, describes Manóbo physical characteristics, surveys the group's material and social culture. A final chapter in Part 2 and all of Part 2 describes the Manóbo material culture in closer detail, including dress, diet, use of narcotics, subsistence means, weapons and craft activities. Part 3 covers Manóbo social life and practices, including domestic life and marriage, childbirth and rearing, management of illness, social affairs, and political organization. Part 4 concludes with a close examination of the Manóbo religion.

Philippines/ Ethnography/ Indigenous and local communities—Farming practices/Indigenous and local communities—Forest land use and management practices/ Indigenous and local communities—Forest products use and trade/ Indigenous and local communities—Land and resource tenure systems/ Indigenous and local communities—Religion and cosmology/ Indigenous and local communities—Social relations/ Agriculture—Shifting cultivation.

857.   **Goeghegan, W. 1977.** "Balangingi' Samal." In *Insular Southeast Asia: Ethnographic Studies. Section 3. Philippines.* Comp. F. M. LeBar, vol. 1, pp. 1–36. New Haven, Conn.: Human Relations Area Files.

Ethnographic account of the Balangingi' Samal, a coastal dwelling linguistic and tribal group, dispersed over the Sulu Archipelago, the Sabah coast, and Sulawesi.

Philippines/ Sulu/ Ethnography/ Indigenous and local communities.

858.   **Goldrick, G., and D. James. 1994.** "The Palawan Regional Development Plan." In *The Application of Economic Techniques in Environmental Impact*

Assessment. Ed. D. James, pp. 217–246. Dordrecht: Kluwer Academic Publishers.

Goldrick and James describe the natural resource status of Palawan island and current plans for development and environment protection on the island, as embodied in the environmental component of the Palawan Integrated Area Development Project, a landmark development approach developed by the Philippine government for Palawan island since 1979. A benefit-cost analysis was the main tool use to asses the environmental impacts of various development strategies proposed under the PIADP, and favored strategies were then synthesized into a Strategic Environmental Plan (SEP). Details are provided on the planning and assessment methodology and on the overall regional development plan. The paper concludes with an analysis of logging, tourism, and fisheries activities in one part of the island, Bacuit Bay, to demonstrate the application of economic valuation techniques at a local scale.

Philippines/ Palawan/ Forest management/ Economic development/ Forest management—Economics/ State policy—Forest and natural resources.

859. **Government of the Philippines. Ministry of Natural Resources. Natural Resources Management Center. 1986.** *Guide to Philippine Flora and Fauna.* Quezon City: Natural Resources Management Center, Ministry of Natural Resources and the University of the Philippines.

13 volumes describe the fungi, seaweeds, mosses, ferns, trees, grasses, corals, insects, zooplankton, barnacles, crabs, fish, amphibians and reptiles, birds, mammals, ectoparasites, as well as poisonous animals of the Philippines. Economic aspects of Philippine flora and fauna are discussed. Bibliographies and indexes are included.

Philippines/ Forest biology and ecology/ Forest flora/ Forest fauna/ Non-timber forest products.

860. **Government of the Philippines. Department of Environment and Natural Resources. Natural Resources Accounting Project. 1991.** "The Philippine Natural Resources Accounting Project (NRAP-Phase I): Executive Summary." Manila: Department of Environment and Natural Resources; International Resources Group, Ltd.

Philippines/ Forest management—Economics/ State policy—Forest and natural resources.

861. **Government of the Philippines. 1991.** "Report on Philippine Environment and Development: Issues and Strategies." UNCED National Reports, Manila: Government of the Philippines, Bureau for Environment Management, Department of Environment and Natural Resources.

Report prepared for the U.N. Conference on Environment and Development, June 1992, in Rio de Janeiro, Brazil.

Philippines/ Deforestation/ Forest management—Forest resource conservation/ State policy—Forest and natural resources.

862. **Government of the Philippines. Department of Environment and Natural Resources, World-Wide Fund for Nature, University of the Philippines Science Foundation, and Foundation for Sustainable Development. 1992.** "Management Plan for Mount Kitanglad Nature Park." Report prepared for the Integrated Protected Area System (IPAS) Project. Photocopy.

Philippines/ Mindanao/ Forest management—Parks and conservation areas/ State policy—Forest and natural resources.

863.   **Granert, W. G. 1983.** "World Neighbors-Assisted Soil and Water Conservation Project, Cebu, Philippines." Paper presented at the De La Salle University Seminar Series III on Participatory Approaches to Development, 18 August 1983, Manila, Philippines. Photocopy.

A comparison of two projects in Argao and in Guba, Cebu City respectively.

Philippines/ Cebu/ Project intervention—Soil conservation/ Watershed management/ Project intervention—Participatory methods.

864.   **Guiang, E. S. 1992.** "Community Forestry Program (CFP): Concept, Vision, Objectives, Strategies, and Future Plans." Paper presented at the International Workshop on Networking for LEISA, 10–15 March 1992, in Cavite, Silang, Philippines. Photocopy.

The Community Forestry Program was launched in 1989 by administrative order no. 123 of the Department of Environment and Natural Resources (DENR). The program formalized terms under which organized communities could now apply for 25-year community forestry management agreements, with the possibility of renewal for another 25 years. As such, the Community Forestry Program (CFP) is viewed as "one of the key alternatives for replacing irresponsible TLA [Timber License Agreement] holders, for canceled and abandoned TLA's, and for many communal residual forests."

At the program's initiation, twelve pilot project sites were selected, representing most regions of the country. Responsibility for managing residual forests at these sites now fall on organized local communities in exchange for the right to extract, process, utilize, or sell forest products. Various tenural arrangements are possible under the program, all extending over a twenty-five year period. These include: community forestry management agreements for residual forests; forest land management agreements for areas under contract reforestation; and certificate of stewardship contracts for individually occupied and cultivated upland farms. The program stipulates that part of the proceeds derived from community forestry agreements will be channeled back into local reforestation and management activities. Specific projects include a number of components such as agroforestry extension, projects in forest product extraction, processing and marketing, contract reforestation, alternative livelihood schemes, and institutionalized linkages with other upland development programs. In theory, NGO's are to figure prominently in the implementation of the CFP at each project site.

At the time of writing, ten CFP-NGO contracts had been signed. Virtually all of the pilot projects already underway started with contract reforestation as their main focus, although some of the "more vision-oriented and committed CFP-recipient NGOs" also made community organizing and training a central focus. The problem of selecting appropriate collaborating NGOs has been a key constraint in CFP thus far. Only three of the NGOs involved have a strong technical background ultimately required for optimal results. This situation may have a number of underlying reasons, namely a lack of familiarity about the CFP among suitable NGOs, a general reluctance among NGOs to work with the DENR, or, alternatively, the existence of a genuine dearth of qualified NGOs in the field. Other problems encountered include: Friction in NGO-community relations, where communities often end up feeling that they are simply providing the labor for an NGO-specified agenda; unprepared and poorly trained DENR field staff in terms of species selection; vested NGO interests in obtaining funding rather than realizing project goals over the long term; and a general lack of integrated social forestry mentality among DENR and NGO staff alike.

Philippines/ Project intervention—Social and community forestry/ Reforestation/ State policy—Forest and natural resources.

865. **Hackenberg, R. A. 1988.** "Upending Malthus: The Household Role in Philippine Food Gains and Fertility Losses, 1970–1980." In *Impact of Modernization on Development and Demographic Behavior: Case Studies in Seven Third World Countries.* Ed. C. Vlassof and Berkat-e-Khuda, pp. 7–20. IDRC Publication, no. 260e. Ottawa, Canada: International Development Research Centre.

> Reporting data on population growth and food production for two municipalities of Davao del Sur, Mindanao in 1970s and 1980 respectively, the authors challenge Malthusian perceptions of population growth. There appear to be two main factors behind the demographic changes in the study areas: 1) rapidly changing economic circumstances in a frontier setting, and 2) large government programs. The study highlights the need for greater local involvement in program design, leading to greater diversity in agricultural production and population growth control arrangements. Partnership between farmers, grass roots groups, research scientists, and policymakers may prove a suitable model for managing an accelerated pace of agricultural development with the Green Revolution.

Philippines/ Mindanao/ Agricultural development/ Population pressure.

866. **Halos, S. C., F. F. Natividad, L. J. Escote-Carlson, G. L. Enriquez, and I. Umboh. 1994.** Proceedings of the Symposium on Biotechnological and Environmental Approaches to Forest Pest and Disease Management, Quezon City, Philippines, 28–30 April 1993. BIOTROP Special Publication, no. 53. Bogor, Indonesia: SEAMEO-BIOTROP.

> Twenty papers discuss current problems in forest pest management in various parts of Asia and highlight recent strategies in biotechnological and environmentally-based pest control. Individual papers include, among others: "Inventory of Forest Damages at the Faperta UNCEN Experimental Gardens in Manokwari, Irian Jaya, Indonesia" by Matheus T. E. Kilmaskossu and Jan Piet Nerokouw; "Incidence of Dieback in Two *Acacia mangium* Plantation Sites in Sabah" by Mahmud Sudin; "Preliminary Observations on Insect Pests and Diseases Problems of *Gliricidia sepium* (Jacq.) Walp. germplasm collection in ViSCA and Its Implications for Genetic Improvement" by Ernesto C. Bumatay; "Biological and Environmental Pest and Disease Control Strategy in PICOP" by Emelio O. Anino; "Forest Pest and Diseases Research in the Philippines: An Overview" by Segundino V. Forondo and Marcelino U. Siladan; "Natural Enemies Associated with Some Insect Pests of Forest Plantations in Peninsular Malaysia" by Ahmad Said Sajap and Jaacob Abd. Wahab; "Preliminary Survey on Entomopathogenic Fungi in the Forest at Khao Yai National Park" by Pimpun Sommartya and Banpot Napometh; "Recent Insect Pest Outbreaks in Forest Plantations in Peninsular Malaysia" by Ab. Majid B. Ab. Rahman and Ahmad Said Sajap; and "Development of *Parmela* sp. in a *Pinus merkusii* stand affected by air pollutants at Puncak, West Java" by Dadang K. Permana, Soetrisno Hadi, and Simon T. Nuhamara.

Indonesia/ Malaysia/ Philippines/ Sabah/ Pest, weed, and crop disease management/ Forest management—Commercial forestry and silviculture/ Timber plantations.

867. **Halos, S. C. 1982.** "Opportunities and Constraints of Agroforestry in the Philippines." *Canopy International* 8 (7–8): 5–8.

> Agroforestry has been practiced in the Philippines for centuries, as evidenced by the famous Ifugao rice terrace system. Agroforestry can play a number of different roles, including 1) forest protection (e.g., the Forest Occupancy Management Program of the Bureau of Forest Development), 2) economic production (e.g., Communal Tree Farming Program of the BFD), and 3) use as a "corporate tool." Various project ventures falling within each of these three categories are described.
>
> Halos points out that while agroforestry can be more cost effective than reforestation programs, recent efforts haven been dogged by various problems, among which BFD's lack

of familiarity with real community participation, delays and inadequacy of project funding, over-reliance on ipil-ipil (*Leucaena leucocephala*), failure to assess local felt needs, and lack of agreement on long term goals have been the most important. Agroforestry has considerable potential but flexibility and the ability to identify, evaluate, and address problems are needed to ensure program success.

Philippines/ Agroforestry.

868.   **Hashim, A. A., J. Kebede, and G. P. Kibira. 1984.** "Farming Systems in the Hilly Areas of Barili, Cebu, the Philippines." Bulletin of the International Course for Development Oriented Research in Agriculture, no. 16. Netherlands: ICRA.

Philippines/ Cebu/ Farm management—Cropping systems/ Agriculture—Shifting cultivation/ Agriculture—Permanent/ Farming systems research.

869.   **Hires, G., and T. N. Headland. 1977.** "A Sketch of Western Bukidnon Man—bo Farming Practices, Past and Present." *Philippine Quarterly of Culture and Society* 5: 65–75.

A study of western Bukidnon Manobo farming practices reveals that contact with lowland farmers has promoted the adoption of lowland farming practices by the Manobo, including extension of the cropping period for cultivated swidden fields. Extended cropping periods on swidden plots are maintained even as the Manobo are pushed onto steeper lands. Among the most significant results of these changes are declining yields of subsistence food crops such as corn.

Philippines/ Agriculture—Shifting cultivation/ Agricultural intensification/ Indigenous and local communities—Farming practices/ Indigenous and local communities—Forest land use and management practices/ Soil erosion and degradation.

870.   **Huke, R. E. 1963.** "Abaca Production in the Philippines." *Philippine Geographical Journal* 7 (1): 18–35.

Prior to Spanish colonization, abaca was long produced and used by indigenous communities of the Philippines for home-based cloth and rope production. At the turn of the 20th century, abaca was also the Philippines' leading export product, accounting for 68 percent of all foreign exchange. This commodity was produced both on plantations and by sedentary and swidden farmers in the coastal lowlands and on the lower slopes of the islands' numerous volcanoes, providing an important source of income for these producers. The author describes the uses and biology of abaca as well as the environmental and agronomic conditions needed for its successful cultivation, which include rich soil and labor-intensive weeding and cleaning of standing plants to avoid disease and pests. A concluding section describes changes in the distribution of abaca production during the first half of the 20th century, citing both intervention by Japanese and American occupying forces as well as increased incidence of disease in several regions of the country as some of the major factors behind these changes.

Philippines/ History—Colonial/ Agriculture—Smallholder tree and perennial crop farming/ Agriculture—Smallholder cash crop farming.

871.   ———. **1963.** "Mindanao . . . Pioneer Frontier?" *Philippine Geographical Journal* 7: 74–83.

Philippines/ Mindanao/ Migration/ Land settlement and development.

872.   **Hyman, E. L. 1981.** "Tree Farming from the Viewpoint of the Smallholder: An Ex Post Evaluation of the PICOP Project." Paper presented at National Confer-

ence on the Conservation of Natural Resources, December 1981, Manila, Philippines. Photocopy.

The author provides an evaluation of a World-Bank financed tree-farming project of the Paper Industries Corporation of the Philippines (PICOP). The setting is Eastern Mindanao (Surigao del Sur and Agusan del Sur). The process of project implementation, a profile of project participants (none of whom could be regarded as kauginero), and various economic parameters are described. In general, the project provided an adequate financial return. Tree farmers who follow typical silvicultural practices "are able to earn good returns in all cases except when low yield is combined with a high wage assumption."

In general, the project was a good example of cooperation between the public and private sectors from the earliest stages of project development through implementation. The success of the project also demonstrates World Bank sensitivity to a pattern of rural development that takes into direct account the well-being of small producers. Reasons for this success, chief among which is "the existence of a well-developed, assured market," are discussed.

Philippines/ Mindanao/ Project intervention—Social and community forestry/ Forest management—Economics.

873. **Industan, E. 1993.** "Detribalization of the Ata Man—bo: A Study of Ethnicity and Sociocultural Change." Ph.D. diss., Xavier University, Cagayan de Oro, Philippines.

Philippines/ Mindanao/ Ethnography/ Indigenous and local communities—Commoditization/ Indigenous and local communities—Social relations/ Ethnicity and ethnic relations.

874. **Intal, P. Jr. 1985.** "The Macroeconomic Policy Environment of Philippine Agricultural Performance." *Journal of Philippine Development* 22 (2): 395–408.

Philippines/ State policy—Agricultural and rural development/ State policy—Economic development/ Agricultural economics.

875. **Intal, P. S. J., and J. H. Power. 1990.** *Trade, Exchange Rate, and Agricultural Pricing Policies in the Philippines.* Washington, D.C.: World Bank.

While the Philippines national economy as a whole fared poorly between 1960 and 1985, the agricultural sector was particularly hard hit by trade and sectoral policies adopted during this period. The authors examine the specific effects of trade and pricing interventions on agricultural output in the Philippines, focusing on rice, maize, sugar, and coconuts. Direct and indirect price interventions are shown to have had differential effects on the production of different crops. Particularly negative effects are noted for the sugar and coconut sectors, which may have contributed to increased social unrest in the main sugar-and coconut-producing areas of the country. Political economic issues relating to the dominance of patronage in formulating policy are emphasized, and the wider impacts of price interventions on food consumption, income distribution, and foreign exchange earnings are noted.

Philippines/ State policy—Agricultural and rural development/ Agricultural development/ Agricultural economics/ Political economy.

876. **Jabla, J. 1990.** Defending the Forest: A Case-Study of San Fernando, Bukidnon, Philippines. Manila: Heritage.

Philippines/ Mindanao/ Timber industry—Logging/ Timber industry—Impacts on local communities and economy/ Timber industry—Environmental impacts/ Social movements.

877.   **Kellman, M. C. 1969.** "Some Environmental Components of Shifting Cultivation in Upland Mindanao." *Journal of Tropical Geography* 28: 40–56.

Philippines/ Mindanao/ Agriculture—Shifting cultivation's environmental impacts/ Land settlement and development—Environmental impacts.

878.   ———. **1970.** *Secondary Plant Succession in Tropical Montane Mindanao.* Department of Biogeography and Geomorphology Publication, BG/2. Canberra, Australia: Australian National University.

Philippines/ Mindanao/ Forest regeneration/ Forest biology and ecology/ Vegetation analysis.

879.   **Kikuchi, M., and Y. Hayami. 1978.** "Agricultural Growth Against a Land Resource Constraint: A Comparative History of Japan, Taiwan, Korea and the Philippines." *Journal of Economic History* 38: 839–864.

Philippines/ Agricultural intensification/ Agricultural development/ Population pressure.

880.   ———. **1983.** "New Rice Technology, Intrarural Migration and Institutional Innovation." *Population and Development Review* 9 (2): 247–257.

In the Philippines, adoption of the high yielding varieties of rice has been limited largely to lowland areas. As a result, work opportunities in agriculture have expanded most rapidly in the lowlands, thereby encouraging net rural-rural migration from upland to lowland areas. Data from Laguna province which support this thesis are presented by the authors. Changes in labor contracts associated with the new rice technology and the resulting migration flows are also discussed in the article.

Philippines/ Migration/ Agricultural development.

881.   **Kinley, D. 1991.** "Ending the Plunder of Palawan." *World Development* 4 (4): 18–21.

Palawan island represents a "growing ecological disaster." The article attributes this situation largely to the environmentally unsound practices being followed by kaingineros. The author suggests reason for some optimism, in large part thanks to the UNDP-financed Palawan Integrated Area Development Program (PIADP). Under this program, upland farmers have been given stewardship contracts and encouraged to grow tree crops and/or soil protecting hedgerows. Moreover, the PIADP is only one part of a larger national response by the Philippine government, as outlined in the Master Plan for Forestry Development. In Ilocos, upland farmers are now growing coffee and other crops. In Southern Luzon, the Integrated Social Forestry Program (also assisted by UNDP) is currently being implemented. Given the government's new approach in forest management, local communities throughout the Philippines will assume a role as primary forest managers and protectors. Reforestation projects have increased dramatically, fueling DENR hopes that the country can become a net reforester some time in the 1990s.

Philippines/ Palawan/ Forest management—Control of shifting cultivation/ Project intervention—Social and community forestry/ Project intervention—Agroforestry/ Reforestation.

882.   **Korten, F. F. 1994.** "Questioning the Call for Environmental Loans: A Critical Examination of Forestry Lending in the Philippines." *World Development* 22 (7): 971–981.

Korten describes problems encountered in the reforestation and resource management programs of the Philippine government over the last several decades. Early government-organized as well as more recent, privatized approaches towards reforestation funded by large ADB loans have fallen far short of expected success. Reasons for this failure include: limited participation by local villagers, poor relations between contracted non-governmental organizations and local communities, expediency-induced over-use of *Gmelina arborea* species in the government-funded programs, and widespread corruption resulting from the large size of the loans involved. A major pressure behind the government's poor management of the its reforestation projects has been its dependence on programs such as the Forestry Sector Loan Program to meet foreign exchange needs. Emphasizing the wastefulness, inefficiency and potential for corruption inherent in loan-based strategies for resource management, Korten recommends the promotion of alternative options, including social forestry and assisted natural regeneration.

Philippines/ Reforestation/ State policy—Forest and natural resources/ Social forestry.

883. **Krinks, P. A. 1970.** "Peasant Colonization in Mindanao." *Journal of Tropical Geography* 30: 38–47.

A 1967 field survey of a random sample of 50 settlers who had settled in the municipality of Mawab in Davao Province between 1931 and 1966 was supplemented with information gathered from previous immigrants, native residents, and government offices to observe processes of land acquisition, land use, and socioeconomic status. Early immigrants and those with significant capital resources when first arriving to the region report noticeable improvement in their standard of living with their move to Mindanao. Many others, however, especially those of more recent immigrant status, have done less well, lacking the necessary capital to buy land. Often, recent and poor migrant farmers resort to squatting on land that is increasingly located on hillside areas, poorly suited for intensive agriculture. While Mindanao island may continue to be able to absorb more new settlers for the short-term, over the long term, "neglect of conservation of resources will reproduce conditions of the depleted environments of the migrant source areas," ultimately helping to "perpetuate the land problems of the Philippines rather than to solve them."

Philippines/ Mindanao/ Migration/ Migrant farmers and farming/ Land settlement and development/ Poverty.

884. ———. **1975.** "Changing Land Use on a Philippine Frontier." *Agricultural History* 49: 473–490.

Philippines/ Migration/ Land use—Patterns and planning/ Land settlement and development/ Agriculture—Shifting cultivation's environmental impacts/ Migrant farmers and farming/ History—Colonial.

885. **Kummer, D. M. 1990.** "Deforestation in the Post-War Philippines." Ph.D. diss., Boston University, Boston, Mass.

Philippines/ Deforestation/ Timber industry—Logging/ Timber industry—Environmental impacts/ Timber industry—State policy and regulation/ Political economy.

886. ———. **1991.** "The Political Use of Philippine Forestry Statistics in the Post-war Period." Photocopy. Worcester, Mass.: Department of Geography, Clark University.

Philippines/ State policy—Forest and natural resources/ Political economy.

887. ———. **1992.** *Deforestation in the Postwar Philippines.* Chicago, Ill.: University of Chicago Press.

A model of deforestation for the post-war Philippines is presented in which the two main agents of forest destruction have been identified as logging and agriculture (both shifting and permanent). It is postulated that logging is primarily responsible for converting the primary forest to secondary forest and that agricultural activities then convert the secondary forest to farmland. The results of cross-sectional analysis indicate that forest cover is negatively related to road and population density. Panel analysis, on the other hand, indicates that actual deforestation from 1970 to 1980 is positively related to forest area in 1970, distance from Manila, change in agricultural area and logging quotas in 1970. The distance from Manila variable is important because it represents the lack of control of the forest removal process and, as such, it is used as a proxy for corruption in the forestry sector and elite control over government and natural resources. It is important to note that changes in population were not important in explaining deforestation. Deforestation is the result of both the failure of the Philippine economy to provide jobs as well as elite control of the government which has concentrated the financial returns from logging in the hands of logging concessionaires and their allies. This conclusion also suggests that deforestation in the Philippines is amenable to policy intervention.

Philippines/ Deforestation/ Timber industry—Logging/ Timber industry—Environmental impacts/ Timber industry—State policy and regulation/ Agriculture—Shifting cultivation's environmental impacts/ Political economy.

888.   ———. 1992. "Measuring Forest Decline in the Philippines: An Exercise in Historiography." *Forest and Conservation History* 36 (4): 185–189.

Kummer examines the available data on the history of forest cover loss in the Philippines. Because most forestry related records dating from the Spanish and U.S. colonial eras have been destroyed or made unavailable, accurate assessments of the exact extent of forest cover loss prior to the most recent decades are difficult if not impossible to make. Nevertheless, approximate estimates of extant forest cover dating to 1876 culled from various sources are available. These are cited to suggest that the forest cover in the Philippines declined from c. 68 percent of the archipelago's total land mass to c. 49 percent by the early 1950s. Estimates made at 7 year intervals since the 1950s, again culled from a number of different sources, suggest continued disappearance of both primary and secondary forests in the country. The most reliable current statistics include those collected by the Philippine-German Forest Resource Inventory Project as well as those derived from the World-Bank funded satellite mapping effort by the Swedish Space Corporation in the mid-late 1980s. Much less reliable have been the Philippine Forestry Statistics as well as measurements collected during FAO's study in the early 1980s.

Notes the author, if the 1980–87 rate of deforestation is extended to the current year, it is likely that only 20 percent of the country's total land mass remains under forest cover, with a far smaller percentage still under old-growth forests. The data indicates that questions of preserving primary forest lands in the Philippines are quickly becoming moot. Concerted attention must now be directed at ensuring the survival of the country's remaining secondary forests.

Philippines/ Deforestation/ Forest management—Forest resource conservation/ History—Colonial.

889.   ———. 1992. "Upland Agriculture, the Land Frontier and Forest Decline in the Philippines." *Agroforestry Systems* 18: 31-46.

Although shifting agriculture and expansion of small-scale farming are usually seen as the main causes of deforestation in the Philippines, available statistics contradict this view. Close examination of land use and demographic statistics strongly suggests that by far most farmers in the uplands practice sedentary rather than shifting agriculture. Neither does the data bear up the view of population pressure as the leading cause of deforestation. The study suggests the need to rethink basic concepts, like that of arable land, in development planning.

Philippines/ Deforestation/ Population pressure/ Land use—Patterns and planning/ Agriculture—Shifting cultivation/ Land settlement and development/ Agricultural intensification.

890. **Kummer, D., R. Concepcion, and B. Cañizares. 1993.** "Image and Reality: Exploring the Puzzle of Continuing Environmental Degradation in the Uplands of Cebu, the Philippines." Paper. Photocopy.

The authors report on observations made during field survey of Cebu island undertaken in May–August 1993. Over the past hundred years, virtually all primary forest cover has been removed from Cebu island. However, the authors find that significant and possibly growing parts of the island are covered with secondary vegetative cover ranging from grassland to dense shrubs and plantations of fast-growing tree species. In many areas, these re-vegetated areas appear to be supporting a thriving, small-scale fuelwood industry critical to local village economies. A review of soils data was also undertaken, suggesting that the problem of soil erosion may at present not be as large-scale as has been commonly represented in the literature. In many areas much of the arable top soil has already been eroded, and significant re-deposition of materials may now be occurring instead. These preliminary observations suggest that while much alarm has been raised about the scale and the pace of environmental degradation on Cebu, this degradation process has been slowed and possibly even reversed in recent years as a kind of "low-level equilibrium" has been reached. The paper raises a number of questions of the appropriateness of current efforts at large scale soil conservation program development by the World Bank and other large funding agencies. These efforts, note the authors, are based on a monolithic view of environmental problems in the Philippines which is not supported by the results of the fieldwork completed. The need for greater attention to be directed to local farmer responses to environmental decline as well as the larger socio-economic structures underlying this process is emphasized.

Philippines/ Cebu/ Soil erosion and degradation/ Deforestation/ Forest regeneration/ Indigenous and local communities—Forest products use and trade/ Indigenous and local communities—Forest land use and management practices/ Fuelwood.

891. **Lamug, C. B. 1989.** "Social and Cultural Factors and Their Effects on Social Forestry in the Philippines." In *Social Forestry in Asia: Factors that Influence Program Implementation.* Ed. N. T. Vergara and R. A. Fernandez, pp. 59–77. College, Laguna, Philippines: Southeast Asian Regional Center for Graduate Study and Research in Agriculture (SEARCA).

Drawing from previous tests of community appraisal methods at three pilot social forestry projects in Luzon, the Visayas and Mindanao, as well as from other forestry related research endeavors, the author discusses the significance of social and cultural factors in social forestry development. Specific factors noted included: the role of local community organizations; the types of social organizations and social conflicts characteristic of the project area; demographic factors; tenurial arrangements; labor constraints; livelihood alternatives; local perceptions and attitudes about land use; the attitudes and interests of influential persons in the area. The paper is instructive for reflecting some of the author's direct field experience. In addressing the issue of land tenure, for example, the author notes that in some cases, even where certificates of stewardship have been awarded, farmers continue to share crop yields with those formerly identified as "owners" of the public land. Official social forestry arrangements thus do not automatically cancel out existing informal tenure arrangements—or asset inequities—among local communities.

Philippines/ Luzon/ Cebu/ Mindanao/ Project intervention—Social and community forestry/ Land tenure.

892. **Lantin, M. M., W. D. Dar, and R. L. Lim. 1994.** "Recent Developments in Philippine Agriculture." In *Upland Agriculture in Asia.* Proceedings of a

workshop held in Bogor, Indonesia April 6–8, 1993. Ed. J. W. T. Bottema and D. R. Stoltz, pp. 61–74. Bogor: Regional Co-ordination Centre for Research and Development of Coarse Grains, Pulses, Roots and Tuber Crops in the Humid Tropics of Asia and the Pacific (CGPRT Centre).

The authors describe key objectives and development emphases of the Department of Agriculture in relation to upland farming. Crop diversification is currently being stressed as a major thrust in rural development efforts, with a focus on maize, coconut, sugar, livestock and poultry, fisheries, tobacco, fibers, fruits, vegetables, and flowers. A shift in investment from research on lowland agriculture to upland agriculture noted, the latter claiming 51% of budget allocations in 1992, as compared with 40% in 1990. Appendices provide data on agricultural production by crop and the percentage share of agricultural crops in total area harvested, production volume and value. The period covered is 1982 through 1990.

Philippines/ Agricultural development/ State policy—Agricultural and rural development/ Agriculture—Smallholder cash crop farming.

893. **Laquihon, W. A. 1989.** "Some Key Determinants of SALT Adoption in the Philippines: Viewpoints of Farmer-Cooperators." In *Social Forestry in Asia: Factors That Influence Program Implementation*. Ed. N. T. Vergara and R. A. Fernandez, pp. 79-116. College, Laguna, Philippines: Southeast Asian Regional Center for Graduate Study and Research in Agriculture (SEARCA).

The author reports on the results of a study on Sloping Agricultural Land Technology (SALT) adoption among Philippine farmers undertaken by the Mindanao Baptist Rural Life Center. The study involved a survey of 71 farmers in Luzon, Visayas and Mindanao, sought to answer a series of questions related to the determinants of adoption, and tested several hypotheses concerning expected differences between Luzon, Visayan and Mindanao farmers. The paper includes a brief review of the existing literature on biophysical and socio-economic determinants of farming systems; description of the methodology used; and discussion of the study results. Major key determinants of SALT adoption were found to include training and exposure to technology; anticipated benefits; seed availability; sincerity and capability of the sponsoring organization; source of outside farm income; land elevation; and market needs.

Philippines/ Mindanao/ Project intervention—Agroforestry/ Farming systems research.

894. **Lasco, R. D. 1991.** "MPTs in Indigenous Agroforestry Systems: The Naaland Case." In *Research on Multipurpose Tree Species (MPTS) in Asia*. Ed. D. Taylor and K. G. MacDicken, pp. 19–23. Bangkok: Winrock International Institute for Agricultural Development; Kasetsart University Faculty of Forestry.

The author describes an indigenous form of multipurpose tree (MPT) use among upland farmers in Naga, Cebu. The system described involves contour hedgerows on sloping farm fields.

Philippines/ Cebu/ Indigenous and local communities—Farming practices/ Agroforestry.

895. **Ledesma, A. J., S.J. 1992.** "Bukidnon: Mindanao's Heartland for Agrarian Reform." In *Mindanao: Land of Unfulfilled Promise*. Ed. M. Turner, R. J. May, and L. R. Turner, pp. 61–74. Quezon City, Philippines: New Day Publishers.

A total of 310,581 ha of Bukidnon province has been slated for inclusion in the land reform program of the Philippines. Most of this area is comprised of old military reserves, land officially classified as public forest land (especially in Malaybalay and Talakag municipalities), large private landholdings as well as commercial plantations. The author provides a broad overview of the geographic characteristics of Bukidnon province, the province's history as an increasingly plantation-oriented economy, the planned models for land redistribution in Bukidnon, the priority ranking of individual municipalities for land reform activity, and major issues in the pending implementation of land reform.

Philippines/ Mindanao/ Land reform/ Agriculture—Plantations/ Land use—Patterns and planning.

896. **Ledesma, A. J., S.J. et al. 1990.** "NGOs in Agrarian Reform: Building Links with the Grassroots." *Solidarity* 127: 87–97.

Included in this paper is a short case study of the Mindanao Support Centre for Agrarian Reform and Rural Development (MINCARRD) as well as a closer examination of efforts undertaken by Xavier University, College of Agriculture in terms of local agrarian reform, cooperatives, smallholder and landless farmers.

Philippines/ Mindanao/ Land reform/ Social movements/ Non-governmental organizations.

897. **Leones, J. P. 1985.** "Forests for Whom?: A History of the Practice of and Policy Response to Shifting Cultivation in the Philippines." Photocopy. Ithaca, N.Y.: Cornell University.

Philippines/ Agriculture—Shifting cultivation/ Agriculture—Shifting cultivation's environmental impacts/ Forest management—Control of shifting cultivation/ State policy—Forest and natural resources/ Migrant farmers and farming/ Political economy.

898. **———. 1987.** "The Impact of an Agroforestry Project on Upland Farming in San Francisco, Cebu, Philippines." Cornell International Agriculture Mimeograph, no. 116. Ithaca, N.Y.: Cornell University.

Leones describes both the farming systems developed by local farmers in the hills of San Francisco municipality on Cebu island and a recent watershed project undertaken in the area. Project objectives included soil and water conservation, and intervention strategies focused on promoting intercropping and fruit-tree planting to reforest the watershed. Project impacts in terms of conservation and food production are assessed.

Philippines/ Cebu/ Farming systems research/ Farm management—Cropping systems/ Farm management—Economics/ Watershed management/ Project intervention—Soil conservation/ Project intervention—Agroforestry/ Reforestation.

899. **Lewis, M. W. 1992.** *Wagering the Land: Ritual, Capital, and Environmental Degradation in the Cordillera of Northern Luzon.* Berkeley, Calif.: University of California Press.

Lewis examines the socio-cultural factors behind recent changes in the farming practices of the Buguias, indigenous inhabitants of the Northern Luzon Cordillera. Agricultural commercialization in the Cordilleras has involved a blend of new and old economic, environmental and religious practices. While these changes have brought about signs of serious environmental degradation—loss of forests and wildlife, increased pesticide use, soil erosion—a corresponding breakdown of traditional society and culture has not occurred. Rather, old beliefs and rituals, particularly the "redistributive prestige feasts" central to indigenous religion in the area have flourished.
Drawing from archival sources and local fieldwork, Lewis describes the economic and social life of the Buguias in the early 20th century, the destruction of indigenous agriculture and livestock management practices in the mid-1940s, and the rapid growth of commercial vegetable farming since. Abundant cash income generated by this new livelihood has served

to strengthen rather than undermine ritualistic communal feasting, which serves the local function of both honoring the dead as well as bringing good luck to the host farmer's enterprises. As the drive to gain ancestral favor discourages environmental prudence, Buguias farmers appear to be "quite literally wagering their lands in the hope of gaining prosperity and prestige."

Philippines/ Luzon/ Indigenous and local communities—Commoditization/ Indigenous and local communities—Economy/ Indigenous and local communities—Farming practices/ Indigenous and local communities—Social relations/ Indigenous and local communities—Religion and cosmology/ History—Colonial.

900.   **Lewis, R. F. 1988.** "Mt. Apo and Other National Parks in the Philippines." *Oryx* 22 (April): 100–109.

Philippines/ Mindanao/ Forest management—Parks and conservation areas.

901.   **Librero, A., and Z. C. Lameyra. 1991.** "The State of Philippine Upland Research: Profile." Vol. 1. Photocopy. Los Banos, Philippines: University of the Philippines at Los Ba–os, IESM.

This report presents results of a survey of 81 researchers from different institutions in the Philippines presently working on the uplands. A major concern voiced by current uplands researchers is the overly narrow definition ascribed to the term "uplands" by official agencies such as the Department of Environment and Natural Resources. Possible improvements suggested by survey respondents are listed: 1) including a wider range of terrain characteristics (undulating, flatlands, sloping, rugged); 2) including a wider range of slope characterizations (3–30 percent); 3) including farming as well as non-farming activities when assessing land suitability; 4) specifying the susceptibility of upland environments to soil erosion and impairment of hydrological systems; 5) including other identifying elements frequently present in upland ecosystems such as rainfed agriculture; marginal farmland; distinct micro-environments; 6) expanding the definition's focus to include not only public lands but also privately held land, ancestral reserves, and parks.

Philippines/ Rural development/ Farming systems research/ Forest management/ Soil erosion and degradation.

902.   **Lockwood, B. 1989.** "The Zamboanga del Sur Development Project; 1975–1985." Paper presented at the Conference on "Mindanao: Land of Unfilled Promise," 2–3 November 1989, at the Australian National University, Canberra, Australia. Photocopy.

This paper reports the achievement and failures of the Australian-funded Zamboanga del Sur Development Project, a rural development project aimed at improving living standards among Zamboanga's rural majority. In all, about 93 million dollars was spent the project's three major components (roads, water systems and irrigation) and its minor foci (agricultural technology assistance, social welfare and training). Agroforestry and hillside farming improvement were added during the second phase of the project.

The construction of additional farm-to-market roads was generally successful, although road maintenance after project termination has been somewhat problematic. In some cases these roads were servicing upland areas of the province. For agriculture, on the other hand, the emphasis upon multiple cropping technology appears to have been somewhat inappropriate, as most cooperators found that except for upland rice the new technology yields were not high enough to compensate for the higher production costs and increased risk. Commercial tree crops were relatively successful but were generally adopted only by the wealthier, market-oriented farmers. In general, the unstable political situation in Zamboanga's hinterlands proved to be an important impediment to a more successful outcome of the agroforestry component of the project.

Philippines/ Project intervention—Rural development/ Project intervention—Soil conservation/ Project intervention—Agroforestry.

903. **Lopez, M. E. 1987.** "Integrated Displacement: The Palaw'an Case." In *Southeast Asian Tribal Groups and Ethnic Minorities: Prospects for the 80's and Beyond.* pp. 127–133. Cultural Survival Report, no. 22. Cambridge, Mass.: Cultural Survival.

This paper draws from the author's field research among Palaw'an swidden farmers in 1982–1983. The author discusses the different factors contributing to systematic displacement of the Palaw'an from their ancestral lands. In one way or another these lands are being gradually taken over by either state agency or immigrant newcomers. Competing interests in local resources result in steady resource degradation. Political "brokers" such as missionaries, community organizers, and Peace Corps volunteers have an important role to play in representing indigenous interests on the regional and national policy-setting levels. The author emphasizes the need for legal measures to protect Palaw'an lands from further encroachment as a matter of cultural, social, economic and environmental survival.

Philippines/ Palawan/ Indigenous and local communities—Commoditization/ Indigenous and local communities—State policy/ Land settlement and development—Impacts on local communities and economy/ Ethnicity and ethnic relations.

904. **Lopez, M. E. Z. 1986.** "The Palaw'an: Land, Ethnic Relations, and Political Processes in a Philippine Frontier System." Ph.D. diss., Harvard University, Cambridge, Mass.

Philippines/ Palawan/ Indigenous and local communities—Social relations/ Indigenous and local communities—Land and resource tenure systems/ Ethnicity and ethnic relations/ Land settlement and development—Impacts on local communities and economy.

905. **Lopez, R. 1968.** *Agricultural Practices of the Manobo in the Interior of Southwestern Cotabato.* San Carlos Publications, Series A: Humanities, no. 7. Cebu City, Philippines: University of San Carlos.

The author reports the results of a study of economic factors, such as productivity and profits, in the development of swidden-based farming systems among the Manobo of Cotobato province on Mindanao. Crop production was measured based on actual yields, while agricultural profits were assessed against production costs and consumption needs. Contrary to conventional theory, the author finds that yields for corn and rice among traditional Manobo swiddeners actually exceeded the national average (that is, before the Green revolution). Manobo farmers generally produced harvests in surplus of subsistence grain and food needs, allowing villagers time for other economic and cultural activities.

Philippines/ Mindanao/ Indigenous and local communities—Farming practices/ Indigenous and local communities—Economy/ Farm management—Economics/ Agriculture—Shifting cultivation.

906. **Lopez-Gonzaga, V. 1983.** Peasants in the Hills: A Study of the Dynamics of Social Change among the Buhid Swidden Cultivators in the Philippines. Diliman, Quezon City, Philippines: University of the Philippines Press.

Philippines/ Mindoro/ Indigenous and local communities—Economy/ Indigenous and local communities—Commoditization/ Indigenous and local communities—Social relations/ Indigenous and local communities—Farming practices/ Ethnicity and ethnic relations.

907. **Ly Tung, and R. V. Labios. 1992.** "Farming Systems Research in the Uplands of the Philippines: State of the Art." Proceedings of the Upland Rice-Based

Farming Systems Research Planning Meeting, 28 April-1 May 1992, Mae Ping Hotel, Chiang Mai, Thailand. pp. 55–70. Bangkok, Thailand; Manila, Philippines: Department of Agriculture; International Rice Research Institute.

The authors provide a brief overview of land use systems in the Philippines, current agencies involved in upland farming systems research, and progress made in promoting improved resource management technologies for upland farms. Philippine land use systems include food crop systems, coconut-based systems, grassland systems (based on livestock production), and forest plantations. Considerable efforts have been made in the Philippines to promote contour hedgerow systems in permanently farmed systems of the uplands. Crop rotation with legumes has also been promoted although phosphorus deficiency continues to be a major constraint for realizing the potential of nitrogen-fixing legumes. Although comprising a widespread farming system type in the Philippines, crop-fallow rotation has received considerably less attention than permanent upland farming among researchers and extension agencies. Citing promising results of a limited number of studies in this area, the authors emphasize the need for more research on effective ways to improve fallow-based systems through increasing nutrient levels and organic matter on fallowed fields. The potential for international collaboration for further progress in farming systems research is also emphasized.

Philippines/ Land use—Patterns and planning/ Farm management—Cropping systems/ Farming systems research/ Agriculture—Permanent/ Agriculture—Shifting cultivation/ Project intervention—Fallow improvement/ Grasslands.

908.   **Lynch, O., Jr. 1982.** "Native Title, Private Right, and Tribal Land Law: An Introductory Survey." *Philippine Law Journal* 57 (2): 268–306.

Philippines/ Land tenure—Legislation and state policy/ Indigenous and local communities—Land and resource tenure systems.

909.   **———. 1984.** "Withered Roots and Landgrabbers: A Study of Research on Upland Tenure and Displacement." In *Uplands and Uplanders.* Proceedings of the First National Conference on Research in the Uplands, 11–13 April 1983, Quezon City, Philippines. Ed. C. P. Castro, pp. 167–230. Quezon City, Philippines: BFD-Upland Development Program.

Philippines/ Land tenure—Legislation and state policy/ Land settlement and development—Impacts on local communities and economy/ Ethnicity and ethnic relations.

910.   **Lynch, O., Jr., and K. Talbott. 1988.** "Legal Responses to the Philippine Deforestation Crisis." *Journal of International Law* 20 (3): 679–713.

Philippines/ Deforestation/ Land tenure—Legislation and state policy/ Forest management—Forest resource conservation.

911.   **Lynch, R. 1955.** "Some Changes in Bukidnon between 1910 and 1950." *Anthropological Quarterly* 28 (3).

Philippines/ Mindanao/ Land use—Patterns and planning/ Regional development/ History—Colonial.

912.   **Maceda, M. 1977.** "Cotabato Manobo." In *Insular Southeast Asia: Ethnographic Studies. Section 3. Philippines.* Comp. F. M. Lebar, vol. 1, pp. 117–147. New Haven, Conn.: Human Relations Area Files.

Ethnographic account of the Cotabato Manobo centered around the Kulamin Plateau and upper Tran River. The description is based on field work carried out between 1962 and 1964.

Philippines/ Mindanao/ Ethnography/ Indigenous and local communities.

913.   ———. **1977.** "The Mamanua." In *Insular Southeast Asia: Ethnographic Studies. Section 3. Philippines.* Comp. F. M. LeBar, vol. 2, pp. 148–164. New Haven, Conn.: Human Relations Area Files.

Ethnographic account of the Mamanua of northeastern Mindanao. Originally inhabiting lowland plains of the region, the Mamanua have been displaced to mountainous areas further inland by the arrival of immigrant and local settlers since the 1920s. Current problems in sustaining Mamanua livelihoods include further encroachment by timber concerns.

Philippines/ Mindanao/ Ethnography/ Indigenous and local communities.

914.   **Madigan, F. C. 1984.** "In Search of a Balanced Agro-Forestry Growth in Northern Mindanao: A Study of Corn, Rice, Sugar, and Cassava Industries in Bukidnon Province." Final report to the Population and Development Research Project, National Economic Development Authority, Region X. Cagayan de Oro, Mindanao: RIMCU, Xavier University.

Sugar production and cassava starch production, two of several plantation industries in Bukidnon Province, comprised the focus of the study reported in this paper. Collected data indicates that a substantial increase in sugar production took place in Southern Bukidnon between 1975 and 1983. A corresponding decrease was also noted for corn and rice production. While it is difficult to prove a cause-and-effect relationship, sugar growing areas experienced net in-migration during the period while a corn-growing area chosen for comparison seems to have declined in population. There is also a modest tendency for the sugar growing districts to show higher rates of family planning adoption, lower rates of infant mortality, and higher incomes. The analysis is repeated for the province's cassava industry.

Philippines/ Mindanao/ Agriculture—Permanent/ Agriculture—Smallholder cash crop farming/ Agriculture—Plantations/ Health and nutrition.

915.   ———. **1986.** "Erosion Control by a Sondeo Approach to Rapid Rural Reconnaissance: Locating and Assisting Farmers Whose Topsoil is Eroding in Region X." Final project report to the International Development Research Center. Cagayan de Oro City, Philippines: RIMCU, Xavier University.

Madigan summarizes the results of efforts to provide practical information about specific factors behind soil erosion and appropriate approaches to deal with the problem. Two barrios were investigated, one in Bukidnon, the other in Misamis Oriental. The research team consisted of eight specialists ranging from a soil technician to a social scientists familiar with issues of upland agricultural development. The report describes findings in each of these different subdimensions, concentrating upon the major constraints faced by the farmers in the two barrios.
Insecurity of land tenure and labor constraints are cited as major factors behind the tendency among landless farmers to practice incipient swidden farming in the uplands. Insecure tenure arrangements also appear to be a major reason for continued soil erosion from the two study sites, since tenants, hired workers, and squatters have little incentive to undertake labor-intensive erosion-control methods that yield only long term benefits. Local residents face a downward spiral in quality of life as use of "slash and burn" farming methods without alternative forms of conservation farming continues to destroy local forests and watersheds, contributing to soil erosion and flooding and a further loss of livelihoods.

A planned demonstration farm encountered difficulties due to 1) declining "peace and order" conditions and 2) the ipil-ipil blight. Plans for further work with farmer cooperators are discussed in a final section of the report.

Philippines/ Mindanao/ Soil erosion and degradation/ Migrant farmers and farming/ Farming systems research.

916.   ———. **1987.** "Where Trees Are Fewer: Attitudes on Forest Development of a Forest Dwelling People." *Philippine Sociological Review* 35 (1–2): 26–38.

Emphasizing the importance of local attitudes for the success of any reforestation project, Madigan presents the results of a survey assessing the attitudes of members of a tribal minority community in northern Mindanao, utilizing a six-dimensional, Likert-type approach to scaling. The study found the respondents aware of the hazards of over-logging to their farms and livelihood, and well disposed to reforestation. Strong objection was voiced, however, to the ownership or control of reforestation projects by business agencies or persons.

Philippines/ Mindanao/ Indigenous and local communities—Forest land use and management practices/ Reforestation.

917.   **Madulid, D. A. 1991.** "The Philippines: Palm Utilization and Conservation." In *Palms for Human Needs in Asia: Palm Utilization and Conservation in India, Indonesia, Malaysia and the Philippines.* Ed. D. Johnson, pp. 181–227. Rotterdam: A. A. Balkema.

This report summarizes the Philippines section of a study of palm utilization in Asia undertaken within a wider, WWF-funded research effort on wild palm conservation. The project's overall aims were to identify the most economically important as well as most threatened wild palm species in Asia, develop appropriate action plans for their conservation, and raise public and policy-maker awareness of current conservation needs. In this report, various aspects of palm utilization in the Philippines are summarize, including the impact of increasing rates of collection on the resource, the potential for cultivation of various palm species, and the potential for sustainable management of wild palm stands.
The status of in-situ and ex-situ conservation of palm resources is discussed. Several tables list the distribution of various palm species across the Philippines, endangered palm species found in the country, and the location of cultivation efforts for various species both in and outside of the country. A recommended action plan focuses on commercial rattan species development, palm ethnobotany, public awareness of palm utility and conservation issues, in-situ and ex-situ resource conservation. A separate appendix lists existing research programs related to palms, which involve mainly coconut and rattan. Similar reports for Sabah, Sarawak (East Malaysia), and Indonesia included in the monograph have been abstracted separately.

Philippines/ Forest flora/ Non-timber forest products/ Rattan—Growth and distribution/ Rattan—Resource management and conservation/ Rattan—Cultivation/ Rattan—Collection and trade.

918.   **Magallanes, J. M. n.d.** "Participatory Resource Development: Improving Hillside Farmers' Quality of Life Through a Soil Conservation Program." IMA Research Report, no. 1. Cagayan de Oro, Mindanao: Institute of Market Analysis, Xavier University,.

A review of current soil conservation efforts using field data on the Mindanao Upland Stabilization and Utilization through Agroforestry Networking (MUSUAN) produced considerable evidence that a significant degree of soil fertility is maintained and soil erosion halted through the cultivation of hedgerows. However, the hypothesis that technology adoption improves the rate of increase in crop productivity was not born out by the evidence. Study results also strongly suggest an important link between household size and the successful application of initially labor-intensive hedgerow technology. In light of these findings, the author suggests the need for greater attention to possible cottage industries that could feasibly supplement marginal household incomes.

Philippines/ Mindanao/ Project intervention—Agroforestry.

919.   ————. **1991.** "Interactions Between Social and Ecological Factors During the Implementation of the MUSUAN Program: The Case of Himaya, Kolombogon, Maramag Pilot Project." Paper presented at First Cagayan Valley Programme on Environment and Development Conference, 26–29 August 1991, Cabagan, Isabela, Philippines. Photocopy.

Drawing from formal assessments of the Mindanao Upland Stabilization and Utilization through Agroforestry Networking (MUSUAN) program, the author notes that even though some improvement in crop productivity, soil nutrient content, and the condition of local flora and fauna were achieved through the program, local participation nevertheless tended to stop once the program was phased out. In particular, although a participatory approach was taken, the program left no strong local community organization as an ongoing medium for farmers' active participation. Drawing from this experience, Phase II of the MUSUAN program has featured active community organizing, including the development of a multipurpose cooperative.

Philippines/ Mindanao/ Project intervention—Agroforestry/ Project intervention—Participatory methods.

920.   **Makil, P. Q. 1984.** "Forest Management and Use: Philippine Policies in the Seventies and Beyond." *Philippine Studies* 32: 27-53.

The decade of the 1970s is often associated with the rise of social forestry approach in the Philippine uplands. A careful look at Bureau of Forestry Development (BFD) guidelines and Presidential Decrees for this period, however, gives a rather different picture. Makil notes the differential treatment accorded different forest users: those who view the forest as a source of profit (i.e., business corporations) are given various incentives and few threats, while those who see the forest as a source of livelihood (kaingineros, tribals) continue to be treated as second class citizens or even criminals. These differences are in turn linked to lack of clarity in the legal status of subsistence activities, to the resources offered by social class and economic position, and to the (Marcos) government's development ideology. Government policy has consistently promoted "large-scale exploitation for profitable ends, such as international trade and increased governmental revenue" over local subsistence needs. Questions are raised concerning land tenure, appropriate scale of "development" projects, and conflicting understandings of the meaning of "public" lands.

Philippines/ Forest management—Control of shifting cultivation/ State policy—Forest and natural resources/ Political economy.

921.   **Malajczuk, N., and B. Dell. 1995.** "Heavy Metals in Philippines Soils Affect Growth and Establishment of Trees." *ACIAR Forestry Newsletter* 18: 2–3.

Philippines/ Mindanao/ Forest management—Commercial forestry and silviculture/ Soils/ Reforestation.

922.   **Malix, S. R. 1991.** "Quirino: A First Exploration of Deforestation Background and Actors." Paper presented at the First Cagayan Valley Programme on Environment and Development Conference, 26–29 August 1991, Cagayan, Isabela, Philippines. Photocopy.

The author describes ongoing research on access to public forest lands in the upland province of Quirino, emphasizing the diversity of land uses and land users present in the research area. The paper first provides a broad outline of Philippine land laws, noting the primacy of managing forest lands for immediate resource exploitation over conservation and long-term development within Bureau of Forestry Development (BFD) policy. Recently however, important shifts in policy and program orientation (e.g. Timber Production Sharing Arrangements and contract reforestation) reveal a new concern for issues of equity within the BFD. The author also describes recent patterns of transformation from primary forest to idle, open grasslands in the Philippines as a whole, drawing from currently available satellite imagery. Accessibility (via rivers and roads) has played a major role in this change. Paralleling the diversity and rapid rate of change in current land uses, a marked diversity in land users—from indigenous tribal people to various in-migrating groups—is noted. Eleven major occupational groupings related to the forestry sector are identified. Logging companies, NGOs, government agencies, etc., also add to the complexity. Forest-dependent tribals, in the meantime, have had to choose between slipping back into the forests and a process of accommodation, acculturation, and enforced exploitation.

Philippines/ Land use—Patterns and planning/ Deforestation/ Land tenure—Legislation and state policy/ State policy—Forest and natural resources/ Land settlement and development—Environmental impacts.

923. **Manaligod, R., ed. 1990.** "Struggle Against Development Aggression." Quezon City, Philippines: Tunay Na Alyansa Ng Bayan Alay Sa Katutubo (TABAK).

Philippines/ Timber industry—Impacts on local communities and economy/ Land settlement and development—Impacts on local communities and economy/ Social movements.

924. **Manalo, F. T. 1991.** "SALTing the Uplands: OTRADEV's Agro-forestry Project." *Phildraa Notes* 6 (2): 7–8.

The article describes a project for introducing improved agricultural farming practices (the SALT technology) to the Iraya-Mangyan tribal group of Puerto Galera, Mindoro Oriental. Problems encountered include the uneasy peace and order situation, drought, unsettled land tenure questions, and political instability. Despite difficulties, twelve demonstration farms are still operational, with cooperators reporting higher yields and decreased soil erosion. The system is very labor-intensive, particularly during the first year, which has proven a significant constraint.

Philippines/ Mindoro/ Project intervention—Agroforestry/ Project intervention—Fallow improvement.

925. **Mandac, A. M., J. C. Flinn, and M. P. Genesilda. 1986.** "Developing Technology for Upland Farms in Northern Mindanao." *Philippine Journal of Crop Sciences* 112 (2): 69–79.

Philippines/ Mindanao/ Project intervention—Soil conservation/ Project intervention—Agroforestry/ Farm management—Cropping systems.

926. **Mandac, A. M., R. D. Magbanua, and M. P. Genesila. 1987.** "Multiple Cropping System in Northern Mindanao, Philippines." *Philippine Journal of Crop Science* 12 (2): 71–85.

Philippines/ Mindanao/ Agriculture—Permanent/ Farming systems research/ Farm management—Cropping systems.

927. **Manuel, A. 1975.** "The Manuvu." In *Insular Southeast Asia: Ethnographic Studies. Section 3. Borneo and Moluccas.* Vol. 1. Comp. F. M. Lebar, pp. 37–78. New Haven, Conn.: Human Relations Area Files.

> Manuel provides an ethnographic account of the Manuvu (e.g. Upland Bagobo) lifestyle and customs, including a description of their swidden-based cropping patterns. The Manuvu population is centered in the region between Southeast Bukidnon through East Cotabato del Norte to Western Davao City. Traditionally, households rotate the use of swidden fields every two or three years and supplement their diet by hunting. In recent decades, contact with lowland migrants has increased, introducing abaca and coffee as major cash crops into the area. As cash exchange has penetrated into local village economies, the Manuvu have altered their farming and food production patterns somewhat, reducing their dependence on hunting while including the cultivation of coffee and abaca along with traditional subsistence crops like rice and corn.

> Philippines/ Mindanao/ Ethnography/ Indigenous and local communities—Farming practices/ Indigenous and local communities—Commoditization.

928. **Mauricio, F. P. 1991.** "Natural Regeneration of Philippine Dipterocarps: Case Study of PICOP's Forests." In *Proceedings of the Fourth Round-Table Conference on Dipterocarps, Bogor, Indonesia, 12–15 December 1989.* Ed. I. Soerianegara, S. S. Tjitrosomo, R. C. Umaly, and I. Umboh, pp. 365–393. Bogor, Indonesia: SEAMEO BIOTROP.

> Information on the composition, structure, volume, utilization and marketing of Philippine dipterocarps is summarized. Discussion also includes data on habitat, growth, and response to harvesting and regeneration treatments.

> Philippines/ Forest regeneration/ Forest management—Commercial forestry and silviculture.

929. **Mauricio, L. S. 1989.** "ISF: What Went Wrong?" *Canopy International* 15 (1): 6–8.

> Participants in two Philippine ISF (Integrated Social Forestry) projects in Panganiban, Camarines Norte and Dona Remedios Trinidad, Bulacan, voice favorable attitudes toward social forestry and the importance of preserving the forest. At the same time, neither ISF project was associated with any significant improvements in local socio-economic conditions, in part possibly because it may still be too early for quantifiable benefits to be noted. Specific problems with the project were, however, cited. These included bureaucratic red tape resulting in the slow release of funds, lack of well-trained and dedicated personnel, inadequate marketing services and weak commitment to the principle of a participatory approach to program implementation. The unsteady peace-and-order situation found in the uplands has also made program success problematic. Recommendations for overcoming these problems are given.

> Philippines/ Project intervention—Social and community forestry/ Project intervention—Participatory methods.

930. **Mednick, M. 1977.** "Ilanon." In *Insular Southeast Asia: Ethnographic Studies. Section 3. Philippines.* Comp. F. M. LeBar, vol. 2, pp. 209–228. New Haven, Conn.: Human Relations Area Files.

> Ethnographic account of a broad ethnolinguistic group once more commonly known as the Ilanon. Today, the Ilanon are often closely associated with the Muslim Maranao and Maguindao of the southern Philippines region. Traditionally a seafaring folk, the Ilano have settled coastal areas throughout the islands of the Sulu and Celebes Seas; among Europeans

the Ilanon were known as sea "pirates," with a pronounced strong tradition of maritime journey and raiding.

Philippines/ Mindanao/ Ethnography/ Indigenous and local communities.

931. **Montemayor, L. Q. 1992.** "Networking for Low-External Input and Sustainable Agriculture: The Experience of the Federation of Free Farmers." Paper presented at the International Workshop on Networking for LEISA, 9–15 March 1992, in Cavite, Silang, Philippines. Photocopy.

The author describes the work of the Federation of Free Farmers, a national organization of small farmers in the Philippines, aimed at mobilizing peasant producers facing a variety of circumstances (i.e., as owner tillers, tenant farmers, forest farmers, and municipal fishermen) into self-reliant associations able to lobby for and implement their own socio-economic development activities. The association is non-denominational and a strong advocate of land reform, including tenure reform in forested areas of the Philippines. Since the mid-1970s the group's leadership training seminars have incorporated organic and sustainable agriculture components. In particular, the association has collaborated with World Neighbors and the SALT training center at the Mindanao Baptist Rural Life Center. In 1981 the association joined other farmers' organizations to form the National Congress of Farmers Organizations to advocate policies promoting the interests of small farmers. Included in the Congress' agenda is a focus on Integrated Social Forestry and active advocacy on behalf of organic farming, diversification of production, appropriate marketing and pricing programs.

Philippines/ Social movements/ Conservation farming/ Social forestry/ Agroforestry/ Non-governmental organizations.

932. **Nava, M. J., and A. J. Ledesma. 1988.** "Rural Workers in a Sugar-Growing Village in Bukidnon, Philippines." *Voices from the Culture of Silence: The Most Disadvantaged Groups in Asian Agriculture.* Ed. I. Getubig and A. Ledesma, pp. 223–267. Kuala Lumpur: Asia and Pacific Development Center.

Major changes in Philippine rural life have resulted in the emergence of landless rural workers as a major segment of the population. Nava and Ledesma summarize findings of a study that aimed to review the plight of landless workers, assess government and non-government efforts to improve their condition, and highlight obstacles faced by this group in achieving a better standard of living. Particular emphasis was also given to understanding the perceptions of landless workers themselves. Results of survey data and interviews conducted in a sugar-growing village of Mindanao are presented. The discussion concludes with policy recommendations.

Philippines/ Mindanao/ Poverty/ Indigenous and local communities—Economy/ Agriculture—Plantations/ State policy—Agricultural and rural development.

933. **Nelson, R. A. 1994.** *Soil Erosion and Conservation in the Philippine Uplands: A Review of the Literature.* SEARCA-UQ Uplands Research Project, Working Paper no. 3. Los Ba–os, Philippines: SEARCA-UQ Uplands Research Project.

Nelso provides a broad review of the problem of soil erosion and conservation in the Philippines. Following an introductory chapter, he presents a background discussion on the general problem of soil erosion, establishing definition for soil erosion, and reviewing common ideas about its causes, effects and most promising technological solution. The focus of the working paper then turns more specifically to the problem as faced in the Philippines, with a description of the Philippines climate, upland soils, farming systems, and current estimates on the state of land degradation in the country. Highlighted as key factors in the soil erosion problem are: Deforestation, population pressure, economic development patterns that have exacerbated upland migration trends, particularly in recent decades, poverty, unequal distribution of land, the failure of agrarian reform, and institutional failure. A review of indigenous and non-indigenous soil conservation technologies in the Philippines uplands follows. Examples of the former include the Banaue rice terraces of northern Luzon, the use of enriched fallows in Naaland area of Cebu, the construction of rock and log walls in Siquijor, Cebu, Nueva Viscaya, Palawan, and the use of agroforestry in Batangas province as well as various conservation farming techniques in Cordillera mountains. Non-indigenous technologies include reforestation, hedgerow intercropping, and the "sloping agricultural land technologies" or "SALT" promoted by the Mindanao Baptist Rural Life Center. The review paper closes with an emphasis on the need for greater understanding of the farm-level constraints to soil conservation adoption.

Philippines/ Soil erosion and degradation/ Indigenous and local communities—Farming practices/ Project intervention—Soil conservation/ Project intervention—Agroforestry/ Conservation farming.

934. **Ocampo, P. 1984.** "Evaluation Report: World Neighbors Soil and Water Conservation Project." Photocopy. Cebu City, Cebu: World Neighbors.

Upland projects in five localities of Cebu are discussed: Pinamungajan, Argao, Adlawon, and Guba. Separate appendices include: Mid-term evaluation report by D. Bagalla; evaluation of the BFD/WN Soil and Water Conservation Project; memorandum by F. Seymour, Ford Foundation discussing the World Neighbors evaluation program; financial statement; and an executive summary.

Philippines/ Cebu/ Project intervention—Soil conservation/ Watershed management/ Project intervention—Participatory methods.

935. **Ofreno, R. E., and M. R. Serrano. 1991.** *Problems and Prospects of Agrarian Reform Implementation.* Diliman, Quezon City, Philippines: University of the Philippines, School of Labor and Industrial Relations; Friedrich Ebert Stiftung.

The monograph provides an overview of progress made in executing the Comprehensive Agrarian Reform Law (CARL) in the Philippines by the third year of its implementation. Major developments occurring between 1988 and 1991 are noted. The analysis is supported by questionnaire and cadastral data collected at several sites, including Bulacan, Sto. Ni-o, and Sibul, Luzon as well as South Cotabato and Basilan, Mindanao. The Basilan case study records the struggle of a labor cooperative to take over a rubber plantation once owned by Sime Darby. A major conclusion noted by the authors is that a considerable portion of the land transfers occurring under CARL have been the result of earlier legislation and resettlement on land previously classified as public, rather than the redistribution of private agricultural land. While common problems in CARL's implementation existed across all sites, there were also problems specific to each area. Of particular relevance for more recent agricultural areas (i.e., recent "frontier" areas like Mindanao) are problems of determining homesteader rights, making education about CARL more widely available, and determining appropriate beneficiaries for mountainous, unirrigated areas previously controlled by corporate livestock owners.

Philippines/ Luzon/ Mindanao/ Land reform/ Agriculture—Smallholder tree and perennial crop farming/ Social movements.

936. **Okamura, J. Y. 1986.** "Community Participation in Philippine Social Forestry." *Participatory Approaches to Development: Experiences in the Philippines.* Ed. T. S. Osteria and J. Y. Okamura, pp. 102–126. Manila: Research Center, De La Salle University.

The participatory approach to upland development means involving the people in more than the simple act of planting trees. Okamura assesses the extent to which this aim has been achieved through a review of five social forestry projects. The case studies suggest that an "only minimal" degree of community participation has been attained in social forestry thus far. Initiated by the government rather than local communities themselves, upland development projects typically "come prepackaged with a previously decided upon overall design."

Addressing this shortcoming, the author outlines a more suitable approach for Philippine Social Forestry, beginning with a review of earlier models proposed by F. Aguilar and S. Fujisaka. The author's approach "represents less a refinement of . . . (these two) models than an emphasis on certain of their principle elements" and their interrelationships. More specifically, particular emphasis is upon community participation and socioeconomic objectives over environmental objectives. Community empowerment through legally-recognized decision-making, strengthening land rights, community associations and a truly collective orientation are all stressed.

Philippines/ Project intervention—Social and community forestry/ Project intervention—Participatory methods.

937.   ———. **1988.** "The Policy of Neglect: Philippine Ethnic Minority Policy." *Southeast Asian Journal of Social Science* 16 (2): 17–46.

Okamura critically reviews ethnic minority policy in the Philippines, assessing relevant provisions in the 1987 Philippine constitution and current state policy on regional autonomy for the Cordillera people in Northern Luzon and to Muslims in Mindanao. Notes the author, little difference appears to be evident between current policies and those of PANAMIN (Presidential Assistant on National Minorities) under the Marcos regime. Constraints posed by export-oriented economic development policy for improving ethnic relations are discussed. Given current trends, it is likely that Philippine ethnic minorities will continue to occupy a subordinated position in the future.

Philippines/ Mindanao/ Indigenous and local communities—State policy/ Ethnicity and ethnic relations.

938.   **Okamura, J. Y., and T. S. Osteria. 1990.** "Operationalizing Community Participation: Primary Health Care in a Highland Community in the Philippines." *Philippine Quarterly of Culture and Society* 18 (1): 3–21.

Okamura and Osteria describe recent efforts to establish a community-based health care system among Hanunuo Mangyans upland swiddeners. Although some village-based workers have been trained and will continue to provide basic health services in the future, the Hanunuo as a whole "did not develop the social capacity or consciousness for collective action to address their health needs and concerns. . . . While the project operationalized the concept of community participation by allocating decision-making authority to the Hanunuo, the latter were not always willing or capable of assuming the duties and responsibilities that accompany such roles." Summarizing the lessons learned, the authors note that empowerment implies not simply decision-making authority, but also active participation in project development. This in turn suggests the critical importance of careful community organizing around collective needs and shared interests that have been clearly identified by community members themselves.

Philippines/ Health and nutrition/ Project intervention—Participatory methods.

939.   **Ole, T. B. 1983.** "Upland Farmers—A Profile." In Developing Tropical Uplands: A Collection of Papers on the Zamboanga del sur Development Project. Photocopy.

The collected papers outline various aspects of the Zamboanga del Sur Development Project. Data showing population growth, mortality/morbidity, ethnic composition, land use patterns, upland farms, cropping patterns and income levels in the region are presented. Investigating specific characteristics of individual participants and livelihood strategies, one paper reports that interest in gaining security and increased income tended to be strongly dependent on farm size. That is, those farmers with small landholdings tended to seek more off-farm employment across longer distances in order to secure income. Major problems perceived by the people relate to government services/facilities, poor transportation facilities, inadequate supplies of potable water, and difficulties in obtaining credit. In conclusion, the authors note, uplanders are "rational" beings, attempting to satisfy at least three major goals: 1) increased income, 2) improved food security, and 3) minimizing risk.

Philippines/ Mindanao/ Project intervention—Rural development/ Poverty/ Health and nutrition.

940. **Olofson, H., ed. 1981.** *Adaptive Strategies and Change in Philippines Swidden-based Societies.* Laguna, Philippines: Forest Research Institute College.

Philippines/ Agriculture—Shifting cultivation/ Agriculture—Shifting cultivation's environmental impacts/ Indigenous and local communities—Forest land use and management practices/ Indigenous and local communities—Farming practices/ Indigenous and local communities—Land and resource tenure systems/ Indigenous and local communities—Commoditization/ Population pressure/ Agricultural intensification.

941. ———. **1985.** "Traditional Agroforestry, Parcel Management, and Social Forestry Development in a Pioneer Agricultural Community: The Case of Jalajala, Rizal, Philippines." *Agroforestry Systems* 3: 317–337.

Olofson describes agroforestry systems that have been developed by a small community of migrant farmers. Case studies of individual farmers are presented to describe landholding and cropping patterns and the role played by agroforestry technologies in managing scattered farm parcels. The paper concludes with implications for further research and the social forestry efforts currently being undertaken in the community.

Philippines/ Migrant farmers and farming/ Indigenous and local communities—Farming practices/ Farm management—Cropping systems/ Indigenous and local communities—Forest land use and management practices/ Agroforestry/ Social forestry.

942. **Olofson, H., and R. Alburo. 1991.** "Strategies for Sustaining Agriculture, Natural Resources, and Communities in the Uplands of the Insular Economies of Southeast Asia." Report prepared for the Working Meeting on the MacArthur Planning Grant on Strategies for Sustaining Agriculture, Natural Resources, and Communities in the Uplands of the Insular Economies of Southeast Asia, 2–11 January 1992, in Cebu City, Philippines. Photocopy.

Philippines/ Cebu/ Deforestation/ Soil erosion and degradation/ Poverty/ Rural development/ Forest management—Forest resource conservation.

943. **Ooi Jin Bee. 1987.** "Depletion of the Forest Resources in the Philippines." Field Report Series, no. 18. Singapore: Institute of Southeast Asian Studies.

Philippines/ Deforestation/ Timber industry—Logging.

944. **Ozbilen, E. 1971.** "The Philippines: Shifting Cultivation." Technical Report. Demonstration and Training in Forest, Forest Range and Watershed Manage-

ment, no. 9. Rome: Food and Agriculture Organization of the United Nations.

This report discusses current problems associated with shifting cultivation in the Philippines. Of major concern on many islands of the Philippines is the problem of upland farming. Particularly problematic has been the role of poverty-stricken lowland farmers forced to seek arable land in the uplands, where they engage inappropriate farming technology causing accelerated soil erosion.

Philippines/ Agriculture—Shifting cultivation's environmental impacts/ Migrant farmers and farming/ Soil erosion and degradation/ Forest management—Control of shifting cultivation.

945. **Pabuayon, I. M. 1991.** "Rattan Resources Accounting." Technical Report, No. 5. Manila: Natural Resources Accounting Project, Department of Environment and Natural Resources (DENR).

Philippines/ Non-timber forest products/ Rattan—Resource management and conservation/ Forest management—Economics.

946. **Paderanga,Jr., Cayetano W. 1995.** *A Review of Land Settlements in the Philippines*. Mindanao Studies Reports, 1995/ No. 2. Quezon City: University of the Philippines, Center for Integrative and Development Studies.

Paderanga presents a historical account of the settlement of Mindanao from 1900 to 1975. The report begins with an overview of various land settlement schemes under U.S. colonial rule, the Commonwealth Period (1935–1946), immediate post-independence (1946–1960), and the more recent, "regional awareness" period of the 1970s during which the government paid growing attention to the spatial dimensions of development. More detailed case studies are provided on the settlement of the Digos-Padada Valley in Davao Province during the first half of the 20th century, the Central Palawan Resettlement project undertaken during the 1950s, and the Nueva Ecija Resettlement Project No. 1, which relocated a number of villages from the area of the planned Pantabangan dam complex to new sites at the border of the Central Luzon plains. A final section attempts to assess the degree of success achieved by various settlement efforts and their impacts on both the migrant supplying and receiving areas. Early resettlement programs aimed at colonizing frontier areas on Mindanao and Palawan proved very successful in this respect, facilitating a major increase in the population density of these areas and a marked shift in the demographic profile of the country more generally. Effects on overcrowded areas and minority groups are of much more ambiguous nature, however. Resettlement failed to reduce in any significant way problems of poverty and landlessness in the country, and in many cases engendered growing land conflicts between tribal inhabitants and new settlers in the receiving areas. Concludes the author, while land settlement may facilitate population redistribution and agricultural growth with the expansion of farm land, solving agrarian problems will require attention to a much more complex range of issues than simply the transfer of tenant farmers or surplus population.

Philippines/ Mindanao/ Land settlement and development/ Migration/ Land settlement and development—Impacts on local communities and economy/ State policy—Land development/ History—Colonial.

947. **Pagaduan, M. C. 1988.** "Mindanao Peasant Women: A Participatory Research Investigation of their Realities and Potentials." *Community Development Journal* 23 (3): 195–201.

Philippines/ Mindanao/ Gender relations/ Gender analysis.

948. **Palmer, J. 1991.** "Interactions Between the Social, Ecological, and Technical Factors Underlying the Success of SALT: The Case of the MBLRC." Paper presented at the First Cagayan Valley Programme on Environment and Development Conference, 26–29 August 1991, Cabagan, Isabela, Philippines. Photocopy.

The Sloping Agricultural Land Technology (SALT) is a "hillside farming system designed with farmers for farmers and by farmers." Experience shows that this approach has proven itself successful in many ways: sociologically, ecologically, and technically. More and more farmers are adopting SALT with the result that "for each one SALT project that is implemented, we win another small battle in the war against hunger, erosion, deforestation, and poverty in the hillsides."

Philippines/ Mindanao/ Project intervention—Agroforestry/ Project intervention—Participatory methods.

949. **Pamplona, P. P. 1987.** "Rubber Intercropping for Small Landholders." *Pcarrd Monitor* 15 (9): 8–9.

Philippines/ Mindanao/ Agriculture—Permanent/ Agriculture—Smallholder tree and perennial crop farming/ Agriculture—Smallholder cash crop farming/ Agroforestry.

950. **Pante, F. Jr., and Mario B. Lamberte. 1989.** "Recent Policy-Oriented Research and Current Policy Issues: A Cursory Review." Working paper, no. 89–17. Makati, Metro Manila: Philippine Institute for Development Studies.

This paper reviews policy-oriented research on the past and future course of economic development in the Philippines. A section on forest resources management covers policies specific to the forestry sector as well as those with indirect effects on forestry such as the tariff system and exchange rates. The need for particular attention to issues of cutting charges, licensing, and halting both illegal and overcutting is noted. There also an urgent need for an improved land classification scheme that can facilitate rational management of national forest lands in order to sustain optimal output from the forestry sector in its three major roles—production, protection, and recreation. A short bibliography on recent (1980 or later) publications pertaining to natural resources and environmental damage is provided.

Philippines/ Economic development/ Timber industry—State policy and regulation/ State policy—Forest and natural resources.

951. **Pava, H. et al. n.d.** "The Himaya Bukidnon: Musuan Experience." Research report. Photocopy. Musuan, Bukidnon, Philippines: Central Mindanao University.

Results of a recent field study are presented to suggest that the lack of soil conservation and appropriate crop management is a key factor behind the poverty of many indigenous farmers in Bukidnon.

Philippines/ Mindanao/ Indigenous and local communities—Farming practices/ Soil erosion and degradation/ Poverty/ Agriculture—Shifting cultivation.

952. **Pava, H. M. et al. n.d.** "Participatory Processes to Upland Development: The Musuan Model." Musuan Program Monogram Series, no. 2. University Town, Musuan, Bukidnon: Central Mindanao University.

Designed to complement the Integrated Social Forestry project, the MUSUAN program aims to resolve specific social and economic constraints encountered at particular ISF sites.

Originally located in Himaya, Maramag, Bukidnon on Mindanao island, the MUSUAN pilot project was later expanded to three other upland areas in the province. Major steps undertaken by the project are outlined in the report, including selection of site and participants, participant trainings, cross farm visits, technology selection, design of individual farm plans and subsequent implementation of these plans. The report ends with a discussion of some of the main lessons learned from the MUSUAN project experience, among which the problem of obtaining sustained commitment by farm-cooperators to the new technologies remains paramount.

Philippines/ Mindanao/ Project intervention—Agroforestry/ Project intervention—Social and community forestry.

953.   **Pelzer, K. 1945.** *Pioneer Settlement in the Asiatic Tropics.* Special Publication, no. 29. New York: American Geographical Society.

Population distribution in the Asian tropics is considered, with particular focus on the Philippines and Indonesia. The author argues that population is poorly distributed in the region, with islands like Java and Luzon suffering increasingly serious over-population and declining person:land ratios, while other islands remain sparsely settled by "primitive" swidden farmers. Government assistance is needed to encourage the migration of households from over-populated areas to areas where arable land is still plentiful. Case studies of government-sponsored resettlement schemes in Mindanao, the Philippines, and Lampung province on Sumatra, Indonesia are presented.

Asia/ Philippines/ Mindanao/ Indonesia/ Sumatra/ Migration/ Land settlement and development/ State policy—Land development/ History—Colonial.

954.   **Peñalba, L. M. 1991.** "Land Use Conversion Policies and the Comprehensive Agrarian Reform Program." IAST Occasional Papers Series, No. 34. College, Laguna, Philippines: Institute of Agrarian Studies, College of Economics and Management, University of the Philippines at Los Baños.

The paper focuses on the problem of conversion of agricultural land to non-agricultural uses around urban centers in the Philippines, as this relates to rising landlessness in the farming population.

Philippines/ Land use—Patterns and planning/ Poverty.

955.   **Pendleton, R. J. 1942.** "Land Utilization and Agriculture of Mindanao, Philippine Islands." *Geographical Review* 32: 180–210.

Philippines/ Mindanao/ Land use—Patterns and planning/ Agricultural development/ Migrant farmers and farming/ Agriculture—Shifting cultivation/ Land settlement and development.

956.   **Philippine Council for Agriculture, Forestry and Natural Resources Research and Development (PCARRD). 1990.** *Rattan: Proceedings of the National Symposium/Workshop on Rattan, 1–3 June 1988, Ecotech Center, Lahug, Cebu City, Philippines.* Book Series, No. 99/1990. Laguna, Los Ba–os, Philippines: Philippine Council for Agriculture, Forestry and Natural Resources Research and Development (PCARRD); International Development Research Center (IDRC).

Philippines/ Non-timber forest products/ Rattan—Resource management and conservation/ Rattan—Cultivation/ Rattan—Downstream processing.

957.   ————. **1990.** *Soil and Water Conservation Measures and Agroforestry*. Proceedings of the Training Workshop on Soil and Water Conservation Measures and Agroforestry, 9–16 July 1989, Los Ba–os, Laguna, Philippines. Book Series, no. 103/1990. Los Ba–os, Laguna, Philippines: Philippine Council for Agriculture, Forestry and Natural Resources Research and Development, Department of Science and Technology.

The first part of this monograph includes a series of papers providing an overview of problems relating to soil erosion and hydrological regimes. A number of papers present data useful for gauging more locally-specific rates of erosion, infiltration, and watershed regeneration in the Philippines. The main measures being deployed through various state agencies are described. Also included are case studies of soil and water conservation experiences in specific localities. The monograph's second half deals exclusively with agroforestry in the Philippines, describing various practices and current research and development efforts being made in the Philippines. A list of completed, ongoing, new and proposed agroforestry projects monitored by PCARRD is also presented. A series of individual papers describe in more specific detail the agroforestry practices found in the different regions of country.

Philippines/ Soil erosion and degradation/ Hydrology/ Watershed management/ Project intervention—Agroforestry/ Indigenous and local communities—Farming practices.

958.   **Philippine Council for Agriculture, Forestry, and Natural Resources Research and Development (PCARRD). 1991.** *The Philippines Recommends for Rattan Production*. PCARRD Philippines Recommends Series, No. 55-A. Los Ba–os, Laguna, Philippines: Philippine Council for Agriculture, Forestry and Natural Resources Research and Development; National Program Coordinating Office.

Philippines/ Non-timber forest products/ Rattan—Resource management and conservation/ Rattan—Cultivation/ Rattan—Downstream processing.

959.   Philippine Council for Agriculture, Forestry and Natural Resources Research and Development (PCARRD) and the Rainforest Resources Development Project. 1991. *State of the Art and Abstract Bibliography: Agroforestry Research in the Philippines*. Forestry SOA AB Series, no. 8/1991. Los Ba–os, Laguna, Philippines: PCARRD, Department of Science and Technology; Rainfed Resources Development Project, Government of the Philippines and U.S.A.I.D.

A 93-page monograph representing one of the most complete and up-to-date reference sources for current research on agroforestry-related issues in the Philippines. Increasingly critical problems of land and resource degradation in the Philippines have promoted the perception that agroforestry may be one of the most appropriate land uses for fragile forest uplands where agricultural activity has been rapidly expanding. An initial summarizing paper of the monograph provides an overview of government programs related to agroforestry as well as a detailed review of the concept of agroforestry, especially as it pertains to current issues on resource management in the Philippines. Subsequent papers discuss the results of past research on various aspects of agroforestry, such as its role and effects on the local environment and agricultural production, the potential of various cash crops, nitrogen-fixing trees and legumes for agroforestry, and the socioeconomics of agroforestry practice. While largely descriptive, the monograph provides a highly useful overview about the kinds of agroforestry-related research which have been conducted over the last two decades.

Philippines/ Agroforestry/ Bibliography/ Project intervention—Agroforestry/ Farm management—Economics.

960.   **Philippine National Task Force, and Population Center Foundation. 1979.** "Population in Asian Forestry Communities Practicing Shifting Cultivation: The Case of the Philippines." Paper presented at Second Intercountry Consultation on the UNDP/ FAO Shifting Cultivators Project, Jogjakarta. Photocopy.

   Demographic and physical characteristics of the Philippines and its upland situation are described. In addition, the paper presents a discussion of kainginero lifestyles and practices along with a typology of kainginero groups. Government plans for shifting cultivators as exemplified by BFD, PANAMIN and Ministry of Human Settlement Policies are described sympathetically, although budget constraints continue to be a problem.

   Philippines/ Agriculture—Shifting cultivation/ Migrant farmers and farming/ Indigenous and local communities—Farming practices/ Demography/ Forest management—Control of shifting cultivation.

961.   **Porter, G., and D. J. Ganapin. 1988.** *Resources, Population, and the Philippines' Future: A Case Study*. Washington, D.C.: World Resources Institute.

   Philippines/ Deforestation/ Soil erosion and degradation/ Population pressure/ Forest management—Forest resource conservation/ State policy—Forest and natural resources.

962.   **Power, J. H., and Tessie D. Tumaneng. n.d.** "Comparative Advantage and Government Price Intervention Policies in Forestry." Working Paper, no. 83-05. Makati, Metro Manila: Philippine Institute for Development Studies.

   Philippines/ Timber industry—Trade and markets/ Timber industry—State policy and regulation/ Forest management—Economics.

963.   **Puhlin, J. M. 1985.** "Integrated Social Forestry Program: Will It Succeed?" *PESAM Bulletin* 5 (3): 9–11.

   The author describes the background, initial accomplishments and common problems of the Integrated Social Forestry Program (ISFP). Specific problems include 1) low income return to ISF projects, 2) a lack of personnel who are qualified to effectively carry out the program, 3) an approach to project monitoring that ignores social and economic effects, 4) limited people-based participation in planning and decision making and 5) some indications that project returns are accruing more to rich and influential persons than to the rural poor. Recommendations for overcoming these problems are suggested.

   Philippines/ Project intervention—Social and community forestry/ Project intervention—Participatory methods.

964.   **Queblatin, E. 1985.** "Upland Agriculture Development: The Central Visayas Regional Project-I. Experience." *Soil erosion management*. Proceedings of a workshop, 3–5 December 1984, PCARRD, Los Ba–os, Philippines. Ed. E. Craswell, J. Remenyi, and L. G. Nallana, pp. 71–76. Canberra, A.C.T.: Australian Centre for International Agricultural Research.

   Problems of soil erosion and conservation in the Central Visayas are examined, with a focus on the implementation of a large World Bank funded project in the region.

   Philippines/ Cebu/ Project intervention—Rural development/ Project intervention—Soil conservation/ Soil erosion and degradation.

965.   **Quisumbing, Ma. A. 1987.** "Land Reform for Forest and Upland Areas: Some Suggestions." Institute of Agrarian Studies Occasional Paper, no. 22. College,

Laguna, Philippines: Institute of Agrarian Studies, College of Development and Management, University of the Philippines at Los Ba–os.

Philippines/ Land reform.

966.   **Raintree, J. B., and H. A. Francisco, eds. 1994.** *Marketing of Multipurpose Tree Products in Asia.* Proceedings of an international workshop held in Baguio City, Philippines, 6–9 December 1993. Bangkok: Winrock International.

Eight sections cover different themes related to multipurpose tree product marketing in different Southeast Asian countries, at different scales of operation, and in connection with different products. Section themes include: 1) Marketing of multipurpose tree products; 2) Woodfuel and timber markets; 3) Marketing of multipurpose food trees; 4) Industrial markets; 5) Impacts of markets on rural development: farm forestry, agroforestry and non-timber forest products; 6) Market information systems; 7) Innovative approaches (including case studies of green marketing, plantation development and marketing in West Sumatra, and MPT product marketing by the Ikalahan in the Cordilleras of Northern Luzon); and 8) Working group reports. Products discussed include fuelwood in Cebu and Asia, timber in Sri Lanka, *Parka speciosa* fruits in Peninsular Malaysia, Jackfruit in the Central Visayas, *Artocarpus* species in Nepal, industrial wood in Pakistan, India, Thailand, and the Philippines, and *kapok* in West Sumatra.

Asia/ Indonesia/ Sumatra/ Kalimantan/ Philippines/ Cebu/ Palawan/ Agroforestry/ Non-timber forest products/ Indigenous and local communities—Forest products use and trade/ Fuelwood/ Agricultural economics.

967.   **Ravanera, R. 1990.** "Impact of an Agri-Based Transnational Enterprises [sic] on Peasants and Peasant Community: The Case of Del Monte in Bukidnon." IAST Occasional Papers Series, No. 33. College, Laguna, Philippines: Institute of Agrarian Studies, College of Economics and Management, University of the Philippines at Los Ba–os.

Ravanera briefly reviews the history of the Del Monte pineapple plantation in Bukidnon province, Mindanao and examines the impact of the plantation on the communities around the plantation area. While taking up much of the arable land in the area, the plantation has brought little long-term benefit to the local population: the amount of labor absorbed into the plantation labor force is limited, and most workers continue to earn very low wages. In one part of the plantation, Del Monte controls 1,822 ha of land while local smallholders control only 307 ha. Presently 80 percent of the labor force in the area are agricultural workers and less than 20 percent of these have an income above the national poverty threshold. Given these statistics, it is likely that rather than offering a viable alternative to smallholder farming in Bukidnon, the Del Monte plantation is exacerbating pressures on local households to move further upland in search of arable land and adequate livelihood.

Philippines/ Mindanao/ Agriculture—Plantations/ Land settlement and development—Impacts on local communities and economy.

968.   **Rebogio, L. L. 1984.** "A Brief Analysis of Socio-economic Constraints to Social Forestry in the Philippines." Paper presented at the EWC/FAO workshop on the Socio-economic aspects of Social Forestry in the Asia-Pacific Region, 18–22 September 1984, Bangkok, Thailand. Photocopy.

Reviewing six evaluation studies of social forestry projects in the Philippines, this paper attempts to identify the most frequently cited constraints to project success. These constraints may be categorized as follows: the environment, poor specification of targets (goals/objectives), lack of appropriate technology options, and need for facilitative agency/strategy.

Philippines/ Project intervention—Social and community forestry.

969.   **Remedio, E., H. Olofson, and L. Batomalaque. 1989.** "Socio-Economic Baseline Survey for Balha-an." Report prepared for the Community Nature Park and Tourism Development Project for Matutinao. Photocopy. Cebu City, Cebu: ARTC, San Carlos University.

Philippines/ Cebu/ Forest management—Parks and conservation areas/ Land use—Patterns and planning/ Demography/ Rural development.

970.   **Remedio, E., H. Olofson, and J. Lendio. 1990.** "Socio-Economic Survey of Solsogan, Badian, Cebu." Report prepared for the Community Nature Park and Tourism Development Project. Photocopy. Cebu City, Philippines: ARTC, University of San Carlos.

Philippines/ Cebu/ Forest management—Parks and conservation areas/ Demography/ Land use—Patterns and planning/ Rural development.

971.   **Remedio, E., H. Olofson, and J. Adlawan. 1991.** "Socio-Economic Survey for Matutinao." Report prepared for the Community Nature Park and Tourism Development Project for Matutinao. Photocopy. Cebu City, Philippines: ARTC, University of San Carlos.

Philippines/ Cebu/ Forest management—Parks and conservation areas/ Land use—Patterns and planning/ Rural development/ Demography.

972.   **Revilla, A. V. 1981.** "Land Assessment and Management for Sustainable Uses in the Philippines." In *Assessing Tropical Forest Lands: Their Suitability for Sustainable Use.* Ed. R. Carpenter. Dublin: Tycooly.

Philippines/ Land use—Patterns and planning.

973.   **Reyes, M. R., and V. B. Mendoza. 1983.** "The Pantabangan Watershed Management and Erosion Control Project." In *Forest Watershed Development and Conservation in Asia and the Pacific.* Ed. L. S. Hamilton, pp. 485–553. Boulder, Co.: Westview Press.

Philippines/ Watershed management/ Forest management—Control of shifting cultivation/ Project intervention—Soil conservation/ State policy—Forest and natural resources.

974.   **Riveria, P. C. 1979.** "Shifting Cultivation: The Asian Perspective." *Initiatives in Population* 5 (4): 26–30.

Attempting to correct past government neglect of forest communities, a regional project (the "Slash and Burn" project) sponsored by the FAO and UNFPA was designed to examine the extent and effects of shifting cultivation in various Asian countries. Riviera focuses on findings from Phase I of this study in the Philippines, which attempted to develop a typology of all kaingineros found in the country based on the field data gathered. Comparative typologies from other Asian countries are also presented. Phase II of the project will be action-oriented, involving more detailed data gathering, development planning, pilot projects, and evaluation strategies.

Philippines/ Agriculture—Shifting cultivation/ Migrant farmers and farming/ Indigenous and local communities—Farming practices/ Forest management—Control of shifting cultivation.

975. **Romero, M. R. 1991.** "Watershed Management: Impacts on Tumauini Irrigation System, Tumauini, Isabela, Philippines." Paper presented at First Cagayan Valley Programme on Environment and Development Conference, 26–29 August, Cabagan, Isalbela, Philippines. Photocopy.

> Sediment discharges in the Pinacanauan de Tumaunini River were measured to estimate the impact of (upland) soil erosion upon the (downstream) irrigation system. The irrigation system's performance was described and assessed in terms of total area irrigated, expenses, collection efficiency, cropping intensity. Collected data reveal that the system's performance has been less than satisfactory. Failing to attain specified targets, the system has also been plagued by steadily climbing expenses. Farmer irrigators generally agreed that there has been a decrease in water supply over time, attributing this poor performance to activities of loggers and/or kaingineros upstream. An economic analysis indicates that a watershed protection/conservation project will significantly increase the economic benefits of the irrigation system.

> Philippines/ Soil erosion and degradation/ Watershed management/ Farm management—Economics.

976. **Rood, S., and A. L. Casambre. 1993.** "State Policy, Indigenous Community Practice, and Sustainability in the Cordillera, Northern Philippines." Paper prepared for the Tenth Annual Berkeley Conference on Southeast Asian Studies, "Examining Sustainability in Southeast Asian Fields, Forests, and Fisheries," 20–21 February 1993, in Berkeley, Calif. Photocopy.

> Written in preparation for fieldwork in the Cordillera region of Luzon island, Philippines this paper aims to illuminate how interactions between state policy and community practice affect sustainability. Initial paragraphs describe past contradictions in Philippine national land policy which on the one hand recognized indigenous people's customary rights over land, and on the other hand negated these rights by declaring all forest lands as public domain under control of the state. Also discussed is the relative weakness of the Philippine state in enforcing its own policies, both in terms of preventing settlement of commercially lucrative forest lands and, more recently, in terms of implementing new sustainability-and land reform-oriented policies.
>
> In a second major section of the paper the authors discuss how these national land policies and the conflicts surrounding them have been played out in the Cordillera region. The authors advocate community-level investigation of these processes, given the diversity among local communities both in terms of indigenous land tenure systems and in terms of the extent to which local farmers are involved in market-oriented production. Such diversity throws considerable doubt on recent assertions of regionally based claims for ancestral domain as well as regionally defined community-based resource management schemes. In reality, note the authors, considerable divisions exists among the local communities concerning a unifying Cordilleran identity. Combined with a general mistrust of government-imposed systems for resource management, these divisions resulted in the rejection of a 1990 referendum proposing regional autonomy for the Cordilleras. The authors hypothesize that sustainable management of local forest and land resources in the Cordilleras will proceed only with the genuine empowerment of local communities to govern their own resources and a devolution of power to indigenous political structures capable of forestalling the rapid commodification of local land resources at the hands of profit-oriented individuals.

> Philippines/ Land tenure—Legislation and state policy/ Indigenous and local communities—Land and resource tenure systems/ Indigenous and local communities—Forest land use and management practices/ Social movements/ Ethnicity and ethnic relations/ Politics.

977. **Roth, D. 1983.** "Philippine Forests and Forestry: 1565-1920." In *Global Deforestation and the Nineteenth Century World Economy*. Ed. R. P. Tucker and J. F. Richards. Durham, N.C.: Duke University Press.

Philippines/ History—Colonial/ Timber industry—Logging/ Timber industry—Development and structure/ Timber industry—Trade and markets/ Deforestation.

978.   **Saito, S. 1968.** *Preliminary Bibliography of Philippine Ethnography.* Quezon City, Philippines: Institute of Philippine Culture, The Rizal Library, Ateneo de Manila.

The monograph offers an extensive bibliography categorized by region and subject. Regions covered are General, Luzon, Visayas and Palawan, Mindanao and Sulu. Subject headings total 48, and include, among others: Agriculture and Animal Husbandry; Agriculture and Food; Anthropology; Community and Community Development; Community Development, Community and Territorial Organization; Demography; Economics; Ethnic Influences; Family and Kinship; Geography and Demography; Health and Sickness; History and Culture Change; Labor; Land Tenure and Land Reform; Law and Justice; Light and Heavy Industries; Mobility and Social Stratification; Nationalism; Political Science; Sociology; Total Culture.

Philippines/ Ethnography/ Bibliography.

979.   **Sajise, P. E. 1972.** "Evaluation of Cogon (*Imperata Cylindrica (L.) Beauv.*) As a Seral Stage in Philippine Vegetational Succession." Ph.D. diss., Cornell University, Ithaca, N.Y.

Philippines/ Forest regeneration/ Pest, weed, and crop disease management.

980.   ———. **1982.** "Social Forestry in Upland Development." Paper delivered during the 72nd Alumni Homecoming, 29 April 1982, at the College of Forestry, University of the Philippines at Los Ba–os. Photocopy.

In the past, upland agricultural practices were well-suited to their ecological setting. Over recent decades, however, population growth and the introduction of inappropriate lowland technologies have changed this. The paper discusses three basic questions which come up in any attempt to address these problems, namely: 1) What really are the goals in upland development and what indicators can be used to measure their attainment? 2) What is the best procedure for developing appropriate and site-specific upland development programs? 3) What is the most appropriate management strategy and institutional structure for promoting and sustaining elements of flexibility, interdisciplinary capability and commitment, while still retaining both an indigenous and interagency character? The author notes four additional issues that will assume increasing importance in the future: population pressure, inheritance patterns, tenure status, and the present educational systems.

Philippines/ Rural development/ Social forestry.

981.   ———. **1984.** "Upland Farming Systems." In *Uplands and Uplanders.* Proceedings of the First National Conference on Research in the Uplands, 11–13 April 1983, Quezon City, Philippines Ed. C. P. Castro, pp. 135–156. Quezon City, Philippines: BFD-Upland Development Program.

Philippines/ Farming systems research/ Farm management—Cropping systems/.

982.   ———. **1985.** "Agroforestry and Land Tenure Issues in the Philippines." In *Land, Trees and Tenure.* Proceedings of the International Workshop on Tenure Issues in Agroforestry, 27–31 May 1985, Nairobi, Kenya. Ed. J. B. Raintree, pp. 273–276. Nairobi; Madison, Wis.: International Council for Research in Agroforestry; Land Tenure Center.

Philippines/ Land tenure/ Project intervention—Agroforestry/ Agroforestry.

983. **Sajise, P. E., and D. B. Magcale. 1987.** "Soil Erosion in the Philippines and Other Asia-Pacific Countries." *Solidarity* 115 (November–December): 79–88.

The authors provide an overview of the results of recent research on soil erosion and soil nutrient loss in various part of the Philippines and other Asian countries. Specific authors are cited although more complete citations of the work described are not provided.

Philippines/ Southeast Asia/ Soil erosion and degradation.

984. **Sajise, P., and D. J. Ganapin Jr. 1991.** "An Overview of Upland Development in the Philippines." In *Technologies for Sustainable Agriculture on Marginal Uplands in Southeast Asia*. Proceedings of a seminar held at Ternate, Cavite, Philippines, 10–14 December 1990. Ed. G. Blair and R. Lefroy, pp. 31–44. Canberra: Australian Centre for International Agricultural Research (ACIAR).

Sajise and Ganapin describe prevailing land uses and land cover classification in the Philippines based on SPOT imagery taken by the Swedish Space Corporation in 1987, which showed only 23.9 percent of forest cover remaining in the country and expanding areas of land under agricultural use. Data on upland population growth and rates of deforestation across the country are presented and discussed. This is followed by a brief discussion of appropriate definitions for the uplands and a review of current state of research concerning upland development. Covered in the review are: the broad characteristics of upland, hilly land, and highland sites, the problems in sustainability faced in these areas, most promising technologies for upland soil conservation and development, factors behind the success of these technologies, and successful strategies upland extension and general upland development. The paper closes with a list of research questions and areas needing further attention by the research and development communities. These are related to land tenure, population, equity, education, empowerment, upland-lowland interaction, armed conflict, and policy reform.

Philippines/ Agricultural development/ Land use—Patterns and planning/ Deforestation/ Soil erosion and degradation/ Conservation farming/ Project intervention—Soil conservation.

985. **Sajise, P., and D. B. Magcale. 1983.** "Status of Soil Erosion in the Philippines and Some Countries in Asia and the Pacific." Paper presented during the UNLP Press Foundation of Asia Seminar on the Environment, 12–18 December 1983, Manila, Philippines. Photocopy.

Philippines/ Soil erosion and degradation.

986. **SANREM CRSP-Philippines. n.d.** "A Participatory Landscape-Lifescape Analysis of the Manupali Watershed in Bukidnon, Philippines: Characterization and Identification of Research Priorities for the SANREM-CRSP." Paper prepared by the SANREM-CRSP Survey Team, Cagayan de Oro City, Philippines. Photocopy.

This 20 pp. paper provides the results of a participatory appraisal exercise undertaken in the Manupali watershed, Lantapan district in Bukidnon province, Nov. 22 through Dec. 6, 1992.

Philippines/ Mindanao/ Indigenous and local communities—Farming practices/ Indigenous and local communities—Forest land use and management practices/ Migrant farmers and farming/ Agriculture—Shifting cultivation/ Agriculture—Permanent/ Agriculture—Smallholder cash crop farming/ Project intervention—Participatory methods.

987.   **SANREM-CRSP, Philippines. 1993.** "Framework Plan." A Research and Development Program for a Landscape Approach to Sustainability in the Tropics (LAST), prepared by the Philippines Program of the Sustainable Agricultural and Natural Resource Management Collaborative Research Support Program (SANREM CRSP). Photocopy.

This draft document describes the action-research framework being developed by the SANREM-CRSP network for the Manupali watershed, Lantapan district, Bukidnon province. A list of network participants is included.

Philippines/ Watershed management/ Project intervention—Rural development/ Project intervention—Soil conservation.

988.   **Sather, C. 1977.** "Bajau Laut." In *Insular Southeast Asia: Ethnographic Studies. Section 3. Philippines.* Comp. F. M. LeBar, vol. 2, pp. 165–184. New Haven, Conn.: Human Relations Area Files.

Ethnographic account of the Bajau Laut, a dispersed ethnolinguistic group found today in coastal areas of islands embracing the Sulu and Celebes seas, most notably on the Sulu archipelago, Semporna District in Sabah, the Kalimantan coast, and Sulawesi.

Philippines/ Mindanao/ Indigenous and local communities/ Ethnography.

989.   **Schlegel, S. A. 1967.** "Tiruray Constellation: The Agricultural Astronomy of a Philippine Hill People." *Philippine Journal of Science* 96 (3): 301–331.

Philippines/ Mindanao/ Indigenous and local communities—Religion and cosmology.

990.   **———. 1979.** *Tiruray Subsistence: From Shifting Cultivation to Plow Agriculture.* Quezon City, Philippines: Ateneo de Manila University Press.

Drawing from field research conducted from 1966 through 1967, this book reports the findings and analysis of subsistence livelihood patterns among the Tiruray, an indigenous cultural minority in Southeast Mindanao. Notes Schlegel, study of Tiruray subsistence requires a close examination of two very different systems: traditional swidden farming still practiced by those Tiruray living in the still forested reaches of the Cotabato Cordillera up the Tan Grande River in southeastern Mindanao, and those living the largely deforested grasslands in the northern parts of the mountain range, closer to Cotabato City, now practicing plow-based, sedentary agriculture, mostly as tenants on lands owned by native Muslim Maguindanaon and immigrant Christian Ilocanos and Ilongos.

For traditional Tiruray in the forested upriver area of the Cordillera mountain range, a combination of swidden farming, hunting, forest product gathering, and some trade with downriver traders provides a secure subsistence base which is preferred to sedentary farming both because of higher returns to labor and the food security it provides. For the Tiruray in the downriver reaches of the Cordillera, a shift to sedentary farming as tenant peasants began with the opening up of the Cotabato Cordillera during American colonial rule in the early 20th century. American administrators at the time encouraged immigration to the valleys of the mountain range by lowland Maguindanaon as well as new homesteaders from other islands. As large areas of northern part of the mountain range were cleared of forest cover by the homesteaders, a shift to plow agriculture among those Tiruray swiddeners who did not retreat from outsider encroachment was strongly encouraged. While some Tiruray were able at first to obtain legal title to land as sedentary farmers, over the years, these titles were lost, and by 1960s, "virtually all plow-farming Tiruray in the peasant areas were working the land of Ilocanos or Ilongos as tenants."

Transformation of the once heavily forested region begun by incoming homesteaders was massively accelerated with the onset of large-scale logging in the region in the 1960s, displacing large numbers of Tiruray, who now faced the choice of either retreating further upriver or becoming tenant,farmers for those able to obtain title to the cleared land. With the forest now virtually eliminated from the landscape, shifting cultivation became increasingly less possible, household diets became less varied, and Tiruray farmers became heavily dependent on the market to procure subsistence goods, with only the "goodwill and generosity of the landlord" to fall back on during bad times. This change from integral, only marginally market-dependent, swidden-based society to market-and landlord-class dependent ethnic group within wider, Filipino society, represents an "externally imposed transformation" that even upriver Tiruray are likely to face as forests of the Cotabato Cordillera continue to disappear and the Tiruray world continues to change.

Philippines/ Mindanao/ Ethnography/ Indigenous and local communities—Economy/ Indigenous and local communities—Commoditization/ Indigenous and local communities— Farming practices/ Indigenous and local communities—Forest land use and management practices/ Indigenous and local communities—Forest products use and trade/ Indigenous and local communities—Social relations/ Land settlement and development—Impacts on local communities and economy/ Ethnicity and ethnic relations/ Agriculture—Shifting cultivation/ Health and nutrition.

991. **Schreurs, P. 1981.** "Agusan's Loggers: Hewers of Wood and Carriers of Water." *Philippine Quarterly of Culture and Society* 9: 261–274.

Schreurs seeks to challenge some of the anti-logging sentiments now being voiced by various sectors. To begin, the paper questions the commonly held notion that deforestation in Agusan has caused recurring flooding in this area. Historical research demonstrates that there were numerous floods which occurred in Agusan during the previous century, that is, even at a time when forest cover was still dense. Heavy precipitation and steeply sloping terrain combine to make regular flooding in Agusan more or less inevitable. Secondly, the author challenges the assumption that trees slow down water flows better than grass or shrubs. Third, areas reforested by "responsible" loggers appear to have a record in flood control which is about as good as that found for virgin forest. Even if loggers are less responsible, secondary growth and plant cover usually come back quickly. Finally, upland farmers are likely doing more harm than the loggers. Continuous cultivation of upland slopes for crops like corn seems to be the real culprit. Argues the author, floods have become an urgent concern in Agusan, not because they are occurring more frequently, but because more people are living in the area than ever before and because media coverage of such disasters has increased. Given these realities, the author urges the application of flood control methods other than logging bans (e.g., dredging of rivers) to deal with the current situation in Agusan province.

Philippines/ Timber industry—Logging/ Timber industry—Environmental impacts.

992. **Scott, W. H. 1982.** *Cracks in the Parchment Curtain*. Quezon City, Philippines: New Day Publishers.

This monograph presents a collection of essays focusing on the history of the Philippines during the Spanish and U.S. colonial periods. Attempting to look through "cracks in the parchment" enshrouding the Filipino history constructed by Spanish and U.S. colonial authorities, Scott constructs an alternative national history developed from the indigenous Filipino point of view. Two essays on "Filipino class structure in the sixteenth century" and "Class structure of the unhispanized Philippines" describe social relations among indigenous Filipinos of Visayas, Luzon, Mindanao and other islands at the time of colonial rule.

Philippines/ Indigenous and local communities/ History—Colonial/ Ethnicity and ethnic relations.

993. **Sealza, I. S. 1984.** "From Staple to Cash Crop: A Survey of the Plantation Industry and Occupational Diversification in Bukidnon Province." *Philippine Sociological Review* 32 (1–4): 91–104.

During the period 1976–81 there was a dramatic increase in sugar cultivation in the hilly province of Bukidnon. This article demonstrates that this trend has had a favorable impact upon job creation in the non-agricultural sector. Indices of occupational diversification in sugar-growing areas are higher than are those for areas where rice or corn is the dominant crop. This, in turn, is probably linked to an increasing monetization of the local economy.

Philippines/ Mindanao/ Agriculture—Plantations/ Agriculture—Smallholder cash crop farming/ Indigenous and local communities—Commoditization/ Rural development.

994. ———. **1985.** "Income Changes and the Antique Upland Development Program." *Philippine Sociological Review* 33 (3–4): 89–93.

Studies have shown upland populations to rank among the "poorest of the poor." The Antique Upland Development Program was initiated to provide assistance to this sector of the population, placing major emphasis upon farmer trainings in the allocation of agricultural inputs with some financial support. Based in Hamtic, Antique for six months for purposes of assessing the program, the author interviewed a total of fifty farmers, split evenly between cooperators and noncooperators. The cooperators were found to have higher incomes, even after controlling for household size and size of landholding. Income increases over time were significant for owner-cooperators but not for tenants.

Philippines/ Antique/ Poverty/ Project intervention—Rural development.

995. **Sealza, I. S., and L. Palma-Sealza. 1985.** "Perspectives from Higher Places: Forest Policies and the Upland Farmer of Region 10, Philippines." Final project report. Photocopy. Cagayan de Oro: International Development Center.

The major purpose of this study is to discover whether or not the "policies, regulations and activity statements" associated with the Integrated Social Forestry (ISF) program of the Bureau of Forestry Development (BFD) "are acceptable to the upland farmers." Most of the interviewed farmers expressed favorable opinions about the new BFD policies. Prohibition of farm expansion, relocation policies and the twenty-five year land tenure policy, however, were still somewhat controversial. Prior knowledge about the ISF policies tended to make the respondents opinions more favorable; farm size however, was negatively associated with this variable.

A few reservations were also expressed about policies which mandated uplanders to suppress forest fires, to refrain from cutting down certain trees and to conserve forest growth. Respondents were generally willing to engage in tree farming; however, they needed technical assistance, capital and seedlings. An improved information campaign is recommended. There is also a need for strengthening community organizations. Overemphasis upon loans and dole-outs, especially during the early states of the project should be avoided. The government should also extend assistance for control of soil erosion in the "non-public uplands."

Philippines/ Project intervention—Social and community forestry.

996. **SEARCA-UQ Survey Team. 1995.** *Soil Conservation in an Upland Farming System in Cebu: A Socio-economic Survey.* SEARCA-UQ Uplands Research Project, Survey Report no. 1. Los Ba–os, Philippines: SEARCA-UQ Uplands Research Project.

Reports results of 3-month socio-economic survey of farmers' responses to promotion of soil conservation in Argao municipality, one of four project sites of Mag-uugmad Foundation, a Cebu-based NGO. The field survey was completed in the fall of 1993 as part of the collaborative SEARCA-UQ Uplands Research project [See separate entry for Robert A.

Cramb and G. C. Saguiguit, Jr. *Socioeconomic Evaluation of Soil Conservation Technologies for Upland Farming Systems in the Philippines: Project Overview*].

Philippines/ Project intervention—Soil conservation.

997.   **Segura de los Angeles, M. 1982.** "Research on Forest Policies for Philippine Development Planning: A Survey." *PIDS Survey of Philippine Development Research* 22: 3–55.

The author reviews forest management and economic development policies in the Philippines to identify how particular aspects of the timber industry are incorporated into decision-making over forest management. Physical, economic, and institutional considerations are treated simultaneously. Factors contributing to over-cutting and specific problems of forest regeneration are examined. Separate sections address possibilities for multiple-use forestry and issues of wood processing. A final section synthesizes the research findings and summarizes key policy "bottlenecks."

Philippines/ Timber industry—State policy and regulation/ State policy—Forest and natural resources/ Forest management—Economics/ Forest management—Commercial forestry and silviculture/ Timber industry—Downstream processing.

998.   **———. 1985.** "Economic and Social Impact of an Upland Development Project in Nueva Ecija, Philippines." *Journal of Philippine Development* 12: 324–394.

Philippines/ Project intervention—Rural development/ Poverty.

999.   **———. 1988.** "Economics of Upland Resource Depletion: Shifting Cultivation in the Philippines." Philippine Institute for Development Studies Working Paper, no. 88-02. Manila: Philippine Institute for Development Studies.

Philippines/ Agriculture—Shifting cultivation/ Deforestation/ Agricultural economics/ Forest management—Economics.

1000. **Segura de los Angeles, M., C. Cruz, and E. B. Corpuz. 1988.** "The Private Costs of Commercial Forestry, Reforestation and Social Forestry." *Journal of Philippine Development* 15 (1): 113-138.

Philippines/ Forest management—Economics/ Forest management—Commercial forestry and silviculture/ Reforestation/ Social forestry.

1001. **Segura de los Angeles, M., and Ma. E. C. Bennagen. 1993.** "Sustaining Resource Use in the Philippines Uplands: Issues in Community-Based Environmental Management." In *Structures and Reforms for Rural Development in the Philippines.* ed. A. M. Balisacan, and K. Nozawa, Pp. 115–138. Tokyo: Institute of Developing Economies.

The authors discuss problems relating to upland forest occupancy and its consequences for the environment and rural development. A brief history of the issue of forest occupancy in the Philippines is provided, followed by a review of recent efforts in upland agricultural development, reforestation, and community forestry. The authors stress the importance of addressing several "macro constraints" on upland resource conservation, including the role of poverty, population pressure, and labor pricing. Within the "micro" environment, the authors suggest the need to reduce transaction costs for upland farmers by devolving power to community institutions, widen the technological choices effectively available to farmers, and facilitate better information flow from social scientists to foresters and biologists.

Philippines/ Forest management—Economics/ Social forestry/ Rural development/ Forest management—Control of shifting cultivation.

1002. **Seidenschwanz, F. 1987.** "Ecological Zones of Southern Cebu: A Gradient Analysis." *The Philippine Scientist* 24: 43–54.

Philippines/ Cebu/ Forest biology and ecology/ Forest flora.

1003. **———. 1988.** "Forest Types of Cebu Island." *Philippine Quarterly of Culture and Society* 2: 93–106.

Philippines/ Cebu/ Forest biology and ecology/ Forest flora/ Land use—Patterns and planning.

1004. **Sevilla, J. C. 1984.** "Indicators of Upland Poverty: The Macro-View." Photocopy. Manila: Integrated Research Center, De La Salle University.

Philippines/ Poverty/ Project intervention—Rural development.

1005. **Seymour, F. 1985.** "Ten Lessons Learned from Agroforestry Projects in the Philippines." Paper prepared for the Ford Foundation. Photocopy.

The author discusses the major lessons learned about the adoption of agroforestry technology by upland farmers in the Philippines. Lessons listed include, among others, the importance of immediate household food needs as well as long-term goals; the importance of *de facto* rather than *de jure* tenure security for farmer adoption; the need to address transportation and marketing problems faced by upland farmers for successful project results; the importance of cash income opportunities to farmers; the need to find ways of working with the Bureau of Forestry Development to promote agroforestry among farmers cultivating officially classified public lands; the need to involve farmers in project-related decision-making; the need for clearly defining project staff roles in relation to the project activities and community; the promising potential of site visits to successful project sites for gaining the interest and support of policy-makers, extension agents and farmers; the realistic potential of voluntary cooperative work groups for implementing agroforestry technologies; and the potential of training and working with farmer-leaders for successful agroforestry extension.

In addition to these major points, the author emphasizes the central importance of ensuring that project leadership is assigned to an insightful and energetic project manager with a strong sense of initiative, good managerial skills and an ability and willingness to inspire enthusiasm for project activities. Another issue critical to project success is that of developing an appropriate phase-out process, including a strong farmer training emphasis. Finally, the author points out the need to place agroforestry projects in their proper perspective: while efforts to promote agroforestry may help to alleviate resource degradation and immediate hardships among upland farmers, "the fact that poor farmers are in the uplands mining the forest and soil resources for their subsistence is a result of unequal land distribution, a stagnated economy, and a high rate of population growth." It is these "root causes of poverty in the uplands" which must be addressed to effect real, long-term solutions. The review appears to draw from published and unpublished accounts of a number of specific project experiences in the Philippines. A bibliography of project materials reviewed is included.

Philippines/ Project intervention—Agroforestry.

1006. **Shively, G. E. 1995.** *Do Farmers Really Underinvest in Soil Conservation?: Theory and Evidence from an Upland Area of Davao del Sur, Philippines.* SEARCA-UQ Uplands Research Project, Working Paper no. 5. Los Ba–os, Philippines: SEARCA-UQ Uplands Research Project.

Shively develops a farm-level economic model to calculate privately optimal rates of hedgerow use under different scenarios. These are compared with observed patterns on sample farms in Bansalan area in foothills of Mt. Apo. Model parameters are based on observed prices, farmer characteristics, and econometric estimations using experimental plot data. The study finds that observed rates of hedgerow intensity often meet or exceed those rates that are privately optimal. A number of factors which may be at work in this pattern are suggested. These include: problems with recommendations by extensionists which remain overly focused on erosion control effectiveness rather than optimizing farmer returns; differences in the shadow price of labor and the market wage or shadow price of produced grain and the farm-gate price; and the possibility that hedgerows provide some economic gain that were not recognized by the author and hence not included in the model (e.g., reduction in the need for fertilizer, sale of hedgerow seed, etc.).

Philippines/ Mindanao/ Farm management—Economics/ Agroforestry/ Project intervention—Agroforestry.

1007. **Siebert, S. F., and J. Belsky. 1985.** "Forest Product Trade in a Lowland Filipino Village." *Economic Botany* 39: 522–523.

Siebert and Belsky report results of a year long study (1983-1984) in a lowland village of Leyte documenting local forest product use. The importance of different rattan and timber species for local survival strategies is noted, and the threat to these resources posed by overharvesting and agricultural conversion of forest lands is discussed.

Philippines/ Indigenous and local communities—Forest products use and trade/ Rattan—Collection and trade/ Rattan—Resource management and conservation/ Non-timber forest products.

1008. **Siebert, S. F. 1987.** "Land Use Intensification in Tropical Uplands: Effects on Vegetation, Soil Fertility and Erosion." *Forest Ecology and Management* 21: 37–56.

Siebert reports results of a study on the effects of agricultural intensification in hillside areas on land use, vegetation, and soil quality in the Bayhang River watershed of Leyte, Philippines. Intensification has involved accelerated forest product collection (mainly rattan and hardwoods), shortened swidden fallows, and continuous cultivation of corn and sweet potato. Effects include decreasing availability of forest products central to local livelihoods, invasion of exotic flora (dominated by *Imperata cylindrica*, *Saccharum sponteneum*, and various *Compositae*), soil nutrient depletion and increased acidity. Analysis results indicate a slower decline in soil quality under sweet potato compared with corn + sweet potato relay intercropping. Serious rates of soil loss within the first 6 months of cultivation are also documented. Emphasizes Siebert, the most promising measures for ameliorating the environmental deterioration associated with agricultural intensification are those which build upon extant land and forest use practices. These include rattan cultivation and a variety of agronomic and agroforestry-based conservation farming measures.

Philippines/ Agriculture—Shifting cultivation's environmental impacts/ Migrant farmers and farming/ Indigenous and local communities—Forest land use and management practices/ Agricultural intensification/ Soil erosion and degradation/ Rattan—Resource management and conservation.

1009. ———. **1990.** "Hillside Farming, Soil Erosion, and Forest Conversion in Two Southeast Asian National Parks." *Mountain Research and Development* 10 (1): 64–72.

Comparing the Bayhang watershed near Leyte Mountains National Park, Philippines and the Sungai Ning watershed near Kerinci-Seblat National Park, Indonesia, Siebert examines the relationship between soil erosion on hillside farms and forest conversion to farmland in adjacent national parks. Evidence of accelerated erosion in both watersheds based on a random sample of hillside farms is noted. In Bayhang, mean soil losses were about 422 t/ha during the first six months of cultivation, while in Sungai Ning loss equaled 3.8 t/ha during the cropping year on continuously cultivated farms. Research also demonstrated declining soil productivity as a result of soil erosion. As farmers' fields become degraded, new forest is cleared for agricultural use in the Leyte National Park. In Kerinci, farmers substituted cassava for crops with higher fertility requirements and also turned to the adjacent national park for access to fresh farmland. Possibilities for the introduction of soil-conserving technologies and alternative livelihood opportunities are discussed.

Philippines/ Indonesia/ Soil erosion and degradation/ Agriculture—Shifting cultivation's environmental impacts/ Migrant farmers and farming/ Indigenous and local communities—Forest land use and management practices/ Agricultural intensification/ Forest management—Parks and conservation areas.

1010. **Simkins, P. D., and F. L. Wernstedt. 1971.** *Philippine Migration: The Settlement of the Digos-Padada Valley, Davao Province.* Monograph Series, no. 16. New Haven, Conn.: Yale University Southeast Asia Studies.

Philippines/ Mindanao/ Migration/ Land settlement and development.

1011. **Stewart, T. 1992.** "Land-Use Options to Encourage Forest Conservation on a Tribal Reservation in the Philippines." *Agroforestry Systems* 18: 225–244.

Economic changes among the Negrito (Ati) tribe of Nagpana in Iloilo, Philippines have deepened their dependence on wage labor for local landowners and cash-oriented permanent rice farming. Loss of residual forests has resulted in soil degradation, declining crop harvests, and diminishing availability of non-timber forest products important for Ati subsistence. Stewart discusses the potential offered by new agroforestry strategies for addressing these environmental concerns. Different land use possibilities are assessed in terms of their economic viability. The superior economic, social and environmental potential offered by a combination of sustainable forest use and incorporating fast-growing tree species in existing farm fields is noted.

Philippines/ Indigenous and local communities—Commoditization/ Indigenous and local communities—Farming practices/ Agricultural intensification/ Soil erosion and degradation/ Project intervention—Agroforestry.

1012. **Stitt, R. E. 1948.** "Mindanao: Key to the Philippines' Future." *Journal of Geography* 48 (4): 150–160.

Philippines/ Mindanao/ Land settlement and development.

1013. **Tacio, H. D. 1989.** "Sustainable Agroforest Land Technology." *Pcarrd Monitor* 17 (10): 9–10.

Philippines/ Mindanao/ Project intervention—Agroforestry/ Agroforestry.

1014. **———. 1993.** "Sloping Agricultural Land Technology (SALT): A Sustainable Agroforestry Scheme for the Uplands." *Agroforestry Systems* 22: 145–152.

Tacio discusses the development of SALT at the Mindanao Baptist Rural Life Center (MBRLC) in Southern Mindanao. SALT incorporates the use of leucaena hedgerows on cultivated hillsides to mitigate soil erosion. Addressing the need to confirm the actual sustainability of the technology, he reports the results of various research efforts conducted both on MBRLC demonstration plots and farmer's fields. Tests measuring soil erosion found a total soil loss from SALT treated plots to be 20.2 tons over a six year period, while soil loss from non-SALT plots totaled 1162.4 tons during the same period.

A ten-year economic study showed marked increases in farmer income with the use of SALT, although the author qualifies this finding by noting that the study accounted only for the costs of seeds, fertilizers, and insecticides, not labor input. Separate labor studies indicated that SALT systems required much higher labor inputs than traditional corn farming during the first years of implementation. Labor requirements decreased both absolutely and relative to traditional corn field management after this initial period.

Research regarding yield productivity suggested a significant increase in per hectare yields with the addition of leucaena biomass with the SALT system. Yield increases were higher, however, with the use of commercial fertilizer even without SALT technology. The use of commercial fertilizer with SALT technology seemed to result in a yield no higher than that documented for commercial fertilizer use alone. No significant improvements in yield were recorded with the use of new corn varieties with SALT, suggesting that farmers would do just as well with traditional corn varieties when deploying SALT. Finally, continuous corn cropping with the use of SALT over a ten-year period resulted in some decrease in yields, though much less so than was experienced on plots cropped continuously for ten years without SALT.

Philippines/ Mindanao/ Project intervention—Agroforestry/ Soil erosion and degradation/ Farm management—Cropping systems.

1015. **Tocmo, B. S. 1991.** "Greed for Money May Spoil DENR's Reforestation Efforts." *Mindanet* 3 (3): 3–7.

Local government officials are getting involved in DENR reforestation projects, either directly or as contractors of private households under the "family approach" program. In either case, these officials become entitled to some portion of the incentives set aside for encouraging tree planting. At the same time, government policies also provide for the participation of NGOs in tree planting. In general, NGOs have a better track record than government agencies and officials, largely because they provide training and follow-up to ensure a higher seedling survival rate. There is evidence, however, that some local government officials are moving to exclude NGOs from reforestation activities since this will ensure them the possibility of garnering a greater share of the reforestation incentives.

Philippines/ Reforestation/ Political economy.

1016. **Tomboc, C. C., and G. A. Mendoza. 1993.** "A Simulation Model for the Philippine Selective Logging System: Case Study of a Timber Company." *Journal of Environmental Management* 39 (2): 89-100.

The authors apply a simulation model developed for the Philippine Selective Logging System to the case of a logging company in northeastern Mindanao. Results of the simulation suggest the unsustainable nature of the company's logging practices and the need to incorporate more strategies like timber stand improvement into its forestry regime.

Philippines/ Mindanao/ Timber industry—Logging/ Timber industry—Environmental impacts/ Forest management—Commercial forestry and silviculture/ Forest management—Forest resource conservation.

1017. **Tucker, R. P. 1988.** "The Commercial Timber Economy Under Two Colonial Regimes in Asia." In *Changing Tropical Forests: Historical Perspectives on Today's Challenges in Asia, Australasia and Oceania.* Ed. J. Dargavel, K. Dixon, and N. Semple, pp. 219–230. Canberra, Australia: Centre for Resource and Environmental Studies.

The author contrasts the history of timber extraction and marketing in the Himalayan forests of northern India and in the Philippines under British and American colonial rule. Catalyzed largely by the policies of U.S. administrators, between 1900 and the late 1960s the Philippines was transformed from a net importer of wood to Southeast Asia's largest exporter. The fortunes of American and Philippine lumber industries became closely intertwined as American administrators recruited U.S. foresters and equipment manufacturers to help the Filipino elite modernize the local timber industry as quickly as possible. After World War II, American companies were reluctant to reinvest directly into the industry, allowing Filipino firms to assume a dominant position in the country's timber industry. By the late 1960s, the Philippines' vast tropical forests were already severely depleted, leading to a rapid decline in timber exports even before 1970. The Philippine experience contrasts with the colonial history of timber extraction in the Himalayas where a modernized and export-oriented timber industry did not evolve. Despite these different conditions, however, severe forest resource depletion occurred in both cases.

Philippines/ Deforestation/ Timber industry—Development and structure/ Timber industry—Trade and markets/ History—Colonial.

1018. **Tung, L. 1992.** "Attempts to Incorporate/Institutionalize an FSRE/ E Approach into the Research Function of an Agricultural University." Paper presented at the International Workshop on Networking for LEISA, 9–15 March 1992, in Cavite, Silanga, Philippines. Photocopy.

In 1987 an independent unit called the Farm and Resource Management Institute (FARMI) was established at the Visayas State College of Agriculture (ViSCA). Staffed by a small inter-disciplinary team, the institute is thought of as an 'inter-disciplinary institutional innovation' to mobilize a significant portion of ViSCA resources towards serving resource poor farmers in the Visayas region. FARMI is itself an outgrowth of the Farming Systems Development Project-Eastern Visayas (FSDP-EV) financed by the Government of the Philippines and USAID which established six research management units in diverse upland areas, all devoted to research and extension and linked to the regional Department of Agriculture for technical assistance. Since its inception, FARMI's mandate has been to 1) use FSR/E in on-farm research to develop, identify, adapt and disseminate farming technologies that can successfully increase agricultural productivity among resource poor farmers of the uplands; and 2) develop, strengthen and extend the institutionalization of the FSR/E approach to the rest of ViSCA as well as the general Visayas region.

Though the institute has developed some substantial programs, a number of problems have been encountered: 1) Question has arisen as to whether establishing FARMI as a separate FSR/E unit has simply competed with existing methodologies rather than institutionalizing and integrating FSR/E methods throughout ViSCA. 2) Criticism has been voiced that FARMI has merely succeeded in institutionalizing the farming systems research label rather than its underlying philosophy, values and beliefs. Failure to make a user perspective the true research starting point has been noted. 3) Efforts must be made to ensure that FSR/ E is simply approached as a separate science within ViSCA and that FARMI's focus on upland farmers growing rice and corn is well integrated into other upland research taking place at the college.

Philippines/ Farming systems research.

1019. **Turner, M., R. J. May, and L. R. Turner, eds. 1992.** *Mindanao: Land of Unfulfilled Promise*. Quezon City, Philippines: New Day Publishers.

The monograph presents an overview of various issues in the socio-economic development and political history of Mindanao and its various sub-regions. Individual papers include: "Introduction: images of Mindanao," Mark Turner and Lulu Respall Turner; "The political economy of Mindanao: an overview," Eduardo C. Tadem; "The demography of Mindanao," Michael A. Costello; "Bukidnon: Mindanao's heartland for agrarian reform," Antonio J. Ledesma, S.J.; "The Zamboanga del Sur development project 1975-85," Brian

Lockwood; "Surigao bypassed," Paul Mathews; "Order and the law in Muslim Mindanao," G. Carter Bentley; "Philippine and Muslim women: their emerging role in a rapidly changing society," Luis Q. Lacar; "The wild west in the south: a recent political history of Mindanao," R. J. May; "Contemporary politics in Mindanao," Michael O. Mastura; "The Moro people's struggle for self-determination," Eliseo R. Mercado, Jr., OMI; "The Organic Law for the Autonomous Region in Muslim Mindanao: contrasting views," Nagasura T. Madale; "'One whole sorry mess': the Zamboanga hostage-taking incident," Mark Turner; "The theoretical problems of insurgency in Mindanao: why theory? why Mindanao?" Kit Collier; "The once and future insurgency in northeastern Mindanao," Peter M. Sales; "Ancestral domain: a central issue in the Lumad struggle for self-determination in Mindanao," B. R. Rodil; "Behind and beyond the Tasaday: the untold struggle over T'boli resources," David Hyndman and Levita Duhaylungsod. Papers by M. A. Costello and A. J. Ledesma are abstracted separately.

Philippines/ Mindanao/ Demography/ Migration/ Indigenous and local communities— Forest land use and management practices/ Indigenous and local communities—Land and resource tenure systems/ Ethnicity and ethnic relations/ Politics/ Political economy/ Land reform/ Social movements.

1020. **Ulack, R. 1977.** "Migration to Mindanao: Population Growth in the Final Stage of a Pioneer Frontier." *Tjidschrift voor Economishe en Sociale Geografie* 68 (3): 133–44.

Philippines/ Mindanao/ Land settlement and development/ Migration.

1021. ———. **1986.** "Ties to Origin, Remittances, and Mobility: Evidence from Rural and Urban Areas in the Philippines." *Journal of Developing Areas* 20 (3): 339–355.

Ulack explores the role of remittances in the local economies of urban and rural localities of Cebu, Philippines. Research findings demonstrate ongoing ties maintained by migrants in urban centers to their village of origin embodied in cash remittances, non-cash gifts, and regular visits. Differences in the size of cash remittances between urban and rural areas are noted, and implications of the study findings for rural development and general economic policy are discussed.

Philippines/ Cebu/ Migration / Household livelihood strategies/ Indigenous and local communities—Economy.

1022. **Ulack, R., M. A. Costello, and M. Palabrica-Costello. 1985.** "Circulation in the Philippines." *Geographical Review* 75 (4): 439–450.

Philippines/ Migration/ Household livelihood strategies.

1023. **United States Agency for International Development. 1990.** Show: A Resource Catalogue of Selected Communities Showcasing Agroforestry and Reforestation Technologies, Participatory Community Organizations, and Development Processes. Washington, D.C.: U.S. Department of State; Agency for International Development.

This brochure lists twelve agroforestry projects currently underway in the Philippines. Of these five are on Mindanao. Each entry profiles the project, its exact location, accessibility, number of participating farmers, various organizations involved, facilities and infrastructure, and area of staff expertise. All but one project appear to be connected to the Department of Environment and Natural Resources of the Philippines.

Philippines/ Project intervention—Agroforestry/ Project intervention—Participatory methods/ Non-governmental organizations.

1024. **Upland NGO Assistance Committee. 1991.** *NGOs in Agroforestry, Land Tenure, and Marketing Activities in Philippine Uplands.* Manila, Philippines: Philippine Upland Resource Center.

Philippines/ Agroforestry/ Land tenure/ Rural development/ Project intervention—Agroforestry/ Project intervention—Rural development/ Non-timber forest products/ Non-governmental organizations.

1025. **Uriarte, N. S. 1991.** "Bamboo Production in the Philippines: Financial Analysis at the Small Farmholder Level." Ph.D. diss., Michigan State University, East Lansing, Mich.

Philippines/ Cebu/ Agriculture—Plantations/ Agriculture—Smallholder cash crop farming/ Agriculture—Smallholder tree and perennial crop farming/ Farm management—Economics.

1026. **Van Oosterhout, A. 1983.** "Spatial Conflicts in Rural Mindanao, the Philippines." *Pacific Viewpoint* 24 (1): 24–49.

Philippines/ Mindanao/ Geography/ Land settlement and development/ Ethnicity and ethnic relations/ Migrant farmers and farming.

1027. **Vandermeer, C. 1963.** "Corn Cultivation on Cebu: An Example of An Advanced Stage of Migratory Farming." *Journal of Tropical Geography* 17: 172–177.

Philippines/ Cebu/ Migrant farmers and farming/ Agricultural intensification.

1028. **———. 1967.** "Population Patterns on the Island of Cebu, the Philippines: 1500–1900." *Annals of the Association of American Geographers* 57 (2): 315–337.

Philippines/ Cebu/ Migration/ Demography/ History—Colonial.

1029. **Vandermeer, C., and B. C. Agaloos. 1962.** "Twentieth Century Settlement of Mindanao." *Papers of the Michigan Academy of Science, Arts and Letters* 47: 537–548.

Philippines/ Mindanao/ Migration/ Land settlement and development.

1030. **Vitug, M. D. 1993.** *Power from the Forest: Politics of Logging.* Manila, Philippines: Philippine Center for Investigative Journalism.

Investigative journalist Vitug chronicles the history of logging in the Philippines over the last several decades. Patronage relations of mutual economic and political benefit between the Filipino timber industry and local, regional and national government figures on the one hand as well as leading insurgent groups on the other are detailed. Disputes between government factions over control of the country's natural resources are reported, and a growing grass-roots resistance movement against further resource plundering is noted. The monograph presents a well-researched narrative account of leading figures, companies and groups involved in ongoing conflicts over forest resources in the Philippines.

Philippines/ Timber industry—Development and structure/ Timber industry—Logging/ Deforestation/ State policy—Forest and natural resources/ Social movements/ Political economy/ Politics.

1031. **Warren, C. 1977.** "Palawan." In *Insular Southeast Asia: Ethnographic Studies. Section 3. Philippines.* Comp. F. M. LeBar, vol. 2, pp. 229–290. New Haven, Conn.: Human Relations Area File.

> Ethnographic account of the indigenous people of Palawan island. Nine distinct language and cultural groups may be identified on the island. A broad description of settlement patterns, kinship, agricultural and/or food gathering practices of each group is given.

Philippines/ Palawan/ Ethnography/ Indigenous and local communities.

1032. **Warren, J. F. 1987.** *At the Edge of Southeast Asian History.* Quezon City: New Day Publishers.

> The monograph presents a collection of essays written between the late 1970s and the mid-1980s. Several essays focus on the role of trade and slave trading in the development of the Sulu Zone under the Sulu sultanate during the 19th century. Incorporating the Sulu archipelago between the Southern Philippines, Northern Borneo and Northern Sulawesi island, the Sulu sultanate commanded great control over inter-island trade throughout insular Southeast Asia during the first half of the 19th century. Warren links vigorous slave raiding by sultan forces throughout the Southeast Asian islands to booming Western demand for jungle products such as gutta-perche (raw rubber) and rattan as well as the infusion of Western-made arms and munitions to the area. Booming trade with the West through Singapore and other entrepot cities made command over adequate labor supplies to procure tradeable goods vital to the economic and political dominance of the Sulu sultanate, encouraging in turn the procurement of labor through slave-raiding. Access to a constant supply of weapons made this procurement possible.
>
> These forces had an impact on local populations and ethnic relations far beyond the area directly controlled by the Sultanate. Also important was the role of Western traders who were able to manipulate connections with coastal sultans in eastern Borneo to establish lucrative trading links with shifting cultivator communities located far upstream in the Borneo interior. Both the Sulu sultanate and these early Western trade monopolies were eventually usurped from their dominant commercial position in the area by the arrival of Arab traders using steamboats. The control exerted by Sulu sultanates in the region was also severely diminished by the end of the 19th century after vigorous military attacks by both Spanish and English naval fleets. A concerted resettlement campaign was started by colonial authorities, aimed at transforming the seafaring coastal communities of the region into sedentary agriculturalists. With these essays, the author seeks to highlight the impact of global forces linked to industrialization in the West on communities conventionally perceived to be on the periphery of modern history.

Indonesia/ Malaysia/ Philippines/ History—Colonial/ Non-timber forest products/ Ethnicity and ethnic relations/ Resettlement.

1033. **Watson, H. R., and W. A. Laquihon. 1986.** "Sloping Agricultural Land Technology (SALT): A Social Forestry Model in the Philippines." *Community Forestry: Lessons from Case Studies in Asia and the Pacific Region.* Y. S. Rao, M. W. Hoskins, N. T. Vergara, and C. P. Castro, pp. 21–44. Bangkok; Honolulu, Hawaii: FAO Regional Office for Asia and the Pacific; Environment and Policy Institute, East-West Center.

Philippines/ Mindanao/ Project intervention—Agroforestry/ Project intervention—Social and community forestry/ Project intervention—Participatory methods.

1034. **Weidelt, H. J., and Valeriano S. Banaag. n.d.** "Aspects of Management and Silviculture of Philippine Dipterocarp Forests." *Schriftenreihe der GTZ,* no. 132. Eschborn, Germany: GTZ.

This report discusses a range of issues related to silviculture of dipterocarp forests in the Philippines. Included is an analysis of the Philippine Selective Logging System, describing typical logging methods, the effect of selective logging on the residual stand, techniques for reducing damage from logging methods, and general problems associated from logging. Argue the authors, "for silvicultural and ecological reasons, a well supervised and carefully conducted selective cutting offers the best conditions for the development of the natural regeneration of dipterocarp and other climax species."

Philippines/ Forest management—Commercial forestry and silviculture/ Timber industry— State policy and regulation/ Forest management—Forest resource conservation.

1035. **Wernstedt, F. L., and P. D. Simkins. 1965.** "Migration and the Settlement of Mindanao." *Journal of Asian Studies* 25: 83–103.

Philippines/ Mindanao/ Migration / Land settlement and development.

1036. **Wernstedt, F. L., and J. E. Spencer. 1967.** *The Philippine Island World.* Berkeley, Calif.: University of California Press.

Philippines/ Geography/ Land use—Patterns and planning/ Land settlement and development/ Agricultural development/ Economic development/ Regional development/ Agriculture—Permanent/ Agriculture—Shifting cultivation/ Agriculture—Plantations/ Indigenous and local communities/ Migrant farmers and farming.

1037. **Western, S. 1988.** "Carrying Capacity, Population Growth and Sustainable Development: A Case Study from the Philippines." *Journal of Environmental Management* 27: 347–367.

Palawan island is presented as a case study to illustrate the concept of human carrying capacity and its role in environmental degradation. Population on the island is expected to rise from 315,000 in 1983 to over 1 million by 2007, due largely to in-migration. Due to land tenure conflicts and technical constraints, settlement is occurring on steep hillsides, where newcomers often practice shifting cultivation, resulting in land degradation and destruction of coastal fisheries. Analysis of the island on the basis of six ecological zones and 20 subzones enabled researchers to identify areas where human carrying capacity has been reached and exceeded to the point of compromising the possibilities for sustainable development. Three strategies are compared to project some possible alternatives to the direction suggested by present trends. This model involves projecting changes in land use, agricultural systems and population capacity for different scenarios over 25 years.

Philippines/ Palawan/ Population pressure/ Migration/ Land settlement and development/ Agriculture—Shifting cultivation's environmental impacts.

1038. **White, S. M. 1990.** "The Influence of Tropical Cyclones as Soil Eroding and Sediment Transporting Events: An Example from the Philippines." In *Research Needs and Applications to Reduce Erosion and Sedimentation in Tropical Steeplands.* Ed. R. R. Ziemer, C. L. O. O'Loughlin, and L. S. Hamilton, pp. 259–269. IAHS Publication, no. 192. Wallingford, Oxfordshire, U.K.: International Association of Hydrological Sciences.

Philippines/ Soil erosion and degradation.

1039. **Wischusen, E. W. 1990.** "The Foraging Ecology and Natural History of the Philippine Flying Lemur (*Cynochephalus volans*)." Ph.D. diss., Cornell University, Ithaca, N.Y.

Philippines/ Mindanao/ Forest fauna/ Forest biology and ecology.

1040. **World Bank. 1989.** Philippines: Environment and Natural Resource Management Study. Washington, D.C.: World Bank.

Philippines/ State policy—Forest and natural resources/ State policy—Pollution control/ Deforestation/ Timber industry—Development and structure/ Timber industry—State policy and regulation/ Forest management—Commercial forestry and silviculture/ Forest management—Forest resource conservation/ Forest management—Economics/ State policy—Agricultural and rural development/ Land use—Patterns and planning.

1041. **World Conservation Monitoring Centre. 1988.** "Philippines [Conservation of Biological Diversity and Forest Ecosystems]." Cambridge, U.K.; Gland, Switzerland: World Conservation Monitoring Centre; International Union for Conservation of Nature and Natural Resources, Tropical Forest Program.

Uncontrolled agricultural conversion, logging concerns bent on short term gain, illegal logging, failed resource management, poor enforcement, and inadequate staffing are cited among the most important reasons for rapid destruction of the Philippines' diverse natural forests. Specific actions are recommended. A 21 page report.

Philippines/ Deforestation/ Forest management—Forest resource conservation/ Forest management—Parks and conservation areas/ Biodiversity.

1042. Yanez, N., and M. Zeegers. "Grassland-Based Livelihoods in Barangay Songsong, Gamu, Isabela." *Agroecosystem Research in Rural Resource Management and Development*. Ed. Percy E. Sajise and T. A. Rambo. College, Laguna, Philippines: Program on Environmental Science and Management, University of the Philippines.

Drawing from 11 months of field research Yanez and Zeegers highlight the distinct factors influencing land use decision making by swidden farmers of an upland community (Lak Balinsasayao) in Negros Oriental. Constraints posed by labor rather than land scarcity are particularly noted. Choices regarding cropping practices, resource and land use are shaped by this constraint as well as issues of risk, site factors, and time allocation. Incorporation of these considerations is likely to improve the design of the agroforestry component in a community development project.

Philippines/ Indigenous and local communities—Forest land use and management practices/ Indigenous and local communities—Farming practices/ Farm management—Cropping systems/ Household livelihood strategies/ Grasslands.

1043. ———. **1991.** "Grassland-based Livelihoods in Barangay Songsong, Gamu, Isabela." Paper presented at the First Cagayan Valley Programme on Environment and Development Conference. 26-29 August 1991, Cabagan, Isabela, Philippines. Photocopy.

The authors report on research intended to assess the different uses, income-generating capacity, and general "relative importance" of cogon grasslands for farmers in Songsong. Grasslands are important to local villagers both as a source of agricultural land and as a source of cogon grass for gathering. The authors attempt to identify the specific conditions under which cogon gathering assumes importance as a source of income to local villagers, In particular, it is noted that while income from agricultural production is the main source of livelihood for most households in the region, supplemented by cogon grass gathering on the side, for the poorest families in the community, cogon grass has become the primary income source. In addition, cogon gathering and agricultural show an important relationship over time during the agricultural cycle, as more labor is devoted to the former during the summer months, when labor requirements for agriculture begin to slack off.

Philippines/ Household livelihood strategies/ Indigenous and local communities—Forest land use and management practices/ Indigenous and local communities—Farming practices/ Pest, weed, and crop disease management/ Agriculture—Shifting cultivation/ Grasslands.

1044. **Yengoyan, A. A. 1964.** "Environment, Shifting Cultivation and Social Organization Among the Mandaya of Eastern Mindanao." Ph.D. diss., University of Chicago, Chicago, Ill.

Philippines/ Mindanao/ Ethnography/ Indigenous and local communities—Forest land use and management practices/ Indigenous and local communities—Forest products use and trade/ Indigenous and local communities—Land and resource tenure systems/ Indigenous and local communities—Social relations/ Indigenous and local communities—Commoditization/ Agriculture—Shifting cultivation.

1045. ———. **1977.** "Southeast Mindanao." In *Insular Southeast Asia: Ethnographic Studies. Section 3. Philippines.* Comp. F. M. Lebar, vol. 1, pp. 79–116. New Haven, Conn.: Human Area Relations Files.

Ethnographic survey of several ethnic groups of Southeast Mindanao. Of these, the Mandaya of the mountainous inland are the largest group. Mandaya customs, settlement patterns and agricultural practices are discussed in some detail. Briefer ethnographies of the Bagobo (Manuvu), Bila-an, Kulamin, Tagakaola, and Ata are provided in a second section.

Philippines/ Mindanao/ Ethnography/ Indigenous and local communities.

1046. ———. **1979.** "The Effects of Cash Cropping on Mandaya Land Tenure." In *Land Tenure in the Pacific.* Ed. R. Crocombe, pp. 362–374. Melbourne, Australia: Oxford University Press.

The author notes important changes in land tenure and social organization among Mandaya households who have moved to the lowlands in Davao Oriental, Mindanao. More specifically, Mandaya households in the lowlands now engage primarily in the cultivation of abaca for cash exchange. Among these households, patterns of land inheritance have changed, reducing fragmentation of family land holdings as well as the independence of the nuclear family from the larger kin group. Although cash crops are also being cultivated by more traditional Mandaya in the uplands, many upland villagers are still engaged primarily in swidden-based rice farming and remain bilaterally organized, thus maintaining the independence of the nuclear family from the kin group of either spouse.

Philippines/ Mindanao/ Indigenous and local communities—Commoditization/ Indigenous and local communities—Farming practices/ Indigenous and local communities—Social relations/ Ethnicity and ethnic relations/ Indigenous and local communities—Land and resource tenure systems/ Agriculture—Smallholder cash crop farming/ Agriculture—Smallholder tree and perennial crop farming.

1047. ———. **1985.** "Memory, Myth, and History: Traditional Agriculture and Structure in Mandaya Society." In *Cultural Values and Human Ecology in Southeast Asia.* Ed. K. L. Hutterer, A. T. Rambo, and G. Lovelace, pp. 157–176. Ann Arbor, Mich.: Center for South and Southeast Asian Studies, University of Michigan.

Philippines/ Mindanao/ Indigenous and local communities—Farming practices/ Indigenous and local communities—Social relations.

1048. ———. **1988.** "Hierarchy and the Social Order: Mandaya Ethnic Relations in Southeast Mindanao, Philippines." *Ethnic Diversity and the Control of Natural Resources in Southeast Asia.* Ed. T. A. Rambo, K. Gillogly, and K. L. Hutterer, pp. 173–195. Michigan Papers on South and Southeast Asia, no. 32. Ann Arbor, Mich.: Center for South and Southeast Asian Studies, University of Michigan.

Drawing on past and current fieldwork in the eastern Davao highlands, Yengoyan analyzes the changing relations between Mandaya, the Mangguangan and the coastal Bisayans. Subsistence swidden farming and collection and trade of game and non-timber forest products sustain the Mangguangan who remain concentrated in the remote forest interior. The swidden farming Mandaya are located in more accessible foothills and upland areas, where land is being rapidly settled by inmigrating coastal Bisayans. Yengoyan applies a hierarchy-framed model to highlight the subordination and displacement being experienced by the Mandaya *vis à vis* the Christian Bisayans. In this process, ethnic relations are being reconstituted along class lines, suggesting future directions of change.

Philippines/ Mindanao/ Indigenous and local communities—Commoditization/ Land settlement and development—Impacts on local communities and economy/ Migrant farmers and farming/ Ethnicity and ethnic relations.

SOUTHEAST ASIA, ASIA, AND GLOBAL

1049. **Anderson, J., and J. Thampapillai. 1990.** "Soil Conservation in Developing Countries: Project and Policy Intervention." Policy and Research Series, no. 8. Washington, D.C.: World Bank.

Noting the widespread attention that soil erosion has garnered among agricultural researchers today, the authors address the problem of providing the relevant information for effecting successful projects and policies. The authors focus more specifically on information needed to assess factors influencing farmer decisions to engage or eschew soil conserving practices. While the issue is particularly salient for marginal farmlands in the tropics, most information on farmer land management decision-making continues to be derived mainly from farming systems in industrialized countries. Some preliminary data does exist from the developing world which suggest that soil conserving agricultural practices are positively linked to a number of specific variables including: net income from on-and off-farm sources, the availability of credit, the ability to perceive benefits (in turn linked to education), secure land tenure, low discount rates, and long-range planning perspectives on the part of local and national governments, access to good technical support. More ambiguous, however, is the link between soil conserving practices and technological development. While certain types of technological innovations may help contain soil loss, others, such as modern cultivars, have tended to accelerate degradation of the system by increasing the need for inputs like fertilizers, irrigation and tillage. The effects of risk attitudes, price supports and taxes on soil management practices also remain unclear. Results of existing studies have been contradictory, showing that these latter factors can both encourage and discourage conservation practices in different study locations.

The contradictory nature of existing evidence suggests that a broad combination of different factors rather than one overriding concern are at work in promoting or discouraging soil conserving behavior among farmers. Further research is needed to shed more light on the exact relationship between different factors. One particular technical constraint in the implementation of rigorous policy-relevant research has been that of accurately assessing the degree of soil loss actually taking place in any given area. Existing assessments taken to have general regional validity are in fact usually based on survey data from much more limited areas, or derived through the application of the "universal soil loss equation" (USLE) which tend to assume away a number of variables, in the end leading to a highly distorted final estimate. (Specific examples of relevant variables include quality of the soil and quality of vegetative cover, each of which is often highly location specific). Also, direct evidence of soil erosion and its effects is available by and large only with the occurrence of extreme events, such as floods and mud slides, meaning that areas in urgent need of soil conserving interventions are often recognized far too late. Appraising the exact value of benefits derived from soil conservation—necessary both for understanding farmer decision-making patterns as well as for recommending appropriate interventions—is also highly problematic.

These issues suggest opportunities for the application of simulation modeling as well as the need for ongoing research to fill in crucial technical information gaps in "the physics of soil erosion," "changes in plant genetics" and other relevant areas. Development of appropriate remote sensing documentation comprises another important research need. Finally, the crucial need for further information from the field also suggests that sincere project efforts to improve land management will require careful, though often expensive ongoing monitoring. Though time and labor intensive, on-farm research completed in connection with project-based extension could offer a critically important spin-off benefit by providing needed information directly to farmers in the process of assessing different agricultural practices. Providing more concrete evidence of the direct upstream benefits rather than simply the downstream gains of soil conservation should be considered a priority, especially for developing countries, where agricultural concerns outweigh those connected with downstream infrastructural works (reservoirs, dams, etc.), still relatively few in number in the non-industrialized world.

The need for completing research on "particular domestic environments" is stressed, given the location specific implications of various factors such as soil type, vegetative ecosystems, etc. While the high cost of such research may be prohibitive to many developing country governments, networking among researchers from different countries who are confronted with "similar ecologies and erosive tendencies" may offer a promising alternative research strategy.

Global/ Soil erosion and degradation.

1050. **Arnold, J. E. M. 1992.** *Community Forestry: Ten Years in Review.* Community Forestry Note, Rome: Food and Agriculture Organization of the United Nations.

Global/ Social forestry.

1051. **Arsyad, S., I. Amien, T. Sheng, and W. Moldenhauer, eds. 1992.** *Conservation Policies for Sustainable Hillslope Farming.* Ankeny, Iowa: Soil and Water Conservation Society.

This monograph presents a collection of papers prepared for an international workshop on "Conservation Policies for Sustainable Hillslope Farming" held in Solo, Central Java in March 1991. Papers deal with a variety of issues related to soil conservation, including World Bank strategy in Asia (W. B. Margrath), recent approaches in soil conservation (D. W. Sanders), links between land tenure, land tenure legislation and soil conservation in Indonesia (S. M. P. Tjondronegoro; I. Soetiknjo; S. Soeromihardjo); experiences of soil conservation in Java (Yuwanti, Suyamni, and J. Levine) and the Philippines (R. Atienza); monitoring and evaluation (K. C. Lai); and forestry policy and soil conservation (N. P. Sharma). Papers are generally brief, providing broad overviews rather than research detail.

Asia/ Indonesia/ Soil erosion and degradation/ Project intervention—Soil conservation.

1052. **Atal, Y., and P. L. Bennagen, eds. 1983.** Vol. 1. *Swidden Cultivation in Asia.* Bangkok: UNESCO.

This volume is part of a larger report on the comprehensive UNESCO study on shifting cultivation in Asia conducted in the early 1980s. A broad review of the literature and summary of research findings are presented. Subsequent volumes describe specific study sites, research methods used, and information gathered.

Asia/ Agriculture—Shifting cultivation.

1053. **Avery, M. E., M. G. R. Cannell, and C. K. Ong. 1991.** *Biophysical Research for Asian Agroforestry.* Arlington, Va.: Winrock International Institute for Agricultural Development.

Current problems, research needs and methodologies in Asian agroforestry are discussed.

Asia/ Agroforestry.

1054. **Baas, P., K. Kalkman, and R. Gersnik, eds. 1990.** *The Plant Diversity of Malesia.* Proceedings of the Flora Malesiana Symposium Commemorating Professor Dr. C.G.G.J. van Steenis, August 1989, Leiden. Dordrecht, Netherlands; Boston, Mass.: Kluwer Academic Publishers.

> The proceedings are organized into six major sections: Progress in Malesian Botany; Vegetation and Flora; Biogeography; Conservation; Economic Botany; and Taxonomy. Papers presented include among others, J. Dransfield, "Outstanding Problems in Malesian Palms"; K. Kartawinata, "Review of Natural Vegetation Studies in Malesia with Special Reference to Indonesia"; J. H. Beaman and R. S. Beaman, "Diversity and Distribution Patterns in the Flora of Mt. Kinabalu"; S. Sukardjo, "Secondary Forests of Tanah Grogot, East Kalimantan, Indonesia". (See separate entries for papers by Beaman and Beaman and Sukardjo in Malaysia and Indonesia sections respectively).

Southeast Asia/ Forest flora/ Non-timber forest products/ Rattan—Growth and distribution/ Rattan—Resource management and conservation/ Forest management—Forest resource conservation/ Biodiversity.

1055. **Bethel, J. S. et al. 1982.** "The Role of U.S. Multinational Corporations in Commercial Forestry Operations in the Tropics." Report prepared for the U.S. Department of State. Photocopy. Seattle, Wash.: College of Forest Resources, University of Washington.

> General aspects of forestry and its environmental impacts in tropical countries are reviewed. Common features of forestry-related joint venture contracts between host country enterprises and multinational corporations are outlined, discussing specific financing arrangements, financing guarantees, problems of labor supply, the nature of forestry-related technology, as well as the international marketing of tropical forest products. The role of United States corporations in forestry activities in seven countries, including Brazil, Colombia, Costa Rica, Honduras, Indonesia, Malaysia, and the Philippines, is studied in closer detail. It is argued that forest conversion by shifting cultivating squatters or by government design, as well as new farming practiced in logged-over areas, are the leading cause of forest cover loss. The authors contend that U.S. corporations represent a "very small fraction" of the total number of joint venture or foreign-owned forestry enterprises in the tropics, and the "commonly held view" that U.S. demand and U.S. MNCs are responsible for much of the world's tropical deforestation "is simply not true." A lack of appropriate technology and trained forestry personnel in developing countries suggests that U.S. MNCs and universities have an important role to play in providing capital and personnel as well as in promoting better research and training facilities in tropical forestry.

Southeast Asia/ Global/ Timber industry—Development and structure/ Timber industry—Environmental impacts.

1056. **Breman, J. 1988.** *The Shattered Image: Construction and Deconstruction of the Village in Colonial Asia.* Comparative Asian Studies, 2. Dordrecht, Netherlands: Fortis Publications.

Asia/ History—Colonial/ Indigenous and local communities—Social relations.

1057. **Brookfield, H., and Y. Byron, eds. 1993.** *Southeast Asia's Environmental Future: The Search for Sustainability.* Tokyo: United Nations University Press.

> The monograph contains papers and responses commissioned for an international conference on securing a sustainable environmental future for Southeast Asia held in Yogyakarta, Indonesia in 1991. Individual papers in the monograph's first section deal with "the

driving forces of change," including population growth, industrialization, urbanization, energy and mineral development, and logging. Part 2 presents papers on different aspects of climate change. Papers in Part 3 address various selected issues, including sustaining the green revolution in rice farming, ecology of rice production (in Indonesia), upland land management, problems of forest fires, issues in coastal, inshore and marine management. Papers in Part 4 deal with issues of place and people, including problems of open access resources, environmental hazards facing different localities, threats posed to the life and livelihood of Southeast Asia's indigenous peoples (with a note on the case of Penan resistance to logging in Sarawak) and urban environmental problems. Issues are largely addressed on a Southeast Asian region-wide basis, and the papers draw from an extensive body of literature. A concluding section by Harold Brookfield synthesizes key findings and presents recommendations for future research and action. An extensive bibliography on a wide variety of environmental issues in Southeast Asia is included.

Southeast Asia/ Agricultural development/ Agricultural intensification/ Agriculture—Shifting cultivation's environmental impacts/ Agriculture—Permanent/ Economic development/ Forest fires/ Population pressure/ Soil erosion and degradation/ Deforestation/ Land settlement and development—Environmental impacts/ Timber industry—Environmental impacts/ Timber industry—Impacts on local communities and economy/ Mining/ Forest management—Forest resource conservation.

1058. **Bruijnzeel, L. A. 1990.** *Hydrology of Moist Tropical Forests and Effects of Conversion: A State of Knowledge Review.* Geneva; Amsterdam: UNESCO International Hydrological Programme; Free University Amsterdam.

Provides a broad overview of current theory and evidence on the impacts of human disturbance on tropical forest hydrology. Includes numerous references to research conducted in Southeast Asia.

Southeast Asia/ Global/ Hydrology/ Soil erosion and degradation/ Watershed management/ Timber industry—Environmental impacts/ Agriculture—Shifting cultivation's environmental impacts/ Land settlement and development—Environmental impacts.

1059. **Burgess, P. F. 1989.** "Asia." In *No Timber Without Trees: Sustainability in the Tropics.* Ed. D. Poore, with contributions from P. Burgess, J. Palmer, S. Rietenbergen, and T. Synnott. pp. 117–153. London: Earthscan Publications.

Asia/ Forest management—Commercial forestry and silviculture/ Timber industry—Logging/ Timber industry—State policy and regulation/ Forest management—Forest resource conservation.

1060. **Cuc, L. T. 1988.** "Agroforestry Practices in Vietnam." East-West Center Working Paper, no. 9. Honolulu, Hawaii: East-West Center.

Southeast Asia/ Vietnam/ Agroforestry/ Indigenous and local communities—Forest land use and management practices.

1061. **Cuc, L. T., K. Gillogly, and A. T. Rambo. 1990.** "Agroecosystems of the Midlands of Northern Vietnam." East-West Center Working Paper, no. 12. Honolulu, Hawaii: East-West Center.

Southeast Asia/ Vietnam/ Indigenous and local communities—Farming practices/ Indigenous and local communities—Forest land use and management practices/ Cultural ecology.

1062. **Daniels, R. 1993.** *Historical Land Use and Carbon Estimates for South and Southeast Asia: 1880–1980.* Oak Ridge, Tenn.: Carbon Dioxide Information Analysis Center.

This numeric data package offers a digital database of land use changes and estimates of vegetational carbon content for South and Southeast Asia for the years 1880, 1920, 1950, 1970 and 1980. Data sources include international and national agricultural and economic statistics, geographic and demographic texts, as well as other reliable news reports and articles. Data are presented for 94 ecological zones in the South-Southeast Asia region, with 1–27 zones per country. Both documentation of methods used and data files (available on magnetic tape, floppy disk and over Internet) are provided with the package. Data files are comprised of 90 Lotus 1-2-3 files, 3 ARC/INFO export files, and 5 ASCII data files. [Summarized from publisher's announcement by J. F. Richards and E. P. Flint].

Southeast Asia/ Land use—Patterns and planning/ Forest cover.

1063. **Davidson, J., Tho Yow Pong, and M. Bijleveld, eds. 1985.** *The Future of Tropical Rain Forests in South East Asia.* Proceedings of a Symposium Organised by the Forest Research Institute, Kepang, Malaysia and the IUCN Commission on Ecology, 1–2 September 1983, Kepong, Malaysia. Gland, Switzerland: International Union for Conservation of Nature and Natural Resources.

Southeast Asia/ Deforestation/ Forest management—Forest resource conservation/ Forest management—Parks and conservation areas.

1064. **de Beer, J. H., and M. J. McDermott. 1989.** *The Economic Value of Non-Timber Forest Products in Southeast Asia.* Amsterdam: IUCN Netherlands.

Southeast Asia/ Non-timber forest products/ Indigenous and local communities—Forest products use and trade/ Rattan—Collection and trade.

1065. **Dent, F. J. 1980.** "Major Production Systems and Soil-related Constraints in Southeast Asia." In *Priorities for Alleviating Soil-Related Constraints to Food Production in the Tropics.* pp. 76–106. Los Baños, Philippines: International Rice Research Institute.

Southeast Asia/ Farm management—Cropping systems/ Agriculture—Permanent.

1066. **Dove, M. R. 1995.** "The Theory of Social Forestry Intervention: The State of the Art in Asia." *Agroforestry Systems* 30 (3): 315–340.

A 1992 review of the Ford Foundation's community forestry program in Asia involved extensive interviews with program officers, academics, government officials, and NGO staff associated with in social forestry development and implementation in Bangladesh, China, India, Indonesia, the Philippines, and Thailand. Drawing from this review and his own extensive research experience in the field, Dove identifies four major issues that have emerged in current policy-related discussions on social forestry as a strategy to arrest forest land degradation: 1) disagreement concerning the cause of deforestation—local communities or government agencies; 2) identifying the most appropriate time for social forestry intervention, with the "receptivity of the forest agency and society" as a key variable; 3) identifying the most appropriate focus for social forestry programs—state lands or community lands; and 4) the need to consider unintended consequences of social forestry intervention, including shifts in intervention focus due to bureaucratic resistance or negative feedback and emergence of new patterns of resource use under social forestry arrangements. Dove concludes that a promising shift from a focus on biological issues to one addressing socioeconomic and institutional constraints has occurred in social forestry development. An appropriate direction now would be greater emphasis on "sensitizing" forestry practitioners to broader issues in theory and reconceptualizing "social forestry intervention as forays in social engineering that have much to do with society and environment, broadly conceived, and little to do with trees or forests in their narrowest sense".

Asia/ Social forestry/ Project intervention—Social and community forestry/ Forest management—Forest resource conservation.

1067. **Fischer, C. 1964.** *South-East Asia: A Social, Economic and Political Geography.* London; New York: Methuen; Dutton.

This general, historical work describes the social, economic and political development of different countries on Southeast Asia. Separate chapters are devoted to Indonesia, Philippines and Malaysia respectively. The work includes numerous pre- and post-independence maps of each country (i.e. from the 1950s and 1960s). A 34-page bibliography is provided.

Southeast Asia/ Geography/ History—Colonial/ Economic development.

1068. **Fisher, L. 1993.** "Changing Landscapes in the Uplands: Issues, Stakeholders, and Institutional Responses." Paper presented at the Workshop on the Status and Development of Dryland Farming in Indonesia, 16–18 November 1993, in Mataram, Lombok.

Upland areas have often been associated with isolated ethnic communities and marginal natural environments. However, over the last several decades, new transportation channels, commercial interests, in-migration and government development programs have brought much change to these areas, linking them in complex and sometimes contentious ways to the outside world and placing increasing pressure on the natural resource base. Fisher outlines some of the key issues and research needs associated with changing conditions in the uplands. These include changes in local farming systems, loss of forest cover, population increase, changing tenure systems, and institutional development needed for improved resource management.

Recent developments in the uplands have ensured that, in addition to local communities, a range of other interest groups, including government agencies, non-governmental organizations concerned with upland poverty and upland environmental degradation, natural and social scientists, and commercial entrepreneurs, have become stakeholders in the upland environment. Each of these stakeholders bring both complementary and competing interests as well as potential contributions to the problem of sustainable development in the uplands. The author stresses the need for new institutional frameworks in order to both tap into complementary strengths and mediate conflicting interests. The experiences of the Nusa Tenggara Uplands Development Consortium in eastern Indonesia is cited as an example of one promising approach.

Southeast Asia/ Forest management—Forest resource conservation/ Project intervention—Soil conservation.

1069. **Fujisaka, S. n.d.** "A Diagnostic Survey of Shifting Cultivation in Northern Laos: Targeting Research to Improve Sustainability and Productivity." IRRI Social Science Division Paper, no. 90–42. Manila, Philippines: International Rice Research Institute.

About 25 percent of Laos' four million people practice shifting cultivation (mainly of rice) on a third of the country's cropped area. Official policy is to eliminate shifting cultivation by year 2000. Diagnostic surveys of shifting cultivation were conducted in Luanag, Prabang and Oudamsay Provinces in northern Laos to understand the practice from a farmers' perspective, to observe fields, and to identify and prioritize problems and research to address problems. Weeds, low and possibly declining soil fertility, intensification of the cropping cycle, rats (plus birds, wild pigs) and insects lowered rice yields or reduced system sustainability. The forest ecosystem has been degraded by logging, burning and rice monocropping; and potentials for environmental rehabilitation through natural succession are minimal. Farmers cannot adopt high labor and cash cost innovations; and improved fallow is needed as an intermediate step prior to crop diversification, adoption of agro-forestry technologies, and sedentary agriculture. [Quoted from paper].

Southeast Asia/ Laos/ Agriculture—Shifting cultivation/ Indigenous and local communities—Farming practices/ Farm management—Cropping systems/ Project intervention—Fallow improvement.

1070. **Gadgil, M., and R. Guha. 1993.** *This Fissured Land: An Ecological History of India*. Delhi, India: Oxford University Press.

Beginning with a brief critique of the modes of production framework for understanding socio-economic change, the transition to and development of capitalism, the authors develop an alternative theory of socio-economic development as ecological history. The framework of analysis proposed remains focused on the sphere of production but recognizes the centrality of natural resources to the trajectory of change in human society. In addition to historical analysis, the modes of resource use framework may be used to examine both the characteristic ideologies and ecological impacts associated with different modes. The authors identify and describe four historical modes: gathering, pastoralism, settled cultivation, and industrialism. The framework is applied to the case of India, with emphasis given to drawing comparisons with the process of ecocultural change in European history.

Asia/ India/ Economic development/ Land use—Patterns and planning/ Forest management/ History—Pre-colonial/ History—Colonial.

1071. **Garrity, D. P., P. Cooper, and D. Bandy. n.d.** "ICRAF's Southeast Asian Programme: Alleviating Tropical Deforestation and Rural Poverty through Improved Agroforestry Systems." Unpublished report prepared for the International Center for Research in Agroforestry (ICRAF), in Bogor, Indonesia.

This 9-page report describes ICRAF's research and dissemination activities in Southeast Asia. Five research programs target a number of areas, including environmental characterization, multipurpose tree improvement, agroforestry component interactions, systems improvement, and policy adoption and impact analysis. Dissemination of research findings will be undertaken through training, education, information and documentation and communication activities.

Southeast Asia/ Project intervention—Agroforestry/ Project intervention—Fallow improvement/ Forest management—Forest resource conservation.

1072. **Garrity, D. P., and P. E. Sajise. 1991.** "Sustainable Land Use Systems Research in Southeast Asia: A Regional Assessment." In *Sustainable Land Use Systems Research*. Proceedings of an international workshop, 12–16 February 1990, New Delhi, India. Pp. 59–76. New Delhi: Oxford and IBH Publishing Co.

The authors briefly describe the major land use systems of Southeast Asia and highlight major areas of current research on sustained productivity at the systems level. Major land use systems in Southeast Asia's lowlands include irrigated rice, rainfed rice, freshwater lakes and ponds, and coastal wetlands. Problems of sustainability include worsening insect infestations with heavy pesticide use following the Green Revolution, a worrisome leveling and even decline in rice yields, shrinking fisheries, as well as a decline in real income levels among farmers. Integrated pest management, combining organic and inorganic fertilizers, and crop diversification are cited as some of the major responses devised to address these problems thus far.

Upland areas in Southeast Asia encompass from 84 to 98 percent of the total land area of the region's countries. Shifting cultivation, other fallow-based dryland crop production systems, coconut-based systems, grassland systems, and forest plantations are among the major land uses in the uplands. High rates of soil erosion (reportedly the highest in the world) and conflicts over land tenure security are the most serious sustainability issues facing resource users in these areas. Hedgerows, zero tillage and social forestry are among the most promising strategies developed by numerous research institutions in the region to address these problems.

The authors also distinguish highland areas of the Southeast Asian region as those lying 1,000 or more above sea level. These areas are characterized by cooler temperatures, cloudiness, lower radiation, subsistence cropping (including irrigated rice, rootcrops and agroforestry) and commercially-based agriculture (mainly vegetable growing), with some animal husbandry. While traditional highland land use systems have proven sustainable under low population densities, numerous problems have been associated with commercial vegetable farming, including pest infestation, chemical pollution, soil deterioration, degrading water regimes, loss of control over factors of production by farmers, and high risks. Very little research has been conducted to address these problems thus far, outside of the Cordillera Studies Center of the University of the Philippines at Baguio.

The paper concludes with a call for greater research to be directed at two priority ecosystems—the coastal lowlands and the uplands—which presently appear to have the "lowest prospect for positive trends in sustainability attributes". In particular, institutional integration and innovation are needed to adequately address the problems of the uplands in their totality.

Southeast Asia/ Land use—Patterns and planning/ Project intervention—Soil conservation/ Forest management—Forest resource conservation.

1073. Government of the Philippines. Department of Environment and Natural Resources, International Institute of Rural Reconstruction, and Ford Foundation. 1990. *Agroforestry Technology Information Kit.* Cavite, Philippines: DENR; IIRR; Ford Foundation.

The kit includes c. 100 sheets containing text and illustrations describing various aspects of agroforestry technology, including different technology types, the specific soil and water conservation problems these technologies can potentially address, other potential benefits, different tree species suitable for different conditions, instructions for establishing and optimizing agroforestry systems as well as troubleshooting. The kit was developed in a workshop held in late 1989, and is intended for use in the training of social forestry technicians and extension workers.

Global/ Project intervention—Agroforestry/ Agroforestry.

1074. **Grandstaff, T. 1978.** "The Development of Swidden Agriculture (Shifting Cultivation)." *Development and Change* 9 (4): 547–579.

Policymakers and scholars have long viewed swidden agriculture as a cropping system inevitably fated to be replaced by sedentary farming. Grandstaff offers an alternative approach to this traditional system of food production, arguing that the specific conditions posed by tropical environments for farming make for serious problems in the wholesale expansion of permanent agriculture in the humid tropics. Given these circumstances, the author cites the need to attempt "comprehensive improvement of swidden cultivation itself, that is, as swidden agriculture, rather than in terms if its being phased out in favor of other forms of land use." Departing from most previous assessments of the long-term viability of swidden farming, Grandstaff approaches shifting cultivation as "a potential modern adaptation, capable of agricultural aid and improvement as are other forms of agriculture today."

Four specific areas are identified where particular attention is needed in order to improve the overall performance of swidden farming: viability (meaning the ability of a particular swidden system to produce food on an ongoing basis); productivity; income; and sociocultural factors. Suggestions for improving system viability include a range of site selection techniques; various soil and nutrient conserving tree cutting and clearing practices; closer controls over the burning process; site-appropriate cropping periods, crop types, crop composition, and cropping sequences; improved weeding practices; and selection of fallow species according to local biophysical and socioeconomic conditions.

Because improving the productivity of swidden farming is constrained by the inappropriateness of conventional yield increasing strategies (such as monoculture farming) to tropical environment, efforts in this area will have to focus on preserving diversity and food self-sufficiency. More specifically, the author suggests careful selection of mixed cropping to ensure maximum sustainable yield and the use of locally available and small-scale fertilizer (livestock and green manure; mulching; low-tech chemical fertilizer applications).

Greater system viability and productivity will allow swidden farmers greater time to devote to cash income earning, in turn improving overall community welfare. Specific strategies for increasing local income opportunities include use of fallow for timber and other cash crop production (i.e., locally controlled taungya systems); integration of cash crops into the swidden cycle; cultivation of permanent cash crop plots where appropriate; animal husbandry; collection of wild forest products; remunerative wage labor; handicraft production and other tourist-related industries.

In attempting to improve existing swidden systems, careful attention must also be paid to the socio-cultural impact of these efforts on local communities. Monitoring for shifts in wealth distribution, trends towards privatization and encroachment from outsiders is essential to make sure that the "development" of swidden farming benefits, rather than undermines, the long-term welfare of different groups within swidden farming communities. Development of appropriate land tenure arrangements is likely to become necessary to ensure equity. Information on current socioeconomic trends and on the various options available to mitigate their negative effects should be made available to local villagers. New institutions are likely to become necessary and constructive ways for government assistance in this must be found. Finally, a more representative "political relationship between the swiddeners and the larger society that claims sovereignty over swiddeners and their territories" must be forged, so as to ensure that local rights to livelihood are not subsumed by the "growing demands" of "national economies" and foreign interests. This latter area, notes the author, is likely to prove the most "problematical" over the long run.

Southeast Asia/ Agriculture—Shifting cultivation/ Indigenous and local communities— Farming practices/ Agricultural intensification/ Agriculture—Shifting cultivation's environmental impacts/ Project intervention—Fallow improvement.

1075.   **Guha, R. 1990.** "Toward a Cross-Cultural Environmental Ethic." *Alternatives* 15: 431–447.

Identifies three major philosophies of environmental history which underpin environmental advocacy in the Western and non-Western cultures, with specific reference to the U.S. and India. "Wilderness thinking", the philosophical basis for radical environmentalism in the U.S., celebrates notions of biocentrism and pristine primitivism, whereby true harmony between humans and nature is best exemplified by hunter-gatherer lifestyles and the preservation of wilderness undisturbed by agriculture, industry, or other manifestations of human activity. "Agrarianism" represents the philosophical underpinnings of much radical eco-activism in India, challenging the value of growth-oriented industrial development and advocating a return to communitarian values, traditional village life, and non-consumerist subsistence production. "Scientific industrialism" may be associated with environmental interest groups (foresters, engineers, development specialists, government policy makers etc.) in each country who remain wedded to the idea that scientific thinking and management born of industrial progress hold the key to maintaining healthy natural and social environments. While agrarianism and wilderness thinking find a common enemy in advocates of modern scientific progress, contradiction and tension characterize the relationship between all three schools of thought. The author suggests the possibility of a promising synthesis of these diverging visions, that is, the possibility of a new environmental ethic built on notions of diversity, sustainability and equity, each emerging from the existing ethics of wilderness, agrarianism, and scientific progress respectively. Works by Lewis Mumford and J. C. Kumarappa are cited to articulate the specific contours of this transcendent ethic.

Global/ Forest management—Forest resource conservation/ Social movements.

1076. **Hurst, P. 1990.** *Rainforest Politics: Ecological Destruction in South-East Asia.* London; Atlantic Highlands: Zed Books.

Southeast Asia/ Deforestation/ Timber industry—Development and structure/ Timber industry—Environmental impacts/ Timber industry—Impacts on local communities and econ-
omy/ Land settlement and development/ Land settlement and development—Impacts on
local communities and economy/ Land settlement and development—Environmental
impacts/ Politics/ Political economy/ Non-governmental organizations/ Social movements.

1077. **Ingram, C. D. 1995.** "Managing Natural Tropical Forests for Income and Diversity: A Model for Mixed Lowland Dipterocarps (Indonesia, Malaysia, Philippines)." Ph.D. diss., University of Wisconsin, Madison, Wisc.

Southeast Asia/ Forest management—Commercial forestry and silviculture/ Forest
management—Economics/ Biodiversity.

1078. **Kartasubrata, J., S. S. Tjitrosomo, and R. C. Umaly, eds. 1990.** *Symposium on
Agroforestry Systems and Technologies.* Biotrop Special Publication, no. 39.
Bogor, Indonesia: SEAMEO BIOTROP.

Reports and papers included here summarize the current status of agroforestry in four
Southeast Asian countries: Indonesia, Malaysia (Sarawak), Philippines, and Thailand.
Papers focus largely on the bio-ecological aspects of agroforestry, including, for example,
the potential application of selected trees in Malaysian agroforestry (A. M. Ahmad and F.
Abood), the potential role of selected non-timber forest plants in agroforestry (K.
Kartawinata), the use of *agathis* in a coffee plantation in East Kalimantan (A. Lahjie and B.
Seibert), the integration of bee-keeping with agroforestry in Indonesia (Kasno), and aspects
of agroforestry for lowland humid areas with low population densities in East Kalimantan
(B. Seibert). Papers on the socioeconomic aspects of agroforestry include, a discussion of
land use by smallholders in East Kalimantan (A. Lahjie), case studies of agroforestry in
Japan, Thailand and Indonesia (J. Kartasubrata), and the prospects for agroforestry in West
Sumatera (M. Jalal). Overall conclusions raise several points, including: 1) The wide
diversity of agroforestry systems in terms of species used and the socio-cultural conditions
associated with them highlights the need for more research on local plant species, indigenous management and tenure arrangements, and traditional beliefs regarding trees and food
production; 2) Forming an agroforestry network among Asian countries to compile a common data-bank would be an important way to increase the usefulness of this kind of
research; 3) Greater support from policymakers is needed in order to better integrate lessons
learned from the study of technical and socioeconomic aspects of agroforestry.

Southeast Asia/ Agroforestry/ Indigenous and local communities—Forest land use and
management practices/ Non-timber forest products/ Farm management—Economics/
Project intervention—Fallow improvement.

1079. **Kemp, J. 1988.** *Seductive Mirage: The Search for the Village Community in Southeast
Asia.* Comparative Asian Studies, no. 3. Dordrecht, Netherlands: Foris Publications.

Southeast Asia/ Indigenous and local communities—Social relations.

1080. **Knight, W. J., and J. D. Holloway, ed. 1990.** *Insects and the Rainforests of
Southeast Asia.* London: Royal Entomological Society of London.

Southeast Asia/ Forest fauna/ Pest, weed, and crop disease management.

1081. **Kunstadter, P. 1987.** "Swiddeners in Transition: Lua' Farmers in Northern Thailand." In *Comparative Farming Systems.* Ed. B. L. Turner II and S. B. Brush,
pp. 130–155. New York: Guilford Press.

Southeast Asia/ Thailand/ Agriculture—Shifting cultivation/ Agricultural intensification/ Population pressure/ Indigenous and local communities—Farming practices.

1082. **Kunstadter, P., E. C. Chapman, and S. Sabhasri, eds. 1978.** *Farmers in the Forest: Economic Development and Marginal Culture in Northern Thailand.* Honolulu, Hawaii: University of Hawaii Press.

Southeast Asia/ Thailand/ Agriculture—Shifting cultivation/ Agricultural intensification/ Population pressure/ Indigenous and local communities—Farming practices/ Indigenous and local communities—Forest land use and management practices/ Health and nutrition.

1083. **Ooi Jin Bee. 1990.** "The Tropical Rain Forest: Patterns of Exploitation and Trade." *Singapore Journal of Tropical Geography* 2 (2): 117–142.

Includes time series data since the 1960s on timber exports from different Southeast Asian countries.

Southeast Asia/ Timber industry—Development and structure/ Timber industry—Trade and markets/ Timber industry—Logging/ Deforestation.

1084. ———. **1993.** *Tropical Deforestation: The Tyranny of Time.* Singapore: Singapore University Press.

The author presents a global account of tropical forest resource use with a particular focus on the problem of deforestation. Rates and causes of deforestation (including logging, shifting cultivation, fuelwood extraction, and organized resettlement) as well as patterns of timber exploitation, trade and forest management are presented in historical and cross-country comparative perspective. Concluding chapters critically assess the feasibility of sustainable tropical forest resource use given the conditions necessary for successful rainforest renewal. It is estimated that at least 60 to 100 years are needed to fully regenerate the timber richness of mature tropical forests, while the time frame needed for restoration of biodiversity is still unknown. Barring a significant reduction in current pressures to exploit land and natural resources in the major rainforest countries, the "tyranny of time" casts considerable doubt on the ability of any management regime to preserve the world's remaining tropical forests over the long run. The monograph features a concise, illustrated synthesis of some of the existing data on tropical resource use and degradation across the globe.

Global/ Deforestation/ Forest regeneration/ Agriculture—Shifting cultivation's environmental impacts/ Timber industry—Environmental impacts/ Land settlement and development—Environmental impacts.

1085. **Ormeling, F. J. 1956.** The Timor Problem: A Geographical Interpretation of an Underdeveloped Island. Groningen; Jakarta: J. B. Wolters.

Southeast Asia/ East Timor/ Geography/ Agriculture—Shifting cultivation/ Agriculture—Shifting cultivation's environmental impacts/ Regional development/ Indigenous and local communities—Economy/ Indigenous and local communities—Farming practices/ Indigenous and local communities—Forest land use and management practices/ Soil erosion and degradation/ History—Colonial.

1086. **Poore, D. 1989.** *No Timber Without Trees: Sustainability in the Tropical Forest.* With contributions from P. Burgess, J. Palmer, S. Rietenbergen, and T. Synnott. London: Earthscan Publications, Ltd.

Based on a study made for ITTO (International Tropical Timber Organization), this book examines the extent to which natural forests are being sustainably managed for timber production. The first chapter discusses the issues and the second presents a case study from

Queensland, Australia, of an approach to successful sustainable development. The next three chapters analyze the results of consultants' field visits and discussion for the continents of Africa (including Cameroon, Congo, Ivory Coast, Gabon, Ghana and Liberia), Asia (including Indonesia, Malaysia, Papua New Guinea, Philippines and Thailand), and South America and the Caribbean (including Bolivia, Brazil, Ecuador, Honduras, Peru and Trinidad and Topago). Chapter Six gives an overview of problems faced in the search for sustainable forest management. Policy recommendations are provided.

Global/ Forest management—Commercial forestry and silviculture/ Timber industry—Logging/ Timber industry—Development and structure/ Timber industry—State policy and regulation/ Forest management—Forest resource conservation.

1087.   **Raintree, J. B., and H. A. Francisco, eds. 1994.** *Marketing of Multipurpose Tree Products in Asia.* Proceedings of an international workshop held in Baguio City, Philippines, 6–9 December 1993. Bangkok: Winrock International.

Eight sections cover different themes related to multipurpose tree product marketing in different Southeast Asian countries, at different scales of operation, and in connection with different products. Section themes include: 1) Marketing of multipurpose tree products; 2) Woodfuel and timber markets; 3) Marketing of multipurpose food trees; 4) Industrial markets; 5) Impacts of markets on rural development: farm forestry, agroforestry and non-timber forest products; 6) Market information systems; 7) Innovative approaches (including case studies of green marketing, plantation development and marketing in West Sumatra, and MPT product marketing by the Ikalahan in the Cordilleras of Northern Luzon); and 8) Working group reports. Products discussed include fuelwood in Cebu and Asia, timber in Sri Lanka, *Parka speciosa* fruits in Peninsular Malaysia, Jackfruit in the Central Visayas, *Artocarpus* species in Nepal, industrial wood in Pakistan, India, Thailand, and the Philippines, and *kapok* in West Sumatra.

Asia/ Indonesia/ Sumatra/ Kalimantan/ Philippines/ Cebu/ Palawan/ Agroforestry/ Non-timber forest products/ Indigenous and local communities—Forest products use and trade/ Fuelwood/ Agricultural economics.

1088.   **Rambo, A. T., K. L. Hutterer, and K. Gillogly. 1988.** "Introduction." In *Ethnic Diversity and the Control of Natural Resources in Southeast Asia.* Ed. A. T. Rambo, K. L. Hutterer, and K. Gillogly, pp. 1–17. Michigan Papers on South and Southeast Asia, no. 32. University of Michigan Press.

Theoretical confusion surrounding the great diversity characteristic of Southeast Asia's ethnic groups persists despite a considerable body of ethnographic work completed in the region. The authors argue that classificatory schemes applied to ethnographic observations in Southeast Asia have been largely imported, reflecting a theoretical underdevelopment in Southeast Asian area studies. Early migration-based theories of ethnic differentiation in the region have been replaced by more refined and less simplistic evolutionary models. More specifically, notions of ecological adaptation have emerged from evolutionary theory, whereby cultural traits are seen as subject to natural selection as well as the selective pressures of any given social environment. Also important are recent theories of intergroup interactions which build upon the link drawn by Fredrik Barth between ethnic differentiation and competitive interactions among groups competing over limited resources. Both ecological adaptation and intergroup interaction theories are represented in the essays compiled within the larger monograph which this paper introduces. However, note the authors, while shedding important light on processes of ethnic identity formation and development, these essays show that no single conceptual approach appears to successfully explain the total ethnic diversity of Southeast Asia. Readers are encouraged to consider the possibility that "different explanations are applicable to different social evolutionary stages".

Southeast Asia/ Ethnicity and ethnic relations/ Cultural ecology.

1089. **Reid, A. 1988.** *Southeast Asia in the Age of Commerce 1450–1680.* New Haven, Conn.: Yale University Press.

Southeast Asia/ History—Pre-colonial.

1090. **Repetto, R. 1988.** "Overview." In *Public Policies and the Misuse of Forest Resources.* Ed. R. Repetto and Malcolm Gillis, pp. 1–41. Cambridge, U.K.: Cambridge University Press.

This overview provides an introduction to a collection of country-specific papers on deforestation and government policy. Preliminary empirical data is provided on regional deforestation rates, international trade in forest products, rents, and economic returns from forest utilization. The analysis is comparative and identifies some of the context-specific reasons for deforestation in tropical countries. Ways in which specific forest sector and non-forest sector policies have contributed to deforestation in different countries are considered. Among the most important of these has been the application of markedly skewed timber royalty and other timber-based revenue generating systems, which have allowed private concessionaires to capture the lion's share of all rents accruing from national forestlands. The author concludes that existing policies have promoted highly destructive logging practices aimed at maximizing short-term gain, resulting in both economic as well as environmental losses for forest-endowed developing countries. More economically sound forestry development policies would help to secure greater national revenues to serve the public good and to sustain an ongoing forest resource base. From this perspective, economic development and forest conservation are not seen as mutually exclusive policy objectives.

Global/ Deforestation/ State policy—Forest and natural resources/ Timber industry—Development and structure/ Timber industry—Environmental impacts/ Timber industry—State policy and regulation/ Forest management—Economics.

1091. **Rerkasem, K., ed. [1988].** Agroecosystems Research for Rural Development: Selected Papers Presented at the Third SUAN Regional Symposium on Agro-ecosystem Research, 22–24 October 1986, Chiang Mai, Thailand. Chiang Mai, Thailand: Multiple Cropping Center, Chiang Mai University and Southeast Asian Universities Agroecosystem Network.

Southeast Asia/ Farming systems research/ Farm management—Cropping systems.

1092. **Richards, J. F., and R. P. Tucker, eds. 1988.** *World Deforestation in the Twentieth Century.* Durham, N.C.: Duke University Press.

Global/ Deforestation.

1093. **Rigg, J. 1991.** *Southeast Asia, A Region in Transition: A Thematic Human Geography of the ASEAN Region.* London: Unwin Hyman.

The author discusses different aspects of socio-economic change characterizing the Southeast Asian region, including its colonial history, the impact of the Green Revolution on rice production in Thailand, problems of deforestation and its relation to indigenous communities in Sarawak, Malaysia and the Philippines, the Indonesian Transmigration Programme, ethnic relations and the New Economic Policy in Malaysia, the experience of urbanization in Bangkok, the role of natural resource exports, the case of export-oriented industrialization in Singapore, and the role of ASEAN. Drawing from recent literature, the book provides an introductory overview to current issues in Southeast Asian development, appropriate for an audience otherwise largely unfamiliar with the region.

Southeast Asia/ Geography/ Economic development/ Deforestation/ Indigenous and local communities/ Ethnicity and ethnic relations/ Land settlement and development/ Timber industry—Development and structure.

1094. **Robison, D. M., and S. J. McKean. 1992.** *Shifting Cultivation and Alternatives: An Annotated Bibliography, 1972–1989.* Wallingford, Oxon, U.K.: CAB International.

Global/ Bibliography/ Agriculture—Shifting cultivation/ Agriculture—Shifting cultivation's environmental impacts/ Forest management—Control of shifting cultivation/ Agroforestry/ Conservation farming/ Project intervention—Fallow improvement.

1095. **Roder, W., B. Keoboualapha, and V. Manivanh. 1995.** "Teak (*Tectona grandis*), Fruit Trees and Other Perennials Used by Hill Farmers of Northern Laos." *Agroforestry Systems* 29 (1): 47–60.

The authors report results of village and household surveys in upland dominated districts of Viengkham, Pakseng, and Xiengngeun, Luang Prabang province, conducted during 1992 and 1993. Survey results reveal that a wide variety of trees are planted on forest fallows and numerous forest products are collected for home consumption and market. Teak appears to be the most favored perennial planted in upland fields, due to its good cash income-generating potential and as a means to secure land tenure. Differences in strategies are noted, however, between farmers of different ethnic background and socio-economic means, largely related to significant differentials in the resources available to individual households. Resource-poor households appear the least likely to maintain combined food, livestock and timber production systems, and are thus least likely to benefit from a booming market in teak. [Summarized with modification from journal abstract].

Southeast Asia/ Laos/ Indigenous and local communities—Forest products use and trade/ Indigenous and local communities—Forest land use and management practices.

1096. **Roder, W., S. Phengchanh, B. Keoboualapha, and S. Maniphone. 1995.** "*Chromolaena odorata* in Slash-and-Burn Rice Systems of Northern Laos." *Agroforestry Systems* 31 (1): 79–92.

Characterizations of *Chromolaena odorata* as a noxious weed resulting from poor farming practices contradict alternative assessments of its role as a beneficial fallow species in intensifying swidden farming systems. To gain a more informed perspective on the issue, the LAO-IRRI research project involved data collection on land use practices, weed problems and soil fertility in various Laotian provinces between 1991 and 1993. Specific questions examined included: 1) the introduction and spread of *C. odorata* in Laos since the 1930s; 2) its role in the rice-growing and fallow phases of extant rice-growing systems; and 3) its possible advantages and disadvantages as a fallow plant. Biomass analysis found that the weed species contributed 16 to 48 percent of total above-ground biomass at rice harvest after 1 to 2 year fallow, though this proportion declined significantly with longer fallow periods as tree and bamboo species became more dominant. Farmers were found to appreciate *C. odorata* as a fallow species for its ability to suppress other weeds, its lack of negative effects on rice yields, the ease with which it is controlled by hand weeding, and other reasons. The research also highlighted *C. odorata*'s importance in quickly establishing a protective cover in early fallow periods, suggesting its suitability particularly for sloping fields. Possible disadvantages of the species for systems involving grazing, crop rotation, fruit, and/or timber production exist, however, and require further study before general recommendations on its role in developing improved fallow systems can be determined.

Southeast Asia/ Laos/ Pest, weed, and crop disease management/ Indigenous and local communities—Farming practices/ Indigenous and local communities—Forest land use and management practices.

1097. **Soerianegara, I. et al., eds. 1991.** Proceedings of the Fourth Round-Table Conference on Dipterocarps, 12–15 December 1989, Bogor, West Java, Indonesia. Bogor, West Java, Indonesia: SEAMEO BIOTROP.

Southeast Asia/ Forest management—Commercial forestry and silviculture/ Forest management—Forest resource conservation/ Timber industry—Logging/ Timber industry— State policy and regulation.

1098. **Spencer, J. E. 1966.** *Shifting Cultivation in Southeastern Asia.* University of California Publications in Geography, vol. 19. Berkeley, Calif.; Los Angeles, Calif.: University of California Press.

Southeast Asia/ Agriculture—Shifting cultivation/ Indigenous and local communities— Farming practices/ Indigenous and local communities—Forest land use and management practices.

1099. **Sun, P. 1989.** *Land and Water Resource Management in Asia.* Economic Development Institute Policy Seminar Report, no. 20. Washington, D.C.: World Bank.

Presents a state-of-the-art review of current theory and practice of soil and watershed management in Asia.

Asia/ Soil erosion and degradation/ Hydrology/ Watershed management/ Project intervention—Soil conservation/ Conservation farming/ Forest management—Economics/ Farm management—Economics.

1100. **Sustainable Land Use Alternatives to Slash and Burn in Asia (SAVE-Asia). 1992.** *A Regional Project Proposal as Part of a Global Strategy on Alternatives to Slash and Burn.* Unpublished Manuscript. Photocopy.

The proposal describes plans for an international Asian project aimed at finding appropriate alternatives to shifting cultivation. Regional issues in shifting cultivation are briefly discussed along with project goals, research model, activities, expected outcomes and the strategies planned for achieving these. Implementing agencies include: International Rice Research Institute (IRRI); International Council for Research in Agroforestry (ICRAF); International Fertilizer Development Center (IFDC); Philippine Departments of Agriculture and Natural Resources; Philippine Universities; Indonesian Ministries of Agriculture and Forestry; Indonesian Universities; Thailand Departments of Agriculture and Forestry; Thai Universities; Asian Coalition of Non-Governmental Organizations in Agrarian Reform and Rural Development.

Southeast Asia/ Forest management—Control of shifting cultivation.

1101. **Tadem, E. 1990.** "Conflict Over Land-based Natural Resources in the ASEAN Countries." *Conflict Over Natural Resources in Southeast Asia and the Pacific.* Ed. Lim Teck Ghee and M. J. Valencia, pp. 13–50. Manila: Ateneo de Manila University Press.

While the ASEAN countries are abundantly endowed with vital natural resources, the region has seen growing tension over their use and control. This paper describes the rapid exploitation of land-based resources in the region and some of the ensuing conflicts which have resulted. The role of big business (logging firms, agribusiness, mining companies) is emphasized and the historical (i.e., colonial and neo-colonial) roots of logging, agricultural modernization, and the mining industry are described. The authors advocate a strong position against the monopolistic control being exercised by large business and the developed countries. It remains unclear, however, that the ASEAN governments possess the political will to take decisive steps in this direction, given their tendency to side with big resource-exploiting companies rather than represent the interests of peasants, workers, and tribal communities.

Southeast Asia/ Deforestation/ Timber industry—Development and structure/ Land settlement and development/ Mining/ Agriculture—Plantations/ History—Colonial/ Political economy.

1102. **Tamin, N. M., ed. 1993.** *Ecological Economics in Relation to Forest Conservation and Management.* Proceedings of the International Conference on Ecological Economics, Pulau Langkawi, 20–22 July 1992. Kuala Lumpur: Syarikat Datar Raya Sdn Bhd.

Contains ten papers dealing with various issues in ecological economics and forest conservation, including biodiversity conservation, economics of conservation, rainforest management in Papua New Guinea, timber resource management in Sri Lanka, forest pathogens in Thailand, forest regeneration in Sabah, natural resource accounting for forest values, ecology and economic role of Toona in Malaysia, and information access and dissemination.

Asia/ Malaysia/ Sabah/ Forest management—Forest resource conservation/Forest management—Economics/ Forest regeneration/ Biodiversity.

1103. **Thai-Tsung, N., T. Yui-Long, and H. Kueh, eds. 1991.** *Towards Greater Advancement of the Sago Industry in the '90s.* Proceedings of the Fourth International Sago Symposium, 6–9 August 1990, Kuching, Sarawak, Malaysia. Kuching, Sarawak, Malaysia: Ministry of Agriculture and Community Development and Department of Agriculture.

As reflected in the Symposium's title, the focus of the papers included in the proceedings is on the technical aspects of increasing sago yields, in line with government efforts in the Southeast Asia region to increase plantation-based sago cultivation. Several of the papers presented also focus on describing the environmental conditions associated with sago production, the ecology of sago in Sarawak, the variety and diversity and genetic importance of sago palms generally, and traditional sago palm management by indigenous communities in Papua New Guinea.

Southeast Asia/ Malaysia/ Sarawak/ Non-timber forest products/ Forest flora/ Agriculture—Plantations/ Agricultural development/ Forest biology and ecology/ Indigenous and local communities—Forest products use and trade/ Indigenous and local communities—Forest land use and management practices/ State policy—Agricultural and rural development.

1104. **Tugby, D. 1968.** "Ethnological and Allied Work on Southeast Asia, 1950–66." *Current Anthropology* 9: 189–206.

Southeast Asia/ Ethnography/ Indigenous and local communities/ Bibliography.

1105. **Vergara, N. T., and R. A. Fernandez, eds. 1989.** *Social Forestry in Asia: Factors that Influence Program Implementation.* College, Laguna, Philippines: Southeast Asian Regional Center for Graduate Study and Research in Agriculture (SEARCA).

This monograph presents papers prepared for a 1987 regional workshop aimed at addressing the question: Why has social forestry not been more widely accepted by farmers in Asia?. For the most part, the papers included deal with the experience of social forestry in individual countries (Philippines, India, Nepal, Malaysia (Sabah), Indonesia) and report on the results of small short-term field studies. Papers presented in the monograph include, among others: Daylinda B. Cabanilla, "Anthropological Studies of Land Use in Project Sites: A Prerequisite to Effective Social Forestry Implementation"; Sharon C. Quizon, "Social Forestry: An Age-old Indigenous Approach to Rural Development"; Corazon B. Lamug, "Social and Cultural Factors and their Effects on Social Forestry in the Philippines"; Warlito A. Laquihon, "Some Key Determinants of SALT Adoption in the Philippines: Viewpoint of Farmer Cooperators"; Antonio Q. Repollo, Jr. and Elvira R. Castillo, "Agroforestry Technology in Hilly Land and Households: Factors Influencing Its Adoption"; Glora R. Diokno, "Participation of Upland Women: A Determinant in the Success of Social Forestry Programs"; Marcelo P. Udarbe, "Social Forestry in Sabah: A Learning Experience"; Charles P. Castro, "Facilitating and Constraining Factors in the Implementation of Social Forestry in the Philippines". Papers by Lamug, Laquihon, Udarbe and Castro have been abstracted separately.

Asia/ Project intervention—Social and community forestry/ Project intervention—Agroforestry.

1106. **Wan Razali Wan Mohd., J. Dransfield, and N. Manokaran, eds. 1992.** *A Guide to the Cultivation of Rattan.* Malayan Forest Record, no. 35. Kuala Lumpur: Forest Research Institute Malaysia.

The background to rattan cultivation, rattan silviculture, and rattan processing are discussed in three separate sections. Part 1 includes chapters on issues related to morphology, ecology and natural history, physiology, phenology, traditional uses, and history of cultivation. Chapters in Part 2 cover selection of species and planting sites, nursery procedures, planting systems for small- and large-diameter canes, field preparation, nutrient requirements, pests and diseases, seed technology, tissue culture, harvesting methods, and economics of cultivation (both large- and small-diameter cane). Part 3 (one chapter) details the procedures and problems involved in rattan processing for further downstream manufacture of rattan goods.

Asia/ Rattan—Cultivation/ Rattan—Downstream processing.

1107. **Watters, R. F. 1960.** "The Nature of Shifting Cultivation." *Pacific View-Point* 1: 59–99.

Asia/ Agriculture—Shifting cultivation/ Agriculture—Shifting cultivation's environmental impacts/ Indigenous and local communities—Farming practices.

1108. **Whitmore, T. C. 1984.** *Tropical Rainforests of the Far East.* Oxford: Clarendon Press.

Asia/ Forest flora/ Forest fauna/ Forest biology and ecology/ Forest management—Parks and conservation areas/ Biodiversity.

1109. **Wong, K. M., and N. Manokaran, eds. 1985.** *Proceedings of the Rattan Seminar, 2–4 October 1984, Kuala Lumpur, Malaysia.* Kepong, Malaysia: Rattan Information Centre.

Southeast Asia/ Rattan—Growth and distribution/ Rattan—Cultivation/ Rattan—Resource management and conservation/ Rattan—Downstream processing.

MAPS AND ATLASES

1110. *Agricultural Land Use in Sabah.* **[1992].** 1:50,000. Kota Kinabalu, Sabah: Agriculture Department, Sabah.

> The Agriculture Department of Sabah has recently prepared a series of maps for the state, showing land being used for different kinds of agriculture.

> Map/ Malaysia/ Sabah/ Land use—Patterns and planning.

1111. *Agroclimatic Map of the Philippines.* **1980.** 1:2,500,000. Los Ba–os, Philippines: International Rice Research Institute.

> One color-coded map shows agroclimatic zones distinguished by length of wet and dry seasons (in months).

> Map/ Philippines.

1112. *Atlas Kalimantan Timur.* **1982.** Hamburg: Transmigration Area Development (TAD).
[Atlas of East Kalimantan.]

> Brief description of mapping techniques used, including remote sensing, aerial surveys, side-looking airborne radar surveys, among others. The following maps included in the atlas are shown by section at a scale of 1:750,000: Topography; geology; mineral resources; geomorphology; soils; vegetation (1974, excluding crop cover, though indicating areas that are "inhabited and developed";) agricultural potentials also showing areas already "inhabited and developed" as of 1978.
> The following are shown at a scale of 1:3,500,000: drainage basins (1:3,500,000) and river profiles (i.e. gradient); forest categories (1980); precipitation; administrative areas.
> The atlas was compiled by the Transmigration Area Development project within the context of identifying soil and land suitability for agricultural conversion in connection with Indonesia's transmigration program.

> Atlas/ Indonesia/ East Kalimantan/ Soils/ Forest flora/ Topography.

1113. **Barrera, A. et al. 1954.** "Soil Survey of Cebu Province, Philippines." Department of Agriculture and Natural Resources. Soil Report, no. 17. Manila: Bureau of Printing.

> Includes 1 soil map.

> Atlas/ Philippines/ Cebu/ Soils.

1114. **Collins, M., ed. 1990.** *The Last Rainforests: A World Conservation Atlas.* New York: Oxford University Press.

> This atlas describes the remaining rainforest areas of the world, providing a brief, popular description of local flora, fauna, ecosystems, and human communities. Maps showing remaining rainforest (montane and lowland), former rainforest and critical drought/forest fire areas are provided for different regions (Amazon, Central America, Caribbean, Philippines and Sabah, Central Indonesia, etc.). Sources of the maps for Southeast Asia include among others: Indonesia—RePPProt "National Overview of the Regional Physical Planning Programme for Transmigration" 1990; Sabah, Malaysia—Sabah Forest Department, "Sabah, Malaysia, Natural Plantation Forests" 1984; Philippines—Forest Management Bureau, "Natural Forest Resources of the Philippines," Dept. of Environment and Natural Resources, Manila, 1988.

> Atlas/ Malaysia/ Indonesia/ Philippines/ Forest cover.

1115. **Collins, M., J. A. Sayer, and T. C. Whitmore, eds. 1991.** *The Conservation Atlas of Tropical Forests: Asia and the Pacific.* With IUCN, The World Conservation Union. New York: Simon and Schuster.

> Several introductory chapters in the atlas briefly review current issues regarding shifting cultivation, land settlement schemes, the timber industry, and government land use policies. Subsequent chapters are devoted to individual countries, showing maps based on available information concerning forest types, forest cover, and existing forest reserves and national parks. Chapters also discuss the characteristics of local flora and fauna. For Indonesia, maps of individual islands are shown, including Kalimantan, Sumatra, Java, Sulawesi and the Lesser Sundas. Forest cover depicted is based on survey data collected through the Transmigration development program. For Kalimantan, Peninsular Malaysia as well as Sarawak and Sabah are shown. Data for the Philippines is drawn from recent satellite imagery and ground surveys by the Swedish Satellite Corporation and the German Agency for Technical Cooperation working in conjunction with the DENR.

> Atlas/ Southeast Asia/ Indonesia/ Malaysia/ Philippines/ Forest cover/ Forest management—Parks and conservation areas.

1116. **Conklin, H. C. 1980.** *Ethnographic Atlas of Ifugao: A Study of Environment, Culture, and Society in Northern Luzon.* New Haven, Conn.: Yale University Press.

> Atlas/ Philippines/ Indigenous and local communities—Farming practices/ Indigenous and local communities—Forest land use and management practices/ Agriculture—Shifting cultivation/ Cultural ecology.

1117. *Forest Inventory of the Philippines.* **[1990].** 1:250,000. [Manila]: German Agency for Technical Cooperation.

> Aerial photography and ground measurement provided the data for this mapping project. Some discrepancies with slightly earlier mapping results by the Swedish Space Corporation obtained. See entry for "Mapping of the Natural Conditions of the Philippines" for further details. Scale is 1:250,000.

> Map/ Philippines/ Forest cover.

1118. **Holm, L. G., J. V. Pancho, J. P. Herberger, and D. L. Plucknett. 1979.** *A Geographical Atlas of World Weeds.* New York: Wiley-Interscience.

> Atlas/ Global/ Pest, weed, and crop disease management/ Grasslands.

1119. **Indonesia. Ministry of Internal Affairs. 1984.** *Atlas penggunaan tanah.* Jakarta: Ministry of Internal Affairs; Agraria General Directorate.
[Land Use Atlas.]

> This atlas includes color-coded provincial maps showing altitude, land under wet rice, dryland crops, plantation, forest, scrub, urban settlements, as well as alang-alang covered and other degraded areas. Paved roads are also highlighted. Derived from data gathered by Agraria between 1978 and 1980.

Atlas/ Indonesia/ Land use—Patterns and planning.

1120. ***Indonesia: luas panen tanaman bahan makanan.* 1976.** 1:7,500, 000. Jakarta: Badan Koordinasi Survey dan Pemetaan Nasional.
[Indonesia: Harvested Area of Food Crops.]

> Color-coded map showing amount of different food crops harvested from different provinces. Includes information on wet rice, dryland rice, cassava, peanuts, soybeans and other legumes.

Map/ Indonesia/ Agricultural development.

1121. ***Indonesia, peta vegetasi.* 1980.** Jakarta: Badan Koordinasi Survey dan Pemetaan Nasional.
[Indonesia, Vegetation Map.]

> Map/ Indonesia/ Forest flora.

1122. ***Kalimantan Timur: tata guna hutan kesepekatan.* 1984.** 1:1, 000,000. [Hamburg]: Transmigration Area Development (TAD).
[East Kalimantan Forest Categories.]

> Single map prepared by the Transmigration Area Development Project (TAD) showing areas of the province set aside for protection, limited production, research production, agricultural conversion and nature reserves. No indication of actual extant forest cover is included. The scale presented is 1:1,000,000. The map's information is based on a forest classification map compiled earlier (1:5,000,000 scale) and available at the Provincial Forestry Department Office in Samarinda, East Kalimantan.

Map/ Indonesia/ East Kalimantan/ Land use—Patterns and planning.

1123. ***Land Capability Classification of Sabah.* 1976.** Land Resource Study, no. 25. Surbiton, Surrey, U.K.: Land Resources Division, Ministry of Overseas Development.

> Results of a land capability classification undertaken in 1975 are presented in three volumes and 9 sectional maps. Individual volumes report on Tawau, Sandakan and West Coast/Kudat Residencies respectively. A series of small (page to half-page size) maps at 1:2,000,000 and 1:1,425,000 scale is presented in the analysis. These show land categories, cultivated areas, land suited for agriculture already under cultivation, land suited for agriculture not yet cultivated, alienated land, land suitable for mining, land suitable for commercial forestry, forest inventory and areas of conflicting potential use between agriculture and forestry. 9 larger maps at 1:250,000 scale are color-coded showing land classed by potential for agriculture, mineral development, forest exploitation, conservation, stateland, alienated lands, forest reserves, government reserves, grazing, drainage and irrigation areas, alienated and gazetted boundaries.

Map/ Malaysia/ Sabah/ Land use—Patterns and planning.

1124. ***Land Status and Recommended Development Areas. 1989.*** 1:250,000. London; Jakarta: Land Resources Dept. of the Overseas Development Natural Resources Institute; Directorat Bina Program, Direktorat Jenderal Penyiapan Pemukiman, Departemen Transmigrasi, Republik Indonesia.

> Detailed maps similar to "land systems and suitability" series though with greater emphasis on showing proposed changes. Specifically, the maps show existing and proposed paved roads, proposed and existing forest protection areas, existing settlements, transmigration areas, proposed settlement areas, and recommended development areas suggesting specific land uses, existing nucleus estate plantations and oil concessions. Olin Library has maps covering a number of provinces, including East Kalimantan. The latter is shown in 20 segments, although library holdings include only 17 of these [not yet cataloged; refer to map librarian to obtain access]. Scale is 1:250,000.

> Map/ Indonesia/ East Kalimantan/ Land use—Patterns and planning/ Land settlement and development.

1125. ***Land Systems with Land Suitability and Environmental Hazards. 1989.*** 1:250,000. London; Jakarta: Land Resources Department of the Overseas Development Natural Resources Institute; Directorat Bina Program, Direktorat Jenderal Penyiapan Pemukiman, Departmen Transmigrasi, Republik Indonesia.

> Detailed maps showing existing and proposed land systems, transmigration areas, indigenous settlements, cities and towns, suroads, logging roads, rivers, navigability. East Kalimantan is divided into 20 segments with one segment displayed per map. Compiled in context of national transmigration program. Covers most of Indonesia. Olin library has all but 1 of East Kalimantan's 20 segments [not yet cataloged, refer to map librarian to obtain access], most of Sumatra and Java as well. The library is receiving additional maps on an ongoing basis. Key is needed to read map completely though it is not clear whether such a key is present in the library holdings. Scale is 1:250, 000.

> Map / Indonesia/ East Kalimantan/ Land use—Patterns and planning/ Land settlement and development.

1126. ***Mapping of the Natural Conditions of the Philippines. 1988.*** 1:250,000. Solna, Sweden: Swedish Space Corporation.

> LANDSAT spot imagery provided the data for this mapping project, commissioned by the World Bank c. 1988. A subsequent forest inventory mapping project engaged by the German Agency for Technical Cooperation (GTZ) and the Department of Forestry of the Philippines revealed some significant discrepancies when compared with the SSC results. In some cases, areas of forest cover differed by as much as 50% between these two projects. An investigation by the Dept. of Forestry revealed the possibility of some error in both mapping efforts. LANDSAT imagery may have been blurred by cloud cover in some areas. In addition, the images obtained did not clearly reveal borders between shrub and forest cover. For these areas, the ground work completed by the GTZ/Forestry Department obtained more accurate data. In other areas, however, the latter suffered from errors in manual map measurement. NMRIA (National Mapping Resources Information Authority) has since completed a 1 km x 1 km reclassification of the areas covered by both projects. Where significant discrepancies arise, the area is reclassified according to which technique appeared to be able to give the most accurate results under the given area conditions. This later data set may be available in digital form from NMREA. The original SSC maps are located at NMREA and the World Bank in Washington D.C. Scale is 1:250,000.

> Map/ Philippines/ Forest cover.

1127. **Marginal Farmer Community Development Project. 1991.** 1:250, 000. Jakarta, Indonesia: Agency of Agricultural Research and Development; Asian Development Bank.

> The packet contains a set of 16 maps prepared for the Marginal Farmer Community Development Project. (See separate entry in Indonesia section of this update for description of the project). Maps show land use and land units in 8 areas of Indonesia, including: western and central Aceh; northern Bengkulu; Sukabumi, Cianjur and Garut in West Java; eastern Sumba; South Kahayan-South Kitingan river area in Central Kalimantan; South Barito river area in Central Kalimantan; western South Kalimantan; and southern South Sulawesi. Data source is culled from the results of the RePPProt mapping project of the late 1980s. Areas displayed in the maps are those identified to be occupied by high concentrations of marginal farmers, as indicated by poverty statistics and biophysical characteristics of the land being cultivated.

> Map/ Indonesia/ Central Kalimantan/ South Kalimantan/ Land use—Patterns and planning/ Agriculture—Shifting cultivation.

1128. **Pengunaan tanah Kalimantan Timur. 1970.** 1:50,000; 1:250, 000. Jakarta: Direktorat Landuse.
[Land Use in East Kalimantan.]

> 19 maps are presented in one grouping at 1:50,000 scale. 2 further maps are at a scale of 1:250,000.

> Map/ Indonesia/ East Kalimantan/ Land use—Patterns and planning.

1129. **Penyebaran penduduk: Kalimantan. 1983.** 1:7,500,000. Jakarta: Badan Koordinasi Survey dan Pemetaan Nasional.
[Population Distribution: Kalimantan.]

> Differing densities of dot shading reveal population concentration in different provinces on one map. Dots reflect population numbers in specific areas of each island. The figure is based on 1978 statistics from the Central Bureau of Statistics. Scale is 1:7,500,000.

> Map/ Indonesia/ Demography.

1130. **Present Land Use and Forest Status. 1988.** 1:250,000. Jakarta: Badan Koordinasi Survei Tanah Nasional (BAKORSTANAL; Coordinating Body for National Land Surveys).

> Detailed maps prepared in connection with the national transmigration program. The maps show specific land use and forest status patterns for different provinces divided into individual sections.

> Map/ Indonesia/ Land use—Patterns and planning/ Forest cover.

1131. **A Provisional Map of Soil Degradation Risks. 1980.** 1:5,000, 000. Rome: Food and Agriculture Organization.

> 1 map on 3 sheets, based on an interpretation of major environmental parameters. According to ARLIN search at Mann Library, within the U.S. this map is available at the U.S. Library of Congress only. Map is at 1:5,000,000 scale.

> Map/ Global/ Soil erosion and degradation.

1132. **Sabah Sarawak: taburan penduduk bandar. 1983.** Jabatan Perangkaan. [Sabah and Sarawak: Population Distribution of Towns.]

Map/ Malaysia/ Sabah/ Sarawak/ Demography.

1133. ***Soils of Sabah.* 1975.** Land Resource Study, no. 20. London: Overseas Development Natural Resources Institute.

A range of maps are presented summarizing the results of a soil classification study conducted in the early 1970s. A series of district maps is provided, c. 11" by 16" in size (fold-out maps), at 1:750,000 scale, each showing 1) towns, villages, roads and major footpaths; 2) vegetation cover (excluding crops); 3) parent materials; 4) land currently under cultivation as well as recommended agricultural expansion and new development areas (available for only part of the study area); 5) soil suitability; 6) land forms. A separate series of much larger maps at 1:250, 000 scale show soil classification for 10 districts in Sabah, including: Labuan, Pulau Banggi, Susut, Kota Kinabalu, Tuaran, Sandakan, Dent Peninsula Pensiangan, Tawau and Semporna. Assessment of land suitability for agricultural conversion is provided in percentage terms. Data for the maps was gathered through aerial photography as well as ground-level fieldwork.

Map/ Malaysia/ Sabah/ Soils/ Agricultural development.

1134. ***Southeast Asia.* 1979.** 1:5,000,000. Soil Map of the World, no. 9. Paris: UNESCO.

One color-coded map shows the countries of Southeast Asia, classified by soil unit and soil phase. 60 soil units and 7 soil phases are represented. Scale is 1:5,000,000.

Map/ Southeast Asia/ Soils.

1135. ***Topographic Maps of Sabah.* 1962.** 1:50,000. [Kota Kinabalu, Sabah]: Sabah Land and Survey Department.

132 maps of Sabah are included in this series, showing the state's topography by subdistrict. Copies are available through the Institute for Development Studies.

Map/ Sabah/ Topography.

1136. ***Topographical Maps of the Philippines.* 1956.** 1:50,000. Manila: Bureau of Coast and Geodetic Survey.

Topographical sectional maps covering most of the Philippines. The maps show topography of the islands as well as roads (both dirt and paved), areas of wood, scrub, tropical grass, swamp and nipa mangrove cover as well as areas under rice paddy, orchards and vineyards. Sources for these maps were primarily U.S. Army maps compiled by photogrammetric methods between 1947 and 1953. Most of Mindanao and Cebu is covered. Scale is 1:50,000.

Map/ Philippines/ Cebu/ Mindanao/ Topography/ Land use—Patterns and planning.

1137. **Ulack, R., and G. Pauer. 1989.** *Atlas of Southeast Asia.* New York: MacMillan.

This atlas reports on various geographic aspects of both mainland and insular Southeast Asia. In particular, it includes two shaded maps showing 1980 population density as well as rate of population change across different countries of the whole region. These are helpful for highlighting relative differences within the region.

Atlas/ Southeast Asia/ Geography/ Demography.

1138. *Vegetation Map of Malesia.* **1958.** 1:5,000,000. Paris: UNESCO.

Color-coded map showing vegetation cover classified by type as follows: rainforest, dipterocarp rainforest, agathis, ironwood, casuarina, pine, swamp, sago, mangrove, secondary forest, savannahs, grassland, alpine grassland, monsoon forest, teak, wet rice, dry fields, and plantations. The map was compiled in connection with UNESCO's Humid Tropics Research Project and includes Indonesia, much of Philippines and Malaysia. Not all areas on Cebu island have been coded, however. Scale is 1:5,000, 000.

Map/ Southeast Asia/ Forest flora/ Grasslands/ Land use—Patterns and planning.

1139. **Whitmore, T. C. 1984.** "Vegetation Map of Malesia at Scale of 1:5,000,000." *Journal of Biogeography* 11: 461–471.

Map/ Southeast Asia/ Forest flora.

1140. **Wong, I. F. T. 1973.** "The Present Land Use of Sabah, 1970." Ministry of Agriculture, Kuala Lumpur.

Aerial photo (1:25,000 scale) interpretation techniques were used to prepare this report, as a joint effort between the Departments of Agriculture of West Malaysia and Sabah respectively. According to the report, the 1970 land use in Sabah were: Urban 22,873 acres (012%); agriculture 774,709 acres (4.24%); forest 13,153,631 acres (72.04%) scrub forest 1,873,747 acres (10.26%) swamps 1,756,568 acres (9.62%); grassland 386,753 acres (2.12%).

Atlas/ Malaysia/ Sabah/ Land use—Patterns and planning.

1141. *World Map on Status of Human-Induced Soil Degradation.* **1990.** 1:15,000,000. Nairobi, Kenya; Wageningen, Netherlands: UNEP; ISRIC.

Includes 3 maps total.

Map/ Global/ Soil erosion and degradation.

Journals

1142. *Asia-Pacific Uplands.* Honolulu, Hawaii: Program on Environment, East-West Center.

> Reports on current research, workshops and conferences dealing with issues in uplands development in the Asia-Pacific. Regular features include reviews of recent books as also a listing of new published and fugitive literature. Published quarterly.

Journal.

1143. *Borneo Research Bulletin.* **1969+.** Williamsburg, Va.: Borneo Research Council.

> Results of current research are presented along with announcements related to the pursuit of scholarly work in Borneo. The journal is multidisciplinary, reflecting work on a wide range of subjects.

Journal.

1144. *Borneo Review.* **1990+.** Kota Kinabalu, Sabah, Malaysia: Institute for Development Studies.

> Articles related to socio-economic and socio-cultural development in Sabah, Sarawak, and Indonesia's Kalimantan provinces are presented.

Journal.

1145. *Buletin Penelitian Hutan.* **c. 1975+.** Bogor, West Java, Indonesia: Pusat Penelitian dan Pengembangan Hutan (Center for Forest Research and Development).
[Forest Research Bulletin.]

> Includes articles reporting on current research on forest products, forest management, agroforestry, and related topics in Indonesia. [In Bahasa Indonesia].

Journal.

1146. *Environesia: A Publication of WALHI.* **1986+.** Jakarta, Indonesia: Indonesian Environmental Forum (WALHI).

> Published Indonesia's largest environmental advocacy groups, this journal covers current news concerning problems of environmental protection in Indonesia, including natural resource management and pollution.

Journal.

1147. ***Flora Malesiana Bulletin*. 1947+.** Leyden, Netherlands: Flora Malesiana Foundation.

> Covers research on botany and flora in Malaysia and Indonesia.

Journal.

1148. ***Gaharu*. 1991+.** Samarinda, East Kalimantan, Indonesia: Lembaga Pengembangan Lingkungan dan Sumberdaya Manusia (PLASMA) (Foundation for Environmental and Human Resource Development).

> A local community-oriented periodical covering issues in forest and water management, pollution, non-timber forest products, indigenous culture, land rights, health and nutrition, appropriate technology, agricultural development, and self-sufficient community development in the Kalimantan provinces. Bimonthly. [In Bahasa Indonesia].

Journal.

1149. ***GFG Report*. 1986+.** Samarinda, East Kalimantan, Indonesia: German Forestry Group and the Faculty of Forestry, Universitas Mulawarman.

> This series is co-published by the German Forestry Group and the Faculty of Forestry, Universitas Mulawarman, Samarinda, East Kalimantan. Articles deal with various aspects of forestry in Kalimantan, including emerging results of research on natural forest management, issues in silviculture, agroforestry, social forestry, and forest use patterns by local communities.

Journal.

1150. ***Indonesian Environmental History Newsletter*. 1993+.** Leiden, Netherlands: Ecology, Demography, and Economy in Nusantara, KITLV.

> Predominantly English-language. Presents reports on recent research activities related to environment, environmental change, and management from different as well as interdisciplinary perspective in Indonesia. In addition to articles newsletter issues feature a bibliography of recent literature. Semiannual.

Journal.

1151. ***Journal of the Sabah Society*. 1960+.** Jesselton, Sabah, Malaysia: Sabah Society.

> Covers the natural history, archaeology, anthropology as well as other socio-cultural aspects of Sabah.

Journal.

1152. *Kajian Malaysia. Journal of Malaysian Studies*. 1982+. Penang: Universiti Sains Malaysia.

> Interdisciplinary journal related to Malaysian studies, including issues of politics, economy, agricultural development, regional development, natural resource development, with both state-specific (Peninsular, Sabah, Sarawak) and Malaysia-wide focus. Semiannual. [Articles in English and Bahasa Melayu].

Journal.

1153. **Kalimantan Review. 1992+.** Pontianak, West Kalimantan, Indonesia: Institute of Dayakology Research and Development (IDRD).

> The magazine emphasizes providing a forum for scholars in Kalimantan to discuss current issues affecting communities in Borneo and to describe and exchange interpretations of local cultural heritage and oral traditions. Publication of the magazine is one of several foci of the Institute of Dayakology Research and Development, which also include research, community education, women and development and fundraising for social, education and socioeconomic development projects in Kalimantan.

> Journal.

1154. **Kinaadman. 1979+.** Cagayan de Oro, Misamis Oriental, Philippines: Xavier University.

> Particular emphasis on Mindanao culture and socio-economic development. Annual.

> Journal.

1155. *Laporan Penyelidikan Hutan Negeri Sabah. Forest Research Center Biennial Report.* 1969+. Kota Kinabalu, Sabah, Malaysia: Forest Research Center, Department of Forestry.

> Covers forestry sector issues in Sabah. Biennial. [Articles mostly in English].

> Journal.

1156. **Malaysian Directory of Timber Trade. 1985+.** Kuala Lumpur, Malaysia: Malaysian Timber Industry Board, Ministry of Primary Industries.

> Presents a directory of timber concession-holders, processing firms, trading agents, and others related to the timber industry in Malaysia. Journal format allows for periodic updating.

> Journal.

1157. **Malaysian Forester. 1974+.** Kepong, Selangor, Malaysia: Officers of the Forest Department, Malaysia.

> Includes articles reporting on various issues and current research in Malaysian forestry.

> Journal.

1158. **PCARRD Monitor. 1973+.** Laguna, Los Ba–os, Philippines: Philippine Council for Agriculture and Resources Research and Development.

> Presents articles and reports on current issues and research results on agricultural development and resource conservation in the Philippines and Southeast Asia. Monthly.

> Journal.

1159. **Philippine Quarterly of Culture and Society. 1973+.** Cebu City, Cebu, Philippines: University of San Carlos.

> Presents scholarly papers and essays on a various aspects of Philippine society and culture.

Journal.

1160. **Philippine Studies. 1953+.** Quezon City, Philippines: Ateneo de Manila.

>   Presents a wide variety of scholarly papers and essays on various aspects of Philippine society and economy.

Journal.

1161. **Rattan Information Center Bulletin. 1982+.** Kepong, Selangor, Malaysia: Rattan Information Center, Forest Research Institute.

>   Covers issues related to development of rattan production and industry.

Journal.

1162. **RIC Newsletter. [c. 1987]+.** Kuala Lumpur, Malaysia: Rattan Information Center.

>   The newsletter reports on recent developments in silvicultural, marketing, and other aspects of rattan cultivation in the Asian region. Recent trade statistics are often provided.

Journal.

1163. **Sandakania. 1992+.** Sandakan, Malaysia: Forest Research Centre, Forestry Department.

>   Reports on recent botanical research and survey findings in Sabah and Sarawak. Irregular.

Journal.

1164. **Sarawak Museum Journal. 1911+.** Kuching, Sarawak, Malaysia: Sarawak Museum.

>   Presents work related to the anthropology, archaeology and natural history of Borneo, with special, though not exclusive, emphasis on Sarawak.

Journal.

1165. **Solidarity. 1966+.** Manila, Philippines.

>   Present articles and essays dealing with contemporary issues in Philippine society, politics and culture, including tensions and conflicts over resource use. Bimonthly.

Journal.

1166. **South East Asia Research. 1993+.** London: School of Oriental and African Studies.

>   Reports on recent research conducted in Southeast Asia.

Journal.

1167. **Tropical Biodiversity. 1992+.** Depok, Indonesia: Yayasan Bins Sains Hayati (Indonesian Foundation for the Advancement of Biological Sciences).

The journal is envisioned as a forum for communicating the results of emerging research on tropical biodiversity with particular focus on Asia. The editorial board notes its particular interest in interdisciplinary approaches to the study of biological species richness. Quarterly.

Journal.

SUBJECT INDEX

Agricultural development

2, 4, 29, 30, 54, 57, 116, 151, 190, 220, 234, 238, 352, 374, 385, 386, 404, 409, 449, 464, 515, 539, 548, 558, 559, 569, 574, 639, 698, 704, 719, 720, 741, 749, 765, 766, 796, 803, 865, 875, 879, 880, 892, 955, 984, 1036, 1057, 1103, 1120, 1133

Agricultural economics

4, 172, 264, 558, 559, 618, 704, 749, 805, 845, 874, 875, 966, 999, 1087

Agricultural intensification

21, 33, 115, 133, 230, 231, 232, 255, 301, 311, 352, 417, 456, 475, 476, 480, 531, 532, 547, 687, 752, 756, 788, 795, 796, 800, 801, 805, 827, 840, 841, 869, 879, 889, 940, 1008, 1009, 1011, 1027, 1057, 1074, 1081, 1082

Agriculture—Permanent

1, 12, 28, 31, 34, 57, 115, 142, 150, 464, 476, 547, 574, 577, 606, 668, 719, 720, 733, 765, 853, 868, 907, 914, 926, 949, 986, 1036, 1057, 1065

Agriculture—Plantations

28, 45, 57, 85, 89, 142, 147, 151, 220, 353, 384, 385, 393, 404, 409, 426, 464, 472, 539, 616, 618, 691, 692, 698, 704, 719, 720, 733, 848, 895, 914, 932, 967, 993, 1025, 1036, 1101, 1103

Agriculture—Shifting cultivation

57, 64, 76, 78, 79, 82, 86, 87, 91, 95, 115, 130, 134, 157, 177, 185, 211, 216, 221, 295, 348, 363, 382, 394, 417, 441, 454, 455, 456, 464, 465, 473, 475, 476, 478, 481, 511, 512, 517, 523, 524, 532, 542, 567, 590, 598, 607, 628, 636, 637, 638, 660, 687, 706, 720, 722, 736, 752, 758, 776, 779, 787, 788, 790, 795, 803, 831, 836, 840, 841, 845, 846, 847, 855, 856, 868, 869, 889, 897, 905, 907, 940, 951, 955, 960, 974, 986, 990, 999, 1036, 1043, 1044, 1052, 1069, 1074, 1081, 1082, 1085, 1094, 1098, 1107, 1116, 1127

Agriculture—Shifting cultivation's environmental impacts

9, 45, 76, 83, 88, 123, 157, 166, 167, 171, 198, 199, 300, 311, 312, 322, 327, 329, 340, 347, 349, 350, 384, 388, 389, 390, 426, 458, 477, 479, 531, 532, 606, 635, 697, 705, 733, 735, 760, 768, 822, 837, 845, 848, 877, 884, 887, 897, 940, 944, 1008, 1009, 1037, 1057, 1058, 1074, 1084, 1085, 1094, 1107

CONTRIBUTORS

René Alburo, Area Research & Training Center, University of San Carlos

Randolph Barker, Cornell University

Christopher Barr, Cornell University

Erlinda Burton, Research Institute for Mindanao Culture, Xavier University

Michael Costello, Research Institute for Mindanao Culture, Xavier University

Shelley Feldman, Cornell University

Eveline Ferretti, Cornell University

Nico Kana, Lembaga Penelitian Universitas, Satya Wacana University

David Kummer, Clark University

John Maluda, Institute for Development Studies

Harold Olofson, Area Research Training Center, University of San Carlos

Stephen Siebert, University of Montana

SOUTHEAST ASIA PROGRAM PUBLICATIONS

Cornell University

Studies on Southeast Asia

Number 1   *The Symbolism of the Stupa*, Adrian Snodgrass. 1985. Reprinted with index, 1988. 2nd printing, 1991. 469 pp. ISBN 0-87727-700-1

Number 3   *Thai Radical Discourse: The Real Face of Thai Feudalism Today*, Craig J. Reynolds. 1987. 2nd printing 1994. 186 pp. ISBN 0-87727-702-8

Number 5   *Southeast Asian Ephemeris: Solar and Planetary Positions, A.D. 638–2000*, J. C. Eade. 1989. 175 pp. ISBN 0-87727-704-4

Number 6   *Trends in Khmer Art*, Jean Boisselier. Ed. Natasha Eilenberg. Trans. Natasha Eilenberg and Melvin Elliott. 1989. 124 pp., 24 plates. ISBN 0-87727-705-2

Number 7   *A Malay Frontier: Unity and Duality in a Sumatran Kingdom*, Jane Drakard. 1990. 215 pp. ISBN 0-87727-706-0

Number 8   *The Politics of Colonial Exploitation: Java, the Dutch, and the Cultivation System*, Cornelis Fasseur. Ed. R. E. Elson. Trans. R. E. Elson and Ary Kraal. 1992. 2nd printing 1994. 266 pp. ISBN 0-87727-707-9

Number 9   *Southeast Asian Capitalists*, ed. Ruth McVey. 1992. 220 pp. ISBN 0-87727-708-7

Number 10   *Tai Ahoms and the Stars: Three Ritual Texts to Ward Off Danger*, trans. and ed. B. J. Terwiel and Ranoo Wichasin. 1992. 170 pp. ISBN 0-87727-709-5

Number 11   *Money, Markets, and Trade in Early Southeast Asia: The Development of Indigenous Monetary Systems to AD 1400*, Robert S. Wicks. 1992. 354 pp., 78 tables, illus., maps. ISBN 0-87727-710-9

Number 12   *Fields from the Sea: Chinese Junk Trade with Siam during the Late Eighteenth and Early Nineteenth Centuries*, Jennifer Cushman. 1993. 214 pp. ISBN 0-87727-711-7

Number 13   *Fair Land Sarawak: Some Recollections of an Expatriate Officer*, Alastair Morrison. 1993. 196 pp. ISBN 0-87727-712-5

Number 14   *Sjahrir: Politics and Exile in Indonesia*, Rudolf Mrázek. 1994. 536 pp. ISBN 0-87727-713-3

Number 15   *Selective Judicial Competence: The Cirebon-Priangan Legal Administration, 1680–1792*, Mason C. Hoadley. 1994. 185 pp. ISBN 0-87727-714-1

Number 16   *The Nan Chronicle*, trans. and ed. by David K. Wyatt. 1994. 158 pp. ISBN 0-87727-715-X

Number 17   *The Vernacular Press and the Emergence of Modern Indonesian Consciousness*, Ahmat Adam. 1995. 220 pp. ISBN 0-87727-716-8

Number 18   *In the Land of Lady White Blood: Southern Thailand and the Meaning of History*, Lorraine M. Gesick. 1995. 106 pp. ISBN 0-87727-717-6

Number 19   *Essays into Vietnamese Pasts*, ed. K. W. Taylor and John K. Whitmore. 1995. 288 pp. ISBN 0-87727-718-4

Number 20   *Making Indonesia*, ed. Daniel S. Lev and Ruth McVey. 1996. 201 pp. ISBN 0-87727-719-2

Number 21   *Interpreting Development: Capitalism, Democracy, and the Middle Class in Thailand*, John Girling. 1996. 95 pp. ISBN 0-87727-720-6

Number 22   *Young Heroes: The Indonesian Family in Politics*, Saya S. Shiraishi. 1997. 183 pp. ISBN 0-87727-721-4

SEAP Series

Number 2   *The Dobama Movement in Burma (1930–1938)*, Khin Yi. 1988. 160 pp. ISBN 0-87727-118-6

Number 3   *Postwar Vietnam: Dilemmas in Socialist Development*, ed. Christine White and David Marr. 1988. 2nd printing, 1993. 260 pp. ISBN 0-87727-120-8

Number 5   *Japanese Relations with Vietnam: 1951–1987*, Masaya Shiraishi. 1990. 174 pp. ISBN 0-87727-122-4

Number 6   *The Rise and Fall of the Communist Party of Burma (CPB)*, Bertil Lintner. 1990. 124 pp. 26 illustrations, 14 maps. ISBN 0-87727-123-2

Number 7   *Intellectual Property and US Relations with Indonesia, Malaysia, Singapore, and Thailand*, Elisabeth Uphoff. 1991. 67 pp. ISBN 0-87727-124-0

Number 8   *From PKI to the Comintern, 1924–1941: The Apprenticeship of the Malayan Communist Party*, Cheah Boon Kheng. 1992. 147 pp. ISBN 0-87727-125-9

Number 9   *A Secret Past*, Dokmaisot. Trans. Ted Strehlow. 1992. 72 pp. ISBN 0-87727-126-7

Number 10   *Studies on Vietnamese Language and Literature: A Preliminary Bibliography*, Nguyen Dinh Tham. 1992. 227 pp. ISBN 0-87727-127-5

Number 11   *The Political Legacy of Aung San*, ed. Josef Silverstein. 1972, rev. ed. 1993. 169 pp. ISBN 0-87727-128-3

Number 12   *The Voice of Young Burma*, Aye Kyaw. 1993. 98 pp. ISBN 0-87727-129-1

Number 13   *The American War in Vietnam*, ed. Jayne Werner & David Hunt. 1993. 132 pp. ISBN 0-87727-131-3

Number 14   *Being Kammu: My Village, My Life*, ed. Damrong Tayanin. 1994. 138 pp. ISBN 0-87727-130-5

Number 15   *The Revolution Falters: The Left in Philippine Politics After 1986*, ed. Patricio N. Abinales. 1996. 183 pp. ISBN 0-87727-132-1

Number 16   *Cutting Across the Lands: An Annotated Bibliography on National Resource Management and Community Development in Indonesia, the Philippines, and Malaysia*, ed. Eveline Ferretti. 1997. 329 pp. ISBN 0-87727-

Translation Series

Volume 1   *Reading Southeast Asia*, ed. Takashi Shiraishi. 1990. 188 pp. ISBN 0-87727-400-2

Volume 2   *Indochina in the 1940s and 1950s*, ed. Takashi Shiraishi & Motoo Furuta. 1992. 196 pp. ISBN 0-87727-401-0

Volume 3   *The Japanese in Colonial Southeast Asia*, ed. Saya Shiraishi & Takashi Shiraishi. 1993. 172 pp. ISBN 0-87727-402-9

Volume 4   *Approaching Suharto's Indonesia from the Margins*, ed. Takashi Shiraishi. 1994. 153 pp. ISBN 0-87727-403-7

MODERN INDONESIA PROJECT PUBLICATIONS
Cornell University

Number   6   *The Indonesian Elections of 1955,* Herbert Feith. 1957. 2d printing, 1971. 91 pp. ISBN 0-87763-020-8

Number   7   *The Soviet View of the Indonesian Revolution,* Ruth T. McVey. 1957. 3d printing, 1969. 90 pp. ISBN 0-87763-018-6

Number 25   *The Communist Uprisings of 1926–1927 in Indonesia: Key Documents,* ed. and intro. Harry J. Benda and Ruth T. McVey. 1960. 2d printing, 1969. 177 pp. ISBN 0-87763-024-0

Number 37   *Mythology and the Tolerance of the Javanese,* Benedict R. Anderson. 1965. Second Edition, 1997. 104 pp. ISBN 0-87763-041-0.

Number 43   *State and Statecraft in Old Java: A Study of the Later Mataram Period, 16th to 19th Century,* Soemarsaid Moertono. 1968. Rev. ed., 1981. 180 pp. ISBN 0-87763-017-8

Number 48   *Nationalism, Islam and Marxism,* Soekarno. Intro. by Ruth T. McVey. 1970. 2d printing, 1984. 62 pp. ISBN 0-87763-012-7

Number 49   *The Foundation of the Partai Muslimin Indonesia,* K. E. Ward. 1970. 75 pp. ISBN 0-87763-011-9

Number 50   *Schools and Politics: The Kaum Muda Movement in West Sumatra (1927–1933),* Taufik Abdullah. 1971. 257 pp. ISBN 0-87763-010-0

Number 51   *The Putera Reports: Problems in Indonesian-Japanese War-Time Cooperation,* Mohammad Hatta. Trans. and intro. William H. Frederick. 1971. 114 pp. ISBN 0-87763-009-7

Number 52   *A Preliminary Analysis of the October 1, 1965, Coup in Indonesia* (Prepared in January 1966), Benedict R. Anderson, Ruth T. McVey, assist. Frederick P. Bunnell. 1971. 174 pp. ISBN 0-87763-008-9

Number 55   *Report from Banaran: The Story of the Experiences of a Soldier during the War of Independence,* Maj. Gen. T. B. Simatupang. 1972. 186 pp. ISBN 0-87763-005-4

Number 57   *Permesta: Half a Rebellion,* Barbara S. Harvey. 1977. 174 pp. ISBN 0-87763-033-8

Number 58   *Administration of Islam in Indonesia,* Deliar Noer. 1978. 82 pp. ISBN 0-87763-002-X

Number 59   *Breaking the Chains of Oppression of the Indonesian People: Defense Statement at His Trial on Charges of Insulting the Head of State, Bandung, June 7–10, 1979,* Heri Akhmadi. 1981. 201 pp. ISBN 0-87763-001-1

Number 60   *The Minangkabau Response to Dutch Colonial Rule in the Nineteenth Century,* Elizabeth E. Graves. 1981. 157 pp. ISBN 0-87763-000-3

Number 61   *Sickle and Crescent: The Communist Revolt of 1926 in Banten,* Michael C. Williams. 1982. 81 pp. ISBN 0-87763-027-5

Number 62   *Interpreting Indonesian Politics: Thirteen Contributions to the Debate, 1964–1981.* Ed. Benedict Anderson and Audrey Kahin, intro. Daniel S. Lev. 1982. 3rd printing 1991. 172 pp. ISBN 0-87763-028-3

Number 64   *Suharto and His Generals: Indonesia's Military Politics, 1975–1983,* David Jenkins. 1984. 3rd printing 1987. 300 pp. ISBN 0-87763-027-5

Number 65   *The Kenpeitai in Java and Sumatra.* Trans. from the Japanese by Barbara G. Shimer and Guy Hobbs, intro. Theodore Friend. 1986. 80 pp. ISBN 0-87763-031-3

Number 66   *Prisoners at Kota Cane,* Leon Salim. Trans. Audrey Kahin. 1986. 112 pp. ISBN 0-87763-032-1

Number 67   *Indonesia Free: A Biography of Mohammad Hatta,* Mavis Rose. 1987. 252 pp. ISBN 0-87763-033-X

Number 68   *Intellectuals and Nationalism in Indonesia: A Study of the Following Recruited by Sutan Sjahrir in Occupation Jakarta,* J. D. Legge. 1988. 159 pp. ISBN 0-87763-034-8

Number 69   *The Road to Madiun: The Indonesian Communist Uprising of 1948,* Elizabeth Ann Swift. 1989. 120 pp. ISBN 0-87763-035-6

Number 70   *East Kalimantan: The Decline of a Commercial Aristocracy,* Burhan Magenda. 1991. 120 pp. ISBN 0-87763-036-4

Number 71   *A Javanese Memoir of Sumatra, 1945–1946: Love and Hatred in the Liberation War,* Takao Fusayama. 1993. 150 pp. ISBN 0-87763-037-2

Number 72   *Popular Indonesian Literature of the Qur'an,* Howard M. Federspiel. 1994. 170 pp. ISBN 0-87763-038-0

Number 73   *"White Book" on the 1992 General Election in Indonesia,* Trans. Dwight King. 1994. 72 pp. ISBN 0-87763-039-9

Number 74   *The Roots of Acehnese Rebellion 1989–1992,* Tim Kell. 1995. 103 pp. ISBN 0-87727-040-2

* * *

Javanese Literature in Surakarta Manuscripts, Nancy K. Florida. Hardcover series ISBN 0-87727-600-5; Paperback series ISBN 0-87727-601-3. Vol. 1, *Introduction and Manuscripts of the Karaton Surakarta.* 1993. 410 pp. Frontispiece and 5 illus. Hardcover, ISBN 0-87727-602-1, Paperback, ISBN 0-87727-603-X

Sbek Thom: Khmer Shadow Theater. ed. Thavro Phim & Sos Kem. 1996. 363 pp., incl. 153 photographs. ISBN 0-87727-620-X.

In the Mirror, Literature and Politics in Siam in the American Era, ed. and trans. Benedict R. Anderson and Ruchira Mendiones. 1985. 2nd printing, 1991. 303 pp. Paperback. ISBN 974-210-380-1

For ordering information, please contact:

Southeast Asia Program Publications
Distribution/Purchase Orders
Cornell University
East Hill Plaza
Ithaca, NY 14850

Telephone: (607) 255-8038
Fax: (607) 277-1904

E-mail: SEAP-Pubs@cornell.edu
URL: http://www.einaudi.cornell.edu/SoutheastAsia/SEAPubs.html

1-97/.6M